AMERICAN MISFITS AND THE MAKING
OF MIDDLE-CLASS RESPECTABILITY

...fits and the Making of Middle-Class Respectability

{≈≈≈W≈≈≈}

Robert Wuthnow

PRINCETON UNIVERSITY PRESS

PRINCETON & OXFORD

Published by Princeton University Press,
41 William Street, Princeton, New Jersey 08540

In the United Kingdom: Princeton University Press,
6 Oxford Street, Woodstock, Oxfordshire OX20 1TR

press.princeton.edu

Jacket illustration: "Strawberries: A New Huckster Song."
Courtesy of the Lester S. Levy Collection of Sheet Music,
The Sheridan Libraries, The Johns Hopkins University

ISBN 978-0-691-17686-4
Library of Congress Control Number 2017938253

British Library Cataloging-in-Publication Data is available

This book has been composed in Miller

Printed on acid-free paper. ∞

Printed in the United States of America

10 9 8 7 6 5 4 3 2 1

CONTENTS

ILLUSTRATIONS

AMERICAN MISFITS AND THE MAKING
OF MIDDLE-CLASS RESPECTABILITY

Introduction

LEGEND HAS IT that sometime in the late eighteenth century a freed slave, manumitted at the death of his owner, married a white woman and together they settled in a remote wooded area somewhere between Philadelphia and New York. They were joined a few years later by several other freed slaves and white people who together formed a small community where they could eke out a modest living. They called the community Zion.

Like many legends, the story's details are not entirely accurate. The freed slave, whose name most likely was Will, did not settle there until 1807. He was not manumitted when his owner, the Reverend Oliver Hart, died in 1795, but eleven years later when he turned twenty-five. The second freed slave, whose name was James, did not arrive until 1811. Some white people did join them, but it was not until later that the community became known as Zion.[1]

Zion is located ten miles from Princeton University. I doubt that many of the university's faculty and students know it exists. To get there you drive past high-end estates through a newer suburb of McMansions until the valley opens into an expanse of horse farms. Then you elevate on narrow, winding roads into rough terrain called the Sourland Mountains covered with rocks and trees, among which are a few houses that have mostly seen better days. Your GPS says you've arrived, but nothing is there. Except a small church called Mt. Zion.

Methodists who came through in the 1830s and held camp meetings in the woods built Mt. Zion church in the 1840s. The church's history tells the story of who was already there when the Methodists arrived. The freed slaves and the white people who joined them came to Zion because it was unclaimed land. It was a "safe haven from the world," whoever wrote the history explained, a world "in which they would have been deemed misfits."[2]

Similar events occurred in many places. People who did not quite fit founded communities and churches and called them Zion. The name signaled an intentional distancing from the surrounding world, a destination to aim for in life, and simply a better place. They were German immigrants in the back reaches of Pennsylvania, Scotch Irish in the Carolinas, and slaves in Alabama. Others sang of Zion, laid their loved ones to rest in cemeteries named Zion, and spoke of finding comfort in Zion. Zion was the holy hill of God. The people of Zion were God's people, strangers and pilgrims, sojourning for a time as they looked toward something higher and purer. As the scriptures said, "The Lord hath founded Zion and the poor of his people shall trust in it."[3]

Poor whites. Freed slaves. Squatters. The ones in central New Jersey certainly had no place in the region's proud history of notable citizens. The slave master Reverend Oliver Hart was a distinguished Old School Baptist from Pennsylvania who pastored a church in Charleston, South Carolina, before moving to New Jersey where his support for the American Revolution was more in favor than it was in the South. His congregation at Hopewell a few miles from Zion had been a rallying place of resistance to the British and included the Honorable John Hart, whose name appeared on the Declaration of Independence. Down the hill a few miles from Zion was the community of Stoutsburg, founded by the Stouts, who owned large tracts of land in the valley. Years later one of the distinguished Americans who would settle nearby was Charles Lindbergh.[4]

Those were prominent people whose stories would be preserved for subsequent generations' admiration. They stood out for their achievements. Theirs was the success that demonstrated what America was all about. The misfits at Zion were not.[5] However, they did share something with their illustrious neighbors. Settling there in the woods on unclaimed land and hoping to secure food and shelter for their families, they aspired to something that would later be called the American Dream.

How did the misfits fit? What was their place in nineteenth-century understandings of what it meant to be a fine, upstanding American? Were they simply the ones who didn't succeed? Did they figuratively live off in the hills somewhere? Or did they play a more important, if relatively neglected, part in the making of middle-class respectability?

The answer to these questions, I argue, is that the misfits did fit, but not simply as people who struggled and failed. My argument is that marginalized individuals and groups served persistently, repeatedly, and often quite prominently as the contrasting cases, the negative comparisons through which middle-class respectability was defined. To be respectable was a high aim that often could not be pinned down precisely. People on the margins who stumbled along in out-of-the-way places played an important role in clarifying what it meant.

What the common American wanted, historian James Truslow Adams wrote in 1931, "was what he thought America stood for—opportunity, the chance to grow into something bigger and finer, as bigger and finer appeared to him." Adams called this aspiration for something bigger and finer "the

American Dream," earning for himself the lasting distinction of having originated the phrase.[6]

Adams viewed the American Dream as a national project more than as the aspiration of any particular individual or class of individuals. It was largely the country's collective effort during the nineteenth century to become a single nation extending from coast to coast, unified from north to south, taming the wilderness, conquering the frontier, and bringing civilization to the continent. Pioneers, soldiers, and statesmen embodied the dream.

Appearing as it did during the Great Depression, the phrase soon took on distinctly economic connotations. Faced with joblessness, Americans apparently dreamed of nothing bigger and finer than food on the table and a steady job, or so it seemed. Indigent sharecroppers and mill hands could best achieve the American Dream by getting a secure job and working their way up. The nation's role was to provide opportunity for those willing to work hard. On the eve of America's entry into World War II, President Franklin Delano Roosevelt emphasized "freedom from want" as being of equal importance to freedom of speech, freedom of worship, and freedom from fear.

Well before Adams and Roosevelt, something akin to the American Dream was articulated in nineteenth-century literature. Horatio Alger's novels were perhaps the most widely read depictions of hardworking native-born and immigrant Americans who rose from rags to riches, pulling themselves up by their bootstraps, resisting swindlers and villains, and climbing from the lowest occupational rungs to the highest. Alger's characters were only the latest in a lineage of rugged, industrious Americans who succeeded across the frontier, on farms, and in business by taking advantage of the opportunities America provided.

Understanding the American Dream as decent-paying jobs, upward mobility, and economic prosperity has remained its most popular interpretation. "We proclaimed a dream of an America that would be 'a shining city on a hill,'" Ronald Reagan stated in accepting the 1984 Republican nomination for a second term as president. The phrase echoed John Winthrop's speech aboard the *Arbella* shortly before reaching New England in 1630. But Winthrop's "city upon a hill" warned that eyes across the world were watching to see if the colonists would observe their covenant with God. Reagan's was a city of prosperity induced by low interest rates, low taxes, small government, and jobs.[7]

Reagan was not the only officeholder to reinforce the idea that the American Dream should be interpreted in economic terms. "The American dream that we were all raised on is a simple but powerful one," President Bill Clinton explained in a 1993 speech. "If you work hard and play by the rules, you should be given a chance to go as far as your God-given ability will take you."[8] A decade later Congress passed "the American Dream Downpayment Act," which President George W. Bush said would help homebuyers "achieve an important part of the American Dream."[9] Taking a theme from the same playbook,

Barack Obama in his 2008 bid for the White House crafted his best-selling book and one of his signature campaign speeches around the theme of reclaiming the American Dream, linking the idea with jobs, health care, and education.[10]

Journalists have described the American Dream in essentially the same terms. Tracing the concept's roots, Kate Ellis and Ellen Guettler observe that something like it was evident in immigrants' quest to escape poverty, Roosevelt's promise of freedom from want, the G.I. Bill, and Americans' post–World War II near obsession with home purchases and new cars. They quote historian David Farber, who explains that the American Dream "became closely linked to material comfort, to the consumer abundance America was producing. 'A better life' started to connote not just an economically secure life, but an abundant life . . . a kind of linkage between mobility, a better life, and the good stuff that would make it so."[11]

Social scientists, while varying by discipline, have given similar emphasis to Americans' striving for upward mobility, better jobs, and economic well-being. Political scientist Jennifer L. Hochschild suggested in her exhaustive 1995 book on the topic that the American Dream is a cluster of tenets affirming that everyone should have opportunities to achieve whatever they wish according to their talents and desires, arguing that the goal to which Americans aspire can aptly be summarized as *success*, which in most cases means attaining an attractive income and working at a desirable job. Hochschild acknowledged that success can be whatever people want it to be but argued that experts and the general public alike view it in measurable terms, such as annual incomes and how the occupations of a cohort of younger Americans compare with their parents' occupations.[12]

Few measures in empirical studies of the American Dream have captured as much attention as upward mobility. Community studies in which crude measures of social status were obtained led to statistical estimates based on indices of occupational status and levels of educational attainment. Surveys asked working Americans about their parents' occupations while large-scale longitudinal studies assessed changes in family incomes and assets over time. Better data and more sophisticated statistical techniques made for more detailed discussions of rates, trends, and comparisons by race, ethnicity, gender, and family background. Between 1975 and 1999 sociology journals alone included more than 2,600 articles discussing upward mobility.[13]

In the twenty-first century this interest has continued. The Great Recession of 2008 and subsequent evidence of rising income inequality prompted new inquiries into the American Dream's status in terms of measurable economic indicators. Pollsters determined that 80 percent of pollees considered the American Dream important but concluded that Americans were frustrated in pursuing it, working harder, and downscaling their financial expectations.[14] A few years later, commentators pointed to rising employment rates as evidence that the American Dream was coming back, while other commentators emphasized stagnant wages as evidence that it was not.

Cast in these terms the American Dream has become a measurable standard by which to assess how the nation is faring. Lawmakers look to economists to document whether certain policies are working. Arguments for particular proposals and their proponents find support not only in statistics but also in personal anecdotes. Especially in the context of electoral politics, the rhetoric of worth based on rising from humble origins appears again and again. Whether in the story of an indigent father who delivered milk for a living, a widowed mother who worked as a seamstress, or immigrant parents who fled to America, the successful offspring they bore become the exemplars of merit.

Claims that the American Dream is achievable by all because a few have experienced remarkable success of course inevitably ring untrue. The realities of poverty and discrimination stand in sharp contrast to the ideal of a nation in which any and all can rise from the bottom to the top. The social science literature on upward mobility is if anything secondary to the literature on these realities. Many of the literature's lasting contributions have dealt with the enduring barriers that inhibit the successful pursuit of the American Dream. Classics such as W.E.B. Dubois's *Philadelphia Negro*, Gunnar Myrdal's *American Dilemma*, and Michael Harrington's *Other America* tell of people and places in which the struggle for upward mobility was quite different from what it was for the few.[15]

The misfits who settled in Zion, New Jersey, would be among those about whom history has had little to report. Were more about them known, they would be an important part of the story of how Americans in the nineteenth century pursued the American Dream. The story would show the enduring effects of slavery, the passage of laws that offered freedom but not for their children and only if they could demonstrate an ability to fend for themselves and prove that they were of sound mind, and how their descendants battled the timber companies and worked for meager wages in the quarries. In these respects, they were like many Americans who never quite made it because they were outsiders—the excluded, the discriminated against, the marginalized who existed at the edges of refined society by virtue of what they did, how they looked, or some other trait that branded them as defective.

One way to think about the marginalized and excluded is to regard them as people who failed in their endeavors to achieve the American Dream and who thus beg for something about their struggles to be included in the story of our nation's past. While others marched onward and upward, they stumbled and fell. The American Dream, though, has always connoted something more than the pursuit of economic success. Adams's 1931 discussion framed the topic not only as Americans' quest for a better life but also as the broad cultural narrative that animated democracy's tensions with wealth, conquest of the frontier, and imperialism. Roosevelt's call for freedom from want was couched in an argument for a "greater conception—the moral order," as he called it, opposed to tyranny and in defense of the supremacy of human rights.[16] Obama considered the American Dream as much about "a set of ideals that continue to stir our collective conscience; a common set of values that bind us together despite our differences; a running thread of hope that makes our improbable experiment in democracy work" as about jobs and prosperity.[17] Alger's rags-to-riches stories communicated a moral ideal of integrity and diligence as well as a struggle for upward mobility.[18]

If the American Dream is about more than upward mobility, the language in which its larger dimensions have been framed, however, is strikingly vague. It is variously described as a vision, a philosophy of life, a myth, and a national culture. Its ingredients are said to consist of values, goals, and ideals. They serve in various descriptions as personal aspirations, measuring sticks, and moral principles. In that, they somehow provide motivation for hard work, affirmations for achievement, and explanations for failure. The question is whether the concept is sufficiently indeterminate that it has to remain vague or whether something more systematic can be said about it.

The tools of cultural analysis that have developed during the past quarter century offer some insights. The tools are conceptual, drawn from cognitive anthropology, literary criticism, the study of discourse, and cultural sociology. They include two emphases: pay close attention to the actual words, gestures, metaphors, and narratives through which meanings are communicated rather than looking past them in search of overarching themes; and ground the analysis of these words, gestures, metaphors, and narratives in observations of social settings, interaction, ritual, networks, and communities.

The American Dream, as many have argued, is less about the aims and aspirations of individuals than it is about the meanings that emerge in social settings and that shape how individuals in those settings behave and relate to one another. To say that individuals' behavior is driven by goals, whether the goal is upward mobility or a happy life, is too simple. We know from personal experience that we engage in real and imagined conversations with others, draw distinctions between those we identify with and those we do not, and make sense of ourselves in the context of these ongoing conversations.

In these respects the American Dream is not so different from the processes through which we construct other understandings of ourselves: family life, for example, or how we think about our friends and the ways we choose to spend our time. Moving the American Dream from the stratosphere in which it is often discussed into the mundane realities of everyday life forces it to be considered differently. The topics of relevance cease to be the long-term trajectory through which protagonists rise from rags to riches and become instead questions about the immediate contexts in which people live.

To shift in that direction I suggest the possibility that what we might call middle-class respectability gets us further than continuing to discuss the

American Dream as an ideal or philosophy of life. "Middle class" can be used as a sensitizing concept for present purposes, not in the narrowly specified sense in which it might appear in theoretical discussions, but in the way that large majorities of Americans do when asked in surveys how they think of themselves. To be middle class in those terms is to suggest that a person is generally self-identified with certain lifestyles and expectations, however diverse those may be. Respectability suggests that the respect a person hopes for and receives from others is important, which in turn necessitates bringing the question into a social context by asking, respect from whom?

Horatio Alger's protagonists, for example, were exemplars of persons seeking middle-class respectability as much as they were hardworking individuals pulling themselves up by their bootstraps. Besides the pluck and good personal habits that distinguish them from indolent and reckless persons, Alger's characters discover and embrace the patterns of behavior they see in persons they admire and who serve concretely as role models. Starting as impoverished youth who are untutored but eager to learn, "Alger's heroes learn to imitate the ways of those who occupy higher rungs on the social ladder," as one writer observes. They "embrace conformity with the mores of a higher social class."[19] Honesty and hard work become habits less because they led reliably to success and more because they earn the protagonist approval from persons the protagonist wants to please.

Alger's stories illustrate further that meanings are expressed concretely in actions as well as in thoughts. "The hero's entry into the world of 'respectability,' which entails acceptance of the rules for succeeding articulated by the benefactors," the same writer notes, "is heralded by getting a new suit." Clothing becomes the observable marker through which the protagonist becomes respectable. The protagonist's physical appearance, including the display of appropriate speech, hygiene, and mannerisms, signals a particularly trustworthy status in contrast with the uncertainties of urban life depicted in the behavior of swindlers, drunks, derelicts, and tramps. The change in the hero's personal appearance is also dramatized by the hero's relocation to a space that is at once more secure and less confining. Success is instantiated in movement that results in finding one's place.[20]

In the late 1880s and 1890s, a decade after Alger's best-selling rags-to-riches stories, publishing houses such as Lake City and Chapman Brothers in Chicago began producing nonfictional "portraits and biographical albums" of well-known citizens in attractively bound volumes organized by counties and states. The accounts resembled Alger's stories in emphasizing the notable successes of self-made individuals. Sketches included descriptions, exclusively of men, who rose from humble beginnings, starting from the foot of the ladder, and through self-reliance, energetic ambition, and force of character with no aid from anyone proved the potency of industry and enterprise in achieving success. But the sketches also displayed many of the social characteristics typical of Alger's heroes.[21]

The self-made men in these depictions may have come from humble stock, but the sketches frequently emphasized parents and grandparents whose occupations and activities augured well for their offspring and set an example of how to behave. The featured descendent then located to a new community that was blossoming with opportunities. And in that new location the industrious person engaged in visible activities that signaled success, such as growing crops, raising cattle, teaching school, holding public office, marrying well, and raising well-mannered children. The person was thus well known and said to have been held in high esteem by equally respected members of the community.

Examples such as these have been identified in advice books of the period, serialized fiction, newspaper columns, primary school readers, Sunday school lessons, and sermons. The common elements include norms for everyday behavior in family life and at work, manners, modes of speech, and examples of dress and grooming. Middle-class respectability was something that people may have aspired to as an ideal, but it was modeled, learned, and exhibited in practice.

Practices, as discussed especially in the writings of Pierre Bourdieu, are routines that become habits through repetition as individuals and groups engage in day-to-day social interaction. Practices are constrained but by no means determined by the social settings in which they take place. They include the aims and aspirations of individuals but also consist of the concrete short-term strategies that people devise to pursue their goals and adapt comfortably to their surroundings. Practices are embodied as well as mental, meaning that they are inscribed in posture, dress, and modes of speaking.[22]

Bourdieu insists that status is always reflected in everyday practices. Practitioners bring to new situations the habits, mannerisms, and language they have learned in the homes in which they were raised and from the schools, communities, and workplaces to which they have been exposed. Status in terms of race, ethnicity, and gender as well as social class is reproduced in these ways. Status is reproduced, but it is also attained, reinforced, and communicated. An aspirant achieves status by displaying the appropriate gestures, words, and material accouterments. Success depends on the relevant reference group implicitly conferring acceptance of the cues provided.

Understood this way, middle-class respectability is a practice that consists in the first instance of distinctions. Distinctions are the categories that identify the differences between desirable and undesirable behavior. Distinctions are in these regards norms, but they indicate that norms are more than the accepted means through which goals are attained. Norms become interpretable through actions and understandings based on explicit comparisons. The proper way to behave is shown as much by criticisms of improper behavior as by exhortations to behave properly. Distinctions can thus be said to function symbolically as the guidelines through which people demonstrate that they understand and accept certain standards. The specific terms in which respectability is defined are dramatized in distinctions.

Distinctions are reinforced through selective social interaction. The criteria of selectivity are sometimes intentional, as in the case of picking friends to invite to a party, but in many instances are contingent on local situations, such as interacting with people who happen to live in the same neighborhood. Interaction may occur more frequently among people who share similar lifestyles and values than among those who do not. However, interacting with strangers and persons with whom one disagrees also reinforces distinctions. Disagreements, conflicts, and situations in which estrangement is felt are often among the most powerful ways in which social distinctions are dramatized.

Although the person-to-person interaction that takes place in daily life is likely to reinforce the distinctions that dramatize differences in statuses and values, the fact that we live in larger public worlds is also important. Interaction of this kind occurs vicariously through the experiences we hear about firsthand from friends and family, such as the story a family member might tell about a run-in with someone at work. It is easy to imagine being in a similar situation and having similar feelings. Listening to questions and answers at town hall meetings, participating in worship services, reading novels and newspapers, and studying texts in school also provide information about social distinctions and statuses.

The distinctions that provide order in everyday life can be the basis for morally neutral decisions, as in choosing to drink coffee or tea. The distinctions associated with differences in social status, though, are likely to include moral valences. The distinction implies not only a difference but also a right way to behave and a wrong way. Failing to let one's tea steep the proper length of time and in water heated to the correct temperature puts the tea drinker in jeopardy not only of having less than ideal tea but also of being viewed as naïve, inexperienced, and perhaps alien among those properly educated in the art of tea.

Distinctions then are social in two respects: they are enacted and reinforced in social interaction, whether in personal relationships or in vicarious experiences, and they are subject to the definitions and evaluations provided by the bystanders and observers who make up the community in which they occur. Drinking tea properly depends on the presence of a real or imagined community that models, defines, and evaluates the meaning of "proper." The relevant communities are sometimes sufficiently isolated that the activities they define as desirable are quite unique, such as in a family that has its own coded words of affection and gestures that no other family would understand. The possibility that something as general as middle-class respectability exists, though, depends on small, localized communities also being integrated into wider contexts in which shared understandings are communicated, such as in schools, workplaces, and the mass media. Overlapping and yet different communities are the basis for diversity, meaning that something as wide-spread as middle-class diversity may be identifiable but will also be composed of variations based on location or race and ethnicity.

The potential for relativizing that occurs in pluralistic contexts is one of the reasons that secondary modes of moral legitimation play an important role in social life. When the question arises of why "we" do things one way and "they" do things a different way, the answer may well involve an appeal to some kind of authority: we do things this way because the law tells us to, because God says so in holy scriptures, because we have discovered that this way causes the least problems and gets things done, because we believe in honoring timeworn traditions, because scientific studies have proven this to be the correct way, and so on.

Distinctions, social interaction, communities of reference, and modes of legitimation all bear on assessments of respectability. A "respectable" show-ing typically means good enough, acceptable, or solid, rather than the very best. While discussions of social practices such as playing chess and boxing frequently emphasize mastery, practices that demonstrate respectability imply having achieved a threshold level of conformity with social expectations rather than having pushed to the very top.

Middle-class respectability further underscores the idea of performing at a satisfactory level and not necessarily at the very highest level. The distinctions that define middle-class respectability distinguish it from behavior below the threshold, such as failing to work hard enough, but they also distinguish it from behavior that is too high, such as putting on airs and purchasing goods that are too expensive. Middle-class respectability is, then, in between, diverse, and defined both by behavior considered acceptable, such as being a respon-sible employee and family member, and by behavior that falls below or above the line.

With these preliminary considerations (which I develop in chapter 1), we can return to the question of how the American Dream constituted a widely accepted and widely practiced understanding of middle-class respectability. The period in which to consider this question is one that historians have iden-tified as the time in American history when something clearly identifiable as a middle class came to be discussed as a growing and achievable reality by a large segment of the population. With roots in antebellum America and in-terrupted by the American Civil War, the idea of middle-class respectability gained popularity in the decades immediately following the war and then adapted to the changing contours of urban and industrial life over the next half century.

The story of *how* Americans became middle class during the nineteenth century has been described in varying levels of detail many times. It included native-born Americans moving west along the frontier that had been taken from its native peoples, immigrants arriving in search of better lives, and families establishing themselves through public education and expanding opportunities for employment. In this telling, the story of the American middle class is understood through the lens of growth, conquest, and expansion. It is a story mostly of the Americans who made it. The ones who did not make it because of misfortune, discrimination, and oppression have received attention as well, but much more needs to be understood. They were the ones who stumbled along on the margins trying to fit in and make a better life for themselves like everyone else but in ways that deviated from the mainstream.

The literature on social distinctions—symbolic and social *boundaries*, as they are termed—has richly described the ways in which distinctions are constructed and how they affect social life. The evidence suggests that people who were marginalized while others successfully achieved middle-class respectability played an important part in the cultural dynamics of the process. They did so less as examples of failure and more as contrasting cases who by negative example clarified the often-ambiguous meanings of respectability. Respectability was defined in the breach as much as it was through straightforward declarations of what it should be. Individuals and groups that served this purpose were enough a part of ordinary communities that they were familiar, frequently interacting with people who attained respectability, and at the same time deviated from how that was defined to the point that they were stigmatized. In many instances the distinctions were reinforced by physical separation and in some instances by policing and other means of legal enforcement. And yet the process of drawing these distinctions was complicated, involving not only persons and groups on the outside, as it were, but also people who transgressed the interstices and whose status was ambiguous.

Much of the literature has dealt with the lines defining middle-class respectability through contrasts with groups marginalized on the basis of social class and race. Although these contrasts are culturally constructed, they are the ones that have characteristically hardened into sharp distinctions that serve as the basis for exclusion, either through informal patterns of behavior or through enforced separation. There is, however, another kind of distinction that plays a subtler role in daily life and is perhaps less easily recognized. These are the symbolic and social boundaries that arise from people crossing them in unexpected ways—coming and going, being on the edge of the community and sometimes straying beyond its borders while still being part of it in other ways, and necessitating discussion by virtue of having an unclear relationship to middle-class respectability. It takes cultural work to figure out who they are, why they behave like they do, and what they imply for how ordinary people who want respect should act. That work necessarily happens in local settings and involves firsthand interaction, even though it usually includes the intervention of persons in positions of authority and sometimes results in laws being passed and punishments being imposed. The discussions are interesting because they communicate messages about the meanings of respectability that imply the complex criteria on which nineteenth-century status determinations were made.

Other than race and gender, *place* was probably the distinction that most often played a role in daily life. The very notion of being an "insider" or "outsider" was based on metaphors of place. Places were "ours" or "theirs," "close" or "distant," owned by "us" or owned by "them," and they were in turn nuanced with feeling familiar or strange and secure or unsafe. Spatial distinctions figured in property ownership, government surveys, placement of roads, parish and township boundaries, municipal identities, and tax codes. Some have argued that places were particularly important to nineteenth-century Americans because they were in fact a mobile population whose ancestors had been less mobile and who wanted to emulate that experience by settling down. Whether that was the case or whether the desire to put down roots was simply a human instinct, the national project clearly encouraged the establishment of new settlements, farms, and towns.

The role of places in the quest for power, status, and respectability has been examined on multiple fronts, with research increasingly directed toward the processes and flows involved in the construction of places and attributing them with meaning.[23] Among the most consequential exertions of dominance and exclusion were the formation of plantations under slavery and the displacement of American Indians. On a smaller scale regional histories document the economic stakes involved in "county seat wars," decisions about the routing of railroads, and contested property rights. A cultural distinction that lasted well into the twentieth century in conjunction with urbanization separated the rural population from the town population and gained expression in political disputes as well as in stereotypes about "country bumpkins" and "city slickers."

The question of how people who may not have fit neatly into any of the generally accepted spatial categories were regarded and what role they may have played in clarifying and dramatizing those categories has received less attention. One such group was composed of hucksters whose presence was widely known to nineteenth-century Americans and who played an important role in the period's economic transactions. Hucksters exemplified what might be called *placeless labor* because they operated not from farms or shops but in between, always in motion, transporting goods from place to place. They were literally the connective tissue that linked farms and cities, vivifying the distinction between the two by crossing it routinely.

To have worked as a huckster was to have occupied a liminal cultural space and thus to have provided an opportunity for discussions of what it meant to be respectable when respectability had so much to do with being located in an established place. There was nothing inherently moral or immoral about being a huckster, at least not in the nineteenth century, but (as I show in chapter 2) huckstering revealed the extent to which morality and such attendant virtues as trustworthiness and decency were associated with being located in a particular place. Huckstering's meanings were negotiated as people in local communities interacted with hucksters and peddlers, told stories about them, and read about them in stories and newspapers. Its meanings, though, were not entirely cultural. Huckstering also had important economic implications and was contested legally and politically.

Like hucksters, lunatics were also legally and politically defined with the intent of constraining their activities and setting them apart from respected members of the community. Lunacy was clearly different from huckstering in most other respects. While it was considered to be an affliction subject to medical diagnosis, its causes were acknowledged even by medical experts to be poorly understood. Insanity could happen unexpectedly in an instant with no known cause or could develop over a long period and be anticipated in the smallest deviations from standard speech and decorum by any who might be watching. There was widespread concern that the insane could and apparently often did commit atrocious acts of violence, which made it a popular narrative through which to account for crime. It was likely enough to be inherited to cast suspicion on siblings and offspring, and whether it was inherited or not, it posed questions about morality, especially in discussions of drinking, promiscuity, and other kinds of intemperate behavior. Religion was useful in deterring these impulses toward immorality, it seemed, but "religious excitement" could also be a leading cause of insanity.

Lunacy reinforced place-based social distinctions insofar as the preferred method of treatment was institutionalization, effectively removing the insane from interacting with respectable citizens and resulting in tragic realities of confinement. If insanity was culturally managed by means of literal displacement, though, its reality and potential remained an aspect of daily life. Its role in defining respectability by deviating from it occurred in two important ways (discussed in chapter 3) that were more public than private. The first was in court hearings that required neighbors and friends to testify about behavior they considered as departures from how persons of "sound mind" behaved. The second was in similarly public information required of families of the insane who hoped to receive financial support from government pensions. Evidence of this kind illustrates the extent to which insanity figured in local discussions that in turn negotiated particular meanings of respectability. Insanity deviated from respectable behavior especially in small departures from ordinary decorum in social relations and in decision making that seemed to observers to betray a lack of rational planning. For the families, respectability figured in the breach through financial difficulties, dependence on relatives, and being drawn into legal and bureaucratic interactions that otherwise would not have been present.

Fanaticism overlapped with insanity to the extent that excessive religious enthusiasm was sometimes considered a source of lunacy and because fanatics and lunatics were often said to exhibit similar characteristics. The interesting aspect of fanaticism for present purposes is not its etiology, about which much has been written, but how it illustrated the limits of respectable displays of religious emotion. For religious leaders and academic observers alike, religion posed a significant quandary in terms of how much or how little emotion was appropriate to display. The pious were supposed to be zealous in the cause of Zion, but they were also expected to avoid putting emotions ahead of clergy authority. The matter had to be decided locally and for that reason varied in what was deemed respectable.

Instances in which fanaticism gained popular attention demonstrated that charges of excessive emotion could be used as a weapon against any person or group that challenged clergy authority. Upstart preachers sparked interest by holding events at which raw emotion seemed to show the presence of the Holy Spirit, but there also had to be limits. If sufficient reason and order were not also demonstrated, enterprising leaders could be branded as heretics. Accusations (discussed in chapter 4) served as well to suggest that certain groups dressed improperly, behaved strangely, and could not be trusted.

Hucksters, lunatics, and fanatics shed light on the question of how certain ambiguously marginalized groups figured in defining middle-class respectability. The lines between "us" and "them" in these cases were negotiated in local contexts that were sufficiently similar to have implications for how ordinary people were supposed to behave. The distinctions demonstrated by negative contrast the value of such small things as having a known address, making reasonable decisions in the conduct of personal affairs, and keeping one's emotions in check most of the time. These were usually not matters that resulted in violence or that subjected entire populations to discrimination, but they sometimes did include those consequences—and did so often enough that cautionary tales resulted.

There are other questions, though, that require considering different groups and different modes of categorization. Hucksters, lunatics, and fanatics were often marginalized as individuals, one person at a time, and the categories into which they were placed were shaped in the process. These examples provide few opportunities to consider how marginalized groups functioned as groups. Among the most interesting of such groups were ones that could have easily moved from the margins into the mainstream but continued to behave as outsiders. The impetus in these instances involved distinctions imposed on the groups from the outside but also was a kind of centripetal force that bound people together from the inside. The pressure against nonconformity from the outside, in short, existed in interaction with an opposing pressure from within.

Immigrant religious groups that adopted a kind of sectarian stance toward their neighbors illustrate this kind cultural boundary work. They held beliefs and engaged in styles of worship that differed from others' practices and in many instances led them to be regarded as outsiders, and yet they continued to adhere to these distinctive practices instead of assimilating. They thrived, as observers would argue about later such manifestations, by maintaining strict standards of behavior and by regarding themselves as embattled. Many aspects of what was involved in maintaining these distinctions nevertheless remain underexamined. Was it simply to keep their doctrines pure that they set up barriers against the outside world, for example, or were there other considerations, and, if so, did they cultivate their own standards of respectability or manage to interact with outsiders on equitable terms?

The reality that native-born and immigrant nineteenth-century Americans faced was that many of them died young. They failed to gain the success of their notable neighbors through no fault of their own. They simply died, and in many instances their loved ones' hopes for success died with them. The value of acknowledging this reality is that it supplies one of the ways of understanding the role that religious communities played. They sustained the bereaved emotionally and provided supportive networks. Their strength depended on more than shared beliefs and obligations. They also had to resolve conflicts among complexly interrelated families, attract newcomers, and deal with attrition. These practices, as discussed in chapter 5, illustrated how distinctions were dramatized through internal solidarity as well as from external characterizations.

If the distinctions defining immigrant religious communities complicate the story, so do the practices through which groups regarded as superior were classified. Although persons of high status are presumably looked up to most of the time, being of high status is by definition to be in a numeric minority and for this reason subject to the drawing of symbolic boundaries that may malign rather than simply adulate the other. Donna T. Andrew's study of aristocratic vice, for example, illustrates how middle-class respectability in eighteenth-century England was crafted through attacks on dueling, suicide, adultery, and gambling.[24] In nineteenth-century America, depictions of how the pursuit and uses of wealth might need to be morally constrained provided additional occasions in which ordinary, nonwealthy people developed an understanding of middle-class respectability. Many discussions described ordinary Americans as sharing the same aspirations as the wealthy and simply being less fortunate in attaining them, but during the latter half of the nineteenth century sharper distinctions that portrayed the wealthy as corporate entities rather than as individuals became increasingly salient.

Although it was relatively short lived, the public outcry against profiteering that emerged during and immediately after World War I, as discussed in chapter 6, significantly altered how the wealthy were depicted and in turn what it meant to be a common person. The common person was more clearly than before a citizen consumer, an identity reinforced by concerns about rapidly rising prices and the need for price controls. The campaign against profiteering had a strong moral dimension but also brought government regulation into the marketplace in ways that demonstrated the difficulties of putting such regulations into effect.

A remaining aspect of the boundary work that defined middle-class respectability by maligning outsiders concerns the nature and extent of the maligning itself. Nineteenth-century Americans learned not only to differentiate themselves from others they considered inferior but also to demonize them. The "others" were dangerous, treacherous, and evil. Understanding the language used and how it was applied requires looking at the stories children learned and the advice parents received about children. The stories and advice communicated the importance of obedience and honesty and showed how children who observed these traits gained approval from all who knew them and generally became successful in life.

Less attention has been paid to the naughty children who also inhabited these spaces of moral instruction. They were present too, often in the persons of more colorful characters who did more interesting things than their milquetoast counterparts. They stole things, told lies, disobeyed their parents, hit their siblings, broke their toys, tortured their pets, pouted, yelled, and played pranks, and as they got older their bad behavior got worse. They demonstrated what not to do and thus by negative example illustrated what good children should do. And, insofar as that was the role they played, their place in the moral culture to which children were exposed was relatively straightforward.

But that was not all. The stories invite closer investigation, and when the nuances are considered, as discussed in chapter 7, it becomes evident that more was being implicitly communicated. Naughty children appeared in illustrated stories wearing particular kinds of clothing and interacting with some adults more than others. Naughty boys misbehaved in different ways than naughty girls. Some of the children were irredeemably bad while others deviated only temporarily. Methods of punishment varied considerably and changed over time, but naughty children frequently suffered severely for their behavior. They experienced illness, died, were attacked by vicious animals, lost their parents, and learned that God did not love them. The stories carried clear implications for parents as well: naughty children became worse as a result of bad parenting and would become bad adults unless extreme measures were taken. In these respects the lines that were sometimes easily transgressed solidified as children grew into adulthood. The lines also became more distinct as older children experienced life outside the family. Good children and bad children were institutionally separate: the good ones went to school and church and joined juvenile temperance associations; the bad ones joined street gangs and had to be removed from the community by being sent to workhouses and placed in penitentiaries.

Those early nineteenth-century settlers in the Sourland Mountains of New Jersey are a reminder that status distinctions are shaped in the cultural imagination as well as in material reality. Zion was the holy hill of God, literally one of the hills in Jerusalem, but figuratively much more. For the predominantly Christian eighteenth- and nineteenth-century American population that lived in communities of faith where they worshipped under the tutelage of clergy, Zion referred to the hope they shared in attaining eternal life as their heavenly reward. It expressed a higher goal, attainable by even the humblest in worldly standards, and was thus an expression of unity and commonality. To be a part of the community aiming for Zion implied a moral commitment to live according to the community's rules. It evoked standards of behavior that earned those who conformed respect, and it stigmatized those who did not conform.

The fact that Zion was a hill was profoundly significant to its metaphorical meaning. Zion's aspirants elevated themselves as they moved closer to Zion. The worthy deemed themselves to be marching confidently toward Zion, never quite making it in this life but gaining in perfection and in the esteem of their neighbors. They were not only marching toward Zion but also working for its mission to be accomplished on earth through pious preaching, evangelism, and upright living. The moral order that Zion symbolized was in this sense deeply religious, giving divine impetus and legitimation to those who best exemplified its holy perfection.[25]

But Zion was also a hill that many found difficult to climb. They stumbled more than they marched. They backslid, sinned, and had to be redeemed again and again. They died before their time. They displayed too much emotion in their quest for faith, or not enough. Their zeal for the kingdom of God left them suffering from religious monomania. Or they simply were on the margins because of the work they did and where they lived. Zion was in these respects a moral order that drew sharp distinctions. It was defined not only by an image of the faithful moving collectively in ascent but also by the outcasts, the stragglers, and the transgressors who sometimes merited redemption and just as often failed to receive it.[26]

A map of New Jersey printed in 1850 amply illustrates the small but important ways in which social distinctions were part of Americans' everyday lives. The path that would later be named Zion Road separated Montgomery Township from Hillsborough Township, sending residents in opposite directions when they had taxes to pay and votes to cast. To the immediate left of Zion was Province Line Road, which marked the state's colonial division between the Dutch part to the north and the English part to the south. And there were two churches, not one: the Methodist Chapel up the road and a hundred yards away the African Church.[27]

The map illustrated some of the distinctions, but in so doing it also shielded others from view. The settlers at Zion did what they could to earn the trust of one another and were undoubtedly looked down on by their more prosperous neighbors. Daily life would have been a matter of negotiating relationships between men and women, parents and children, and with strangers. Perhaps a huckster came through from time to time selling produce, and perhaps someone went insane. Respect would have been an aspect of all those relationships. We can imagine some of the dynamics. We can do so by asking how nineteenth-century Americans in other contexts dealt with the neighbors who did not quite fit and who thus provided the occasion for thinking about respectability.

CHAPTER ONE

A Relational Approach

THE SOCIAL CONSTRUCTION OF
RESPECT AND RESPECTABILITY

HANS JAKOB OLSON with his wife Bertha and three children emigrated from Norway in 1871, settling on a scrubby forty-acre farm in western Wisconsin where three more children were born over the next few years. On November 24, 1889, following the community's Sunday evening church services, Olson was seized from his bed and hanged from a tree outside the family's home by a vigilante mob of more than two dozen local residents. A journalist who covered the ensuing investigation described Olson as a ne'er-do-well who roamed the neighborhood at night scaring people by peeking in windows and then running off. The investigation suggested that Olson may have spent time in prison, been abusive toward his family, and on one occasion threatened to burn down the house. The vigilantes' ringleader was Charles Johnson, a neighbor who served as president of the Farmers' Trading Association and had business ties with the old-stock Yankee establishment. An account of the trial reported that Johnson "was so well respected that he had the trust of the community, and the fathers and mothers of the young boys who were members of the mob believed that he wished only to lead the children into good deeds."[1]

Questions about respect and respectability appear in a wide variety of contexts. Twenty-first-century advocates of uplift for poor families and of greater inclusion for gays and lesbians, for example, have argued that gaining respectability by putting aside distinctive personal habits, styles of dress, and demeanor may be the key to accomplishing these tangible goals. Critics of such proposals, in contrast, argue that the politics of respectability expects disadvantaged groups to police their own behavior instead of challenging prevailing social norms.[2] In electoral politics similar discussions have hinged on whether particular candidates and officeholders have blatantly transgressed accepted standards of respectability and whether others in high office have stayed too narrowly within these confines.[3]

Historical research illustrates the varied contexts in which questions about respect and respectability arise as well. A recent study of the American abolitionist movement demonstrates, for example, the extent to which the movement sought to enhance its reputation for respectability through "sane and decent" meetings and "good manners" in the face of critics who branded abolitionism as "crazy," "wild," and "promiscuous."[4] The mid-twentieth-century struggle for respectability by southern country musicians posed a similar challenge because of racial divisions and was waged through professionalization, musical innovation, and marketing that ran against the region's poor-white rural reputation.[5] Woodruff D. Smith's wide-ranging history of consumer goods during the seventeenth and eighteenth centuries similarly emphasizes respectability, viewing it as the key to their meaning and how they signaled the modernization of social relationships. Nineteenth-century obituaries and news stories such as the ones about Charles Johnson frequently described the perpetrators or victims of crimes as respected members of their communities.[6]

Respect and respectability are topics of continuing interest because privileges and resources flow so often to those deemed respectable, while disrespect goes hand in hand with disadvantage and discrimination. Respect is valued in its own right but is also deployable in negotiating for political and economic power. Examples abound of disgraced public figures seeking to regain respect and of marginalized groups—speculators, pawnbrokers, sex workers, circus barkers, survivalists, migrant laborers, among others—pursuing respectability and being called on by higher-status groups to do something different in hopes of acquiring it.[7] Whether for these or for other reasons, respect and respectability are traits that families and schools endeavor to cultivate in children and that organizations consider essential to good employee and customer relations.[8] Attaining and maintaining respectability is said to be one of the reasons people attend religious services and is perhaps a consideration in religious organizations' efforts to promote decency and decorum.[9] Other discussions emphasize society's mechanisms for facilitating conformity by stigmatizing groups that insiders regard as lacking respectability. Another context in which the topic receives attention is the management of self-respect.

Respect overlaps with but is distinguishable from concepts such as trust and prestige. Trust is an expectation based on past performance in role-specific activities, whereas respect refers to an assessment of the more diffuse qualities of persons.[10] A person who is respected is likely to also be trusted, but with notable exceptions, as in the case of scoundrels in public office who are not respected but are trusted to make bad laws, or members of a stigmatized ethnic group who are trusted to serve faithfully in menial jobs. Respect and prestige often go hand in hand as well but differ in that prestige indicates occupancy of a highly valued position in a social hierarchy, whereas respect may include relationships among persons of equal status.[11]

Efforts to study the meanings and manifestations of respectability have taken a wide variety of approaches, including practical interests in self-improvement and those stemming from therapeutic, religious, and medical authorities claiming to know how to determine who was respectable and who was not. A method of assessing women's respectability that gained interest in conjunction with phrenology in the 1890s, for example, consisted of reading character from inspection of the vagina. As a "genitologist" reported in the *Journal of Orificial Surgery* about one of his recent patients, she was "a woman of great power" who could "accomplish anything she undertakes . . . with great determination and energy . . . has the power of an organizer and campaigner [and] possesses wonderful powers of observation." He was certain that she exhibited "extreme force of character." This method's popularity was brief.[12]

The social science literature has often considered respect and respectability as culturally conditioned attributes of persons, such that a person who behaves in certain ways is respectable while another person who behaves differently is not respectable. In this view respectability is a trait that individuals learn or aspire to learn, usually as children and in early adulthood, and, once learned, becomes a stable personal attribute that can be carried from place to place and can serve the individual in attaining coveted goals in life, such as a good job and desirable friends. Melvin L. Kohn's research on child-rearing values in the 1950s, for example, argued that working-class parents were especially concerned about honesty and neatness because these were "qualities of respectable, worthwhile people" and would thus be important to their children's success in life.[13]

As an enduring attribute that individuals either manifest or aspire to, respectability could then be understood as a characteristic of large segments of the population. Middle-class respectability in this view referred to relatively fixed attributes and values shared by the large number of individuals who composed the middle class. It represented in various formulations a stable, well-defined normative structure, collection of rules, or value system that reinforced and rewarded certain kinds of behavior, such as honesty and neatness, and served as a standard against which "deviance" could be measured. Juvenile delinquents, for example, were said to deviate from the norms of middle-class respectability for various reasons that included improper socialization, personality defects, and economic disadvantages.[14]

Much research, of course, has challenged the view that respectability was simply a value system to which some adhered and from which others deviated. Research has paid closer attention to the contested nature of respectability, including the strategies that groups seeking respectability use to attain it and the strategies through which dominant groups ground claims of superior respectability. Respectability emerges in these studies as not only contested but also changeable and negotiable. Evelyn Brooks Higginbotham, who coined the phrase "politics of respectability" in her study of late nineteenth-century African American Baptist church women, for example, observes that the "talented tenth" who played important leadership roles promoted racial pride by encouraging fewer displays of emotion in worship, emphasizing cleanliness and disciplined home management, and discouraging women from wearing gaudy colors as well as advocating for economic and educational opportunities.[15] The conclusion is not that something that might be called middle-class respectability is nonexistent but that its existence is situational, diversely understood and attained, and contingent on multifaceted activities and cultural constructions. *How* honesty and neatness are constructed and communicated is more the issue than simply knowing *that* they are valued. Respectability is understood not only as a value but also as an encounter. Dress and demeanor matter in gauging how deviance is interpreted. Architecture and extravagance suggest respectability in some instances as much as professionalism and skill.[16]

Following in this line of research, the approach taken here emphasizes that respect and respectability are relational. They are best understood in terms of a contrast between what counts as respectable and what does not, either as the absence of respectability or as its antithesis. A respected person or group contrasts with one that is variously shifty, unrefined, wicked, or simply disgusting. The binaries of metaphor—high vs. low, light vs. dark, close vs. distant, and so on—come into play in making these contrasts. To say that someone is respectable necessitates asking, respected by whom and in comparison with what? There is in addition a performative aspect to the literal and figurative relationships involved. As Amy Laura Hall observes, "Respectability is not just a status; it is a performance, for an audience [and] these performances are ritualized in order for them to be correctly understood."[17]

Relational approaches that have gained popularity in studies of topics as diverse as economic sociology, microsociology, and the sociology of social networks derive from several theoretical traditions, perhaps the most notable of which is Émile Durkheim's emphasis on the categorical principles through which social life is organized and particularly the ritualization of the distinction between that which is sacred and that which is profane. In subsequent contributions by Mary Douglas, Clifford Geertz, Susanne K. Langer, Norman O. Brown, and Pierre Bourdieu, among others, relationality emphasized that categories exist only to the extent that they interact with one another. Words and numbers have meanings, Langer argued, "in terms of relationships, not of substance." Power lies in the interstices, Brown observed, and in the transgressions, as Douglas suggested.[18]

While the human cognition involved in constructing categories is important as a starting point, relational approaches emphasize the social interaction through which categories such as respect and disrespect are created and maintained. Categories in this understanding are more than mental schemas through which individuals organize information. They are part of a dynamic process in which people in real life relate to one another in ways that sometimes affirm social boundaries and at other times violate those boundaries. The boundary work includes social practices in which names and labels are communicated, idioms are deployed, and understandings about what is appropriate to do and say are negotiated. Investigating these practices necessitates paying close attention to the transactions involved and doing so without emphasizing social boundaries as reified pre-existing categories but by examining why the parties are interacting in the first place, what is at stake, and the scripts that explain how what they are doing is legitimate. Relational approaches, Mustafa Emirbayer argues, "reject the notion that one can posit discrete, pregiven units such as the individual or society as ultimate starting points . . . [persons] are inseparable from the transactional contexts within which they are embedded." And if that is true of persons, it also pertains to personal attributes.[19]

Approaching respectability from a relational perspective contrasts especially with viewing it as a variable. In that view, some people are simply respectable to a greater degree than others. The topic of interest is inequality, period. What are the social conditions that facilitate some people acquiring respectability while inhibiting others? The image is of a gradient along which autonomous individuals and groups can be placed, each striving to move up, attaining respectability that associates them with something already identifiable as the middle class. Relationships among the parties involved may be present but are incidental. A relational approach, in contrast, makes them central. Respectability is less of an attribute that someone simply has and more of an outcome implicitly negotiated in relationships that simultaneously constitute the meanings of middle-class refinement and middle-class moral expectations. Respectability is a process of compare and contrast. What counts as respectable behavior is defined by negative example. Those who are maligned as the "other"—as outsiders, misfits, ne'er-do-wells, defectives, degenerates—are as essential to the social construction of respectability as are its exemplars.

The relationality of respect and respectability can be examined at four levels that bring to focus distinct aspects of social life: practices, discourse, organizational arrangements, and machineries of enforcement. The boundary work involved in drawing distinctions between the "us" that manifests respectability in various ways and the "them" that perhaps even more clearly demonstrates what respectability is by its absence, I argue, is best understood through the multiple lenses that these aspects of social life illuminate.

Practices

Practices are routines of social interaction that include among other things physical and discursive acts that serve as markers of respectability. The literature on social practices emphasizes that they involve activities that occur repeatedly rather than on a one-off basis and for this reason can be examined in terms of recurring patterns. As the parties engage in a practice over time they adapt to changing circumstances and innovate and yet follow rules that may or may not be formalized, in the process developing skills that facilitate their interaction. Examples of practices include such activities as playing chess and practicing the piano, which illustrate activities that take place over time, involve rules, and require skill. Some discussions also regard such practices as the methods through which personal virtues, such as patience and courage, are learned.[20] A relational approach understands practices less in terms of patterns and skills and more as the unfolding interplay of which social interaction is composed: chess is less about the rules of the game and more about the moves and countermoves of the two contestants; piano playing is not only the solitary student repeating the scales but also the relationship between student and teacher and between performer and audience.

Practices establish the contexts in which respect and respectability are attended to and displayed, in the first instance, by circumscribing what Alfred Schutz termed "domains of relevance."[21] Master chess players earn the respect of other chess players by deploying innovative strategies. An amateur pianist may be judged to have performed respectably by doing about as well as others at the same level. But practices are interlaced, which suggests that respectability requires consistency across domains of relevance and boundary work to separate public and private domains. An otherwise respectable British college professor, for example, whose sideline was privately performing in pornographic films was a case in point. Practices also establish the social horizon in which activities relevant to respectability are defined. What counts as respectable and what contrasts with it differ from place to place and from time to time. Gaming at private clubs and on country estates was a mark of respectability for English aristocrats in the seventeenth century, for example, but by the end of the eighteenth century was widely criticized as a dissolute use of time.[22]

The social interaction of which practices are composed occurs both in concrete, face-to-face situations, such as chess matches and piano recitals, and in larger "imagined communities," such as between groups with different ethnic identities. Generalizations about who is respectable and who is not typically emphasize conformity, skill, or status. Respectability accrues from relationships in which the parties show by their behavior that they understand and accept how practices are conventionally performed, as in the case of people saying prayers together, paying respects at a funeral, or standing while the national anthem is being sung. It accrues in other settings as a spillover to the parties involved when skill is demonstrated, as in weather forecasters earning respectability as a profession by discussing scientific evidence of atmospheric conditions and by grassroots preachers gaining respectability by quoting scriptures in ancient languages. In other instances respectability depends less on conformity or skill than on status, as in social events hosted in lavish venues and requiring expensive attire.

How respect emerges varies from situation to situation. The interaction sometimes includes verbalizations that what is happening is respect, as when a meeting at which different opinions are discussed includes the statement, "With all due respect," or at a funeral when the statement, "I just wanted to pay my respects" occurs. Absent verbalizations, respect is the result of the parties interacting in ways that give off an impression that both parties take to be a satisfactory aspect of the interaction, even though conflict and disagreement may be present. Erving Goffman's discussion of sidewalk behavior in which strangers passing each other make eye contact at a certain distance and then avert their eyes, for example, suggests that respect is negotiated in the interaction in this small way. One of the parties would likely feel disrespected if the other hogged the center of the sidewalk.[23] Studies of turn taking in conversations suggest another way in which respect is negotiated. Turn taking follows patterns that conversation partners know in advance from many previous conversations; and yet each conversation establishes or fails to establish mutual respect in particular ways that vary with the topic under discussion, seating arrangements, whether a bystander is present, and the ages and genders of the conversationalists.[24]

The sense that the interaction has been satisfactory has less to do with having accomplished an instrumental goal, such as negotiating an agreeable price of a consumer good, than with having performed in ways that the parties communicated to each other fit their definitions of what should happen. Acquaintances meeting for coffee would likely be satisfied that respect was present if they exchanged pleasantries about the weather and acted interested in hearing each other's gossip. A meeting between an employee and employer would likely result in the two feeling that respect was present if the employee exhibited deference to the employer, perhaps by standing or waiting to be invited to sit, and if the employer was clear in giving instructions and refrained from displaying anger or annoyance. Bodies and the management of bodies, as these examples suggest, often play an important role in the relationships through which respect is constructed. Clothing, grooming, posture, eye contact, facial expressions, hand movements, and the positioning of bodies in relation to other people and objects, as well etiquette concerning the discussion of gender and sexuality, are among the ways in which studies suggest that respectability is negotiated. Something as seemingly minor as the cut of a broadcloth coat, for example, served as a marker of respectability among postbellum clerks seeking a satisfactory niche between store owners and customers.[25]

Describing someone or something as "respectable" implies generalizing beyond a particular situation to multiple situations and thus imputing that a person acting within the range of these situations has a reputation for respectable behavior. Respectability implies not only that particular people engage in respectable behavior but also that an element of reflexivity is present, such that certain ways of behaving are done with the explicit aim of demonstrating respectability and that the interaction includes a discussion about what constitutes being respectable. Reflexivity occurs with regard to particular acts as well as broad categories of activities. For example, a Facebook photo of a ninety-two-year-old woman kneeling in prayer that was shared 35,000 times and generated 320,000 comments and nearly a million "likes" included the statement that "every day before bedtime she will pray and thank God for another day," adding "she deserves our respect." What prompted such interest on Facebook can only be imagined, but the statement about respect invites thoughts about a specific kind of behavior that may be—and in the view of the person posting the photo should be—considered respectable.[26]

What discussions of respectability based on mutual assent miss is the frequency with which negative comparisons play a role in defining and communicating its meanings. Edward W. Morris's ethnographic study of a low-income rural high school, for example, found that students based their definitions of peers' respectability on small impressions gained from interaction during and after school, such as whose teeth were brushed, how recently clothing had been washed, and what brand the clothing was. Students drew inferences about fellow students' self-respect and made moral assessments about personal responsibility, attitudes toward school success, and whether they were desirable as friends on these grounds. Students who did not fit the profile of respectability in these terms were called "rutters," an insult that Morris discovered referred to the surname of an impoverished family in the area whom the community looked down on as not only poor but also morally deficient.[27]

Lorena Garcia's ethnography of a Puerto Rican neighborhood in West Chicago identified a similar practice of defining respectability among teenagers, in this case drawing a sharp distinction between "good girls" and "bad girls." As one example, Garcia reported that during an outing one afternoon at the neighborhood grocery store a girl named Magdalena appeared, was greeted by several friends who politely complimented her on her pregnancy, and asked how things were going; then when Magdalena left, one of the girls remarked, "Guess some females just don't know how to handle their business." This was one of many instances in which Garcia observed that "handling your business" was the key to being considered respectable among one's peers. As far as sex was concerned, respectability did not require chastity but did imply practicing safe sex to avoid STDs and pregnancy.[28]

A notable feature of the interaction Garcia observed is that the teens were friendly to Magdalena and offered the comment about her lack of respectability in her absence, rather than avoiding her. The interaction in this instance provided the occasion for the comment, which was made for the ethnographer's benefit as much as for the participants'. The participants affirmed their own respectability by criticizing Magdalena's failure to "handle business." Liza Steele's study of unwed teen mothers being assisted by Pentecostal churches in Rio revealed a similar way in which inclusion provided more of an occasion for demonstrating respectability than exclusion would have done. Although they disapproved of premarital sex, the Pentecostal pastors helped the unwed mothers, showing by doing so that the women were trying to be respectable and were in fact more respectable than the boyfriends who had abandoned them.[29]

The importance of interaction that publicly offers opportunities for participants to demonstrate their respectability while distancing themselves from less respectable others was also a prominent feature of Mitchell Duneier's *Slim's Table*, which described conversations at a café in a predominantly African American neighborhood in Chicago. Duneier observed that respectability was defined in small behavioral cues having to do with dress, demeanor, the length of time considered appropriate to occupy a table, and how loudly a person was supposed to speak. The interpretation of these cues as marks of respectability was communicated in critical comments about people who didn't fit or who didn't seem to understand how the participants thought about themselves.[30] These interpretations and the expressions of disapproval that went with them in turn provided a standard of respectability against which subsequent behavior was judged.

In my research on small towns I found another interesting dynamic at play. Residents naturally thought of themselves as respectable citizens and insisted that they appreciated living in a community where everyone respected everyone else; they did, however, identify "riff-raff" they did not respect, naming individuals who did not hold jobs, failed to keep their property looking neat, or were known to have come from bad families. Riff-raff tended to distance themselves or be excluded from community activities, but another category of people who were disrespected were rich people who were disliked because they "put on airs" or showed off or looked down on other people. As in Duneier's research, cafés were the places where respectability across status lines was negotiated. Ordinary townspeople said they felt respected when a rich person sat and engaged them in conversation at the café; they said they respected the rich people who did that; the rich people in turn said they did that on purpose in order to earn the fellow townspeople's respect. They also understood the importance of serving on committees, appearing to be working hard, and getting out of town if they wanted to do something extravagant.[31]

Discourse

The foregoing examples demonstrate that respectability is negotiated by what people say as well as by what they do. Discourse consists of dialogic constructions that are the mental, verbal, and written interpretations of social interaction that, among other things, sort activities, events, and people into categories that vary in terms of respectability, thus defining them and providing accounts that give these definitions legitimacy. "Dialogic," following Mikhail Bakhtin's use of the term, emphasizes the relationality of these interpretations and accounts. Although they consist of cognitive schemas that organize raw information into meaningful categories, their meaning occurs in relation to other categories. A face can be recognized as a friendly face, for example, not only by the brain's instantaneous organization of stimuli about the positioning of eyes and nose and mouth but also because of comparisons with facial patterns that are not friendly. Dialogic constructions moreover interpret relationships in terms of narratives that describe a temporal contrast between before and after as well as in symbols and myths that add moral valences beyond sheer description.[32]

The dialogue implied in this emphasis includes three manifestations of social interaction: first, the relationship between a concept and a contrasting concept, such as the relationship between "favorable" and "unfavorable"; second, the relationship between the speaker and a real or implied audience, such as political candidates to prospective voters or journalists to potential readers; and third, the relationship between persons about whom an account is given, such as a story about a boy who hit a girl or a nativist who discriminated against an immigrant. All three were evident, for example, in David Goodhew's study of working-class respectability in 1930s through early 1950s Johannesburg. Respectability was popularly defined in contrast with the concept of "rough," which meant anything from drinking to sexual unions outside of marriage to a lack of religiosity. Second, it was a topic of discussion between British and African residents and between different segments of the working class, the common denominator of which was that "respectability was defined against other people." And third, the discourse included narratives in which real-life characters played dialogic roles, such as in a nativity pageant involved Mary and Joseph being arrested by African police.[33]

Dialogic constructions provide shorthand ways of talking that summarize the normative evaluations interacting parties attach to their activities. "Respectable" itself may be the operative word, as in "she is a respectable member of the community," although "respectability" appears to be an abstraction supplied by external observers more often than the term that occurs naturally in social situations. The naturally occurring shorthand for respectability appears to develop through local usages that communicate shared understandings. "Handling their business" had meaning in West Chicago because people used the phrase frequently in everyday life. Similarly in Morris's study high school students' perceptions based on differences in grooming and clothing crystallized into "moral boundaries of social differentiation" that were as strong as or stronger than economic distinctions. As some students became stigmatized as "rutters" who "don't care" and "don't want to work," further distinctions were drawn between "good families" and "bad families." As one student explained, "Family name is everything here," meaning that in a rural community in which everyone claimed to know something about everyone else, being identified simply as a Smith or as one of the Johnsons, for example, signaled a lack of respectability.[34]

Whereas in the case of "good families" and "bad families" the normative contrast is specified in the language itself, the meanings of discursive distinctions are often more like the "rutters" example in being determined by social interaction. An example illustrating how this occurs in face-to-face situations is present in Vanesa Ribas's study of a slaughterhouse in which some of the cutting-floor employees were Hispanic and others were African American. When the word *moyo* came up in a conversation between Vincent and Rosa, it was immediately interpreted as a racial slur. As several other employees joined the conversation, though, it became clear that the word might or might not have that meaning, in which case it was important to clarify whether something disrespectful had been said. As an employee named Thomas explained, "You gotta look at the person and be, like, 'Hmm, you and me, are we cool?' I guess like when someone calls you a *moyo*, you need to check the person out and see in what way are they saying that word."[35] In larger settings in which face-to-face interaction is absent, such as media reports, similar ambiguities are of course frequently present, requiring that meanings be established through the narratives involved.

Bakhtin's interest in dialogism emphasized the flexibility through which the competent uses of speech could express multivocality, ambiguity, and nuance. Multivocality in particular opens numerous possibilities for interlocutors to assert distinctions while seeming not to or at least qualifying the assertion. In my research on late twentieth-century volunteering in the United States, for example, I found that volunteers presented themselves as respectable members of their community who deserved commendation for their activities but at the same time were somewhat self-interested like everyone else and did not want to appear immodest.[36] As another example, an analysis of late twentieth-century American evangelical apocalyptic fiction found "ostensible reticence" in texts' conspiricism, which made it possible to appear respectable, reasonable, and rational. In these instances the relationality of dialogic constructions softened the symbolic boundaries present.[37] Yet in practice many of the ways in which respectability is signaled appear to be crystallizations resembling the sharp binary contrasts that interested Claude Lévi-Strauss. The good is differentiated from the bad, the clean from the impure, and the raw from the cooked. A study of an impoverished community in Cape Town, South Africa, for example, found that respectability was constructed almost literally in these terms. To be respectable was to be cultured, formed, orderly, and decent; to be unrespectable was to be raw, unformed, disorderly, and vulgar.[38]

Dialogic constructions are the key to understanding how respectability can at once be the product of firsthand social interaction in local settings and something about which broad generalizations can be made, as in references to "middle-class respectability." Generalizations are transmitted from one situation to the next through the labels that group activities into categories and assign valences to these categories. Conversations replicate the labels in local settings. The media do so in wider settings. The making of middle-class respectability in nineteenth-century America was clearly a process in which newspapers, periodicals, sermons, and schoolbooks played an important part. During the twentieth century radio and television increasingly became the media through which respectability was defined. Whether it was television or insecurities driven by the Cold War or the rising numbers of families with small children, the 1950s has been regarded as a time in which respectability gained or regained new importance. As Beth Bailey observes, "A great many Americans saw respectable behavior as the foundation of a moral, civil, and legitimate social order. And a great many Americans saw respectability as the *natural* price of admission to the expanding American middle class."[39] The terms in which respectability was defined were perhaps not so different from what they had been in the past, particularly with regard to sex, work, and parental responsibilities, but the discussion played in wider venues because of mass communications. And it was as relational as ever, with good behavior being defined through highly publicized counterexamples. The predominantly white middle class defined its respectability in contrast with the poor, African Americans, atheists, and the occasional musician or movie star who lived promiscuously.

In many cases the dialogic constructions reinforce the practices, accentuating the distinctions that are present in social interaction, but instances also occur in which the practices soften or subvert the cultural distinctions. Grace Yukich's study of the Catholic Worker House in New York City, for example, provided an illustration of a group that defined its respectability by drawing critical distinctions with other groups such as secular social service providers, the Roman Catholic hierarchy, Wall Street banks, the military, and defense contractors. The group's antiwar advocacy and efforts to assist the poor were practices that reinforced its internal solidarity and distinctive sense of itself. However, the group also thought of itself as an inclusive organization that wanted to be respectful toward everyone. Yukich argued that the group's small rituals were how it maintained this conviction of itself as inclusive. Members shared Holy Communion with anyone who would take it, physically embraced the strangers who participated, shared food and clothing, and spoke often of conversations they may have had in which they found common ground with people with whom they otherwise disagreed.[40]

Organizational Arrangements

Besides the practices and discourses through which respect and respectability are defined—and which often are most evident in local settings—organizational arrangements structure where that interaction takes place and what kinds of interaction can routinely happen in those places. Organizations are relevant to questions about respectability in two ways: first, organizations became known as places in which respectable behavior occurs and thus confer respectability on the people and activities that are associated with them (hospitals and universities would be examples); and second, organizations solidify the distinctions and in many cases increase the distance separating people and activities that are considered respectable from those who are not (as a resident of one nineteenth-century town recalled of the community's slum, "there . . . lived people of drunken, worthless and disreputable lives who were shunned by their respectable neighbors and with whom little or no intercourse was possible").[41]

While the symbolic boundary separating respectable insiders from outsiders may be reinforced informally through discursive distinctions and patterns of association, these patterns often become more salient, visible, and enduring when organizations develop around them. Organizations are the reason people congregate in certain places and interact with some people more than others. They compete with other organizations by proclaiming competitors' products and personnel to be inferior. They formalize the rules about who is expected to interact with whom and under what circumstances, sometimes requiring or encouraging members to abide by the rules for the sake of enhancing the organization's respectability as well as their own (dress codes, decorum at meetings, expectations about the kinds of affect that should be displayed, and voluntary participation in community service would be examples). The rules not only specify what can and cannot be done but also provide accounts of why they are legitimate, such as in arguments that segregated lunch counters are the best way to prevent racial conflict or that separating first-class from coach passengers is necessary for airlines to earn the highest profits. Organizations are one of the settings in which rituals of inclusion and exclusion routinely occur as well. The rituals make public what otherwise might remain private, giving newspapers a reason to report, for example, that so-and-so has joined the firm of such-and-such. Organizations also perpetuate definitions of respectability in their role as preservers of collective memory—telling school children about the atrocities committed against their ancestors by foreigners or reminding a firm's newcomers about an incident in which a member of a minority group caused trouble.[42]

The extent to which simply being part of an organization confers respectability is suggested in comparisons with those who are not members of organizations. A study of peddling among the deaf, for example, found that peddlers were considerably more likely to be stigmatized by other deaf people than counterparts employed in ordinary businesses or working at organizations for the deaf. The reason was that peddlers' status was ambiguous as to whether they were earning too much or too little, working too hard or too little, truly deaf or not, and perhaps conveying negative signals about deafness to the public. The stigma attached to peddling suggested that respectability may be of particular concern among groups that are already subject to marginalization because of race, gender, social class, or disabilities, and that persons are more likely to be respected if what they do takes place in a space set aside for that purpose and is understood to put constraints on moral or potentially immoral behavior.[43]

Research on churches, temples, and other places of worship shows the several ways in which organizational arrangements dramatize particular meanings of respectability. Max Weber's essay on Protestant sects, which was informed largely by his visit with relatives in North Carolina, emphasized that ascetic Protestantism did more than simply encourage believers to work hard and be thrifty (as he argued in *The Protestant Ethic and the Spirit of Capitalism*); it also banded people together in small congregations where they were accountable to one another. They were respectable in one another's eyes, in this sense, and being respectable was backed by vouchers of sorts that they could use in applying for loans and conducting business. "What was decisive," he wrote, "was the fact that a fairly reputable sect would only accept for membership one whose conduct made him appear to be morally qualified beyond doubt."[44] Not only was respectability a condition of membership, but also the fact that people who considered one another respectable came together regularly for meetings, which provided occasions for publicly affirming that common identity. In addition, coming together meant physical separation from nonmembers. As S. D. Clark observed in studying Protestant sects in Canada in the late 1930s, "Respectability was a condition of membership in the church, and respectability was maintained by ignoring undesirable characters of the population. The puritan taboos of Protestantism, particularly, prohibited any recognition of the fact that such people as slum dwellers, criminals, or prostitutes existed in the community."[45]

Subsequent research has added nuances to these observations. The boundary separating "us" and "them" is also dramatized by religious organizations' methods of engaging with "them." Omar M. McRoberts's study of African American churches in Boston, for example, found that members' sense of respectability was defined in contrast with "the street," but that the reality of the street was affirmed in one instance by a kind of embattled avoidance of it, in another by limited engagement with it through service, and in another by evangelistic recruitment from it into the church.[46] Yet another mode of interaction surfaced in Allison Schnable's study of youth at an African American church in Trenton, New Jersey. Youth members of the choir were incorporated into the church's traditions, history, and leadership structure through the lyrics and by singing together, having respectability conferred on them in these ways, but meetings also spread that self-conception into other aspects of the youths' lives as they ate meals at the church, played, and interacted with grownups.[47]

If churches—not to mention other examples such as clubs, lodges, fraternal associations, and professional societies—are organizations that aim to confer respectability, other organizations, whether by design or in terms of unintended consequences, serve as places of disrespect. The asylums, hospitals, and houses of correction established in the seventeenth and eighteenth centuries were such places—places that "confined," as Michel Foucault observed, "the debauched, spendthrift fathers, prodigal sons, blasphemers, men who 'seek to undo themselves,' libertines."[48] They separated the people whose ways of thinking, ideas, and morals did not fit with respectable people. Confinement set them physically apart and made them more visibly the examples of what to avoid.

Even that was something organizers understood could be managed to some extent, though. Against the perception that poverty and debauchery inevitably went hand in hand, organizers of a charitable organization in 1813 named it the New York Association for the Relief of Respectable, Aged, Indigent Females, proclaiming it to be for women "who once lived respectably." A decade later New York's Asylum for Lying-In Women offered respectable but destitute women a place to avoid contact with degraded almshouse women. These and similar early nineteenth-century asylums held Bible studies and organized sewing circles as activities aimed at reinforcing clients' image of respectability.[49]

While studies of churches and asylums show how respectability is shaped by structured interaction within organizations, other research demonstrates the importance of *where* organizations are located. Brian Hoffman's study of early twentieth-century nudist camps offers an interesting illustration. Nudism was hardly a promising venture in that regard because of its sexual connotations. Nor was it obvious that a location in rural Indiana would help. Yet when Alois and Lorena Knapp decided to start a nudist camp in 1933, they selected a site near Roselawn, Indiana. Deflecting criticism was uppermost in their minds. The site was Lorena's family farm. She'd grown up in the community and figured she could deal better with people she knew than with people she didn't. The farm's isolation was important but so was the prevailing sentiment that rural areas were more wholesome than places like Chicago and New York. Nudism, the Knapps claimed, was really just about being healthy and enjoying nature, and if that were not enough, they insisted that the camp's members be married, hold jobs, and attend church.[50]

Hoffman's study suggests that connotations about respectability are sometimes associated with particular kinds of places—for example, rural places—because of the interactions and organizations perceived to exist in those places. The Knapps may have considered it more respectable to be in a rural area than in a city, while residents of Chicago and New York probably would have thought the opposite. The dynamics of compare and contrast are of course evident. The association of places with respectability also is the basis for asking about people that are between places: the "middleman," brokers, mediators, traders, itinerant preachers, the homeless, and hoboes, among others. Being without a place is necessarily to be marginalized, not as a true outsider who occupies some other space, but more as what Georg Simmel described as the "stranger," who is both near and remote because of physically being in a place but not belonging there. Simmel argued that the stranger experiences freedom and is often able to assess situations more objectively than true insiders can but is also likely to feel estranged.[51] Whether the stranger is considered respectable is harder to know because respectability is again relational. Traders and itinerant preachers are likely to benefit by their relationship as representatives of respected organizations. Hoboes and the homeless are not. Sherri Broder's study of the urban poor in nineteenth-century Philadelphia, for example, found considerable variation in social reformers' views of the poor based on the kinds of relationships the poor were assumed to have. Tramps were among the least respected: they were men with no attachments to families, jobs, or homes. Prostitutes were disrespected by the location of their work ("street trades") and their illicit relationships with customers. Unfit mothers were disrespected because they did not perform responsibly in the role they had, whereas "fallen women" continued to benefit to some extent from the respectable families from which they had fallen.[52]

The stranger who is present in a place and yet remains marginal poses a larger question about organizations' roles in defining respectability. On the one hand, organizations harden the boundaries separating "us" and "them" by formalizing the distinction, creating physical separation, and setting up standards of inclusion. Educational requirements, entrance exams, admissions committees, certificates, and identity cards—the grist of what Randall Collins termed "the credential society"—all represent these organizational gatekeeping mechanisms.[53] For those who qualify, respectability is partly defined by having qualified. On the other hand, organizations are processes in which the criteria of inclusion and exclusion are continuously modified as organizations adapt to changing conditions. Changes in the etiquette of corporate management styles, including such matters as work schedules, vacation time, the kinds of jokes considered appropriate to tell, and how much emotion to display, as larger numbers of women have become corporate executives would be an example. Such changes moreover evoke complicated responses, as a survey of office workers in which a significantly higher proportion of women than men reported having cried at work during the past year—but were also more likely to disapprove of doing—demonstrated.[54]

Like strangers, persons on the margins of organizations, especially when the boundaries of inclusion and exclusion are being contested, become the focus of what is considered respectable and whether they are doing an appropriate job of upholding it or being too lenient or too strict. It is as if their own status as insiders or outsiders is precarious.[55] In *Inventing the Feeble*

Mind James W. Trent, Jr., for example, shows how the superintendents of asylums for the feeble minded, reformers, public officials, and clergy were cast into prominent and controversial roles during discussions of what feeblemindedness was, whether the feebleminded could be considered a distinct category at all or were on a continuum with everyone else, how they should be treated, and how they were in fact perceived and assisted. Questions about respectability, such as whether respected families could have feebleminded children and if so why, whether providing financial support for asylums was something respectable members of the community should do, and whether superintendents were abusing their authority or behaving respectably all became important aspects of the public discussion surrounding asylums for the feebleminded.[56]

Enforcement Machineries

Enforcement machineries are the arrangements through which power is applied to social behavior. Coercive power ultimately rests with the state, through which laws are passed, regulations applied, taxes levied, and punishments inflicted. Enforcement machineries include noncoercive enactments of power as well, ranging from the power of employers to hire and fire employees to the power of parents to reward and punish children. Enforcement machineries strengthen the distinction between those considered respectable and those considered disrespectable in a number of ways. They shape the contexts in which the distinction becomes important, for example, by holding elections that prompt groups to take different sides and engage in mutual mudslinging. They sometimes provoke violence in the name of protecting respectable people—the refined, the native born, the defenders of freedom, the law abiding—against intruders. They can identify certain categories of people as worthy of political rights and resources and others as unworthy, thus doing the political work, as Bourdieu put it, of "imposing a vision of divisions."[57]

The state's coercive power is frequently a factor in the sharpening of social boundaries that define respectability as a comparison between those on one side and those on the other. Andreas Wimmer has emphasized this role in discussing the making and unmaking of ethnic boundaries, arguing that ethnic identities are often nonexistent or unimportant until they become salient because of political action. The actions through which salience is increased include the formation of political parties that compete by attempting to cater to different ethnic factions, educational policies that exclude persons speaking a minority language, and differential suppression of dissident movements based in particular locations or grounded in different religions. Wimmer observes that ethnic minorities' efforts to overcome marginalization often include attempts to regain respect through such cultural means as having their heritage honored in national museums and their language taught in schools.[58]

Enforcement brings squarely into the picture the extent to which respectability informally supports—and is supported by—mechanisms of oppression. Slavery, apartheid, serfdom, and debt peonage are durable inequalities maintained in part by expectations demanding—often on pain of violence—that the oppressed pay obeisance to the oppressors in deportment and manners of speech, showing that they "know their place," and that respectability be upheld in ways that curtail indolence, intemperance, and sexual immorality. Respectability specified in these ways is said to be good for the oppressed as well as for those in control and is defended in terms of moral uplift and upward mobility. As such, it constitutes a form of "emulation," in Charles Tilly's terms, that serves as a template for accepted behavior and valorizes norms present among those at the top while denigrating the disorderliness that may be inescapable for those at the bottom.[59]

Research on these coercively supported forms of oppression demonstrate the frequency with which discussions of respectability accompany the otherwise heavy-handed actions of states. Hannah Arendt's discussion of British colonialism, for example, suggested that colonial administrators earned the respect of their superiors by behaving aloof and dispassionately toward their subjects because this style of administration was considered rational, economically sound, selflessly sacrificial, and as such the best safeguard against corruption and the best protector of human dignity.[60] Mona Oikawa's study of Canada's internment of citizens of Japanese origin during World War II, as another example, shows that the Canadian government upheld the notion that the Canadian people were more "respectable" than other nations' citizens, especially those in the United States, because the internment was done more slowly and involved fewer people, which made it more "humane" and thus legitimate.[61] The history of lynching in the United States, as yet another example, provides numerous instances in which perpetrators' claims to respectability—and to be upholding respectability—allowed them to escape the punishment they would otherwise have received.[62]

A relational approach further suggests the importance of considering the effects of enforcement that stem from individuals and groups being deprived of the resources needed to behave in ways that meet expectations about respectability. Goffman's discussion of mental hospital patients being deprived of the clean clothing, grooming equipment, and freedom of bodily movement to appear respectable constitutes an extreme example. Susan Crawford Sullivan's study of mothers living in poverty who did not attend church because they did not have the appropriate clothing to appear respectable was another case in point. While coercion was not direct, as it was for Goffman's subjects, its role was indirect through the fiscal policies and welfare regulations that affected the women's lives.[63]

Transgression

A remaining consideration is what to make of the person or group who transgresses the lines that separate the respectable from the nonrespectable. These are the people who challenge the conventional wisdom: instead of rising into the ranks of respectability, they question the meaning of respectability. Many instances of such persons exist: the Lone Ranger who rides into the sunset, the renegade who voluntarily leaves town, the charismatic leader, the reformer, the hipster, the émigré, the person who simply picks up and leaves. Russell Banks says the only version of the American Dream in which he believes is flight.[64]

Scandalous transgressions, as Ari Adut calls them, "consist of willful wrongdoings that, when made public, make the transgressor look like a bad person."[65] They differ from scandals that arise unintentionally on the part of the transgressor from sheer incompetence, such as a doctor who operates on the wrong patient or a lawyer who falls asleep during a trial. Scandals of this kind are especially shocking when they occur among otherwise respectable people: more shocking than when a petty thief bungles a burglary. Willfully committed transgressions, as in the case of a respected attorney who commits fraud, pose additional questions about why such acts occur and whether steps need to be taken to protect respectability. Besides the scandalous transgressions that put the transgressor in ill repute are the ones that might be termed heroic. Heroic transgressions intentionally violate the boundaries of respectability in the name of some higher value. They are the charismatic leaders, the revolutionaries, and the prophets—the "supernormal deviants" who exhibit unusual imagination and are often admired as larger-than-life mythic figures but are often criticized for their violations as well.[66]

The most likely result of heroic transgression is the further dramatization of the distinction between respectability and nonrespectability. The Lone Ranger temporarily dramatizes the struggle between good and evil but leaves the settlers to contend with the next round of villains on their own. The reason the distinction is dramatized lies in the process of "mythification" through which the figure of a larger-than-life character is created. An ordinary trapper who does not fit neatly into any of the established categories can over time become legendary. The itinerant peddler who quietly transports goods between farms and cities and in so doing quietly transgresses the cultural boundary separating the two can evolve into an entrepreneur or a sharper who cleverly violates customary standards of business. The sharper does not subvert the conventional meanings of respectability but reinforces them by making it all the more important to be vigilant.

But transgression is also the source from which subversion arises. The making of American middle-class respectability consisted not only of denigrating those at the margins who seemed inferior but also of challenging the pretension of those at the top who claimed respectability as their exclusive preserve. The way this happened repeatedly was by challenging the social horizon in which respectable behavior was considered to be relevant. Elites that cornered the meaning of refinement fell before arguments that it was rather "the people" whose homespun ways more truly exemplified virtue.

In the end, transgression comes full circle to the point that respectability is at heart relational. Its meanings are negotiated in social interaction through which agreements and disagreements occur about what should and should not be done if a person or group is to enjoy the respect of significant others. The lines separating the respected "us" from the disrespected "them" are not fixed. They are nevertheless not entirely situational as well. They take on meaning as they are upheld and as distinctions are affirmed. They are also upheld as they are transgressed. While generalizations about respectability refer in many instances to patterns of behavior evident among large swathes of population and apparently present over long periods of time, closer inspection demonstrates that it is constructed in practices and discourse and in conjunction with organizational arrangements and enforcement machineries. An understanding of respectability as it may pertain to social classes and particular places requires examining especially how it is constructed through relationships with those who serve as negative examples.

CHAPTER TWO

Worked as a Huckster

MORAL CONNOTATIONS
OF PLACELESS LABOR

SAMUEL M. HUEY WAS SEVENTEEN when his brother John joined the Union Army. John was twenty-two when he died. The Hueys might have sided with the South when the southern states seceded in 1861. Before they moved to southern Illinois, they lived in South Carolina and Kentucky. However, the brothers belonged to a religious community that opposed slavery. John enlisted in Company A of the 31st Illinois Volunteer Infantry Regiment on August 21, 1861. The regiment participated in Ulysses S. Grant's "first great victory" at Fort Donelson, Tennessee, on February 16, 1862. More than four thousand soldiers were killed or injured. "So thickly was the battlefield strewn with the dead and wounded," an officer recalled, "that he could have traversed acres of it, taking almost every step upon a prostrate body." John was one of the wounded, dying two weeks later.[1]

Samuel joined the same regiment as his brother, enlisting on January 7, 1864, and mustering out on July 19, 1865. The regiment's action included the Siege of Vicksburg, the Atlanta Campaign, and Sherman's March to the Sea. The conditions under which the soldiers fought caused nearly as many casualties as the fighting did. Huey contracted typhoid fever in July 1864 and spent much of the summer and fall with hundreds of other soldiers too ill to fight or badly wounded at a field hospital in Marietta, Georgia. "Day after tomorrow will be two months I am in this darned hospital," a fellow soldier wrote. "A lot of the time here I have had the blues and still I am among the lucky ones to get away at all. On the hill the other side the railroad hundreds of poor fellows lay under the little mounds newly made. They will never answer to bugle call anymore and to them all troubles in this world are over."[2]

When the war was over Huey became one of the tens of thousands of men and women who earned meager livings as hucksters and peddlers. They peddled farm produce in towns, brought town goods to farms, and went from place to place selling books, maps, jewelry, newspaper subscriptions, and sewing machines. Although most of them were literate, they were rarely well educated, and only a few left written traces of their activities. Compared to the large numbers of Americans who farmed, operated stores, and worked in factories, their ranks were small. They were diverse in the goods they sold, geographically scattered, and more mobile than most of their fellow citizens. They were interesting enough to have made cameo appearances in widely divergent literary accounts. They appeared in Aesop's Fables, in Balzac's story of the old Neapolitan huckster, as the humble huckster of thread and cotton handkerchiefs in *Crime and Punishment*, as Professor Marvel in the *Wizard of Oz*, in theologian Charles Hodge's commentaries on the Bible, and in nineteenth-century arithmetic books. Hucksters and peddlers nevertheless have been relatively neglected in historical treatments.[3]

Huey began huckstering in 1868. He'd spent the fall after his discharge recovering from a severe case of inflammatory rheumatism and then helped on his father's farm, working with his father and a younger brother. In 1867 he and a cousin traveled to Missouri, worked on a farm for a month, and went on to Kansas, walking part way and working as farm laborers. Back in Illinois, he canvassed for books and took classes in hopes of finishing high school. In 1869, suffering again from chronic rheumatism, he picked and peddled strawberries. The following year he and another cousin tried traveling the countryside soliciting orders for maps and pictures.[4]

Huey's career as a huckster was occasioned by a farm accident. In 1867 he worked during the summer as part of a threshing crew, going from farm to farm threshing almost three times as many bushels of wheat than had been grown in the area in 1850. Crude wooden, horse-driven threshing machines had been in use in Illinois since the 1830s, but at the end of the Civil War larger machines costing as much as $500 came into use as farmers planted more acres in wheat and shipped grain over longer distances by rail. Threshing machines, operating as they did with rapidly moving exposed parts that could not be immediately stopped, were dangerous enough that states passed laws requiring boxed coverings over some of the parts and inventors filed patents promising to enhance safety. Nevertheless, newspapers carried frequent stories of farmers, farm laborers, and children being killed or losing limbs in threshing machine accidents. Huey's job included tending the team of horses, measuring the grain, and oiling the machine. While brushing dust off the machine's boxing, his left hand was caught in the cogwheels. The badly mangled hand had to be amputated.[5]

During the next two decades, Huey's itinerant peddling continued. In 1870 he journeyed again to Kansas and found part-time work as a farm laborer. He worked the following year as a schoolteacher and canvassed for book subscriptions. In 1872 he returned to Illinois, took odd jobs, and once again worked at canvassing. Marrying in 1873, he and his bride took over the family farm from his father, who died that year. In 1878 they migrated to Kansas and after six months settled on a farm in the center of the state. Over the next decade, with farming barely supporting their growing family, Huey peddled fuel to farmsteads, canvassed for books, and took orders for fruit trees. In 1890, when he applied for a Civil War pension, his acquaintances knew him as a person engaged in light employment, part-time farming, and huckstering.[6]

The social role of the huckster offers an exceptional opportunity to probe the moral ambiguities of American culture as the nation transitioned from an agrarian to an urban economy. In simplest terms, hucksters occupied a liminal space that was neither fully rural nor fully urban, connecting the two as they passed goods from one to the other. They served as a significant commercial link antecedent to the establishment of large-scale wholesale and retail markets. As important as this role was economically, its cultural significance was equally important. Hucksters were the marginal figures who stood in the interstices of established cultural categories. Neither fish nor fowl, they served as moral curiosities by their differences from what a good respectable American was supposed to be, whether that person lived in the country or in a city. By their own account and in the many accounts that contemporaries gave of them, hucksters transgressed familiar occupational and spatial categories and in so doing dramatized both in negation and in affirmation the shifting meaning of those categories.

In their coming and going, hucksters were both known and unknown. They played a familiar enough role in peddling and canvassing that the people with whom they interacted did so on the basis of previous encounters and neighborhood gossip. At the same time, hucksters were here today and gone tomorrow, unlike the resident that could be identified at a fixed location in the cultural landscape. Existing as they did on the margins of ready categorization, they became objects of discussion as observers imagined who they were and what they did.

Hucksters rarely provided the occasion for nineteenth-century Americans to draw sharp contrasts between entire categories of the population. The cultural work in which they participated was unlike the stark divisions that separated white Americans and black Americans. Hucksters did not become the targets of sweeping categorical distinctions of the kind that marked southerners in the mind of northerners or Indians in the minds of settlers. They were instead like the cowboy, newsboy, barmaid, siren, or tramp about which individual attributions of virtue and vice could be discussed. In that, they contributed to Americans' sense of the individual as the defining feature of moral evaluation.

The most large-scale division in which hucksters figured was the contrast between country life and city life. Although the differences between those who lived on farms or in small towns and those who lived in cities was a topic of frequent discussion, the fact that it was never an easy distinction to make cast hucksters in a mediating role. They stood out because they brought rural goods to the city and city goods to the farms. They became not only a management problem in terms of how to organize markets but also a cultural opportunity for considering what it meant to be a good person in rural America and a person of worth in urban America.

Hucksters deviated from the conventional expectation that people could be known and identified—placed—by their attachment to a specific geographic location. Despite, or perhaps because of, the fact that America was a country populated by people on the move, the people who moved, following the frontier into the Midwest and beyond, were called settlers. The presumption was that they came to settle the land. And even though many of them moved on, either because they failed or because they could sell their land at a profit, it was their place in the land that defined them. Their neighbors knew where they lived, what they did there, and how to find them.

Americans' geographic placement was shaped by the fact that land was mostly what the emerging nation had to offer. Surveyors staked out townships and divided them into sections, further divided them into quarter sections, and homesteaders took occupancy of the quarter sections by living on them, improving them, fencing them, and gaining the right of patent, or by purchasing the land from previous settlers. Towns proliferated as entrepreneurs divided space into lots and sold them to merchants and prospective residents. To be a merchant was to have a store at a particular location, preferably on Main Street and near the town square.

Hucksters lacked the spatial anchoring that defined those who farmed and operated shops. "There are many such beings in our land who wander about as if belonging nowhere and as if the Almighty had sown and then forgotten them," one account of hucksters declared. "They seem like the sea gulls . . . that roam about without ever resting."[7]

Hucksters differed from peddlers in this regard. Hucksters' movement typically occurred within a relatively delimited space. If they grew their own produce and a family member who worked as a huckster took it to market, at least the family and the source of the produce were known. That was true as well of hucksters who routinely trucked produce to a nearby market house or carried it from there to town residents by cart. And yet merchants' criticisms of hucksters emphasized the value of having a fixed location. Peddlers are "nobody from nowhere," one critic observed. The contrast was with the "home merchant" who sits in one place and could say, "I have been here a long time, and everybody knows me."[8]

Peddlers' circuits were larger than the typical huckster's. Peddlers appeared less often or at least less regularly. And that made them more mysterious. Nobody knew quite who they were or where they had been when they were absent. Uncertain that the peddler might ever return, residents interacted with

them cautiously. Perhaps they were swindlers or thieves. If a crime was reported, gossip spread that perhaps the peddler was to blame. Peddlers were
sometimes suspected of engaging in witchcraft and casting spells. The mysterious goods in their bags might not be good at all. "The peddler was often
chased and hooted at in the streets," a story that circulated in several versions
explained. "When the children pelted him with stones, he would whip up his
pony and make off so meekly that everyone knew he had a bad conscience."9

Hucksters and peddlers were thus the strangers who nevertheless were familiar enough to be objects of fascination. They existed, as it were, outside the
gates but in close enough proximity that they were as much like those inside
the gates as those on the margins. The familiar stranger in literary depictions
and popular culture is a person whose identity and activities require consideration because of their differences as well as their similarities. As a person
of opprobrium, a huckster's faults and failings were a reminder of the moral
standards communities held dear. What observers said they disliked about
hucksters was an indication of what they did like about themselves and their
neighbors. As a person sometimes admired, a huckster's accomplishments occasioned commentary about the changes and challenges communities were
facing as well.

Hucksters stood out from the crowd in several interesting ways. They were
just different enough from rural residents to show what *was* expected of rural
Americans and different enough from city residents to provide that contrast as
well. These were topics not merely of descriptive interest but of moral concern
insofar as they dealt with questions about honesty, trustworthiness, character,
and square dealing. Why hucksters could not be trusted offered instruction in
how important trust was and how it was understood. As transients, hucksters
demonstrated the particular extent to which trustworthiness depended on
geographic stability. In addition, hucksters evoked commentary about proper
behavior for men and women, providing a distinct angle on nineteenth-
century understandings of gender. Hucksters played a part in broader discussions of moral character as well, especially in the clues that emerged in discussions of the nuanced public mannerisms through which something as deeply
interior as a person's character could be discerned.

The fundamental characteristic of huckstering was its ambiguity. Although
huckstering was a word widely used to describe a certain kind of work that
resembled but was not quite the same as peddling and canvassing, the activities to which it referred were so varied that the term in fact referred to
many different things and was used differently in different places. It was an
old term, much older than America, which meant that its origins and exact
meanings were obscure. One interpretation suggested it derived from early
Dutch or German words similar to hawking or haggling. Another interpretation associated it with the act of squatting or of carrying something on
one's hip. An 1865 edition of *The Slang Dictionary* noted that huckster had

in earlier times carried meanings similar to cad, chap, fogger, and fogey, all of which referred to persons of low or questionable social standing. Another source suggested that huckster was the modern derivative of the Anglo-Saxon hawkestere, which referred to the female companion of a hawker who, like a hawk, went around the country dealing in petty goods. Some authorities believed the "ster" ending implied contempt, as in "gamester," "punster," "trickster," and "shyster."[10]

Apart from its etymological ambiguities, huckstering evolved in different ways in different circumstances. Hucksters in nineteenth-century cities such as Philadelphia and Baltimore collected produce at markets and went from door to door reselling the produce. Hucksters in small towns typically purchased fruit and vegetables from local farmers or grew their own produce and sold it directly to townspeople. Hucksters who drove wagons in rural circuits to purchase produce from farmers typically brought town goods to sell to the farmers in return. But hucksters invented their own practices based on what worked or did not work in particular locations.

An early twentieth-century agricultural pamphlet illustrated the myriad ways in which huckstering could be practiced. A huckster could be an independent traveling peddler. A huckster could purchase a load of produce, haul it to the nearest city, and sell it house to house or to city grocers. A huckster could be an employee of a grocery store, trading merchandise for produce. A huckster could work for a produce wholesaler, working on salary or commission. And a huckster could be a kind of wholesaler who collected produce in small towns and shipped it by rail to cities. The pamphlet's author observed all these patterns among hucksters in Indiana and southern Michigan dealing in eggs.[11]

While huckstering usually involved farm produce, peddling more often pertained to manufactured goods. Peddlers appear in fiction and historical accounts with greater frequency and in a wider variety of locations than hucksters. They walk the countryside, hunker on cold mornings in crowded city streets, and peddle everything from pencils to washing machines. They are old, young, male, female, poor, rich, maimed, able bodied, and nearly everything in between. Canvassers and traveling agents resembled hucksters and peddlers in variety and itinerancy. They solicited for newspapers, publishers, and companies that conducted business by taking orders and selling on commission.

Hucksters, peddlers, and canvassers prefigure the modern era of salesmanship, advertising, and consumption. They can easily be taken as remnants of a simpler time that for better or worse signaled all that was to come. They can just as easily represent the struggling but adventuresome nineteenth-century entrepreneur who rises from rags to riches. And yet, as harbingers of modern consumerism or exemplars of the American dream, these handy depictions are too linear. They tell a story of straightforward ascent from past to present, from old to new, but miss the cultural significance of lived experience along the way.

Antebellum Huckstering

Huckstering in colonial America followed patterns in England that had been in existence since the fourteenth century, if not before. As market towns were established, hucksters functioned as petty traders linking peasant producers to villagers. Besides meat and vegetables, hucksters supplied grain, flour, eggs, butter, and cheese and sometimes specialized in bread, wine, ale, and used clothing. The line separating hucksters from chandlers, butchers, brewers, and dealers in petty merchandise of other kinds was often unclear. Typically hucksters were excluded from the rights enjoyed by burgesses, and village ordinances restricted their activities. Although they rarely earned more than meager incomes, huckstering included both men and women who secured goods from wholesalers at a discount and resold them at a profit. By the sixteenth century peripatetic traders peddled goods door to door in larger towns and traveled circuits among smaller villages.[12]

In the American colonies specified market days and market places preceded huckstering as the arrangement through which townspeople purchased produce from surrounding farms. Councilors in 1656 of what would be New York City observed that farmers were bringing a wide variety of "veal, pork, butter, cheese, turnips, roots, straw, and other products of the land for the purpose of selling them" but at such varied times and places that residents frequently did not know that goods were available and farmers frequently lost revenue from unsold goods and spoilage. To remedy the problem, the councilors decreed that Saturday of each week would be the official market day and that the market would be held at the Strand. That ordinance remained in effect until 1676, when a second marketplace was added, and Wednesday was declared as a second weekly market day in 1679. A 1683 ordinance that prohibited the sale of stale victuals also banned hucksters from purchasing goods from the market houses with the intent of monopolizing them for resale at higher prices.[13] By 1738 the city had five market houses open every day from sunrise to sunset except Sunday. Hucksters were prohibited from purchasing produce at the market houses before noon so that housekeepers could "pay moderate rates for their provisions, upon pain that every such huckster and retailer shall for every time offending herein forfeit ten shillings."[14]

Philadelphia's market house, which opened in 1728, had thirty-two numbered stalls leased on an annual basis to butchers and was open on Wednesdays and Saturdays. Its regulations stipulated that "no hucksters buy more than shall be judged necessary to last their family from market day to market day before our town clock strikes ten [after which they were] at liberty to buy as much as they please." The ordinance further required that the stalls be kept "sweet and clean" and that meat "unfit for Christians be thrown in the river."[15]

New Jersey's provincial government passed a law requiring anyone traveling from house to house as a peddler, hawker, or "petty chapman" to (a) be an

FIGURE 1. *First Market House*, St. Louis, 1812, showing huckster wagons.
Drawn under the direction of Fred L. Billon. Library of Congress
Prints and Photographs Division, Washington, DC.

inhabitant of the province, (b) obtain a license from the governor, and (c) post
a bond of twenty to fifty pounds with the county clerk. Anyone peddling without a license would be fined forty shillings, and anyone without a certificate
from the county clerk would be fined twenty shillings. The problems these
laws aimed to solve included peddlers giving false identities, absconding with
their masters' goods or money, drinking excessively, and selling unsuspecting
housekeepers faulty goods. New York's officials found it necessary to take New
Jersey's law a step further, publishing the names of peddlers who were appropriately licensed. Boston disciplined unlicensed peddlers simply by setting
them in the stocks, exposed to pelting from anyone so inclined.[16]

Boston's north market house was in operation by the early 1730s, and its
better-known market house, named for its donor Peter Faneuil, was built in
1741 and rebuilt in 1762 after a fire destroyed it. The first market house in
Newport, Rhode Island, was in business by 1732, and its Old Brick Market
was completed in 1772. Providence's opened a year later. Smaller eighteenth-
century communities typically constructed market houses as soon as the population's size warranted something more than temporary stalls and tables in
the town square on market days. By 1786 market houses existed in places as
varied as Albany, New York; Middletown, Delaware; New Haven, Connecticut; Alexandria, Virginia; Fredericktown, Maryland; Carlisle, Pennsylvania;
Charleston, South Carolina; and Augusta, Georgia. "In all well regulated cities
and towns," a resident of Williamsburg, Virginia, explained, an established
market house was necessary lest goods be sold by "vagrant strangers [who]
generally turn out a pest to society."[17]

In southern towns the market houses sometimes included slaves who conducted huckstering under the control of merchants and plantation owners.
The practice in Charleston by the late 1700s was for copper tags or badges to

be issued to slaves identifying them as licensed hucksters. While annual day laborer badges went for two dollars, huckster badges commanded up to six dollars. Badges further distinguished hucksters specializing in meat, fish, fresh produce, fruit, and baked goods.[18]

Philadelphia, as the nation's second largest city with a population of 28,000 in 1790, was an attractive location for hucksters as well as shopkeepers. Huckstering required no training and was not yet subject to stiff licensing fees, which made it an appealing vocation for those who would otherwise have been unable to earn a living. Of more than four hundred people who worked at least temporarily as hucksters between 1791 and 1805, two-thirds were women. Many of the hucksters were too old or too young to work at other vocations. They included widows and orphans who had no other means of support. Some were disabled. Their ranks included both blacks and whites.[19]

By the 1830s it was common for towns with populations of three thousand or more to have market houses built at public expense and open on particular days of the week for the convenience of residents wishing to purchase meat, poultry, eggs, fruit, and vegetables. Town councils appointed market house committees to oversee the construction and operation of these buildings and passed ordinances regulating the activities of persons using the market houses. Amending and expanding earlier acts of incorporation, the ordinances dealt with a broad range of topics related to the goods that could be sold, who could sell them, and how the market houses were related to the activities of growers, butchers, vendors, street peddlers, and hucksters. Philadelphia's ordinances were revised in 1823 and again in 1834, Raleigh's in 1838, Baltimore's in 1839, and Portland, Maine's, in 1842. In southern towns, the ordinances typically included provisions for the sale of slaves and clauses about when and under what other conditions Negroes could be present in the marketplace.

The establishment of market houses defined not only the specific rules governing hucksters but also their place in the antebellum cultural milieu. The public debate from 1769 to 1773 involving plans to construct a market house in Providence, Rhode Island, was particularly revealing in this regard. The plan's proponents emphasized that bringing sellers and buyers together in one place would induce competition among the sellers, reduce the prices buyers would have to pay, and make it easier for sellers and buyers alike to determine fair prices. House-to-house peddling, the plan's advocates argued, lacked these advantages. As one writer observed, "The inconvenience of calling at every door, answering questions, disputing about the price, the fatigues of heat, cold, rain and snow, joined to the damage which the provisions must suffer by being carried about, is enough to convince the country, as well as the town, that a market house would be of singular advantage to both."[20]

In short, huckstering became what market houses were not, even though the two were intimately related. The central idea of a market house was to establish a *place* in which business was regularly transacted. Huckstering,

FIGURE 2. *The Huckster*, Philadelphia, 1851, described as a "fat old lady who
has a stall in the market which she rents by the year." *City Characters, or,
Familiar Scenes in Town* (Philadelphia: George S. Appleton, 1851).

in contrast, was business that did not operate at a place. Bringing sellers together in a place was the key to ensuring that market competition would be
the factor that determined prices. The uncertainty as to whether hucksters'
prices were fair, whether hucksters were swindlers, and the haggling buyers
had to do with hucksters were all contingent on the fact that they operated on
their own away from the market house. In addition, market houses were supposed to be the places in which produce was fresh, which left the connotation
that hucksters' produce might not be. As far as convenience was concerned,
householders could count on market houses being open at certain times and
plan their day accordingly, while hucksters' visits happened sporadically and
as interruptions. Such were the advantages of selling at a single location, the

proponents of market houses argued, that farmers, householders, and hucksters alike would understand them.

Market houses literally and figuratively became the centers of town life, serving as an expectation that a place respectable enough to call itself a town would have one. Built at public expense, market houses were a collective good that required bonds and taxes to be levied on their behalf. Adjacent locations were purchased or leased at a premium. Shops conveniently located near the market house sold dry and packaged goods, such as kitchen utensils, knives, locks, clocks, candles, cloth, jewelry, Bibles, and psalters. The fact that shops had established locations made it possible for them to post notices in local newspapers about their wares, which meant that advertising too was contingent on selling from designated places.

Hucksters whose licenses did not include a stall inside the building vied for contested space at the edges of the market house, sometimes finding shelter from inclement weather under the market's awnings and more often jockeying with farmers' wagons for locations at the curb or hitching posts. Hucksters in this position had their carts confiscated by the police, stolen by other hucksters, and displaced by unhappy farmers. Municipal ordinances to curtail the difficulties varied from specifying the size of tables that could be placed in the immediate vicinity of the market houses to enjoining auctioneers from entering the space. Concerned not only by who was there but also by what they might have left behind, St. Louis decreed that no huckster, peddler, or other person in the immediate vicinity of the market house was allowed "to throw, place or deposit in, or upon said market square, or in the market house, any melon rinds or parings, nor the rinds or parings of any fruit, potatoes, turnips, or other vegetables; nor shall any person be allowed or permitted to place or deposit on said square, or in said house, any refuse, putrid or offensive animal or vegetable matter."[21]

Unlike landowners and merchants whose identities could be known from the property they owned and occupied in particular places, hucksters were a miscellany that defied easy classification. In 1842 a writer for the *New York Union* pondered the question of who the many people were who earned their livings from the street. The writer contrasted them with persons with "ample acres," on the one hand, and with "mercantile" pursuits, on the other. Those who fell into neither category were men, women, and children who "traverse the streets with coarse empty bags on their shoulders or baskets on their arms," rough-clad people who "start at early day to gather the rags, papers, old shoes, pieces of glass, bones, or any other refuse substances they find in the streets or gutters." They were also the hucksters who purchased "the fruits and vegetables they daily vend, and from the profits of which they eke out, not only a living, but lay by something for a rainy day."[22]

By the 1840s huckstering and peddling had grown to the point that in larger cities, like New York, Philadelphia, Washington, DC, and Baltimore, community leaders felt it necessary to pass new ordinances on, further restrict, and develop more detailed understandings of hucksters' and peddlers' activities. *New York Tribune* editor Horace Greeley concluded from talking with them that there were at least two kinds. Country hucksters lived on farms, produced their own eggs, and grew their own fruit, cabbage, beets, turnips, and other vegetables. A family member then brought the produce to town, selling it from door to door or at a stall on market days. City hucksters, in contrast, purchased farm produce and other items from wholesalers and resold them on the streets. Country hucksters generally operated at a larger profit margin than city hucksters, sold to a less disadvantaged clientele, earned as much as thirty dollars a week compared with four or five dollars a week among city hucksters, haggled less, and less often engaged in fraud and deception.[23]

When a proposal to suppress hawking and street peddling came before the municipal government in New York City in 1843, Greeley wrote, "We will go heart and hand for the clearing of every huckster or peddler out of the streets just so soon as the City has provided honest, un-degrading labor for every person who, not being able to do better, is willing to work for the public for a bare subsistence until he can do better. Until that is done, great as is the nuisance of street peddling, and hardly as it bears on those who pay rent for stores and are deprived of custom by peddlers, we will not assent to any measure of the kind proposed."[24]

It was more the nuisance than the needs of street peddlers, though, to which ordinances were directed. In 1843 Baltimore's city council considered an ordinance prohibiting the huckstering of wood within the city limits following five years of complaints from boat captains who preferred having the exclusive right to sell directly to consumers. The measure's merits seemed indisputable, but it was unclear whether the committee on markets, the police, or the state legislature should handle the matter.[25]

The fact that farmers' and merchants' interests were at stake compounded the difficulties of regulating huckstering. The key was finding a way to bring order to the huckstering business without infringing on the well-established activities of persons more clearly identified with farming and mercantile interests. Baltimore, for instance, considered cheese vendors subject to huckstering license fees if the vendors had not produced the cheese but exempted vendors who did produce cheese, just as they did farmers who delivered milk and eggs from their own farms.[26]

Councilors in Washington, DC, introduced what they regarded as a relatively straightforward bill in 1854 to regulate huckstering through licensing enforced by the police, only to be confronted with such thorny technicalities as whether hucksters would be required to place the word "Huckster" on their wagons, how modest in value items had to be to qualify for huckstering, whether tradesmen as well as produce peddlers could apply for licenses, whether a huckster could purchase more than one license, and whether the established annual rate should be $15 or $25 per license.[27]

One of the commonest concerns was forestalling, which literally referred to the practice of hucksters buying up farmers' produce early in the day or the previous evening—before the market stalls were open—in order to resell the produce at higher prices. In Cincinnati several dozen farmers and hucksters were arrested in 1853, fined, and jailed for violating an ordinance against forestalling.[28] In other towns, farmers complained that huckster regulations were preventing farmers from selling directly to customers in town, householders worried that license fees would elevate the price of fruits and vegetables, and merchants argued that hucksters would still get away with selling rotten produce.

Besides passing ordinances, towns that had not previously had market masters established such positions and appointed officials to oversee the complexities of farm produce and other goods offered for sale in municipal markets. Market masters were charged with supervising what was sold in market stalls, on huckster's wagons, and by peddlers. Details to which masters were held responsible included the accuracy of weights and measures, the appropriate quantities in which articles could be sold (such as corn by the barrel, flour by the bag, and potatoes by the half peck), the days and hours during which sales could be transacted, penalties for selling spoiled or diseased meat, and where hucksters' carts should be parked when not in use. A town in Maryland gave its market master the right to set aside six benches for children's use as long as the children's items were priced less than a dollar.[29]

The accounts hucksters gave of themselves indicated not only that they existed in humble straits but also that some explanation for the straits they were in was necessary. A peddler named John Gilbert who traveled through Maryland in 1859 said he had been "reduced," like thousands of others, "owing to the late commercial panic."[30] A girl in Ann S. Stephens's *Fashion and Famine*, published in 1854, peddled strawberries with the help of a huckster woman because the girl's grandparents were too old and feeble to support themselves without the girl's assistance.[31] Other descriptions suggested that hucksters suffered from illness, bereavement, the loss of a farm, a business failure, or some other catastrophe. They were too poor to eke out a living in any other way, could not make it or had not made it in the country, had children to feed, and were doing what they could instead of begging or turning for help to the almshouses. They were the working poor whose morals and activities were debated as to whether they were hardworking or lazy, honest or dishonest, did or did not serve a useful purpose, and did or did not deserve respect.

Westward Expansion

Notwithstanding the difficulties municipal authorities faced in determining what counted or did not count as huckstering, the U.S. Census Bureau decided in 1850 that the time had come to affix precise numbers to the population's principal occupations, including huckstering and peddling (which it opted to combine). The 1850 census determined that 11,254 Americans worked as hucksters and peddlers. By 1860 the number doubled to 22,339. The average age was thirty-three, and nearly everyone so classified that year was male (94 percent).[32]

Although the next figures were not collected until 1870, anecdotal evidence suggested that women and children carried on most of the huckstering and peddling that was done during the Civil War. Soldiers' letters indicated that women gathered at rail stops and near field hospitals to sell farm goods that had not been plundered or commandeered and that others canvassed in noncombat neighborhoods to gather supplies. "Little huckster stands were everywhere—apples, oranges, peaches, watermelons, everything," a wounded soldier at a depot in Alabama recalled. "I know that I never saw a greater display of eatables in my whole life. I was particularly attracted toward an old lady's stand; she had bread, fish, and hard boiled eggs."[33]

Appreciation for hucksters' provisions diminished when prices were inflated and peddlers were suspected of swindling. On more than one occasion soldiers confiscated and helped themselves to peddlers' goods. "Our men are not civil to these huckster men," a lieutenant from Iowa wrote in his diary in 1863. "Today, March 17th I saw them accidentally, as they said, overturn a barrel of apples that was brought in on a cart with a team of oxen. In the excitement the oxen were detached from the cart and driven off while the huckster was gathering up some of his apples. Then his box of pies was accidentally turned over, and more than thirty [men] were readily and willingly helping him to gather them up. Unfortunately, the box was carried away and most of the pies too."[34]

Peddlers traveling in slaveholding areas took care to avoid being identified as deserters, spies, and agents working for the Underground Railroad. Several of the residents John Gilbert approached in rural Maryland suspected him of being an abolitionist intent on stealing slaves. He was accosted at gunpoint, threatened with arrest, and chased by dogs. The citizens in one community accused him of organizing an insurrection. "By some unfortunate means the idea of a peddler and an insurgent had become blended together in the minds of the people as being one and the same thing," he wrote. "I was covered with insults as I called at the houses and met with incivility and rebuff on every hand. Civilization seemed to be getting scarce."[35]

When the war ended, the ranks of hucksters and peddlers swelled as displaced, indigent, wounded, and disabled veterans returned to civilian life. The 1870 census counted 34,152 hucksters and peddlers, an increase of approximately 50 percent since 1860. Besides the large number of disabled Civil War veterans, men and women who suffered from farm accidents, like Samuel Huey, and from mishaps with horses, train crashes, fires, and amputations took up huckstering. Although soldiers' homes cared for many of the seriously wounded and families assisted others, those who could find work in less

FIGURE 3. *The Peddler's Wagon*, 1868. Drawn by C. G. Bush for *Harper's Weekly*.
Library of Congress Prints and Photographs Division, Washington, DC.

physically demanding occupations tended shops, worked as clerks, served as
postal carriers and book agents, and turned to teaching and peddling.

Newspapers portrayed crippled workers sympathetically, especially if they
were veterans, noting instances in which they were assaulted, robbed, taken
ill, compelled by poverty into begging, tempted to commit suicide, or in other
cases performed courageous deeds, but they also carried stories of disabled
persons charged with crimes, fights, drunkenness, and disorderly conduct.
They printed cautionary tales as well about able-bodied peddlers falsely claiming to be selling on behalf of disabled relatives. By 1880 nearly all states exempted disabled peddlers from the licensing fees required of other peddlers.

When the 1880 census was taken, there were 53,734 hucksters and peddlers. The number grew to 59,083 in 1890 and reached a high point of 68,739
in 1900. The 1910 figure of 67,394 was slightly lower, and the 1920 figure of
47,566 represented a significant decline. Relative to the overall population,
though, huckstering and peddling peaked in 1880. The number of hucksters
and peddlers per 100,000 population rose from 56 in 1850 to 82 in 1860, 89 in
1870, and 107 in 1880. The comparable figures then declined to 94 to 1890, 91
in 1900, 73 in 1910, and 45 in 1920. The figures also reflected the population's
westward movement. In 1850, 59 percent of the nation's hucksters and peddlers were concentrated in four states (Massachusetts, New York, Ohio, and
Pennsylvania), but by 1880 that figure had declined to 51 percent and by 1900
to 48 percent. The majority of hucksters and peddlers were located in rural
areas, which the Census Bureau defined as farms, open country, and towns of

less than 2,500 people. That proportion declined only from 74 percent in 1880 to 61 percent in 1900.

Descriptions of hucksters and peddlers resembled earlier ones in most respects. Huckstering was still a placeless occupation that differed from the spatially located identities of farmers and merchants. Hucksters' and peddlers' activities were sufficiently varied that it was difficult to know exactly how to regulate them, which meant that debates about the details of municipal ordinances continued. If they were difficult to place in the hierarchy of rural or urban life, they remained notably inferior, doing work that self-respecting citizens would not do if they could help it. "The cities and towns are full of men who once had visions of a business success that would in monthly profits put to shame the small savings of a farmer's lifetime," an essay praising farm life explained. "On the home stretch of three score and ten they find themselves dependent for a livelihood on a salaried position which they hold by a dismally uncertain tenure, or on the precarious commission of a canvasser or commercial traveler."[36]

How persons might be forced into huckstering through circumstances no fault of their own was the most common interpretation but by no means the only one. In a frontier world emphasizing freedom and self-determination, making bad choices was also a reason to have fallen into a lowly occupation like peddling. Kansas senator John J. Ingalls, whose statement *ad astra per aspera* (to the stars through difficulty) became the state's motto as well as his personal creed, illustrated the point in a commencement oration at Kansas University in 1873. Ingalls insisted that modern life required "harmonious action of all the faculties which constitute true manhood or womanhood" combined with the "practical knowledge" needed to prosper in an age of specialization. A classical education built character and disciplined the mind but had to be supplemented with knowledge of the "hurly-burly of Western life" if a person was to prosper. A person who clung to the classical texts and failed to become self-reliant would not succeed. "When he discovers that he has been leaning upon a broken reed, he succumbs at once, becomes a book canvasser or a life insurance agent, and fades out of existence."[37]

Ingalls's audience would have understood book canvassing and insurance peddling as less than desirable occupations. The peddlers who visited their homes selling tonics and farm produce were not in charge of their own destinies. Peddlers' subordinate status was evident in the fact that the peddler's box or wagon was filled with goods the peddler's master owned, and any money the peddler might be carrying was the master's minus whatever commission the peddler was due. Peddlers could also be identified by their clothing, gait, complexion, and manner of speaking. Whereas a gentleman was considered a proper man because of his refined clothing, fresh complexion, and qualities of speech, a peddler deviated in these respects, noticeably with a swarthy complexion, a pockmarked face, and a boisterous affect.

Hucksters delivering goods in rural communities in the 1870s imitated patterns from earlier in the century. A journalist who rode a huckster's circuit in the far southwest corner of Pennsylvania in 1875 described embarking at six o'clock in the morning in a wagon loaded with two barrels of sugar, half a dozen chairs, a pair of scales, and boxes of packaged groceries. The first stop was eight miles away at a village of a dozen houses, the second was two miles further at a village of twenty-five dwellings, the third and fourth were several more miles down the road. After lodging with a family at a fifth town, the tour continued through a second circuit of towns, and then the return trip took two more days. The wagon's load now consisted of five hundred pounds of butter, two hundred dozen eggs, three calves, a hundred chickens, and nineteen gallons of raspberries.[38]

John Frank Turner, who recalled working as a huckster in rural Indiana in 1890, described a similar pattern of activities. The owner of a general merchandise store who also had substantial landholdings employed him. At nineteen and with only a grade school education, Turner was glad to have the job. The work consisted of making a two-day circuit covering more than thirty miles to the north and west, a two-day circuit on alternate weeks of more than twenty miles to the south, and shorter trips on the remaining days. At each stop Turner exchanged yard goods, tinware, brooms, and groceries for eggs, poultry, butter, and vegetables. He also delivered fruit crates, twine, and farm equipment and took orders for washing machines.[39]

Although hucksters like this traveled regular enough circuits to be known in their communities, huckstering was not the kind of work that involved settling into a community for a long period of time. Of the 106 Kansas hucksters identified in the 1880 federal census who could be tracked in the 1885 state census, only 34 percent were still living in the same county, 10 percent were living in Kansas but in a different county, and 56 percent had left the state. Farm families moved too, far more than anecdotes about settlers who sunk roots for a lifetime suggested, but a study of farmers at several locations in Kansas at the same time showed that 52 percent remained in the same township, compared with the third of hucksters still in the same county. Hucksters' family characteristics also suggested why they might have been particularly mobile. A quarter of the ones in Kansas were single and another 10 percent were widowed or living apart from their spouse. In the national data, 41 percent of hucksters and peddlers in 1880 were unmarried.[40]

In addition to residential mobility, hucksters and peddlers traveled in wider circuits as the items they offered shifted from agricultural produce to manufactured goods. Lightning rod agents expected to saturate a particular rural community and then move on to a new community. Peddlers selling durable items such as scissors, knife sharpeners, and sewing machines knew the necessity of calling on new customers rather than returning too often to the same ones. Canvassers taking subscriptions for a biography of Ulysses S. Grant or an engraved portrait of Abraham Lincoln could return to the same house-holds only when a new book or picture was available. Firms like J. B. Burr in Hartford and the National Publishing Company in Boston advertised for men and women who did not work as general agents carrying other items but as canvassers who would devote their time to subscriptions for particular books. Canvassers were assigned to large territories and given the exclusive right to solicit in these territories.

Notices in newspapers appealed to farmers whose crops might have failed and teachers who may have lost their jobs or young people hoping to get started in a business by advertising that agents and canvassers could earn handsome commissions. Advertisements proclaimed that agents could earn $10 a day, receive higher commissions than from competitors, and be in the enviable position of selling new inventions (unspecified) or popular books that were selling rapidly. Energetic canvassers were particularly needed, and book agents especially could take pride in playing a small role in spreading civiliza-tion. "The very art of salesmanship is to appear thoroughly conversant with the work and goods," a canvasser in Kansas City explained. "Impress the cus-tomer politely with your ability; let her see, while you seemingly hold it back, that you know more than she."[41]

Canvassers working circuits spanning multiple counties and states had to be not only energetic and knowledgeable but also willing to embrace danger and adventure. Annie Nelles, who canvassed for book subscriptions in Illinois, Indiana, and Michigan, took pride in "the dissemination of light and knowl-edge among the masses" and claimed to enjoy "the excitement, the constant variety, and the abundant opportunity for studying human nature afforded by the energetic pursuit of this calling." Although the details she published about her personal life were mostly fictionalized, she offered credible accounts of the difficulties involved in tramping the streets of entire towns without making a single sale, dealing with pawnbrokers when cash ran low, negotiating with postal clerks about packages, taking rides from strangers, and boarding with less than hospitable farm families.[42]

What compensated for having to sell in unfamiliar territory to complete strangers was cultivating social networks. Samuel Huey's book canvassing in southern Illinois benefited from the fact that he was related to dozens of families across several counties and belonged to a church that had close ties with other churches of the same denomination and whose members prided themselves on reading, sending their children to school, and stocking their homes with books. Annie Nelles learned from initial setbacks to cultivate con-nections among freemasons, selling subscriptions to a history of freemasonry, and working networks among members of the Grand Army of the Republic, Quakers, and church members.

While most canvassers worked alone, larger publishing companies and manufacturing firms also began experimenting with a form of organized

canvassing involving a number of canvassers working together. The plan
included a manager, chaperone, and dozen or more women canvassers who
traveled by train to a large town, took rooms in a hotel, and worked out a
division of labor by which to canvass the entire town. At six o'clock the next
morning, the canvassers would commence contacting the town's business establishments, and they worked until nine o'clock in the evening, spending additional days as necessary. The canvassers spoke from a uniform memorized
script and were monitored by spotters who timed their visits at each firm and
reprimanded any canvasser whose visits were too long.[43]

But organized blitz-style canvassing was the rarity rather than the norm.
When Americans in the nineteenth century encountered peddlers and canvassers, the experience in most instances involved either a stranger or a person
who traveled a regular circuit but who nevertheless came and went. They were
enough like everyone else that it was possible to be curious about them and
even to imagine that through some unfortunate circumstance a person who
had expected to farm, manage a store, or go to college could be forced into
huckstering. It was not the happiest of prospects and it was preferable to being
sent to the poorhouse, but it was certainly imaginable.

Moral Meanings

The hucksters and peddlers of the nineteenth century that took shape in their
own sparse writing and in the more ample narratives about them depicted
not only a peripatetic occupation but also a moral landscape. The huckster
inhabited a world in which assertions about respect, work, honesty, and trust
rose to the surface. The peddler populated a narrative in which commentators thought about what it meant to be a person of worth, whether that person lived on a farm or in a small town or city. The ambiguities attached to
huckstering and peddling provided interpreters with opportunities to argue
about definitions of appropriate behavior in themselves and their neighbors.
These discussions occasionally took the form of explicit preaching and teaching about morality. They more often surfaced as implicit expectations of the
kind that later came to be understood as mores and at the time composed the
commonsense morality that widely prevailed.

Few topics were as closely associated with understandings of commonsense
morality as discussions of character. Sermons, tracts, and nineteenth-century
advice books for young men and women counseled that being a person of good
character was to be prized above all else. To be a person of character was to
have an inner strength composed of natural and cultivated virtue, including
such traits as discipline, generosity, and courage. Character was supposed
to be evident not only through such exterior activities as working hard and
speaking honestly. It was also expected to reside in a person's heart—indeed,
in the soul—as a kind of interior resolve or a disposition toward honest work

and speech. "Character," an 1856 sermon explained, "is not any appendage nor on the outside, but is internal."[44]

The question was how to know what a person's character truly was if character was in essence interior. Did not the Bible warn that the heart could be deceitfully wicked even though a person appeared to be righteous? The warning was sufficiently serious that religious organizations administered written and oral examinations to assess the character of aspiring clergy. Lay members underwent at least routine religious instruction, and congregations were supposed to know their members well enough to vouch for their trustworthiness. Explicit instruction of this kind went a long way toward defining the outer boundaries separating good and evil. They depended in practice, though, on people learning by example from observing people like themselves and people who differed—learning less what the Ten Commandments or the Golden Rule dictated and more what it meant to be accepted as a good neighbor and citizen.

Besides its more obvious behavioral manifestations, were there signals that might reveal a person's true character from such clues as one's facial expression, posture, mannerisms, and bearing? These were the subtle indications that persons of good upbringing were supposed to display and in turn were expected to be attentive to in their interaction with others. Teachers were expected to be adept at both cultivating the appropriate mannerisms in pupils and discerning their strengths and weaknesses. Phrenology and physiognomy, through such articles as "Signs of Character and How to read them" and "Signs of Character as manifested through Temperament and external forms," were popularly entertained as tools in this endeavor. In addition, teachers were instructed to read the character of a child from "the expression of the face, by the actions, and by the various variations in form and position of the nose, eyes, lips, forehead, and ears."[45]

In other contexts the phrenology and physiognomy of good character may have been reinforced by the kinds of etiquette governing the aristocracy of Victorian England or the protocol of the Prussian military. But in America the mixing of social classes and ethnic groups and nationalities had made it harder for the proponents of good manners to specify widely shared understandings. Deciphering a person's inner character from small external clues was all the more problematic as the nation urbanized, included a wider variety of immigrant groups, and dealt with the complexities of market transactions between farms and cities and across regions. Suitors pondered the difficulties under such changing conditions of determining how to identify and court a person of interest. As a story about one such who was keeping his eye on two young ladies explained, he was "observing them of late, striving to learn the true character of each." But this, he found, to be "rather a difficult matter" in an urban context. "How he yearned to see through the false surroundings into the true and inner life beneath!"[46]

FIGURE 4. *A South Carolina Huckster*, 1904. Library of Congress
Prints and Photographs Division, Washington, DC.

While it was possible and indeed desirable for any well-bred person to read
character from subtle cues, it was also possible to imagine that hucksters and
peddlers were particularly adept at these skills. To the extent that something
about a peddler might be admirable, it might be this ability on which success
in dealing with people so obviously depended. Illustrations of this impression
of peddlers were evident in comments such as, "He studies life and human
nature" and "His knowledge of character is often thorough, for to be successful
he has to be able to read his customer almost instantly."[47]

The peddler who could read character so adeptly in this manner was
sometimes called a Yankee peddler, implying that he knew by heart the appropriate ways to deal honestly with people and thus succeeded by virtue of
his own character and his understanding of others. In contrast, peddlers who
succeeded only by talking loudly, behaving aggressively, and overpricing their
goods were sometimes referred to as Jews or Bohemians. By implication, their
ethnic origin made it impossible for them to discern the marks of good character as well as a Yankee could. Nor could a novice or child peddler be expected
to read character this well. They were classed as street gamins or urchins.

Just as a peddler could be admired for an ability to read character, so a
peddler could be viewed as an example of faulty character. The same sermons

and publications that called on young persons to be of good character warned of the special difficulties faced by those who moved, who lacked the stability of a fixed residence and spent their days mingling with strangers. Amid such changing conditions, it was difficult to continue the good habits of one's upbringing. The small moorings that held those habits in place were gone. The people who jostled for business in the streets and byways were particularly at risk of falling short of high moral standards. They were free-floating individuals, adrift from the "familiar and stable landmarks of good morals."[48]

If good character meant behavior that sincerely reflected one's intentions, peddling could serve as an illustration of artfulness, as crafty behavior that deceptively displayed motives that were not sincere. A person of character was reserved, patient, and careful in entering into relationships, but a huckster regarded those traits as timidity. It was better to move quickly, putting oneself forward aggressively, even swaggering a bit. Always on the go, looking ahead to the next deal, one could easily lose track of one's roots. Character was best described in words suggesting the opposite of a peddler's transience. Character was a matter of habit, an unchangeable standard, a firm conviction, a fixed determination, a grounding discipline, an anchor, a place to stand.[49] An ordinary person reserved certain topics and expressions of emotion for intimate conversations while a peddler might reveal or play on intimacies to make a sale. If nothing else, character was to be read through enduring interactions with friends and neighbors, whereas a peddler's character was unknown because the peddler was a stranger.

Accusations of cheating reinforced the view that hucksters functioned in a liminal reality ungoverned by the rules under which trustworthy citizens operated. Hucksters were wily enough to have figured out how to circumvent the rules. Transgressing the rules illustrated what the expectations of ordinary life were to be. Hucksters who put rotten fruit at the bottom of the basket violated the expectation that surface appearances in everyday life could normally be trusted. Deviations from standard weights and measures provided occasions for observing the value of having such standards. A story to this effect circulated about an elderly woman who, while purchasing peaches from a huckster, noticed not only that the price (four cents a quart) was cheap but that the quart measure the huckster was using seemed small. When questioned, the huckster acknowledged that he also had a six-cent quart that was considerably larger than the four-cent quart. How was it possible to call them both quarts, the woman wondered? It was the only way he could attract business, the huckster explained.[50]

For boosters of agrarian values, hucksters provided an instructive lesson in what could go wrong when people, goods, and farm produce transgressed the symbolic boundary separating country life from city life. There were numerous ways of putting the country in a better light than the city. Simple contrasts pitted clean air against polluted air, bright fields against dark streets, and simple living against disorienting strangeness. Farm families in these accounts were strong, humble, patient, and hardworking compared to greedy, pretentious city dwellers. The symbolic boundary, though, was clearer when it was transgressed than when it merely represented a division. A farm person who moved to the city constituted one such transgression, the ill rewards of such movement being counted in failure and disappointment if not crime.

Huckstering illustrated transgression of a different kind. It was the fresh farm produce that crossed the line in the huckster's hands. The president of an agricultural society in Michigan explained it this way in an 1857 address: "The fruits of the garden, which come to the farmer's table all crisp and fresh from their native soil, reach the city epicure after they are wilted and withered on the huckster's bench, and changed by the destructive processes of nature from wholesome into health destroying substances." In the speaker's mind, the shift from wholesome to spoiled that inevitably took place at the huckster's hand resembled a change in the air itself. "Even the pure breath of the fields, sweeping along the heated thoroughfare, gathering up the thickly rising dust, absorbing ten thousand fetid exhalations, steals at length through the open casement not to breathe refreshingly upon the fevered brow within, but to plant insidiously the seeds of death."[51]

Despoiled freshness became a recurring theme in descriptions of hucksters' trade. An 1877 sociology text contrasted life in rural townships with existence in crowded cities. Rural residents enjoyed "fresh vegetables from the earth and fruits from the tree." City dwellers "live on withered and rotten fruits, with a half dozen hucksters' profits upon them." How much better it was, the writer thought, for people to live on farms than amid the "putrid gases and fetid slums, obliged to subsist upon the musty articles of diet vended at the hucksters' stalls."[52]

The more explicit expectations associated with good character were reinforced in narratives in which hucksters and peddlers served as negative examples. Perseverance was one such trait. A person of good character was supposed to demonstrate perseverance by sticking to the task at hand, working from sunup to sundown. Hucksters and peddlers might well have provided examples of people who persevered, making their calls early and late despite frequent rebuffs. As one subscriber to a book about blood circulation and disease explained about the canvasser who wore him down, "He is a man whom you can't escape any more than you can your own shadow; he follows his victim like a ghost and hangs around him grinning like an undertaker."[53] But canvassers' persistence was the kind that kept other people from getting their work done. They illustrated the sort of interruption that truly hardworking individuals had to resist, much like a person of determination needed to ignore an affliction of stomach cramps. A good farmer, rural commentators observed, was known for staying on the job, regularly paying the bills, and working hard, whereas peddlers wasted farmers' time and lived by smooth talking instead of hard work. "I have not had a moment's respite from canvassers this day," Samuel Clemens remarked. "I have bought a sewing-machine which I did not want; I have bought a map which is mistaken in all its details; I have bought a clock which will not go; I have bought a moth poison which the moths prefer to any other beverage; I have bought no end of useless inventions, and now I have had enough of this foolishness."[54]

Smooth talking and huckstering had nearly identical connotations. A good peddler was glib, a fast talker, who could sell anything through the guile of saying just the right thing, flattering the prospective buyer, and talking up the product while talking down its competitors. Hucksters contrasted with the plain-speaking person of few words whose character was evident in good deeds. Plain speaking had as much to do with character as it did with talking because a plainspoken person was humble enough and sufficiently secure to keep quiet when the situation called for action rather than words. In contrast, hucksters and canvassers were known for being cheeky and brassy. There was, however, the grudging admission that the reason peddlers succeeded was that plain-speaking people rather enjoyed being smooth talked and liked to imagine themselves doing it too.

The notion of shoveling smoke was a colloquial way of expressing common folk's tendency to deviate occasionally from the norm of down-to-earth, practical speech. Besides the contrast they provided about perseverance and hard work, peddlers illustrated a kind of moral weakness in the people to whom they sold goods. In some discussions, the weakness was gullibility, a trait that seemed to characterize farmers more than townspeople. The more subtle weakness was the impulse to talk and think in a fanciful way for the sake of entertaining one's imagination instead of being consistently in touch with reality. Shoveling smoke was the weakness that led people to waste their time talking to lightning rod agents and book canvassers, letting themselves imagine the great benefits that the peddler described, rather than staying sufficiently grounded in reality to say "No."[55]

Humorous anecdotes were one of the commonest ways in which peddlers' deviations from expectations about ordinary social relationships were popularized. What made an anecdote humorous was turning the tables, such that the peddler's supposed superiority was outdone or undermined. The humor in stories about dogs chasing peddlers up trees or canvassers scrambling for their lives over back fences was that a person who initially was better dressed, more carefully groomed, and cleverer in talking than the ordinary householder was now in disarray. Similarly, the huckster told to stop talking and get walking or out-talked to the point of slinking away in silence was the butt of the joke because of being cut down to size.

The less humorous ways of cutting hucksters and peddlers down to size involved ethnic slurs. The same slurs that native-born white Protestants and Catholics directed toward outsiders whom they regarded as inferior were directed at hucksters and peddlers. The traits considered offensive in ethnic minorities included being pushy, talking too loudly and aggressively, behaving deviously and with cunning, and not fitting in. Skepticism toward canvassers was said to be necessary because they were "foreign," implying that they were somehow alien compared with local merchants. Saying that a huckster would try to "Jew" a customer meant the same thing as haggling and swindling. In Baltimore "arabing" was used synonymously with huckstering. In California it was said that the only way to insult a "Chinaman" was to call him a huckster.

The fact that hucksters and peddlers sometimes were ethnic minorities contributed to the stereotyping associated with them. Historian Lee Shai Weissbach's account of Jewish life in small-town America describes a number of instances in which Jewish merchants started as peddlers and grew their businesses into prominent commercial establishments. Examples could be found in locations as varied as Fitchburg, Massachusetts; Lafayette, Indiana; Patchogue, New York; Erie, Pennsylvania; Danbury, Connecticut; and Leavenworth, Kansas. Starting with modest horse-and-wagon enterprises selling produce, groceries, and household goods, the peddlers became known in their communities to a greater extent than other peddlers did because they stayed and opened stores bearing their names. Well into the twentieth century "resentment of them as middlemen" perpetuated anti-Jewish stereotypes characterizing them as marginal to the mainstream of small-town culture. They were viewed particularly as "avaricious, domineering, untrustworthy, and clannish," traits that contrasted specifically with the norms of self-deflection, mutuality, trustworthiness, and neighborliness that were supposed to prevail in small towns.[56]

Commentary that usually passed as genderless sometimes emphasized specific expectations about appropriately gendered behavior. As liminal persons, hucksters' liminality resulted in ambiguous descriptions of their gender characteristics, which further emphasized their marginality to familiar cultural categories. Critics questioned if male hucksters were manly men who could be proud of their masculinity or were like eunuchs who spent most of their time among women dealing with domestic items or like cuckolds who were powerless in their own homes and on the street in relation to the strong men who farmed or operated respectable businesses. Male canvassers were called Lotharios who engaged in ungentlemanly conduct toward women, wooing them with some exceptional magnetism, attempting to seduce them or lure them into unpleasant alliances with artful skill.

The same talents canvassers used to make an effective sales pitch for a book or sewing machine could be used to violate the norms governing polite relationships between men and women. "The very business of a canvasser gives him a certain personal charm, an ease and confidence and an address that are good capital," a Kansas City canvasser acknowledged. "I know of more than half a dozen who have quietly become the husbands of fifty-thousand, hundred-thousand, and even a quarter of a million dollar girls."[57] A story that resembled later "traveling salesman" escapades featured a peddler tempting housewives with jewelry, fine handkerchiefs, linen, and perfume, whereupon the victim unable to pay for the desired item was asked to fulfill the peddler's desires. In one version of the story, the peddler was the victimizer, leaving the unfortunate woman's reputation in tatters and her husband a cuckold. In another version, the peddler was victimized, outwitted by the woman who refused to compromise her virtue, set fire to the peddler's wares, or turned him over to the police.

Other variations on the theme of victim or victimizer typically located the male peddler in an unfamiliar, insecure space in which events out of the ordinary and usually under a man's control could happen. Peddlers appear alone on dark country roads or in wooded areas, traveling between towns, unnamed and unknown to local residents, either being set upon by ruffians or attacking and robbing innocent passersby. As cautionary tales, the events cast the peddler as a person outside of and unprotected by the routine expectations of ordinary life and thus as a figure surrounded by danger. The peddler's precarious situation is evident in such small details as being alone, sleeping out-of-doors or in a stranger's barn, having no money or carrying too much money, foolishly discussing money or gambling, and feeling afraid or being overly confident.

Descriptions of the relatively smaller number of women who worked as hucksters portrayed them as nervy, deceitful, and willing to exploit their feminine wiles to make a sale, and in other settings as less honest than the typical housewife, dirtier, coarse, and abrasive. "Her features are rigid with care and calculation," an essayist observed about a huckster in Vicksburg in the 1840s. She had a "strong, grasping, masculine" propensity for business, rather than "that sweet smile of loveliness which plays about the sweet countenance of woman." Everything about her contrasted with the usual womanly virtues. "Her voice has assumed a hard and commanding tone, instead of the soft cadences of love and kindness." Her step was "hurried, instead of light and graceful," and her "look and air is that of business instead of the graces of lovely woman."[58] Fictional accounts also put women hucksters in an unfavorable light. A story about a huckster woman named Mrs. James who exploited a servant girl named Mabel characterized Mrs. James in terms nearly as sour as the wicked stepmother in Cinderella. Unlike a proper woman who would care for children and empathize with their emotions, Mrs. James worked Mabel early and late, gave her too little to eat, scolded her, beat her, and clothed her only in rags. Worse than the harsh treatment itself, "the huckster woman never seemed to think that Mabel could feel pain or cold or weariness."[59]

Later accounts, perhaps shaped by criticisms of suffragists, described women canvassers as somewhere between the artful seductress of the past and the self-reliant woman of the future. An essay for the *New York Herald* in 1886 characterized women canvassers as combining the more traditional talents of the harlot with the forward-looking skills of someone especially adept in persuasion and the art of selling. Instead of claiming to solicit on her own behalf, the canvasser cleverly made the sale seem to benefit some charitable or worthy civilizing cause. Older canvassers could "get in more vocal work in a given space than any male agitator of the organ of speech extant." Younger canvassers used a different tactic: "Her strong points are her eyes. Once her tongue has set forth her business it suspends and her eyes begin to issue dividends." The man writing the story quailed in her presence. "He thought of Amazons going to war and trembled for the storekeepers and office clerks upon whom all those resources of rhetoric and optics would soon be brought to bear." But a conversation between the writer and the advertising agency's manager who employed women canvassers also enabled the essay to include a different interpretation of the canvassers. In the manager's positive assessment, women canvassers differed from the stereotypic rural or urban housewife in being independent. Instead of looking for support from their families, they struck out on their own. They were typically well educated or at least had educated themselves and were well read. Instead of being forced into the labor market, they in fact worked because they wanted to and happily spent their earnings on luxuries for themselves. They were energetic, mentally gifted, courageous, and at the same time patient and courteous. The proper masculine response, he argued, was to treat them with respect.[60]

Another positive appraisal of women canvassers suggested that they could succeed where men failed because men had to affect a less than masculine style to secure cooperation. Women were more easily invited into people's homes, could sell without being impolite, and could play up some aspect of themselves as being the weaker sex and in need. "Female canvassers are a pretty well-educated class," one observer explained. "They have been to school or are music teachers or they are poor gentlemen's daughters. In dress they are neat, not gaudy, and have a reserved, modest style of manner [that] always commands attention. If she is middle-aged she is perhaps a widow lady who lived in Southern affluence before the war, or a forsaken wife, or an ex-opera singer; and should she find the listener in the melting mood, she will drop a few remarks about financial or domestic troubles."[61]

Besides the deviations from gendered and other societal norms they often illustrated, peddlers and canvassers sometimes provided occasions for specifically positive moralizing. Americans who were familiar with biblical narratives extolling the hidden virtues of the stranger and of those showing strangers kindness could imagine the visitors who came to their doors hawking petty goods in this light. Blessed are the poor in spirit, Jesus taught. The widow's mite was more worthy than the gifts of the rich. The Samaritan cared for the injured sojourner when the other passersby did not. The key to such narratives was that the person who at first glance is an object of derision becomes the character who reveals a higher understanding of moral virtue. The tables are turned. The last shall be first. The person at the margins shows the moral standards to which the insiders have fallen short.

A true-to-life account of a fictional book canvasser circulated in small-town newspapers in 1877. In contrast to the usual narrative in which a beleaguered resident tries to get rid of the wily bookseller, the story put the reader in the bookseller's shoes. After losing his job and looking in vain for other employment, John hopes to care for his wife, Lizzie, and their children by selling books. Her care-worn face and the small glimmer of encouragement in her eyes linger in his mind as he sets forth canvassing, only to meet one rebuff after another. Servants slam doors in his face, women give him hard looks, children say nasty things when he appears, business managers cut him off before he can say three words, clerks refuse to speak with him. He is thoroughly defeated. Lizzie throws her arms around him that evening and tries to comfort him. "I am not the man I was when I left you this morning," he says. "I have been made to feel that I was a scalawag, a leper, an outcast, a scoundrel, and a thief. I have been shut out of houses, bullied from shops, and shunned in the street." "All for my sake and the children's, dear John," she says with tears in her eyes. "God bless you." Lizzie's response was like a "benediction" that in expressing such love helped the burden fall from John's shoulders, the writer explained, underscoring the moral meaning of the story. John was an outcast, a leper, not because of who he was but because of how he was treated, despite his good intentions. The higher value that the story emphasized was love, evident both in John's efforts on behalf of his family and in Lizzie's love for John at the moment of his despair.[62]

Huckstering in Decline

By the end of the nineteenth century, the ambiguities involved in huckstering had been reduced by the establishment of more clearly defined methods of commerce and by a long progression of legal efforts to subject huckstering itself to licensing ordinances and regulations. As important as the legal constraints were, huckstering and peddling became less important mostly because of changes in the nature of economic transactions. Farm-to-market roads that were maintained better at first with sand and gravel and then with paving made it easier for farmers to bring produce directly to towns and cities and to purchase household goods there instead of waiting for the peddler's wagon. Railroads significantly expanded during the first years of the twentieth century, making it possible for eggs, cream, milk, and butter to be shipped directly to urban markets.

The peddling that continued consisted mostly but not exclusively of canvassers and traveling salesmen selling on commission for large firms headquartered in cities such as Chicago, St. Louis, and Kansas City. In the few short years before mail-order catalogs replaced them, traveling salesmen continued to be the most important connection between the large manufacturing firms and the consumer. Whether it was brushes or chicken feeders or life insurance, consumers could discuss what they needed with the traveling salesman who came knocking at their door.

In farming areas remote from towns or in small towns without rail service, though, hucksters continued to be important channels for farm-to-market transactions well into the 1930s and 1940s. "Southern farm women," historian Lu Ann Jones observes, "proved adept at producing and selling a variety of goods and pursuing a range of marketing strategies. Delivering eggs or butter to a local merchant, trading with a huckster, selling at the curb market, or supplying individual customers was but the first step in a complicated trade network."[63] A farmwoman in Blount County, Tennessee, recalled the peddler coming every week at the same time, usually around lunch, feeding his horse and collecting produce to be sold in town.[64] A farmwoman in Jefferson County, Indiana, remembered the huckster who came once a week as well, in her case driving an old school bus with shelves for groceries and cages for chickens. "If you had chickens but didn't have enough money to pay for the groceries," she recalled, "the huckster would buy your chickens and you could take that amount out in groceries."[65]

As huckstering faded from public consciousness, it was replaced by discussions of a new kind of person about whom ambivalence also prevailed: the middleman. Observers saw the middleman as the key to understanding both the advances shaping economic relationships in the new century and its problems. On the positive side, middlemen served vitally as the connective tissue in an increasingly interdependent society composed of different parts that needed to be brought together. If a community offered investment opportunities and an investor off at a bank in a distant city was looking for opportunities, someone had to forge the connection. The middleman who played the role of intermediary was the answer. The middleman would thus help the community to prosper. The intermediary might even be effective in bringing prices down, as in the case of arranging for cheaper shipments of coal from mines in West Virginia to homes in New York City.

On the negative side, the middleman reflected the exploitative aspects of industrial capitalism that worried its critics. Was it not the middleman who arranged for entrepreneurs to lure young men and women from the farms into the cities' sweatshops? Weren't the middlemen who imported tea from India and chocolate from Latin America interlopers spreading colonialism and imperialism? "Through the beguilements of advertisements the middleman stimulates the imagination of the consumer to the degree that purchases are made of illy adapted articles," a sociologist wrote at the turn of the century.[66]

For better or worse, middlemen were the critical link connecting rural and urban America. "Large towns and small cities throughout the United States generally live not directly off the land about them, but indirectly through the middleman," an observer explained in 1912. "These towns in most cases have no market. The farmers of the country round about cannot sell in these towns the produce of their lands." The absence of "natural and normal intercourse between town and country" necessitated intermediaries such as grain marketers and shippers of produce. At the same time, the very existence of these mediating roles signaled a sharper distinction between the local norms of social and religious life in rural places and the pace of daily life in cities. That which was formerly produced and consumed locally on farms and in country towns was now symbolically alienated from the community by the distance and by the intermediaries through which it passed to terminals in the cities.[67]

In broader terms, the middleman became a metaphor for that which could not be classified and was thus troublesome for that reason alone. A book could be criticized on grounds that it hit somewhere in middleman territory rather than hitting its target. "The thought is that of a middleman," a reviewer explained in dismissing Henry Wood's *Political Economy of Humanism*, "not technical enough to be classed as research . . . nor popular enough to hold the attention of minds below a somewhat select grade of culture. One feels that those who can read the book do not need it, while those who need it will hardly be up to reading it."[68]

Unsurprisingly, the middleman came to be viewed as an alien "other." Nativist resistance to the large numbers of eastern and southern European immigrants who flooded to America from the 1890s to the 1920s attached ethnic labels to the middlemen who could not be easily categorized but were nevertheless disliked. Middlemen especially displayed foreign "Jewish characteristics" of slyness, greed, and a particular affinity for making money. The "middleman minority" theory, as it was dubbed later, argued that ethnic minorities who existed in the interstices of society perhaps had no alternative other than to become skilled in middleman roles. Excluded from the stable positions in society occupied by landowners and business leaders, the sojourners and strangers composed in one era of Jews or in another era of Asians and Latinos had no choice but to trade, travel, and carve out a precarious space in the middle.[69]

As the middleman role became more clearly defined as an institutionalized aspect of the modern economy, the hucksters, peddlers, canvassers, and agents who had previously played these mediating roles became less visible as symbols of societal marginality. They were, after all, less prominent numerically. They were harder to view as a large, influential class of people who could be described by singularities of ethnicity and national origin. Their very diversity protected them from classification, individuated their idiosyncratic characteristics, and even perpetuated some romantic impressions of their colorful past. Like the cinematic romanticization of the cowboy on a much larger stage, the huckster remained in American lore as a sometimes disreputable character who nevertheless was a humble wanderer surrounded by families and communities who mostly kept their distance but who were also intrigued.

And in real life, other itinerants took their place. The moral valences attached to placeless labor shifted to other persons—the migrant farm worker, the vagrant, the impoverished elderly person, and the homeless.

In 1882 Samuel Huey, with his wife and four young children, gave up farming, leaving behind the small grave of a son who died in infancy. Farming was hard enough for everyone, let alone a farmer with one hand who suffered for months at a time from inflammatory rheumatism. The Hueys sold the land they had tried without much success to farm for four years and moved their belongings by train to eastern Kansas, where Samuel had worked a decade before. Samuel resumed peddling, moved to another small town where he tried unsuccessfully running a grocery store, moved twice more, and then settled in a town of three thousand close enough to Kansas City that he could grow vegetables, plant fruit trees, and continue peddling.[70]

The family who purchased the farm from the Hueys made a go of it, staying and expanding their holdings over the next two generations. Huey's Civil War pension increased from $12 a month in 1890 to $27 a month in 1925. His wife died of tuberculosis in 1890, and one of his daughters succumbed five years later. Another daughter lived with him and cared for him until he died in 1935. His other daughter married a salesman. In old age, Huey took pride in tending a small orchard of fruit trees. His son followed in his footsteps, sharecropping, planting vegetables, picking fruit, working at odd jobs, and selling produce.

CHAPTER THREE

An Incurable Lunatic

PENSION POLITICS IN THE STRUGGLE FOR RESPECTABILITY

YOU COULD BE A RESPECTED MEMBER of the community if you lived in nineteenth-century America—you could earn your neighbors' respect if you worked hard, plowed your fields on time, operated a small store in town, kept your children clothed and fed, and showed up regularly for worship at the local meeting house—you could do all that but lose it all if you were suddenly stricken with insanity. You were then a cautionary tale to your neighbors about what not to do.

Insanity meant having abandoned the rational faculties governing the routine social relationships of ordinary life. In popular descriptions it meant having lost one's mental faculties and no longer being of sound mind. A person's status in the community shifted. You became an outsider—a defective, a mind-sick person, one of the nation's poor outcasts. And it could happen in an instant. One moment a person's mind was there; the next moment it was gone. Normal people suddenly "snapped," "broke," "broke down," sometimes flying into a fit of rage and in other cases sinking into a pit of despair.

Anyone in any community could be afflicted, or so it seemed. Even in quiet, out-of-the-way places where well-intentioned people struggled to achieve the American Dream, insanity happened. In one publicized instance a businessman rose from his bed at one o'clock in the morning apparently overcome with insanity and slit the throats of his two children. A similar incident occurred a few miles from Lawrence, Kansas, when a well-respected doctor slit the throats of his wife and daughter before slashing his own. Neighbors decided he must have gone insane. A year later a wealthy farmer living a few miles from Osawatomie, Kansas, "in a fit of insanity" murdered his daughter and dangerously wounded his wife and son-in-law. Later that fall Horace Greeley's *New York Tribune* announced its editor's death, attributing his demise to melancholia—"the most incurable form of lunacy." The following year a highly publicized assassination attempt on Kansas Senator Samuel C. Pomeroy was described as the result of a sudden seizure of insanity on the part of the assailant.[1]

Citizens and public officials looked to specialists to explain how such events could happen. What they learned was hardly reassuring. In an 1871 book on diseases of the nervous system, Dr. William A. Hammond of the Bellevue Hospital Medical College in New York argued that insanity could overtake an otherwise healthy person at any moment and for any number of reasons. Insanity could result from cerebral anemia, hemorrhage, mental exertion, sunstroke, congestion of the brain, the ingestion of bromides, and apoplexy, among other things. The onset could be preceded by such barely noticeable symptoms as irritability, crying, and inappropriate laughter.[2]

Insanity was clearly a social problem. Lunatics needed to be kept from hurting themselves and their families. Communities needed to protect themselves, lest some inhabitant become deranged and terrorize the neighbors. Procedures developed to determine when someone constituted a danger to the community. Legislatures passed laws, raised money, and constructed asylums for the insane.

The vast literature on insanity has dealt with the complexities of diagnosis and the search for effective treatments. Sociological studies have investigated the social conditions affecting rates of insanity. The historical literature has examined how mental institutions came into being and how they changed. The information detailing what life was like for the populations inside these institutions—the horrors of confinement and abuse—has been described in disturbing detail. Little doubt has been left about the difficulties involved in managing these institutions and being treated at them.[3]

What is far less understood is how the families of people who were declared insane got on with their lives. What did it take in the first place for a family to decide that proceedings should be initiated that might result in a loved one being confined to an asylum? What did that imply for the family's ability to sustain itself economically? How did their relationships with neighbors change? Who did they turn to for help?

The historical literature on insanity has recognized the need to pay greater attention to the families. In a well-argued essay in 1997 historian David Wright observed that studies too often focused on medical practitioners, superintendents, and asylums, drawing information from institutional records, rather than examining families' role in decisions about confinement. Subsequent studies suggested that families might have often been implicated in placing loved ones in asylums who they assumed would recover quickly or who they truly wanted to be rid of, while in other instances they may have been better able to provide care at home and in still others may have been reluctant to have relatives institutionalized because of the stigma involved.[4]

Shifting the focus to the spouses, children, and neighbors of persons de-clared insane necessitates addressing questions about respectability. The sharp distinction that society drew to separate its sense of civilized rational behavior—of functioning with a "sound mind"—from those it deemed insane was less sharp when it came to the people most closely associated with the in-sane. They were not themselves insane but stood most directly to lose by being associated with it. Their loss had to be calculated not only in the physical re-moval of a breadwinner, mother, father, or loved one but also in the questions the neighbors asked. Was there a biological problem that ran in the family? Would the insane person's children be next? Was the family simply attempting to rid itself of a nettlesome domestic problem? Were tensions in the family the problem? Would the family become a burden to the community? And whether those questions were ever uttered publicly or only harbored in private, the families' respect in the community could become seriously compromised as they dealt with the economic consequences of loss and learned how to navi-gate the complexities of relationships with asylum superintendents, medical professionals, lawyers, and government agencies.

These questions suggest the extent to which insanity needs to be under-stood less as a sharp boundary separating the insane from the sane and more as a wide gray band of menacing stigma, shame, and embarrassment casting doubt on the respectability of family members and requiring them to do all within their power to reclaim a respectable identity. Insofar as the insane be-came an "other" against which respectability was defined, the same was true of family members who bore the taint of being related to an insane person and thus were the focus of rumors that they too might be or become insane, violent, or an unwelcome presence in the community.

In the postbellum nineteenth century institutional support for the fami-lies of the mentally ill was far less available than it would be a century later. People in these circumstances had only their own resources to depend on and perhaps the assistance they could draw up from relatives and friends. There was, however, the potential of securing governmental support from Civil War pensions. And that put ordinary citizens in contact with attorneys and agents and bureaucrats in utterly unfamiliar ways. The result was a struggle not only to secure the meager resources that would help financially but also to maintain their sense of dignity. This was one of the borderlands on which middle-class respectability was defined.

This chapter examines the cultural work involved in that process. Princi-pally through the previously unexamined history of one such family I demon-strate the extent to which insanity not only separated individuals so identified from the rest of the community by institutionalizing them but also placed the families of the insane in an ambiguous status that required cultural and or-ganizational negotiation. The details of this particular case are unique and yet illuminate many of the challenges that other families, individuals, and communities faced at the time. The story traces the life of a man who like many others fought for his country, moved west with the expanding frontier, experienced a modicum of success, raised a family, and then became an incurable lunatic.

Becoming a Lunatic

William Hall was born on January 10, 1829, near Fairmont in the part of the state that would become West Virginia. He died at the Kansas State Insane Asylum in Topeka, Kansas, on July 20, 1899.[5] One of the small details of his birth that would later become a consideration in understanding his insanity was the fact that he was the youngest of eight children. His parents owned an 80-acre farm located at "Scotch Hill" a few miles southwest of Newburg, where his father held an elected office in local government, which put them squarely in the lower echelons of the rising middle class. Most of the farms in the area were small and the land was hilly, but it produced decent crops of corn and hay. In the 1850 U.S. Census, Jesse and Sarah Hall reported property valued at $2,500, which was among the most of any of the farm families in the township. The Halls were apparently descended from various Scotch-Irish and French Huguenot families that came to America in the late seventeenth and early eighteenth centuries, settling in Delaware, and then migrating west at the end of the century with veterans receiving land grants for serving in the army during the Revolutionary War. Being the youngest put William in line to care for his parents until they died, but being the youngest of eight meant little chance of inheriting enough to earn a living. If he was going to match his parents' economic status, he would have make it on his own.[6]

A second aspect of the story that would become important later was that the family were devout Methodists. According to a local source, William's father "was a justice, a Methodist class leader, and a model in morality and sobriety." One of William's brothers became a prominent member of the Methodist clergy. The brother's obituary stated that he "was blessed with pious parents, who gave him an early religious training, both being devoted members of the M.E. [Methodist Episcopal] Church." William would follow in their footsteps.[7]

The most crucial event in William's path to insanity was his service in the Civil War. When war broke out in 1861, he left almost immediately to support the Union cause, returned home for a year or so, and then served with the West Virginia Cavalry for nine months in 1863 and 1864. As a veteran, he would eventually qualify for a pension based on disability from his time in service. But that came later and dealt as much with his family as it did with him.[8]

In 1853 at the age of twenty-four William married Cynthia Ann Scott, the nineteen-year-old daughter of a well-established Virginia farming family.[9] Between 1856 and 1865 she gave birth to five children, never fully recovering from the fifth and dying in 1867.[10] The children were sent temporarily to live with relatives, and in 1868 Hall married Ann Gallahue, a thirty-six-year-old woman who lived nearby. In the interim William made a brief visit to Kansas, and in 1869 he emigrated with Ann and the five children from West Virginia to claim a quarter section of land in southeastern Kansas.[11]

Hall's visit had given him a firsthand look at the challenges settlers faced on the expanding frontier. Stories circulated of farm accidents, prairie fires, and skirmishes with Indians, but land was waiting to be settled, and already the impression given in local newspapers was one of civilization and progress. Churches were being built, Masonic lodges were being established, druggists and dentists were advertising their services, and shops were well stocked with lumber and dry goods. The hardest times were over, boosters said. Soon the fields would yield the choicest fruits of the land. The prairie was the place where hardworking, respectable people could better themselves.[12]

A letter published in western Pennsylvania newspapers in August 1868 typified the glowing reports to which readers were exposed. "Fertile bottoms with even surface which never overflow spread out on either side of the rivers and their tributaries from one mile to four miles in width," the correspondent said. "Nothing can surpass the transcendent beauty and grandeur of the natural scenery in Kansas." Readers should migrate before it was too late: "A mighty tide of immigration opened into Kansas this spring and newly arrived thousands are now building themselves homes within her limits." His advice: "To all I would say who are living on those poor farms in the Eastern States, come to Kansas and get good farms, land is cheap here varying from $5 to $10 for raw prairie land and $15 to $20 for improved land."[13]

Arriving in southeastern Kansas in 1869 meant being there when hopes for a bright future were high. Plans for not one but two major rail lines to come through the area, linking it with Kansas City to the north, Missouri to the east, and the Gulf ports to the south, raised hopes so high that three towns—one calling itself New Chicago—were laid out and within a few years merged to form Chanute. Settlers who came at the same time and lived on farms near the Halls were from Indiana and Illinois and Ohio and New York and as far away as Sweden, Ireland, and Germany.

The Halls set to work building a small house and erecting stone fences to corral farm animals. William opened a store, calling the place Mound Springs, and established himself as the postmaster. A Cumberland Presbyterian Church opened down the road in one direction and a Methodist Episcopal Church not far in another direction. Settlers "flocked in like the children of Israel into Canaan," a local writer observed a few years later. By 1875 the Mound Springs school was one of seven that provided rudimentary education to the township's growing number of children. Besides the five that came with them from West Virginia, the Halls produced six more children between 1869 and 1878.[14]

But William was not well. Documents indicate that he was initially taken ill shortly after the First Battle of Bull Run and spent three months in the General Hospital in Washington, DC.[15] Whether Hall was present during the battle itself is unclear, but as a "wagon master just after" the battle, he would have been among the bystanders whose service was called on to transport the wounded and bury the dead. Histories of the battle and its aftermath emphasize the raw devastation that the carriers experienced, including the stench of decomposing flesh and the contamination of water in the area. Medical care and ambulance services were so disorganized that rotting corpses remained on the battlefield for several days. It is not surprising that many like Hall spent time recuperating.[16]

Hall returned to Preston County sometime in late 1861, where he remained through the following year tending the farm and caring for his family. As the war escalated and the need for additional troops increased, Congress passed the Enrollment Act, also known as the Civil War Military Draft Act, on March 3, 1863, which required men ages twenty through forty-five to register as persons subject to do military duty. Hall, like many of the men who enrolled, chose to enlist voluntarily rather than be conscripted. By the time he enrolled in October, he had been on active duty for three months.

Hall's service in the 4th West Virginia Cavalry in 1863 and 1864 contributed to his health problems. The regiment consisted of eighty-four men, including Hall's twenty-year-old nephew and his nineteen-year-old brother-in-law.[17] Hall was one of six sergeants. The regiment's leader was the Reverend Jeremiah L. Simpson, a Methodist Protestant pastor who served initially as the regiment's chaplain, recruited many of its members, and then held the rank of captain.[18] The regiment guarded the B&O railroad along the West Virginia and Maryland border, engaging in combat against Confederate troops in late January 1864.[19] A few days later as the troops struggled to stay warm against the bitter cold, measles swept through their ranks, claiming the life of twenty-one-year-old Caleb Zinn, whose marriage three years earlier had been performed by Reverend Simpson. Zinn died of hemorrhaging lungs before he could be transported to a hospital. Hall's fellow sergeant Michael Bradshaw contracted measles a few days later. Suffering from exposure during the 150-mile journey to the nearest hospital at Wheeling, he died on March 8, leaving a widow and five children.[20] Hall was fortunate in comparison to suffer only from lingering illnesses. An affidavit submitted on January 10, 1890, stated, "I remember him as a stout healthy man when he entered my company and I also remember he lost his health in said service and was excused from duty quite often." An affidavit submitted about the same time by Sergeant Abram R. Shriver, who served in the same company, stated, "I remember William A. Hall was sick in said service not down but moping around not able for duty; perhaps he had diarrhea as we had a great deal of that. But the exact nature of his disease and the time and place of said sickness I cannot exactly tell."

Hall's health problems continued when the family moved to Kansas. Dr. M. A. Alexander wrote in an affidavit submitted on November 16, 1889, "I was said William A. Hall's family physician mostly from about the year 1868 or1870 to 1880, during which time I frequently treated said soldier for chronic diarrhea and its results."[21] In a letter of April 29, 1890, Ann Hall stated, "He was taken sick in year 70 in July with Chronic Diarrhea. The doctor that treated him is Dr. Alexander, which his affidavit you have. Six months. He was troubled with the chronic diarrhea until 1874." Another doctor, Peter Julian, recalled treating Hall in 1878 for "chronic diarrhea and rheumatism." "Of his complaints, he told me he had never been clear of rheumatism and chronic diarrhea since he was affected while in the Army."[22]

Hall suffered a nervous breakdown in 1874 when he was forty-five years old. "First day of January 74," Ann's letter continued, "he went insane and was for a time not able to do any thing for his family." On February 21, 1874, Hall's physician, Dr. Alexander brought an affidavit to the Wilson County Probate Court in Fredonia stating that Hall "is a lunatic and incapable of managing his own affairs." The court directed the county sheriff to "summon twelve good and lawful persons to serve as jurors to make inquiry touching said alleged insanity." A few hours later the sheriff returned with twelve jurors who upon being duly sworn in heard testimony from Dr. Alexander and three witnesses, farmers who lived near the Halls. The jurors deliberated briefly and returned a verdict that Hall was indeed "a person of unsound mind and incapable of managing his affairs." Nothing suggests that the jurors had reason to be biased, although they were undoubtedly persuaded by the testimony of Hall's neighbors and a physician: four were farmers, two were carpenters, one was a blacksmith, one was a stone mason, and four were visiting the town. Three days later the court appointed a guardian to take charge of Hall's affairs, for which the guardian posted a bond of $800. The guardian delivered Hall into the custody of the superintendent of the Kansas Insane Asylum at Osawatomie on February 26.[23]

By 1874 asylums in which to institutionalize the insane temporarily or for long periods were common. Although insanity was not well understood, its reality as a medical condition had come to be accepted to the extent that lawmakers initiated efforts to provide publicly funded institutions for the insane, just as they did for the deaf, blind, and feebleminded. Other than the Eastern Lunatic Asylum at Williamsburg, Virginia, begun in 1773, the first wave of asylum founding took place in the 1820s and 1830s, by the end of which a dozen were in existence. Thirteen more were constructed in the 1840s, seventeen were added in the 1850s, and by 1874 sixty-four were in existence, located in thirty-two states and the District of Columbia.[24]

The Kansas Insane Asylum at Osawatomie opened in 1866 and included two wings with space in each for twenty-four patients.[25] Its first patient was a prisoner who arrived under duress and escaped the following day. Three years later, still struggling with how to treat the insane, the asylum received an unexpected visit from reformer Dorothea Dix, who left a box of books and stern advice about the need to improve.[26] In 1870 seventeen men and nineteen women were inmates at Osawatomie. They ranged in age from a boy of ten and another boy of eleven to a man age sixty-seven (the average age of men was thirty-five and of women thirty-two). None of the inmates had been born in Kansas and all but four could read and write. Eight of the men were farmers. The other men's occupations varied from physician and lawyer to stage driver and shoemaker to miller and day laborer. Most of the women listed their occupations as keeping house, but two were teachers and one was a milliner. The asylum's staff consisted of a doctor, a druggist, an engineer, a cook, six housekeepers, and four laborers.[27]

Counties initially paid for the expenses associated with public patients from the county of residence, but in 1874 the state assumed responsibility for these expenses if the court determined, as it did in Hall's case, that the patient's family could not cover them. The asylum also accepted private patients who were admitted simply on a recommendation of a doctor with no court order required. Although the asylum was planned by well-meaning reformers who considered themselves at the forefront of progressive social innovations, it resembled a prison more than it did a hospital, serving to protect society from persons considered dangerous for whom only custodial care was possible.[28] In February 1874 when Hall arrived at Osawatomie, the asylum was emerging from a month of turmoil during which half of the attendants resigned in protest and one of the patients escaped.[29] "The buildings are already so overcrowded with patients that proper classification is rendered impossible," the superintendent acknowledged in his annual report, "and the unhappy inmates but jostle and irritate each other while the necessary appliances for their care are so defective that the supply of properly cooked and prepared food even is questionable." He considered the institution a failure.[30]

Hall's first stay at Osawatomie lasted approximately six weeks. On March 14 the steward at Osawatomie wrote to the probate judge stating that Hall was "restored to his right mind," had been ordered discharged, and should be "removed at once or send him means to go home with." The court did not meet again until April 8, but on that day it convened a new twelve-person jury, which considered the case and declared Hall "of sound mind and capable of managing his own affairs."[31] During the weeks that Hall was a patient at Osawatomie, the most colorful person with whom he would have had contact was the Reverend Samuel L. Adair, who had served briefly as the asylum's director and was now its chaplain and in that capacity preached the asylum's regular Sunday services. Adair's wife was abolitionist John Brown's sister, and, like Brown, Adair and his wife were vehement abolitionists. In the late 1850s they gave refuge to escaping slaves, and, like other Congregational pastors, Adair was active in the free state cause.

His apparent recovery in 1874 notwithstanding, Hall's struggle with mental illness continued. On May 24, 1878, the Wilson County Probate Court again received a statement that Hall was of unsound mind and incapable of managing his affairs. The court initiated the same procedure as in 1874, summoning a twelve-person jury. This time Hall was "brought into court and questioned by the said jurors and the court and the evidence of sundry witnesses was then given to the jury." The jury determined Hall to be insane; the duration and cause were said to be unknown but not due to heredity or epilepsy and not indicative of homicidal or suicidal tendencies. Having appointed a guardian, the court then sent Hall for confinement to Osawatomie. This hospitalization lasted until August 20, when Hall was discharged "restored to his right mind."[32]

On July 28, 1879, Hall once again appeared before the Wilson County Probate Court as a person accused of unsound mind. This time a jury of six heard testimony from a "physician in regular practice and good standing" and determined that Hall was insane. "His disease is of unknown duration," the court recorder wrote. "The cause of his insanity is from religious excitement and family trouble. His disease is not hereditary and not produced from any epileptic tendency. He does not manifest any suicidal, but does manifest homicidal tendencies." A week later Hall was admitted at Osawatomie, although his guardian thought Hall's condition had improved. On August 20 Hall was once again released and declared to be of sound mind.[33]

In January 1880 Hall was admitted to the Kansas State Insane Asylum in Topeka, where he spent the rest of his life.[34] This asylum opened in 1879 and was in a better position to take new inmates than the Osawatomie asylum, which was already overcrowded. A history of the Topeka asylum in this period says it "consists in a central section used as an administration building, on either side of which are three ward buildings. Those on the east are for men and those on the west for women. A detached building with a capacity of two hundred and eighty-nine beds was constructed shortly after the main group and used exclusively for chronic male patients."[35]

The Hall case, from his initial breakdown to permanent institutionalization six years later, demonstrates the significant extent to which becoming a lunatic was a matter not only of clinical diagnosis but also of social relationships. The legal procedures requiring a court hearing were specified in lengthy detail passed by the Kansas Legislature in 1868. The legislation, which pertained to "lunatics and habitual drunkards," stipulated that a panel of at least six jurors should be assembled by the judge and that testimony should be heard by a physician. Whether the person accused was required to be present was optional, but the person had the right to be represented by an attorney. At the conclusion of the hearing the jurors were required to sign the verdict, the wording of which was to include the duration of the accused's insanity, its likely cause or causes, and whether it was determined to be hereditary or associated with epilepsy. Much of the legislation was concerned with the ac-cused's property, which a person of unsound mind was considered incapable of managing. An inventory of the person's assets was to be made, and if suf-ficient assets were available, the cost of the hearing and subsequent confine-ment were to be borne by the person, and if not, by the county or state. A guardian was to be appointed, the responsibilities of whom were described in detail. Additional details dealt with contingencies associated with property held jointly with the person's spouse, the disposition of the person's property at death, and procedures for restoring the person's rights and property if a recovery occurred. The legislation, however, did not attempt to specify what it meant to be of unsound mind, leaving that to the determination of the physi-cian and the jury.[36]

The Kansas statutes resembled those enacted previously in other states, but with notable differences. Unlike Kansas, most states did not treat the in-sane under the same heading as "habitual drunkards." Illinois, which under legislation passed in 1845 categorized "idiots, lunatics, insane, and distracted persons" together, required that a jury be summoned but did not specify the number of jurors or what they were supposed to do.[37] Missouri's 1866 legis-lation similarly specified that a jury be convened and devoted the bulk of its statutes to questions of guardianship.[38] Indiana and Iowa, in contrast, under legislation enacted in 1818 and 1839, respectively, required that twelve jurors be summoned and that they be "intelligent and disinterested." The statutes further required that three guardians rather than one be appointed for the "safety and preservation" of the property of any person judged to be insane.[39] Massachusetts and several other states included as qualifiers the words "repu-table," "respected," or "respectable" in indicating which physicians and citi-zens were allowed to bring formal accusations of insanity. New Hampshire required that the hearings be conducted by the duly elected selectmen of the town in which the alleged lunatic lived.[40] Revisions in several other states sought to overcome earlier shortcomings in the statutes. For example, New York required that certifications of lunacy be made by two reputable physi-cians not related to the accused and provided that any relative or coresident of the accused could call for a public hearing.[41]

The requirement of a jury hearing had as its principal purpose protecting the property of someone judged to be temporarily or permanently incapable of managing such matters on their own. Putting the alleged symptoms and causes of a person's insanity before a panel of witnesses and jurors aimed to prevent persons being declared insane and institutionalized simply because a spouse, child, neighbor, landlord, doctor, or some other member of the com-munity wanted to quietly be rid of them. That was of concern because a person legally insane could not buy or sell property or revise a will, and in some in-stances the person's marriage could be annulled. Judge and jury had to agree that the evidence warranted institutionalizing the person, just as in a criminal case. Further, the witnesses and jurors received a small fee for their service, and, because the fee was charged to the county budget, the names of the witnesses and jurors and the fees paid, along with the name of the person accused of insanity, were usually published in the local newspaper. The less desirable consequence of the proceedings was that a person accused of insanity was known as such by the entire community, which meant that the shame and embarrassment of having been declared insane and of having a family member so declared was public.

Small-town newspapers routinely carried the names of witnesses, jurors, doctors, sheriffs, guardians, and judges involved in legal proceedings against persons accused of insanity. What may have preserved the accused's anonymity in some cases was that the hearings were held in the county seat and enlisted jurors who may not have lived near the accused or may only have been visiting. Not everyone read the newspapers either. But the witnesses had to be acquaintances of the accused. The notices indicated who had been appointed guardian and who had been paid to transport the insane person to the asylum. And residents who may have cared about their taxes knew that a portion was perhaps being used to cover the cost of someone being insane.

Lacking further details about the substance of the hearings, the public was left to speculate about why a respectable member of the community had been declared insane. In Hall's case the "family trouble" mentioned in the court report would likely have been discussed in sufficient detail at the hearing that the witnesses and jurors would have had plenty to gossip about in the days following. Was it that William and Ann were not getting along? Had he abused her? Had she become exhausted from tending a sick husband while mothering a large family? Perhaps they were still fighting the war: they'd come from West Virginia where families were divided, after all, and William's service had been with the Union while one of Ann's brothers had fought for the Confederacy. Or was the trouble between the older children from the first marriage and the younger children from the second?

Family troubles led often enough to violence that physicians and jurors were remiss if they failed to take any hint of them seriously. The physician, witnesses, and jurors at Hall's first hearing in 1874 would have been keenly aware of the report two years earlier of the insane farmer near Osawatomie who killed his daughter and wounded his wife and son-in-law. The hearing in 1878 occurred just six months after an "estimable citizen" in Indiana became violently insane, threw his two-year-old daughter to her death from a second-story window, chased his wife and family from the house with an ax, chopped up the furniture, and held a squad of law officers at bay for three hours before being overpowered and taken in manacles to the insane asylum. Had Dr. Alexander or one of the witnesses heard Hall making angry threats toward his family? Did Ann initiate the proceedings because she feared for her life? At a time when authorities rarely dealt with spousal abuse until it was too late, one of the few recourses for women was to have their husbands sent to an insane asylum, even if it meant financial disaster for the family. Who then in these circumstances retained the community's respect? Was it the wife because she was the victim? Or did the victim also come under suspicion? Was she perhaps like a young woman in Ohio whose father went insane and killed her because she was sleeping around? Or like a woman in Indiana who plotted with her son to kill her husband? [42]

Domestic problems notwithstanding, family relationships played an important role in physicians' and jurors' deliberations for additional reasons. Detailed stipulations about guardianship were included because the disposition of lunatics' property affected their families, as did responsibilities in some instances for the expense of their care and maintenance. Whether the insanity was brought on by epilepsy or was hereditary provided an indication of the likelihood that institutionalization would be short- or long-term but also was conducive to speculation that the lunatic's children might be tainted. Surely insanity was as rooted in biology as any other disease, psychiatrists argued, and if it was physical then it most likely could be inherited. And if it was, the children of lunatics needed to be watched not only for practical reasons but also to see if the problem stemmed more from fathers or mothers and why it seemed to affect some children more than others. In the interest of learning more, asylum directors and legislatures sometimes decided to investigate. Massachusetts, for example, in 1877 expanded the information it required for anyone being admitted to an insane asylum to include the previous or present existence of insanity in the person's family, whether the person in the case of women had borne any children, and the names of children and other relatives. [43]

Religious excitement of the kind Hall's physician said he exhibited would likely have seemed less important to a family's reputation and well-being than questions about inherited insanity, but it was also as much a matter of public perception as it was of private devotion. Reared as he was in a devout Methodist family, Hall would naturally have been interested in reading and hearing about religious developments. In 1872 readers of religious periodicals learned that "the greatest series of revivals which have ever taken place west of the Mississippi" were occurring in Kansas City, Leavenworth, and Lawrence. "Hundreds of hardened sinners, among them drunkards, gamblers and prostitutes, yielded to the power of the gospel," a Methodist writer observed. "Very few even of the smaller towns" had missed having similar revivals. "Religion has been the prevailing topic of discussion in the newspapers, on the streets, in the hotels and railway cars. Not only have whole families been renewed, but villages, towns and cities wear a new aspect." It was true, a writer reflecting on the revivals acknowledged, that there was probably a bit too much zeal, excitement, and even fanaticism, but perhaps that was the price to be paid for getting rid of vice and shame. [44] Two years later a Kansas Methodist presiding

elder wrote that despite the harsh weather and poor crops the religious climate was "decidedly cheering." The state was experiencing "powerful revivals" resulting in some 500 new church members.[45] In 1877 Methodist leaders
again reported that "revival influences were very earnest," with crowds gathering across the southern part of the state for afternoon preaching services and
extending well into the night.[46] And in 1879 newspapers in the Halls' vicinity
carried the story of a Methodist revival in another state at which the fervor of
religious enthusiasm was "rapidly growing to fever heat."[47]

Religious excitement could be regarded, as it often was, as a source of insanity, resulting in delusions, convulsive trembling, and fits of ecstasy. Medical journals discussed patients obsessed with their own sinfulness, disposed
toward constant prayers and exhortations, and believing themselves to be the
messengers of divine revelations.[48] Reports of religious excitement also circulated in newspapers, such as the story in 1879 of a man who attended a series
of Adventist revival meetings, went home, fasted, and killed his five-year-old
daughter, believing he was following the Lord's command and that his daughter would be resurrected in three days.[49] But religion could also be understood
as a hedge against insanity, curbing habitual drunkenness and whatever other
vices might contribute to an unsound mind. It could provide an explanation
for family troubles, illness, and financial reversals, deepening one's sense of
shame or absolving a person of guilt, and it could provide hope in the midst
of adversity. To think of it only as a cause of insanity and not as a response
that provided meaning and solace was clearly too narrow. It was in any case a
matter of belonging to a congregation, having an identity to uphold there as a
family, hearing sermons, and participating in worship with one's neighbors or
even with one's asylum mates as Hall undoubtedly did at Osawatomie. To have
gone insane from religious excitement and to have had that reported to a jury
was grist for communal interpretation among one's coreligionists: evidence
that faith could easily lead to fanaticism, an argument that revivals should be
conducted responsibly and within respectable limits.[50]

The public nature of the hearings opened questions that sometimes
prompted the very controversies they were intended to avoid. In 1879 as Hall
was being institutionalized for the third time a controversy that illustrated
how an extended family and their neighbors could become involved erupted in
an adjacent county. Deacon Ephraim Fisk and his wife Elizabeth were among
a colony of Congregationalists and Presbyterians from Connecticut and New
York who migrated west in 1857 in hopes of founding a large settlement in
the Neosho Valley. In the late 1870s when Elizabeth died, Fisk married Mary
Curtis, a widow living nearby. Mary's son Alroy, Alroy's wife Lena, two young
children, and Alroy's sister Addie, a mentally challenged spinster who required
the family's supervision and care, also lived nearby. Fisk and one of his sons
were among the community's wealthier landowners, while Alroy was struggling on eighty acres, only seven of which were under cultivation. Fisk decided

to help his step son by securing public assistance for Addie. A six-member jury that included a physician and the justice of the peace assembled for a hearing at the offices of the probate judge, and Addie was determined to be insane. Instead of sending Addie to an asylum, the judge opted for the legal alternative, which was to grant a fifty cent per diem to the family to provide home care.

But this decision did not sit well with some of the local citizens, who were already mired in other difficulties: of the three hundred families the original settlers expected to arrive, fewer than a quarter did; crops were not good; and hopes for better days were dashed when plans for a railroad fell through.[51] A petition crying foul about Addie's support circulated through the community, and a few days later an anonymous letter appeared in the local newspaper claiming that Fisk had engineered a "dirty disgracing swindle." Addie was a poor girl who had been "for years shamefully handled," the letter declared, "but [we] do not consider her crazy." The county commissioners should disallow the payment for her care, the letter concluded, "and thus fifty cents per day ($182.50 per year) of our toil stained, hard earned taxes can be more appropriately used elsewhere."[52]

Two weeks later Fisk published an angry reply. "Addie's insanity had reached a state that it became difficult during her insane fits to manage her," he said, "making it necessary to watch her day and night, sometimes obliging Alroy, when she would give him the slip, to get up in the coldest of nights and to go out on the prairie and hunt her up and get her into the house." This was the reason for applying to have her declared insane so she could be admitted to the asylum where her insanity might be cured. "The jury was doubtless selected of men supposed to be fully competent to be judges of such cases; moreover, the examining physician pronounced her to be 'insane, imbecile, and incurable.'" Only because the asylum was not ready to take her was the fifty cents per diem granted, "which was the price fixed upon by the state authority." Surely the petition had been gotten up from "envy and spite," he charged, by people, some of whom were fellow church members, who had it in for Alroy and his mother. Fisk wanted the church to conduct an investigation, he said, but his efforts "were opposed and defeated by those that had signed the protest. From what motives, the community must judge for themselves." As the controversy continued to simmer, Addie was sent to the asylum at Osawatomie, where she spent the remaining thirty years of her life.[53]

The difference between a dirty swindle and a person truly deserving care was never as easy to determine in practice as in theory. Efforts to instruct jurors in what exactly they should consider demonstrated the difficulties. New Hampshire, for example, published detailed guidelines and provided sample forms that judges, lawyers, jurors, and asylum superintendents were supposed to use in communicating with persons alleged to be insane and their families. The guidelines, however, observed that confusion prevailed in distinguishing lunacy from idiocy and both from cases in which persons' capacity to manage

FIGURE 5. *Kansas State Insane Asylum at Topeka*, ca. 1900.
Kansas State Historical Society, Topeka, kansasmemory.org.

their affairs was compromised by illness or old age. Witnesses and jurors were
advised to be unequivocal in their conclusions as to whether the alleged de-
rangement of mind was interspersed with lucid intervals, in which case specific moments of insanity should be identified, or was evident in habits over
time. Ultimately the verdict depended on determining whether an action observed would have been performed under similar circumstances by a sensible
person.[54]

The procedure of requiring juried hearings came under increasing criticism both for spreading misgivings toward the insane and their families and
for putting the definition of insanity in inexperienced hands. Dr. B. D. Easton,
superintendent of the Kansas State Insane Asylum at Topeka, in an 1895 statement on "The Rights of the Insane" argued eloquently for a newer, more humane concept of mental illness. "Taking the insane person into court, forcing
him to hear the testimony often coming from members of the patient's family
[and] obliging him to listen to the necessary statements regarding his mental
infirmity and a recapitulation of his delusions," he wrote, "may be likened to
a case of severe gunshot wound brought into court. Six men from store, shop,
or stable, successively push their bacteria-laden filthy fingers into the wound,
the lawyers do the same thing, the sheriff takes his turn and the janitor has his
opportunity and then the case is turned over to the surgeon, who is expected
to do an aseptic operation."[55]

Hall's family left southeastern Kansas shortly after he was sent to the asylum at Topeka. They did not go to Topeka where they could be near him but to
eastern Kansas and eventually to Kansas City, where Ann worked as a washer
woman and took a job at a carpet-weaving plant. The children from the first
marriage took jobs in other towns in Kansas and Oklahoma. One joined the

Salvation Army. Whether the move was driven by economic necessity or by a desire to escape the embarrassment of remaining in the community, it succeeded in putting them in a new location where few would know about William unless they needed to know.

Confinement

The 1880 U.S. Census listed most Americans only once, but it listed William A. Hall, age fifty-one, four times. One was with his family in Johnson County, presumably reported residing there by Ann, who assumed his absence was temporary or hoped it would be. The second was as an inmate at the Topeka insane asylum. The third was in a special list of "defective" persons at the asylum in Topeka. And the fourth was a list of "defective" persons in Johnson County. The Topeka list showed him suffering from "melancholia," while the Johnson County list said it was "mania." The difference was probably an indication that neither list was precise—or it may have been that Hall suffered from both, vacillating from one to the other, as a later report would suggest.

Among all the inmates at Topeka and Osawatomie in 1880, 51 percent were said to be afflicted with mania, 19 percent with melancholia, 24 percent with dementia, 4 percent with epilepsy, 1 percent with paresis, and 1 percent with imbecility.[56] Melancholia appears to have distinguished those who were quiet and depressed from those suffering from mania, who were loud, excitable, and sometimes in need of physical restraint. Fifty-six percent were men and 44 percent were women. While the majority of men were single, the majority of women were married. The average (mean) age of men at Topeka was 37.2 years and at Osawatomie 35.4 years. Women's ages were nearly the same, averaging 38 at Topeka and 35.3 at Osawatomie. The most commonly listed occupation for men was farming and for women keeping house, but other occupations ranged from doctor, lawyer, and teacher, to real estate agent, railroad worker, and day laborer.

What the exact source of Hall's "melancholia" or "mania" may have been is impossible to know, although several factors may have contributed to his troubles.[57] The Kansas Census of 1875, which included information about agriculture, showed that William Hall owned 160 acres of land with an assessed value of $576 and that he had $282 in personal property associated with the farm. Consistent with the later evidence, the farm included approximately 1,200 feet of stone fencing, probably to corral animals. During the previous year, the farm had grown six acres of winter wheat, thirty acres of corn, seven acres of castor beans, half an acre of sorghum, and half an acre of Irish potatoes.[58] By those indications, the farm was doing well. Among the seventy farm families in Pleasant Valley Township, twenty-eight owned at least 160 acres and only five owned more than that. Land that had been purchased for an average of $2.50 an acre was now valued at an average of $3.00 to $3.50 an acre.

But inmates at Osawatomie and Topeka who suffered from melancholia or mania, according to histories of the institutions, spoke of being particularly afflicted by the trauma and tragedies that were commonly experienced at the time. Many of the men suffered from what they had witnessed during the Civil War. Others spoke of losing their health, the death of a spouse or child, or financial setbacks.[59] According to his doctor, Hall was one of the patients whose illness was compounded by financial embarrassment. Whether the more than $3,000 in personal assets he reported in 1870 had diminished to the less than $1,000 in land and property shown in 1875 or was simply a matter of differences in reporting, a loss of that much could have been a source of his distress. The multiple locations in which he took residence between 1864 and 1867 suggest that he may have been struggling to find a place to settle down and earn a living. The store that he opened in spring 1870 apparently failed, and the Mound Springs Post Office for which he served as postmaster that fall closed before the end of 1871. And, despite the acreage of corn and other crops he reported having planted in 1874, the chances were high that the results were disappointing.

Settlers' expectations of high profits from farm produce had already been dashed by the financial panic of 1873, causing many to have mortgages foreclosed. Winter that year was "unusually severe" and protracted, causing a large number of stock to perish.[60] "To add to the distress," the official history of the county observed, "came in 1874 a drouth, hot winds, chintz bugs and the grasshopper." For the farmers in Pleasant Valley like Hall, whose land was planted mostly in corn, this may have been especially devastating. Wheat matured sooner and largely escaped, but the problems "precluded the raising of the usual crop of corn." The grasshoppers came in August, "dropping as from a great cloud, wide spread wings glancing white in the sunshine." "As far as the eye could penetrate into the sky could be seen the flying pests. At first thinly veiled, then fairly darkening the sun. At first dropping one here, one there, then many hundreds here and thousands there until the surface of the earth was a blackish-gray mass of moving, active hoppers."[61] In April 1874 Hall mortgaged the farm for a loan of $600, clear evidence that things were not going well.[62]

Financial worries may have been particularly vexing for Hall because of the growing size of the family for which he was responsible. By 1880 Ashford, the oldest son, was in his twenties and may have owned an adjacent farm before moving to Chanute and working as a stonemason. Findley and Bertha may have also been employed. Sophie was to join the Salvation Army. Grant was still in the household, but left that year with one of his brothers to work in Oklahoma. And the second family now included Kate, Tom, Eddie, Mame, Emma, and Elinor. The usual solution to providing for large families on meager incomes was to put the children to work. Still, when the Halls settled in Pleasant Valley, they were among the few families with such a large number of children to support.

FIGURE 6. *Patients at the Kansas State Insane Asylum*, ca. 1900.
Kansas State Historical Society, Topeka, kansasmemory.org.

The family's new worry, now that William was institutionalized, was whether he was safe and receiving proper care. Word spread from time to time of contagious illnesses, fires, and deaths at other asylums. Families worried that their loved ones might be in the presence of violent inmates or neglected owing to overcrowding. If Dr. Eastman believed the mentally ill should be treated better, his years as the asylum's director were nevertheless marked with controversy about how the patients were actually treated. As an able-bodied man in his early fifties who did not suffer from digestive illness all the time and who was given to occasional bouts of excitement, Hall would have spent his days doing hard labor, shoveling dirt, hoeing, and weeding the asylum's large garden and tending its farm animals, mowing grass and scooping snow, or providing unpaid labor during the construction of new buildings, interspersed with days and evenings of abject boredom when patients sat lined in wooden rocking chairs with no reading material and nothing to occupy their minds.[63]

The difficulties Eastman encountered in providing healthy, humane treatment were compounded by a rapid increase in the number of inmates. At Topeka the number jumped from 124 in 1880 when Hall was admitted to 508 in 1886 and climbed steadily to 842 by the end of the century. At Osawatomie, the comparable increase was from 200 in 1880 to 400 in 1886 to 1,026 in 1900.[64] The administrators at both institutions spent much of their time appealing to the legislature for additional funds and more buildings and overseeing the construction of buildings. Journalists occasionally posted stories of overcrowding, although their reports generally described the asylums as suitable locations for people who would otherwise pose danger to the public or be exploited in private clinics.

The principal reasons for Eastman's on-again, off-again tenure as superintendent, serving from 1879 until 1883, from 1885 until 1893, and from 1895 until 1897, were accusations of mismanagement and outright corruption among the asylum's staff. Located so close to the state capital, the asylum became a political football that legislators used to reward their cronies and that journalists and legislators' opponents reveled in disclosing whenever the worst abuses came to light.[65] Despite Prohibition being the state law, orders for gallons of whiskey occasionally showed up on the asylum's inventory, and on at least one occasion an inmate who had been declared dead from natural causes was shown to be the victim of murder when his body was exhumed.[66]

The worst charges of corruption against Eastman's administration came in the 1890s when Populists swept the long-dominant Republican Party from office and for a brief period replaced the asylum's administrators with officers and staff of their own.[67] In a June 10, 1895, letter to the secretary of the American Medico-Psychological Association, Eastman took the occasion of explaining why he could not attend the association's annual meetings to vent his spleen against his Populist replacements. The asylum's new officers, he complained, consisted of a seamstress, teamster, baker, and several housekeepers, "no one of whom had ever had any asylum experience [and] were totally unfitted by natural bent, habits, and previous occupations for their duties." Insubordination and pandemonium ensued.

> Ere long the matron and superintendent would not speak to each other, the clerk and the superintendent came to blows, the engineer and clerk were at war, the bookkeeper ignored the steward; some of the board remained continually at the asylum and incited insubordination against the superintendent they had been anxious to elect; the members of the board quarreled among themselves; the female assistant superintendent brought suit against the superintendent for assault and battery; the matron brought suit against him for slander; the superintendent brought suit against the assistant superintendent and matron and two of the trustees for conspiracy, and the assistant superintendent and matron obtained an injunction against the board to prevent the acceptance of resignations said to have been obtained by fraud.[68]

The effect of such pandemonium on inmates whose mental health was impaired and whose well-being depended completely on the asylum's administration cannot have been good. The asylum's perfunctory biennial reports to the legislature chronicled the construction of new buildings and quantified the inmates who had been admitted, released, and died. The reports stated that robust dinners of mashed potatoes, fresh vegetables, and ample servings of meat were being served, leaving it to discerning readers to observe that evening meals consisted only of bread and butter or crackers and cheese.[69] Eastman himself acknowledged that inmates were frequently moved from room to room, resulting in emotional breakdowns, or were awakened in the middle of the night with a new inmate being asked to share what in better times was supposed to be a private room. Only after they were released did some of the inmates disclose instances of being beaten and witnessing inmates being sexually abused.[70]

With hardly anything known at the time about mental illness, asylum superintendents and physicians vacillated from arguing that insanity was probably inherited and incurable to suggesting that it could come on unexpectedly from something as minimally traumatic as being in the sun too long, to implying that it was probably attributable to moral depravity—or, if not caused by moral failure, then a source of it. As another asylum superintendent explained: "That an abnormal condition of the moral powers is a frequent effect of insanity, is now one of those well-settled facts that nobody thinks of questioning. It may be a simple perversion of some sentiment or propensity, or a morbid irritability of the affective powers, under certain causes of excitement. It may be a loss of those fine sensibilities which make the family relations a source of active interest and self-sacrifice, or a feeling of hatred and hostility as bitter as it is unfounded."[71]

The prevailing view held that institutionalization was the only preferable alternative to incarcerating lunatics or letting them go free to harm (or be harmed by) the public. If life on the open frontier was not already dangerous enough, news stories stoked fears of lunatics on the loose by attributing otherwise inexplicable acts of violence to perpetrators' sudden attacks of insanity. How else was it possible to understand a husband killing his wife, a mother killing her children, or an esteemed member of the community killing himself? In the 1870s and 1880s readers learned of insane men and women mysteriously disappearing from their homes, drilling holes in their heads, shooting their spouses and children, committing grisly hatchet murders, and attempting to assassinate public officials.

The Topeka and Osawatomie asylums adopted what was known as the "colony" model, which isolated the insane from the public but provided patients with opportunities to work.[72] Reformers hoped the colonies would protect the public while restoring the insane to health, but nearly every report mentioned escapees and revealed that the numbers released and fully restored to health were markedly low. Nor did the colony system relieve the mentally ill from suffering similar consequences to those imprisoned. Like convicted felons, patients in insane asylums were locked in their rooms at night and were not allowed to vote or testify in court, and on several occasions legislation was introduced denying unmarried patients and former patients the right to marry.[73]

If being institutionalized was devastating for patients, it was no less traumatic for patients' families. In addition to suffering the absence of a loved one, the family itself sometimes bore the responsibility for having asked that the loved one be declared insane. When the patient was the breadwinner, the family was left with only the help of neighbors and relatives to sustain itself. But if insanity was assumed to run in families, and when most of the news stories about insanity associated it with violence, neighborly support may not have been forthcoming. Veterans' pensions were unhelpful except on rare occasions as well because the asylum covered the veteran's care, and the spouse who otherwise would have been eligible was not yet a widow.

The economic consequences of a male breadwinner being institutionalized were sufficiently devastating that institutionalization was usually the option of last resort in those cases. Of the 324 patients institutionalized at the Topeka and Osawatomie insane asylums in 1880, only 52 were married men, and of this number, 21 were old enough (in their fifties or sixties) to have adult sons or daughters capable of taking the role of breadwinner for the family.[74] Nor was this pattern unique to Kansas. Of more than 1,300 patients admitted to insane asylums in Missouri between 1874 and 1885, only 21 percent were married men.[75] And by 1910, when U.S. Census officials compiled statistics for more than 187,000 inmates at insane asylums, the overall proportion of the total that were married men had fallen to only 14 percent—among men 26 percent were married compared with 40 percent of women—prompting the report's authors to speculate that the insane were simply incapable of marrying, rather than acknowledging the obvious economic consequences families incurred if a married man was institutionalized.[76]

The stigma associated with mental illness put family members in the awkward position of ignoring their loved ones, sometimes pretending that they were dead, or keeping friends and neighbors in the dark about the reality. Although Ann Hall and the children were close enough to Topeka once they relocated to Kansas City that they visited William several times a year, his presence at the asylum appears not to have been widely known outside the family.[77] When the census takers came in June 1880, Ann listed William as a member of the household, even though he was no longer living there, and gave his occupation as "merchant." When they came again in 1885, she listed herself as a widow despite the fact that William was alive.[78]

The families of institutionalized men made do in their various ways, depending on the circumstances they were in and the resources on which they could draw—which in the best of situations included veterans' pension support. Walter Kirkland's wife Kate, for example, was left with three children under the age of five when he was institutionalized at Topeka for nine months about the same time as William Hall in 1880. Like Hall, Walter came to Kansas

FIGURE 7. *Visit to the Lunatic Asylum*, 1884, associating insanity with drunkenness and immorality. Lithograph by M. Marques. Library of Congress Prints and Photographs Division, Washington, DC.

in 1869, settling in the same county as Hall, grieving the death of his young wife in 1871, and then moving to Leavenworth where he remarried and taught school. Walter recovered enough in 1880 that he was able to teach school the next two years, but during the winter of 1882 he was institutionalized again for five months and soon after for another four months. He was a Civil War veteran, and in 1885 Kate, with Walter unable to work even part time at her father's grocery store in Leavenworth, filed for a pension on her husband's behalf. Forced to sell their home, she opened a small store of her own and appealed to the pension commissioner to expedite the case. But to no avail. With Walter institutionalized yet again in 1886, she continued the process, filing numerous depositions and affidavits. The chief difficulty was linking Walter's insanity to his service during the war, which he claimed resulted from sunstroke on June 25, 1862. Asked to verify his account, now twenty-five years later, two of his fellow soldiers remembered the incident but three others could not. And if it had happened, had Walter suffered lasting effects? His sister recalled him visiting the school where she was teaching and laughing as she pronounced the spelling words. Her husband remembered Walter mumbling to himself on one occasion and sometimes acting a bit strange. A physician testified that a casual observer probably would notice nothing unusual but that a "peculiarity" could sometimes be observed in "the expression of his eyes" and that he sometimes seemed unable to express himself "while seeming to study what word he shall use." But was he insane? Now that he was institutionalized, it was clear enough that he was, at least temporarily. Dr. Eastman believed he would have "recurring attacks of mania" and they would "become more frequent and eventually become permanent." But was it perhaps an inherited problem? His doctor didn't think so, but an affidavit from a neighbor noted that Walter's father had also been insane. Finally the pension board was persuaded, and Kate began receiving a small monthly payment in 1887 as Walter's guardian.[79]

When pension support was not available, families did as best they could to fend for themselves. Soloman McCall, who spent the last decade of his life at the Osawatomie asylum, was not a veteran, but by the time he was institutionalized his wife Mary was able to look to their grown children for support. Charlotte Bailey's experience was similar. She was sixty-two when her husband Erastus was institutionalized at Topeka. While he was there, she lived with an adult son, and when Erastus was released five years later, they continued this arrangement.[80]

Phebe Millender's experience illustrated a different course. Several years before her husband Martin was institutionalized at Topeka, Phebe separated from him, declared herself a "widow," and returned with her son, daughter, and a stepson to live with her parents in Missouri. Although Martin served in the Kansas Cavalry, he was twice charged with theft in 1864 and with desertion in 1865, which left Phebe ineligible for pension support. Lillie Swingley's experience was different as well. Married in 1869, her husband Leonard was institutionalized at Topeka in 1879 after suffering from paresis for two years. They had no children, but he was a veteran who served as a lieutenant in the Kansas Cavalry, which made Lillie eligible for a pension when he died in 1883.

The stories buried in pension files illuminate both the common struggles and the varied circumstances that families experienced. One of the more interesting cases was that of John Studebaker, who joined William Hall at Topeka on July 9, 1889. John and his wife Emma were married in 1871, six years after his service with Company B of the 46th Indiana Infantry. By the time they moved to western Kansas in 1887, they had four children, a fifth had died at age four, and Emma was pregnant with the sixth. A year later John shot and killed their neighbor Thomas Andrew during an argument about a missing fence post. When a hundred neighbors threatened to lynch Studebaker, the sheriff enlisted a larger force armed with Winchesters to guard the courthouse. Claiming insanity and arguing that the victim had been the aggressor, Studebaker received a divided verdict and was sent to Topeka. In 1891 Emma and the children began receiving pension support of $12 a month.[81]

Securing Pension Relief

Standard histories of Civil War pension support tell of developments that in retrospect seemed remarkably simple. From fewer than 100,000 disabled pensioners representing merely 5 percent of Union veterans in 1870, the numbers climbed steadily to nearly 750,000 representing 74 percent of veterans by 1900.[82] The thousands of veterans who received support while they were alive, statistics suggest, simply submitted papers from a military surgeon stating that they were in fact disabled and thus in most instances had their applications approved. The widows who received pensions when their husbands died filed papers demonstrating that their husbands had in fact served.[83] The standard accounts, written largely from the standpoint of legislation, administration, and public finances, observe that the pension system was massive, costly, and sometimes inefficient but characterize it as a straightforward means of provision for hundreds of thousands of deserving beneficiaries.[84]

For the veterans and widows who applied, however, the process was anything but simple. Besides a standard surgeon's report, it frequently required notarized affidavits and written depositions, letters from doctors and attorneys, court appearances, and testimony from fellow soldiers and neighbors— all with the intent not only of establishing that the veteran had in fact served and suffered war-related injuries and disabilities but also to prevent fraudulent claims. The process was complicated by the fact that different rates of payment applied to different injuries and different standards pertained to different kinds of disability. Evidence of what had happened when depended on memories of events decades in the past. The relevant soldiers and former neighbors often had died or could not be found. Testimony from close relatives might be considered biased. Further complications occurred in instances of remarriage, adoption, and when marriages and birth dates could not be established. Throughout the process veterans and widows and persons submitting official affidavits had to make the case as never before that they were honest, upstanding, respectable citizens.

Wives whose husbands were institutionalized faced several additional challenges in securing pension support. One was that service-related disability was difficult to establish if the claim involved insanity. Unlike a missing limb or well-documented physical ailment, insanity was harder to diagnose and even in the opinion of the best experts was often transitory. A second difficulty was that a veteran in an insane asylum was already being cared for, which could invalidate his need for pension support until he died. A third was that some other person, presumably the wife, had to prove that she was the veteran's legal guardian and in need of support. Compounding the difficulties was the Pension Bureau's generally skeptical attitude toward insanity, which caused it to reject a majority of insanity-based claims and to assume in other cases that the problem was due to heredity, alcoholism, or moral depravity and to disregard testimony that came from "unsound" and "excitable" minds. Veterans and their families that already suffered from the embarrassment of dealing with insanity—such as one in Indiana, for instance, that neighbors said "for the most part managed to keep their problems to themselves"—now had to call on relatives, fellow veterans, and distant acquaintances to vouch that they were truly afflicted and needed help.[85]

With William institutionalized at Topeka, and in view of the daunting complexities of applying for support, Ann sought the assistance of Noah Moser, a pension attorney from Indiana whose associates traveled widely soliciting claims from old soldiers in Kansas, Missouri, and other states. By the 1880s pension processing had become a lucrative practice despite regulations restricting the fees attorneys could charge and prohibiting them from negotiating kickbacks. Many of the pension lawyers advertised regularly in urban newspapers and contributed to political candidates who favored expanding the pension system, and a few were known to have thousands of claims pending at any one time.[86] Moser charged a hefty fee of $25, which was triple the monthly sum that most pensioners received, and for which his tasks required little more than submitting an occasional letter and supplying blank affidavit forms.[87] Moser nevertheless guided Ann through the process, on one occasion arguing that she was in fact destitute and that the pension should come to her directly because it would be of no personal benefit to William if it went to the asylum and would benefit nobody if Ann were to predecease William.[88]

Over the next two years with Moser's assistance Ann demonstrated the exceptional fortitude and personal resolve it took to surmount the hurdles involved in securing pension support. That she waited nearly a decade after William was institutionalized to begin the process suggests that she may have considered her chances nil and took up the challenge only with the encouragement of Moser, who stood to benefit from the process whether it succeeded or not. In letters from her relatives in West Virginia, she would likely have learned that veterans there were applying for pensions in increasing numbers.[89] And, living as she was in Kansas City, she would likely have been privy to the fact that pension attorneys were aggressively soliciting new business as well as the possibility of new legislation being passed, as finally happened on June 27, 1890. Following his successful promotion of the 1879 Arrears Act and subsequent revisions in 1884 and 1885, Kansas senator John James Ingalls with leaders from other northern states pushed for a new law that would grant pensions to Civil War veterans in honor of their service irrespective of claims about service-related disabilities. Benjamin Harrison's victory in the 1888 presidential election and the Grand Army of the Republic's lobbying made it almost certain that new legislation was imminent.[90]

The sequence of events indicates that with Moser's assistance Ann applied for an invalid pension on October 14, 1889, arguing that William had contracted chronic diarrhea while in the army and that chronic diarrhea was in turn the cause of his insanity. Evidence submitted in support of the claim included the date of her marriage to William, her narrative of his service and illnesses, a statement from Moser, and notarized affidavits from two doctors, three fellow soldiers, and William's brother. Several months later the Pension

Office accepted the evidence about diarrhea but sought additional information about the allegation that diarrhea was the cause of William's insanity.

In hopes of securing that evidence, Moser wrote to Eastman at the Topeka asylum, to which Eastman replied that he would only respond to inquiries from the Pension Office.[91] Several months later the Pension Office sent Eastman the following request:

> It is desired in this case that the examination be made with special reference to chronic diarrhea and alleged resulting insanity. His physician states that he treated him also for rheumatism. The object of this examination is to ascertain his exact mental and physical condition and to determine the degree of disability from each of above causes. Please note his general appearance and nutrition, actual height and weight and temperature, respiration and pulse rate. Describe the condition of all abdominal organs. Any evidence of rheumatism in joints or muscles. Has he disease of heart? State apparent condition of brain and its membranes. Any evidence of injury to cranium? Is there dementia, melancholia, or a homicidal or suicidal disposition? Is he dangerous or destructive? Does he require sedatives or mechanical restraints? Is he in front or back high or low ward? Has he lucid intervals? What is the probable cause of his insanity? Any evidence of syphilis? Sunstroke? Give full history of the case from your records. Does he require the constant watching or attendance of another person and why?—Thos. D. Ingram, Medical Referee[92]

This request prompted a lengthy statement from Eastman, dated May 21, 1890, in which he addressed each of the medical referee's requests, stopping short of stating that William's insanity was caused by chronic diarrhea.

> Pulse rate per minute, 100; respiration, 18; temperature, normal; height, five feet ten inches; weight, 136; age, 55 years.
>
> He makes the following statement on which he bases his claim for original pension: He acquired "chronic diarrhea" while wagon master just after battle of Bull Run (1st) and was in General Hospital Washington for 6 weeks but got entirely over it before enlisting about a year or more thereafter. Never received any wound. He continued to have digestive trouble consequent upon chronic diarrhea as above.
>
> Upon examination we find the following objective conditions: He has been an inmate at this asylum since January 10, 1880, having previously been in Osawatomie Asylum. He has had occasional rheumatic attacks and complains of rheumatic pain. He has also had occasional attacks of acute indigestion with diarrhea. Indeed is not today quite as well as usual having had an attack of diarrhea ten days ago. Condition of abdominal organs good. No enlargement of joints or heart disease, no injury to cranium.

[Written in margin] He himself says his digestion is now better than for years. The cause of his insanity is set down as religious excitement and I understand financial embarrassment as cause of much worry. If it is shown that chronic diarrhea followed him from the army, it would be probable with such general recurrence of bouts naturally resulting. How much to do with his breaking down now or suffering insanity, about such is not within my knowledge.

This is a case of chronic insanity. He is totally unable to take care of himself, and if wasn't in the asylum would require the constant attention of at least one person. He is subject to periods of excitement requiring seclusion and restraint when he is dangerous and destructive. At other times quiet then talkative and emotional with many delusions. No history of sunstroke or syphilis.

From the existing condition and the history of this claimant, as stated by himself, there is no evidence, neither in his commitment papers to show that the disability of insanity was incurred in the service as he claims, and that it has not been prolonged or aggravated by vicious habits. He is, in my opinion, entitled to a full rating for the disability caused by insanity provided it be shown that insanity originated in line of duty or sprung from a sickness thus arising.[93]

Eastman's letter dampened the possibility of basing Hall's claim on insanity, leaving chronic diarrhea as the most available option—one that many claimants chose. Among Civil War veterans anywhere in the United States who held pensions in 1888, the most common forms of disability (other than wounds) were chronic diarrhea and rheumatism: 117,947 had gunshot and shell wounds, 55,125 had chronic diarrhea, 41,049 had incised and contused wounds, and 40,790 had rheumatism. In contrast, only 1,098 were classified as having "disease of the brain, including insanity."[94] Hall's claim was consistent with evidence that chronic diarrhea afflicted a number of the veterans from West Virginia. Of the 157 Civil War veterans still living in the Lyon and Valley Districts of Preston County, West Virginia, in 1890—most of whom served in the same regiment or at the same time as Hall—49 listed rheumatism as their primary disability, 19 listed chronic diarrhea, 12 had been wounded, 7 had been imprisoned during the war, and 48 listed other conditions such as heart disease, lung disease, piles, catarrh, deafness, and blindness.[95] Affidavits submitted on Hall's behalf by fellow soldiers and family members were also supportive. The December 17, 1889, affidavit from his brother Ashford attested that William "was often complaining of chronic diarrhea contracted while in the service of the government and he was bad off with same." The January 25, 1890, affidavit from Sergeant Abram Shriver noted, "Perhaps he had diarrhea as we had a great deal of that."[96]

Hall's case was pending when Congress passed the new Pension Act of 1890 with broader terms of eligibility, upon which Ann resubmitted her application. The Pension Office quickly approved a pension of $12 a month, apparently now satisfied. But the pension was held up and nearly five months passed. The problem now was that the payment could not be made to William, since he was institutionalized, but could not be made to Ann either without further proof of who she was. Ann requested help from people able to attest to her marriage and notified Moser. Three people submitted notarized affidavits stating that Ann was indeed William's wife and was destitute.

After seven months delay, the Deputy Commissioner at the Pension Office informed Moser, "Favorable action cannot be taken in said claim until a guardian is appointed who should furnish a certified copy of letters of guardianship under seal of the court."[97] Had proper procedures been followed under Kansas law, Ann would likely have been appointed as William's guardian in 1880, but either the procedures had not been followed or the documentation the Pension Office required could not be obtained.

Moser responded to the deputy commissioner hoping to make the case that since Ann was William's wife she should not be required to be his legal guardian as well: "This soldier is hopelessly insane and has been confined in Insane Hospital for years. Mrs. Ann Hall is his wife. This pension could be paid to this soldier's wife as provided Sec. 4766." To underscore the point Moser added, "The soldier himself is insane and the pension money will do him no good. If a guardian is appointed the money I suppose will be held for benefit of soldier, and his wife will not get the money. Hence the payment of the money to guardian will lock up the money and do neither the soldier or his family any good while the soldier lives. And his wife may die first and then when soldier dies the accumulated pension money in hand of guardian then be hired by some one foreign to the service and distant relation to soldier."[98]

But Moser's appeal was unsuccessful. On July 24, 1891, Ann appeared before the probate judge petitioning to be certified as the guardian for "W. A. Hall, a person of unsound mind." The court recorded the following on her behalf:

> Your petitioner Ann Hall responded and shows, first, that she is a resident of Johnson County, Kansas, and has been a resident of said city for more than three years last passed; second, that she is the wife of W. A. Hall and that she and said W. A. Hall were married in 1868 in Marion County, West Virginia; third, that said W. A. Hall on or about July 28th 1879 in the County of Wilson and the State of Kansas under proceedings duly had in the Probate Court of said county was duly declared and held to be insane and that the said W. A. Hall by virtue of the findings of said court has been duly confined in the Asylum for the Insane in Topeka, Kansas, since on or about January 1st 1880 and that said W. A. Hall is still confined in said asylum for the insane and is declared to be incurable; fourth, that said Ann Hall is the owner of certain real estate in her

own right and name situated in the County of Johnson and which the
interest of your petitioner requires to be conveyed; fifth, that the said
W. A. Hall is entitled to a pension as a soldier of the U.S. during the War
of the Rebellion and for the purpose of conveying said real estate and securing and caring for said pension money it is necessary that a guardian
be appointed by this court—therefore, your petitioner Ann Hall prays
that she may be appointed the guardian of said W. A. Hall.[99]

The judge responded by appointing Ann as William's guardian, asking her to
post bond, and requiring her appointment to be published in the newspaper.
Finally, in September 1891, twenty-four months after Ann made the initial application, the pension payments began.

Aftermath

Meanwhile, the administrative turmoil at the asylum continued, extending
during the last years of William Hall's life, and finally having an inadvertent
effect on the family as well as those who were under the asylum's care and
necessitating yet another round of correspondence and affidavits with the Pension Office. Eastman's third stint as superintendent ended June 30, 1897. His
successor, Calvin H. Wetmore, served only until October 1, 1898, when acting
superintendent L. D. McKinley took his place. At the time of William Hall's
death on July 20, 1899, the new superintendent, Thomas Coke Biddle, had
been in the position only since April 1.

The documents surrounding William Hall's death indicate that if there was
any change in his health, the family in Kansas City was to be notified immediately by telegraph. But Biddle sent a telegram to Ottawa, Kansas, where none
of the family had ever lived, only to have the telegram returned undelivered,
upon which Biddle made no further efforts to locate the family. Three months
after her father's death, Emma Hall finally received a brief typed letter from
Biddle, explaining: "The only record I could find of friends was Mrs. Ann Hall,
Ottawa, Kansas, and I sent a telegram to that place informing her of his death.
The office reported that they could not deliver the telegram, as the person was
unknown. I knew of no other friend, and consequently buried the remains in
the asylum cemetery." Two days later, Biddle also responded to an inquiry from
James G. Young, an attorney from whom the family had apparently sought
advice, stating: "We have received no letters from Ann Hall. If she has written
us, as you state in your letter, they doubtless have been returned to her, as they
have not been received here. I recently wrote the daughter relative to his death
and burial. The notice of his death was sent to the Probate Court of Franklin
County as required by law at the time it occurred."[100]

Thus when William Hall died the family was not immediately notified,
and, having received a pension check several days later to which they were

not entitled, the family found itself in legal jeopardy. The family then engaged in filing another series of affidavits with the Pension Office. On file at the National Archives, these documents on the surface suggest that Ann and the children were greatly embarrassed by the possibility of being accused of having broken the law on purpose. What was left unstated but real was the possibility that the Pension Office would deny Ann the support she deserved and needed as William's widow.

Ann's affidavit explained that she "had made arrangements with the officers of the Insane Asylum at Topeka Kansas that if anything occurred that was unusual with [William], or if he should die, that they would promptly notify me by wire and mail." She added, "Counting on that arrangement and believing that I was perfectly safe to do so, I had no hesitancy to execute my voucher as I had done for years and my family who were familiar with the facts certified as witnesses. Having drawn $36 and not being entitled to but $30, he having died as stated, I herewith return the $6 and announce myself ready so far as in my powers to make any further amends of me by the laws of the government."[101]

Two of the daughters wrote that

at our special request, that if anything should happen to our father, or if his malady should take an unfavorable turn that the superintendent would notify us by wire or mail as the case might be. We were neither aware of the change to the one now in office, T. C. Biddle. From what he writes it seems he had no actual or ready knowledge of our address. We sometimes corresponded with our father and sometimes he answered and sometimes not—just as he happened to feel at the time. Again our being so near to the asylum and he having been there so long and as we assumed intimate relation with the officers, we felt perfectly safe any one of the family in swearing that he was there and alive any day during the last ten years. No such thought ever entered our heads as false swearing, misrepresentation or in any manner wronging the government. No intentional wrong was thought of or would we knowingly permit it.[102]

The Pension Office also received an affidavit from a twenty-one-year-old woman named Bessie Boggs, who described herself as a near neighbor of Ann Hall and a chum of the daughters. "I know them all to be honorable, upright and truthful without exception," she wrote. "They are good people, respected by all who know them and have the very best associates."

The documents illustrate in small measure the layered meanings embedded in nineteenth-century concerns about respectability. In an era when veterans and their families were having to deal with distant government agencies as never before and at a time when official documents were increasingly required without always being available, the testimony of relatives, neighbors, and acquaintances played a critical role in substantiating that a person was a respectable member of the community. The Hall case further illustrates the complexities of the symbolic demarcations that communities drew to set themselves apart as respectable citizens from the insane. Not only the insane but also their families became the "other," subject to questions about their involvement in the family troubles associated with insanity, possibilities of burdening the community with financial needs, and having to prove themselves above reproach in appealing for support.[103]

During the twenty years that William Hall was institutionalized, the Topeka Insane Asylum housed more than 4,500 patients. Only 35 percent were considered to have recovered. Twenty percent died during their confinement. Superintendent Biddle's report in 1900, like those of his predecessors, tallied the number of patients who had been admitted, released, or died. It begged the legislature for additional funds to repair the greenhouse and provide for a suitable library. Otherwise, it painted a rosy picture of life at the asylum. The patients amused themselves with summer lawn concerts and throughout the year with twice weekly "dancing entertainments," he said. "Baseball, croquet and other pleasant games and amusements have been liberally indulged in."[104]

CHAPTER FOUR

Not a Fanatic

ZEAL IN THE CAUSE OF ZION

ONE OF THE MORE DIFFICULT ASPECTS of middle-class respectability has been getting it right when it comes to displays of emotion—too little and a person seems stoical, indifferent, cold; too much and a person is likely to be accused of wearing their feelings on their sleeve, incapable of self-control, being dangerous, overzealous, a fanatic. A person or group that fails to get it right, by some unspoken local or regional code, runs the risk of public censure, which in turn becomes a marker by negative example of how a respectable person should behave.

Durkheim's notion of collective effervescence offers a way to think about displays of emotion. On special occasions when people come together in a particular place with some shared objective in mind, emotions run high. It is more appropriate to display emotion in these instances than it is in everyday life. Effervescence signals that the people involved feel empowered, uplifted, transported, one might say, into the presence of something sacred, the realm of the gods. Emotion makes the event special, memorable, marking it as a reminder of the norms and values that bind people together. Why a holiday reminds people of their commitment to their family, religion, or nation is, in this view, because the food and fellowship generate strong feelings that are publicly displayed.

That argument is well and good, but it sidesteps the question of *how much* emotion can be appropriately displayed and *to whom*. A bit of frenzied abandon is one thing in an isolated space; quite another in pluralistic settings where others are watching, discussing it, writing about it, taking photos, and giving it their different interpretations. These are the occasions for drawing "us" and "them" distinctions. "We" are the reasonable people who keep our emotions in check. "They" are the people who get carried away. It is not hard to think of examples in which racial, gender, and generational distinctions were drawn in this way.

Deciding how much emotion is problematic frames the question clearly as a topic of cultural construction. The answer hinges on context: profuse weeping is socially more acceptable in certain settings than in others. It also depends on the wider norms that may characterize an epoch, nation, or region, which is why it matters to know not only what was done but also the response it evoked. As Stanley Milgram once observed, excessive commitments are exemplified in extreme beliefs and feelings that are *condemned*.[1] They are denounced, ridiculed, and in some instances violently repressed on particular grounds. It is the basis on which they are condemned that gives vital information about the beliefs, activities, and modes of emotional expression that are to be upheld. Is the problem that excessive displays of emotion suggest impulsiveness, close-mindedness, and an absence of civility, impending danger, or what?

Religion is a particularly interesting context in which to consider the display of emotion. On the one hand, religion provides ritual occasions in which emotion is expected. Participants in rituals commemorating the dead, honoring the saints, and putting people in touch with God should be able to express emotions; indeed, it would be odd if they did not. On the other hand, religion is supposed to be reasonable. If it bends too much toward emotions, it can cross the line into fanaticism and even insanity.

Religious traditions vary of course in terms of how much emotion is considered appropriate to display and under what conditions. Some traditions incorporate weeping, shouting, and expressions of ecstasy into their services; others encourage silence, quiet meditation, and sober reflection. And those variations have often been the basis for criticisms across religious lines. "We" have the appropriate mixture of reason and emotion. "They" are the "frozen chosen" who couldn't share an emotion if they had one. Or "they" are fanatics; you can tell by how emotional they are.

In this chapter I examine how accusations of zealotry populated nineteenth- and early twentieth-century discussions of American religion. Zealotry was a contested idea that religious leaders, public officials, scholars, and the popular press discussed repeatedly. It was good, many commentators argued, for Americans to be zealous. Zeal was the ingredient that inspired evangelism. The Lord expected good Christians to be zealous in the pursuit of righteousness. But it was not good to be labeled a zealot. Zealots were led too much by their emotions. They were easily confused, frequently irrational, and sometimes dangerous.

The conflicting meanings of zealotry were embedded in Jewish and Christian teachings thoroughly familiar to America's clergy. Jesus's apostle called Simon Zelotes or Simon the Zealot was understood to have been part of a group that obstinately defended the temple and Jewish law, prosecuted offenders, and refused to pay Roman tribute. Characterized in some treatments as an example of wrong-headedness, he was praised in other discussions for having exemplified the same zeal in energetically spreading the gospel of Christ.

In both its positive and negative connotations, zealousness held implications for discussions of the American dream. Doing well for oneself with the opportunities that the nation provided necessitated an investment of zeal up to a point. A person who zealously pursued the benefits America offered earned respect for working hard and being committed to the tasks at hand. This was the restless, energetic vitality in which Americans took pride. But zealotry was another matter. Zealots overdid it, became too emotionally invested in what they thought was right, and let things get out of hand. Zealots who followed the fanatical teachings of prophets and priests and who heard the voice of God speaking to them pursued a different vision of Zion that had little to do with the American dream.

The sharpest criticisms of zealotry were directed toward small fringe groups of religious adherents. Adventists who believed in the imminent end of the world were frequently on the receiving end. Holiness and perfectionist groups that anticipated the Pentecostal movement that emerged at the start of the twentieth century also frequently found themselves attacked as zealots. But discussions of zealotry occurred in other settings as well. Protestants and Catholics accused each other of zealotry, and factions within Protestant denominations did the same.

Academic discussions of fringe religious groups have focused almost exclusively on trying to describe these groups, categorize them, and explain why people found them appealing enough to become members. The literature has correctly understood that these groups deviated from the ways in which members of mainstream majority religious traditions believed and behaved. The categorizations described these deviations in terms of other-worldliness, mysticism, and militancy. The emphasis on why people join has attributed their interest to being gullible and thus easily preyed on by fanatical leaders, seeking to overcome some feelings of inadequacy or inferiority, being economically disadvantaged, and merely having happened to be connected to members through informal social networks.[2]

Compared with the attention that members of fringe groups have received, far less interest has been directed to the question of what this attention suggests about the expectations governing mainstream behavior. How zealots and fanatics are understood, though, necessarily implies something about what it means to *not* be a zealot or fanatic. Indeed, how deviant behavior is understood, explained, ridiculed, and warned against is in this respect a mirror in which to examine what implicitly or explicitly is favored as the ways in which normal respectable people should act.

A closer look at well-known academic arguments about fringe religious groups suggests some of the ways in which these discussions have said as much about prevailing expectations as about deviations from those expectations.

Groups characterized as otherworldly have been of interest because mainstream culture is supposed to be this worldly and organized around the rational pursuit of means and ends. Adherents under the spell of prophetic leaders contrast with an expectation that ordinary people should think for themselves. The authoritarian structure of some fringe groups serves as a reminder that the rest of us are supposed to favor and benefit from democracy. Similarly, a society worried about drug use may find it interesting to think about fringe religious groups that produce altered states of consciousness and a moment in history when brain science is popular might also consider it interesting to interpret fringe groups as the result of brainwashing.

A focus on zealotry and especially the criticisms expressed in discussions of fanaticism, religious excitement, and excessive displays of emotion puts the development of mainstream religion in nineteenth-century America in a different light. The consensus forged in those years around the idea of quiet, reasonable, respectable, civilized individual piety was only in part the work of theologians and clergy who wrote treatises and preached that faith should be understood this way. It was also communicated in frequently repeated dismissals and denunciations of religious fanaticism. To see the extent to which this was the case does not require suggesting that fanaticism would have had to be invented if it had not existed. Fanaticism did exist or was said to exist often enough and in sufficient extreme manifestations, including violence, that it was always there as the contrast with which arguments about good behavior could be framed.

Zealotry became one of the important discursive topics through which a mainstream, centrist understanding of how middle-class religious beliefs and practices should participate in American culture took shape. There was never complete agreement, which was the reason the discussions continued. Even today, the terms in which discussions about spirituality, atheism, religion and science, and religion and politics are cast bear an affinity with those earlier debates.

Religious Enthusiasm in Antebellum Discourse

On September 30, 1724, a colonist named Peter Rombert, who lived in St. Thomas Parish about twenty-two miles from what is now Charleston, South Carolina, was tried for murder, found guilty, and sentenced to die. His four codefendants—Michael Boineau, Peter Dutartre, Daniel Dutartre, and John Dutartre—were also found guilty and sentenced to die. During the two-day trial the prosecution established that the Dutartres had come under the conviction that God was speaking directly to them, first through visions and revelations, and then through Rombert as a prophet called to warn the world of its wickedness. Heeding only the voice of God, the family refused to comply with laws requiring their support in repairing the highways and maintaining the militia, which prompted the constable to swear out a warrant for their arrest. The attempted arrest resulted in the constable and a local woman being killed.

The bare facts of the case were sufficiently shocking that writers repeatedly reflected on its meanings. The Dutartre Affair, as it came to be called, became a cautionary tale about the dangers of religious fanaticism. But how the story was told and what its implications were changed over the years. Its interpreters used it to illustrate what they considered to be the important lessons that their audiences needed to understand. Writing in 1988, historian Jon Butler, for example, saw the incident as part of the lay-led Huguenot resistance to religious Americanization, extreme in its specific manifestation, to be sure, but an outgrowth of tensions simmering in the colonies for a generation between Huguenot refugees from France after the revocation of the Edict of Nantes in 1685 and the Anglican establishment in England and the English colonies.[3] Historian Bertrand Van Ruymbeke interpreted the incident similarly but described it as "a violent tale of gun battles, murder, executions, and fantasized resurrections" inspired by the apocalyptic prophesies of Huguenots in London.[4] In 2005 a book about the history of murder in America, written for a popular audience, cast the incident as a story about a charismatic preacher named Christian George persuading the Dutartres to establish a "love commune," fathering a child that the residents of Charleston called "the devil's child," and resulting in the outraged citizens burning the commune to the ground.[5]

Anglican minister Alexander Garden in a sermon preached at the Parish Church of St. Philip's in Charleston on July 13, 1740, gave the only firsthand account of the Dutartre Affair. Garden had come to South Carolina from England in 1720, attended the trial in 1724, and attempted to counsel the defendants. But it was significant that Garden's account was given sixteen years later, in 1740. In March of that year George Whitefield, who had been preaching and stirring revivals along the Atlantic seaboard, visited South Carolina. As a member of the Anglican clergy and as "commissary for the Carolinas and Bahamas," Garden was tasked with keeping fellow clergy and their constituents in line. Garden deemed Whitefield a troublemaker preaching gibberish, published a series of letters challenging his theology, and in 1742 tried to get Whitefield's appointment as an Anglican preacher suspended. Among other issues, the two differed vehemently about slavery: Whitefield accused the plantation masters of widespread slave abuse; Garden denied the accusation. The broader theological transformation taking place at the time was also important. The Great Awakening of which Whitefield was one of the most prominent leaders emphasized religious conversion through a new approach to truth gained through emotional experiences in which feelings preceded believing and knowing. This was the context of Garden's 1740 account of the Dutartre Affair.[6]

Without mentioning Whitefield or slavery, Garden's rendition of the Dutartre Affair emphasized the travesty of people getting carried away with their own ideas about God, led astray especially by false teachers, and ignoring the wise precepts of the established church. "The Dutartres," he said, were "of honest repute and for many years behaved themselves regularly and blameless in all outward instances of religious and moral duty." Then an "enthusiast pietist" came and "filled their heads with many wild and fantastic notions," causing them "to withdraw from public worship and all outward ordinances of God in his church." When word of their impending arrest arrived, the family "consulted their prophet [Rombert] who soon told them that God commanded them to arm and defend themselves."

As a representative of the church, Garden tried to reason with the Dutartres once they had been sentenced, but they were immune to reason. "They had the spirit of God speaking inwardly to their souls; who was I to pretend to talk to or instruct them; they had obeyed the voice of God and were about to suffer martyrdom for it." Daniel and John Dutartre a few days later did "become sensible of their delusion, at least professed themselves so, and were pardoned." But one of the two subsequently committed murder and was executed.

Lest the listeners in Charlestown miss the contrast between reason, ecclesial authority, and church ordinances, on the one hand, and the excesses associated with feelings and false prophets, on the other hand, Garden concluded: "And thus ended this tragical scene of enthusiasm, in which no less than seven persons lost their lives; one killed, two murdered, and four executed for those murders; a remarkable instance to what heights of extravagance, folly and wickedness this turn of head or imagination will hurry the poor souls of men."[7]

Garden of course was hardly alone in identifying religious enthusiasm as the antithesis of respectable church-sanctioned expressions of morality and faith. The religion of enthusiasm exemplified by Quakers in America, Anabaptists in Germany, Levellers in England, and Covenanters in Scotland, David Hume wrote in 1741, inspired "the deluded fanatic with the opinion of divine illuminations, and with contempt for the common rules of reason, morality, and prudence." Religious enthusiasm "produces the most cruel disorders in human society," Hume believed, but in small measure he took heart in observing that over time "all fanatical sects sink into the greatest remissness and coolness in sacred matters."[8]

Whether enthusiasm of the kind that led people to defy the dictates of reason, morality, and prudence was ever a significant part of American culture is a question historians have continued to debate.[9] But incidents like the Dutartre Affair stuck sufficiently in the public's imagination to serve as reminders of how respectable people should behave. In the 1780s periodicals recounted the Dutartres' story anew but with clearer instructions about what to do and what to not do. Religion rightly understood was beneficial to society. It encouraged respect for authority, benevolence, gentleness, and peace. The appropriate attitude toward life was to be reasonable, refrain from moral corruption, and pay attention to the examples provided in history for public instruction that

spurs virtue. Religious enthusiasm, in contrast, was pernicious, mistaken, de-
plorable, and attended with melancholy and dismal effects. The path to wrong
behavior was to follow one's wild fancies, to pursue the giddy heights of extravagance, to be guided by a distempered brain, an inflamed imagination.[10]

Discussions couched in less extreme language characterized ordinary
people as having (or needing to have) appropriate levels of zeal and enthusiasm and referred in contrast to persons and groups who were dangerous and
should be feared as zealots. Although zeal referred more often to beliefs and
behavior than to emotions, it was considered good when it conformed to commonsense moral expectations, was balanced by reason, and benefited the community. Zeal was bad when these attributes were absent, especially when it led
to public conflict, disagreements that could not be resolved reasonably, and an
immoral or unconstrained exercise of power. In religion, good zeal promoted
an active, committed faith, while bad zeal was narrowly sectarian. In the context of America's experiment with democracy, zealous citizens took an active
role in civic affairs, while overly zealous persons posed threats to democracy.

"Those who are truly zealous in good works will seek opportunities of
doing good," an essay published in the *New York Evangelist* in 1839 counseled.
"Those who are zealous for the acquisition of property will be on the watch
for every chance of obtaining it." Similarly with the pursuit of pleasure, and so
with the person "who is zealous of the cause of Zion and the souls of sinners."
That person would be on the "look out for ways and means of promoting that
welfare." A zealous Christian would be busy, active, and vigilant in the search
for opportunities to do good works. To follow Jesus was to be like the woman
at the well who listened to the Savior, wondered, believed, and then immediately hastened to the city to invite her fellow citizens to come and listen.[11]

Good works that contributed either to the welfare of others or to propa-
gating the faith were easier to classify as a desirable form of zeal than the
more subjective feelings, attitudes, and convictions of which religion was also
composed. Writers struggled especially with the distinction between feelings
that would seem appropriate to fellow believers and the same feelings that
would be misunderstood by nonbelievers. "To speak feelingly of divine things
seems folly or mere fancy to them who have no knowledge or taste thereof in
themselves," a late seventeenth-century sermon that was widely reproduced in
the eighteenth century explained, adding, "To express with zeal or vigor such
things as seem to others incredible, though they be most true and excellent, is
taken for madness."[12] In this understanding, zeal was in the eye of the believer,
not as an individual seeking the divine alone, but within a community of believers. Heart-felt emotion expressed in word and deed was expected to draw
ridicule from unbelievers, just as the writers of the Bible had said it would.

How zeal could be disruptive reflected the same understanding of it as active goal-oriented behavior, only exercised to a greater degree. Zeal was undesirable if it was exercised by a person in power, which meant an ability to carry

out activities beyond what others could do and that might be harmful. Zeal of this kind needed to be constrained by laws, morality, and social arrangements. It could be present in any setting, including the home and religion, but was especially troublesome in the political sphere and when religion's role in that sphere was strong.

Thomas Jefferson's notes on the state of religion in Virginia from 1785 warned of conditions under which rulers could become corrupt and "a single zealot" becomes a persecutor of others with differing religious and political views. Jefferson's advice of how best to keep that from happening illuminated his understanding of zealotry. Zeal gone wrong was taking one's beliefs too seriously. Convictions were problematic when they were held so seriously that they subverted commonsense morality and could not be subjected to reasonable discussion. "If a sect arises whose tenets would subvert morals," he wrote, "good sense has fair play, and reasons and laughs it out of doors." And in instances of less serious disagreements, "the way to silence religious disputes is to take no notice of them."[13]

Jefferson's interest in religious disputes was well founded in his knowledge of European history and his familiarity with religion in the American colonies. Criticisms by religious leaders like Alexander Garden of alien religious groups and practices were common locations for complaints about fanaticism. In 1820 an account circulated widely about a group in central Pennsylvania called the Pilgrims. From a writer who claimed to have spent an evening with them in 1816, the account described the group as fanatics and stated that they were known among local residents as "the most abject creatures of the vilest fanaticism." How their fanaticism set them apart from well-mannered society, the writer observed, was in the fact that they could not be reasoned with but followed the teachings of their own prophet, which included mortifying the flesh and living communally. In addition, the account dealt in considerable detail with how the group's appearance deviated from generally accepted expectations about dress, cleanliness, posture, and language. The group's quarters were strewn with dirty blankets, the people wore rotten garments, and their hair was matted. They were disgusting compared with a visitor who was "dressed genteelly and like a Methodist." The leader "leaned as if oppressed by an infirmity," made "an emphatic motion of the right hand and body," and spoke with a loud "hoarse throat like the bellowing of a bull." The miserable, inexplicable appearance of the group contrasted sharply, the account noted, with that of another visitor, a young woman "whose features and countenance were very good" and who "spoke in a manner elegant and eloquent."[14]

When Moravian missionaries began preaching to native people in North America in 1740, other European settlers accused them of zealotry, just as they had been in Europe, because of their emphases on prayer, worship, inward spirituality, simplicity, and communal living. Garden's account of the Dutartre

Affair said the enthusiast who led the group astray was a Moravian, Dutch, or Swiss pietist; other accounts asserted that the troublemaker was definitely a Moravian. But accusations of zealotry could be met in the same terms in which they were given. In 1753 an anonymous writer accused the accusers of flaming, barbarous zeal. "The pulpit scold is the most despicable scold in the world," the writer asserted. It was not the Moravians with plain, simple practices that exhibited zealotry but the religions of "human contrivance for the sake of power and wealth [that] convert religion into a divinity shop [and] ever be misrepresenting and vilifying those pestilent heretics who lower the price of their commodities."[15]

Like Jefferson, Robert Owen observed the vast diversity of religious groups and beliefs that vied for public attention. In a Fourth of July speech in 1829 at the Hall of Science in New York City, Owen praised the nation for its religious diversity. "Ye may declare yourselves Presbyterians, Methodists, Catholics, Socinians, Universalists, Friends, Deists, Materialists, Christians, Jews, Mahometans, or pagans," he observed. "Ye may reverence the first or the seventh day of the week or no day at all; ye may sacrifice to Allah or to Jehovah or to Juggernaut's idol or ye may abstain from all sacrifices." Freedom of conscience and freedom of speech permitted diversity of these kinds and more with no cause for the "strong arm of the law" to take cognizance of the words and actions being wise or foolish, tolerant or fanatic. Such freedom, he believed, protected the public against even "the most zealous bigot."[16]

But Owen offered a different warning about zealotry from Jefferson's. Without mentioning his own followers, Owen acknowledged that religious enthusiasts frequently came under attack for deviating from conventional norms, and those norms could be shaped too powerfully by public opinion. "The wayward offspring of fashion and fear, whose law is caprice, and her decisions injustice . . . weighs actions by their popularity." Doing what was customary instead of what was right was the serious danger to be avoided. Public opinion of that kind, he warned, "sits like an incubus on our boldest thoughts and best exertions."

Owen pressed the issue in the remainder of the speech. Zealous religionists and zealous skeptics alike posed threats to the stifling consensus embraced in public opinion. When public opinion demanded compromise, the wise course was not always to capitulate. At the same time, people whose very livelihoods depended on conforming to public opinion should be respected. The very diversity that freedom of conscience sought to uphold should enable public opinion to be reformed when reform was needed. What was customary always tended toward corruption and thus required not only adherence but also reasoned dissent. "Let us not fear to be called, nor even to be thought, religious enthusiasts or irreligious heretics, but let us fear to be deceitful or depraved in word or action. While we insult not public opinion, neither let us cringe to her. Let us yield obedience only when we can yield respect."

Alexis de Tocqueville's tour of America in 1835 convinced him that public opinion, as Owen argued, could be too powerful an influence in dictating what was considered normal. The trouble with public opinion, Tocqueville thought, was its connection to the seamless democracy that he so much admired among the Americans he visited. Lacking the inherited statuses that supported the different relationships among individuals in Europe, Americans looked to one another too often for moral guidance. Public opinion became the standard-bearer of least-common-denominator values guided by the self-interested pursuit of material gain. American democracy was better served, he believed, by citizens who worked together in local communities, understanding that self-interest depended on cooperation, and whose ideas were shaped by those relationships rather than by individuals whose insecurities prompted unthinking conformity to public opinion in general.

Having heard about and witnessed firsthand the religious revivals sweeping the country at the time of his visit, Tocqueville registered more approval than disapproval of the zeal involved. Momentary outbreaks occurred, he wrote, "when souls seem suddenly to break the restraining bonds of matter and rush impetuously heavenward." While it was true, he acknowledged, that religious enthusiasm of this kind sometimes ran "far beyond the bounds of common sense," it was also the case that people whose thoughts were directed mostly toward earth would sometimes turn their attention toward heaven. On the one hand, he met enough people "filled with an enthusiastic, almost fierce spirituality" that he could only conclude that "forms of religious madness are very common" in the United States. On the other hand, social circumstances confined Americans' attention so closely "to the pursuit of worldly welfare" that it was only to be expected that they would also "turn their looks to heaven." Senseless as it may have been at times, religious enthusiasm was part of the restless spirit that drove Americans toward something that was forever on the wing.[17]

By the 1840s the religious disputes associated with the Second Great Awakening prompted discussions of zealotry to be little more that undefined epithets hurled by religionists toward other religions. Calvinists and Methodists called each other zealots. Congregationalists and Unitarians did the same. Protestant publications continued to refer to popish fanatics, and Christian sermons spoke of Jewish zealots. Apparently it was still possible to be zealous in good ways, although that was evident mostly from the addition of clarifying words with negative connotations, such as *fanatical* zeal, *furious* zeal, *enthusiastic* zeal, *flaming* zeal, and *bilious* zeal.

The case of excessive religious zeal that attracted some of the most widespread attention at the time and in subsequent discussion was the Millerite movement that emerged in response to Baptist preacher William Miller's prediction that the world would end with the second coming of Christ in 1843. Miller's followers abandoned their homes and waited expectantly for the Lord's return. Some became ecstatic with joy, a few became violent, and several were taken to insane asylums in Massachusetts and New Hampshire. Many suffered from despondency when the advent failed to happen on schedule.[18] The Millerites gave generations of writers grist to speculate about the disturbed psychology of cult leaders and their followers. But few of the published accounts in the incident's immediate aftermath drew practical lessons for ordinary citizens. Millerites more often provided material for lighthearted stories, such as the one about the Boston Millerite, who woke from a sound sleep at three in the morning thinking the end had come, mistakenly thrust his head into an old cheese cupboard, and cried, "By thunder, this is very singular weather for the end of the world—the night is as dark as Egypt and smells confoundedly of cheese."[19] Perhaps the lesson was simply to take religious predictions less seriously than the Millerites had.

The Millerites illustrated a kind of religion that could easily be considered beyond the pale from the bizarre actions of its followers. As writers criticized the teachings and practices of religious groups they disliked, though, accusations of excessive zeal focused less on behavior and more on emotions. Zealots were people caught up in ecstasy and pious excitement—"brain-sick giddiness," as one writer put it.[20] Fanatics displayed excessive zeal, meaning excessive displays of emotion. They were carried away in fervor, engaged more in holy rapture than in good works. Their fervor kept them from calmly inquiring into the teachings of scripture. Instead of pondering the weightier matters of divine law and judgment, they blindly followed superficial forms of worship and in daily life made foolish, reckless decisions in business and managing their households.

Besides encouraging individuals to make bad personal decisions, emotion signaled something to be avoided in the life of the nation. Emotion could flare to the point that citizens felt the need to support a cause, but emotion was short-lived, self-interested, potentially divisive, and difficult to coordinate into anything productive. Emotion was like a tempest that temporarily took over the mind, a passion that became a momentary obsession. The better path to good citizenship was a reasoned commitment to the common good that included respect for differing views and willingness to work together. "Congenial sentiments, common objects and common pursuits with the same general principles and views can alone produce and support a combined effort and a substantial coalition," a commentator editorialized, adding, "nothing less than the interest of the country can be a proper object and a sufficient bond of union."[21]

Zeal tainted by excessive emotion was discussed increasingly in these years under the rubric of religious fanaticism. Fanatics were driven not only by emotion that spilled into embarrassing public displays but also by feelings, intuitions, and quick responses that clouded their thinking. Strong leaders who claimed to have special divine revelations easily led them astray. Fanatics symbolized in their excess a form of deviation from the social norms that ordinary

FIGURE 8. *Camp Meeting*, 1829, showing heightened emotion among
some of the participants. Drawn by Hugh Bridport. Library of
Congress Prints and Photographs Division, Washington, DC.

citizens were expected to follow, especially respect for justice, benevolence toward others, and a love of truth. Whereas fanatics were guided by superstition,
respectable religious adherents were to be guided by a sense of responsibility
to the truths agreed on in conventional religious teachings. Fanatics became
emotional in public settings, claiming to have a higher morality and engaging
in rancorous disputes while nonfanatics upheld the prevailing moral consensus, which leaders of established churches considered best expressed in biblical teachings—as one explained, "Most devoutly is it to be desired that there
may exist in the churches, especially in their younger members a disposition
and habit of thoroughly investigating the sacred Scriptures."[22]

Isaac Taylor's *Fanaticism*, initially published in 1833, was widely discussed,
both favorably and unfavorably, as an exposé of the inherent tendencies in
religion toward wild irrational displays of emotion. Taylor was in many ways
ahead of his time in attempting to parse the nuances of emotion that distinguished good zeal from bad zeal. Good zeal was composed of feelings that
were benign in their consequences, sentiments of good will, love of God, charitable inclinations, and hatred of evil. Bad zeal arose from anxieties concerning
the truth of religious teachings, misgivings about them, rancorous disputes,
conceit, and infatuation with the authority present in the teachings. It was
difficult, though, to discern concretely the difference except in the context
of religious leaders who provided theological interpretations—which Taylor

conceded led frequently to rancorous disputes. Good zeal was thus Christian or godly to the extent that it accorded ideally with the scriptures, while bad zeal was exemplified by fractious Protestant sects, Catholics during the Inquisition, Jews, and Muslims.[23]

The more interesting—and controversial—part of Taylor's discussion focused on the relationship of fanaticism to social class. There was a fanaticism of want, he argued, but also a fanaticism of plenty, and, contrary to popular opinion, the latter was more acute than the former. Those in poverty were predisposed toward fanaticism by their ignorance and misery; yet the poor rarely violated the public peace, whereas the wealthy seemed inclined toward a "sleek and well-bred religious delirium." The evidence, Taylor said, was in his native Britain, where excitements of politics and religion seemed the order of the day. Still, he hoped that British character, cultivated by rank and high culture, would diminish fanaticism and elevate piety and virtue. And when all was said, biblical religion was not fanatical as long as it was filled with common sense and good morals and was true to the gospel.[24]

Finding the right balance of common sense and personal zeal was the challenge that religious leaders intent on spreading the gospel faced as their ministries grew. Appealing to the poorly educated who worked on farms and in factories and at the same time attracting shopkeepers and skilled artisans aspiring to the civilizing moral uplift that the gospel promised added to the challenge. No group illustrated the challenge more clearly than the Methodists, who, under John Wesley's leadership in England and Francis Asbury's in America, achieved unparalleled numeric success while also experiencing the attacks of critics who described them as hotheaded fanatics, agitators, and enthusiasts. Wesley's and Asbury's meetings included instances of people tearing their clothes, groaning, shouting, trembling, and suffering from temporary blindness. George Bell, an early follower of Wesley, claimed to have healed the blind, become infallible and above temptation, and subject only to his own counsel. London's Bethlem Royal Hospital (better known as Bedlam) included dozens of patients admitted in the 1770s and 1780s for "religion and Methodism."[25] But as Methodism grew, it gained respectability through the good conduct of its members and by cautioning against "extravagant expressions and actions" and favoring the methodical teachings implied in the movement's name. As a widely reprinted editorial in the *Christian Advocate and Journal* explained, "It is to be feared that unless good order, Christian decency, and much heavenly and useful knowledge can be infused, or rather preserved in the mighty mass which is crowding into our Zion, we shall be like a house too hastily built; it may fall by its own weight."[26]

The association of zeal with emotionalism came fully into its own in the discussions of slavery that led up to the Civil War. To the opponents and defenders of slavery, the other side was not only zealous in advancing its claims; it was also degraded, crazy, fanatical, and villainous. Critics on both sides pointed to meetings of emotionally aroused citizens as evidence of fanaticism. The meetings' participants were accused of being licentious, driven by passion, and lacking in scruples. They were especially dangerous when they appeared to be calling on God to justify their actions. Fanaticism signaled a lack of respect for the law. Its opposite involved not only respect for the law but also restraint and perhaps something ingrained in the person. If zealotry had not been sufficiently theorized before, it was now a topic that demanded reflection about its sources in human nature. Zealotry became less an emotion that came to the surface in the heat of the moment and more a symptom of deeper flaws of character. Zealotry was at best the result of circumstances that excited evil passions and at worst the manifestation of those passions under the dominance of prevailing evil itself.

Flaws of character were of two kinds. The first stemmed from some lack that the person could overcome. A person raised in a good family and properly attentive to religious instruction as well as public education was likely to be of good character. Failing to have taken advantage of those opportunities put one at risk of fanaticism—easily led astray by passions of the moment or a fanatical leader. The second kind was inborn. Race provided the principal axis on which discussions of inborn flaws were based. The prevailing argument among white writers was that whites were intellectually superior, more vigorous, and more energetic, meaning active and yet disciplined, while blacks, in contrast, were driven by passions they could scarcely contain. "In mind and body they are inferior," an apologist for slavery wrote in 1850, "this is the law of God—the law of nature, reason and necessity; and if tomorrow, or next year, or a thousand years hence, they were placed on the top of the pyramid of society, they would slide to the bottom, and there remain until they underwent a physical and intellectual transformation." In the meantime blacks would be more susceptible to fanaticism in religion and in approaches to work and other aspects of family life.[27]

If zealots suffered from an underlying flaw of character, it was possible to imagine that the problem could also be diagnosed in physiological terms associated with the biological functioning of the human body. Although psychiatry was yet to be widely recognized as a profession, several of the founders of modern psychiatry as well as physicians and amateur scientists discussed religious fanaticism as a kind of insanity. In 1835 Hartford psychiatrist Amariah Brigham published a critique of religious fanaticism under the title *Observations of the Influence of Religion upon Health and Physical Welfare of Mankind* that drew widespread attention because of the scope of beliefs and practices the book discussed. Brigham's condemnation fell not only on witchcraft, human sacrifice, and mutilation but also on fasting, penance, revivals, and protracted evangelistic meetings. The effects of these activities, he argued, were similar to the ones seen in hysterical epidemics and during experiments with animal magnetism. Brigham's influence on subsequent thinking about

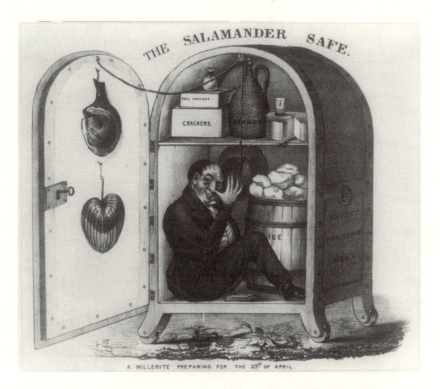

FIGURE 9. *A Millerite Preparing for the End*, 1843, satirizing the possibility of preparations including worldly provisions. Drawn by Thomas S. Sinclair. Library of Congress Prints and Photographs Division, Washington, DC.

the religious bases of insanity continued in 1842 when he became the superintendent of the newly founded New York State Lunatic Asylum at Utica and in 1844 as founding editor of the *American Journal of Insanity*. In 1845 Brigham responded to the flurry of concern about the Millerite movement by calling all religious denominations to curtail their sponsorship of protracted religious meetings.[28]

In 1850 S. Hanbury Smith, professor of medicine at the Starling Medical College and superintendent of the Ohio Lunatic Asylum in Columbus, published the results of research conducted in Sweden in 1841 and 1842 during an epidemic, as he termed it, of "religious monomania." Smith's interest in the topic stemmed from historical accounts of religion-induced "psychical contagion" in which people danced, convulsed, handled venomous snakes, participated in orgies, uttered prophecies, and engaged in other "extravagant ceremonies." The common feature of these activities, in Smith's view, was that they differed so markedly from normal behavior and were similar enough to symptoms occurring from physical maladies that he could classify them under the heading of disease and thus investigate their causes. An inquiry into the details of seven people, all young adults, six of whom were women, Smith concluded, demonstrated that paroxysms, spasms, anxiety, and loss of appetite were present, suggesting that certain medical remedies (zinc, castor oil, saline purgatives, camphor) might be effective, but that social factors also needed to be considered. The social practices most likely to prevent religious monomania read like a recipe for middle-class respectability: provide public education, educate young people with religious knowledge adequate to protect them from superstition, keep people away from radical sectarian prophets and fanatic priests, discourage them from reading inflammatory religious pamphlets, encourage good diets and physical health, and limit the consumption of alcohol; in short, "as much common sense, as little emotion as possible."[29]

It was in this context that efforts to rediscover an understanding of zeal that could be reconciled with an emerging sense of middle-class respectability surfaced. True zeal, as some called it, was to be differentiated from bitter zeal that led to enmity and violence. True zeal was to be tempered with charity and love. It stood against wickedness, against heresy and falsehood, and yet was fair and practical in dealing with disagreements. True zeal was to be expressed in modesty rather than in self-conceit. But if true zeal was temperate, oriented toward achieving a balance between too little conviction and too much, it was an aspiration difficult to achieve in practice. After the Civil War as the nation tenuously tried to pull itself together and push its borders west, zealotry continued to provide the grist for division.

Fanaticism on the Expanding Frontier

The postwar, post-Reconstruction optimism that gained a footing in popular culture in the 1870s and continued through the end of the century held that America was at the cutting edge in the inevitable advance of civilization. Crossing the continent by rail, producing an abundance of grain and livestock, establishing public primary schools in newly settled counties, pacifying the Indians by placing their children in government run schools, attracting immigrants, founding towns, and bringing technological innovation to bear on manufacturing provided ready evidence for writers convinced that civilization was moving rapidly ahead. In the context of those developments it seemed unlikely that religion would diminish in importance because religion too was part of the civilizing process. Certain kinds of religion, though, seemed destined to fall by the wayside.

The kinds of religion that advocates of the civilizing motif considered inconsistent with the times became the focus of concerns discussed under the rubric of fanaticism. Fanatics were like the false prophets of old who claimed to have heard God's voice. Whatever prophecies had been given legitimately were understood to have been enshrined in scripture. New prophecies were not to be believed. Fanatics were like people in less civilized parts of the world who believed in magic. It was possible even in contemporary America to worry that camp meetings and revivals were stoking emotions to the point of crazed behavior resulting. And for leaders who advocated that temperance was the key to advancing civilization, fanaticism was like being intoxicated.

Preachers in respectable middle-class denominations walked a fine line between soft-pedaling evangelism to the point that nobody did it and promoting it so aggressively that it bordered on zealotry. Canvassers and books agents were sufficiently familiar to serve as examples of how to pitch the gospel energetically without stoking the fires of excessive emotion. When Topeka Congregationalists dedicated a new church building in 1871, the guest preacher cautioned against the Stoic example practiced by Ralph Waldo Emerson of retiring within oneself to cultivate the quiet, austere virtues of contemplation. Instead, "Christians must at least show as much zeal as does the canvasser for an insurance company or a publishing house." Had not Jesus himself encouraged believers to "Go out into the highways and hedges and compel them to come in"?[30]

As organized religion encouraged zeal in spreading God's kingdom, zealotry seemed at times to be the plight of deranged individuals more than the work of entire groups. Stories circulated in local newspapers about such individuals killing themselves and their families, committing heinous acts in the name of the Lord, and threatening their neighbors. Fanaticism seemed so often to afflict individuals that the case could have been made that individualism itself was the problem, leaving the mentally vulnerable too often to their own devices. The more likely explanation, though, was the proliferation of local newspapers, filling pages with stories of scandal and intrigue. When local incidents provided too little, the telegraph wires supplied the rest.

In 1875 the wires carried from coast to coast within a few days of it happening the death of a young woman near Honesdale, Pennsylvania, said to be under the influence of extraordinary religious fanaticism. Crissy Hacker, the daughter of a prominent farmer who was widowed, frequently became so convicted of her sins that "her Immanuel" required her to appease the wrath of her deity by offering burnt sacrifices, which sometimes included lambs or household items, and worried her father to the point of trying never to leave her alone. But on January 14, while both he and the hired man were away, Crissy left off reading her Bible, constructed a pyre of quilting frames and carpet, lit the combustible altar, and burned herself to death. She left a note explaining that the cleansing fire had been the only way of finding forgiveness for her unpardonable sins and asking her father to bury her ashes near the northwest corner of the house.[31] Four months later the wires again hummed with news of self-immolation, although this time of a servant girl in France who rose in the middle of the night during an apparent bout of religious fanaticism lit an immense fire in the oven and burned herself to death.[32] Readers would have seen that fanaticism could be deadly.

The efforts begun earlier in the century to identify religious fanaticism as a kind of physiological or psychological malady continued. Religions and religious manifestations that did not fit the expectations of what thoughtful, moderately well-educated members of the middle class should do and believe were treated as a kind of disease. As such, adherents of those religions could be described sympathetically in the same way that a person suffering from heart disease or pneumonia could but at the same time be categorized as alien. Epilepsy offered a particularly appealing category with which to make sense of people who heard divine voices, saw angels, fell into trances, and had seizures.

An example of how epilepsy could be used in this fashion occurred at an 1872 meeting of physicians in which Shakers, Swedenborgians, and Muslims were so classified on the basis of their leaders having claimed to have had divine revelations. Epilepsy, one of the physicians argued, could have been the reason the leaders became fanatics and were considered by their critics to have been crazed or possessed by the devil. "Need we wonder," the physician explained, "that the ignorant Arabs, 1300 years ago, living—as far as a knowledge of nature's law was concerned—in a state of heathen darkness, should have been attracted to the moslem faith, which, while it held out bright hopes for a future life, consorted well with their inclinations in the present."[33]

Besides its interest in epilepsy, the medical community's interest in hallucinations provided another category in which to place persons excessively enthusiastic about religion. Hallucinations provided an explanation for religious experiences involving visions, apparitions, and supernatural voices. They implied that religious fanaticism was either a mental malady or an ignorant response to episodes that clearly were beyond ordinary reality. The cultural space available for persons not suffering from hallucination-induced delusions was in effect broadened at the same time that the severity of the diagnosis of the sufferers increased.

Nearly all discussions of the topic argued specifically or suggested by implication that women were more subject to religious delusions than men. Medical arguments added to stereotypically gendered ideas about female emotionalism by positing connections with reproduction, childbirth, and mothering. Puerperal conditions of interest included not only postpartum bleeding and infections but also depression and inexplicable mood swings. Religious yearnings, visions, spiritual anxieties, and excessive talking about religion came under the same heading. Medical writers cautioned male colleagues to be particularly careful in dealing with female patients suffering in these ways.

At the annual meetings of the American Association of Medical Superintendents of Institutions for the Insane, held at Staunton, Virginia, in 1869, Toronto Asylum superintendent Joseph Workman offered the story of a "pious young lady" recently treated by a colleague for a uterine disorder as a case in point. The uterine specialist had found it necessary "in order to arrive at exact knowledge of the state of the affected organ, that a certain process of examination, not very compatible with virgin delicacy, should be instituted, and a repetition of this process was called for at each appliance of the topical remedy employed." The process, Workman said, surely must have been irksome to the physician; nevertheless the physician did what was necessary. What the physician did not understand was "the peculiar susceptibility of women of fine toned nervous temperament and religious emotionality suffering under uterine disturbance." He therefore innocently engaged the patient in frequent and extended lively conversations in hopes of cheering her. And as a result her "religious anxieties" increased, as did her need for a "spiritual comforter," and she fell "grievously in love with him." This, said Workman, was but one of many such examples he could cite. Emotional religious insanity might not always be associated with disturbances of the female reproductive system, but it was often enough to suggest caution: "It is wise to observe, in our professional intercourse with the subjects of it, a prudential distance."[34]

Ordinary religion as practiced by the major denominations—Protestants, Catholics, and Jews—was by the 1880s firmly located in middle-class communities large and small. The accepted manner of practicing religion was to attend weekly worship services and participate in special activities such as Bible classes and committee meetings. Methodists had become the largest Protestant denomination, overcoming for the most part the reservations about it that led critics earlier in the century to accuse it of fanaticism. But Methodists' growth occurred through mass meetings, revivals, and fiery preaching, and the denomination's emphasis on holiness as the pursuit of personal purity and perfection through spiritual redemption put it at risk of being associated with fanaticism. "It is not a pleasant admission, but doubtless correct," a Methodist writer noted, "that Methodism is afflicted with more cranks than any other denomination." The cause of this affliction, he thought, was the church's teaching about possibilities of being "transferred to a higher region of thought and feeling." Proper preaching and teaching, church discipline, and well-trained ministers were the best antidote. Exhortations were especially needed against "following impressions, special revelations, faith healings, and other vagaries of mysticism." In his mind, "wide cautions against bigotry and rant and cant" would always be needed.[35]

Reverend James Mudge, a Methodist preacher who served churches in New England, had been a missionary in India and wrote extensively and tried in his preaching and writing to distinguish as clearly as he could what he called the delicate line between fanaticism and acceptable religious behavior. He agreed that Methodism had been afflicted with "wild, extravagant notions" held by people under the influence of a "heated imagination." Fanaticism in these respects was similar to insanity. The more interesting argument was his attempt to specify how an ordinary person who was not a fanatic should behave. The principal traits, absent among or violated by fanatics, were "mental discipline, intellectual culture, and scholarly attainments." In addition, a nonfanatic would be guided by reason and common sense, including the laws of health and making practical judgments based on experience.[36]

News accounts of individuals who appeared to be religious fanatics illustrated the kinds of behavior that could result in persons being so classified. A religious fanatic in Seattle committed suicide. A religious fanatic in Michigan was killed after threatening on God's order to kill another man. A religious fanatic in Indiana died from handling a rattlesnake. A religious fanatic in California who was thought to be crazy caused a public disturbance by preaching loudly and blocking traffic. In Illinois a religious fanatic, believing he had received instructions from God, lost his feet by placing them on a track in front of a train. In Missouri a young woman became violent at the train station. In the nation's capital a fanatic torched two of the city's largest Catholic churches. So it went. The actions themselves constituted the classification. Nothing else needed to be known besides the tragic outcome. Religion presumably could easily send people over the edge. The Missouri woman was a "devout student of the Bible" who "showed signs of mental failing." The Washington, DC, incendiary was a "fanatic whose brain has been affected by constant attention to religion."[37]

The possibility that any person could become a fanatic from too much exposure to religion served notice to believers everywhere that religious convictions had to be expressed in orderly ways that did not endanger those holding the convictions or their neighbors. A somewhat different lesson could be drawn from stories about whole groups of fanatics. The danger they presented was not exactly more serious despite the fact that larger numbers were involved. It was rather like stories of outlaws and renegades who somehow lived at the edges of civilization, perhaps in isolated backwoods locations where law and order still needed to be imposed. The moral of these stories was that upstanding citizens needed the protection of better law enforcement.

In September 1876 stories circulated about an incident involving strange religious behavior in central Arkansas about fifty miles northeast of Little Rock. Hearing that an itinerant minister from Tennessee had attracted a group of converts who believed the end of the world was at hand, two men from a nearby town went out to investigate. One was allegedly beheaded, the other escaped, a posse was organized, a shootout ensued, several people were killed or wounded, and the surviving members of the group were tried and found guilty as principals or accessories. Many of the newspapers reported the story as a factual narrative featuring specific names, places, and such details as how the beheaded person was held down, who swung the ax, what was said, where the head was displayed, and what the posse did when it arrived. It was an extraordinary event, all agreed, that happened in a "wild-looking place." Most of the accounts also drew moral lessons from the incident. It demonstrated "that we are living in the land of heathenism," one commentator wrote. "There is practically no limit to the possibilities in the invention of new religions,"

FIGURE 10. *A Seeker Getting Religion*, 1873, suggesting African American religious emotionalism. Drawn by W. L. Sheppard for *Frank Leslie's Illustrated Newspaper*. Library of Congress Prints and Photographs Division, Washington, DC.

said another, complaining that the Arkansas judge had been too lenient on the perpetrators because religion was involved, just as the U.S. Congress was in failing to pass stronger laws against other criminal acts being committed in the name of religion.[38]

In the 1880s and 1890s few religious groups generated as much attention to fanaticism as the Beekmanites, a congregation that began in 1877 at Rockford, Illinois, when Dora Beekman, the wife of Congregational pastor J. C. Beekman, experienced a vision persuading her that she was now the physical embodiment of Christ's second coming. She died in 1883 and failed to rise from the dead, but a follower, George Jacob Schweinfurth, who was a former Methodist minister, claimed that he was now Christ incarnate, and under his leadership the group grew and spread to new locations before it disbanded in 1900. Journalists, clergy, and elected officials all visited the group at Rockford and wrote their interpretations not only of what they saw but also of what the group implied for people who would never dream of becoming members. Clergy took the occasion to warn that Christians should always put their faith in Jesus and in Jesus alone instead of being misled by anyone claiming the sole position that Jesus should occupy. The principal moral lesson was to be on guard against sexual indiscretions (Schweinfurth was said to have an illicit interest in the ladies) and against swindlers who might come along and secure inheritances for themselves in the name of religion. By the 1890s journalistic accounts in Chicago, New York, San Francisco, and other cities also noted that Rockford was a small, rural place and implied that perhaps the followers there were simply naïve. "Naturally these delusions thrived best among the ignorant classes," ethnographer James Mooney observed in an 1896 report to the Bureau of American Ethnology surveying the history of "religious abnormalisms, based on hypnotism, trances, and the messiah idea."[39]

Popular accounts that illustrated the dangers of fanaticism rarely tried to identify any particular emotion that ordinary people should be especially vigilant against. The trouble with emotion was more a matter of degree than of kind. It was almost as if emotion and reason vied for the same cranial space, such that the more emotion predominated the less possible it was for reason to govern behavior. The one exception consisted of discussions in which fanaticism was said to be the result not only of excessive emotion but also of hatred or envy. It made sense that perhaps these negative feelings were the root problem because fanatics frequently seemed to expend their energy criticizing those they disagreed with rather than seeking common ground. As a lecturer in Chicago explained in 1893, "Fanaticism is the wicked daughter of a virtuous mother. Enthusiasm wedded to love gives birth to religion. Enthusiasm wedded to hatred begets fanaticism. It is the same sweet-scented flower becoming honey in the bee and poison in the serpent."[40]

As it had during the Civil War, fanaticism continued to be an epithet used frequently in political as well as in religious discussions. Prohibitionists called the liquor industry fanatics, and the liquor industry returned the favor. Advocates of the various causes rarely thought it necessary to state explicitly what a fanatic was. A fanatic was simply someone on the other side of the issue. By implication, though, the meaning of being or not being a fanatic was sometimes communicated. Fanatics were driven unthinkingly by their emotions. Nonfanatics paused to consider a larger range of options, or in other instances they were in the majority. They were somehow more democratic in their opinions rather than being led by special interests.

It remained the religious community, though, to which fanaticism continued to be of greatest and most frequent concern. Religious leaders who sensed that faith and adherence to accepted teachings were declining under the onslaught of science, Darwinian theories, and materialism argued that upstart religious groups and individual proponents of heretical practices were symptomatic of a continuing desire to know God but an inadequate response on the part of religious authorities to guide and instruct this desire. Catholic writer and founding president of the Catholic Historical Society John Gilmary Shea, for example, contributed a compelling example of arguments in this vein. Respect for civil authority, public opinion, and above all ecclesiastical authority, he contended, was slipping away. In its place an incalculable and growing number of unfettered ideas about God had been promulgated by individuals and groups. The "residuum of Catholic truth" that Protestants retained during the Reformation had been fading ever since. It was now possible during the tenure of Pope Leo XIII to see fanatical sects appearing on all fronts, stirring up dissension and prejudice. But this kind of extremism was nothing new, he said. One could point to false prophets fomenting trouble even in colonial America: to wit, Peter Rombert, who led the Dutartres astray in 1724.[41]

A Shift in Focus

As writers pondered the sources of fanaticism and what became discussed in broader terms as extremism, the relationships of these phenomena to questions of social order rose increasingly and more explicitly to the surface. Just as crime did, deviations from ordinary expressions of religious and political commitment provided a lens through which to examine what in fact constituted normality and could therefore be offered as good counsel for the benefit of individuals and society. Instances of excessive zeal and emotion were frequent enough to offer an opportunity to consider by way of exception what was not only usual but also apparently conducive to the good of society. Writers who imagined that they provided informed scholarly guidance for the kind of social order they hoped would be realized as the nation became better educated and economically developed were especially interested in offering such counsel.

By the 1890s a growing consensus was emerging in popular discussions that the era of trappers, hunters, pioneers, trailblazers, and adventurers in which the rugged life of the open frontier led to occasional outbreaks of fanaticism was over. The largest cities could point to an abundance of tree-lined avenues, department stores, and conservatories as evidence of the new era, but smaller places boasted of the latest in civilizing amenities as well. "Now the former times," a Lutheran pastor in Abilene, Kansas, wrote, would be seen no more. "In their place have come a beautiful city, a flourishing community and great population of noble, intelligent, God-fearing and thankful people who love the state of their adoption and are determined that their children shall engage in honorable business, enjoy refined and educated society and worship God."[42] The time had come, writers with similar views argued, for Americans to prosper by leading quieter, informed, and settled lives on farms and in towns. The dream of that happening was nevertheless continuously buffeted by the realities of fin de siècle excess. The Gilded Age seemed to breed less serenity than agitation, which, if it did not consist of fanaticism as such, came close to it in activism for prohibition, temperance, woman suffrage, union rights, and populist economic reforms. Americans looked to Europe and saw secessionists and fascists. They turned to their solemn places of worship and found contention between fundamentalists and modernists and across denominations. The cautious argument that had always called for moderation in the presence of excess acquired added urgency.

Without exactly condemning the reforms that seemed to be consistent with the nation's economic advancement, arguments for the good life to which average Americans were to aspire resurrected Aristotle's concept of the golden mean as the principle to be followed. A life attuned to the golden mean was not a timid life spent avoiding excess. It instead took into account different points of view, thereby adapting to the broader range of opinions, arguments, and interests to which people living in a more urbanized, ethnically diverse society were exposed. It nevertheless hewed to the middle in terms of whatever majority views might be present, especially on matters of commerce and taste—as a writer reflecting on disagreements about home appliances observed, "Extremists are what their name implies—a little too far from the base of popular opinion, which in most cases is just about correct."[43]

Had opinion polls been taken, avoiding extremism by hewing to the middle would have meant responding "somewhat" agree or disagree to questions about current issues rather than "strongly" agree or disagree. It would have meant approving mildly of the nation's leaders and expressing modest confidence in their decisions. That was not all, however. Religious leaders, as they had done earlier, still expressed the view that faith should be different from simply following the crowd inasmuch as they also thought the crowd was basically right. Revival meetings happened often enough that emotionalism continued to be a problem that clergy in established congregations felt they needed to address while also conceding that faith should not be devoid of emotion. "The emotional, impulsive Christian, who requires frequent conversion, and the cold formalist who is wedded to rites and ceremonies," a writer in *The Advance* explained, were both "superficial in their Christianity." Superficiality, he feared, led people to be swayed by charismatic leaders, on the one hand, and to be content, on the other hand, with outward respectability instead of studying the scriptures and coming to a deeper understanding of divine grace and love.[44]

If the golden mean implied avoiding the extremes of emotionalism or being emotionless, it also meant being a respectable member of one's community without becoming too wedded to or obsessed with respectability as an end in itself. "Respectability and good morals are essential," a writer in *Zion's Herald* observed, but he thought they encouraged churchgoers to fret about being on time, wearing the right clothes, flocking to fine-looking church buildings, and avoiding anything that might be in poor taste instead of ministering to the poor and welcoming strangers. They were like the pilgrim in Nathaniel Hawthorne's "Celestial Railroad," he said, who journeyed to the Celestial City in comfort by train instead of struggling on foot through the many trials and persecutions suffered by the protagonist in John Bunyan's *Pilgrim's Progress*.[45]

William James, in his Gifford lectures, published as *The Varieties of Religious Experience* in 1902, contributed an understanding of religious extremism that also argued for the wisdom implied in the concept of the golden mean. James's interest in the topic reflected the thinking in which he had been engaged since the early 1880s about the nature of emotion. Emotion in his understanding was prompted by physiological stimuli, as in the famous example he gave of running from a bear, which he said was the source rather than the result of fear. Whether pleasurable or unpleasurable, emotion could result from extreme physiological sources and thus be excessive. Religion was one such source, especially when it involved physiologically exceptional activities such as dancing, shouting, fasting, meditating for long periods, and listening at great length to fiery rhetoric. James's well-known distinction between healthy-minded and sick-souled religion allowed for religion to be uplifting, redemptive, and vivifying of an interior world, and for it to result in heroic and saintly behavior toward which admiration was generally conceded, but he also cautioned that few could be expected to effectively engage in such behavior. In his remarks on saintliness, he suggested that the traits so often admired in saints included emotions to which ordinary people rarely aspired. Saintly virtue consisted of extreme passion, strong affections, and strong sympathies that often led to an imbalance of single-mindedness. Fanaticism on the part of devout believers, he said, was loyalty carried to a "convulsive extreme," a phrase meant to suggest a loss of bodily control. As much as saintliness might be admired, he cautioned, it should not be imitated: religion should instead be "subject to the law of the golden mean." Conduct that "lies nearer to the middle line of human effort," he counseled, "wears well in different ages, such as under different skies all judges are able to commend."[46]

Early twentieth-century discussions in mainstream religious periodicals frequently expressed views about moderation similar to James's—sometimes to the extent that the positions taken would later be regarded as naïve, overly optimistic, and too indebted to a kind of postmillennial theology that smacked of Social Darwinism and American exceptionalism. If nothing else, centrist arguments praising the golden mean instantiated an accommodation with popular opinion about the commonsense virtues to which most Americans presumably aspired and, in this, could be regarded as part of the broader secularizing tendencies evident at the time in higher education and the professions. Extremism that deviated excessively from the golden mean, in this understanding, included not only the overt fanaticism of radical sects but also mysticism that focused obsessively on the interior life and legalism that tried too hard to uphold the letter of biblical mandates about such issues as Sabbath observance and modesty in dress.

Charles Monroe Sheldon, the Congregationalist preacher in Topeka, Kansas, who operated a kindergarten for African American children, became widely known for his bestselling *In His Steps* and popularization of the phrase "What would Jesus do?" and a few years later would be an outspoken critic of American involvement in World War I—certainly no stranger to movements for social reform—was another voice encouraging Americans to embrace the good so readily available already in the popular religious and moral sentiments in their communities. The presence of a divine spirit was clearly evident, he told his congregation in 1904, referring to the many people in the community who lived, he believed, according to the "priceless fact of a good reputation" and a "spotless character." "It makes no difference what men call it—public opinion, ethical judgment, a sense of what is right and wrong—it is here as it was not present in the world when Christ first stepped into it and it is one of the marks of a saved world."[47]

The idea of a centrist, moderate approach to religion and morality that could be broadly agreed on despite the religious, ethnic, and regional diversity characteristic of the American population left unanswered the question of why some Americans seemed so easily swayed by fanaticism. The approach that had earlier addressed the question by considering particular maladies of individuals such as insanity and epilepsy became the focus of new inquiries by psychiatrists, psychologists, and scholars of religion with kindred interests. One of the more extensive studies, published in 1892 by Methodist minister James Monroe Buckley, examined faith healing, astrology, dreams, visions, mind cures, and witchcraft, drawing on case studies, court testimony, historical sources, and practitioners' accounts. Buckley held that religious experiences of conversion, forgiveness, and communion with God were conducive to joy, tears, trances, and even lunacy, but he insisted that the reason some people experienced emotional excitement to such extremes had more to do with their temperament than anything else. They were simply susceptible, and for this reason alone charismatic leaders and crowd contagion easily aroused their emotions. In a follow-up essay published in 1903 addressing the notion that the United States was a "hot-bed of fanaticism," Buckley expanded on the same interpretation, arguing again that some people were simply by temperament excitable, acutely sensitive, and hyper-suggestible. Fanaticism represented a danger to the society, he believed, but the impossibility of ever fully eradicating it meant that nonfanatics should avoid making it worse by overreacting. Cautious legislation and sound judgment would ultimately carry the day.[48]

The view that society would always be afflicted in some measure by fanaticism at the edges of common life, as it were, found expression in another argument that reflected the more diverse, urban realities of the early twentieth century. This argument held that fanaticism was inappropriate less because of the emotions involved and more because of its narrow-mindedness. The understanding of appropriate middle-class behavior implied in this view emphasized willingness to be considerate, to be agreeable, and to fit into the normal give-and-take that modern life required. John Wilbur Chapman, the Presbyterian evangelist who held mass urban revival meetings from 1895 until his death in 1918, emphasized this understanding against critics who viewed revivals as the seedbed of fanaticism. Educated in Quaker and Methodist schools, holding a graduate degree from Heidelberg University, employed by the Presbyterian Church, funded by a wealthy Presbyterian philanthropist, and holding evangelistic meetings in cities around the English-speaking world as well as in America, Chapman appreciated the importance of being able to adapt to diverse circumstances. Emotionalism and the potential for fanaticism that might stem from religious awakenings, he argued, were problematic only if they prevented believers from behaving better in meeting the practical challenges of daily life. A fanatic, Chapmen said, was someone who "shuts from his view every other interest and forces his preferences on others in such a way as to make him a disagreeable companion to get along with." Fanatics cared too much about their own opinions, whereas the more desirable expression of religious faith was "in the home, in fairness and honesty in business, in the spirit of its profession, [and in] commonplace duties and normal spiritual joys."[49]

Although it had always been implied, discussions of fanaticism that contrasted it with getting along collegially with other people suggested in addition that *discussion* was the best way to avoid fanaticism. In this view, it was not enough just to be agreeably in the presence of others; it was better to talk things over. Fanatics might talk at you; nonfanatics would talk with you, listening to your opinions as well as sharing theirs. The kind of reason with which fanaticism contrasted was more than the subjective commitment to good reasons it had often been understood in the past to be; it was more popularly the ability, as one would do in business and the professions, to articulate those reasons and improve them by communicating them in the diverse settings of everyday life. The trouble with fanatics was that they coddled a single idea instead of exposing it to alternative points of view. It was the give-and-take that strengthened arguments in contrast to fanaticism that shielded weak arguments by refusing to discuss them.

The Pentecostal movement that gained wide visibility through the Azuza Street revival meetings in Los Angeles in 1906 provided grist for commentators who took the view that ordinary people should engage in social interaction requiring them to entertain and defend multiple points of view. The worrisome aspect of Pentecostalism, critics claimed, was not only their conviction of being in direct communication with God through the Holy Spirit. It was also their belief in the gift of tongues. Glossolalia literally closed off communication with others rather than facilitating an open exchange of arguments. Observers who lacked the gift of tongues were literally left out of the conversation; only those with the gift could provide a translation. Pentecostalism negated the basic understanding of common sense based on an exchange of diverse opinions.

As common as it was for discussions of fanaticism to focus on fringe religious groups, some groups that might have been subject to this criticism never (or hardly ever) were—and the fact that they were regarded differently illuminated something important about the prevailing social norms. Commentators

FIGURE 11. *Panorama of Zion City, Illinois*, 1904. Photograph by George R. Lawrence. Library of Congress Prints and Photographs Division, Washington, DC.

that accused the Millerites of practices bordering on insanity less often expressed the same criticisms toward Robert Owen's followers or those of John Humphrey Noyes, and, in later years, the small colonies of immigrants who brought their own distinctive practices mostly escaped these criticisms as well. The difference had less to do with beliefs that deviated from the mainstream and more to do with staying within the lines of acceptable displays of emotion. Shouting, dancing, ranting, hearing divine voices, and engaging in violence all suggested that people were being driven by impulses instead of being in control of themselves. Groups that settled down, organized themselves, worked hard, and supported themselves might be considered strange, but they were less likely to be called fanatics.

One of the clearest early twentieth-century cases in point was Zion City, a community forty miles north of downtown Chicago founded in 1900 by Reverend John Alexander Dowie. Dowie was a faith healer who considered himself the modern-day equivalent of an Old Testament prophet and sometimes referred to himself as Elijah the Restorer. By 1902 Zion City was a community of some 6,000 people who belonged to Dowie's Christian Catholic Church, which claimed to have between 50,000 and 60,000 adherents nationwide and in Europe. Located as close to Chicago as it was, Zion City regularly attracted visitors, journalists, and interested religious writers who talked with Dowie, attended meetings at the community's large tabernacle, and reported on the community's activities. The reports included sensational accounts not only of conversions and healings but also of scandal and intrigue. The community was afflicted with criticism from without and by conflict and controversy within. Residents in nearby Waukegan worried about the kind of neighbor it would be. Local clergy unsuccessfully petitioned the group's leaders to let them more biblically instruct the faithful. Solicitors traveled the country in hopes of persuading enough people to join and struggled to attract investors to help pay for the land. Several of the solicitors barely escaped mob violence during their travels. Illinois officials questioned Dowie's finances and business dealings. Dissension and dismissals routinely occurred among the overseers Dowie appointed. Dowie, claiming to fear being assassinated, began traveling with bodyguards. A leadership crisis occurred that involved Dowie leaving for Mexico, returning only to die a year later, and followed by divisions within the community and the formation of factions. Charles Parham, the charismatic leader from Kansas who moved on to minister unsuccessfully in Houston and then with William J. Seymour played an influential role in popularizing the Pentecostal movement, led one of the factions. At Dowie's funeral, hundreds of seekers came to touch his burial clothing in hope of being healed.

Under Dowie's successor, Wilbur Glenn Voliva, Zion City's troubles continued: investigations of its finances and property resulted in highly publicized lawsuits, its rigid dress codes sparked criticism especially in view of several sex scandals, and several deaths occurred that were directly attributable to its religious practices. Dowie's sister died refusing medical attention in lieu of hope for divine healing. A year later a mother and baby died in childbirth when the husband believed her wish for a doctor was inspired by the devil. Another husband claimed his wife developed a fiendish temper from attending Dowie's meetings. A few years later a woman suffering from cancer died during a forty day fast. About the same time five members of the community were arrested, accused of torturing a woman suffering from paralysis and rheumatism to death by stretching her limbs and breaking her neck.[50]

But, for all its troubles, discussions of Zion City treated it more as an interesting business venture than as a fanatical sect. It helped that the community *was* a municipality, and it was good that Dowie referred to himself less often as Elijah II than as Dr. Dowie, emphasizing that he had been trained in theology at the University of Edinburgh and ordained as a Congregational minister in Australia. The worst of his excesses, as far as the popular press was concerned, was not his faith healing, which earned criticism more toward a few of his followers than of him, but his money. He lived lavishly, traveled extensively, and was thought to have pocketed several million dollars by the time he died. His wealth, though, inspired as much admiration as criticism. Zion City was a boomtown, admirers said, because it was well planned, was well organized, and had good laws. The 6,500 acres Dowie purchased he leased at a profit; he founded a machine-operated lace factory and brought in immigrants to do the work; and there were strict laws against alcohol and tobacco. Zion City had a post office, depot, bank, hotel, well-stocked general store, and school. The community's children struck observers as the kind they would like their own offspring to be. "They are good, healthy, normal-looking youngsters who seem to be interested in baseball and kindred sports," one visitor wrote, "and who are not so awed by the spirit of religion which is supposed to dominate the community that they take off their hats on weekdays when they enter the house of worship." And if the children were well behaved, the adults were too. "If one is willing to obey the Ten Commandments plus Dowie's additions and to live according to the sanitary code of the old Jewish law," another visitor observed, "he will find Zion City a home among a kindly and industrious people, who, because they spend nothing on drink and tobacco are unusually prosperous."[51]

Early assessments predicted that Zion City would never experience dissension, but despite those predictions going unrealized, Zion City continued to be the fringe community that more often symbolized virtue than vice. Especially Voliva, the new overseer, exemplified all that a respectable business leader should be, observers said. He was in vigorous health and came from a good farm family in which he had learned to work hard and developed good instincts. He was modest and cautious but also forceful. He understood human nature, was energetic and systematic in his use of time, and believed in conducting business on a cash basis. In his comportment he had the dignity and manner appropriate to his position, and above all he believed in and practiced the simple life.[52] Under Voliva's leadership, Zion City became known as one of the nation's strict religious communities that stood for grassroots common sense against the scourge of immorality that seemed to be emanating from places like Paris and New York and Washington. When necklines dropped and hemlines rose, Zion City passed new dress codes for its female residents and sent emissaries to counsel New Yorkers of their wicked ways. When male employees at a nearby electrical company began smoking, Zion City women launched a war on tobacco. And when Uncle Sam required Zion City's draftees to be vaccinated, Voliva said he would sooner cut off relations with America than have the government shooting germs in their arms.[53]

Zion City was never the model of hardworking grassroots moral contentment that its admirers claimed it to be: Dowie's eccentric teachings and the community's tortuous authoritarian leadership continued under Voliva. In the 1920s Voliva gained international notoriety for claiming that the earth was flat, and Zion City's children learned in science classes that evolution was a hoax. Voliva was twice convicted of slandering a rival leader, lived on a peculiar diet of Brazil nuts and buttermilk, and repeatedly predicted the end of the world.[54] For all of that, it was surprising that the community was not more often cited as an example of fanaticism. What saved it was the planning—indeed, the imposition of authority—that impeded impulsiveness and undergirded a regimen of rigid moral control.

In subsequent decades it was less often impulsiveness than rigidness that would earn condemnation under the rubric of fanaticism. Fanatics no longer needed to be excessively emotional; it was enough to be closed minded, set in one's ways, dogmatic. A fanatic could cling to a particular point of view without expressing emotion at all. Narrow-mindedness had always been the trait associated with fanaticism, but now the problem was not too strong an emotional attachment but a failure to reckon with opposing arguments. What was once called dogmatism now became fanaticism. Fanatics were bigoted; they illustrated by negative example that persons schooled appropriately in the wisdom of common sense were tolerant. They could live peaceably in a complex world by adapting as situations changed.

Fanaticism and Moral Order

Fanaticism provides an interesting case in point for considering how the symbolic distinctions we draw in ordinary life serve to affirm a sense of moral order. Some of the most commonly discussed distinctions appear at first glance to be sharply defined and relatively enduring over long periods of time. Racial distinctions, for example, draw such sharp and enduring boundaries between blacks and whites that they reinforce residential segregation, homophilous friendship patterns, and income inequality. But racial boundaries are also maintained by the very fact that they are not always sharp and enduring. They are reproduced through periodic transgressions, testing, and negotiation. Fanaticism was, on the one hand, a recurring accusation that seems to have been meaningful enough for those who used the term to have understood its negative connotations. But, on the other hand, fanaticism was a distinction that shifted from context to context, especially in reference to religious beliefs and practices. "One may easily step across the border without being conscious that he has passed into an enemy's country," a writer for *Zion's Herald* observed in 1896. "This is nowhere seen, perhaps, more frequently than in the facile transition that is so often made from faith to fanaticism."[55]

The value of a boundary so unclear that it can be crossed unwittingly is that it can be—perhaps *has to be*—discussed again and again. The line between faith (or reason) and fanaticism can never be drawn once and for all. A person or group can be accused of fanaticism at one moment and defended the next. The discussion provides the occasion for negotiating the distinction between conventionally accepted standards of moral behavior and deviations from those standards. A respectable display of zeal can be defined as good works, listening to the counsel of reason and reasonable people in positions of authority, speaking with conviction, and exhibiting appropriate demeanor through one's posture and mode of dress. Fanaticism deviates from respectability by following too ardently the private dictates of one's conscience, engaging in violence, violating the law, or hearing the voice of God.

And yet, despite deviating in these ways, fanaticism over the years was discussed in ways that warned people against it without particularly blaming those who experienced it. From the Dutartres and Millerites, who mostly illustrated people who fell under the sway of charismatic leaders, to the epileptics and sufferers of uterine disorders, excessive religious emotion was characterized as the result of conditions over which those involved had little control. Like insanity, it could happen to people who might be least expecting it, coming over them in an instant, and clouding their thinking. As an ever-present danger, it made good copy for cautionary tales. Nobody was safe, which meant that fanatics could be criticized without entirely locating them in a different moral universe, but their existence also encouraged people who did not want to be accused of fanaticism to fit in, restrain their emotions, and use reason.

Margaret Mead, in an essay published shortly before her death in 1978, described fanaticism in terms that any thoughtful person at the time could have appreciated. A fanatic was someone, she wrote, who needed to somehow be transformed "back into a temperate, moderate, self-critical human being." For Mead, the recurring presence of fanaticism in the world was a reminder that the rest of us did well by virtue of temperance, moderation, and self-criticism. There was also something more. Fanaticism not only defied reason. It also represented the negation of progress, the forward-looking attitude toward social change that reasonable people embraced. It was, she felt, the Ku Klux Klan, the John Birch Society, and the extreme McCarthyite anticommunists of her time that most clearly exemplified fanaticism. "Those who hold out for an outworn system in our own society by refusing to let a road go through, or a subway be built, or an archaic law be repealed," she wrote, "may have a comparable deleterious effect upon effective and needed change in other matters such as abortion, birth control, or sex education."[56]

The concerns about fanaticism that surfaced so often in nineteenth- and early twentieth-century discussions of religion are no less evident in the twenty-first century. Only the focus in the American media has shifted, more often discussing fanaticism among Muslims than among Christians, but also continuing to identify it with small sects that deviate from the lifestyles and habits of the respectable middle class. From considering the discussion of fanaticism in earlier periods, one lesson of continuing relevance is that accusations of fanaticism usually make their case by spelling out specifically how it contrasts with the norms of respectable society. Narratives about fanatics do not simply charge an alien group with being fanatics and leave it at that. The narratives employ the rhetorical devices of compare and contrast. If a fanatic presumes to hear the voice of God directly, the contrast is a person who listens to the counsel of reasonable people and considers the conventional wisdom superior to the voice of God. A fanatic that commits violence certainly provides an occasion for stating that others with similar attachments to similar traditions do not condone violence.

Predictions that fanaticism would disappear from the world as science, education, and clinical expertise prevailed clearly have not been realized. The one transformation that should be taken note of is the shift in meaning of one connotation of the term. In milder versions fanaticism merely connotes fandom, as in being a sports fan. Sports fans may be criticized for how they spend their money or time and, except for sports violence and hooliganism, escape much else in terms of public censure.[57] The word's original association with sacred places, sacred voices, and sacred sentiments, though, persists. Fanaticism about religion continues to be of considerable interest and concern.

The moral order that fanaticism symbolizes by standing as a rejection of that order implies something about social status—indeed, status is conferred on people who conform to the moral order and is denied those who deviate from it. To be a person of status—a person who exemplifies middle-class respectability—is to toe the line against tendencies toward fanaticism. In many instances that means behaving reasonably, which in turn requires not only that a person be thoughtful in terms of paying attention to the empirical realities of conventional daily life but also appears to be thoughtful by virtue of his or her mode of speaking and manner of dress. A person who prays for rain must also be known for paying attention to the weather forecast.

Understanding fanaticism in dialogic terms as the language through which religious groups negotiate the respectability and status of their members casts the history of religious movements somewhat differently from the way it is often portrayed. Calvinist Protestants did not have only an elective affinity with rational ascetic financial accumulation, Methodists and Mormons did not simply become more methodical and better organized, and Catholic immigrants did not just become more Americanized as they assimilated into the American middle class. Religious leaders in each of these cases adapted to prevailing norms of respectability by differentiating themselves from groups they described as fanatics. Religious movements were always in play within larger fields of competing movements. The ones that became known in retrospect as accepted representatives of middle-class norms repeatedly distanced themselves from groups they criticized for excessive zeal, excessive displays of emotion, and inadequate conformity to church teachings about doctrinal interpretations.

In the contrast between reasonable religion and fanaticism, the line was always negotiable. On one account, Methodists and Mormons were the reasonable opponents of religious fanatics, while on another account they were bedfellows. To proponents of purely rational thought, whether in philosophy or politics, religion in all forms provided the contrasting case that could be constructed as irrational, especially if instances of religious fanaticism could be included. The meaning of rationality in those discussions, though, was framed in terms of particular conceptions of logic, empirical proof, and natural explanation, unlike popular understandings that contrasted it with thoughtful, moderate common sense.[58]

Religious movements that deviated from established middle-class expectations did so in full awareness that theirs represented a contrasting style of belief and practice. Groups that heard the voice of God speaking directly to them, groups that emphasized the indwelling of deeply emotional spiritual experiences, and groups that favored public outpourings of joy, sorrow, and praise found authority in manifestations of divine truth that explicitly differed from the respectable mainstream versions of piety. The rhetorical logics of compare and contrast worked for those who rejected prevailing conventions just as it did for those who embraced conventionality.

The first question that fanaticism evokes is always why do people become fanatics. The why question is important because it generates answers in the interest of protecting the body politic from the dangers fanaticism presents. Understanding it as religious delusion argues for a reasoned approach to faith; regarding it as disease begs for medical intervention. But the second question that fanaticism should evoke is equally important: what do our complaints about fanatics tell us about ourselves?

Fanaticism in the twenty-first century is rarely about just one thing, any more than it was in the past. Fanatics come in all shades of religious conviction and political persuasion. They are worrisome when they claim to speak with divine authority, refuse to compromise, and fail to listen to reason. They also represent subtler worries about generally accepted ways of life, such as commitments to fair and equitable treatment, mutual respect, tolerance, and common standards of decency and decorum. Fanatics worry us because they remind us of ideals to which we easily give lip service but too often fail to uphold in practice.

CHAPTER FIVE

Dying Young

IMMIGRANT CONGREGATIONS
AS MORAL COMMUNITIES

THE QUESTION THIS CHAPTER ADDRESSES is an old one: what role did religion play—and how did that role change—as immigrants assimilated into American culture? Although the question has been examined many times and from many different angles, relatively little attention has focused on the tensions that often developed between the supportive roles congregations performed for their members and the conflicts that emerged within and among congregations as ethnic traditions evolved. How congregations dealt with these tensions and how they maintained solidarity were integral to how they functioned as moral communities. And that in turn provides an important perspective from which to understand the role that respectability played in the nineteenth century. Immigrant congregations supported their members' sense of being respectable, God-fearing Americans while adhering to distinctive beliefs and practices that also put them at risk of being perceived as outsiders.

The great waves of immigration that brought millions of people from Europe to America in the nineteenth century constructed the religious mosaic that characterized the nation through most of the twentieth century and even today. Roman Catholics emigrated from Ireland, Italy, France, Germany, and Poland, populating ethnic parishes that reflected those origins. Protestants came from England and Scotland, Germany, and Scandinavia, forming the various branches of Episcopal, Presbyterian, Lutheran, and Baptist denominations. Jews, African Americans, Mennonites, Mormons, and various other racial, ethnic, and religious groups added to the diversity.

The image of a melting pot made sense to twentieth-century writers who saw the earlier configurations of race, ethnicity, and religion being reshaped. Swedish Lutherans merged with German and Norwegian Lutherans to become American Lutherans. Irish, Italian, and German Catholics increasingly worshipped at parishes lacking ethnic distinctions. Methodist churches absorbed their German and Swedish congregations under the umbrella of larger regional denominations. What had once seemed separate and at times even divisive came increasingly to be understood as broad-based generic manifestations of something truly American refracted through the lens of such unifying labels as Protestant, Catholic, and Jew.[1]

The questions that interested twentieth-century writers reflected the view that assimilation inevitably stripped the nation of its ethnic diversity. The central question was how immigrants came to think of themselves simply as respectable, middle-class Americans rather than as hyphenated Americans. How did they become integrated into nonethnic occupations, communities, families, lifestyles, and religions? Straight-line assimilation, as it came to be called, saw ethnicity as a relic to be abandoned or at most preserved in moments of nostalgia.[2]

This view of assimilation fit neatly with stories of the American Dream. Immigrants came to America, the narrative went, in search of upward mobility. They embraced the freedom in their new country to pursue their aspirations in whatever way they chose. At first they encountered difficulties because of the foreign traditions and language barriers that held them back. But gradually they broke free of these barriers, abandoning their traditions, learning a new language, and shoving their children from the ethnic enclaves in which they lived. In the process, religious bodies underwent significant transformations. From tightknit communities bound by a common ethnic heritage, they adopted the uniform of individual piety. Religious communities thus ironically facilitated middle-class respectability at the same time that these communities lost their distinctive traditions.

Of course the reality was not so simple. Ethnic enclaves proved to be surprisingly resilient, attracting newcomers and adapting to changing economic and political conditions. Congregations resisted being pulled into denominations born of mergers with other traditions and beliefs. Individuals and families who found themselves displaced formed new congregations and gravitated to others in which they felt more at home. Racial distinctions were by far the most difficult to transcend. People dug in their heels to protect the ethnic and racial customs, local traditions, and family ties they cherished so deeply, and they frequently faced discrimination and exclusion that reinforced these distinctions.

Immigration in the late twentieth century and into the twenty-first century has necessitated paying closer attention to the racial, ethnic, and religious diversity that is now understood as the inescapable reality of American culture. Evidence suggests more clearly than ever that the mythic melting pot was never fully realized. New and old ethnic identities underscore a more segmented pattern of assimilation in which diversity is continuously negotiated and reshaped.[3] Politics, marketing, and the media have, on the one hand, created large categories with which to simplify the diversity. Asian American, African American, Latino, liberal Protestant, Catholic, and evangelical are some of the categories that have become familiar. They confer identities that pundits and pollsters find useful for describing the broad contours of public opinion. On the other hand, investigations of congregations, in communities, and among families show how much is missed when only the broad contours of public opinion are considered. Identifying whole populations as Latino, African American, or white evangelical masks the fact that the people so classified bear multiple identities. Not only can they be Latino *and* African American *and* evangelical; they can also strongly identify as Baptist, gay, and Arizonan.

Such diversity expressed in multiple identities tempts the focus of discussion to shift from organizations and groups to individuals. It is the individual, after all, who represents the location where multiple identities come together. How that happens, how identities are shaped, how they gain expression in personal narratives, and how they change are all interesting and important questions. But they are not the only questions that need to be asked—and indeed they cannot be adequately addressed without also considering the organizations and groups in which individuals participate.

It may be that the organizations and groups in which we currently participate are the product of forces over which the vast majority of us have only limited control—corporations, political parties, and government bureaus, for example—or are so completely the product of individual discretion—hobby groups, clubs, and online social networks, for example—that they reflect only the fungible affinities of likeminded individuals. It is tempting to think about religion as a particular example of the latter, especially in view of evidence that people in growing numbers identify themselves as spiritual but not religious, as having no particular religious identity or affiliation, and as having switched among or participated simultaneously in multiple religious groups.

If that is an accurate description of the present, though, it poses the interesting and important question of how we got to here from something different in the past. In particular, what was that past reality and how did it change? This is the question to which discussions of assimilation have typically been addressed. But looking back in terms of what we now know requires rethinking those discussions, many of which reflected a view of America that no longer seems as adequate as it once did.

To that end, I want to invite attention to aspects of nineteenth-century congregations that on my reading have been relatively neglected and yet shed light on basic questions of how congregations functioned amid the conflicting tensions of ethnic assimilation, economic constraints, kin-based social networks, and negotiations about the meanings of middle-class respectability. Doing so casts doubt on the view that individuals in that era maximized their choices about religion in the same way that individuals do now, only with fewer options available. The evidence instead suggests that congregations' existence in the form it took depended in large measure on the broader social relationships with which they had to contend. When those ties changed, congregations had to undergo major changes as well—changes still under way today.

The key to understanding these changes is to reckon with two basic features of nineteenth-century America: first, that people died young, whether as infants or from giving birth or from contagious diseases and accidents; and second, that individuals were embedded in large co-ethnic networks involving complex family relationships that depended on and shaped their participation in congregations. Understanding these characteristics of the social contexts in which religious leaders and their constituents organized congregations provides a way to think not only about religion but also about the moral lines, obligations, and relationships that influenced how individuals behaved and thought they should behave. It will be helpful if we personalize the topic by briefly introducing two immigrant families.

First, the Kohmans: Henry and Mary Kohman were married in Dodge County, Wisconsin, in 1872. Dodge County is about fifty miles northwest of Milwaukee. English-speaking families settled the area in the 1840s, but by the end of the Civil War it was predominantly German. Except for Milwaukee, it had the largest concentration of Germans of any county in the state. Mary came to America with her parents and several siblings from a rural area north of Berlin in 1862 when she was nine. Henry emigrated by himself from a farming community near Hamburg in 1869 when he was twenty-six. For the next three years he worked as a day laborer for a wealthy farmer named Chancey Parrish who purchased land in Dodge County in 1849.[4]

Without land to farm, Henry and Mary did like thousands of other families and migrated west, settling in Kansas, where their first child was born in 1873. With Henry's savings they purchased a 160-acre farm in Dickinson County along Turkey Creek about fifteen miles south of Abilene. Abilene had become the destination for cattle drives from Texas along the Chisholm Trail when the Kansas Pacific Railway reached it in 1867, and over the next five years dozens of families from Michigan, Illinois, and Tennessee established farms.[5] The township where Henry and Mary settled was not exactly a German enclave— only 37 of the 171 families living there in 1875 were of German origin. But there was a connection with Wisconsin.

That connection was the Baptist church. In 1860 a German immigrant named Hans Heinrich Nottorf arrived in Dickinson County with his wife and three children. Nottorf left Germany in 1848 in search of religious freedom and settled near Lebanon in Dodge County, Wisconsin, where he worked as a butcher, farmed, preached, and helped organize German Baptist churches at Lebanon and Watertown in 1854. In Kansas he farmed and continued to preach, baptizing nine persons in 1863, seven more in 1866, and that year organizing what became known as the First German Baptist Church of

FIGURE 12. *Henry and Mary Kohman and Children*, 1892. Personal collection.

Dickinson County. The church met in homes for more than a decade. When the first church building was constructed in 1880, Henry and Mary Kohman donated the land.[6]

The Kohmans lived out their lives there, raising a large family, and experienced both the opportunities and heartaches of other immigrant families. In many ways they epitomized the American Dream, starting from nothing, working hard, gaining the respect of their neighbors, and doing well. They are buried in the church cemetery. Five of their children and their spouses are also buried there. More about them later.

The second family was named Kruse. They were also German immigrants. Henry and Anna Kruse were married on August 19, 1871, in a small town called Hillsboro in Montgomery County, Illinois. Henry emigrated from Westerstede, a farming community near Oldenburg, Germany, in 1869 at the age of nineteen, settling in Walshville, about twelve miles from Hillsboro, and working as a day laborer for a farmer named Thomas Kirkland. Anna, who was eight years older than Henry, emigrated from near Oldenburg about the same time and went to Mt. Olive, Illinois, which was about six miles from Walshville.

Like it did for the Kohmans, the Baptist church played an important role for Henry and Anna Kruse. Both had been raised as Lutherans, but Henry converted when he was eighteen and subsequently joined the Baptist church

FIGURE 13. *Henry Kruse and Friends*, ca. 1890, showing crew
dressed in coveralls for wheat harvest. Personal collection.

at Walshville, and Anna appears to have converted by the time they were married. The couple's first home was near Burlington, Iowa, where newly arrived
German immigrants formed a Baptist church in 1869. Then in 1878 Henry and
Anna moved to a farm in Kansas near a place that a few years later would be
named Lorraine, where another German Baptist church was being organized.[7]

Two families, then, so similar they could almost be one: Germans who
came to America in the 1860s, married at about the same time, moved to Kansas, settled among other German Americans, purchased land, farmed, and
belonged to German Baptist churches. In many ways they were like thousands
of others who left their countries of origin seeking opportunities in America,
settling among co-ethnics, participating in ethnic churches, marrying, and
having children. Both families were large. The Kohmans had fourteen children; the Kruses had eighteen. There was one other similarity. Both women
died young. Mary Kohman was thirty-nine when she died of complications
from giving birth; Anna Kruse was forty-nine. The two Henrys remarried.[8]

There were also differences, which for present purposes are as instructive
as the similarities. The similarities—ethnicity, location, and historical period—
make it possible to hold those aspects of what we want to consider constant.
The differences make for interesting comparisons. Why did the two families

assimilate in different ways? What kinds of support did they receive from their congregations? How did ethnicity, language, family ties, and religious convictions come together in their lives and in their communities?

It would be easy to fit these families into a larger narrative about assimilation and American exceptionalism. In this telling, the two Henrys and their wives would be rugged individualists who struck out on their own at an early age, worked hard, lived simply, kept their heads down, and raised large families that went on to become successful farmers, teachers, scientists, and public officials. How the wives who died young might fit that story of upward striving, though, is less clear. Maybe it could be jiggered into a conventional American Dream narrative about mothers sacrificing for their children, even to the point of giving up their lives, and illustrating in death that America would see a better day in which lower fertility rates, medicine, and birth control were the keys to longevity and well-being. This version of their lives might be compelling. But it misses a great deal about the details of their families and communities.

Shifting attention to the congregations in which they participated could prompt an equally linear narrative of America and American religion. That would be a narrative about the successful churching of America bringing to fruition the godly city on a hill the nation's founders envisioned. This narrative would tell how the congregations grew from modest beginnings into large churches that were successful because they preached the gospel, projected an entrepreneurial style of competitive administration, retained their youth, and attracted newcomers. The two congregations in this account would exemplify the work of thousands of enterprising pastors turning a small number of believers into a nation of Christian citizens.

The difficulty with these standard renditions is that they leave out almost everything that mattered to the people themselves. The social relationships that sustained individuals as they bore children, saw some of them die, dealt with joy and pain, negotiated the respect of their neighbors, and simply lived their lives from day to day and from week to week have almost no place in the linear history of American progress. To be sure, it was important to families that their children and their congregations succeed. But those aspirations were secondary to putting bread on the table and to breaking bread on special occasions as they gathered at their places of worship. The vertical story of winners and losers needs to be replaced with a horizontal story in which the relations between husbands and wives and with children and neighbors come into view. It needs to pay closer attention to the question of how congregations complemented those relations and were shaped by them.

What we know about the actual details of congregations in that era of national expansion after the Civil War comes largely from two sources. One is the census of religious bodies tallied by the federal government in conjunction with decennial censuses from 1850 to 1890 and then as special reports from

1906 to 1936. Aggregated by counties and states and by denominations, those figures provide an overview of how many congregations of various kinds and in various locations existed and how many people they claimed as members. Absent much else, the numbers have contributed to discussions of overall growth and comparisons of winners and losers. They show that thousands of congregations were founded and that church buildings were constructed, all taking place as the population grew and migrated west and happening in such numbers that America was ostensibly more religious at the end of the nineteenth century than at the start. But the numbers reveal little about actual congregations. The other source consists of historical accounts of particular churches and the ministries of particular pastors. These accounts make for interesting reading but rarely offer more than names and dates associated with the congregation's founding, its buildings, and its most prominent pastors.

Taking the time to reflect on the lives and deaths of a few ordinary people like Mary, Anna, and the two Henrys—standing at their graves, reading the inscriptions on their tombstones, and wondering about the people who gathered there when they were laid to rest—forces attention to shift from large metric generalizations to the particularities of men and women known otherwise only as statistics. The questions that beg for answers then have to do with ordinary members, their families, and their relationships.

This chapter addresses these questions in an attempt to suggest some ways of thinking about congregations as moral communities—as places in which people practiced their faith and formed understandings of what it meant to be good family members and neighbors. Starting from the observation that people did found congregations and gathered all too often to bury their dead and share their grief, what can we learn from considering the role that congregations played in their lives? Is it possible to piece together from the sparse evidence that remains insights about congregations' relationships to families and communities in that era that may have value for us living more than a century later?

My argument is that congregations did function as supportive communities but that the way to understand this role is only in part through considerations of what was distinctly religious about them. Although religion offered hope of eternal life and thus the solace of believing that departed loved ones were in heaven, it was also necessary for the bereaved to live out the rest of their days on earth and deal with the practicalities of earning a living when a breadwinner had perished and parenting children when a parent had died. Congregations were moral communities in this tangible sense. They helped. But it is also important not to leave it at that. Congregations differed from one another, and these differences hold the key to seeing in closer detail how they functioned.

One of the most important differences among congregations was the extent to which they were held together by familial relationships. In what follows I suggest that familial relationships not only varied but also held important implications for the ways in which nineteenth-century congregations functioned as moral communities. I want to consider particularly how congregations contributed to a common culture and experience that spanned family relationships, how congregations functioned in relation to the competing pressures of settling down and moving on, and what the implications were of differing patterns of growth, risk, and trust. For nineteenth-century congregations, these variations emerged with particular salience in relationship to pressures for assimilation and in the differences between churches founded as colonies and churches originating in pastoral circuits.

These considerations also point to several implications for understanding churches and voluntary organizations as moral communities in the twenty-first century. Today, just as in the nineteenth century, congregations are part of an ethnically diverse landscape in which identities are constantly being negotiated. Identities are no less social than they ever were even though the nature of social relationships has changed. Examining the social and symbolic sources of identity has implications for thinking about the constraints governing shared activities, the role of strictness in defining and policing symbolic moral boundaries, and what may be necessary for diverse social networks to heighten tolerance of diversity.

In saying that congregations can be viewed as moral communities, I mean to suggest that they did so in several obvious ways. They were communities because they were composed of members who understood themselves to be members and who in practice met for worship and interacted with one another on a regular basis. They were moral in the conventional sense of that term because they taught people by word and example how they should and should not behave, whether in admonitions about loving their neighbor or in strictures regarding covetousness and greed. Congregations were also moral communities in the less obvious ways that social theorists have argued were basic to the orderly conduct of social life. In the same way that distinctions separating hucksters and lunatics from ordinary people did, congregations drew lines between "us" and "them." The lines congregations drew were of course different from those defining lunatics, criminals, tramps, and other undesirables. The lines varied in degree and in connotation, though, sometimes labeling outsiders as infidels and sometimes regarding them only as neighbors who happened to gather at a different place of worship. In either case, the lines could be viewed as moral boundaries that identified who belonged, who did not belong, and how the one should relate to the other.

Moral Communities and Social Boundaries

Before turning to the Kohmans and Kruses and their congregations, we need to consider more systematically than I have done thus far what exactly we mean by moral communities and the vectors along which comparisons can be made. Discussions of ethnicity and assimilation are helpful in this regard. The activities and beliefs that give an ethnic enclave—or a congregation—a strong identity as a cohesive unit consist importantly of categories or lines or distinctions—call them *social boundaries*—that differentiate the group's members from nonmembers and promote a sense of loyalty to the group.

Social boundaries are in the first instance the mental lines we draw to make sense of the raw, complicated realities of our everyday lives. We sort the living into plants and animals, distances into near and far, and elevations into low and high. The distinctions in turn become metaphors for other aspects of our experience: criminals and degenerates rank low in our esteem, while the rich and famous rank high. In addition the mental maps become the basis for distinctions in actual behavior. The out-group is not only "far" or "low" conceptually but also distant in how we talk about it and how frequently we interact with it.

Social boundaries play an important role in ethnic identities. An ethnic community with strong social boundaries includes members who interact with one another socially, conduct business with co-ethnics, marry co-ethnics, and take pride in the rituals and traditions that define them. An ethnic community's social boundaries may also be reinforced by how others treat it. Ethnic identities are maintained by exclusion and discrimination as well as by in-group loyalties.[9]

Social boundaries are useful for thinking about religion's relationship to ethnicity as well. Congregations' identities depend in part on social boundaries that distinguish them from other congregations. The distinction can be based on theological arguments specifying who should be considered a true believer and who should not. It can reflect traditions in styles of worship, styles of preaching, and styles of conducting sacred rites. Ethnic and religious distinctions overlap when congregations' traditions reflect the practices, language, and kin relationships of an ethnic group. Ethnic and religious distinctions can also pull in different directions. For example, the ethnic tradition suggests maintaining the language of a group's national origin, but the congregation wants to attract new members by shifting to a new language. This is why assimilation involving ethnicity and religion frequently takes place in different ways. One may resist assimilation while the other accommodates it.[10]

Social boundaries are commonly assumed to be most interesting and most consequential when they involve symbolic distinctions *and* social interaction. People can say, well, sure, it is possible to distinguish men from women, but it matters more if that distinction leads to women being discriminated against or is reinforced by organizations that cater only to men. Similarly it matters more if Protestants and Catholics fight each other, exclude each other from voting, and refuse to marry or conduct business with each other than if they merely check different boxes when asked to indicate their religious preference. A case can also be made that social boundaries are more important if they involve symbolic as well as social distinctions. An example would be race relations that involve not only residential segregation but also accusations that the minority group is inferior or evil.

The criterion for what counts as important in these examples is inequality. Social boundaries in these instances matter because the distinctions reinforce inequality between entire segments of the population based on gender, race, or ethnicity. But social boundaries can also be viewed from a different angle. If we ask how an ethnic group maintains constructive loyalty among co-ethnics, then its social boundaries provide a way of answering that question. Its distinctive identity is facilitated by in-group social interaction and by symbolic categories that distinguish it from other groups. Viewed this way social boundaries are important because they provide a way to understand the social cohesion undergirding the moral commitments that bind members of a community together.

Moral commitments refer to the obligations that members of a group feel toward one another and to the group as a whole. People who are part of a moral community interact with one another sufficiently to share a common identity and to value that identity. A social distinction exists between the people who share the same identity and those who do not. There is also a symbolic distinction undergirding a greater sense of loyalty to the in-group than toward outsiders. The cohesion that reinforces this sense of mutual obligation is likely to be greater if it is reinforced by both kinds of distinction: by social and symbolic distinctions. Tightly knit extended families, small towns, ethnic enclaves, and congregations would be examples.

A focus on assimilation, though, necessitates considering instances in which social and symbolic distinctions vary in strength and in relative importance to one another. An immigrant group that is isolated from other groups and composed of members who routinely interact with other members may experience few occasions in which the need to set themselves apart with symbols and rituals is important. The group's cohesion in those situations maintains itself. But put the group in a more diverse context where its social boundaries are porous and interaction occurs more often with outsiders—in that context symbols and rituals that intentionally or inadvertently help the group maintain its identity will probably play a more important role.

Cohesion based on strong social boundaries is arguably difficult to sustain. Families shrink in size and live farther apart from one another. Ethnic groups that for a while benefit from networking with co-ethnics find it necessary over time to branch out and work, live, and interact with people from diverse backgrounds. As much as the very plausibility of their beliefs may depend on interacting exclusively with fellow believers, religious groups confront diversity as well.

Symbolic bases of cohesion might then be expected to diminish in proportion to the weakening of social ties. But there are reasons to think otherwise.

For one thing interaction involving insiders and outsiders elevates the visibility of whatever symbolic distinctions are present. For another, a group that feels weakened, less cohesive, and threatened may increase its efforts to tell its stories, commemorate its traditions, and affirm its identity. Its relationships with outsiders may also become the basis for conflict that inadvertently shores up its identity. The process in these respects is counterintuitive. The symbolism of group identity becomes stronger just as the social bases of the group's identity weaken.

The two Kansas congregations, I suggest, provide an instructive comparison for considering the differences and similarities between cohesion based on social distinctions and cohesion based on symbolic distinctions. The congregations shared similar beliefs and practices, functioned as cohesive moral communities for their members, attracted new members, lost members, and experienced pressures to assimilate and yet maintained their identities in different ways that shed light on the larger processes through which immigrant groups assimilated and responded to diversity.

Understanding these processes requires being clear about what we mean by cohesion and how it may be facilitated or weakened. The term *social cohesion* can be used to indicate the ways that social arrangements hold a community together. The term *symbolic cohesion* can indicate how a community is held together through various beliefs and ideas. Considering each suggests that both can be facilitated in multiple ways.

Social cohesion consists of strong in-group ties, relative to weaker out-group ties, and typically including social interaction that reinforces a sense of interdependence and feelings of solidarity within the group.[11] Holding other things constant, it can be facilitated by the following:

> *Geographic concentration* may occur by choice, through inadvertent circumstances, or be imposed. Examples include ethnic enclaves in which people of the same ethnic background compose the majority population of a neighborhood, town, or community. Other examples include housing developments, college towns, and company towns. Prisons, insane asylums, concentration camps, military installations, and communities based on racial segregation illustrate concentration resulting from coercion.[12]
>
> *Geographic proximity* generally varies in proportion to geographic concentration but can be present when geographic concentration is low. An organization composed of a hundred members scattered among fifty parts of a city, for example, could include a pair of neighbors in each location. Proximity has been one of the important sources of cohesion in ethnic communities. Its role has also been noted in studies of apartment complexes, dormitories, farmsteads, and high-rise office buildings.[13]

Prior experience. A person meeting someone for the first time is arguably more likely to feel a bond—some sense of cohesion—upon learning that the other person grew up in the same city, went to the same college, worked for the same previous employer, or had a mutual acquaintance. Ethnic identity stems to an important degree from having grown up in the same country, having had similar experiences there, and perhaps knowing some of the same people.

Kinship provides a sense of shared identity based on inherited traits and dispositions. It includes shared stories and experiences as well as shared responsibilities and opportunities, such as caring for aging parents and divvying up family heirlooms. Kinship ties vary in frequency of association, warmth, and shared interests and are shaped by fertility rates.[14]

Marriage-based relationships. Endogamous choices reflect in-group identity and reinforce it while exogamy weakens it. Opportunities for endogamy depend in turn on the availability of suitable marriage partners.[15]

Shared economic interests include working in the same occupation, depending on supplies from the same source, and shopping at the same store. Emile Durkheim's well-known distinction between mechanical and organic solidarity differentiated economic relationships based on similarity from those based on difference and interdependence. In local settings it is rare for one to exist without the other.

Institutional concentration is the extent to which a group exercises authority over businesses, schools, and government offices. Concentration raises the chances of interacting to conduct business, having access to organizations, and feeling that organizations represent the group's interests. Ethnic-owned businesses and ethnic political representation can be important sources of cohesion.

Trust is reinforced by shared pasts, economic interests, and proximity and can serve additionally as an underlying orientation that facilitates cohesion. Trust may be particularly important in high-risk situations, such as among combat soldiers or in undertaking risky business ventures. Trust encourages participants to throw in their lot with other participants on whom they depend and with whom they identify.

Enforceable norms are expectations that encourage people to behave in the same way and conform to the same rules. Examples include compulsory school attendance, paying taxes and union dues, showing up at community meetings, and keeping one's lawn mown. The mechanisms of enforcement range from legal sanctions to peer pressure.[16]

Social arrangements that facilitate social cohesion vary from context to context and are influenced by the exogenous relationships present in those contexts. At one extreme, a group isolated physically and socially from other groups is likely to be cohesive because there are no alternatives. At the other extreme, a group in an environment with many competing attractions may experience those attractions pulling the group's cohesion apart. Groups are rarely isolated from other groups and thus must work to prevent loyalties from being dispersed but at the same time allow for members to interact with outsiders.

In addition to the social arrangements that facilitate it, symbols, idioms, beliefs, and narratives about a group's identity also function as important sources of cohesion. Symbolic cohesion consists of an imagined entity such as a nation, an ethnic group, or a community with which people feel an affinity and toward which they owe a sense of loyalty. It typically includes:

Emblems of commonality, such as mascots, flags, national anthems, town halls, capitols, temples, monuments, amulets, and photos, which are physical artifacts that have special meaning as tangible reminders of shared identity.

A shared language, including language itself but also idioms, colloquialisms, accents, registers, and the inflections in which language is spoken. Language is critically important in ethnic groups' identity and how they assimilate.

Collective rituals that consist of people coming together on special occasions to participate in activities symbolizing the collectivity as a whole or in which people participate vicariously as spectators. Collective rituals are a form of symbolic cohesion insofar as they focus attention on shared activities and in many instances promote heightened states of emotion.

Myths of origin that tell a version of the history of a collectivity, highlighting formative moments, heroics, and powerful persons. Such narratives make sense of why the collectivity exists and who can rightfully be considered its members.

Symbolic distinctions that focus specifically on the distinction between insiders and outsiders. "Us" and "them" classifications are often based on popular understandings of race, ethnicity, social class, age, gender, sexual orientation, and religion. Political divisions, elections, and definitions of citizenship sometimes reinforce symbolic distinctions.[17]

Symbolic cohesion is mental, consisting of stories and classifications, but it is also produced and reinforced in the behavior of groups and individuals. Conflicts that generate discussions of the stories and classifications are critically important. Conflict in turn characteristically involves the deployment of power, whether through the mobilization of grassroots activities or through the work of public officials. Ethnic identities and religious distinctions frequently take on meanings in the context of political activity.

Having in mind the social and symbolic ways in which groups such as ethnic enclaves and congregations hold together as moral communities with clear identities makes it possible to examine the similarities and differences between the two congregations to which we now turn.

Two Congregations

William Least Heat-Moon's 1991 bestseller *PrairyErth* brilliantly described the quiet landscape, rustic folkways, and grassroots history of a small town in the Kansas Flint Hills called Cottonwood Falls.[18] If one were to embark from Cottonwood Falls driving half an hour or so west past large expanses of grassland through the Mennonite communities of Hillsboro and Marion and then north a half hour toward a miniscule spot called Elmo, the drive would cross Turkey Creek near the farm where Henry and Mary Kohman lived in the 1870s.

A modest one-story house has replaced the large two-story farmhouse they built as their family expanded, but the view of tall prairie grass flanked by trees along the creek is the same. The land they donated for the church in 1880 is a half-mile down the road. The congregation that met there for nearly a century and a half has diminished and dispersed. It held its last meeting in 2002. The large frame building with soaring bell tower and stained-glass windows that the people built in 1907 to replace the earlier one has been razed. The cemetery is all that remains. More than three hundred people were laid to rest here over the years.

A visitor today would have the best chance of finding the cemetery by exiting Interstate 70 at Abilene, driving nineteen miles south on Kansas Highway 15 and then three miles east, if dry weather permitted, on County Road 400. The neatly mown cemetery lies north of the road on a ridge overlooking the creek to the west and rich parcels of wheat, corn, and pasture in fertile terrain to the south. The closest town is a nearly shuttered village of fewer than four hundred people two miles north and four miles east called Hope. Like many such towns with similar histories, the entrepreneurs who founded Hope in the 1870s expected it to flourish into an important commercial hub—an aspiration that never happened. It was nevertheless the town's good fortune to be where Dwight Eisenhower's father opened a store in 1885. It now attracts the occasional tourist who has visited the Eisenhower museum in Abilene.

The congregation the Kohmans helped start went by different names over the years. In 1866 its founding name was "The Church of believing, baptized Christians of Dickinson County, Kansas." Later on people called it the Baptist Church at Turkey Creek, Turkey Creek Baptist Church, the German Baptist Church, the Dillon Baptist Church, and eventually the First Baptist Church of Dickinson County. Other churches in the vicinity with similar names contributed confusion about exactly which church was being described. For present purposes, the simplest way of referring to it is to call it the Hope congregation.

FIGURE 14. *First German Baptist Church, Dickinson County,*
Kansas, 1908. Personal collection.

The other congregation—the one that Henry and Anna Kruse helped start in 1878—is farther west in central Kansas where the land is noticeably flatter and grows fewer trees. The technical location of the church is Section 16 of Green Garden Township in Ellsworth County. A capacious white-frame church building appropriately fitted with classrooms and a steeple was constructed there in 1893 when the congregation outgrew its 1880 stone building a mile west at the southeast corner of Section 17, which is the site of the congregation's cemetery. A well-constructed brick edifice replaced the frame building in the 1930s and is the largest structure in town except for the towering white cement grain elevator a few blocks away. The town is called Lorraine, named for the daughter of a railroad official, and has a population of approximately a hundred people, which is about half the number it reached in 1940. Founded in 1888 at the intersection of two railroad spurs, it took the place of two earlier attempts to start towns in the immediate vicinity.[19]

The cemetery west of Lorraine is well populated with more than seven hundred graves. Like the surrounding fields, it is nearly treeless, exposing weathered gravestones to the strong Kansas winds that blow in all seasons. A visitor looking for the cemetery would exit Interstate 70 north of Ellsworth, angle to the southwest at Ellsworth on Kansas Highway 156 for five miles, and then drive south for six miles. Had that visitor first stopped to

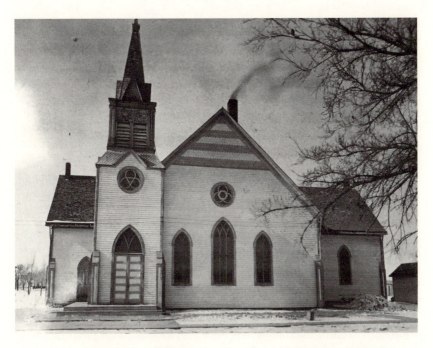

FIGURE 15. *German Baptist Church, Lorraine, Kansas*, 1908. Personal collection.

walk the cemetery near Hope, the shortest route to Lorraine would have been west along Kansas Highway 4, a distance of approximately eighty miles. Like the Hope congregation, this one also went by several names over the years, which means for our purposes referring to it simply as the Lorraine congregation.

Besides having been founded at approximately the same time and in the same state, the two congregations shared other similarities, which is useful for the topics we want to examine. Most of the farmland south of Abilene in Dickinson County was settled in the early 1870s following the arrival of the railroad in 1867 and after range laws were passed in 1872 to prohibit Texas cattle from crossing farmers' land and spreading disease. In 1875 the county's population was 6,841, up from 3,043 in 1870. Banner Township where the Hope congregation was located was home to 523 residents in 1880.

Like Dickinson County, Ellsworth County's settlement depended on the Kansas Pacific Railway, which reached it later the same year and prompted the founding of Ellsworth as the county seat. Like Abilene, Ellsworth became a magnet for cattle drives, saloons, and prostitutes as well as shopkeepers and farmers. The county's settlement lagged Dickinson's by several years, though, which was to be a significant difference in the two congregations' development. Ellsworth County's population in 1875 was 1,758, an increase of only 573 since 1870. The railroad and federal government owned nearly all the county's land, whereas that was true in only the three southwest townships and one southeast township in Dickinson County.

Both counties attracted settlers looking for opportunities to acquire land at rates of 50 to 75 percent cheaper than in eastern states, assuming that land in those states was available at all. Land in Dickinson County in 1875 sold for $7 to $10 an acre and in Ellsworth County for $3 to $3.50 an acre. The southern half of Dickinson County, with trees, creeks, low hills, and rich bottomland, was well suited for corn, wheat, cows, and other farm animals. Much of Ellsworth County, in contrast, was hilly and more suitable for large ranches than for small farms, but the southern third was flat, with rich topsoil ideal for wheat. The largest share of settlers in Dickinson County in 1875 was from Illinois, Indiana, Iowa, Michigan, Missouri, and Ohio. Similarly, the largest share in Ellsworth County was from Illinois, Iowa, Missouri, Ohio, and Wisconsin. Although few in either county came directly from other countries, many were foreign born or had parents who were. Many were ethnically German—so much so in fact that later discussions of immigration in Kansas typically included both communities as centers of German settlement.

The characteristics of German American farm families that historians observed in Wisconsin and Illinois were evident in Kansas as well. German American farmers benefited from having ancestors who farmed in similarly temperate regions in Germany; they had large families, were frugal and hardworking, and liked to acquire land they could pass to their heirs. "The ambition of the German-American father," Marcus Lee Hansen wrote in 1940, "was to see his sons on reaching manhood established with their families on farms clustered about his own." It was not unheard of, Hansen observed, for extended German American families to own much of the land in an entire township. In a study of farm families in Illinois Sonya Salamon noted that German Americans held more strongly to ethnic traditions than neighboring non-German families did, mingling deep loyalties to their families and churches with networking conducive to acquiring land and keeping families intact.[20]

Hans Heinrich Nottorf is considered the founder of the Hope congregation. In 1858 he and his family left Dodge County, Wisconsin, with three wagons, traveling through Missouri where his brother-in-law was seized for several days by proslavery militants, settling along the Kansas-Missouri border, and then, because of the violent skirmishes there between Free Staters and Southern sympathizers, moving to Dickinson County.[21] By 1870 Nottorf had acquired 400 acres of land valued at $5,000 and over the next five years added another 137 acres, which he farmed with the help of two adult sons while also conducting baptisms and preaching. His baptisms of several believers in 1866 came to be regarded as the official founding date of the Hope congregation. But until a building was constructed in 1880, the congregation consisted of families scattered some fifty miles apart to whom Nottorf traveled and preached as often as weather conditions and farming responsibilities permitted. The clusters or "stations," as they were called, were located at upper and lower Turkey Creek in Dickinson County, upper and lower Lyon Creek in Dickinson and Geary County, and Mill Creek in Wabaunsee County.[22]

The Lorraine congregation's origins were quite different. In 1877 a farmer from Illinois named Henry Stassen, who was also engaged in banking, and a preacher named E. C. Janzen visited Kansas with the idea of starting a German Baptist settlement there. A brother who had settled in Kansas sparked Stassen's interest. Janzen's stemmed from pastoring fledgling churches in Wisconsin, Ohio, and Illinois, and having tried unsuccessfully to start a school in Illinois.[23] The best option at the time for securing large tracts of land in central Kansas was to purchase it from the railroad companies. The U.S. government, as an inducement for train transportation to the far West, had given the major railroad companies every odd-numbered section (640 acres) of land ten miles on both sides of the completed tracks. Stassen and Janzen's first effort was with C. B. Schmidt, the Atchison, Topeka, and Santa Fe agent. Schmidt, who was German and had aggressively advertised in Germany and in German-language newspapers in America, contacted church leaders and by 1877 had negotiated agreements with groups from Prussia, Bavaria, Austria, and Bohemia, including Mennonites and Catholics. But Schmidt's negotiations with Stassen and Janzen fell through. On June 9, 1877, Schmidt wrote to land commissioner Colonel A. S. Johnson, "One party of German Baptists, who intended to locate on our lands in Cow Creek near Ellinwood, I lost, because they found that they could purchase K.P. lands, half way between Ellinwood and Ellsworth (on Plum Creek) at about half of our prices, with no apparent difference in the quality of the soil."[24]

"K.P. lands" were owned by the Kansas Pacific railroad company and extended south from Ellsworth to Plum Creek, where the town of Lorraine would be located a few years later. Land in that part of the county struck Stassen and Janzen as ideal for farming. "I shall never forget the impression I received when getting out of the hilly country we for the first time saw the beautiful prairie called Plum Creek Flats," Janzen recalled. "I thought, 'Surely this country is well adapted for a German Baptist colony.'" The soil was rich, the land was flat, there was plenty available, and it could be purchased for $3 an acre cash or $3.60 an acre on payments. The hitch was that the agent in charge of sales was skeptical of the prospective buyers' plans to create an entire settlement so stipulated that ten sections totaling more than six thousand acres had to be purchased to consummate the deal, which would include eighty acres for a church and cemetery at no cost. The agent further stipulated that purchases be contracted within a month's time, in which case additional land would be reserved for future purchases by the colony. Stassen contacted friends and relatives, Janzen posted announcements in the German-language Baptist newsletter *Der Sendbote* (The Messenger), and within a year the first settlers were in residence. By 1880 the Lorraine congregation had done in less than three years what it had taken the Hope congregation nearly a decade and a half to accomplish. It was a thriving congregation with its own house of worship.[25]

Composed as they were of German Baptists the congregations fit the definition of what students of religion call "sects." The congregations held strongly defined beliefs, followed distinctive practices in worship, and, unlike Lutherans, Anglicans, and Catholics that were recognized as state religions in Europe, did not receive government support and were relatively small in total membership. The Baptist movement in Germany dated only from the 1830s and was attributed largely to the efforts of Johann Gerhard Oncken (1800–1884), a fiery preacher who was raised Lutheran, became a Methodist convert while working in England, was baptized by an American missionary in Germany in 1833, and started churches in Hamburg and scattered locations throughout Germany that met in homes and struggled to attract large enough gatherings to construct houses of worship.[26] Over the next decade they persisted in the face of persecution from Lutheran and government authorities and were forced to call on fellow believers in the United States for financial assistance.[27] Following the political upheavals of 1848, which increased the Baptists' freedom to make converts, persecution subsided moderately, and by 1853 the three regional associations in Germany included sixty congregations with a total membership of nine thousand.[28]

German Baptists in the United States were a mixture of immigrants who had become Baptists in Germany and immigrants who converted after they arrived. The first German Baptist church in America was organized in Philadelphia in 1843. As German immigration continued, churches organized in New York, Illinois, Michigan, Minnesota, Wisconsin, and Canada. The members kept in touch with fellow believers in America and Germany through correspondence. They also maintained contact through pastoral visits, including American leaders traveling to Germany and Oncken preaching in Illinois, New York, Vermont, Maine, Massachusetts, and Virginia in 1853 and 1854.[29] In the United States, pastors from established congregations typically gave inaugural sermons at new congregations. When the church in Burlington, Iowa, that Henry and Anna Kruse joined held its inaugural meeting on Sunday, November 7, 1869, for example, pastors from Racine, Wisconsin, and Davenport, Iowa, addressed the audience. The new pastor at Burlington, Reverend John Kohrs, would move on to serve at Hope and give the inaugural sermon at Lorraine.[30]

Like other sects, German Baptist congregations were moral communities that defined themselves in tension with their surroundings through the distinguishing beliefs and practices to which they adhered. They held that eternal salvation could be found only through a positive commitment of a believer's life to Jesus Christ, rejected infant baptism and confirmation, and instead practiced "believer's baptism," which restricted the sacrament to those who had come to an age of accountability and had publicly accepted Jesus Christ as their savior. Meetings sometimes included demonstrable outpourings of emotion; as one participant recalled: "Such weeping and sobs, and crying for mercy, arose, that there was no more any order. The stream was beyond all human control. The whole house was moved." People wrestled with God, fell on their knees, and prayed. He added, "It seemed as if we saw God face to face."[31]

The sect further set itself apart by prohibiting members from marrying unbelievers or adherents of other religions, preached against infidelity and worldliness, and decried the persecution its founders received from religious authorities in Germany. Conversion in these respects was a matter not only of adopting private beliefs but also of severing ties with the established church to which most of one's family and neighbors belonged. Baptisms were outdoor spectacles that included singing and preaching, marking the occasion for all to witness. As a letter describing one such event observed about the woman being baptized, "Her separation from the state church and union with us have produced a great commotion among the ministers and her former friends and will be the means of much discussion."[32]

Doctrinal distinctions that set them apart also reinforced members' loyalty to their congregations. Adherents in America were expected to attend worship services regularly, could be banned from fellowship if they did not or if they played cards or profaned the Sabbath by working, could also be banned if they did not support the congregation financially, and well into the twentieth century had their donations recorded down to the penny in annual reports for all to see.

While setting themselves apart, German Baptists nevertheless adapted in other ways to the social norms of the wider communities in which they lived. They did not wear distinctive clothing, did not prohibit the use of tobacco, sent their children to public schools, held that marriages contracted prior to conversion remained valid, sometimes held services in English as well as in German, and stopped short of embracing pacifism even though they preached against the use of armed violence. Members decamping to other denominations simply disappeared from church rolls, but members in good standing who departed to Baptist churches received letters of transfer whether the transfer was to a German- or English-speaking congregation. Displays of emotion notwithstanding, they considered faith as they practiced it to be reasonable, practical, and devoid of zealotry.

Adhering to distinctive practices and at the same time adapting to prevailing customs resulted in ambiguities that had to be resolved through deliberation and negotiation. Among these was the basic ambiguity of what to be called. Although they gradually became known as German Baptists, they worried that calling themselves Baptists would result in being confused with Anabaptist groups that had been persecuted in Europe during the Reformation and with smaller groups in Germany, such as the "wrangling, mystical, heretical set here calling themselves Baptists" from which Oncken's follow-ers hoped to distinguish themselves.[33] The congregation in Philadelphia that organized in 1843 referred to itself simply as "The Church of the Lord that Meets on Poplar Street." Similarities with other groups, such as Old German Baptist Brethren and German Baptist Dunkards, plus the fact that early Ger-man Baptist congregations rarely had buildings or regular meetings, created further ambiguities.

The German Baptists' unique history put them in the vortex of conflict-ing tendencies with respect to assimilation. On the one hand, they were suf-ficiently small and close knit and held distinct enough beliefs that they could resist assimilation. They were composed almost exclusively of immigrants from Germany and a few German speakers from Switzerland and Russia, and they considered ministering to German immigrants their primary mission. These characteristics augured well for maintaining a German identity. On the other hand, their origin and strength had nearly as much to do with America as Germany. They received support from the American Baptist Home Mission Board, pastors went to the same seminaries as pastors of American Baptist churches, and the much larger American Baptist Convention was in a strong position to start English-speaking churches in locations that would attract German immigrants and the children of German immigrants.

The extent to which one or the other of these competing tendencies pre-vailed was thus shaped by local conditions, of which the most important were how a congregation originated and the relationships among its core constitu-ents. A moral community with a clear identity and strong in-group social rela-tionships could withstand pressures toward assimilation better than a moral community with an unclear identity and weak in-group social relationships. However, as we will see, there is also reason to argue that strong in-group relationships could ease what might otherwise be a more tortuous process toward assimilation.

Information about the two congregations comes from multiple sources, none of which is definitive, but which together make possible a detailed ex-amination of the memberships involved. Names of the congregations' found-ers and brief accounts of what they did are from short histories compiled for each congregation on the occasion of its fiftieth, seventy-fifth, or hundredth anniversary. The Hope congregation's history includes the names of several lay members who served as deacons and on the building committee with Henry Kohman. The Lorraine history lists the names of its twenty-five charter mem-bers. Both histories give the names of pastors and dates during which they served.

Additional information was possible to reconstruct from partial mem-bership rolls, baptismal lists, attendance reports at women's missionary so-ciety meetings, federal and state censuses, land records, cemetery indexes, obituaries, biographies, and personal contacts with local residents. While membership lists would seem to have been particularly useful, complete lists were not available, and the partial lists that were illustrated the weaknesses of such information. Names were abbreviated, misspelled, or illegible; dates of joining were not included; death dates were often inaccurate; and departures were not systematically recorded. Because the congregations practiced adult baptism, children's names were generally not included, although in several instances they were. Information supplied by recent members permitted some of these discrepancies to be identified, and for the Hope congregation information was also available for a few years about tithing and service on committees.

Information from the U.S. decennial censuses for 1850 through 1940 (1890 having been destroyed by fire) and from the Kansas censuses conducted every ten years from 1865 to 1925 provided the best source from which to identify the names, dates, family relationships, and locations of persons who had probably participated in each congregation. In addition, complete lists of persons buried in each congregation's cemetery were available, in many instances providing maiden names as well as married names of women, and in a few cases obituaries had been preserved and brief biographical accounts had been published in books and local newspapers.

Piecing together the information from these various sources made it possible to construct a list of persons for whom there was a high probability of having participated in each congregation based on having lived within a radius of six to eight miles of the church and having been an immediate family member of someone buried in the church cemetery or listed as having been a member on a membership list, obituary, or biographical sketch. Each criterion required considering on a case-by-case basis. Transcriptions of census information had to be checked against the original handwritten entries to correct errors in spelling, dates, and ages. The exact month or year when families arrived or left could rarely be determined but in most cases could be estimated within several years by comparing the federal and state censuses and noting the birthplaces of children. The criterion of six to eight miles criterion was based on information about decisions in the history of each congregation about its location and about competing congregations in each area. Cemetery records had to be checked against census information because people who had not lived in the area for years were sometimes buried in the cemeteries and in other cases buried elsewhere as a result of retiring to another location. For individuals having left the vicinity of each congregation, cemetery indexes also provided information about where they had moved.

In all, information was obtained for 1,154 people for whom there was a high probability of having participated as adults or children in one congregation or the other between its inception in the 1860s or 1870s and 1918, the end point being selected to include World War I and to increase the likelihood of information being available in the relevant sources. Of this number, 445 were associated with the Hope congregation and 709 were associated with the Lorraine congregation. In addition to their names, each person's birth year, death year, gender, family relationship (husband, wife, son, daughter), year of probably having started participating in the congregation, year of probably having ended participating in the congregation, place of residence immediately prior to participating in the congregation, and (if applicable) location having moved to upon leaving the congregation was recorded. With this information it was possible to construct additional information, such as lifespan and age at which participation in the congregation began or ended, as well as comparisons by gender, congregation, and time period.

The statistical profile that emerges from this information indicates that participation in both congregations peaked in 1910, at which time the Hope congregation included 69 adults and 209 children and the Lorraine congregation included 112 adults and 329 children. The total number of adults and children at Hope increased gradually from 19 in 1870 to 61 in 1875, 123 in 1880, and 141 in 1885, while the number at Lorraine jumped from only 2 in 1875 to 168 in 1880 and 301 in 1885. After 1910 the number of adults and children at Hope fell to 258 in 1915 and 220 in 1920 and at Loraine from 415 in 1915 to 370 in 1920. Average (mean) lifespan was 68.4 years at Hope and 67.3 years at Lorraine. Average (mean) number of years participating in the congregation was 34 at Hope and 32 at Lorraine.[34]

How the two congregations managed the task of becoming and behaving as moral communities for their participants was a function of their location, size, pattern of growth, and the attendant demographics of births, deaths, arrivals, and departures. It was equally a function of relationships among families and of occupations and land, none of which could be understood from statistics alone. To understand those dynamics we must return to the particularities of families like the Kohmans and Kruses, Nottorfs and Janzens, and Stassens.

Moral Ambiguities of Death and Bereavement

Mary Kohman died at home in Dickinson County on a Saturday evening in 1893 from complications incurred giving birth to her eleventh child. The baby also died. Anna Kruse's death two years earlier on a farm seven miles west of the church at Lorraine left six children without a mother. A seventh died as an infant before the Kruses moved to Kansas. Both husbands remarried. Lizzie, Henry Kohman's second wife, had four children. Hulda, Henry Kruse's, had eleven.

At thirty-nine and forty-nine, respectively, Mary Kohman and Anna Kruse were by no means the youngest women in their communities to die. One of the first was Caroline Mollhagen. Caroline Henning and William Mollhagen were married the day after Christmas in 1855. Both had been born in Germany and were now living in Wisconsin. Caroline's sister Dorothy was married to Hans Heinrich "Henry" Nottorf, whose forty-acre farm modestly supported the family while he traveled and preached. Two of William's brothers and their wives moved to Michigan, where they started a fishing business at St. Joseph and became founding members of its German Baptist Church. Instead of joining them, William and Caroline moved to Kansas Territory in 1858, where they homesteaded a farm on Lyon Creek and he served as government commissioner of the first district of Dickinson County, which had been organized a year earlier. Henry and Dorothy Nottorf joined them in 1860, and together the couples formed the nucleus of what would become the Hope congregation.

William and Caroline's first son was born in Wisconsin, a second was born shortly after they moved to Kansas, and Caroline gave birth to a daughter in 1862. With rail service still in the future, securing supplies required trips of more than 150 miles by ox team that could take a month. "These trips were not often made, probably once or twice a year," a person who lived in the area recalled, "but when the 'old man' went to market or mill, the whole family had to go, because the country being so sparsely settled, and settlers being so far apart, and Indians so plenty, it was not deemed safe to leave the family behind."[35] In 1864, though, William was away from the family on business when word spread of an imminent Indian attack. Caroline fled into the woods with the children. She died from exposure a few days later. She was twenty-nine. Later settlers said a baby might also have died.

Histories of frontier America rarely fail to emphasize the prevalence of dying young. Immigrants contracted contagious diseases, suffered from malnutrition, and died during or shortly after the six- to eight-week trips coming to America by ship. Early settlers like the Mollhagens and Nottorfs lived in crudely constructed log or sod cabins that poorly shielded them from the harsh plains weather. The great grasshopper invasion that spread across the central plains in 1874 left recently arrived families destitute. Doctors, pharmacists, and midwives were in short supply. Dentists were so scarce that Nottorf was said to have added fixing teeth to his repertoire. Streams and shallow wells frequently became contaminated with typhoid, causing tragedies like the death of a young man at Hope just days after his wedding, and men, like the twenty-six-year-old preacher's son at Lorraine whose shirt got caught in a machine, were killed in farm accidents. Women and babies were especially vulnerable. For the nation as a whole, statistical estimates based on demographic information suggest that 18 to 21 percent of babies born from 1860 to 1880, 15 to 17 percent born from 1880 to 1900, and 10 to 13 percent born from 1900 to 1920 died before their first birthday. Estimates of average life expectancy for persons born in those decades ranged from only forty to fifty years.[36]

By that standard, the Hope and Lorraine communities fared considerably better. Average lifespans of sixty-seven or sixty-eight years were markedly longer than the national average, and rates of infant and child mortality were lower. Of 628 people associated with the two congregations who were born between 1880 and 1918, only 38, or 5.7 percent, died as infants. A total of 75, or 11.3 percent, died before their eighteenth birthday, and a total of 140, or 21 percent, died in their forties or younger. As was true elsewhere, mortality rates were higher among women than among men, but only slightly so: 21.9 percent of women died younger than fifty compared with 20 percent of men.

The two communities' relatively low mortality rates reflected characteristics identified in national data. While child mortality rates were higher among German-born than among native-born women, they were lower than among women who remained in Germany. They were lower among American-born women whose mothers were German than among German-born women. In addition, they were lower among women in rural areas than in cities, and they were lower in the northern central states than in other regions. Nutrition was the principal factor in these differences, including child spacing, which in turn reflected duration of breastfeeding. Although Hope and Lorraine women had large families, children were rarely less than two years apart.[37]

But if mortality rates were lower than national averages, death and bereavement were still the stark realities of lived experience, and they were the realities that religion in particular sought to address. When social scientists of the period pondered why religion was a prevalent feature of human societies, it was religion's unique provision in the face of death that offered the most persuasive answer. Surely it was reason enough to be devout when life was so often cut short. Religion's promise was that life continued beyond the grave. It was also evident that religion served a social as well as a psychological role. For the living it provided assurance that the departed were in God's presence. It offered hope of seeing them again in heaven. Gathering for burial services helped to comfort the bereaved. Grief was less painful when it was shared.

The prevalence of dying young and religion's relationship to the fear of death were thus plausible reasons for the abundance of churches in nineteenth-century America. As the population moved west, people needed religion, which meant that immigrants brought their familiar religions with them, built new churches, and flocked to whatever other churches that might be available, perhaps selecting especially the ones that stoked their fears of death with hellfire-and-brimstone revival meetings and those that in turn told clearly how to find assurance of eternal life. Aggressive evangelism, entrepreneurial leadership, and above all a persuasive theology were the keys.

As moral communities, congregations offered not only hope but also support. An interesting example occurred in 1870 when Eliza Brownsworth, a daughter of the Kinderdicks, who had come to Kansas with the Nottorfs, died at the age of twenty-two, leaving two little girls ages one and two. There was no church and no cemetery near their farm at Woodbine; Eliza was buried on her parents' farm. But the Kinderdicks were part of Nottorf's Baptist circuit, and while the girls' father put his life together, Nottorf's half-brother William Stegen, who had come from Germany with Nottorf in 1848 and now lived on an adjacent farm, cared for the girls. Stegen died nine years later but in the meantime became the second husband of a widow with three young children who was also part of the Baptist circuit.

Less obvious perhaps than the support they provided, congregations were also a source of stability. Frontier life was transient. People came and went. The ones who stayed were often the exceptions, the survivors that lasted when drought, prairie fires, failed crops, grief, and simply the belief that new ventures would be more rewarding prompted others to move on. In practical terms religion provided a way of leaving something behind, of creating something public that would last, whether in boards and brick or in the hearts of those who stayed. Among other things it facilitated remembering the dead, serving not only to give believers hope for a life in heaven but also to provide a place for those who died to be remembered.

Caroline Mollhagen died before the Hope congregation started. She was buried in a lonely grave in a field near her home. A year later William married again—the second wife's identity obscuring the first because her name was also Caroline. Seeking to start a new life, William and Caroline II left Kansas in 1866, joined his brothers in Michigan for a few years, lived briefly in Wisconsin and Illinois, and then in 1878 became charter members of the new congregation at Lorraine. Other than his family, few knew that William's first wife had died. The farmer who purchased the land when William left knew only to avoid plowing where someone was buried. It was 1996 before descendants located the grave and erected a marker. Her story was not unusual. It illustrates how congregations increased the chances that the dead would occupy a public space in which to be remembered.[38]

Congregations' role in founding cemeteries and conducting funerals is a reminder that they functioned not only for the individuals who participated but also as moral communities. Cemeteries were tangible symbols of respect, as historian Brian Young has shown in his study of "respectable burial." They were to be tended properly; the gravestones were meant to last; and sacred space in which the graves were placed communicated that the families and their loved ones were respectable people.[39] So with the funerals. They brought people together, rendering their separate lives periodically public and shared. That was particularly important as families experienced death, illnesses, tragedies, and misfortunes. Those were events that had large ramifications beyond the relatively small percentages of children and young adults who actually died. A death like Mary Kohman's had an immediate impact on ten motherless children. Its emotional impact would certainly have extended to her sister Anna and her brother-in-law Otto who lived nearby.

Having a cemetery of its own in which a congregation's families could bury their dead was particularly important to German Baptists. Unlike many of their neighbors whose families populated nondenominational municipal cemeteries, Baptists had learned the value of having their own cemeteries in Germany during the years when they were persecuted. Officials in some areas prohibited them from conducting any public meetings, including funerals, while in other areas Baptists were charged high fees for interments in public cemeteries. "Under these circumstances," a leader observed, "we thought it necessary to purchase land for a churchyard of our own and here our departed brethren and sisters will from henceforth rest."[40]

While it was comforting to gather collectively with fellow congregants to bury the dead, the extent to which families were affected by death and bereavement was always uneven. Despite the fact that death was certain, it befell some families sooner than others, leaving children without mothers or fathers and causing hardship while cousins and neighbors benefited from longer lives. Caroline Mollhagen died when she was twenty-nine, but her sister Dorothy lived until she was fifty-two. Mary Kohman was thirty-nine when she died, but sister Anna lived until she was eighty-four.

Death struck not only sooner for some than others but also more often. The Seidel sisters—also members at Hope—were a vivid example. Dolly Seidel came to America from Germany with their parents and seven siblings in 1852 when she was six. Her father, a skilled hostler in Germany, took up farming near Columbus, Ohio, where the family lived for seven years before moving to Whiteside County in Illinois. The Seidels were Lutheran, but in 1865 nineteen-year-old Dolly married Carl Schrader, a German Baptist widower twenty years her senior with four children. Dolly and Carl moved to Dickinson County and became part of the Hope congregation in 1877, raising two of the children from Carl's first marriage and six of their own. In 1889 at age forty-three Dolly died. One of the daughters from the first marriage died the same year. She was twenty-six. Her half-sister died of complications from childbirth five years later. She was twenty-seven. Dolly's sister Mary's experience was sharply different. Born in Columbus in 1854, Mary followed her sister to Kansas, marrying Harvey Abelson in 1879 and becoming part of the Hope congregation the same year. Mary had ten children. She lived forty-five more years after her sister died.

Neither community fell victim to the contagious diseases that killed entire families and sometimes wiped out entire cohorts of infants and children. The congregations were sufficiently isolated that even the influenza epidemic of 1918 passed them by with only one exception. But infrequent as it was in statistical terms, more than half the family groups were affected by someone dying young. Of seventy-five extended families with children living at one or the other community during the community's first half-century, forty-three lost at least one child or infant and twenty lost more than one. And yet thirty-two families were not affected, while at the other extreme four or more children died in four families, and in one family ten children died.[41]

Besides the unevenness in these comparisons, the fact that deaths of spouses frequently resulted in second marriages raised the chances of inequities and possibilities for strained relationships between stepchildren and stepparents and among half siblings. The family of Lizzie Kohman, Henry Kohman's second wife, for example, lived on an adjacent farm and was German but was not German Baptist, which meant cross-denominational relationships for the second family that had not been present for the first family. In contrast, the family of Hulda Kruse, Henry Kruse's second wife, did not live near Lorraine but was German Baptist with ties to congregations in Iowa, Nebraska, and Hope, including Hulda's sister Bertha. Only three of the fourteen Kohman children married German Baptists, compared to ten of the fifteen Kruse children who lived to maturity.

Differences resulting from deaths and second marriages sometimes accentuated inequality in economic status as well. Henry Kohman's marriage to the daughter of a wealthy neighbor, for example, appears to have facilitated several of the children's careers, including one that became a prominent scientist, another that became a research chemist, and a third that founded a conservatory in Chicago. Henry Kruse's marriage to the daughter of a farmer with sparse holdings did not have the same effect, but as Henry aged his own holdings increased to the benefit of the second family more than to the first.

While it is reasonable to argue that a supportive congregation shared the grief when one of its families was bereaved, it is also reasonable to imagine that families felt relief when they were spared and questioned why when they were not. Indeed, it was the observable reality of people they knew being unequally affected by death and misfortune that prompted the biblical cry, "Why do the righteous perish?"

The theological answer that religion provided dealt with the inscrutable justice and mercy of God. The biblical response, though, came in narrative form that provided examples of people struggling with invidious differences. If Dorothy Nottorf blamed William Mollhagen for her sister's death, if Carl Schrader envied Harvey Abelson, and if the Kruse offspring's relations with their half-siblings were strained, there were the stories of Cain and Abel, Rachel and Leah, and Jacob and Esau to ponder.

Strained relationships suggest the importance of cross-cutting ties as well. Instead of thinking of congregations as aggregates of individuals, it helps to view them as shared identity-conferring relationships layered on top of other relationships based on kinship, proximity, ethnicity, and economic conditions. The families at Hope and Lorraine were all of these: Kohmans and Kruses and Janssens and Abelsons and Schraders, neighbors living within a few miles of one another, Germans by national origin and language, and for the most part farmers. Some of these identities divided them and some united them. Death and bereavement had the same effects, creating unity among some who were similarly affected and dividing them from those who were not. Religion's role was to add another important layer to those identities and social relationships.

The regular coming together that the two congregations obliged of their members meant that when they gathered, they were still divided but also united. The family that had lost a loved one was no less bereaved compared to the one that had not, but for the moment they shared an identity as German Baptists, reading the same Bible, singing the same hymns, and worshipping the same God.

The stark realities of death and bereavement, happening as they did so unequally among families that otherwise shared so much, meant that congregations were at their best when they could exert a unifying force. They were moral communities that did not come close to equalizing the differences among their participants. They were moral communities nevertheless in reinforcing both in belief and in practice an identity that superseded the differences.

Sources of Cohesion

The ambiguities associated with death and bereavement illustrate the role that supportive congregations could play but also the potential tensions that could weaken them. Besides death affecting families unequally, congregations dealt with strains from some families faring better than others financially, from conflicts between old-timers and newcomers, and from people coming and going.

The geographic dynamics of frontier congregations were always important. William Mollhagen's departure from Kansas en route to Michigan, Illinois, and Wisconsin, for instance, was a serious setback for his brother-in-law's efforts to start a congregation in Dickinson County. His return to Kansas in 1878 represented a small benefit to establishing the congregation at Lorraine.

America in the nineteenth century was a nation in flux. Millions of immigrants arrived, and millions of Americans who were already here moved west. The years immediately following the Civil War were particularly a time of migration-driven population growth for the Middle West and West. The railroads advertised in eastern newspapers and sent agents to Europe to persuade buyers to leave their homes in hope of turning the nation's recently "pacified" grasslands into productive farms. Entrepreneurs bought land they hoped would become towns. Kansas's population of 107,000 in 1860 tripled in the 1860s and nearly tripled again in the 1870s.

The impetus driving this massive migration was the desire to settle down, build homes, put up fences, grow crops, and, for townspeople, set up shops, open stores, build houses, plant gardens, attract railroads, and prosper as their towns grew. The end-goal for settlers was to settle—an impetus seemingly rooted in an innate propensity to be in a particular place and enjoy the security of occupying a familiar space. This was the propensity against which the unsettledness of rogues, bandits, and hucksters seemed shifty.

But the same freedom—the same restless quest for individual expression and opportunities to travel and acquire land—that beckoned settlers to settle also facilitated movement. People who moved once frequently picked up and moved again. Those who failed whatever they were doing at one location could imagine themselves doing better somewhere over the next horizon. Feeling cramped or crowded or hedged in and restless, they could relocate.

Relocating not once but two or three times typified the settlers at Hope and Lorraine. Although nearly all the 208 settlers born prior to 1860 were born in Germany, only 36—17 percent—came to Hope or Lorraine directly from Germany. The pattern illustrated by the Nottorfs and Komans coming from Wisconsin and the Kruses coming from Illinois via Iowa was typical. Families moved, settled temporarily, and then moved again.

The story of Americans establishing churches has mostly been understood in terms of settling. Church buildings rising across the land were a sign that people had come to stay. They wanted a fixed location in which to raise their children, praise God, and remember their dead. But that was not the whole story.

Churches may have connoted settling down, but much about them was unsettled, temporary, portable, and even ephemeral. Inexpensive frame buildings burned down, blew away, fell apart, and had to be replaced. Priests and pastors moved on. Charter members left, died, and raised children who moved on. It was one thing for churches to commemorate tradition, symbolically re-enacting it, keeping the old ways intact. But churches also had to stand pat without standing too much in the way of people moving.

The extent to which Hope and Lorraine had to deal with moving on is evident in the difference between average lifespan and average duration of involvement with the church: people who lived sixty-seven or sixty-eight years on average were involved with the church for only thirty-two or thirty-three years on average. The difference was not because they arrived in midlife and stayed until they died. Approximately half of those who were involved at some point in their lives left and went to live somewhere else. That was the attrition the congregations experienced *despite* being in rural communities and holding strong beliefs that encouraged members to stay.

Attrition of that magnitude required congregations to cope with it if they were to remain viable. The standard account that imagines congregations simply keeping members for a lifetime and growing by attracting newcomers gets it wrong. The principal fact was transience, not stability, and the principal dynamic was not outreach but reproduction. Reproduction was the reason that congregations held their own or grew. It was also the reason people left. Large numbers of children benefited farm families by providing hands to help with chores and by increasing the chances that one or more of the children would take over the farm and take care of aging parents. But land was scarce, and farm families anticipated that many of their children would need to depend on education rather than inherited land and would need to relocate to find jobs.

Whatever else they may have been, the Hope and Lorraine congregations were baby mills. Children outnumbered adults by a ratio of three to one. To be sure, the congregations included men and women who remained unmarried or were married but childless. But on average the number of children born to women who had any children was four. And, as was true nationwide, the numbers were higher earlier in the period than later. Among Hope and Lorraine women who had any children, women born in the 1840s and thus becoming mothers in the 1860s and 1870s had 7.5 children on average, and that number declined to 7.1 among women born in the 1850s, to 5.8 among women born in the 1860s, to 3.9 among women born in the 1870s, and to 3.2 among women born in the 1880s.

Congregations with birth rates like this could hold their own or grow as long as they did a decent job of retaining members' children. But large numbers of children also set congregations up to decline unless economic conditions were just right. In farming communities like Hope and Lorraine, a few children could stay in the area and continue to farm, but many could not. The ones who did farm lived in neighboring counties closer to different churches, while others took jobs in surrounding towns that provided opportunities to attend different churches, and a few moved to western Kansas, Oklahoma, Oregon, and California—sometimes in sufficient numbers to form the nucleus of a new Baptist congregation.

The broader implication is that congregations with high birth rates and close-knit intermarried families had a good chance of growing, but congregations functioned best when they could also make newcomers feel welcome. The value of strong in-group ties and yet an ability to absorb outsiders was evident at both congregations. The sources of cohesion I discussed earlier, though, differed in the two congregations.

While both enjoyed numeric success and functioned well as supportive moral communities, social cohesion was stronger at Lorraine than at Hope, and Hope perhaps inadvertently relied more on symbolic cohesion than Lorraine. The difference was one of degree only. Social cohesion was by no means absent at Hope or symbolic cohesion lacking at Lorraine. But the difference was important enough that it affected how the congregations adapted to and resisted assimilation.

The principal difference stemmed from the fact that Hope began as a circuit and Lorraine began as a colony. Colonies were settlements founded by groups of individuals who collectively and in coordinated ways planned to migrate to a particular geographic location and take up residence in relatively close proximity to one another. In many instances, clergy and lay members supplied the leadership involved in initiating a colony, and the resulting colonies became identified with a specific congregation or denomination. Circuits, in contrast, were loose, sometimes sporadic, geographically dispersed relationships through which one or more leaders attempted to found congregations. Both were practiced widely as ways of starting congregations on the expanding frontier.

Colonies of historical interest were often characterized by distinct religious beliefs and by living communally or practicing modes of work, dress, or worship that set them apart. Notable examples were the Oneida Community founded in upstate New York in 1848 by John Humphrey Noyes, the New Harmony colony founded by Robert Owen in Indiana in 1825, and the Mormon settlers who colonized Utah under Brigham Young's leadership in 1846. Kansas's colonies included the abolitionist Beecher Bible and Rifle Colony founded in Wabaunsee County in 1855, the Berea Colony founded by Associate Reformed Presbyterians from Pennsylvania in Franklin County in 1855, the Gnadenau [Meadow of Grace] Colony founded by Jacob Wiebe in Marion County in 1874, and numerous Mennonite, Swedish Lutheran, Dunkard, and Russian Catholic settlements throughout the state—many of which had been recruited by Santa Fe agent C. B. Schmidt. In Dickinson County, the settlers who gradually succeeded in forming the church at Hope were in close proximity to groups that had migrated to the area as colonists. Immigrants from Michigan and Illinois founded small colonies of forty to sixty settlers each in 1871 and 1872; Presbyterians from Tennessee came as a colony about the same time and settled within a few miles of the German Baptists; and River Brethren from Pennsylvania founded one of the largest colonies in 1879, bringing some 300 people and fifteen train carloads of freight estimated at $500,000.[42]

Circuits contrasted with colonies in being relatively low-key networks forged by professional and lay preachers who traveled from place to place, identified families that might have shared similar religious backgrounds or interests, and held worship services in their homes or outdoors on their farms. When clergy were scarce and when populations were too sparse and widely dispersed to start congregations by other means, circuits provided an economical alternative. Denominational offices coordinated the efforts to ensure nonduplicative coverage and paid pastors small fees, while the recipient families provided food and lodging. Methodists were particularly known for circuit riders founding churches but Baptists, Disciples of Christ, Roman Catholics, and Presbyterians also supported clergy charged with ministering to scattered families.

When Kansas became a territory in 1854, circuits quickly became the means through which itinerant preachers held worship services and started churches. Baptists, Catholics, and Methodists had established Indian missions in the 1830s, which along with fledgling towns like Atchison, Lawrence, and Leavenworth became hubs for pastoral circuits. One of the first circuits that included settlers in Dickinson County started in 1854 when Methodists sent Reverend James Sayre Griffing from New York to minister to a circuit that took in settlements around Fort Riley and Manhattan.[43] "The immigrant . . . no matter whence he comes, has hardly erected his cottage," a Methodist writer observed at the time, "when the itinerant knocks at his door to 'reprove him of sin, of righteousness, and of judgment' and under his faithful ministry, long before a house has been erected, or a public altar consecrated to the worship of the Most High, the praises of redeeming grace are ascending."[44]

Colonies had particular strengths and weaknesses, as did circuits, which meant that the two complemented each other and both contributed to the spread of new churches as the nation's population moved west. Colonies ensured that a sufficient number of people would relocate together that a full-time pastor could be supported and a church building constructed. Colonies also ensured that like-minded people would be neighbors and provide assistance to one another as might be needed. But colonies were high-risk ventures. Many failed because of adverse weather conditions, poor crops, inadequate planning, and internal dissension. Circuits were low-risk ventures in comparison. By connecting small numbers of families in scattered locations, they could maximize the chances of being able to form a congregation in at least one of those locations. If the entire venture failed, the pastor or pastors involved could simply move on.

Nottorf's efforts in Dickinson County began as what could almost have been a colony but quickly became a circuit. The trip to Kansas from Wisconsin included not only the Nottorfs and their children but also Nottorf's half-brother William Stegen and two other large German Baptist families—the Kinderdicks and Rubins. Land was still sufficiently available that the families could have settled in close proximity. A few years later when the 1865 state census was taken, there were only fifty-four farm families in the entire county, so the problem for Nottorf and company was not finding available land; it was rather finding land they considered desirable along the creeks.

The Smoky Hill River bisected the county from west to east, leaving approximately two-thirds of the county south of the river with attractive bottomland along the several branches of Turkey Creek and Lyon Creek and less subject to flooding than north of the river. The bottomland, however, was separated by hills with thin, rocky soil ill-suited for crops. Seeking the best land, the Nottorf party spread out rather than settling in close proximity to one another.[45] Nottorf claimed land seven miles from his brother-in-law William Mollhagen. The Rubins settled about five miles north of the Nottorfs, and the Kinderkicks settled almost twenty-five miles away. Over the next decade as more German Baptist families arrived, the settlements continued to be dispersed across the southern half of Dickinson County, south in Marion County, east in Geary County, and farther east in Wabaunsee County. Geographic concentration in consequence was low.

Stassen and Janzen's efforts in Ellsworth County contrasted sharply with those in Dickinson County. The one similarity, besides their Baptist beliefs, was that Lorraine, like Hope, depended on a circuit preacher for a year until it called a full-time pastor. The intent from the start at Lorraine was to create a settlement on the model of a colony. The railroad agent's insistence that the settlement purchase ten sections of land necessitated a sufficient number of families to make that happen, and the availability of sections in close proximity to one another facilitated geographic concentration. The government's agreement with the railroad was that it would receive grants of half the land on strips ten miles wide on each side of the track for each mile of track, with the government keeping the even-numbered sections and the railroad the odd-numbered sections.[46] That arrangement kept Stassen and Janzen's settlers from buying up parcels from the railroad that were all adjacent, but it did allow the Baptists to settle near one another and essentially to dominate the township. Although the two counties were only eighty miles apart, the land and expectations about farming were also different. The Dickinson settlers were used to smaller farms in Wisconsin best suited for dairy production, while the Ellsworth settlers were used to dry-land farming in Illinois, considered the large flat acreage for sale by the railroad a good investment, and started planting wheat as soon as they arrived. Facing wet conditions, cinch bugs, and grasshoppers, the Dickinson farmers struggled to grow wheat, whereas the Lorraine colonists found their land well suited for wheat.[47] By 1886 the differences were clearly in evidence in agricultural statistics. Dickinson County was home to nearly 10,000 milk cows and produced nearly 600,000 pounds of butter, while Ellsworth County had fewer than 4,000 cows and produced only 200,000 pounds of butter. Dickinson County produced twice as much corn as Ellsworth County, but Ellsworth County produced twice as much wheat.[48]At century's end, the clearest indication of differences in geographic concentration was that families affiliated with the Hope congregation owned 5,707 acres or 24.8 percent of the land in Banner Township where the church was located, whereas families affiliated with the Lorraine congregation owned 14,005 acres or 60.8 percent of the land in Green Garden Township where the church was located. A similar pattern was evident in another measure of geographic concentration: Hope families owned at least some land in twenty of the township's thirty-six sections, while Lorraine families owned land in thirty-four of the township's thirty-six sections. Insofar as large holdings by individual families may have mattered, only three of the Hope families owned 640 acres or more, while six of the Lorraine families did.

The differences in geographic concentration meant that German Baptist families in Green Garden Township were more likely to live near fellow German Baptists than were their counterparts in Banner Township. For German Baptists who did not live in these townships, it was also less likely for the ones near Hope to have German Baptist neighbors than for the ones near Lorraine. In Hope Township to the east of Banner Township, three of the four German Baptist families did not live close to one another, and to the north in Jefferson County, the German Baptist families were also geographically separated. At the same time, what did matter was that another German Baptist family settled near the Kinderdicks, and in Wabaunsee County three large German Baptist families settled near one another. Although the concentration of kindred spirits was dispersed, it at least included enough proximity among small clusters of families to keep the circuit going. In contrast, the Lorraine congregation included three German Baptist families near one another to the west in Valley Township and six in close proximity to the north in Lincoln Township.

I suggested earlier that prior acquaintance—or, lacking that, similarities of prior experience, such as having lived in the same location—is often conducive to social cohesion. The fact that nearly all German Baptists had roots in Germany (the few who did not were from German-speaking sections of Switzerland and Russia) was a significant source of common prior experience, even for ones who came from different parts of Germany. Relatively few of those who settled near Hope and Lorraine came directly from Germany, though. Of 141 people associated with the Hope congregation in 1885, only 13 had come directly from Germany, and of 301 associated with the Lorraine congregation in 1885, only 30 had. By that date many in the two groups had been born locally (56 at Hope and 66 at Lorraine). The remainder (72 at Hope and 205 at Lorraine) had come after having lived at some other location in the United States. At Hope, only the 13 from Dodge County, Wisconsin, would likely have known one another before migrating to Kansas. At Lorraine, 32 came from Will County, Illinois, 17 from Woodford County, Illinois, 17 from McLean County, Illinois, and 10 from Montgomery County, Illinois. On that basis, it would appear that Hope, where only 18 percent were from a common location, benefited less from prior experience than Lorraine, where 37 percent were from locations in which a significant number of fellow members had lived. Viewed differently, though, the differences were not as great. The 13 migrants from Dodge County linked nine different families, while the ones at Lorraine from various locations in Illinois linked thirteen different families.

Where the differences in total numbers and prior locations had the greatest impact was in kinship and marital relationships. Of the 141 people at Hope in 1885, three extended families had ten or more members each, and those three families made up 26 percent of the total. Of the 301 people at Lorraine, eight extended families had ten or more members each, and those families made up 37 percent of the total. Stronger differences were evident when families with 8 or more members were compared: five such families at Hope made up 38 percent of the total, while seventeen such families at Lorraine made up 62 percent of the total. On average, 4.5 persons at Hope shared the same surname in 1885, while 5.9 persons did at Lorraine.

Endogamy is more likely, all else equal, in a large congregation than in a small one because the larger one provides more possibilities for identifying a suitable marriage partner. Both congregations had high rates of endogamy, but in this respect Lorraine had a clear advantage because of its size. Of 102 couples at Hope between the congregation's inception and 1918 for whom the wife's maiden name could be identified, 54 percent represented endogenous marriages; that is, both spouses' families were part of the congregation. Of 147 such couples at Lorraine, 71 percent were endogenous marriages. The same pattern was evident when only couples present in 1885 were considered: 50 percent of 38 couples at Hope were endogamous, compared with 76 percent of 83 couples at Lorraine.

To the extent that marriage linked families together, the potential for cohesion of this kind was significantly greater at Lorraine than at Hope. Of twenty-nine families (by surname) at Hope in 1885, only twelve were related by marriage to at least one other family, and only four were related to two other families. Of forty-six families (by surname) at Lorraine in 1885, thirty-eight were related by marriage to at least one other family, and eighteen were related to two other families. One family was linked to six other families, another to seven other families, and yet another to twelve other families. In all, there were ninety-one pairwise links at Lorraine compared with only sixteen at Hope.

Besides the fact that it was smaller, the Hope congregation's potential for interfamily ties was weakened by the fact that the three largest families had fewer connections than the large families at Lorraine. Two of the large families at Hope had no marital connections with other families, and the third had only two. Marital connections were further weakened by the fact that the Kinderdicks and Rubins, who came with the Nottorfs from Wisconsin, were not involved with the Hope congregation and by early deaths in three of the core families.

Some of the other indicators of social cohesion I discussed earlier were indistinguishable at the two locations, while several were significant. Shared economic interests were similar at Hope and Lorraine: nearly everyone farmed, and most of the ones who farmed owned their own land. But institutional concentration differed. The Hope congregation had the good fortune of the Kohmans' land for its location, but that put it in the country instead of in town. The Lorraine congregation's decision to relocate the church put it in town. By 1885 German Baptists at Lorraine not only farmed but doubled in most of the town's professions: shoemaker, wagon maker, miller, mason, carpenter, tailor, postmistress, schoolteacher, merchant, and minister. In contrast, the Hope congregation's members lacked these positions and instead conducted business with nonmembers three miles north at Dillon, four miles west at Banner City, or six miles east at Hope. Another significant difference was the schools. Both communities had primary country schools and valued education, but Lorraine became one of the first districts in the state to consolidate its schools into a single primary school and a secondary school at Lorraine, while the Hope congregation's access to secondary education in the 1890s was twenty miles away.

How differences in institutional concentration affected daily life was evident in small ways. Although the members of both congregations dealt regularly with nonmembers (traveling to Abilene and Ellsworth to conduct business at county offices, dealing with the railroad to ship cattle, going to town for supplies, and interacting with neighbors), the institutional boundaries at Lorraine were well defined by members of the congregation while the ones at Hope were relatively porous. The grain elevator at Lorraine that played a central role in farmers' lives not only for grain but also for coal, flour, and feed, for example, was owned by August Groth, who sold land in Illinois to move to Lorraine in 1881, and his son Henry, born in 1872. The Groths were related by marriage to the Heitmans, Janssens, Nausseds, Schroeders, Steinbergs, and Willms—all members of the church. The other business central to the community was the farm implement dealership, which also provided blacksmith services, sold wagons and buggies, and supplied households with groceries, dry goods, and hardware. Peter Miller, who moved his family to Lorraine from Wisconsin in 1886, operated the business with fellow church members Paul Peters and Anton Schmidt.[49]

Hope's members dealt almost exclusively with nonmembers for essential goods and services—the Crosbys from Vermont, Hardins from Iowa, Kochs from Pennsylvania, Lowes from West Virginia, Reaughs from Indiana, and so on. The Mosleys from Tennessee ran the nearest grain elevator, and a Lutheran family named Brinkman operated the nearest implement dealership. The German Baptists sometimes combined farming with doing masonry or carpentry work for their neighbors, just as farmers did at Lorraine, but the interaction at Hope was more likely to be with people from different denominations, a notable example of which was the death of Charles Schmidt, a fifty-five-year-old member of the Baptist church, killed by lightning in 1887 while building a Lutheran church.[50]

Trust, as I mentioned, is difficult to assess except in relation to considerations of risk, which means being able to speculate only about the differences that may have been associated with colonies and circuits. The advantage of circuits that perhaps accounted for their popularity as a method of founding churches was that they hedged against risk. If families moved away, the circuit could adapt. If the entire circuit failed, the pastor could move on and an eventual church could be built in another location. For the families involved in a circuit, the risk attached to individual families rather than to a collectivity. The Mollhagens and Nottorfs and Rubins and Kinderdicks sought to minimize their individual risks by selecting the best creek-bottom land despite being geographically dispersed. Colonies, in contrast, are high-risk ventures. Many of them failed because of not being able to attract enough families in the first place or because of crop failures and deaths. A colony of Ohio Methodists a few miles south of Lorraine, for example, disappeared almost as soon as it began because of a murder in the community.

If colonies were indeed high risk, the way to minimize risk was to recruit participants who had reasons in addition to economic incentives to trust one another. Colonies based on religion had the advantage of shared beliefs and rituals; they also had disciplinary mechanisms they could use to ostracize members violating the common trust. Colonies sometimes specified in detail the rules members were to follow. An abolitionist group composed mostly of Congregationalists that met in Lawrence, Kansas, in 1856 to form what it called the Pottawatomie Colony, for example, passed resolutions prohibiting liquor, swearing, desecrating the Lord's Day, and anything considered immoral. "We hereby pledge ourselves to each other," they resolved, "to aid and assist one another in all matters pertaining to social society and endeavor to live in peace with all men whilst engaged in the improvement of our claims when selected."[51]

Recruiting families with reasons to trust one another was clearly the case with the Lorraine colony. Although several of the initial families may have come strictly from reading notices in *Der Sendbote*, nearly all of them had prior connections from kinship, marriage, or having lived in the same place. Besides that, Lorraine's advantage was the selectivity involved in having to fulfill its contract with the railroad agent. Not just any family had the wherewithal to purchase land on short notice. Those that did had mostly established themselves already by owning land in Illinois. An acre of land in Illinois in 1880 covered the cost of three to four acres at Lorraine. Of the forty-four families at Lorraine that owned land in 1885, twenty-six owned more than 160 acres, eleven owned at least 480 acres, and one owned more than a thousand. Members of the colony purchased from the railroad or homesteaded all of eighteen sections and parts of sixteen others, totaling more than 14,000 acres. Land purchased for $3.00 an acre now averaged $13 an acre. It was evident from land transactions that the colony played a collective role in its members' dealings as well. "E. C. Janzen et al." appeared frequently as grantors, grantees, and holders of mortgages.[52]

I mentioned earlier that enforceable norms about participation and conformity frequently contribute to groups' social cohesion. Hope and Lorraine resembled each other in terms of enforceable norms, particularly on the crucial matter of baptism that was the mark not only of being a member but also of being saved. The congregations required late adolescent and adult members to be baptized again even if they had been baptized as infants at other churches. They would have rejected parents' requests to have children baptized unless the children were old enough to make an independent profession of their own faith. Families that might have been tempted to do farmwork other than the routine care of animals on Sundays would have received a visit from the preacher and been talked about by their neighbors. Women who were healthy and not too late in pregnancies achieved almost perfect attendance at women's missionary society meetings. The denomination's leaders could remove preachers that strayed from German Baptist teachings, and preachers could refuse to perform marriages unless the man and woman were believers.

The rule against marrying unbelievers was one of the reasons endogamy was so high in both congregations. Members also went outside the congregation, relying on broader networks among German Baptists, to find a suitable partner. Mary Kohman's sister Anna, for example, became Otto Ihde's wife because Otto wanted to marry a good German Baptist and on Mary's recommendation traveled to Wisconsin to meet Anna. When Anna Kruse died, Henry Kruse went to Burlington, Iowa, where the couple had lived before moving to Kansas, and among the German Baptists there found Hulda Gnuschke to be his second wife.

But enforceable norms are always subject to interpretation, and that was true even of something as important as the rule against marrying unbelievers. The strictest interpretation prohibited German Baptists from marrying anyone other than German Baptists. A less strict interpretation held that marriages with non–German Baptists were permitted as long as the non–German Baptist became a German Baptist. At Hope, perhaps because of smaller and more geographically dispersed numbers of German Baptists, conflict over the prohibition against marrying unbelievers erupted in 1876 and nearly tore the congregation apart. Whether the less strict interpretation became the rule in principle or only in practice, a significant number of subsequent marriages involved a spouse who was not a German Baptist. Henry Kohman choosing a non-Baptist as his second wife was one example. Other marriages included Lutherans, German Reformed members, Presbyterians, and in one instance a Roman Catholic.

Exogenous marriages were but one of the ways in which Hope was more exposed to external relationships than Lorraine. Both congregations had competitors with which to contend for members' loyalties, but the differences were notable. The Lorraine church was the only church in town until the 1890s. At the end of the century a small English-speaking Baptist church began holding services a block away, but the church was short lived, perhaps because the German Baptist church also conducted some of its services in English. A Methodist church on Main Street had more success but was different enough in worship, teachings about baptism, and ethnic composition that it posed less of a threat. North of Lorraine the population was almost entirely composed of Catholic immigrants from Bohemia. West of Lorraine at Holyrood, the German Lutheran Church's members farmed near some of the Lorraine members, but intermarriage was nonexistent, and the German Reformed Church did not begin until the end of the century. Lorraine's only significant competitor was the English-speaking Baptist Church seven miles to the south and east at Frederick, which functioned more as an outlet after the turn of the century for Lorraine offspring farming near Frederick than as a competitor.[53]

The Hope congregation in contrast competed with the two other German Baptist churches that emerged from Nottorf's circuit, three fellowships of German Baptist Brethren, a flourishing German Reformed congregation of German-speaking Swiss immigrants, the River Brethren, a German Lutheran Church, a Christian Church, several country churches, and churches at Dillon, Banner City, and Hope. The area was so religiously diverse that each creek and each section along the same creek could be identified by a different church, as a resident named Frank Klingberg who grew up there in the 1880s recalled: "Upper Turkey Creek had a large and flourishing German Baptist church; middle Turkey Creek had a German Reformed church; upper Lyon Creek had two large German Lutheran churches; lower Lyon Creek a large German Methodist church, to which was added another flourishing German Methodist church in Woodbine, five or six miles away."[54]

Geographically identifiable as they may have been, the congregations near Hope shared a common ethnic heritage and language, did business at the same towns, and sometimes married across denominational lines. They also interacted at weddings and funerals, on holidays, and during community-wide "union services" and revival meetings. The Methodists were especially keen on holding revival meetings, advertising them, and bringing in traveling preachers to attract large audiences. So were the Presbyterians from Tennessee who tried repeatedly to attract new members through "protracted" evangelistic meetings. "It is to be hoped that some of our people," a correspondent wrote about one such event, "will be brought to a realization of the state of their moral depravity ere it is eternally too late."[55]

On the whole, social arrangements were more conducive to cohesion at Lorraine than at Hope. The Lorraine congregation was larger, more geographically concentrated, and more in control of local institutions, and its members were more likely to be linked by kinship and marriage to other members. Hope was smaller, with more geographically dispersed members whose relationships were more likely to include dealings with nonmembers on the farms in their vicinity. While Lorraine benefited from having started as a colony and thus bringing a relatively prosperous group of large families to the area at the same time, Hope's origins as a pastoral circuit brought fewer families with fewer prior connections over a longer period to more scattered locations. Both congregations grew by producing large numbers of children, and the numbers were sufficiently large that many of the offspring left to find work in other areas. But Lorraine's identity on the basis of its large, interconnected families was relatively more secure while Hope's was less secure.

What Hope may have had less of than Lorraine in terms of firmly bounded cohesion-facilitating social arrangements, it nevertheless had in what I have called symbolic sources of cohesion. Symbols and rituals are important features of any church's definition of itself. Both congregations were affiliated with what became known as the North American Baptist Conference, and they retained that affiliation over the decades while ethnic-origin congregations were being absorbed into large, nonethnic national denominations. Both had distinctive church names and buildings, and each had its own

cemetery. Preaching, communion, and baptisms functioned as regular reminders of members' shared identity as German Baptists, and those identities
were reinforced with periodic visits by German Baptist preachers from other
congregations. Both congregations held revival meetings, celebrated major
congregational anniversaries, told stories about the pioneers who founded
the congregation, and produced congregational histories. As more of their
members spoke English at home and as more neighboring churches held services in English, services in German were important to maintaining their
identity.

By the 1890s language had become one of the most contested issues among
German Baptist leaders. Those arguing for services in German held that the
mother tongue was not only dear to the hearts of German Baptists but also the
key to the denomination's success in ministering to recent immigrants of German origin. Those contending for English believed it was only a matter of time
before assimilation, Americanization, public education, and upward mobility
would diminish preferences for German-language services. Relationships with
the American Baptist Convention continued to be critically important. Would
German Baptists be absorbed into the larger denomination if German services
ceased, or were their days numbered even if they did not? Would younger,
better-educated, and more affluent members seek fellowship in thoroughly
assimilated English-speaking Baptist churches or perhaps abandon the faith
entirely?[56]

Rural and relatively isolated as they were, Lorraine and Hope were not
immune to these considerations. Neither congregation attracted immigrants
directly from Germany after the 1880s. Growth depended on retaining the
congregations' children, but even the children who stayed in the vicinity
spread into surrounding towns and townships and went to English-speaking
churches closer to where they lived. Kinship within the congregations, youth
groups, and pastoral exchanges with kindred congregations exercised centripetal pulls, but members mostly used English in conducting nonchurch business, and church leaders attended regional Baptist association meetings where
they mingled with leaders whose congregations were well on the path toward
Americanization.

Lorraine and Hope were similar in favoring services in German, but they
also differed. On its inaugural Sunday in 1878, Lorraine held a German-
language service in the morning and an English-language service in the afternoon. It then held an English-language service once a month and gradually
switched to English-language services three times a month, conducting and
recording the minutes of its business meetings in English in 1920, and dropping the German-language services entirely in 1925.[57] In 1900, when the U.S.
decennial census asked if people could speak English, only three of Lorraine's
members and only three of Hope's said no. Yet in 1916, when Hope celebrated
its fiftieth anniversary, the services were conducted in German, and despite

pressures during World War I that prompted many German-speaking congregations to switch to English, the Hope congregation did not change until later. It conducted its business meetings and kept the minutes in German for another decade. In 1928, when a vote was taken on whether to conduct Sunday school classes in English or German, a third of those voting preferred German. Preaching in English began the same year on a trial basis in which the preacher spoke in English for half the time allotted for the sermon and in German the other half. Two years later communion services began alternating between English one month and German the next. The congregation did not give away its German hymnbooks until 1937 and held some of its services in German until 1939, when a new constitution was adopted and "German" was dropped from its name.[58]

Diversity and Assimilation

The similarities and differences evident in the two congregations pose an interesting complication for discussions of diversity and assimilation. The standard interpretation would argue that a cohesive congregation or ethnic group with strong internal ties and strong symbolic markers distinguishing it from other groups would have the best chances of maintaining its identity in the face of pressures for assimilation and thus be a prime example of how best to facilitate diversity. Hope and Lorraine largely support this interpretation. They further support another standard argument about assimilation: as economic conditions and larger changes in the culture inevitably force ethnically distinct communities to assimilate, it is the symbolism of a distinct heritage that remains. Being members of German Baptist churches despite speaking English and shifting to modern methods of farming illustrates that kind of symbolic ethnicity. But the argument about symbolic ethnicity may be wrong if it suggests that symbolism survives because it doesn't matter as much to what people actually do or to how they are viewed.

The value of thinking about symbolic boundaries is that it suggests the importance of considering how those boundaries are maintained and how they may function. The point can be made by imagining the differences between a highly cohesive community based on social arrangements like those at Lorraine and a community based on less cohesive social arrangements like those at Hope. The tight-knit community is arguably more secure in its identity. It can interact with outsiders in relative confidence that its identity will not be compromised. Insofar as it faces pressures to assimilate, it can be imagined to shift with relative ease in that direction because the social relationships at its core remain intact. That may not be the strong position from which many tightly knit ethnic communities confront assimilation, but it has characterized some, especially in ethnic neighborhoods and in ethnic congregations that benefit from geographic concentration, a shared past, institutional concentration, and relationships based on kinship and marriage. In contrast, a community lacking that degree of cohesion from social arrangements has to work harder to maintain its identity. Its rituals of remembrance and the symbols it uses to set itself apart may need to take on greater importance.

One of the most effective ways in which rituals and symbols increase in salience is through conflict. A group that is attacked or that perceives itself to be under attack by powers over which it has no control is likely to shore up its identity against those attacks. Especially if the attackers are powerful, standing up to them even in small ways reinforces the group's identity. The basis for the attack may well be real or it may be imagined, but in either case the attack can portray the group as a cohesive unit and increase the salience of the group's identity. Groups sometimes do nothing to instigate an attack and in other instances foment conflict without quite realizing that what they are doing is reinforcing their distinctive identities. Witch hunts that remind people of the importance of their values by accusing someone of violating those values are an example. Rituals that remind people of evil that had to be overcome and persecution that had to be endured in the past are examples as well. The symbolic boundary becomes clearer and more salient by an act or narrative that transgresses it.

World War I necessitated a serious reexamination of the symbolic boundaries that had set German Americans apart as a distinct ethnic population. In large part the response was for German-speaking schools, churches, community organizations, and families to quit speaking German, which was the most public marker of being German, and for German-language newspapers to go out of business or switch to English. To the extent that a distinctive ethnic identity continued, it went underground and located itself in innocuous private activities such as eating German-style food, speaking German at home, or interspersing English with German idioms. But in other ways conflicts involving German-origin communities heightened the symbolic boundaries identifying them.

Local German American communities that had differed from one another in terms of region of origin, date of immigration, location of settlement, dialect, and religion were treated as a single entity unified by a common language.[59] Legislatures passed laws against German-language schools and in a few instances against the use of German in all public settings, including churches. Newspapers editorialized about German Americans needing to be more patriotic in supporting the American war effort. In several instances patriotic groups attacked the homes, schools, businesses, and churches of German communities, thereby highlighting that the attacked were alien and the attackers were not. Mennonites, Amish, and Hutterites were targeted because they were pacifists as well as German, but German speakers in communities previously identified as Russian, Swiss, Bohemian, Catholic, and Reformed also came under suspicion.[60]

German Americans sometimes took active roles in accusing co-ethnics of disloyalty, identifying themselves in that way as patriotic Americans and arguing that they had long been proponents of total assimilation. German American clergy in many instances supported calls to hold church services only in English. German Americans sometimes responded defensively to the attacks as well, siding with groups arguing for neutrality during the war and in a few instances proudly affirming their German identity—as a German American farmer a few miles east of Dickinson County did by hoisting the German flag to the top of a windmill and declaring his land part of the German Empire.[61]

Common sense would suggest that a tight-knit ethnic community would be the one attacked under the kinds of uncertainties World War I involved. But common sense would be wrong if attacks of that kind had more to do with symbolic identities than with social arrangements. A community with cohesive social arrangements would have less need to affirm its identity in symbolic ways, and it could either isolate itself or interact easily with other groups in ways that demonstrated its patriotism. A less secure community might intentionally or inadvertently do things to protect itself or become the target of outsiders intent on demonstrating their own patriotism. That was the case at Hope.

In 1918 the U.S. government required all nonnaturalized males age fourteen and older of German birth and their wives to register as "alien enemies." On pain of being charged with a felony and imprisoned or sent to an internment camp for the duration of the war, each person so categorized had to appear in person at the post office, have one's fingerprints and photo taken, and supply information to a designated public official such as the postmaster or sheriff about one's birthdate and place of birth, length of time in the United States, relatives, and any relatives who were currently in the military either in America or in Germany.[62] Many registrants found the process deeply embarrassing, especially if they had lived in America for decades, were American-born wives, or had family members serving in the U.S. Armed Forces. Few of the German Baptists at Hope or Lorraine by that date had been born in Germany and had not become naturalized citizens. If anything registration fell harder at Lorraine, where five men and seven women, all from the congregation's founding families, had to register, than at Hope, where only two men and three women did. Registration at Lorraine could also have been eased—or been more embarrassing—by the fact that the postmaster there belonged to the church.

Besides registering them as alien enemies, many states including Kansas formed militia-like cadres of "home guards" to monitor German Americans and take action against them if any indications of supporting the enemy became evident. German Americans eager to demonstrate that they were above suspicion sometimes joined the home guards and voiced complaints against members of their own families. Reportable offenses could be as serious as withholding grain that was supposed to be sold to assist America's allies or

FIGURE 16. *Round Up the Traitors*, 1918, characterizing passage
of the Sedition Act. Drawn by W. A. Rogers. Library of Congress
Prints and Photographs Division, Washington, DC.

acts as minor as expressing doubts about the war. Authorities were particularly vigilant toward anything in the way of organized opposition to the war,
such as the Nonpartisan League, a grassroots antiwar movement that gained
a following among farmers in North Dakota and then across the Midwest and
West, including an office in Topeka, Kansas, established in December 1917.
The Nonpartisan League drew criticism from Kansas's farm organizations that
viewed it as the work of outside agitators and warned farmers to stay clear of

it, but authorities cautioned that German Americans might nevertheless be attracted.[63]

The home guard played an active role in communities near Lorraine. "Was ready at all times to put down any pro-German argument; put German schools out of business and incidentally saw that German sympathizers kept their place or left town," a guard member in a town north of Lorraine reported. At a town east of Lorraine, the guard forced a German preacher, accused of teaching German music, to leave. At the town of Ellsworth, the high school dropped German from the curriculum and offered Spanish in its place. West of Lorraine near Holyrood, neighbors of the Kruses agitated so vehemently that an elderly German woman fell into a deep depression and committed suicide a few years later. Surprisingly, the home guard levied no accusations against the Lorraine congregation. Hope's experience was different.[64]

The trouble at Hope stemmed from a cousin of Henry Kohman's second wife, Lizzie Rumold. The Rumolds were one of the most prominent extended families in the vicinity of the Hope congregation. With the exception of Lizzie, who became a German Baptist by marriage, the Rumolds were not German Baptists. The person in charge of the Kanas Home Guard in Dickinson County was Lizzie's cousin William J. Rumold. Born in 1875, six years after his parents settled in Kansas, William was the son of John Ferdinand Rumold, who came to America at the age of fifteen in 1851, and Elizabeth Dewald Rumold. William had three older sisters, an older brother, and two younger brothers. Two other siblings died as infants. The Rumolds' first home was a crudely constructed log cabin, but by the time the father died in 1917 the family was well established in the community and relatively successful, farming 200 acres in Section 12 of Banner Township about a mile north of the German Baptist Church. The Rumolds' barn—46 feet wide and 72 feet long with a built-in granary—was one of the most impressive in the area, a neighbor recalled, and John Rumold was known for raising large herds of steers, which he marched to the depot at Dillon for a final ride to the Kansas City stockyards.[65]

But the John Ferdinand Rumolds were neither as successful nor as prominent in the community as the Jacob J. Rumolds. Jacob was four years younger than his half-brother John. Coming to America in 1855 as a fifteen-year-old, Jacob went to Detroit where he worked for a year, then to the Lake Superior area where he worked for a year and a half mining copper, and then for a year as a hotel porter in New York and a sailor on ships to Liverpool. In 1860 he became a skilled glass blower, pursuing that career for five years in New York and Pennsylvania before marrying in New Jersey. In 1868 he and his bride purchased a farm in Dickinson County, only to move a year later to Illinois, where Jacob pursued his trade as a glass blower for another four years. Returning to Dickinson County in 1873, the family gradually increased its holdings to more than 600 acres by the time he died in 1893.[66]

By 1918 Jacob and Mary Rumold's daughter Lizzie had become the second wife of Henry Kohman, who was one of the wealthiest farmers in the township, and several of the Kohman children were in college or had married well in the community. Her brother Christian had become a college science teacher, and her younger brothers John and Henry were expanding their father's farming operations.

William Rumold and his siblings had been less fortunate than their cousins. William's oldest sister Kate was widowed, his next oldest sister had moved to Missouri where her husband was trying to earn a living farming, his brother Ferdinand had moved to a town in Riley County where he was working with cattle, the youngest brother Carl was farming the home place following their father's death in 1917, brother George was working as a traveling salesman in the grocery business, and William was selling real estate in Hope where he and his wife were coming to terms with being childless. Whatever they may have thought about their more fortunate cousins, the potential for strained relationships was certainly there.

If there was a weak spot in the more fortunate Jacob Rumold family's appearance of success, it was John, the cousin who was the same age as William and was farming an entire section of land about twenty-five miles away in the next county. This John Rumold was an embarrassment for two reasons. His most serious offense was that he illegally hoarded some 4,000 bushels of wheat, corn, and oats for four years during the war, storing the grain in bins hidden from the road, and when questioned on two occasions by the authorities declaring that he did not wish to have his grain shipped to any of the allies that were fighting against Germany. Both incidents received publicity in newspapers locally and throughout the state. After the first incident, the local *Hope Dispatch* editorialized, "It is a bad time to not be truly loyal to the government, and the most of that class of fellows will be caught sooner or later." Following the second, the paper said Rumold was also wrong for his hoarded grain attracting mice and rats. The minor offense was that publicity naming him as John F. Rumold and suggesting that perhaps he was merely suffering from old age confused him with William's recently deceased eighty-year-old father, whose name was also John F. Rumold.[67]

Holding a highly visible office in the Kansas Home Guard functioned for William Rumold, like it did for many others of German descent, to ward off any suspicions about their own patriotism toward America. Why he turned his attention where he did, though, is impossible to know. Perhaps he heard rumors through his dealings in real estate. Perhaps his dealings were disagreeable. Perhaps he did what he did to deflect attention from his cousin's grain hoarding or to get back at him for embarrassing the Rumold name.

William's target was the German Baptist Church. Despite the fact that he was related to the Kohmans, and despite the fact that nearly everyone in the congregation was an American-born or naturalized citizen and several of the members owned nearly as much land as the Kohmans, the congregation was vulnerable. The church held all its services in German, was located in the country and was composed almost entirely of farmers, and belonged to a denomination that was smaller and more distinctly German than any of the larger denominations in the county. Its near-pacifist Baptist heritage put it at odds with American appeals for war but put it equally at odds with German military expansion.

A year earlier when the U.S. government required males to register for the draft and asked if they wished to claim exemption, several of the congregation did. One of the men claimed exemption to support his wife and child. One of the Kohmans claimed exemption to care for his crops. A Kohman nephew said he had a wife to support. Another Kohman nephew asked exemption on grounds that he was farming. Those instances were few, though, and a year later the government provided no options to claim exemption.

William Rumold was in a good position to know who was naturalized or nonnaturalized and who was eligible for the draft. Besides his real estate dealings, he had been active in the Kansas National Guard for two decades and served as enumerator for the 1900 and 1910 federal censuses for the township in which many of the members of the German Baptist church lived. Census enumerators visited every family in their township, recorded everyone's name, listed when they had immigrated, and indicated whether they were naturalized citizens.

On March 11, 1918, in his capacity as "Captain of the Hope State Guards," William Rumold wrote to the Kansas Adjutant General in Topeka suggesting that the "large country German Baptist church" near Hope be investigated on grounds of disloyalty and seditious remarks. An agent of the Nonpartisan League, Rumold claimed, had been recruiting sympathizers from the church. He further suggested that the church's pastor was spreading German propaganda and sparking opposition to the war effort. The pastor, Rumold charged, "was very bitter against our government and preached very strongly against the government in his sermons." That was before the war, Rumold conceded, but could have sown the seeds for the Nonpartisan agent's recruiting. "Whether he has spread German propaganda I am unable to say but the above named conditions make it look suspicious." Not only that, Rumold continued, but also some of the farmers had claimed exemption from the draft and "are not buying Liberty Bonds as they should." It was urgent, he said, that the government send someone out to conduct a thorough investigation. "We have too large a German settlement to take any chances," he warned.[68]

The witch hunt Rumold tried to initiate failed. No evidence indicates that the adjutant general took the action Rumold suggested. By the time Rumold posted his letter, the pastor who concerned him had moved to Cincinnati. None of the congregation hoarded grain. None was charged with sedition. The congregation, though, did preserve its language and its German identity.

Understanding Diversity

A couple of nineteenth-century congregations in the middle of Kansas seem a long way from anything relevant to now. I have suggested, though, that a better understanding of diversity then can give us a clearer picture of diversity now. The social and symbolic cohesion on which the diverse identities of individuals and groups depend remain the same. Only the ways in which they are achieved have changed. Then, as now, people looked to the communities with which they identified—and in many cases to the congregations to which they belonged—for cues about how to behave as respectable friends and neighbors as well as camaraderie and support. The German Baptists at Hope and Lorraine considered themselves respectable, hardworking people of faith who valued their families and expressed that value through the close ties that bound them to their congregations and their communities. Being a good middle-class American depended not only on individual striving but also on adhering to the standards of the social contexts in which a person lived.

Geographic concentration now is more relevant to considerations of national identity and the identity of towns and cities than of rural enclaves. It still matters that people who imagine themselves to be a moral community occupy a territory they consider their own. Religious congregations are local whether the locale of their members is a small neighborhood or a large suburb. Geographic proximity is achieved not only with next-door neighbors but also through travel and in cyberspace. Institutional concentration, trust, and enforceable norms are important underpinnings of group identities as well.

The sharp reduction in family size and the attendant possibilities for relationships through intermarriage bear the most significant implications. Congregations, towns, and ethnic enclaves are rarely linked so complexly together in these ways as they once were. The burden of such encumbrances being lifted gives individuals the freedom to make of themselves what they wish. It also poses the need for substitute connections, whether in more intense commitments with fewer relationships or in less intense commitments to more.

The notion that symbolic cohesion may be present when social cohesion is weak continues to be an interesting feature of American life. It squares with the idea that ethnicity tends often to be symbolic, continuing in festivals, heritage centers, congregations, and family traditions long after it ceases to bind co-ethnics together through intermarriage and ethnically homogeneous neighborhoods. It also suggests that symbolic boundaries are more than mental categories. Symbolic boundaries are better understood as practices that groups negotiate and that through the negotiations are reinforced, dramatized, and made salient. To be sure, the salience of ethnic boundaries shifts dramatically in many instances because of large-scale political developments, just as it did for German Americans during World War I and as it has more recently for Latinos and Asian Americans. However, changes in markers of identity as important as language cannot be understood by associating them only with sudden political events. The gradual changes at Hope and Lorraine were not unusual in this regard. It took years of meetings, experiments, discussions, and votes for one language to replace the other.

Congregations function as moral communities to the extent that they generate enough social and symbolic cohesion to play a significant role in members' lives and to be a significant part of members' identities. Congregations are like charitable organizations, neighborhood associations, clubs, political party affiliates, work groups, and committees in these respects. They are the substrata of society on which diversity depends. It is important that they be cohesive but not so cohesive that they become insular. Congregations as tight knit as the ones at Hope and Lorraine had to be sufficiently porous to welcome newcomers.

Limited cohesion is the reason organizations are so often composed of a tight-knit core that contributes extensively and a periphery of the less engaged. The less engaged demonstrate the possibility of being involved and yet contributing only a little. It is a calling card for people with external commitments to contribute while also maintaining those external connections.

The same is true of the strictness that is so often a characteristic of religious sects. Extreme strictness may be beneficial to a group's identity. It prevents free riders who benefit from the group but contribute nothing from becoming a burden. But moderate strictness may be more in the group's interest than extreme strictness. Moderate strictness allows the rules to be bent. Moderate strictness is also better understood when it is viewed as the result of multiple characteristics of the group and the group's relationship to its environment. Strictness is as varied as the grounds on which social and symbolic cohesion is based.[69]

Diversity is ultimately about the relationships between insiders and outsiders as much as it is about insiders' identities. Assimilation alters those relationships. It suggests a common path toward which all can aspire. But it is shaped by the diverse relationships that function from day to day as supportive communities.

This understanding of diversity challenges the view that religion flourished in America simply because the nation provided a kind of free market in which organizations competed with one another for market share. The reality of American religious history was more complicated than that. It was true that some denominations grew faster and larger than others. But that was not because some were more inspired by competition than others. Nor was it the case that denominations were like firms that either gained or lost market share but otherwise stayed the same.

Competition among religious organizations, to the extent that it existed at all, occurred at multiple levels: national, regional, and local. The local level throughout the nineteenth century was quite local indeed, defined by the relatively short distances people could travel with ease. Those distances changed not only as transportation changed but also in conjunction with assimilation. People formed moral communities based on social and moral distinctions that reflected their changing understandings of themselves, their families and neighbors, and their ethnic identities. Being a respectable middle-class American meant earning the respect of one's extended family, neighbors, and fellow congregants.[70]

When religious beliefs and practices are the basis of those moral distinctions, as they continue to be for many Americans, they need to be considered in relation to other social relationships instead of in a vacuum. It may be important to know that some religions draw strict or sharp distinctions between their adherents and other people. But it is equally important to consider the likelihood of disagreements and the necessity of mechanisms for resolving or transcending those potential conflicts.

To say that religion brings people together in ways that spread and thus reduce the fear of death and the trauma of bereavement is too simple. If it works that way for the victims of misfortune, it also puts a burden on the more fortunate and potentially draws attention to unpleasant considerations of why some people's misfortune is worse than others. Funerary rites may be the occasion for redefining the roles of those involved. But part of that redefinition involves accepting the distinction between the bereaved and the nonbereaved and emphasizing in ritual and in belief that the two are bound together in other ways.

At the present time when social relationships undergirding a sense of moral cohesion are changing, it is probably not surprising that symbolic ways of drawing moral distinctions remain as important as they do. Accepting diversity never comes easily. People hunker down, doing what they can to keep intact their sense of who they have been. Differences interpreted as threats set the wheels of fear in motion, triggering suspicions and prompting conflicts. Painful as those conflicts may be, they also serve as the occasions for self-examination, redefinition, and renewal.

CHAPTER SIX

Excessive Profits

WEALTH, MORALITY, AND
THE COMMON PEOPLE

ONE OF THE HIGHEST-PROFILE ARRESTS ever to take place in New York City occurred on Saturday, June 19, 1920. That morning a task force of government agents assembled at the Federal Building in Lower Manhattan, traveled to the Gimbel Brothers department store at Thirty-third Street and Sixth Avenue, made their way to the store's eighth-floor executive offices, and arrested Frederick A. Gimbel on 185 counts of profiteering. They also arrested Joseph J. Dowell, general merchandise manager of the store, and C. D. Slawter, its clothing buyer. The warrant charged Gimbel and his associates with selling clothing at exorbitant profit margins of 90 to 275 percent.[1]

The arrests came at the peak of public outrage over the high cost of living that had developed during World War I and showed no signs of declining now that the war was over. A later cost-of-living index would reveal that overall consumer prices had doubled between 1914 and 1920, with the steepest increase having occurred between 1918 and 1920, reaching a level that would not be met again until 1947.[2] Contemporary evidence showed that household items worth $100 in 1904 cost $230 in 1919. During that time the price of clothing increased 149 percent, bread increased 184 percent, and meat increased 329 percent.[3] Another report showed that during roughly the same time period the average price of pork chops in U.S. cities increased from 13 cents a pound to 39 cents, eggs increased from 22 cents a dozen to 57 cents, and milk increased from 28 cents a gallon to 56 cents.[4]

On August 8, 1919, President Woodrow Wilson made a widely publicized speech before Congress asking for legislation to curb the soaring prices that he said were "in many cases artificially and deliberately created by vicious practices."[5] Wilson argued that the regimen of price controls imposed during the war should be extended until peace in Europe was fully restored. Without

FIGURE 17. *Give Me Back My Clothes*, 1919, satirizing the profiteer
exploiting the consumer. Drawn by William Hanny for the *St. Joseph
News-Press*, reprinted in *Cartoons Magazine* 16 (1919), 517.

controls, prices could be expected to spiral upward as civilian employment
returned to normal, wages increased, and the demand for consumer goods
grew. Consumers and retailers purchasing and hoarding goods as a hedge
against further inflation and wholesalers hiking prices on surplus wartime
goods contributed to the problem. Wilson urged the public to engage in self-
examination and to call forth the "strong fiber of self-control" that would put
an end to selfish and sinister practices.

Profiteering was but one of a long list of complaints about the wealthy. If
they were not directly engaged in price gouging, they had surely ramped up
interest in going to war, critics charged, because war was good for the bottom
line.[6] It was further evidence that the rich were corrupt, and even if they were
not, that they enjoyed the kind of luxuries to which any greedy person in candid moments might aspire. In subsequent studies countless efforts were made

to describe the extent of America's economic inequality, ascertain its sources, and chronicle its effects. Investigations considered whether the wealthy owned the right amount or too much of the nation's wealth and if the latter what could be done about it. But it was also true that the wealthy held a significant spot in the nation's cultural imagination. The wealthy were an "other," a category of comparison with which to make observations not only about the rich but also about the common people—who they were, by what moral standards they should live, how they should view the wealthy, and whether they were beholden to the wealthy in ways they might not fully understand. Profiteering heightened the contrast between the wealthy and everyone else, evoking old and new arguments about the meanings of wealth, the pitfalls of pursuing it, and the terms in which people lacking it could understand themselves.

It fell to the Justice Department under the direction of Attorney General A. Mitchell Palmer to bring whatever methods of enforcement the federal government could muster to bear on postwar profiteering. Palmer's office operated on an annual budget of nearly $10 million, of which $2.5 million was spent on special investigations.[7] Besides the usual business of prosecuting cases involving alleged crimes against federal statutes, Palmer was preoccupied with ridding the nation of anarchists, communists, and suspected subversives. In April 1919 three dozen packages containing dynamite and labeled as Gimbel Brothers Novelty Samples had been mailed to prominent business leaders, newspaper editors, and government officials. On June 2 Palmer's family narrowly escaped when their house in the nation's capital was bombed. Over the next six months Palmer used the full force of his office to threaten coal strikers, intimidate union leaders, and deport suspected radicals. Fueled by widespread fears of terrorism and assassinations, Palmer's agents rounded up, arrested, and deported tens of thousands of suspected anarchists and communists.[8]

"Palmer's raids," as they were called, served as the model for the Justice Department's efforts to combat postwar profiteering. The raids depended on two sources of information. The Justice Department through its regional offices solicited tips from the general public about persons possibly engaged in hoarding, price gouging, and other potentially criminal activities. Any citizens who felt they had been overcharged or who simply wanted to cast suspicion on a neighbor or competing storeowner could file a complaint. Palmer's office received thousands of complaints dealing with matters as small as a few cents on the price of potatoes to as large as thousands of dollars on the resale of surplus war supplies. The Justice Department also organized teams of undercover agents in large cities who scouted local stores, took note of prices, made purchases, and asked questions about pricing decisions and profit margins.[9]

The teams of undercover federal agents were known as flying squadrons. The name resonated with the popularity of aviation during the war but had nothing to do with airplanes and the war. The phrase originated in reference to squadrons of ships used by the British in the 1860s and 1870s and was adopted

FIGURE 18. *Attorney General Alexander Mitchell Palmer*, 1919, at his home
after it was bombed on June 2, 1919. Photograph by Harris & Ewing. Library
of Congress Prints and Photographs Division, Washington, DC.

by the U.S. Navy during the Spanish-American War. By World War I flying
squadrons still referred to naval vessels but also to teams of traveling speakers
who stumped the country on behalf of temperance and prohibition. The key to
being a flying squadron was to travel as part of a coordinated effort—to swoop
in quickly, get the job done, and move on.

The person in charge of the Justice Department's flying squadron in New York City was Armin W. Riley. Riley was a thirty-seven-year-old German immigrant who had graduated in 1904 from Princeton, where he sang with the Glee Club, participated in summer geological expeditions, and represented his class in the annual "cane spree," a peculiar campus tradition consisting of wrestling one's opponent for control of a hickory walking stick. In 1920 Riley's position as special assistant to the attorney general put him in charge of enforcing laws regulating the sale of imported Argentine sugar and investigating complaints about steep increases in the price of bituminous coal as well as tackling similar increases in food, clothing, and other retail goods.[10]

Riley's efforts aimed to curb profiteering not only by threatening profiteers with fines and jail sentences but also by publicly shaming them. Shaming fit well with public sentiment at the time. The administration's Committee on Public Information had used it during the war to encourage citizens to purchase liberty bonds. Persons who opposed the war or who might in any way seem indifferent about supporting it risked being labeled "yellow" or "red." Shaming reflected the view that a lack of patriotism was not only illegal but also immoral. The same logic applied to profiteers. Editorials declared that disgracing them, rather than levying fines of a few hundred dollars that they could easily pay, was the way to stop wealthy profiteers. As one writer observed, "To a man of pride disgrace is the severest of all punishments."[11] Public information director George Creel cooperated by including among his weekly press releases the names, locations, and offenses of business leaders accused of profiteering. Cartoonists and essayists took up the challenge as well. From 1918 to 1920 *Life* magazine filled its pages with pithy jibes at profiteering, such as "A fool and his money are soon parted by the profiteer," "A profiteer is a man who follows the long green line," and "One half the profiteers don't know how the other half profits." The magazine included dozens of essays, short stories, and cartoons about profiteers and embellished its Thanksgiving issue cover with a sinister profiteer. One of the most notable cartoons depicted a uniformed soldier with a missing leg and a crutch sitting on a park bench adjacent to an overly large, well-dressed, cigar-smoking profiteer who says, "The war is over, my boy. Forget it!"[12]

Bringing moral pressure to bear on profiteers was a significant aspect of the Justice Department's overall strategy for another reason. Palmer was not at all certain that criminal charges could be brought that would stand up in court. The Lever Act of 1917 under which the federal government assumed control of the coal industry provided for only limited regulation of food, beverages, and fuel, and Congress was still debating whether it could be applied to the postwar pricing of food and clothing. Besides the legal uncertainties, Palmer believed criminal law was an "imperfect instrument" for curbing profiteering because sound business practices and economic considerations also had to be respected so as not to retard the operation of "economic laws." The practical difficulties of investigating large corporations further complicated the task. "It is a simple matter to detect a corner groceryman in the act of profiteering," he declared, but "the investigation of a big corporation means the employment of numerous accountants, auditors, and agents for many months, careful analysis of the evidence secured, and exhaustive presentation of a vast array of figures to the grand jury."[13]

That shaming could work—sometimes all too well—became evident when one of Riley's first flying squadron raids led to the arrest of Brooklyn haberdasher Joseph Nichthauser. Nichthauser was a fifty-year-old Jewish immigrant of Austrian and Polish descent who had come to America in 1890, established himself as a haberdasher specializing in "Gents' Furnishings," and in 1920 was living with his wife and three children in a modestly upscale apartment building across the street from Prospect Park. On Wednesday April 7, 1920, Riley's office received a tip that Nichthauser was charging excessive prices. Riley dispatched an investigator to the store who reported that the markup could be determined from a code attached to each item in the store. Two days later the flying squadron examined the store's books and charged that a raincoat initially priced at $23 had been increased to $45. Nichthauser was arrested the following day and held on $2,500 bail, which he posted the same evening. Sunday editions of the *New York Times* and *New York Tribune* reported the details of the arrest, declaring that Riley was well satisfied and that further arrests would be made within the week. The stories went to press without the knowledge that at 7:35 that morning Nichthauser took his life by shooting himself in the right temple with a .32 caliber revolver. Nichthauser may have already been troubled with worries about his business and family, but accounts left no doubt that his suicide was the result of his arrest.[14]

Nichthauser's death notwithstanding, Riley's office declared it would pursue and arrest profiteers as relentlessly as before. The June 19 Gimbels raid aimed to bring maximum notoriety to profiteering. Twenty reporters armed with notebooks and cameras, including a motion picture camera, accompanied the flying squadron through the store to the eighth floor and then followed the officers and arrestees back to the Federal Building. Spectators witnessed a melee at the store and a second fracas outside the Federal Building when a brief fistfight broke out and a camera was broken. Newspapers across the country carried the story with banner headlines such as "Wealthy Merchant Held as Profiteer" and "Flying Squadron Men Charge New York Store with Profiteering." The coverage included examples of how much the store had been charging for selected items and emphasized that the Justice Department's flying squadrons were at work in other cities.[15]

It was hardly surprising that the raid drew national attention. Gimbels was one of the best-known department stores in the country, rivaled only by Macy's in New York and Wanamaker's in Philadelphia. Founded in 1842 by Adam Gimbel, the business launched a chain of stores in Indiana and Illinois and then expanded into other states under the direction of Gimbel's seven sons. By 1920 Gimbels stores were located in Philadelphia, Milwaukee, New York, Pittsburgh, Richmond, and Trenton. Newspapers in these cities regularly published quarter-page advertisements of clothing and housewares and entertained readers with holiday greetings and homey advice. Although customers could only speculate how profitable the family-owned business might be, the stores' upscale ambience and frequent claims that business had never been better gave the impression that it was profitable indeed. So did the society columns, which described the Gimbels' business and family connections with prominent Jewish families such as the Sulzbergers, Loebs, Hamburgers, and Guggenheims and reported frequent outings to London and Paris. When the company went public in 1922, its net sales exceeded $66 million, and by 1930 they totaled $123 million, making it the largest department store corporation in the world. At the helm of the New York store, Frederick Gimbel, who lived at a coveted address on the Upper East Side with his wife Lucille—a granddaughter of mining tycoon Meyer Guggenheim—was the scion of the family.[16]

Profiteering charges threatened the company's reputation with its customers and were profoundly embarrassing for the company's owners. Against the reality that prices were indeed high and rising, the store proudly proclaimed that they would have been even higher had it not been for the company's success in securing goods in volume at reasonable prices. The arrests were doubly embarrassing because they happened at the exact moment when the head of the company's closest competitor, Nathan Straus of Macy's, was being hailed for his generosity to charitable causes—including war relief, support for Jewish settlements in Palestine, and campaigns for pasteurized milk to lower infant mortality—all inspired, it was said, by the untimely death of a brother and sister-in-law aboard the *Titanic* in 1912. As the public absorbed the news of Gimbel's arrest, Straus was making headlines by saying he was trying to give away all his money with the intent of dying poor, and his wife, Lina Gutherz Straus, was in the news for donating some $18,000 in jewelry for postwar relief.

What exactly constituted profiteering and who specifically should be charged were questions open to debate. The Food and Fuel Control Act that went into effect on August 10, 1917, stated as its intent the prevention of "hoarding, injurious speculation, manipulations, and private controls" and gave the president broad powers to determine when and how to impose sanctions to that end.[17] Arguments for the legislation pitted patriotic, hardworking farmers and consumers against heartless and unpatriotic speculators, manipulators, and intermediaries.[18] The law under which the Justice Department pursued profiteering after the war defined it as making an unjust or unreasonable rate or charge or conspiracy to exact excessive prices. But legislators debated the meanings of "unjust," "unreasonable," and "excessive."[19] Different conclusions could be drawn if current prices were compared with prices in 1913, 1914, 1915, or 1916. It mattered if seasonal variations in prices were

considered, if prices for single items or categories of items or entire invento-
ries were considered, and if increases in labor costs were taken into account.
Newspapers carried stories suggesting that department store prices were not
excessive at all, given these additional considerations. Pundits suggested that
ordinary housewives stocking up on sugar and flour before prices increased
were the true profiteers.

It was nevertheless the wealthy profiteer toward whom the greatest indignation was directed. The flying squadrons were just as interested in the
unpretentious corner grocer as in the moneyed elite, Riley told reporters after
Nichthauser's arrest, but he said his investigators were keeping a lookout especially toward people who were making money in carloads. Three months
after the Gimbel arrest, Riley's flying squadrons brought charges against firms
owned by two of the nation's wealthiest families—Armour and Company and
Sugarland Industries. The trouble with wealthy profiteers, columnists contended, was that they were already rich and for that matter had not contributed enough to paying for the war. They knew how to manipulate the markets
to their advantage and could obfuscate their bookkeeping. Legislators naturally took differing sides depending on the constituencies they represented but
rarely failed to make front-page news by assailing the heads of meatpacking
companies, Wall Street bankers, and unnamed millionaires. "Do you suppose
that the people who pinch, skimp, and are being forced to do without many
of the things they need are thrilled to see the number of millionaires double?"
Republican Arthur Capper of Kansas asked his colleagues in the U.S. Senate.
Profiteers, he declared, were more dangerous than "Reds."[20]

The Gimbel case was important not only because of the publicity it generated but also as a turning point in the history of American understandings of
wealth. Until World War I the problems that excessive wealth might cause for
the society at large were dealt with mostly in moral terms. Wealth was problematic to the extent that it was immoral, and it was immoral to the extent
that it involved fraud, greed, exploitative business practices, deceptive marketing, or an overweening obsession with self-interested accumulation. Discussions of wealth in moral terms continued after World War I but increasingly
were accompanied by efforts aimed at controlling the worst excesses of wealth
through public policy. The price controls instituted during the war established
the grounds for such policies on an emergency basis. Never before had average
citizens been affected on such a wide scale and in such intimate financial details
as through the federal government's regulation of prices, its efforts to mobilize
the sale of savings bonds, and its calls to produce more and consume less.[21]

The campaign against postwar profiteering of which the Gimbel case
was a part represented an attempt to combine policy measures with moral
accusations—a practice that would be repeated in public officials' attempts to
mobilize public support for policy proposals by emphasizing the basic honesty
of average citizens in contrast with morally questionable practices of the rich.

The campaign itself was short lived, brought to an end by declining prices and the Supreme Court's March 1921 ruling that the Lever Act was too imprecise in its definition of profiteering to be enforced and was thus unconstitutional. Within days of that ruling a federal judge dismissed the Gimbel case and the cases against Armour and Sugarland. The campaign against profiteering in this respect demonstrated the weaknesses as well as the possibilities of efforts to mobilize moral restraint against market relations. As efforts shifted toward other issues and then in the 1930s moved dramatically toward public policy, characterizations of wealth and the wealthy changed, and with those changes, a new conception of the common middle-class American also came into being.

Wealth and Morality

Whatever else ordinary, nonwealthy Americans may have thought about wealth and those who possessed it, the wealthy could be characterized by two indisputable facts: they were a minority and they were different. It was not that ordinary, nonwealthy Americans had reason to think a lot about the wealthy. It was entirely possible, as a farmer who lived in rural Indiana in the 1920s explained, to have no exposure at all to wealthy people, except, as he also recalled, on the rare occasion when business took him to Indianapolis, where the magnificent mansions in one section of the city suggested grandeur befitting of royalty.[22] It was possible for people like that to cling to the belief, as ethnographers discovered in studying small towns in the 1920s and 1930s, that the livelihoods of everyone in one's own town were pretty much the same. And yet when Robert S. Lynd and Helen Merrell Lynd collected information in Muncie, Indiana, for their widely read study *Middletown*, they found that money was very much on people's minds and that incomes among the few at the top exceeded those at the bottom tenfold.[23]

Were there no immediate exposure to the wealthy, the literate public had ample information to prompt the imagination. Newspapers large and small entertained readers with stories of the rich being robbed, being murdered, committing suicide, dying by other means, or partying, sponsoring debutante balls, marrying, and traveling abroad. "It is easier for a needle to go through a camel's eye," Mark Twain quipped, "than for a rich woman to sprain her ankle and keep it out of the papers."[24] In the decade before World War I, exposés treated the details of fortunes amassed in the conglomerates having arisen in railroads, oil, meatpacking, insurance, and banking and through the corruption of Tammany Hall. Readers before that would have been entertained with Horatio Alger's "Luck and Pluck" and "Tattered Tom" books. And before that, lessons about wealth could have been learned from reading the Bible and listening to sermons.

While it was true that commentary about wealth and the wealthy insofar as these were topics of interest to the American public could be found throughout the nation's history, discussions of wealth were of greater interest and thus more common at times when economic conditions warranted particular concern. Understandings of wealth in America were grounded in political arguments about the comparative advantages of democracy for treating persons with varying amounts of wealth the same and providing opportunities for anyone who worked hard to acquire wealth. They were also rooted in theological arguments about the exercise of moral responsibility in attaining wealth and in the uses of wealth. By the mid-nineteenth century most of these arguments were evident in popular discussions that dealt with wealth and the wealthy largely as unproblematic topics except for concerns expressed occasionally about the concentration of wealth and its political implications. Later nineteenth-century discussions situated the pursuit of wealth in the context of industrial expansion and posed questions about the widening gap between the wealthy and the poor. The economic crisis of 1873 sparked discussions about the social implications of wealth that continued through the Gilded Age and included populist arguments in the 1890s that set the stage for early twentieth-century discussions of plutocracy, monopolies, and profiteers. In the 1930s the Great Depression brought new arguments to bear on the social role of the wealthy that also reflected many of the ideas put forth during the previous century.

That the wealthy in popular understandings constituted a distinct minority—"different from you and me," as F. Scott Fitzgerald famously observed—went almost without saying.[25] To be wealthy was to be set apart from the rest of the population, occupying a distinct category however ill defined that distinction might have been. To be wealthy was a cultural category as much as it was an economic concept. "The thing itself is altogether relative," a writer noting the difficulties of defining wealth remarked in the 1870s. "Its standard varies according to time and place [and] its substance depends on the opinion of mankind at large."[26] Those variations, the writer observed, pertained even to such standard measures of wealth as money, property, and investments. In addition the temporal and spatial variations reflected judgments about lifestyles, consumption, and the meanings of luxury. As later discussions of social class would argue, the distinction between wealth and the lack of wealth depended on subtleties of appearance and comportment and the control of space and social relationships as well as material assets. Like classifications based on race and gender, the distinction between the wealthy and nonwealthy was culturally constructed, metaphorically embellished in contrasts between upper and lower, large and small, soft and hard, and fat and thin; negotiated, enduring but also fungible, and reinforced through public discussions about who the wealthy were and what they did.[27]

Statistical estimates, such as they were, underscored the extent to which the wealthy constituted a small minority of the population and yet held a significant share of the nation's wealth. U.S. Department of Agriculture statistician George K. Holmes compiled figures in 1890 for more than twelve million farm families showing that 9 percent who could be considered wealthy owned 71 percent of total farm family wealth. From other data Holmes concluded that the nation's four thousand millionaires who made up 0.03 percent of the nation's population owned approximately $12 billion, or 20 percent of the nation's wealth. The wealthy, Holmes contended, were different from the rest of the population not only in the extent of their wealth but also in its sources: they overwhelming earned interest from the nation's debts and amassed wealth from commerce and manufacturing.[28] Three years after Holmes's results, *Outlook* editor Charles B. Spahr drew similar conclusions using additional data. The wealthy classes with estates of $50,000 or more, he concluded, made up 1 percent of the population but owned 51 percent of the nation's wealth.[29]

Like other categories of the population that were conceptually set apart, the wealthy provided occasions for moral reflection. They were like hucksters and lunatics and fanatics in this regard, except that it was more common for the wealthy to be admired than reviled. They were like other groups toward which the majority public distinguished itself, too, in that the symbolic boundaries separating the wealthy from the nonwealthy were never simply straightforward and thus were negotiated in discussions about how to define wealth and how to distinguish its consequences in the lives of those who had a lot of it and those who did not. The same observations that described who the wealthy were and what they did cast these descriptions in moral terms, arguing variously that the wealthy exemplified standards toward which the nonwealthy should also aspire or suggesting that the wealthy were somehow morally deficient in ways that other people should guard against. While much of the attention the wealthy received in both popular and scholarly media focused on how they attained their wealth and how it was used, there were always implications about the moral lessons that ordinary people should come away with from considering the rich. The lessons could rarely be understood simply as justifications that the wealthy used to legitimate their elevated position or that the nonwealthy used as a kind of sour-grapes rationale for their lack of wealth. The moral language in which wealth was discussed more often suggested by implication that the nonwealthy should behave in certain ways—and in this the moral language played a role in defining who ordinary Americans were and what was common about them.

The moral terms in which wealth was discussed in the early Republic set the pattern for much that was to follow. The distinction between the wealthy and nonwealthy was often elided in religious and political discussions by referring instead to prosperity, prospering, and being prosperous. To prosper could be taken as an indication of having become wealthy or simply as doing well whether financially or in other ways. A person could prosper in gaining knowledge of God, for example, or in producing children. Being prosperous

implied that a person was probably doing something right and thus held positive moral connotations. Insofar as the wealthy provided an example of those
who were prospering, wealth and morality were positively joined. A sermon
widely published and republished in the 1780s and 1790s by the theologically
moderate Scottish minister Hugh Blair illustrated this connection. "You see
that those who are born with the same advantages of fortune," Blair observed,
"are not all equally prosperous in the course of life. While some of them by
wise and steady conduct attain distinction in the world and pass their days
with comfort and honor, others of the same rank by mean and vicious behavior
forfeit the advantages of their birth, involve themselves in much misery, and
end in being a disgrace to their friends and a burden to society." The difference,
he argued, was that prosperous people early in life gave serious attention to
planning their conduct, engaged in self-reflection, and sought good counsel
while the nonprosperous did not.[30]

Blair's argument could be interpreted as counsel for ascetic frugality, sobriety, and diligent devotion of the kind that attracted Max Weber's attention
in perusing the writings of Richard Baxter and Benjamin Franklin.[31] The intent was certainly to caution young people against the dangers, as Blair put
it, of "giddiness and levity." There was also the implication that the prosperous achieved prosperity through upright living and in so doing exemplified
the fruit of abiding by such standards. To that extent, the prosperous were
an exemplary category not only in wealth but also in moral character. As another writer explained a few years later, success and fortune that might at first
glance appear to be the result of good luck could in most instances be the outcome of sound judgment. And while it might be true that misfortune would
befall the wise in ways that seemed to defy the idea "that providence regulates
the affairs of men by a well-ordered economy," the proper response should
be to stimulate one's efforts and improve one's circumspection.[32] That was a
strand of thinking about the wealthy that would continue.

But it was tempered by two related arguments. One was that the wealthy
owed a responsibility not only to themselves through sober living but also to
the poor through acts of charity. "May the wealthy enjoy happiness and ease,"
a writer in the *Independent Ledger* advised in 1784. "May the prosperous enjoy
the blessings of prosperity, but in their enjoyment, let them not forget the liberal hand of Providence, which bestows on them their abundance." The writer
continued, "May they esteem all the children of men as their brethren. May
they not forget the poor and the naked, without fire and without victuals."[33]
The other argument, also drawn from biblical admonitions, cautioned that
the relationship of wealth and morality was far from perfect. "The wicked who
break through all the laws of God and man are often prosperous," Presbyterian
minister Thomas Reese counseled in a 1785 sermon, "while the righteous are
oppressed and borne down with the heaviest afflictions and calamities."[34] The
wealthy could lose their wealth through no moral failing of their own, and

they could be seduced by their desire for wealth into valuing it too much and devoting too much effort to attaining it. Nor was it lost on audiences of such preaching that the scriptures frequently held the wealthy in contempt. "Does not the Bible often present to us the very worst men in the most prosperous circumstances," a preacher asked in an 1811 sermon, "as if, by bestowing wealth on them, God meant to show how little value he sets upon it?"[35]

Although it was less common, writers occasionally went beyond assertions about the positive or negative characteristics of the wealthy to instruct those lacking wealth in what their attitudes should be toward the wealthy. An example was a version of Psalm 131 that was popular in late eighteenth- and early nineteenth-century America. The fifth verse declared, "With humane [or generous] pleasure let me view the prosperous and the great; malignant envy let me fly with odious self-conceit."[36] It was important not only to avoid being envious of the rich but also to keep one's efforts to be like them in perspective. "A moderate desire for riches is unquestionably what we ought to have," a writer observed in 1816. "It excites emulation and industry in a fair and honorable way; it destroys many a violent passion that idleness might foster."[37]

That was undoubtedly how the wealthy hoped they would be viewed. Biographies, obituaries, and directories put them in the best possible light, not only as captains of finance and industry but also as models of respectability and examples of what ordinary people might try to achieve. An 1845 biographical directory of some 300 New York City residents with wealth estimated at $100,000 or more, for example, spared nothing in emphasizing the extent to which all who knew them respected these citizens. They were beloved and esteemed by their friends and acquaintances, and in wider circles it seemed evident that the directory wanted them to be known for their vigor, purity, good judgment, hard work, independence, and sparkling brilliance.[38]

These arguments together provided the broad parameters in which subsequent discussions of wealth's relation to morality took place. The parameters as such were necessarily broad, providing a basis for thinking that wealth could be a conceptual space in which high morals could be found and thus emulated or could be a location for behavior that served only as a negative example of what to do. It was rarely the case that the wealthy were simply admired or simply despised. It was more common, as with other groups that symbolized differences from the cultural majority, for specific moral associations to be attached to the wealthy, which in turn provided messages about desirable and undesirable behavior for ordinary people.

The wealthy as a social category were different, though, in important respects from most other minority groups that were set apart from the majority. The wealthy had resources that carried implications for the rest of society. The wealthy could be a threat to society in the same way that lunatics and fanatics could be, but the threat posed by the wealthy was different. It was primarily the threat of using their wealth to exercise political power and to manipulate economic affairs to their advantage. The wealthy also differed from other minority groups in bearing special responsibilities to society. They were a social category that was not only different but also integrally related to the wider society.

These questions about the potential threats and moral responsibilities of the wealthy were the ones that surfaced again and again as the population increased, the economy grew, and the distribution of wealth changed. The view that the wealthy were moral exemplars by virtue of good planning and hard work did more to suggest that other people should look up to them than it did to specify anything else that the society might expect or demand from the wealthy. The starting point for those other considerations was the argument that the wealthy should help the poor through charitable contributions. An additional argument was that the wealthy should be of service to the society. Those arguments took the form of moral appeals but stopped short of suggesting that the wealthy should be coerced into doing more. Coercion required a different understanding of the ordinary, nonwealthy person who could make political claims on the wealthy. That was the challenge the nation faced as wealth became increasingly concentrated and the wealthy became increasingly powerful.

The Gilded Age

The half-century preceding the profiteering scandals during and immediately following World War I featured three arguments about the wealthy and their relationship to common, ordinary people. The first appealed to a common sense of basic underlying morality. This argument held that the wealthy were fundamentally like everyone else, only more so in the sense that they were moral individuals whose wealth reflected their moral instincts and whose resources enabled them to be good citizens like everyone else except to a greater degree. This was the argument on which appeals to the wealthy to engage in charity and public service were made and on which the claim was made that the wealthy fulfilled a public service simply by producing and transporting goods. It required no sharp distinctions to be made between the wealthy and nonwealthy and for that reason reflected the view that people could move up or down a kind of open, continuous scale of financial success. The second argument resembled the first insofar as the wealthy and nonwealthy were considered to be essentially the same, but this argument held that human relationships were more often governed by immorality than by morality. This was the view in which concerns about selfishness, greed, miserliness, hoarding, manipulation, and corruption came to the fore. The implication for ordinary people was that they needed to be cautious in their own behavior, support laws against the ill effects of inevitable immoral behavior, and be particularly vigilant toward the rich whose riches could be associated with immorality and perhaps inflict greater damage to society because of the resources at their disposal. To the extent that laws and law enforcement applying especially to the wealthy could be proposed, this argument required identifying immoral behavior of which the rich might be accused, such as fraudulent bookkeeping and whatever side effects might be associated with greed.

The third argument differed from the other two in being neutral with respect to the question of whether the wealthy and ordinary people were more likely to exhibit moral behavior or immoral behavior. This argument allowed for the possibility that wealth attained in perfectly moral ways could nevertheless constitute a moral problem because it contributed negatively to the collective well-being of the society. It was a difficult argument to make and thus was most often voiced in the context of concerns about the wealthy having undue political influence, such as in being used to shape elections, trade, and economic policies. Although it was grounded in democratic assumptions about the rights of common people for self-government, it surfaced with greatest emphasis in discussions of the economy and especially of remedies that might be needed to recover from and prevent economic crises.

One of the most remarkable aspects of the Panic of 1873, which sunk the nation in an economic depression that lasted for five years during which some 18,000 businesses failed and unemployment rose above 8 percent, was the number of editorials, commentaries, and essays that interpreted it in moral terms. *The Gilded Age*, published to great acclaim that year by Mark Twain and Charles Dudley Warner, in which the authors satirized greed and corruption, undoubtedly contributed to this interpretation. Twain and Warner spared nothing in ridiculing the fickle, gullible, speculative get-rich-quick schemes of protagonists in the far reaches of Missouri and on Wall Street and in the nation's capital who anticipated fortunes from sketchy investments in land and railroads and in contrasting them with sober-minded persons (many of them women) who behaved conservatively, made cautious decisions, and worked hard with few expectations of acquiring wealth.[39] But serious writers who drew no connections between the novel and the events on Wall Street viewed the panic as the result of some deficit in the American soul that had been festering during Reconstruction and that now needed to be diagnosed and quickly excised. It was appropriately termed a panic, they said, because it arose from an era of melancholy and greed, a time of moral decay that undermined the basic trust and spirited optimism on which the nation's prosperity depended.

Calling it a panic put the onus of responsibility for the collapse on the general public instead of the wealthy few. The general public in this instance was by no means the entire population but the relatively large number of farmers, shopkeepers, and small-town merchants who had been coaxed with promises of high returns and threats of financial losses into purchasing the bonds on which further expansion of the nation's railway system depended. It was the small-time investor on whose goodwill the economy rested, and it was the lack of judgment on the part of these investors that accounted for unrealistic expectations in the first place and a failure of nerve when difficulties arose. To the extent that the wealthy who principally owned and controlled the railroads and the banks were culpable, theirs were mistakes of the same kind as those of the general public and, indeed, in some interpretations the result rather than the cause of the public's mistrust.

In the first days of the panic the discussion about responsibility focused on whether the moral decay from which the panic presumably arose was broadly characteristic of the public, such that the panic was likely to continue and worsen, or whether there was enough goodwill that it would likely be brief. Instead of focusing on differences between the wealthy and nonwealthy, the discussion drew on contrasts that were familiar in other contexts. The trouble was identified as conflict between, on the one hand, reasonable people who took the ups and downs of life in stride and, on the other hand, excitable people who, like religious enthusiasts and fanatics, followed their passions. If only the public would quit acting like maniacs and return to its right mind, critics said, all would be well. It was a difference between people who understood that life was imperfect but who stayed the course and those who expected moral perfection and lost all hope when that was not achieved—"a difference," *Appleton's Journal* editor Charles Henry Jones declared, "as wide as between reason and lunacy."[40]

The side that anticipated the worst had already been warning that something bad was likely to happen. "The great battle of our day," Henry Ward Beecher wrote in anticipation of the panic that would occur seven months later, "is to be the battle of money. The combinations of capitalists, the consolidation of railroads, the enormous concentration of money in comparatively few hands, is raising up a plutocracy which threatens to overmatch legislatures, courts, and all private interests that may stand in the way of these gigantic corporations." The years Beecher had spent fighting for abolition left no doubt in his mind about the importance of politics and that any reforms to curb the rise of plutocracy would require political intervention. And yet the role that moral persuasion had played in the abolition movement convinced him that the battle of money was also basically to be fought on moral grounds. What was most urgently needed, he said, was a "home sentiment of honesty." That was the antidote to the deterioration of moral convictions he believed was evident in the daily "evasions, overstatements, understatements, prevarications, [and] misrepresentations that like dust settle on everything." Honesty was needed both at the centers of power and among the common people. "The moral education of the whole community," he argued, "must, after all, be the grand remedy." [41]

Once the panic had taken place, the tone of moral arguments shifted. While the moral climate of the nation at large remained of interest, it became more likely for distinctions to be drawn between the wealthy and those lacking in wealth. If greed that led to financial speculation was the specific offender, its source was the wealthy—especially the newly wealthy—whose example caused ordinary people to become greedy and invest too readily in get-rich schemes. The wealthy and nonwealthy were also distinguishable in terms of the panic's consequences. Expressing mock sorrow for financier Jay Cooke, who was at the center of the panic and "has to give up his marble palace," an editorial published shortly after the panic began lamented that "thousands of families who were comfortably off before are in poverty now, and, through all the coming years of their earthly pilgrimage, aged men and women who have been thus deceived or misled will have to struggle with extreme want and its attendant miseries."[42]

The sharpest contrast to moralizing interpretations that attributed the panic to greed was one that conceptualized both the wealthy and the general public as participants in a wider, integrally connected system of social relationships. This approach advanced an understanding of society as a moral order and in so doing was able to posit what was socially desirable or undesirable in ways that were not reducible merely to considerations of economic productivity. One of the clearest expositions of this approach was an 1876 essay on the centenary of American politics by William Graham Sumner. Sumner, who went on to become a president of the American Sociological Association and be remembered for his work on folkways and ethnocentrism, had spent the 1860s after graduating from Yale as an Episcopal priest before returning to Yale in 1872 as a professor of political economy and in 1876 offering the nation's first course in sociology. Sumner's essay did not attempt to offer a full-blown sociological account but did include several key arguments that cast the current economic crisis in a distinct light.

Sumner described the wealthy as a "class," using the term that had become common in British and German social theory but was rarely employed by American scholars. The presence and prominence of a wealthy class in America, he suggested, derived from a characteristic of the society rather than simply from industriousness and upright living; namely, the fact that America offered few opportunities for men of ambition to serve and gain respect in other ways such as holding public office. The pursuit of wealth in Sumner's view was clearly an inferior alternative. "Wealth offers no honorable social power," he wrote, "it awakens no intellectual or political ambition . . . it means simply the ability to buy what they want, men or measures, and to enjoy sensual luxury." And as an inferior pursuit, "the dominion of wealth over the energies of the nation" was excessive; it "absorbed far too much of the ambition of the nation." In short, the wealthy class was problematic not because of particular moral failings on the part of wealthy individuals but because its size and composition were not in the best interest of the nation.[43]

Sumner's view of the general public differed from descriptions of it as being guided strictly by greed or being victimized by the wealthy. He conceded that the people were currently "demoralized" but meant that in the sense of being discouraged rather than in the sense of deviating from high moral standards. He disagreed with arguments suggesting that public morals were degenerating. The words he used to describe the nonwealthy did not focus on their lack of wealth or their moral character. Instead, the public was the "public will"—the "political will of the nation." It was in need of instruction and guidance but was basically pure and characterized by sound judgment. Cast in these terms the people were the electorate, the citizens in whom democratic constitutional government entrusted political rights. They were the public to whom the wealthy were ultimately responsible to serve or to be criticized for not serving. In defining the terms in this way, Sumner placed the discussion of wealth squarely in the tradition of democratic theory and in so doing suggested that a political response to the wealthy class was appropriate.[44]

Sumner's *What Social Classes Owe to Each Other* (1884) presented in greater detail and with added complexity his understanding of the wealthy class's place in society. Rejecting what he regarded as an outmoded view of society based on fixed estates rooted in sentiment and governed by relationships of patronage and fealty, he regarded contractual relationships among free and independent citizens who respected one another's self-reliance and dignity as the basis of society. Sumner insisted that ordinary individuals were ultimately responsible for their own welfare. It was as if the community said to them, "We give you every chance that anyone else has. Now come along with us; take care of yourself, and contribute your share to the burdens which we all have to bear in order to support social institutions." Citizens' expectations about the state's involvement in their lives should thus be minimal. "The state gives equal rights and equal chances just because it does not mean to give anything else. It sets each man on his feet, and gives him leave to run, just because it does not mean to carry him." It followed, Sumner argued, that, contrary to what one might hear from the pulpit, "it is not wicked to be rich." Indeed, he believed, everyone would like to be rich, and it was only natural to be envious of the rich.[45]

If there was nothing inherently wrong with the wealthy monopolizing sectors of the economy and accumulating huge fortunes, Sumner nevertheless regarded the wealthy arrogating power to themselves and becoming a plutocracy as a potential threat to democracy. "The wealthy class has attempted to merge itself in or to imitate the feudal class," he wrote. "The consequence is that the wealth-power has been developed, while the moral and social sanctions by which that power ought to be controlled have not yet been developed." There needed to be a moral code that upheld truth and fidelity and despised lying and stealing with as much gravity as the code of honor on which the feudal system had been built. Moral resolve capable of producing good legislation was sorely needed. "The task before us . . . calls for fresh reserves of moral force and political virtue from the very foundations of the social body."[46]

Sumner's discussion attempted only briefly to outline how the moral resolve he thought the nation needed was to be called forth. It had to consist of
something more than denunciations of the wealthy from pulpits and in newspapers, he believed, perhaps including an awakening of citizens through cooperative efforts and organizations to elect better legislators. The real strength
of the nation lay in its ordinary people who enjoyed their freedom and somehow took care of their families, but beyond that it was hard to say much more.
Sumner called them "the forgotten man and the forgotten woman." They
worked, voted, and prayed. They sometimes grumbled at the dinner table but
rarely talked politics. Their names did not get in the newspapers except when
they married or died. They were obscure—forgotten.[47]

But it was the forgotten men and women who did organize in hope of
bringing political pressure to bear on the rich. By 1884 stirrings of what was to
become the populist movement were already evident in scattered grassroots
antimonopoly organizations. The antimonopolists, as their name implied,
identified the "other" against whom they were organized less as wealthy individuals or as a wealthy class but as the large corporations, particularly the railroads and banks, over which ordinary people had little control. Antimonopoly
sentiment was strongest in the midwestern states and took on a rural and
regional cast in opposing corporations located on the East Coast. Antimonopolists distinguished farmers and small-town residents as their primary
constituents in opposition to urban consumers, differentiated themselves as
native-born Americans from immigrants who they claimed were undercut-
ting established wage rates, and defined themselves as law-abiding citizens
against criminals who were no better than moral lepers. They favored government regulation of the railroads and currency and wanted public lands to be
disposed of only to settlers instead of to absentee landlords.

Although the antimonopoly movement was short lived, it gave rise to arguments in the 1890s that focused less on the morality or immorality of individuals and more on the moral implications of economic inequality itself.
It was in this context that statistics about the distribution of wealth began
being included systematically in discussions about equitable government policies. Kansas populist William A. Peffer, who served in the U.S. Senate from
1891 to 1897, exemplified the use of such statistics in an 1891 publication in
which he observed that the average wealth of the top 1.4 percent of families
was $238,135 while the average of the next 9 percent was only $6,250, and that
of the bottom 90 percent was a mere $968. Peffer further provided statistics
showing that farm incomes were decreasing while income derived from farm
mortgages and government bonds was increasing. Deep, dark lines between
the wealthy and everyone else were already visible, he argued, and were "becoming more and more conspicuous from year to year."[48]

Viewed in those terms, the nation's wealth was a zero-sum game: the more
the wealthy got, the less there was for everyone else; and if everyone else was

becoming poorer, it was because the wealthy were becoming wealthier. Peffer called it a "gigantic system of spoliation" that had to be stopped.[49] The reason for calling it that, in his view, was that the "money power"—holders of great wealth—was always consulted whenever financial legislation was discussed. It had been that way during the Panic of 1873 and it remained so regardless of which political party was in power. Peffer left no doubt that the problem was not only political but also moral. The wealthy, he said, were devoid of conscience; they preyed on the failures of others; they were a pampered aristocracy living in splendid homes and masquerading as philanthropists and patriots while despoiling the nation and robbing the poor.[50]

Peffer's arguments were typical of the ones that circulated widely in populist newspapers and pamphlets, many of which were inflected with deeply moral and religious language. What could account for the present discontent, a contemporary of Peffer's asked; was it "a wave of mere fanaticism" or a desire to be rich and live at ease? It was instead a growing awareness that the present "degradations and sufferings" were the result of "legalized spoliation practiced by many of the wealthy-independent few." Their very souls were controlled by an "intense unconquerable and almost infinite passion for accumulation." It was the usurper under which "all the nobler qualities and attainments of the soul" perished; the passion that caused "the finer and truer sympathies and reciprocities of being and of life, and the grand principles of truth, virtue, honor, religion, hope, faith, [and] charity" to die. If the problem, as the writer claimed it to be, was the fault of the entire economic and political system and thus required a political solution, the wealthy were nevertheless guilty of "satanic idolatry."[51]

An alternative view that could be advanced in equally biblical terms held—perhaps facetiously—that the wealthy should be pitied rather than condemned. Why, after all, would anyone aspire to be wealthy, Pulitzer Prize–winning editor William Allen White asked. The average citizen in White's hometown of Emporia, Kansas, he argued, could live happily on an income of $75 a month, which was plenty to pay for a good house, supply meals and clothing for the family, and leave enough extra for reading materials and an occasional vacation. In contrast, the wealthy person was consigned to a life of grief: purchasing more clothing for the children than was good for them, fretting about their failures, spending nerve-shattering evenings at community meetings, and facing scandals if tempted to engage in politics. The last thing a person should want, he declared, was wealth. Wealth was "no longer a badge of respectability."[52]

Closer to the nation's centers of wealth, two arguments about its uses and abuse vied for attention as the Gilded Age drew to a close. One justified the accumulation of wealth as long as it was devoted to charity and not allowed to accumulate too long. Andrew Carnegie's "gospel of wealth," which he articulated in an 1889 essay, drew praise from the many who hoped it would stimulate the largesse of others in the philanthropic community.[53] "His doctrine of the surplus is sound," a Methodist writer declared, stating that the possessor of great wealth should administer it for the good of the community from which it derives.[54] Besides encouraging philanthropy, the gospel of wealth promulgated the view that wealth is a burden for the person who possesses it and a source of debauchery for that person's children. For the wealthy and nonwealthy alike, Carnegie's principal advice was modest, unostentatious living.

The other argument focused less on the wealthy than on the political uses of wealth. Concerns about plutocracy emphasized that the common people were served by democracy and endangered by plutocracy. Popular discussions of plutocracy, though, provided more colorful descriptions of the faults and foibles of the rich than they did of how ordinary people contrasted with the rich. The implicit contrasts were expressed mostly in criticisms of plutocracy. The plutocrats were shallow, pretentious, and snobbish. They tried to appear well versed in the arts and literature but were not. They overdid it in purchasing fine houses and lavish jewelry. They desperately wanted the respect that the aristocracy of Europe had once commanded, but they were more like mongrels than blue bloods.[55]

Arguments against the political uses of wealth took tangible form in efforts to curb corruption. One of the more interesting was led by Reverend Dr. Charles H. Parkhurst of the Madison Square Presbyterian Church in New York City against the graft and organized crime associated with Tammany Hall. Although Tammany Hall's influence in New York politics continued long after reforms were instituted in the 1890s, Parkhurst's campaign, which involved the newspapers, women's organizations, and churches, emphasized the possibility of arousing moral indignation against the worst excesses of money and power. The single, simple unifying element in the movement against Tammany Hall, Parkhurst argued was that the common people—men and women, educated and uneducated, foreign born and native born—shared a conscience that distinguished right from wrong.[56]

Parkhurst's understanding of conscience was at heart theological. To the extent that ordinary people were defined and united through a shared conscience, it was from the God-given human capacity to respond to the "reviving spirit" of divine grace and as a result to be instructed and encouraged in moral purpose. People could fail to respond because of having turned away from God—Parkhurst said there were situations and pursuits that could become "conscience pulverizers"—but for the most part a shared conscience, he believed, was common among ordinary people. It pertained equally to the wealthy except in instances of corruption such as those practiced by Tammany Hall.[57]

In addition to this theological understanding of conscience, discussions grounded in the emerging fields of psychology and sociology were beginning to define another feature of the common people that also implied ideas about the wealthy. This was the idea that human behavior was basically driven by what could variously be called common sentiments, a collective consciousness, shared feelings, sympathy, or a tendency toward imitation—what sociologist Franklin Henry Giddings called a subjectively shared "consciousness of kind." Scholars debated whether these shared feelings were an inevitable, perhaps biological, aspect of human evolution or whether they could be guided through education and research. There was, however, a way to imagine that these shared sentiments were the key to understanding the public's relationship to the rich. It was only natural that sentiments toward the rich should be favorable, even envious, the argument went: simply put, the common person looked up to the rich and looked down on the poor. That was socially beneficial to the extent that it encouraged the average person to work hard in hopes of becoming financially successful; it was harmful to the extent that it increased the power of the wealthy.[58]

The Progressive Era

The distinctions popularly drawn between the wealthy and ordinary Americans during the first years of the twentieth century were as mixed as the ones preceding them. Evidence pertaining to the concentration of wealth demonstrated that the wealthy were indeed a small minority of the population, and, despite Carnegie's argument that the wealthy should live inconspicuously, it was apparent to anyone who might be thinking about it that the wealthy were different from everyone else in where they lived, how they lived, and the influence of the corporations they owned. If there were lessons to be learned and identities to be gained for ordinary people through the contrasts with the wealthy, it was mostly that the public should avoid greed, mind their own business, and be honest. In so doing the public would inevitably ensure that democracy would remain strong and that whatever excesses the wealthy might exhibit would be kept in check. This was one of the hopes undergirding the pervasive optimism of the Progressive Era.

The sense of common moral purpose among ordinary people was reinforced by frequent discussions about the dangers posed by the wealthy engaging in corrupt practices and becoming a plutocracy. The wealthy may have been admired, but newspapers, sermons, and fiction castigated them as cold, heartless persons who ran soulless corporations and pursued superficial pleasures.[59] The nonwealthy increasingly acquired a collective identity in contrast to the wealthy as the "common man" and through leaders who sought public office by describing themselves as commoners. The emerging identity of a respectable middle class was in this sense a political as well as a cultural project. Nonwealthy persons as the common man were a constituency that could be appealed to for political purposes that sometimes included arguments against the political influence of the rich.

The basic characteristic of the common, ordinary American, as contrasted with the rich, was not the average family's relatively meager standard of living; it was said to be a superior appreciation of commonsense morality, which included such simple virtues as caring for the good of one's family, neighbors, and community. The wealthy, in contrast, were driven by greed, which was an overriding, singular passion that displaced these simple virtues. Few descriptions drew the contrast as sharply as *The Common Lot* (1904), the widely acclaimed novel by realist writer Robert Herrick, most of whose career was spent in Chicago and whose previous work included *The Memoirs of an American Citizen*, which chronicled the rise of a predatory meatpacking tycoon. Herrick patterned *The Common Lot* on the biblical story of the prodigal son. The novel's protagonist Jackson Hart is a young architect who has failed to receive a substantial inheritance from a wealthy uncle, devotes himself to earning his own fortune, becomes corrupt, builds a flimsy apartment building that catches fire and causes a large loss of life, narrowly escapes a grand jury indictment, and in the end returns to the "common lot" as a poorly paid draftsman. Critics hailed the book because it depicted a character with whom any reader could identify. As an example of how important symbolic boundaries are dramatized by movement back and forth across them, the protagonist's rise into the ranks of the wealthy and subsequent fall allowed his experiences and his reflections on them to instruct the reader in the moral dilemmas involved. The personal transformation associated with the return to the common lot includes the veritable return of his soul, which replaces his parasitic self, and a cleansing of his greed induced debasement. The story, one of the book's reviewers observed, was "a vivid example of the numbing process which goes on in the soul in our greed for success and the symbol of that success, money."[60]

William Allen White's novel *A Certain Rich Man* (1909) drew a similar contrast in its fictional cradle-to-grave account of financier John Barclay. Like *The Common Lot*, the book sold well, was widely reviewed, and served as grist for Sunday sermons. Social gospel preacher Washington Gladden went so far as to compare it favorably with *Uncle Tom's Cabin*. "In its ethical and its social significance," he wrote, it "is the most important work of fiction that has appeared lately in America." The book was less adroitly plotted than *The Common Lot*, but White's prominence as a spokesperson for the Midwest allowed the book to be understood as a commentary on the rich from ordinary people. The protagonist's small-town roots particularly invited that interpretation, providing an element of simplicity and homeliness as well as an intimate commitment to the townspeople that contrasted with the unscrupulousness and selfishness associated with Barclay's financial success. Toward the end of the book Barclay experiences a moment of self-reflection in which the biblical statement from Proverbs, chapter 14, verse 34, "Righteousness exalteth a nation, but sin is a reproach to any people," comes to mind, prompting him to articulate his commonplace understanding of righteousness. It "was not piety—not wearing your Sunday clothes to church and praying and singing psalms; it was living honestly and kindly and charitably and dealing decently with everyone in every transaction."[61]

No figure in public office did more to cultivate that sense of the common people having a distinct, fundamentally moral identity than William Jennings Bryan. Remembered for his role in the 1925 Scopes trial, Bryan was better known during and after his years in Congress as the "great commoner" who championed the interests of the common people by opposing the gold standard, favoring free silver, and challenging the power of big money. He richly embellished his speeches with religious language that contributed to its popular appeal. The moneyed interests in his view were an abominable evil against whom a holy war had to be waged. The common people were not only the victims in that scenario but also the warriors. To a greater extent than many of his contemporaries, Bryan praised the common people by associating their courage with the sacrifices of fallen soldiers. "We cannot afford to degrade the common people of this land," he declared. "They are the people who in time of war bare their breasts to a hostile fire in defense of the flag. Go to Arlington or to any of the national cemeteries, see there the plain white monuments which mark the place where rest the ashes of the nation's countless dead."[62] Anticipating the arguments against war profiteers during World War I, Bryan contrasted the nation's countless dead with the wealthy whose wealth excuses them from military duties. "They are the ones who make contracts, carefully drawn, providing for the payment of their money in coin, while the government goes out, if necessary, and drafts the people and makes them lay down upon the altar of their country all they have." In contrast to the wealthy, "the people who fight the battles are largely the poor, the common people of the country; those who have little to save but their honor, and little to lose but their lives."[63]

In 1901 Bryan founded a newspaper that he continued to publish from Lincoln, Nebraska, until 1923 under the title *The Commoner*. The inaugural issue provided one of the clearest expositions of his understanding of the common people. They were the people who fight the nation's battles in time of war, he said, returning to his earlier theme. They were "the great body of the population" as distinguished from "the comparatively few, who, for one reason or another, withdraw themselves from sympathetic connection with their fellows." They were industrious, intelligent, patriotic, self-reliant, and independent. At the same time they recognized in their daily lives the ties binding them together with people sharing a common lot and a common hope. They were sometimes called "the middle classes," meaning that paupers and criminals, on one hand, and, on the other hand, those who considered themselves too high were excluded. He conceded that a person of wealth could be included among the common people if the wealth had been attained honestly and legally. But that caveat implied a more aspersive view of wealth. Bryan defined the common people as much as by whom they were not as by whom they were. They

FIGURE 19. *The Little Boy and the Big Boys*, 1901, showing the common people bullied by giant trusts. Drawn by Frederick Opper. Library of Congress Prints and Photographs Division, Washington, DC.

were not the ones Jesus denounced for devouring widows' houses while offering longwinded prayers. They were not the people who excluded themselves because of money or birth. They were not the aristocracy or the plutocrats toward whom the public sometimes fawned. They were "not seeking to get their hands into other people's pockets." They did not "imagine themselves made of a superior kind of clay." In short, they were not the wealthy.[64]

During the following decade as muckraking journalists exposed scandals about the nation's trusts and corporate monopolies, the common people served as a point of reference for that which was homey and wholesome, democratic, and pure. Bryan spoke and wrote of them constantly in his numerous stump speeches, lectures, and editorials. The common people, he said, included about 95 percent of the population: farmers, artisans, mechanics, laborers, physicians, teachers, and most merchants, newspaper publishers, and lawyers. He reminded audiences that Abraham Lincoln said the Lord must have loved the common people because he made so many of them. The common people had gladly listened to Jesus, he claimed, and now gladly read their Bibles. It was the goodness of the common people that ensured the goodness of the nation's democracy and indeed its very survival. Arrayed against the common people were the trusts and the plutocrats.

Moneyed interests controlled the big newspapers, Bryan contended; they chloroformed their readers while the corporations picked the people's pockets. But the smaller newspapers popularized the idea of the common people by printing Bryan's speeches, reprinting his essays, and publishing their own editorials. Papers in places like Willmar, Minnesota; Burlington, Vermont; Logan, Utah; and Sacred Heart, Oklahoma, reminded readers of how the common people had opposed tyranny in biblical times and in the history of Europe. The common people were now an army engaged in a money battle against the gold army's soldiers. Other countries might be ruled by aristocrats to the point that the common people were demoralized, but in America the common people were bold, spirited, energetic, forceful, vigorous, stout of heart, and filled with purpose.

If Bryan popularized the common people as an ideal, the person who most closely came to be viewed as its fulfillment was Theodore Roosevelt. A person in reality born to wealth, Roosevelt's struggles with asthma, his cultivation of a robust western persona, and the fame he earned with the Rough Riders at the Battle of San Juan Hill, as well as the progressive policies he articulated during his years as president, fashioned him into an epitome of the common people. Although he cultivated that image and used it many times to his advantage, it was not until he was out of office that he gave his most candid reflections on the topic of wealth. In 1911 at the Pacific Theological Seminary in Berkeley, California, Roosevelt delivered the Earl lectures on the topic of "Realizable Ideals," published the following year as a book. Tasked with speaking as a fellow Christian to an audience composed mostly of Christian preachers, Roosevelt took the occasion to engage in sermonizing of his own and to urge the assembled clergy to speak forthrightly about the pressing ethical and social issues of the day.

Roosevelt began the lectures by challenging the notion he believed was present in many houses of worship that money was too unimportant or too improper a topic to be discussed. It was his view that money was essential to life and therefore should be considered carefully and openly. It was further evident as he explained his views that they were complicated. In an anecdote reminiscent of Marx's observation that a family living in a hut was likely to be content until a mansion went up next door, Roosevelt recalled a family of modest means that made itself miserable by trying to imitate the finery of one of its wealthy neighbors. The trouble with multimillionaires, he said, was not so much that they formed powerful trusts but that ordinary people spent too much time and effort trying to be like them. Ninety-five percent of the damage the wealthy person could do to the rest of the population, he figured, "rests with us and not with him" because the damage was subjective rather than objective. "I shall preach as an ideal neither to truckle to nor to hate the man of mere wealth, because if you do either you admit your inferiority in reference to him." The 5 percent of damage remaining Roosevelt attributed to the wealthy who made money without contributing to the social good. The ones who built up great businesses and completed railroads across the continent he held in high regard. The others did need to be reined in both by laws and by public opinion. They were scoundrels and should be regarded as such. "In addition to the law and its enforcement we must have the public opinion which frowns on the man who violates the spirit of the law even although he keeps just within the letter."[65]

Roosevelt's remarks expressed the major arguments about wealth and the wealthy that preceded the discussions of profiteering during World War I. First was that the wealthy were a small percentage of the population that was recognized as different, elevated, and generally envied if not also admired. Second was that the wealthy were unproblematic as long as they stayed within the law and contributed positively to the general good. Third was that the wealthy sometimes did break the law and needed to have the law enforced and public opinion mobilized against them. The conception of the common person evident in these arguments was that ordinary people were similar to wealthy people in that both desired to accumulate money; ordinary people needed to guard against feeling inferior to wealthy people; and, as Roosevelt spelled out in the rest of his lectures, men needed to be good husbands and fathers and sons, displaying character that included virtue, decency, and strength, and women needed to be good mothers and wives and daughters, understanding their main responsibilities to be realized in the home.

The stance from which Roosevelt viewed America, standing as it were above the society and looking down on all its components, conditioned his views with an appearance of ambivalence but also illuminated the complexities involved. In his 1916 autobiography Roosevelt acknowledged the frequency with which attacks on the rich had occurred during his administration, almost as if those attacks underscored the symbolic importance of the divide between the wealthy and nonwealthy. "The loud-mouthed upholder of popular rights who attacks wickedness only when it is allied with wealth," he complained, "has either a warped mind or a tainted soul, and should be trusted by no honest man." But almost in the same breath Roosevelt acknowledged the plight of workers living in tenement houses and conceded that his administration had not gone far enough in exercising government control of corporations. It was too often true, he said, that the desire for respectability turned into snobbish worship of swollen, effortlessly attained wealth.[66]

The complexities of wealth evident in Roosevelt's views resembled the ones that religious leaders articulated as well. That Christianity should be "muscular," led by strong men of the kind that Roosevelt personified, suggested that men of all ranks should be taking an active leadership role in congregations. Preaching that emphasized the "social gospel" of ministry to the urban poor stressed the importance of churches advocating for social justice and the alleviation of poverty. It was possible but difficult to embrace the work of organized labor and to endorse government controls of industry when churches depended as heavily as they did on the support of wealthy donors. It was safer to frame criticisms in moral terms, noting the disparities separating the wealthy from everyone else and decrying the excesses of outlandish wealth. True Christianity in these terms could be "manly" in its respect for brotherly love against a world "intoxicated with lust of power and greed."[67]

These were among the arguments and contentions in which the questions of war profits and price controls emerged during the half-decade prior to the Justice Department's raids in 1920. As the American public contemplated the nation becoming involved in the war, the contrast between the common people and the wealthy that had been expressed in populist appeals and in muckraking journalism became more sharply articulated, especially in media geared toward working- and middle-class readers. Bryan's *Commoner* newspaper was one such outlet. Another was *The Day Book*, a daily penny-per-issue newspaper published in Chicago starting in 1911 and targeted specifically to the 95 percent of the population that comprised laborers, farmers, and shopkeepers. *Commoner* and *Day Book* editorials cast the war as an adventure benefiting the rich at the expense of ordinary people. A 1914 *Day Book* essay, for example, explained: "The men who provoke war, prepare for war and levy taxes on the people to pay for war don't do the killing and getting killed. That is done by the young men who come from the loins of workingmen on farms and in cities."[68] In 1916, as Congress debated "preparedness" appropriations, *Commoner* pages supplied readers with dozens of editorials and letters expressing "the people's" opposition. Writers cast the topic as conflict between "Big Business," the wealthy, an ammunition trust, the steel trust, bullies, braggarts, and pistol-toting militarists, on one side, and, on the other side, millions of toiling, peace-loving common people in danger of being maimed and dying, guided by reason, following the "Prince of Peace," and minding their own business.[69] Another voice was the Nonpartisan League, the Midwest and Pacific Northwest organization of farmers, laborers, and small-town business leaders that opposed America's entry into World War I and for its efforts was charged with harboring pro-German sentiment bordering on sedition. The league's *Nonpartisan Leader* published numerous news articles, editorials, and political cartoons accusing its opponents of being pawns of East Coast profiteers. Readers received advice on how to cut out profiteers when purchasing shoes, tires, and farm equipment and were treated to homespun verse, such as "Little pig, don't go to market;/Stay at home if you can,/For there you will meet the profiteer—/The hog that walks like a man."[70]

One of the more interesting expressions of support for the Nonpartisan League's arguments was a letter written to House Ways and Means chair Claude Kitchin on August 10, 1918, by Amos Pinchot, a Yale-educated New York attorney who became a member of Theodore Roosevelt's inner circle, only to fall from grace by voicing strong criticisms of big business and then becoming a supporter of Woodrow Wilson and serving in 1917 as chair of the administration's War Finance Committee. In his frequent criticisms of profiteers, Pinchot conceded that they probably considered themselves patriotic but were basically driven by a stronger desire to make as much money as fast as possible and by that means separate themselves from the common lot; they should, for that reason, he argued, be encouraged to voluntarily limit their profits or, failing that, be subject to a high war profits tax. In his letter to Kitchin, Pinchot defended the Nonpartisan League's proposals to conscript wealth to support the war and its arguments against excessive profits by the large meatpacking and flour milling companies. "Many [Nonpartisan] leaders were arrested and in some instances indicted for sedition," he wrote. "Their houses were painted yellow, their business integrity was generally attacked; and a real doubt was injected into the minds of many readers of metropolitan newspapers as to whether the Nonpartisan league was better than a nest of anarchists and traitors." The attacks, he believed, represented a notable instance of "profiteer drum fire."[71]

Clearer articulation in stories about profiteers of who the common people were included discussions identifying them as miners and steelworkers and members of labor unions, as tenant farmers and sharecroppers, as suffragists, and as African Americans and recent immigrants as well as white native-born Americans. Descriptions of common people sharing the burdens of the war included appeals for workers in America to seek common ground with workers in England, France, Germany, and Russia—appeals that resonated with communist arguments and earned condemnation from the mainstream press and public officials. Calls for the common people to organize added numbers to union rolls and led to the organization of groups such as the Nonpartisan League. But these efforts failed to enlist anything close to a majority of the 95 percent that could be classified as common people. The difficulty, as later analyses of class consciousness and the comparative weakness in America of collectivist efforts suggested, lay in the vast economic, occupational, regional, ethnic, and racial diversity that characterized the American population.[72] It was true, as Thorstein Veblen observed in 1919, that "the great distinguishing mark of the common man is that he is helpless within the rules of the game as

FIGURE 20. *My Lad, I Envy You*, 1919, satirizing the heartless profiteer.
Drawn by Charles Frederick Peters. Library of Congress Prints
and Photographs Division, Washington, DC.

it is played in the twentieth century," but the "common lot" was also a "variegated mass" that could rarely stand up for itself "without getting on the wrong side of the established run of law and morals."[73]

The emerging imprint that became increasingly applicable to the common people was federally mandated, imposing an identity that reached into the lives of ordinary families more effectively than anything voluntarily associated with the diverse locations in which people worked. That was an identity of the common people as consumers. Wartime price controls, rationing, and voluntary food conservation drives solidified the public's identity as consumers that had already been emerging since the turn of the century in conjunction with mail-order catalogs, advertising, mass marketing, retail chains, and department stores.[74] The government's efforts to regulate domestic consumption in order to provide goods to Europe while also combating inflation touched the lives of ordinary women and men across all parts of the nation. The efforts generated conflicting accounts of whether the effects were better for the wealthy or for common people, but if anything the ensuing discussion did more to increase than reduce the salience of that division. Writers praised the price controls in particular for curbing the activities of speculators who seemed to be earning high profits while other writers complained that the regulations were being shaped by the rich to protect their own interests. Both arguments brought long-standing moral claims into the discussion, urging common people to obey the laws and voluntarily cut consumption because it was the virtuous thing to do and criticizing speculators on equally moral grounds.

Whether the effect of price controls on the lives of women was as significant for the passage of women's suffrage in 1920 as the effect of women's involvement in the paid labor force during the war is difficult to know. There was no question, however, that rising prices and the debate about how to control them affected women directly. Particularly in the role of primary purchasers of domestic goods and keepers in most instances of household budgets, women participated in the discussions about profiteering, wealth, and consumption. One of the clearest commentators on these issues was Mary Doane Shelby, who published regular essays from the perspective of a city-bred countrywoman living on a farm in the Ozarks region. "When we ceased to become producers," she wrote, referring to the fact that household goods and services were produced outside the home by canning companies and tailors and dressmakers, "automatically we became buyers." As prices increased, she said the response among women she knew was to blame trusts and intermediaries and expect that men in government would do something about it. But she soon realized that government was more intimately involved in women's lives. She found it necessary to read government bulletins, learn about statistics and the economy, and understand the need to organize. "The helplessness of the purchaser is easily understood and points directly to the strength of organization," she wrote. It was impossible for individual buyers to oppose profiteering because the profiteers were organized. "The profiteering system could not have so submerged us if it had not been for our primitive methods as unorganized consumers."[75]

Nevada suffragist Anne Henrietta Martin, who shared Shelby's concern about profiteering, took the next step toward gaining greater influence and in 1918 and 1920 ran as the first woman to do so for a seat in the U.S. Senate. Although her candidacy failed, she played a prominent role as an advocate for government reforms to reduce the high cost of living as well as to eliminate discrimination against women. The proposals on which she ran included government controls of the railroads and meatpacking industry to protect consumers from business profiteers, and a system of progressive taxes aimed at millionaires. "Taxation of wealth in proportion to ability to pay," she argued, was necessary to prevent "the continued shifting of taxes to the backs of the people in higher prices and increased cost of living."[76]

Bringing government regulations of the marketplace and moral considerations together in these ways nevertheless posed a challenge that would confront discussions of wealth and inequality in the coming years to a greater extent than at any time during the nineteenth century. Legislated regulation required precision in measurable dollars-and-cents calculations, unlike moral arguments that were usually made in terms of broad generalizations about such matters as greed or selfishness or public service, and through narratives illustrating particular examples of virtue or vice. Emergency World War I price controls set the precedent for greater government intervention in the market-place when moral arguments alone were insufficient but also demonstrated the difficulties of defining policy prescriptions in measurable economic terms. The differences between legal and moral claims had significant implications for the implicit identity of the common people that emerged in relation to discussions of wealth. Moral claims could be made—and frequently were made—in support of legal claims. But the balance between the two shifted increasingly toward legal claims as government policies played a larger role in regulating the economy. A form of resistance to those policies was to assert the value of commonsense morality as the best definition of the ordinary person's stake in the marketplace. The contrasting argument allowed that moral claims might be important in private life but regarded legal claims as being more important in public affairs, including economic transactions. The common person in this understanding was supposed to exercise moral discretion in private life but to a much greater extent became a citizen whose rights and responsibilities were defined by relationships to legal claims and mandated regulations.

The Great Depression

How the identity of the common people changed—again in contrast with the wealthy—became most evident during the 1930s as the federal government responded to the Great Depression. As had been the case during the economic crisis following the Panic of 1873, popular discussions of wealth as a problem emerged in the 1920s in conjunction with occasional bank failures and then increased with the stock market crash of 1929 and continued during the 1930s. By the time the first New Deal policies went into effect, expressions of moral outrage against the rich had again become familiar ways of defining who the common people were by negative example. Popular accounts said the wealthy took their money too seriously, while, in contrast, the common people knew how to hunker down and make the best of hard times. Families of modest means might be victims of wealthy landlords and might be viewed as people who lost everything through no fault of their own, but they were people who wanted to work and who loved their homes and families. These were familiar ways of thinking about the common people. Popular discussions did not focus as much on common people's relationship to the federal government as would be evident by the time the Great Depression was over.

In 1923 an exhaustive attempt to identify the nation's wealthiest persons demonstrated that their numbers had grown but that they were still a small minority of the population. The study identified 8,000 who were assumed to be millionaires. By 1926 estimates put the number closer to 11,000. The 1923 figures confirmed popular impressions that the wealthy were mostly concentrated in the Northeast. More than half lived in New York, Pennsylvania, and Massachusetts. Only 12 percent lived west of the Mississippi or in the South. Not only were the wealthy different in where they lived; they also were different in what they did. While the average person earned money needed to spend on consumer goods, the wealthy earned fortunes producing those goods. They produced heating oil, fuel, cars, and meat, and they owned the railroads, mines, and banks.[77]

Observers differed in how they thought the public viewed the wealthy. One interpretation—popular in New York—said the earlier animus toward the rich was gone. "With the increase in the number of millionaires, the public attitude toward them has changed," a writer for the *New York Times* explained. "Not so long since sermons on the rich man, the needle and the camel were very popular. Now it is taken for granted that the average millionaire has gained his wealth by rendering service. He has given the people something they wanted."[78] An opposing argument said the public disliked the wealthy more than ever. Essays by Arthur Train, the New York attorney whose novels became best sellers in the 1920s, typified this argument. Early in the nation's history, Train argued, the wealthy were few, were known by their neighbors, and served the public more than they harmed it. But the ones who became wealthy by founding large corporations were a different story. Corporations often harmed the public and earned the public's distrust. They were machines for making money without regard to pride and a sense of decency. It was not surprising, he said, that Theodore Roosevelt's administration had found it necessary to attack the evils of law-defying wealth and to produce much-needed reforms. Those reforms encouraged the wealthy to give more generously to charity, Train believed, and yet the public remained skeptical, questioning the wealthy's motives, morals, and religious convictions.[79]

It was arguable, too, that the wealthy were simply managing better to protect themselves from public scrutiny and thus from moral censure. "Where are the kings of yesteryear?" a writer for the *Independent* mused in 1925, referring to the captains of industry who a few years earlier were pilloried by muckraking journalists. "Bitter days [those were] when a man of great wealth was assumed to be a malefactor of great wealth, when a million-dollar bank account ceased to be a sign of virtue and became a symbol of corruption. A sad sight it was to see so many freshly dethroned potentates, their occupation gone, all dressed up and nowhere to go." It wasn't that they were any less corrupt, the writer thought. It was just that they were less visible. "Silently they shuffled out of the limelight into the shadows; they became collectors of objects of art, builders of suburban palaces, country gentlemen in Long Island, owners of tax-exempt securities."[80]

The banking failures of the 1920s were an instance in which the wealthy for the most part avoided public scrutiny. On October 7, 1925, the Central State Bank in a small midwestern town where depositors had entrusted their savings since 1887 with the bank's guarantee of their assets closed its doors, causing the loss of some $141,000 to a community in which the average family earned less than $1,000 a year. It was one of 440 state banks nationwide to close that year with liabilities in excess of $118 million. Since the end of World War I, more than 2,700 state banks with liabilities of more than $780 million had failed. Over the same period 420 national banks with liabilities totaling $225 million failed. Bank failures in Europe resulted in well-publicized arrests of high-level financiers and public officials in Germany, Hungary, Italy, and Portugal, while in the United States the failures led to a series of state and federal laws regulating the chartering of branch banks, the expansion of which was deemed to have been a principal source of banking's problems. But there was little outcry against the banks' wealthier owners. Instances in which particular individuals were blamed usually attributed bank failures to unscrupulous cashiers.[81]

The surest way for wealthy people to make news was not to cause other people to lose money but to lose their own. Robberies were certain to make news if the victims were wealthy. One of the most widely publicized was the theft of approximately $100,000 in jewelry from the Southampton home of wealthy oil operator James Hastings Snowden. Another was the brazen holdup of two wealthy couples in Los Angeles who were routed from their limousine and stripped of their cash, jewels, and clothing. It was equally newsworthy to learn of rich people brought low from unsuccessful business ventures—like the New York silk merchant forced to work as a stevedore and the wealthy real estate broker who died penniless.[82]

Lost wealth yielded ample occasions for moral commentary. When Senator Frank Brandegee of Connecticut committed suicide after losing his fortune through bad real estate investments, some saw the event as a lesson in the folly of seeking wealth. "Its slimy form broods over life like a huge eagle over a carcass, and its influence is felt in the ideals, judgments, decisions, and actions of men," one commentator wrote. "From its subterranean path issue its clouds of doubt and confusions which upset our modern life; and from it come the streams of iniquity which poison the very fabric of our civilization." Fictional accounts of wealthy people experiencing loss also provided grist for moral instruction. There was Peggy, the rich woman who lost her money but continued to invite friends for quiet conversations on Sunday evenings, demonstrating that companionship was better than money. There was Flora, the poor woman who made enemies of former friends by bragging about her daughter who married rich, only to be humiliated when her daughter left the husband for a poor man. And there was Jay Gatsby, whose corruption and demise symbol-ized the era's moral decay.[83]

The stock market crash in 1929 increased the number of opportunities for negative commentary on the wealthy. Stories of despondent millionaires com-mitting suicide filled pages alongside news about robberies. The more charita-ble accounts implied that business owners killed themselves from having to let employees go instead of from losing their money. Novels and films told of heirs and heiresses accustomed to lavish lifestyles having to work at menial jobs—and becoming better persons for their effort. As one heroine exclaimed, "Real happiness comes not in spending but in earning." True enough, others said, but the rich would probably become rich again while the jobless and home-less would continue to struggle.[84] New York University economist Lewis H. Haney offered one of the more thoughtful accounts. The trouble to be avoided next time, Haney counseled, was not the pursuit of wealth but pursuing it the wrong way. Bull markets tempted business leaders to seek "adventitious profits" at the expense of sound business practices. Then, too, were the worries and losses incurred from "wasteful and luxurious living." The chief difficulty of stock market booms was "the encouragement they give to thousands of people who desire to live without work."[85]

The wealthy's troubles were teaching them a lesson, writers like Haney sug-gested, and perhaps the lesson for everyone else was that wealth was not as de-sirable as it once may have been thought. Families that survived the Depression would be known for their thriftiness, and they would recall making do with little while struggling to hold their families together. They sometimes praised the local banker who extended their loans, but hard times made it harder to respect those who prospered. It was difficult to learn of rich investors purchas-ing dirt-cheap land, to hear of neighbors striking it rich from oil wells, to think of easy money flowing to bootleggers, and for evicted farmers to forgive the wealthy bankers who evicted them. As a farmer in Texas facing the loss of his land explained, "The law is take from the poor devil that wants a home and give to the rich. Big fish eat the little ones." Or as Woody Guthrie's "I Ain't Got No Home" put it, "Rich man took my home and drove me from my door."[86]

Indignation toward the wealthy dominated the 1933 debate in the U.S. Senate about funding for World War I veterans. The debate hinged on sup-porting or opposing the administration's proposal to reduce the federal budget by, among other things, cutting veterans benefits. Supporters argued that the measure would help Depression-ridden families by lowering taxes. Opponents argued that failing to help disabled veterans not only was callous but also would weaken incentives for future participation in the armed forces. The pre-vious administration's attack on the Bonus Army's Hooverville shantytown in the nation's capital, during which hundreds of veterans were injured or killed, was still fresh in legislators' minds. The wealthy became a target because the National Economy League, which supported the balanced budget measure, was widely viewed as a tool of wealthy individuals and corporations that were said to be hoarding capital and expecting to gain the most from lower taxes. "Their hearts are hardened by greed," one senator declared. "To promote their own interest and add to their enormous wealth they are willing to see others, no matter how worthy, endure the cruelest of hardships." Said another, "These interests are naturally selfish, and if they could shift the burden of taxation to the shoulders of others, would be glad to do so." The rich would benefit, he argued, at the expense of "the forgotten man"—the men who had worn the uniform and defended the nation, the farmer and small property owner, the person who believed in mercy, generosity, and decency.[87]

Although its supporters succeeded in passing the Economy Act of 1933, animus toward the wealthy became the rhetorical stance of the Roosevelt administration as well as of its opponents. Secretary of Agriculture Henry A. Wallace served as one of the administration's chief spokespersons. A talented scientist who became wealthy from successfully breeding high-yield hybrid corn, Wallace was nevertheless the product of his Presbyterian grandfather's social gospel preaching, a tinkerer with theosophy, and an Iowan who could speak the language of small-town residents and farmers. Unlike critics of the wealthy who inveighed mostly against corporate monopolies, Wallace took the unusual step of describing them as old-style individualistic business leaders whose nineteenth-century economic philosophy was outmoded. In its place he urged something akin to the social creed advocated in Rerum Novarum in 1891 by Pope Leo XIII and by the Federal Council of Churches in 1908. The social creed, he said, would bring agriculture and industry together through a practice of fair prices, a living wage, arbitration in labor conflicts, insurance for the unemployed and elderly, and the abolition of child labor.[88]

Having written about the moral foibles of the rich and having arguably become "the incarnate voice of the American middle class," as one commentator remarked, it was perhaps fitting that William Allen White would be an intimate observer of one of the most colorful true-life scandals involving the wealthy, and that his son would turn the event into a moral tale of his own.[89] With so much of the country struggling and so many ways to think about the gap between the rich and the poor, it took an exceptional convergence of wealth and scandal to focus the nation's attention on what it all might mean. The scandal was far less notable than the ones that had swirled around Tammany Hall, but it affected just enough of one state's prominent citizens to capture wider interest. In 1933 a prominent wealthy banker, the banker's son, and the state treasurer were indicted on conspiracy to trade in fraudulent bonds. The case, which involved the discovery in the state treasury of $1.25 million in forged bonds and warrants, prompted Governor Alf Landon (who would run for president three years later) to call out the militia and resulted in a lengthy prison sentence for the banker's son and a sentence that the banker escaped serving by killing himself. The bank was located in Emporia, Kansas, where

White lived and was friends with the banker, and the banker's son and White's son, William L. White, were about the same age and had gone to school together. In 1938 the younger White published a thinly disguised book-length fictional account of the episode.[90]

During a vacation back in Emporia while a student at Harvard, the younger White had gotten drunk, sexually assaulted his date, and only with the intervention of his father and the city attorney managed to escape arrest. The character in the book cast as the younger White is Junior, who wrestles with the moral questions raised by the bond scandal and his own experiences as a young man from a small town facing an era in which the old rules seem to be changing. "In college you drank. You shouldn't, but you did," Junior says toward the end of the book. "If you didn't get drunk and hurt someone, maybe it wasn't so bad. And about girls, of course you shouldn't do that either. It was probably wrong. But hell!" It was the same with lying and stealing. You probably shouldn't do it, but maybe you just needed the money. Nobody wanted to think about it. "Nobody was a saint!"[91]

Wallace Stegner described the book as "eloquent and powerful." It added "a chapter to the story of America, a chapter full of the twistings and turnings of men bred to a philosophy of progress and get-rich-quick dreams." Its depiction of sharpers, dubious promotion schemes, fantastic wealth, and disaster was "essentially the story of America." Junior, as the central character, represented the common person, reared to believe in the American Dream in both its economic and moral meanings, wanting to do good and live well, and yet having "lost the knack of marching up the road to perfection by a series of regular steps."[92] Moral uncertainty seemed to capture the mood of the coming generation better than the moral certitude that sometimes characterized earlier discussions of wealth. But those discussions had also been fraught with ambiguity. Wealth was always a topic that left room for differences of opinion, which meant that Americans could want it and pursue it and at the same time condemn its pursuit and its uses.

It was hard for anyone to anticipate how long the Depression would last or how deeply it would affect the public's attitudes toward wealth. Least imaginable at the start was how the massive economic reforms instituted by the New Deal might affect ordinary Americans' understandings of themselves. They were still the nonwealthy who worked for a living, or hoped to again, and they were consumers who participated in the marketplace in small ways, but they were also citizens who arguably felt victimized by the wealthy and whose lives were variously related to the federal government as never before. They were farmers who the government told how much land they could plant and harvest, they were householders who stood in breadlines and looked for employment from the Works Progress Administration, they were self-sufficient workers who wondered if what the government was doing was constitutional, and they were taxpayers who hoped the administration's tax reforms would help the poor by soaking the rich. Whether they looked to the government for jobs and assistance or worried that the government's deficits would increase their taxes, they were inextricably connected to it.

For those who believed the federal government under Roosevelt's leadership was helping them, being citizens in this newly expanded way put the government in their corner against the wealthy whom they mistrusted as swindlers, financiers, monopolists, and chiselers. "Wealth in the modern world does not come merely from individual effort," Roosevelt declared in calling for higher taxes on the rich, "it results from a combination of individual effort and of the manifold uses to which the community puts that effort." It was the "people in mass" who helped make large fortunes possible, and it was thus for their benefit that the government should impose stiff taxes on great accumulations of wealth.[93] The common people in this understanding were citizens whose commonality was expressed not only in their individuality or in their lack of wealth but also in the rights and protections they received from the federal government and the responsibilities they owed to it. They were no less diverse than before in terms of region and race and ethnicity, but there was a more centralized and standardized definition of what that meant for the average person's expectations and obligations.

Roosevelt's commanding victory in the 1936 election gave reason for later interpreters to imagine that most people viewed the federal government as their champion against the rich. In reality the public was divided, which increased the salience of how to consider the government's role in questions of wealth. A Gallup poll in 1936 showed 43 percent of respondents favoring and 57 percent opposing a constitutional amendment transferring power to the federal government to regulate agriculture and industry. A year later Gallup found respondents almost evenly divided (43 percent to 46 percent) on whether they favored or opposed the "trend towards centralizing power in Washington" by giving the federal government "greater power to regulate business, labor, and agriculture."[94]

For many Americans the federal government's involvement in their lives symbolized a reality that was not entirely welcome. To them, the government was in league with the rich, doing everything it could to keep the well heeled happy while preventing common people from following the timeworn dictates of common sense. Critics of the New Deal described a divide between working members of the middle class and public officials catering to the rich. The people in these depictions were productive and frugal farmers, small merchants, and manufacturers unified by government policies that, as former president Herbert Hoover put it, taxed, harried, and demoralized them. Even the people receiving government assistance were being hurt psychologically, as a man in Brooklyn who said he hated "government coddling" declared: "It has become very disheartening to live in these times," he said. Or as a man in Virginia put it, "Mr. Roosevelt's New Deal has been a swell deal for the rich, but a swill deal for the poor man."[95] Other descriptions likened the federal government to fascist Germany and the Soviet Union, images that put the middle class in tension with government, an inherently diverse aggregation of individuals politicized and endangered by the specter of oppression. The common people in this view were political entities whether they wanted to be or not. They were the endangered guarantors of freedom and democracy.

In 1937 Robert and Helen Merrell Lynd published a follow-up to their earlier ethnographic study of beliefs and values in Muncie, Indiana. *Middletown in Transition* reported that the Depression had done little to alter the people's basic values. The people they talked to were cautious, relatively tolerant, and intent on making the best of whatever situation they were in. They were more connected with national issues because of radio and through the same media more exposed to advertising. There was a kind of grassroots vitality that persuaded the Lynds of common folks' fundamental optimism despite living in hard times. But one difference from their earlier study was notable. Basic values were more often defined in conjunction with comments about the role of government. On the one hand, there was an "aroused conception of the possible role of government in bolstering the exposed position of labor by social legislation, including direct relief for the unemployed," and, on the other hand, an "intense suspicion of centralizing tendencies in government."[96]

An Ambiguous Legacy

These examples illustrate some of the ways in which the wealthy provided a contrasting category—an "other"—that offered ordinary, nonwealthy Americans ways to think about who we were by discussing who we were not, much like the insane helped people to define what it meant to be sane and fanatics helped to clarify what it meant to be reasonable. The wealthy differed from the rest of the population not only in having more money but also in the assumptions that pundits, preachers, columnists, public officials, and social scientists made about them. The wealthy were an unusual category because it was harder simply to look down on them than on the insane and fanatics or hucksters and certain immigrant groups. The wealthy had what everyone else presumably wanted: money, power, lavish homes, the wherewithal to live in luxury. They could be the standard to which ordinary people aspired, the most respected members of society, the best evidence that the American Dream could be attained. But popular discussions frequently set them apart negatively. Their wealth and power seemed excessive, undemocratic, perhaps immoral, and at times harmful to the well-being of society. Criticism increased during economic crises and when concentrated wealth seemed to be accumulating at everyone else's expense. The criticisms usually included moral as well as economic and political arguments. Critics said the wealthy were greedy, shallow, unfair, manipulative, perhaps guilty of fraud, and on occasion guilty of profiteering.

The criticisms reflected ideals to which ordinary people were expected to adhere. Diverse as they were economically, regionally, and ethnically, ordinary people were supposed to be honest, thrifty, charitable toward their friends and neighbors, happy to live unpretentiously, and fair in their dealings. That much they were supposed to have in common. The wealthy illustrated what could go wrong if the common people deviated from these basic values. A person obsessed with making money might appear prosperous in the short run but would surely suffer the consequences in the long run. Wealth could crowd out the simpler joys of life.

Changes in popular depictions of the wealthy had more to do with the enlarged scale of the population and the growth of industry than with the ways in which moral claims were made. Better information about assets and incomes made it possible to count the number of millionaires and to speak of skewed wealth distributions. Earlier discussions that likened the wealthy to an aristocracy shifted toward characterizing them as a plutocracy. Criticisms of individuals who happened to be wealthy became criticisms of aggregations—the wealthy class, moneyed interests, monopolies, trusts, and big business. The popular saying that corporations did not have souls expressed the difference between ordinary people and the large, impersonal machinery through which wealth was produced.

Government intervention to regulate prices, prevent profiteering, and combat plutocracy facilitated new discussions of who the common people were and how they differed from the wealthy. The common people increasingly became citizen consumers whose everyday lives were affected for better or worse by the decisions government agencies made. In addition to the basic values they shared, the common people acquired an identity in terms of the rights and responsibilities these influences implied.

How the public that started to acquire this identity during the Great Depression mobilized during World War II, how the New Deal reforms set the stage for the civil rights movement, and how Democrats and Republicans continued, respectively, to embrace and resist government intervention in the marketplace are developments that have been extensively described and debated.[97] It was possible to argue, as some did, that ordinary, middle-class Americans gradually became so used to the realities of economic inequality that the symbolic distinction historically provided by the wealthy no longer mattered. Surely it required the highly mobilized efforts of trustbusters, antimonopolists, and antiprofiteers to keep that distinction alive. And yet the evidence suggests that these mobilizations came often enough and tapped sufficiently into familiar moral scripts that discussions of who the wealthy were played a continuing role in defining the common people.

CHAPTER SEVEN

Naughty Children

MORAL INSTRUCTION BY
NEGATIVE EXAMPLE

AS MUCH AS MIDDLE-CLASS respectability may have been defined by nega-tive contrasts with hucksters, lunatics, fanatics, and people who were deviant in other respects, these were by no means the only ways in which ordinary people learned what it meant to be good and decent. Anyone who might have been asked how that was learned would have said it came from parents and teachers and other adults telling children how to behave. This was the reason for including moral instruction in the storybooks parents read to their chil-dren, in the lessons children learned in school, and in the messages religious leaders hoped children would absorb at their families' places of worship.

The question I want to explore in this chapter is whether and, if so, to what extent and how negative examples played a prominent role in the stories and lessons through which children were expected to learn what it meant to be a respectable member of society. Studies of nineteenth-century children's lit-erature leave no doubt that educators hoped children would learn the positive virtues of good living. Children's literature was above all moralistic, providing in didactic form a moral code that narrated basic values.[1] Children were ex-pected to be honest, obedient, considerate, and pleasant to be around. They learned the importance of good manners, cleanliness, doing their lessons, and dutifully performing whatever work they were asked to do. Stories of good children behaving in these ways exemplified the ideals to which boys and girls were supposed to aspire. But what about the negative examples: If the good gained clarity in contrast with the bad, how was the bad depicted? Who was cast in these negative roles? What did they do that served as examples of what not to do?

Stories about naughty boys and girls appeared routinely in nineteenth-century children's literature. Fables and rhymes intended for young listeners

featured them. Schoolchildren read about bad boys and girls. Religious magazines for young readers and periodicals for pastors and parents taught lessons about wicked children. Newspapers and magazines carried cautionary
tales about real and fictional children who went astray. Naughty children were
the "other"—the exception that illustrated the norm just as the marginal statuses of hucksters, lunatics, immigrant sectarians, fanatics, the poor, and the
wealthy did. Naughty children dramatized the symbolic boundary separating
the good from the bad by transgressing that boundary. They interacted with
good children and adults, on many occasions started out good and turned bad,
and on other occasions repented from their miscreant ways and became good.
Naughty behavior nearly always earned its own punishment either in corporal form or in misery. Depictions of naughty behavior ranged from minor to
major offenses. But naughty boys and girls nearly always stood out and assumed more interesting, colorful, and emotion-laden roles than their well-
mannered counterparts. Misbehavior was the constant reminder of what to
avoid, even as understandings of childhood evolved. Naughtiness kept up with
the times in these respects, adapting to an America that became less rural and
more urban. And by the early twentieth century naughtiness started to acquire
meanings quite different from its more traditional depictions.

The literature in which bad children were featured fell mostly into one
or another of three genres that targeted three specific audiences. The first
genre consisted of stories about boys and girls written for children who were
of *nursery* age—which meant old enough to be read to (not infants) but not
old enough to be in school (age five or six), whether they in fact were in school
or not. The second genre consisted mostly of books and periodical articles
written by clergy and educators for *parents*, offering advice about the duties
of responsible parenting. The third genre consisted of newspaper articles and
reports from civic organizations written for the general public and focusing on
juveniles, which meant children from as young as five or six to as old as fifteen
and sometimes eighteen. Each of the three genres was written for a middle-
class audience, meaning the kind of readers who would have read and perhaps
purchased books and periodicals for themselves and their children, sent or
wanted to send their children to school, may have participated in the activities
of religious organizations, and wanted their children to become respectable,
law-abiding members of the community.[2]

The history of nineteenth-century understandings of childhood has paid
considerable attention to punishment. Studies have emphasized the gradual
shift away from authoritarian styles of parenting based on the use of corporal punishment toward democratic approaches emphasizing reason, discipline, empathy, and psychological rewards and punishments. Research on
specific topics has examined schooling practices, the roles of women writers,
changing perceptions of gender, attitudes toward race, shifts in understandings about the value of children, and variations in arguments about food,

nutrition, clothing, and home furnishings. Less attention has been devoted to the question of who served as negative examples and what middle-class children learned about distancing themselves from the wrong kinds of people and activities. But those lines—those demarcations between "us" and "them"—were an important part of the learning process. Children learned not only what it meant to be good but also whom and what to consider despicable and depraved.[3]

The stories, advice books, and media accounts in which nineteenth-century readers learned about naughty children contributed to the broader tendencies in American culture to define what was respectable by maligning particular people and activities that did not conform to those expectations. Narratives featuring naughty children communicated more than simple truths about the value of being well mannered. They went a great deal further toward instilling fear and revulsion. The dark side inhabited by bad boys and girls was dangerous. It inflicted its own punishments in tears and misfortune. Those who strayed into its alien territory were an embarrassment to their parents and in ill favor with God. The danger was present for young children even in well-tempered middle-class homes. And as children matured, the lines became sharper, separating the bad from the good by location, forms of social interaction, and education.

In the Nursery

Poems, songs, picture books, and short stories for the entertainment and moral edification of young children came to be known in the late eighteenth and early nineteenth centuries as nursery rhymes and nursery tales in part because the nursery itself was coming to be an identifiable space in well-appointed middle-class homes. Nurseries were to be the places where young children slept in physical separation from their parents, kept their toys, played, and enjoyed the relative comforts of a safe environment.[4] Ideally the nursery should consist of two high-ceilinged, well-ventilated rooms, a writer in Philadelphia advised, such that children could retire to one while the other was being cleaned and could have ample space in which to play despite inclement weather. The room temperature should be carefully monitored, the furniture should be selected and arranged to avoid accidents, and the children should be supplied with age-appropriate games, maps, slates, and pencils.[5]

Whether it was possible to provide an ideal space that met these standards or not, the nursery symbolized the care that should be taken in any event to ensure that children avoided bad habits that would damage them for life. Children should be encouraged to get out of bed and dress as soon as they awakened, for example, lest they become fretful and the real evil of an injured disposition be induced. Their intake of liquids should be carefully monitored to prevent them from bedwetting. They should of course be punished, but care

FIGURE 21. *The Purloiner*, 1811. Illustration of a naughty boy in Elizabeth Turner, *The Cowslip, or More Cautionary Stories* (London: J. Harris, 1811).

should be taken to do that in a different room so as not to inadvertently associate the nursery with acts of delinquency.

Stories for and about boys and girls young enough to be in the nursery were remarkably rich in portrayals of bad children and bad behavior. The narratives featured boys and girls who were quarrelsome and wicked. They pinched, struck, and pushed other children, made life miserable for their mothers and siblings, fretted, complained, and developed bad habits.[6] They disobeyed their parents and persistently caused trouble. By the 1820s periodicals printed sermons, essays, and stories in which the behavior of children who were simply bad served as stark evidence of what good children and their parents should avoid. The story of Little Louisa, published in *Youth's Companion* in 1834, was typical. Louisa, the daughter of a poor, intemperate, ungodly man, was "very wicked." She told lies, played on the Sabbath, and stole things. A neighbor described her as "one of the worst children" he ever saw.[7] An unnamed boy rivaled Louisa's wickedness by playing where he shouldn't, making up a false story about it, and from that moment habitually telling naughty wicked lies.[8] And there was Skulking Dick and Lying Harry, whose names betrayed their evil ways.[9] Good children were warned to keep away from such company: as a poem for children in the *Episcopal Recorder* advised, "I cannot love to walk the way / Where wicked children go, / Who fear not God, and never pray— / More sinful daily grow."[10]

Although it might have seemed that children this young were too innocent or too sheltered to do much that was wrong, the stories painted a darker picture. Sweet cherubs who should have played happily and laughed agreeably were in reality sourly disposed children who pouted and said wicked words. They stamped their feet, scowled, and hit their siblings. They told lies, stole cookies, and abused their toys. The writers who wrote the stories and the parents who read them clearly had in mind that young children not only could be naughty but often were. It followed that they needed to be instructed in the error of their ways. Children who did not learn to behave when they were little would be ruined for life. Stories about bad children and about otherwise ordinary children doing bad things served to show what could happen.[11]

Late eighteenth- and early nineteenth-century messages about bad children were often communicated in sermons at worship services and prayer meetings that children were expected to attend with their parents and in religious periodicals that reprinted sermons and included essays by clergy. An example was a sermon preached to children at the Congregational Church in Greensborough, Vermont, in 1819 and reprinted in a periodical called *Youth's Religious Instructor*. The pastor began by telling the children that he was old and might die soon and that "some of you may [die] before another meeting." Children should think of the Bible, he said, as God's mighty sword, like the sword a strong man would use to kill bears and wolves that killed children, only God's sword killed children's sins instead of children themselves. "In this bright sword, the Bible, you may see your own face. How ugly and bad it will look by the side of God! He is so holy and good and you are so naughty and sinful." So much wickedness: "lying, stealing, not minding their parents and good people, breaking the Sabbath, swearing, and quarrelling."[12]

A story the same year emphasized the wickedness of naughty children who misbehaved during worship services. "When they are at meeting, they move, and laugh, and whisper, and stare, and play the whole time. When the Sabbath returns, these wicked children are sorry. They are unwilling to leave their sports to read the Bible and learn the catechism. And sometimes these wicked children get away from under the eye of their parents and begin their play before the end of the Sabbath." These wicked children were even known to avoid bedtime prayers or leave the table before their father gave thanks for the Lord's mercies. "Now my dear children, I hope you are not so wicked."[13]

"No man may put off the law of God," Webster's spelling book declared. "My joy is in His law all the day. O, may I not go in the way of evil men." Abolitionist Tayler Lewis, who memorized these words at a school near Northampton, New York, around 1808, recalled years later that the last line "brought up the idea . . . of the great divergency—the two roads then beginning to part, but with their ends so immeasurably distant; the 'way of virtue,' and the 'way of vice,' the 'upward toiling and the smooth downward path' . . . the way of danger . . . the one in which our feet might so easily incline to run."[14]

The bad behavior stories about nursery age children described aimed to show specifically by negative example what constituted good behavior. The most notable examples of bad behavior involved dishonesty. Naughty children lied to their parents about what they ate, what they may have been playing, and whom they may have hit. Lying was like a disease that started small and then spread. "Lying is a vice that grows with the growth and strengthens with the strength as soon as a child begins to know the difference between good and evil," a writer observed in 1797, "the first lie he tells is spoke with hesitation, and his countenance is crimsoned with the blush of shame; if this passes without detection he soon becomes an adept; a little, a very little practice gives him assurance, the blush is no more to be seen, the faltering in his voice is no longer heard, he finds that by cheating and deceiving his youthful companions he has sometimes benefitted himself."[15]

A popular children's book titled *Good Advice for Boys and Girls* that went through multiple publications from 1842 to 1853 mostly encouraged the well-dressed boys and girls its illustrations depicted to love and obey their parents, be nice to their siblings, read the Bible, pray, and love God. Its most serious warning, though, was about the mean, wicked foolishness of telling lies. "God himself has said that we must not lie; that he abhors liars, and that he will punish them," the author warned. "Ananias and Sapphira were struck dead for telling lies."[16]

The story of Little Henry, published in 1820 for *Weekly Recorder* subscribers to read to their children, described a pious woman attempting to persuade Little Henry what a sinful boy he was. "There is a little boy in this very room, called Henry," the woman said. "A very few months ago that little boy used to tell lies every day." Henry interjects, "I know it was very wicked." The woman presses the issue. Henry replies, "Oh! I know that I am not good. I have done many naughty things, which nobody knows of. And God only can know the naughtiness of my heart." Woman: "Then you think yourself a sinner?" Henry: "A very great one." Woman: "Where do sinners go when they die?" Henry: "The wicked shall be turned into hell."[17]

In other stories naughty children broke their toys and lied about it, ate sweets and said they hadn't, and denied speaking rudely to a nanny or maid who may have been part of the household. Stealing was arguably harder for children of nursery age to accomplish than lying, but many stories focused on petty theft, often with lying as part of the cover-up. In a narrative about siblings William and Jane, the two are simply playing along the walk by their house when a gust of wind blows some cherries from the cherry tree. Momentarily forgetting that their mother has told them to save all the cherries for their father, who is expected home from a trip that day, William eats several of the cherries and Jane eats the rest. Realizing how they have succumbed to temptation, the children decide to confess to their mother, who forgoes punishing them but warns, "A very trifling fault often leads to a great one."[18] In another story Little Charles steals a coin, lies about having found it, is scolded by his father, who calls him a "most wretched wicked child," and sobs that he has indeed been "a very wicked boy."[19]

Bad children stood out as the stories' memorable characters less because of the severity of their misdeeds than because of the detail with which their behavior was described. An 1839 story about a spoiled child named Darling Petkin, for example, included the following scene:

> "[The guests came] into the drawing room, with Darling Petkin in the center, mounted upon the left shoulder of Uncle Benjamin, where he sat with a drum slung round his neck, which he furiously beat with both sticks, screaming in vain glorious delight, and never caring to perceive that each blow of the drumstick in his right hand took his uncle's left ear in its way upwards. At length the general tumult ceased, and the shrill voice of Darling Petkin enunciated, with all the air of a little god just come to light, 'Only look at me!'"[20]

An 1833 story about an angry child in a column called "Children's Friend" in the *Episcopal Recorder* was no less detailed in describing the behavior of four-year-old Little Harriet:

> One day as her mamma was passing the nursery door, she heard a great noise within, and her little Harriet's voice speaking in a tone that made her sure she was bad; so she opened the door, and there she saw Harriet, with her little face swelled and distorted with rage, her curly hair all torn into disorder, while with feet and hands she was kicking and striking with all her force at one of the servants, and crying out, "I don't love you, Mary, I don't love you; I hate you."

Little Harriet's mother then has the girl pray: "Oh, my heavenly Father, look down in mercy, with pardoning mercy, on my poor little silly wicked heart, at this moment throbbing with such dreadfully bad feelings as only the spirit of all evil could put into it; oh, my heavenly Father, drive away this bad spirit."[21]

While the characters were fictional, the stories invited the listening child to identify with one or more of the characters in the story. The characters had common names, such as Mary, Jane, William, and Henry, or were nameless. Their ages were sometimes mentioned, in which case they were usually three, four, five, or six. If illustrations were included, the children were white, well dressed, at home, and shown in rooms with toys. The more didactic narratives included an adult as a narrator who interrogated the child in the story, or who told the child a story, and at the end of the story offered a statement of moral principle or in some instances invited the listening child to render a judgment about the character's behavior. In the Little Harriet narrative, for example, the mother tells Harriet a story about a girl the same age as Harriet who became angry with the new baby brother in the house: "Harriet, like as you did to Mary just now, she struck it with all her force—struck it on the little tender head—it gave one feeble struggling cry, and breathed no more."

The exception to this pattern of bad children being admonished by an adult was the occasional story in which the bad protagonist was a teenager or adult who had started toward evil as a child. "The Awful Death of a Profane Actress," which appeared as a story for children in the 1824 edition of *Zion's Herald*, for example, recounted an incident that supposedly took place in 1763 in Salem, New Jersey, and involved a theatrical troupe that decided to entertain the community by satirizing religious revival meetings. "One night a young actress stood up on one of the benches, pretending to speak her experience, and with mock solemnity cried out, 'Glory to God, I have found peace; I am sanctified; I am now fit to die.' Scarcely had this unhappy girl uttered these words before she actually dropped dead on the floor and was taken up a lifeless corpse." Were the moral of the story not clear enough, the writer concluded, "May such awful examples prove a warning to others, that they may never ridicule religious people or religious exercises."[22]

Although young children's offenses usually involved interaction with an adult, bad behavior also illustrated how not to act with one's siblings and playmates. Naughty children, such as Mary the angry child in the nursery rhyme about the "little girl that beat her sister," hit their siblings and did not share their toys with playmates. They sometimes served as bad role models as well. One example was the story of Eliza, who took her younger brother, Little Charley, for a walk, during which she taught Charley to slap another child and yell at the ground for making him fall. The moral of the story was that Charley would grow up to be selfish, disobedient, and cruel, and it would be Eliza's fault. So much better it would have been if Eliza had taught Charley to be pleasant, obliging, and conversant with little hymns and prayers.[23]

The umbrella offense was disobedience. Children learned that they were expected to obey their parents in all things, never varying and never questioning the voice of authority. Stories of errant children demonstrated how easy it was to be disobedient and what the consequences should be. Little Jane, a four-year-old who lived in Connecticut, was very fond of flowers, according to the story, so much so that her little fingers plucked the petals even though it was forbidden. "This of course displeased her mother very much, who wanted her little daughter to be perfectly obedient." At length the mother slapped Jane's hands quite severely, which "proved an effectual cure of the disease in Jane's busy meddling fingers."[24] Similarly, Little Tom, a character in an 1825 illustrated primer of three- and four-letter words, refused the nanny's command to go to bed, asking instead to sip tea, upon which the nanny scolded, "If you do not go to bed as you are bid, Ann [Tom's sister] will tell your Ma that you are a bad boy, and she will not love you."[25]

The stories suggested that any child—boy or girl, younger or older, churched or unchurched—could engage in bad behavior. However, specific misdeeds varied significantly by gender. Naughty girls disobeyed their mothers, failed to perform household chores, pouted, cried, argued, and used saucy

FIGURE 22. *Good Girls Reading a Children's Book*, 1879, showing pleasant demeanor and fashionable clothing. Chromolithograph by P. O. Vickery. Library of Congress Prints and Photographs Division, Washington, DC.

language. An 1819 story about a girl named Mary Ann illustrated the faults typically ascribed to naughty girls. Mary Ann was a high-spirited, obstinate girl, given too much to gaiety. When she was older and began attending Sunday school, she "became sedate, meek, and submissive, and carefully attentive to the commands and wishes of her parents." But earlier, when she was four or five, she was "thoughtless, peevish, and self-willed."[26] Girls in other stories pouted, frowned, and disobeyed their mothers; they were cross, ill natured, and overly given to tears. The events usually took place inside the home, as girls played, looked at books, and helped with household chores. "My dear little girls, here is a lesson for you," an essay in *Youth's Companion* about daughters helping mothers care for babies explained.

> I fear that some of you, when you are told to take the baby, pout and cry, and say you want to play, and make many more excuses, and your mothers are obliged to insist upon your doing it, and to make you take the child. Now how naughty this is! Think what trouble your anxious mother took with you when you were a babe; how she fed you and attended you day after day, and month after month, and how she was wearied by stooping to teach you to walk, and how she comforted you when you fell, and yet you object to do the least thing for her. Oh, unkind child![27]

Boys' misbehavior frequently involved interacting with their mothers as well. The story of bad-tempered Charles Goodwin, for example, featured the boy's kind mother reading him a long bedtime story while rocking an infant in the cradle, only to have the fretful boy begging for the story to be read again and then a third time, upon which he is punished by being locked in his room for an hour.[28] However, boys also had greater freedom to play outside the home, which occasioned wider opportunities for mischief. Little Frederic was one such boy. Away from his home in the country during a visit with his aunt in the city, Frederic proved what a troublesome child he was by running to the neighbors and repeatedly ringing the doorbell. Closer to home was another boy whose misdeed while playing one day in the yard was drowning the kittens: "Most likely, when he grows a man, a cruel man will be. And many a wicked thing he'll do, because his heart is hard."[29]

Another way in which gender norms were reinforced was by categorizing girls who behaved like boys as naughty. An 1860 essay in *Youth's Companion*, for example, which argued that girls should be "kind and gentle," illustrated the point by describing a girl named Elsie who screamed, talked boisterously, pushed and pulled, and hit her playmates. She shrieked at her brother, shouted at her sister, screamed like a steam whistle, and, in short, roared "like a naughty boy."[30] The much-quoted rhyme about the little girl who had a little curl—"and when she was bad she was horrid"—presented a similar example. The girl got spanked when her mother heard her making noise upstairs and thought it was "the boys" playing in the attic.[31]

Although the stories more often depicted boys than girls as thoroughly bad, many of the narratives described otherwise good children doing bad things for which they were punished and about which they felt guilty. Protagonists that were basically good increased the likelihood that children listening to the stories would identify with the protagonists and thus understand more clearly what it meant to be bad. At the same time the line separating good behavior from bad behavior was dramatized—highlighted—by virtue of being symbolically transgressed. Bad behavior put the child in a separate symbolic space from which it was possible to look back across the line, as it were, with regret. Redemption in the sense of returning back across the line from bad to good was also possible.

There were many contrasting stories, however, in which good children were advised not only to avoid engaging in bad behavior but also to keep away from other children who were thoroughly bad. A bedtime prayer for children published in 1815 in the *Christian Monitor*, for example, said in part, "May I be kept from everything that is bad and wicked, that I may not lose thy favor, and cause thee to punish me." And "may I remember the Lord's Day and not go with wicked children that break it."[32] An 1817 story about Mary the Milk-Maid, which appeared in the *Christian Herald*, described her as a "very good girl" who was respectful and went to Sunday school, in contrast with the neighbor boy who didn't go to Sunday school, was wicked, and had to be sent away from home. Similarly, an 1831 story in the *Episcopal Recorder* about a "bad boy" who did not attend Sabbath school said he was dishonest, stole from his playmates, and endeavored to make others as bad as himself. "I wish to say a word to you about keeping bad company," the author concluded. "If you associate with those who disobey the laws of their Maker by profaning the Sabbath day and taking his name in vain, you will soon get habituated to the same bad practices and it will be very hard to leave them off."[33]

The stories varied in suggesting whether naughty children were rather easily guided from the error of their ways or were so common that extreme vigilance was needed to protect the good from the bad. The latter view was rooted in the argument that everyone, adults and children alike, was fundamentally evil as a result of original sin and thus could be saved from evil only by the divine intervention of a merciful God toward the chosen few who, in turn, were called to resist as best they could the evil deeds of everyone else. An 1819 sermon on depravity graphically described what the righteous were up against. "All men universally in Adam were nothing else but a wicked and crooked generation, rotten and corrupt trees, stony ground, full of brambles and briars, lost sheep, prodigal sons, unprofitable servants, unrighteous stewards, workers of iniquity, the brood of adders, blind guides, sitting in darkness and in the shadow of death; to be short, nothing else but children of perdition and inheritors of hell fire." There was ample evidence, the speaker added, that this was an accurate description of current affairs. According to an educator he knew whose thirty-year career involved working with at least a thousand children, not a single child exhibited a virtuous "native character." Their natural disposition was toward selfishness, fraud, backbiting, and eventually theft, extortion, and even murder.[34]

The punishments children experienced reinforced the message that bad behavior was not only bad but also had bad consequences. The consequences could come from parents, the child's emotional struggles, some natural sequence of events, and God. Isaac Watts's much-repeated poem encouraging obedience to parents warned, "Have you not heard what dreadful plagues are threatened by the Lord to him that breaks his father's law or mocks his mother's word?"[35] John Witherspoon considered it important to caution parents against merely punishing their children, telling them not to be mean spirited, or attempting to reason with them. Bad children should instead be warned, he said, "that they will thereby incur the displeasure of their Maker."[36] Other stories included naughty children being told that God considered them wicked and did not love them.[37]

One of the clearest examples of children facing the emotional consequences of misbehavior was another episode in the life of bad-tempered Charles Goodwin, whose misdeeds included throwing clothes on the floor, kicking the door, and being disagreeable with the chambermaid. His sister

Catherine was naughty as well. In the most vivid episode, Charles is left to tend Catharine while their mother and a neighbor walk to the top of a nearby hill. The children have been enjoying cherries from a tree at the foot of the hill and are instructed to eat no more. Catharine disobeys, her disobedience frustrates Charles, and after an angry exchange he hits her. She runs, falls, hits her head on a rock, faints, and Charles is overcome with guilt thinking that she is dead. "My dear, dear little sister. I have struck you and killed you! What will become of me?" he says. He then washes the blood from her head, she revives, and their mother scolds her but praises him for helping her. He feels worse than ever, and as he grows older he continues to struggle with his bad temper, feeling incapable of controlling it and yet becoming all the more convinced that he will have to suffer the consequences.[38]

Mentions of death, guilt, and fears of death among the consequences of bad behavior were not uncommon. Religious periodicals such as the *Christian Monitor, Christian Herald,* and *Zion's Herald* frequently published "memoirs" in which the testimonies of recently deceased children and adults cautioned the living against evil deeds. The 1819 memoir of Rebecca M. Coit who died at age eleven, for example, described her as a God-fearing girl who began reading the Bible at age four but was nevertheless so distressed by her sinfulness that she wished to die. Other memoirs appealed directly to the deceased's children. Betsy Henderson's dying words as written and published by her husband warned each of her children by name to avoid wickedness so that they would see their dear mother in heaven someday. For children reared on Bible stories, warnings about disrespecting their elders routinely included the story of God sending bears to kill the children who insulted the prophet Elisha.[39]

The likelihood of mental and emotional trauma, misfortune, estrangement, broken limbs, illness, and death befalling naughty children and their loved ones was standard fare in many of the stories. Mark Twain inimitably captured the narratives' formulaic quality in the satirical "Story of the Bad Little Boy" (1865)—the mischievous adventures of a boy named Jim who managed almost magically to escape the usual consequences. Despite the fact that Jim did not attend Sunday school, his pious mother did not die of consumption. He stole the pantry key, ate the jam and replaced it with tar, and did not feel the least bit guilty. He climbed the apple tree and stole apples without falling and breaking his arm or being attacked by the farmer's dog. And he committed many other naughty deeds—stealing the teacher's penknife, going boating on the Sabbath, and giving the elephant in the menagerie a plug of tobacco—all without being thrashed, drowning, shooting his fingers off, or being struck by lightning.[40] The consequences Jim escaped implied that naughty children ordinarily suffered misfortune as a result of their misbehavior. The stories could also be interpreted to suggest that people who happened to be ill, bereaved, poor, and victims of tragedy somehow were responsible for their own misery.

FIGURE 23. *Little Johnny Green*, 1879, "What a naughty boy was that to drown poor pussy cat." *Goode's Infant's Instructor* (London: T. Goode, 1879).

As fewer of the stories in passing years emphasized the prospect of direct or indirect punishment from God, moral understandings continued to support the idea that naughty children would and should reap misfortune. Writers pondered why it was that children, sometimes even in the same family, behaved so differently. Some children seemed cooperative and good natured from infancy, while others were ill tempered and seemed inclined toward mischief from the start. Still, the good and the bad were morally distinct. Bad behavior was immoral even though it might occur naturally in infancy because children early in life chose to misbehave. They willfully did what was wrong and continued doing it despite being punished and despite experiencing remorse. While many of the stories included messages about the possibility of turning from bad to good, they also warned of the particular dangers of failing to do so.

Nowhere were these dangers more dramatically described than in the writing of Alice Corkran, the prolific British writer whose stories circulated widely in the United States during the last quarter of the nineteenth century. The children in Corkran's narratives willfully behaved badly in ways they should have been able to avoid but chose not to and thus reaped the severely unpleasant rewards of self-inflicted misery. For example, in *Down the Snow Stairs* eight-year-old Kitty, whose disobedience has caused her little brother to be critically ill, dreams of traveling to Naughty Children Land. Hearing weeping and seeing broken toys and torn picture books, Kitty is confronted by a group of little frowning, woe-begotten girls who look so angry that Kitty thinks a good whipping is all that would brighten them up. The girls seem destined to live in Naughty Children Land forever, and although Kitty eventually wakes up determined to be a better girl, she wonders during her dream if she too may ever escape.[41]

The panorama of social life communicated in stories for and about nursery-age children divided the world into two separate and contrasting categories: the one populated by good children and the other occupied by bad children. The stories nevertheless implied a subtler connection between the two as well, such that any well-meaning child could slide into depravity almost at any moment. The narratives warned in no uncertain terms that some people behaved badly all the time or so much of the time that they routinely had to be corrected and certainly should be avoided. Their misdeeds were often so commonplace that later interpreters would classify them simply as the way young children naturally were. Interpreters at the time, though, spared nothing in describing misbehavior as thoroughly wicked and the consequences as frighteningly severe. The stories conveyed a precariously achievable realm of respectable activities and emotions surrounded by powerful temptations and vile tendencies to be feared and profoundly rejected.

Parents' Duties

The main character in many of the stories about naughty children was not the child but an adult, usually a parent and most often the mother, whose duty it was to govern, control, punish, instruct, and otherwise guide the child. With the few exceptions in which parents knowingly committed heinous acts, the stories showed well-meaning parents chastising naughty children and in some cases inadvertently contributing to children's misbehavior.[42] Advice manuals and essays about the proper management of children similarly featured parents' moral responsibilities. When infants died as often as they did, it was incumbent on thoughtful parents to read and heed such advice. Even the smallest, seemingly trivial mistakes could have dire consequences. Infants' cribs, for example, were to be positioned so that the child did not turn its head to see the light from a window because doing so could cause squinting or weakness in one eye. A child that appeared to be intellectually gifted should be discouraged from mental exertion for fear of bringing too much blood into the brain and causing dropsy or death.[43]

Cyrus Comstock's *Essays on the Duty of Parents and Children* (1810) amply illustrated the kinds of advice parents received from writers whose thinking adhered closely to biblical teachings. Comstock was raised in Connecticut by strict Puritan parents and taught school for a number of years in New York State before becoming an itinerant evangelist in later life for the American Home Missionary Society. One of his students, who otherwise remembered him fondly, said Comstock brooked no frivolity and solemnly inflicted corporal punishment using a firm rod that produced a stinging pain on the flesh for any falsehoods or use of obscene language. However small their offense, the offenders learned that evildoers must suffer because their immortal souls were in peril. Comstock believed that young children were like "dumb beasts" that knew the difference between right and wrong only as parents instructed them. It was thus parents' duty to command children's absolute obedience, impress on them the need for subordination, and guide them toward truth and righteous living. A child that told lies or disobeyed or harmed animals was not properly trained, and parents were advised even to avoid speaking falsehoods in jest lest it encourage children to lie.[44]

If children were understood to be naturally disposed toward sin, parents' obligation was to guide them away from sin, and if children were considered to be naturally innocent of inclinations toward wrongdoing, parents were at fault if bad behavior then resulted. In either case stories of bad children held important implications for parents. The presence of bad children in the home suggested that parents were not doing a proper job of parenting. It was especially important to halt any sign of willfulness on the part of the child or to cater to such disobedience as excessive crying, which would only worsen over time. Bad children were like a disease that could infect other children, and it would undoubtedly get worse unless something was done to root it out.

Just as stories about children did, admonitions for parents in many instances stressed the dangers of evil to a greater extent than the possibilities for good. Bad parents produced children who tortured animals, roamed the streets, used profane language, and grew up to be killers. One wretched mother, according to the report of a pastor who visited, stubbornly refused to send her daughter to Sunday school, only to have the daughter become violently sick and die.[45] "Dost thou, in the name of this child, renounce the devil and all his works, the vain pomp and glory of the world, with all covetous desires of the same, and the carnal desires of the flesh, so that thou wilt not follow nor be led by them?" the Episcopal *Prayer Book*'s vows for children's baptism asked; to which parents responded, "I renounce them all; and, by God's help, will endeavor not to follow, nor be led by them."[46]

While good children were said to engage occasionally in bad behavior that could be corrected, the result of bad parenting was more likely to be children who were always bad, mostly bad, or bad in serious multiple ways. "Their minds are subject to no principle or rule, and therefore always in disorder," a writer in the *American Journal of Education* observed in 1827. "They are selfish, irritable, passionate, long pleased with nothing, and fretted to impatience and violence at the most trifling accidents which cross the present momentary wish of the mind." They were, in short, a "most melancholy picture of perversion."[47]

If children resembled farm animals, as Comstock believed, parents needed to be as careful about training children as they were with cows and horses. That meant keeping them clean, feeding them proper food, ensuring that they kept warm in winter, seeing that any illnesses were treated, and, as some forward-thinking writers argued, having them vaccinated. It also meant taking special care with ill-tempered children who pushed their siblings, disobeyed their parents, and showed every proclivity to grow into a violent adult like a vicious animal. It was incumbent on parents to walk a fine line between scolding a child too much or too little. Perhaps it would be better, some educators argued, to have infant schools where distraught parents could find assistance.[48]

Compounding the difficulties parents faced was the fact that good families were surrounded by bad influences, both from poorly managed families and from the general tenor of the day toward worldly amusements and extravagance.[49] Abolitionist and women's rights activist Lydia Maria Child, for example, worried that girls not learning to sew and perform other household duties demonstrated a great cause of mischief in society. Irresponsible parents, she feared, were "apt to let children romp away their existence till they get to be thirteen or fourteen."[50] Indolence and inattention to the proper learning of industrious habits posed more serious dangers than might at first be assumed because small matters carried larger implications. "Do not forget that your children, as they are coming into life, are coming into danger," an 1807 essay for parents cautioned. "Ten thousand temptations solicit their incautious minds, and their very steps are amid snares in which multitudes before them have been entangled to their ruin." Not only was there danger, but also the time was short. "What you do in training your children must be done speedily."[51] Nor could it be assumed that bad influences came entirely from the outside. "A great proportion of mankind is cruel, vindictive, revengeful, envious, deceitful, etc.," an 1813 essay observed. The reason? Parents and nannies inadvertently taught children to be naughty. They learned cruelty to animals as a form of amusement. They learned about fear and revenge from stories about "boo boo's coming to take them." They learned to fight, prevaricate, and swear. They learned superstitions about ghosts and apparitions from "foolish tales." Without understanding what they were doing, parents instilled such bad examples "into the mind of the tender infant, which it can never shake off as long as it lives."[52]

A sermon preached at Christ Church in Cincinnati in 1831 illustrated the warnings God-fearing parents heard from the pulpit. Parents undoubtedly wanted their children to be good when they grew up, the speaker argued, which made "the lamentable extent to which the duties of parents are neglected or very imperfectly performed" all the more troubling. Such children would live in sin and misery, burden and pollute their families, and become a fountain of evil, all because of the folly and negligence of their parents. "You wish, parents, that your beloved children should be a credit and a comfort to you—should attain to respectability as members of the community," he observed. "But have you ever considered that, whether their character and condition shall be such or directly the reverse, depends, under heaven, almost altogether upon *yourselves*?" Families were nurseries for heaven or for hell. "Parental influence embraces all time and reaches forward through eternity."[53]

In a sermon published in 1835 Reverend Doctor Gardiner Spring of the Brick Presbyterian Church in New York City cautioned parents against similar problems that carried implications for time and eternity. The gravest danger, he believed, stemmed from failing to teach children the habit of subordination, which was commanded by God, served as the basis for pious behavior, and was probably the reason women were more inclined toward piety than men. He thought parents in cities like New York failed so often in keeping children from vice because they did not give them enough work to do and, to make matters worse, were not native citizens. Refinement, courtesy, and elegance needed to be combined with habits of industry and enterprise. The "use of ardent spirits" represented another danger, not simply to be mentioned in passing but graphically likened to sliding over a precipice, falling into a yawning abyss, succumbing to distress and ruin, and ending in disaster.[54]

The homes at issue were in most instances middle class, marked as such by mentions of schooling, books and other reading material, and servants. Middle-class parents were supposed to bring knowledge, forbearance, and thoughtful approaches to the tasks of parenting. Parents from lower social strata provided the contrasting illustrations of what not to do. For instance, John Witherspoon bolstered the argument that nothing was quite as disgusting as the "impotent rage" of a parent incapable of asserting absolute authority over a child with this example: "Among the lower ranks of people, who are under no restraint from decency, you may sometimes see a father or mother running out into the street after a child who is fled from them, with looks of fury and words of execration; and they are often stupid enough to imagine that neighbors or passengers will approve them in this conduct, though in fact it fills every beholder with horror."[55]

Exhortations of this kind followed the familiar rhetorical pattern of sermons in which the importance of living right was underscored by dramatic descriptions of rampant evil in the world. Reverend Otis Ainsworth Skinner, for instance, who taught school, preached, edited a monthly religious publication, held Unitarian pastorates in four states, and became president of Lombard University in Illinois, was known for his liberal theology and interests in social reform, and yet his *Letters on the Moral and Religious Duties of Parents* (1844) painted the grimmest picture of contemporary parenting and youth. Wherever he went the problems struck him as utterly severe. "Not a month passes in any city or important town which does not present instances of the ruin of the young," he observed. "Our streets are blockaded with profane and dissolute youth." Why? "I believe the evil can be traced to the improper management of them."[56]

Besides the parenting advice that seemed steeped in concerns about pervasive wickedness, a line of argument appeared in antebellum literature that focused on the demands of better parenting for the future of a better society. "The cultivation of refined taste, noble feeling, and general literature certainly belongs to a state of society advanced beyond the mere acquisition of necessary knowledge," an 1829 essay in the *American Journal of Education* declared. "Has not our country arrived at this state?" The writer considered it a new era in which the privations endured by the first settlers were a thing of the past. A spirit of improvement that included manufacturing, trade, and an expansion of agriculture now characterized the nation. Education was the key to further improvement. And for education to achieve that goal, better effort in the home for the management of children was necessary.[57]

Few writers exemplified the arguments for progressive parenting as clearly as Susan Huntington, a Connecticut Congregationalist whose thoughtful correspondence, essays, and memoirs in the 1820s engaged the era's major questions about theology, gender roles, and parental responsibilities. Huntington argued for greater understanding of gender equality and at the same time believed that the responsibility for good parenting fell primarily to mothers. "If children are not under the government of their mothers," she wrote, "they must necessarily be left very much to their own guidance, and exposed to early associations unfriendly to virtue." Fathers, she feared, too often inadvertently encouraged habits of "trifling," "dissimulation," and "rebellion." Mothers for their part needed to cultivate a home atmosphere in which children learned the absolute importance of obedience and yet were not subjected to petty rules and angry language.[58]

Catharine Beecher's *Treatise on Domestic Economy*, published in 1841 and republished nearly every year until 1856, popularized advice similar to Huntington's. Beecher encouraged mothers of young children to attend closely to their nutritional needs, employ rewards more than punishment, avoid anger and inconsistency, and cultivate moral habits in children by modeling the love and mercy of Jesus Christ. Beecher advocated a reasonable pattern of moderation in parenting that facilitated the long-term benefits of honesty, modesty, propriety, benevolence, and self-denial. Her advice nevertheless in many ways reproduced albeit in gentler terms the strict New England moral emphasis of the times. Children were to conform absolutely to their parents' authority. Obedience in all matters, from happily consuming the food set before them to remaining silent during meals, was required. Self-denial and submission to parents' will was the path to understanding the importance of always submitting to God.

The model family Beecher's readers were to aspire to consisted of children who happily and obediently submitted to the commands of parents who rarely needed to raise their voices and never did so in anger. Children knew from a young age that happiness in this life and the life to come depended on the moral habits their patient mothers instilled in them. The model family was a picture of domestic tranquility, populated mostly by wise models and dutiful apprentices of good behavior. The ideal family nevertheless was surrounded by moral danger—"peculiar temptations"—against which it was necessary to constantly be on guard. Children were to be cautioned by frequent reminders of these dangers. "The records of our insane retreats, and the pages of medical writers, teach that even in solitude and without being aware of the sin or the danger, children may inflict evils on themselves, which not infrequently terminate in disease, delirium, and death. Every mother . . . should teach the young that the indulgence of impure thoughts and actions is visited by the most awful and terrible penalties."[59]

Beecher's reference to "medical writers" reflected the increasingly popular view among educated readers that moral principles were not only biblical but also scientifically grounded. Medical opinion likened the mind to a muscle that required an appropriate level of exercise in order to properly cultivate the moral imagination. Inactivity was understood to be a leading cause of nervous disease while excessive mental action was a source of evil thoughts. Children who wasted time reading fiction, building castles in their imagination, sitting idly, or failing to obey their parents were in danger of disease, delirium, and death. Besides disappointing their parents and God, this was an added reason to learn self-denial. Even children who appeared to be obedient could be entertaining evil thoughts in their minds, in which case punishment by severe penalties was required.

As schooling became more common for middle-class children, advice to parents about how to avoid raising bad children came increasingly from educators and dealt with the problems teachers faced when parents failed.[60] Jacob Abbott, who preached, wrote juvenile fiction, tutored, and served as founding principal from 1829 to 1833 of the Mount Vernon School for Young Ladies in Boston, was one of a growing number of educators who sought in lectures and publications to instruct parents about these problems. Acknowledging the subtleties required of modern parenting, Abbott cautioned that all children were prone to insubordination, were given to bias, and would likely bring home tales about what happened at school that should not be taken seriously: "They are all peculiarly exposed, in case of strong temptation, to conceal or to prevaricate, and there are not a few whose word is worthy of no confidence whatever." Parents needed to understand this not only in their children but also in their own behavior. Bad parenting consisted not only of blatant misbehavior, such as lying and stealing, but also of the smaller failures that stemmed from inconsistency and inattention. Parents whose homes were messy and whose emotions were unchecked raised children who caused trouble in the classroom, were heedless and rude, and became an embarrassment among their parents' peers. "If you are passionate, unsteady in your government, impatient and irritable, they will be so too, and thus you communicate to your offspring a moral contamination which is far worse than any hereditary physical disease."[61]

Lenient, ill-managed parenting was also the focus of a lengthy discussion published in 1835 by John Hall, principal of the Ellington School in Ellington, Connecticut, under the title *Education of Children While under the Care of Parents or Guardians*. Hall considered all children to be natively equipped with irascible tempers, selfish dispositions, and propensities toward evil. The trouble worsened when parents failed to understand these tendencies. Assuming their children would naturally turn out good, parents became slack and indulgent in the management of their children. The result was far worse than the occasional lie or theft that children had committed in the past. If such behavior was unchecked, "moral desolation would come over the land." Soon there would be a frightful generation, an upsurge of vindictive passions, a "spectacle of slothful effeminacy."[62]

It was not without reason that *management* was the operative word. Child-drearing was to be done systematically, rationally, according to the knowledgeable application of rules, just as the management of crops, farm animals, and businesses were. Bad parents who raised bad children did so because they were ill informed. They gave in to their emotions rather than thinking about the consequences of what they did and said to their children. They behaved inconsistently, guided only by the moment instead of thinking in longer terms. A woman he knew who he said had little practical skill in domestic management, attorney Sylvanus Urban wrote in the *New York Mirror*, lived in a kind of purgatory with her husband and children. "If she is in a good humor or feels lazily inclined she will overlook a hundred things in her children, which, although not very serious, still ought not to be allowed to pass unnoticed, and for which, the very next day, perhaps if the mood is changed, she will scold them, scream at them, and box their ears."[63]

Bad children who reflected the results of ill-informed parenting, according to this line of interpretation, mostly illustrated an unsatisfactory disposition and objectionable demeanor rather than overtly mischievous deeds and wicked behavior. Respectable people learned by negative example to disapprove of people who were ill mannered, ill tempered, inconsistent in how they modulated their behavior, unrefined, overly passionate, or simply unpleasant to be around. A dislikable disposition would arise from children learning to think too highly of themselves. Perhaps they were irritable because of having been exposed to too much excitement in the nursery or too little discipline from their mother. A bad child was too often angry, ill-tempered, fretful, boisterous, or disagreeable; did not laugh enough; was ill humored; was not sufficiently grateful; was too readily expressed fear; talked too much or talked too little. Boys would sulk about their work, and girls would develop coarse manners unsuited to the gentleness of their sex. Boys and girls alike could appear awkward, vain, simpering, and rough rather than refined. They could lack agreeable manners and develop improper deportment. Any and all of these faults fell to the parents. It was above all parents' inability to conduct with firmness and yet moderation the parenting that would keep their off-spring from perverseness. Parents should of course mete out punishments but guard against communicating that their children were irreparably naughty, modulate the punishments to have the most decisive effect, and set a positive example but ensure that children knew the folly of a reprobate life.

It was certainly the case that advocates of good parenting had in mind a positive image of the ideal home in which children learned good manners, were even tempered and obedient, and did what they were asked to do. Descriptions of behavior that fell short of these ideals could be taken as little more than rhetorical embellishment. There was another message, though, that warned parents to be on guard against people they might know who deviated from the respected standard. Bad parents, like bad children, were a constant danger. They embodied all that was wrong or that could go awry, from the trifling misapprehensions of thoughtless emotion to the inadvertent nurture of offspring who would became a burden on society.

Problem Juveniles

The principal difference between children in the nursery and children age five or six and beyond was that the older ones—"juveniles"—spent time out of the house. They went to school part of the year or were expected to, played in the yard or on the street, sometimes attended church or Sunday school and belonged to clubs, and, depending on their gender and social class, ran errands for their parents, helped on the farm, held menial jobs, and worked in factories or begged. The spaces themselves carried moral connotations, signaling that youngsters in particular places were probably good and in other places probably bad. The adult characters the protagonists interacted with varied as well. While parents populated the stories about juveniles as much as they did for younger children, the larger cast of adults in the role of authority included teachers, preachers, employers, superintendents of correctional facilities, and the police. Community leaders and public officials became relevant in these narratives, as did a wider variety of juvenile age mates.

Jacob Abbott's message to parents of school-age children cautioned especially about the dangers of mingling with juveniles who apparently were not in school. He considered the "company of bad boys abroad" one of the greatest sources of evil. "What folly to think that a boy can play with the profane, impure, passionate boys which herd in the streets six days in the week and have the stains all wiped away by being compelled to learn his Sunday school lesson on the seventh." He warned: "KEEP THEM OUT OF THE STREETS." Otherwise, they would be contaminated with vice, much to their parents' regret. "You must expect to spend your old age in mourning over the ruins of your family," he warned.[64]

Similarly, Gardiner Spring advised his middle-class audience to spare nothing in expense, even if it meant self-denial, to purchase amusements for their children to discourage them from spending any more time outside the home than necessary for school. "Every family ought to be a little world within itself," he suggested. The outside world teemed with ruinous potential. Most to be avoided were "companions that are idle and vicious, ignorant and skeptical." Those would "be sure to poison the unsuspecting mind of youth."[65]

Much the same emphasis was evident in Otis Ainsworth Skinner's arguments. A "pleasant home" was the ideal space in which to expose children to moral training, by which he meant one with appropriate amusements, interesting books, and a piano. Absent that, children would seek amusement in other places, "mingle with children running in the streets," and become "corrupted" by the "vulgarity and profaneness" of "idle and wicked" children who were the "worst of characters." Boys around the ages of ten to twelve were especially vulnerable to these evil temptations, he warned, and would plague their parents with requests to spend evenings out of the house. "Such requests should never be granted," he advised. "More youth are ruined by such indulgences than in any other way. The darkness of the night serves to throw off restraint and embolden them to the commission of acts from which they would shrink in the light of day."[66]

The bad examples that served as warnings to older children described the consequences of misbehavior as severely as stories did for younger children. Older children who were bad did not tell simple lies hoping to get away with them; they practiced a more subtle kind of deceit, smiling and telling half-truths. What they did in youth was preparation for worse acts as adults. "Dissimulation in youth is the forerunner of perfidy in old age," an 1812 essay in the *Juvenile Portfolio* counseled. "Its first appearance is the fatal omen of growing depravity and future shame. It degrades parents and learning; obscures the luster of every accomplishment; and sinks you into contempt with God and man."[67]

The inclusion of varied places and characters in discussions of juveniles reflected the fact that social institutions were involved to a much greater degree than they were for younger children. Schools, churches, jobs, the courts, and especially a growing number of voluntary and charitable organizations constituted the spheres in which juveniles interacted. That had an important implication for the distinction separating good and bad children. The distinction was no longer merely symbolic; it was also the reality of how social relationships were organized. Bad children, in addition to being a maligned "other" in stories, became a separate population that figuratively and literally occupied different spaces and was attended to by different authorities.

An indication early in the nineteenth century of the importance of place in identifying good children was that bad children were described not necessarily as being in a bad space but as being "displaced" or "outcast," as if they did not have a place at all. What they lacked straightforwardly was the kind of middle-class home that writers considered essential to the upbringing of good children. To be outcast meant being homeless, living in the street, possibly as an orphan, but the word also implied more than that. It suggested sympathetically that society in the form of local communities had cast out some of its children, and, less sympathetically, that indigent or irresponsible parents had cast out their own children, leaving them with no alternative but to roam the streets.[68]

The location of juveniles within or outside of certain social institutions carried clear implications about social class. Middle-class juveniles were expected to be good children because they learned how to be refined in schools, churches, and youth associations. Bad children—the ones who caused trouble for the community—were more often assumed to be lower-class juveniles who existed outside these institutions and needed help. That at least was the argument early in the century for promoting public schools, private charity schools, and Sabbath schools that would combat the problems caused by uneducated children.[69] New York mayor DeWitt Clinton, for example, in an 1805 lecture to the trustees of the Society for Establishing a Free School in the City, described the urgency of providing instruction during the week and on Sundays to a larger number of the city's children. Many children, he said, were "living in total neglect of the religious and moral instruction, and unacquainted with the common rudiments of learning, essentially requisite for the due management of the ordinary business of life." He believed the problem stemmed mostly from parents' extreme indigence, intemperance, vice, and indifference to their children's best interests. "Children are thus brought up in ignorance, and amidst the contagion of bad example are in imminent danger of ruin." Many of them, he feared, "will become the burden and pests of society."[70]

The category of bad children that provided the sharpest contrast with expectations governing good middle-class families was composed of children commonly referred to as "boys in the street" and "street urchins." As historian David Floyd observes, street urchins gained popularity in middle to late Victorian literature and among American readers in stories about orphans and children whose parents had for inexplicable reasons abandoned them. The narratives depicted outcasts who came from poor families and generally lived in large cities, appearing in popular narratives and in charitable appeals mostly out-of-doors and in unsupervised spaces. Although some of the characters were portrayed as admirable if unfortunate, many of their counterparts, especially in later narratives, were villains whose ominous nature tended toward degeneracy. In this regard their rough lawless behavior stood in sharp contrast with the emerging genteel and feminized ideal of middle-class domesticity.[71]

The emphasis on streets in much of the literature reflected growing concerns about problems associated with cities, including the stark realities of slum neighborhoods such as Dandy Hill in Philadelphia and Five Points in New York—notorious, sinister, menacing places of "decaying tenements, stinking hovels, and damp cellars [breeding] vice, drunkenness, crime, and pauperism," in historian Paul Boyer's words.[72] These were actual places in which juvenile misbehavior existed and toward which those in safer middle-class locations could look with horror. The view from afar, as it were, was no less frightening because of its distance. At the same time, country youth were not exempt from descriptions about misbehavior in those communities. Commentators assumed that some of the problems stemmed from delinquent youth being sent to farms and small towns by urban reform organizations. Observers also noted the rural temptations to which juveniles—boys at least—frequently succumbed. Taverns were of particular concern to temperance activists. Country stores where youth could idle away the time, engage in gambling and tippling, and learn profane discourse were another.[73] These were places where country boys became indolent, ill informed, and unsuccessful instead of developing the kind of manly gentility expected of the respectable middle class.

Efforts to provide temporary supervision for street urchins included Sunday schools, charity schools, and evangelistic campaigns. Religious periodicals appealed to churchwomen—"Daughters of Zion"—to bring little ones from the streets to instructional meetings on weekends and evenings.[74] Proponents argued that Sunday schools could be a powerful corrective to the problems increasingly evident in the more troublesome parts of the nation's cities. The hope was to bring bad children into the institutional confines in which good children learned to be good. The reality, though, was that sermons and instructional guides for Sunday school teachers focused frequently on the disruptions bad children caused. They came late or did not come regularly at all, made noise, and disobeyed the teachers. Some congregations went so far as to sort the bad children into a "bad class"—the unintended consequence of which was to embolden disobedience and strengthen vice, as one teacher observed.[75]

Bad children of school age acquired publicity beyond the concerns expressed by clergy and teachers through the arrests and court appearances in which local newspapers characterized them as "juvenile offenders" or "juvenile delinquents." Their offenses ranged from loitering and using profanity to more serious crimes such as theft and burglary. They dressed shabbily, begged, picked pockets, ran in gangs, and posed what proper citizens considered a public nuisance. Already separate from the organized spaces in which

FIGURE 24. *Reform School Boys*, 1910, illustrating the ill effects of
street life. Photograph by Lewis Wickes Hine. Library of Congress
Prints and Photographs Division, Washington, DC.

middle-class children spent their days, they became the focus of efforts for
their removal. Municipal codes hardened against them, and public officials
called for them to be relocated. The mayor of Philadelphia issued an order in
1855, for example, requiring the police to take more concerted action against
the vagrant children who filled the streets and haunted the barrooms of hotels
selling toothpicks and soliciting coins. "All these wretched children must be
taken into charge and properly disposed of," the mayor declared.[76]

The charitable interpretation of "properly disposed of" meant sending the
"wretched children" to an asylum, house of refuge, or reformatory. Advocates
of social reform considered neglected children a particularly potent symbol
in making appeals for charitable organizations, poor relief, and child-labor

laws.[77] Sympathetic descriptions of neglected children, however, included less than sympathetic discussions of their misbehavior. They symbolized not only the need for social reform but also the "other" that middle-class families hoped to distance themselves from. Distancing was better achieved when problem juveniles could be removed from the streets and placed in separate locations.

Efforts to organize institutions for the reform of juvenile delinquents in the 1820s stemmed from concerns that placing young offenders in ordinary prisons and penitentiaries increased their chances of becoming hardened criminals. Appeals for charitable intervention asked potential donors to think kindly about the poor but frequently employed extreme language in discussing juveniles' offenses. New York City's Society for the Prevention of Pauperism, for example, declared that hundreds and thousands of children were degraded, degenerate, intemperate, given to dishonesty and obscene language, routinely engaged in criminal activity, and consigned to lives of infamy and desperate villainy. They were like an infestation of pests, the committee said. Little wonder that the problem was so great when the innate perversities of human nature were enticed toward deeper corruption by wicked associates.[78]

Appeals for the support of similar institutions in Boston cast juvenile offenders in less critical language, calling them indigent waifs and victims of neglect, but in so doing attributed blame to the misbehavior of parents. As much as the problems may have been associated with poverty, they were just as often described as moral failures. Offenders' parents failed to instruct their children to be honest and obedient and in the worse cases encouraged them on vicious courses of behavior and profited from the depredations committed by their children.[79] The role of correctional institutions was thus to impose standards of obedience and industry that parents failed to provide.

Besides being defined by their institutional locations, bad juveniles were described in ways that respectable middle-class youth would want to avoid if they possibly could. The inhabitants of these institutions were shifty-eyed, unkempt, set apart by being of different races and ethnic origins, and even in the most sympathetic accounts miserable. Charles Dickens, visiting the House of Reformation for Juvenile Offenders in Boston in 1842, reported favorably on the kind and judicious treatment the boys received and yet observed that the offenders "had not such pleasant faces by a great deal" and that the establishment included "many boys of color."[80] Juveniles who public officials thought should be placed in these institutions bore similar characteristics: they not only wandered the streets but also pilfered, plundered, destroyed property, and corrupted the morals of law-abiding children. They were dissolute, debased, unhappy, ill tempered, and thriftless, embodied the lowest of all passions, and were likely to be of foreign birth.[81]

The distinction separating good and bad juveniles was reinforced by the simultaneous formation of youth organizations for well-mannered middle-class youth. Inspired by the success of such organizations in London, clergy in

New York City organized a Female Juvenile Tract Society in 1816 that enlisted churchgoing girls in monthly prayer meetings at which tracts were read and testimonials were heard about the tracts' beneficial effects.[82] In the 1820s temperance organizations formed juvenile chapters for children between the ages of five and fifteen who signed pledges of abstinence from intoxicating liquor, solicited pledges from other children, attended regular meetings at churches, and, as the adult organizers at least hoped, tried to persuade drunken parents to turn sober. By most indications these were children from churchgoing families and were often recruited from the private academies attended by middle-class children. As early as 1827 the American Board of Commissioners for Foreign Missions organized similar juvenile associations to spark interest and solicit money for missionaries. By the mid-1830s juvenile antislavery societies were also in operation.[83] Like the organizers of reform schools, leaders of these juvenile associations hoped their efforts would help the poor, and yet the terms of discussion emphasized a sharp distinction between good and bad children. "Consider how much good you may do!" an appeal on behalf of the Female Juvenile Tract Society proclaimed. "Wicked children . . . by their evil example, scatter fire brands, arrow and death, like the madman described by Solomon."[84]

Although they were institutionally separate as a result of these organizations, bad juveniles nevertheless sometimes represented a way to think about redemption, just as naughty nursery-age children did who repented of their misbehavior. Redemption could occur from evangelism, Christian charity, and public education. It would have been an overstatement to say that the reforming zeal of the era required the existence of street urchins and juvenile delinquents as a population to be reformed, but there was some truth in that assertion. It was equally true that stories of individual redemption emphasized the transformation juveniles seemed capable of making on their own if they tried hard enough. Street urchins could pull themselves up by their own bootstraps. They could turn out well and become useful citizens if they only worked hard and saved their meager earnings. The story by Horatio Alger, Jr., of Ragged Dick, the New York bootblack who smoked and drank before deciding to turn over a new leaf and grow up respectable, was one example.[85]

But as time passed commentators on the "juvenile problem," as it was increasingly called, exhibited less confidence that street urchins could be successfully reformed. Street urchins instead posed a continuing problem, a more obvious public danger that had to be more strenuously guarded against by means of stiffer laws.[86] Discouraged reformers wrote of neighborhoods and extended families that seemed to epitomize wickedness from one generation to the next. Writers floated the idea of criminal inheritance and speculated that biology might be involved.[87] Waifs became lawless troublemakers and bad boys became hoodlums. "Oh, I hope my boy will never be as they are!" a "refined woman" was quoted in 1894 as saying in reference to street urchins she had seen playing in a poor section of the city. "Their lawless play, rude behavior and obscene talk" contrasted with how she wanted her boy to behave. "They may be seen any day smoking cigarettes, stealing fruit, climbing on passing vehicles hoping to steal a ride, and indulging in coarse, ill-bred remarks." The narrator of the story, after noting several other instances of concern about street urchins, concluded, "I believe the mothers of such boys as we see on the street are both thoughtless and selfish."[88]

Spirited Naughtiness

The naughtiness that categorized certain activities and their instigators as aliens to be maligned proved perhaps unavoidably to be a source of fascination as well. By the end of the nineteenth century stories circulated in increasing number in which the hero or heroine was bad or at least had been as a child and yet displayed a kind of spirited naughtiness that contrasted with the pale featureless terrain of middle-class life. The naughty person in this rendition had spunk enough to set a different course, violate the norms of conventionality, and bring new life to the community. To be spirited was to exhibit the natural playfulness of childhood, even if it temporarily landed the boy or girl in trouble, and to defy authority when it was too harsh or unreasonable. The naughty person who garnered interest in this way was a renegade whose willfulness could be admired as long as there was some redeeming value present in the person's eventual accomplishments or underlying motives or inadvertent contributions to the common good. The "bad boy" in particular became a figure who could be viewed with admiration for having sown his wild oats before settling into a respectable adult role, while the "lively girl" grew up to be a gracious hostess, refined wife and mother, and on occasion an enterprising careerwoman.[89]

Spirited naughtiness symbolized an intriguing departure from life in the quiet, tree-lined communities—the "superficial and artificial" middle-class neighborhoods, as Alfred Stieglitz called them—where children spent their days attending school and lived too comfortably to develop the energy that had conquered the frontier and inspired a great industrial nation.[90] Unlike the children of an earlier generation who had risen from hardship and learned to do physical work, the emerging cohort of middle- class children was soft. They had every advantage at their doorstep, learned to "dress in good taste," learned "the courtesies of polite society" and "the art of companionship." They were pleasant, alert, smart, and attractive—but not very interesting. They were destined to become clerks, bookkeepers, and housewives.[91] The urban middle class and its youth was not only uninteresting; it was also somehow inauthentic. It lived in a human-made environment, a world of contrivances that served its needs for convenience but deprived it of having to grapple with the uncertainties of nature. The ambience protected children, but they became "the little bottle babies of civilization." Artificial devices, manufactured toys, and fairy tales entertained them. They looked at pictures of butterflies instead of actual butterflies. Quiet homes sheltered them from the noise and bustle of the street.[92]

But the mild allure of spirited naughtiness played better in fiction and art than in real life. Stories of bad boys and lively girls served up antics that were mostly amusing. Protagonists got their way by scheming and playing innocent tricks. The extreme reproach they often earned only added to the fun. Children could play at being outlaws, and adults could imagine the wild exploits of gangsters and the exotic lives of showgirls. High-spirited children could be forgiven for youthful vanity and brashness and for occasionally straying into temptation. It had long been understood that immaturity and bad judgment went hand in hand. And that was all the more reason to draw the distinction between good middle-class behavior and the activities of those who deviated. The naughtiness that might be appealing was still a world apart, taking place in secret or in unrecognizable places and being performed by people who dressed differently and spoke differently.

Conclusion

For the generations of Americans that had been raised on stories of naughty children, the task of being a respectable member of the middle class meant continuing to raise their children as they had been raised, hoping to instill positive behavior by inculcating fear of the consequences of bad behavior. Whether that fear included corporal punishment or consisted only of harsh verbal instruction, the danger of straying across the line from good to evil was an ever-present reminder. It could be a strong message indeed to think that an unguarded moment of anger was evidence of a bad temper that could ruin one's life. The message that God could not possibly love a child who failed in any respect to obey the parent's every command could fill an impressionable youth with lasting terror. For the grownups the stories offered little solace as well. Naughty children reflected badly on their parents. It was parents' duty to correct and to correct again and again any child that strayed from the narrow path.[93]

These were not the messages that only the children of stern Puritan parents learned. Religious magazines and Sunday school materials across many denominations and traditions communicated harsh moral ideals by negative example. The ones that did not—the ones that portrayed children as innocents who were basically good—nevertheless put children in the uncomfortable position of struggling emotionally with shame, guilt, and frustration. Naughty boys and girls in these respects were powerful examples. If it was unclear exactly how good children should behave, it was crystal clear that bad behavior was to be avoided at all costs. Bad behavior was heinous, despicable, wicked.

It was as dangerous as a contaminant that could affect an unwitting person through mild exposure. Whatever else a person did to behave respectably, it was necessary to be vigilant against such danger.

The narratives communicated a view of human nature and an outlook toward society that instilled a watchful, if not also wary, orientation toward the many ways in which a person aspiring to be good could go wrong. Danger was present in the physical harm that could be inflicted by hoodlums, in the moral torpor that naughty children symbolized, and in the dark side of the human soul to which any person could be drawn. The activities and negative consequences that naughty children represented were more than rhetorical devices illustrating the values a good society wished to embrace by occasionally mentioning their absence. Narratives about well-behaved children were remarkably bland. Good boys and girls might be loved by God and approved of by their parents, but the tangible details of this love and approval were sparse. Good children paled in comparison with the richly embellished lives of bad children whose misbehavior led to illness and death and eternal damnation. Bad children were the dangers to be avoided in life because they occupied dark, disorderly spaces and dangerous streets. They signaled the looming degeneracy of the age and the pervasive depredations of evil. They were troublesome enough when they were out there in other places. They were more troubling as reminders of the vile thoughts and emotions that could happen within.

Stories of naughty children clearly served as cautionary tales for parents as well as for children. Twentieth-century parents learned just as their predecessors had that bad-behaving offspring reflected badly on their parents. And it became harder, if anything, to know exactly how to recognize bad behavior and prevent it from getting out of hand. As children became fewer and more likely to live to adulthood, they also became less economically crucial to the typical family, a greater cost in terms of educational investment, and of greater value to the family's sense of subjective well-being. Good parenting demanded that closer attention be paid to the expert opinions of doctors, educational specialists, and child psychologists. Little wonder that parenting became a source not only of gratification but also of anxiety. Examples of the bad children that bad parenting produced were not hard to find. They failed at school, broke the law, populated the jails and reformatories, and burdened the community.[94]

If naughtiness sometimes came to be regarded as a kind of harmless tomfoolery in which adventuresome adults could engage, it was also a trope that could be used to shame its target. An adult who behaved like a naughty child was twice scorned: once for acting like a child and once for misbehaving. A naughty child was in popular parlance a person who was spoiled, peevish, choosing to do something based on emotion instead of reason, and failing to take the appropriate actions that any normal person would. Adults who behaved like naughty children certainly should not, in these understandings, be rewarded for their behavior. If what they did was pardonable in children, it was clearly shameful for adults. As one observer noted, an adult who behaved like a naughty child was either a "hick" or a "smart aleck" who was "not yet completely civilized."[95] And given the right circumstances, any group could be targeted and thus maligned as naughty children: women who might be accused of peevishness, teenagers who failed to fulfill their parents' aspirations, campus protesters, immigrants, and racial minorities.

CHAPTER EIGHT

Othering

CULTURAL DIVERSITY AND
SYMBOLIC BOUNDARIES

TRACES OF HOW nineteenth-century Americans defined respectability continue to be present in the twenty-first century. Although the nation's population is much larger and more diverse and communication technologies are
vastly different, we still as individuals and groups desire to be respected and
negotiate what that means in our interactions with others. Deciding what respectability means is still a matter of drawing distinctions between "us" and
"them," even though the bases of these distinctions may have changed and
been influenced by a greater awareness of the realities of diversity and the
importance of tolerance. To call someone a huckster, a con artist, or a fanatic
is still a way to express disrespect. We do not respect them quite as much as we
respect ourselves. They cannot be trusted, they talk too fast and too loud, and
they are too emotionally caught up in what they are doing. Despite significant
changes in understandings of mental illness, stigma remains significantly attached to the topic. Immigrant groups are widely and repeatedly subjected to
abject bigotry and discrimination. In other quarters whatever the difficulties
may be, the problems are laid to the evils of the millionaire and billionaire
class. And if the rich are not to blame, isn't the trouble that too many parents
are on welfare and are failing to properly discipline their children?

Othering is the process through which a person or group is turned into
somebody different from us, an "other" from whom it is possible to distance
ourselves. It is at heart a relational process that occurs in social interaction,
real and imagined, as a person or group defines itself in contrast with and
in opposition to someone else. The other, Julia Kristeva writes, is the for-
eigner, the stranger, the exile, the rebel who nevertheless lives within us and
is the "hidden face of our identity."[1] The other is deemed not only distant but
also inferior, less respectable than we are, perhaps degenerate, more readily

stigmatized, and thus more easily abused. The distancing in this sense is both figurative and literal. It carries moral connotations as well. The other is less simply a victim than someone who hasn't quite made the proper effort to fit in or who lacks the mental and emotional timber to behave respectably.

Assertions about a person's own respectability can certainly be made without othering someone else. It might in fact be supposed that being respectful toward other people would be a hallmark of respectability. In practice, however, othering appears to be a common way in which claims about respectability are made. Who qualifies as a respectable person or group and what it means to be respectable are socially constructed by identifying someone who seems deficient. The other's deficiencies may give a clearer sense by way of negative example of how respectable people should behave than anything else. The other is often maligned because of race, ethnicity, social class, gender, or sexual orientation. The other may also be marginalized in less obvious ways, such as because of not grooming properly, speaking too loudly, displaying emotion in inappropriate ways, or appearing to have temporarily lost one's mind.

On a larger scale American politics is one of the principal arenas in which othering takes place. The two-party system provides the occasion and incentive for candidates and supporters of each party to distance themselves from the other party. Numerous instances occur in which differences on the issues escalate into name calling, rumor mongering, and character assassination. In the twenty-first century studies suggest that othering of the opposition is rooted in widening polarization between Democrats and Republicans. Unfavorable ratings of the opposing party have dramatically increased, and some research suggests that turnout is driven more by voters' hostility toward the opposing party than by support of their own. While the etiquette of electoral politics has mostly encouraged candidates to be respectful toward one another and, in the interest of preserving the dignity of holding elected office, to keep things respectable, these norms appear to be easily broken, as illustrated in candidates' spreading innuendo about opponents' sexual indiscretions, using racial epithets to cast aspersions, and calling one another liars and cowards.[2]

The most salient instances in which othering occurs are ones in which a cultural distinction based on a power differential or struggle for power exists. The othering that colonizers inflict on the colonized amplifies the differences separating the two by treating the colonized as members of an inferior culture. Their otherness, which is geographically and politically delineated, is further distinguished by sharp, homogenizing contrasts based on language and style. Racial stereotyping and discrimination and stigmatization based on gender and sexual orientation function similarly. Cultural distinctions and evaluations are mapped onto phenotypical characteristics and perceived differences in biological, psychological, emotional, and intellectual capacities. The other is inferior, abnormal, and immoral, and in the extreme the othering process results in violence. Similar dynamics are evident in the othering of the poor, who in many instances have been discursively classified as dirty, diseased, depraved, and dangerous and in more recent contexts as criminal, undeserving, and welfare dependent.[3]

The inadvertent effect of discussions that for obvious reasons focus on the stark inequalities, discrimination, and violence associated with othering is to locate the topic elsewhere. The problem occurs among colonizers and slaveholders or among bigots and rednecks, not among ordinary people in everyday life. Recent discussions have paid greater attention to this bias. Robert A. Orsi, for example, has noted the tendency in postcolonial scholarship to otherize the colonizers and in academic religious studies to do the same toward devout members of evangelical and fundamentalist groups.[4] The anthropological and ethnographic literature similarly has devoted significant attention to how the subjects of field research are often otherized by being treated as representatives of radically alien cultures and in less alien settings only as victims, recipients of charity, or underprivileged and stigmatized minorities.[5]

The common template for these discussions, however, has been the othering that occurs along relatively sharp distinctions such as race, class, gender, and sexual orientation. While these are understood to be socially constructed divisions, the focus of analysis starts with a distinct categorical separation—a "social fact"—that can be treated as a symbolic boundary and then examines such questions as how it manifests itself, when it becomes salient, why it is or is not associated with behavioral patterns, and what its results are in terms of inequality, intolerance, and misunderstanding.[6] What is missing from consideration is how vague, blurred, ill defined, or nonexistent a potentially important symbolic boundary may be in the first place.

Examples taken from the nineteenth century in which ordinary people negotiated the meanings of middle-class respectability demonstrate that significant symbolic boundaries often were not sharply defined and often did not fall neatly along major cultural fault lines. The hucksters who peddled goods from farms to towns and from towns to farms and who were often regarded with suspicion by their customers and became the trope for later references to fast-talking, slick, conniving, con artists were hardly the persons who could be understood in terms of simple well-established symbolic boundaries. To the extent that such boundaries were important, it was the boundary between town and country that was dramatized as hucksters traversed it, and it was their own lack of place—the placelessness of their labor—that set them apart from the settled populations of town and country. And it was this placelessness that contrasted with arguments claiming that market houses were the preferable places in which respectable pricing processes could occur without threat of immoral impulses taking over. The lesson huckstering communicates is that othering is specific to the times and places in which—in this case, commercial—interaction occurs. It need not result in extreme rejection or exclusion and indeed may be reinforced by the fact that regular interaction exists.

At first glance the lunatic, as another example, might appear to represent the kind of othering that occurs along sharply defined boundaries: the person locked away in an asylum, concealed from public view, physically confined in a separate place away from the normal daily activities of respectable people. If the distinction was well defined in these terms, it was nevertheless the result of a definitional process. Determining that someone was insane was a matter of collective authoritative categorization, just as decisions were about persons of mixed race and ambiguous occupational status. It was in fact a difficult designation to make because it referred to qualities of mental soundness that could be disputed and were in any case understood to be sudden and often temporary occurrences. The sharp distinction between the insane who were institutionalized and ordinary people who were not, moreover, was not sharp at all when it came to the many whose lives were ambiguously affected. That number included the persons who were suspected of lunacy or had even been diagnosed as temporarily insane but for whom there was no space in the asylums. It included the spouses of institutionalized persons who struggled to make ends meet and whose neighbors wondered if something unspoken or even fraudulent was taking place. And it included the children of the insane who were widely suspected of being in line to inherit insanity. If lunacy illustrates anything about othering, it underscores the fact that seemingly sharp symbolic boundaries have wide margins that put those who are close to the margins at risk.

Accusations of fanaticism represented an even harder to define symbolic boundary along which othering could occur. Terming a political opponent a fanatic was tantamount to suggesting that the person was obsessed to the point of irrationality—and yet it was a commonly made allegation. Saying that an entire religious group was composed of fanatics was a more serious charge. Fanaticism illustrates how othering can be based on relatively subtle behavioral cues, such as the display of emotion, which under many circumstances is expected and even encouraged in religious settings but also risks challenging the authority of religious leaders and can result in observers claiming that the fanatics are not properly rational about their religion or are dangerous. Othering on grounds of fanaticism demonstrates that symbolic boundaries are context specific but depend on broader interpretations as well. Heightened displays of emotion may be an important part of what makes religion—or sports events or political rallies—meaningful, but people also have to decide how much or how little is appropriate.

Besides the ways in which symbolic boundaries may be ill defined and context specific, another complication stems from assumptions about who is doing the defining. Discussions of othering usually treat it as a phenomenon imposed by a dominant group. But that may not always be the case or at least may not fully capture the relational dynamics involved. One argument, for example, suggests that race and ethnicity should be distinguished on grounds that race is a category over which people have no control, whereas ethnicity can more often be a matter of self-assertion.[7] This argument in more nuanced form has been made in studies showing that the making of Hispanic identity in the United States has resulted from strategic political and cultural organizing among Hispanics even though this organizing has taken place within the context of highly structured external power relations.[8] Another example is research on the exoticization of art and on enclaves of artists who intentionally marginalize themselves from mainstream patterns of behavior.[9] Immigrant religious congregations are yet another example, which, as nineteenth-century examples as well as recent studies suggest, are sometimes self-marginalizing because of distinctive beliefs and are able to preserve their identity through strong in-group solidarity. The difficulty with many of the discussions of symbolic boundaries, though, is that they fail to distinguish the specific kinds of behavior to which they apply. Immigrant congregations illustrate the complexities involved. They were sometimes able to separate themselves on the basis of exclusive worship practices and adherence to strict marriage policies, for example, but mingle readily with nonmembers when engaging in economic transactions. In short, othering may be all encompassing in some instances, distancing groups from one another in every regard, while in others limited to only specific kinds of interaction.

If, as studies suggest, othering usually occurs in asymmetric relationships where the otherized has less power than the otherizer, a further complication that merits attention is how, if at all, the reverse may happen. A few studies suggest that it does. Research among working-class men, for example, suggests that African Africans sometimes set themselves above white coworkers who they claimed were not as loyal to their families or less moral, and African Americans and whites alike criticized upper- and middle-class men for being shallow and materialistic. The case of Gilded Age and Progressive Era profiteers, however, suggests that more has to happen for large-scale othering to be mobilized. Wealthy individuals could be criticized for moral failings such as greed and engaging in fraud, but collective entities such as power interests, moneyed interests, monopolies, and the plutocracy had to be identified for othering to occur that included demands for political intervention. Bringing politics to bear on othering may in turn sharpen the symbolic boundary, as it did in that case, but also significantly shift the nature of the distinction from moral criticism toward measurable bases on which to impose regulations.

A remaining aspect of othering that requires clarification is the extent to which it refers to an out-group that is relatively stable and thus permanently marginalized or whether it applies to symbolic boundaries that are relatively permeable. Othering people on the basis of race and gender suggests that the categories are fixed, with only their salience and implications varying in interesting ways. But other cases do not fit this pattern. Examples might include an atheist who has been maligned for being an unbeliever who then undergoes a conversion experience and becomes a member of a respected church, a convicted felon who serves a full sentence in prison and then rejoins the community, a member of an ultraconservative religious group who defects, or a gay person who comes out of the closet. In each case a symbolic boundary has been crossed, and its crossing both reveals that it exists but also implies that something about the person who has been (or who might be) otherized is likely to change. In the nineteenth century discussions of naughty children held the same implications. It was important that the child not be an outsider who was evil from the start, but that the child became an outsider by virtue of a particular act and then could be redeemed through some act of contrition or punishment. The othering that occurred in these instances was important even though it was temporary because it permitted the difference between good and evil to be taught.

Whether they are crisp or vaguely constituted, the symbolic boundaries around which othering revolves vary in salience and thus pose the question of why they are more important under some circumstances than others. Studies provide a variety of explanations, which on closer inspection turn out to be more about different perspectives than about testable empirical propositions. The perspectives range from ones focusing on cognitive, discursive, and psychological factors to ones concerned with large-scale social conditions.

Cognitive, discursive, and psychological perspectives get us to the point of understanding that we do process information by organizing it into categories, which we reference as alterity in speech, and which sometimes relate to anxiety, as in instances of scapegoating others when feeling under duress. In these perspectives othering is in the first instance the imposition of differences, as Saussure argued, on which meaning depends.[10] The perspectives focusing on societal conditions tell us that othering is likely to be directed toward groups that are already in the minority because of race, ethnicity, and national origin, and that othering may erupt into violence or become more vicious because of struggles for power, such as during hotly contested political campaigns. Discussions of societal conditions also suggest that othering becomes more salient when a society's members feel threatened. Kai T. Erikson's *Wayward Puritans*, for example, showed the relationship of New England colonists feeling under threat to the outbreak of the Salem witch trials.[11] Research on purges in Stalinist Russia and anti-immigrant hysteria in the United States following the Pearl Harbor and 9/11 attacks serve as similar examples, suggesting the effects not only of feeling threatened but also of being committed to the nation's collective interests.[12]

Less attention has been given to the possibility that othering is a response that helps people feel respectable when the diversity to which they are exposed makes it difficult to stipulate in more positive ways what respectability is. This possibility would pertain to situations in which well-intentioned people want to get along with others with whom they differ and simply find it easier to target some out-group as exemplifying what not to do than to work out the details of what respectability actually is. For example, a devout African American Baptist and a devout Italian American Roman Catholic who were friends and had mutual friends might find it awkward to talk about their churches' different doctrines and hierarchies or their different ethnic and racial lineages but easily fall into discussing how terrible it is to have Hispanic immigrants living in America. The point is not that their othering of immigrants is "caused" by the lack of theological agreement but that it allows them to have something in common with each other without having to specify in much detail what that is. The logic is similar to saying that "the enemy of my friend is my enemy" except that it becomes "I consider X my friend because we have a common enemy."

Several lines of argument point to the possibility of cultural diversity being associated with a tendency to find solidarity by identifying an outside group as the "other." One possibility is that communication across a diverse population becomes harder and thus changes in quality, leaving the option of communicating more easily about an objectified outsider. Émile Durkheim, for example, suggested that in larger, more voluminous societies, "the common conscience is itself obliged to rise above all local diversities, to dominate more space, and consequently to become more abstract." A theological system in a large complex religiously diverse society, for instance, might refer abstractly to God or a higher power, whereas the sacred in a small isolated context might refer to a particular animal or ancestor.[13] An abstract symbol capable of speaking to the common conscience, such as references to God, pride, or freedom, might serve as a unifying principle, Durkheim argued, but only if it could be revered as especially powerful or sacred—which was the function of the "negative cult," the taboo, the forbidden fruit, the impure that, by contrast, defined the pure.[14]

A related argument is suggested by recent scholarship on whiteness. Whiteness in this understanding is an empty cultural category that masks the diversity it contains. It is the default, the center, the majority that supposedly is homogeneous and requires no further specification, whereas in reality it is composed of much diversity. Lacking in detail, it is, as Cornel West has observed, a "constructed category parasitic on blackness." It "expels its anxieties, contradictions and irrationalities onto the subordinate term," West argues, "filling it with the antithesis of its own identity; the Other, in its very alienness, simply mirrors and represents what is deeply familiar to the center, but projected outside of itself."[15]

It would be inaccurate to say that nineteenth-century definitions of middle-class respectability were similarly empty. Writers advocated for parents to responsibly teach their children good morals and for children to obey. There were efforts to link middle-class membership not only with schooling and indoor jobs but also with appeals for good taste and refinement in character. However, it was not always easy to specify the meaning of these abstractions. The nation was ethnically and racially and culturally diverse from the beginning and became increasingly so. Respectability as an ideal had to be specified in practice. It was specified relationally. The good guys gained specificity in relation to the bad guys. The bad guys were puzzling, interesting, different, and often ambiguous, and they attracted attention for that reason. Whether it was the stranger who came as a huckster with wares to sell or the neighbor who went berserk or the German farmers who seemed to be promoting sedition, they sparked discussion of what was not quite right. The profiteers and the plutocrats played a similar cultural role. If it was hard to say who exactly the "common man" was, it was at least possible to claim that ordinary people were not like those scandal-ridden millionaires.

In 1922 G. K. Chesterton hinted at something like this when he wrote about America being a "nation with the soul of a church." More than nearly anything else from his visit, the phrase caught the imagination of subsequent observers. Yes, it seemed, America was founded on religious principles; yes, the nation was exceptional in the extent of its religious beliefs and participation; and yes, the United States embraced the ideal of religious freedom. If there was something practical to be remembered from Chesterton's observation, it was the idea that America was engaged in a continuing quest to uphold its principles of inclusion, pluralism, and tolerance. Surely this was the challenge that good-hearted Americans would face again and again as the nation sought to retain its moral character at the same time that it dealt with successive waves of immigrants.[16]

But there was an irony in all of this that not even Chesterton fully appreciated. What American culture fundamentally stood for, he argued, was citizenship and nothing more. Everyone should be treated as citizens, full stop. That was the meaning of equality. In all other respects the principle of equality meant that differences should be embraced, or at least tolerated, and that in treating one another as equals, citizens proved themselves worthy of public respect. And yet that was not the reality of America at all. It was not the reality Chesterton observed in 1921 when his visit prompted him to comment critically on rampant racism, anti-Semitism, political conflicts, and religious divisions. It was not the reality when he visited a decade later, and it was not the reality that later commentators observed.[17]

The irony was actually a paradox. Citizenship and citizenship alone may have been the ideal, but if the nation did in any way have the soul of a church, its soul was an impetus to define what good citizenship should involve. It was the desire to identify common values and to instill them in children and uphold them through legislation. The notion that citizenship should be minimally defined and the fact that in reality there was considerable diversity in ideas of good citizenship, though, meant that it was difficult to spell out much more than the abstract terms in which values and character could be discussed. Honesty, integrity, and fair play, to be sure, but beyond that it was harder to elicit agreement.

And that was the connection with Americans' penchant for disagreement and exclusion. In the breach, when it was difficult to say with much specificity what the values on which good citizenship should be based were, it was easier to say what they were *not*. Criticizing, castigating, stereotyping, finding fault with, and excluding those who were different was not simply the problem with which Americanization had to deal; it was part and parcel of the Americanization process itself.

Nearly a century later the nation's soul would less aptly be described as a church—perhaps more as a mosaic, a cacophony, a nation in search of itself, or a dissonant space. Calls are made from time to time for common ground to be identified and for a middle way to be affirmed somewhere between the radical right and the radical left. In the name of reason, elected officials call on the citizenry to show respect and to uphold basic values. They caution against mudslinging and vulgarity. That's not who we are, they warn when bigotry and violence erupt. That betrays our values. We're better than that. But it is far easier to say what we are against than what we are for.

Introduction

1. Anne Hart, widow of Rev. Oliver Hart: Will (age fourteen), bound to James Ewing, to be manumitted after a term of eleven years, Hopewell Twp., 29 April, 1796; Anne Hart, widow of Rev. Oliver Hart: James (age ten), bound to Peter Gordon, to be manumitted after a term of fifteen years, Hopewell Twp., 28 April, 1796; copies of original manumission papers, Clerk's Office, Hunterdon County, Manumissions of Slaves, 1788–1836; New Jersey Department of State, accession numbers 1977.013 and 2005.08. Another manumitted slave who lived nearby was Sylvia Dubois; see DoVeanna S. Fulton Minor and Reginald H. Pitts, eds., *Speaking Lives, Authoring Texts: Three African American Women's Oral Slave Narratives* (Albany: State University of New York Press, 2010).

2. "A Brief History," Mt. Zion United Methodist Church, Hillsborough, New Jersey, undated; the history of the region is described in T. James Luce, *New Jersey's Sourland Mountain* (Hamilton, NJ: White Eagle Printing, 2001); additional information courtesy Hopewell Museum, Hopewell, NJ.

3. Isaiah 14:32, KJV; published accounts of such communities include Shelly O'Foran, *Little Zion* (Chapel Hill: University of North Carolina Press, 2006); Dale Edwyna Smith, *The Slaves of Liberty: Freedom in Amite County, Mississippi, 1820–1868* (New York: Routledge, 2012); and Erskine Clarke, *Our Southern Zion: A History of Calvinism in the South Carolina Low Country, 1690–1990* (Tuscaloosa: University of Alabama Press, 1996).

4. "The Baptist Meeting House, Hopewell, Mercer County, NJ," *Trenton Evening Times*, May 12, 1901.

5. Oliver Hart's diary, which was used in H. A. Tupper, *Two Centuries of the First Baptist Church of South Carolina* (Baltimore: R. H. Woodward, 1889) and transcribed by Loulie Latimer Owens in 1949 and later made available online, details Hart's involvement with other patriots during the American Revolution but makes no mention of his ownership of slaves; however, Tupper devotes a chapter to "Work among the Negroes," in which he recalls services in the 1830s when there was an "immense crowd of negroes in the north gallery, whose faces beamed with intense interest in the preached word, and whose lips made the house to resound with their singing of the old songs of Zion" (315).

6. James Truslow Adams, *The Epic of America* (Boston: Little, Brown, 1931), 174.

7. Ronald Reagan, "Remarks Accepting the Presidential Nomination at the Republican National Convention in Dallas, Texas, August 23, 1984; https://reaganlibrary.gov/archives/research.

8. William J. Clinton," Remarks to the Democratic Leadership Council," December 3, 1993; http://www.presidency.ucsb.edu.

9. George W. Bush," Remarks on Signing the American Dream Downpayment Act," December 16, 2003; http://www.presidency.ucsb.edu.

10. Barack Obama, *The Audacity of Hope: Thoughts on Reclaiming the American Dream* (New York: Random House, 2006); Barack Obama, "Speech on the American Dream," November 7, 2007; http://cnn.com.

11. Kate Ellis and Ellen Guettler, "A Better Life: Creating the American Dream," American Public Media, 2015; http://www.americanradioworks.org.

12. Jennifer L. Hochschild, *Facing Up to the American Dream: Race, Class, and the Soul of the Nation* (Princeton, NJ: Princeton University Press, 1995), 15–38.

13. The number refers to articles and reviews in sociology journals included in the JSTOR online database.

14. Martha C. White, "American Dream Deferred: We Now Embrace More Modest, Personal Goals," *Time*, December 1, 2011; Sandra L. Hanson and John Zogby, "Attitudes about the American Dream," *Public Opinion Quarterly* 74 (2010), 570–84.

15. W.E.B. Dubois, *The Philadelphia Negro: A Social Study* (Philadelphia: University of Pennsylvania, 1899); Gunnar Myrdal, *An American Dilemma: The Negro Problem and Modern Democracy* (New York: Harper & Row, 1944); Michael Harrington, *The Other America* (New York: Macmillan, 1973).

16. Franklin D. Roosevelt, "State of the Union Address," January 6, 1941; http:// voicesofdemocracy.umd.edu.

17. Obama, *Audacity of Hope*, 12.

18. Roy Schwartzman, "Recasting the American Dream through Horatio Alger's Success Stories," *Studies in Popular Culture* 23 (October 2000), 75–91.

19. Quotes from Schwartzman, "Recasting the American Dream," 81, who references Glenn Hendler, "Pandering in the Public Sphere: Masculinity and the Market in Horatio Alger," *American Quarterly* 48 (September 1996), 415–38, and Alex Pitofsky, "Dreiser's *The Financier* and the Horatio Alger Myth," *Twentieth Century Literature* 44 (Fall 1998), 276–90.

20. Schwartzman, "Recasting the American Dream," 82.

21. Examples of these volumes include *Portrait and Biographical Album of Lenawee County, Michigan* (Chicago: Chapman Brothers, 1888), and *Portrait and Biographical Album of Racine and Kenosha Counties, Wisconsin* (Chicago: Lake City Publishing, 1892).

22. Pierre Bourdieu, *Outline of a Theory of Practice* (New York: Cambridge University Press, 1977).

23. Linda M. Lobao, Gregory Hooks, and Ann R. Tickamyer, "Introduction: Advancing the Sociology of Spatial Inequality," in *The Sociology of Spatial Inequality*, ed. Linda M. Lobao, Gregory Hooks, and Ann R. Tickamyer (Albany: State University of New York Press, 2007), 1–27; Thomas F. Gieryn, "A Space for Place in Sociology," *Annual Review of Sociology* 26 (2000), 463–96.

24. Donna T. Andrew, *Aristocratic Vice: The Attack on Duelling, Suicide, Adultery, and Gambling in Eighteenth-Century England* (New Haven, CT: Yale University Press, 2013).

25. Nineteenth-century references to Zion by Christian leaders were related to the idea that America was the "New Israel" foretold in biblical prophecy, some of the most prominent examples of which are included in Conrad Cherry, ed., *God's New Israel: Religious Interpretations of American Destiny*, 2nd ed. (Chapel Hill: University of North Carolina Press, 1998). The idea that America was divinely ordained attached moral fervor to leaders' calls for it to enlarge itself and bring about God's kingdom on earth; Ernest Lee Tuveson, *Redeemer Nation: The Idea of America's Millennial Role* (Chicago: University of Chicago Press, 1968); J. Larry Hood, *Visions of Zion: Christianity, Modernization and the American Pursuit of Liberty Progressivism in Rural Nelson and Washington Counties Kentucky* (Lanham, MD: University Press of America, 2005). Critical reflections on these and related ideas form the basis of Robert N. Bellah, *The Broken Covenant: American Civil Religion in Time of Trial*, 2nd ed. (Chicago: University of Chicago Press, 1992). At the local level one of the best illustrations of America being described as the New Israel is a sermon preached at Gallipolis, Ohio, in 1864 by Reverend Robinson Breare, a fifty-three-year-old Unitarian pastor who had been a Wesleyan Methodist earlier in his career. The sermon stated: "By comparing the events of our history as a nation, from the first settlement of New England by the Puritans, from the old home up to the present day—with certain of the prophetic statements we have already cited, we think we have a right to the conclusion—that the

portion of this western continent occupied by the United States, is the promised land of the future, as designated by ancient prophecy; that the American people, native, and adopted, or naturalized, are the modern Israel" (Breare, "The Union Soldier," *Gallipolis Journal* [Gallipolis, Ohio], February 25, 1864). References to America as the fulfillment of biblical prophecy can also be found in twentieth- and twenty-first-century discussions; for example, Joseph D. Brandon, *America A Staggering Nation: A Vision of the Future, Recovery or Demise* (Bloomington, IN: WestBow Press, 2010); see also examples in Todd Gitlin and Liel Leibovitz, *The Chosen Peoples: America, Israel, and the Ordeals of Divine Election* (New York: Simon & Schuster, 2010). Zion typically referred to specific places rather than to the nation or the American people at large, as in Brigham Young's plans for building an earthly Zion in the valleys of the Rocky Mountains, *Discourses of Brigham Young*, ed. John A. Widtsoe (Salt Lake City, UT: Deseret Book Company, 1954), 119–21; the Mount Zion Society's efforts in Winnsboro, South Carolina, the Mount Zion Association in South Carolina, and church leaders' efforts in Alabama, Illinois, Kentucky, Missouri, Pennsylvania, Tennessee, Texas, and West Virginia, among other locations. Jewish understandings of the relation of America to Zion are discussed in Henry L. Feingold, *Zion in America: The Jewish Experience from Colonial Times to the Present* (New York: Dover Publications, 2002).

26. The multiple meanings of Zion are evident in Christian hymns, sermons, and advice columns that likened congregations to Zion and counseled Christians to march, pursue purity, attend revival meetings, engage in evangelism, aspire to life in heaven, be progressive, support charity, avoid being at ease in Zion, understand that God welcomed the destitute to Zion, and take courage in knowing that Zion was a steep and rugged climb for people with feeble steps and trembling hearts who would face the snares of the enemy along the way. While most of the counsel about Zion spoke to individuals and congregations, a World War I hymn entitled "Zion America" (Lawrence Harper, "Zion America," Cincinnati: Willis Music Company, 1918) asked God's blessings on the soldiers who had "gone after the Hun" and were "fighting for Jesus" and "Christ's Kingdom" and "the Red, White, and Blue."

27. J. W. Otley, L. Van Derveer, and J. Keily, *Map of Somerset County New Jersey Entirely from Original Surveys* (Camden, NJ: Lloyd Van Derveer, 1850), from the collection "Nova Caesarea: A Cartographic Record of the Garden State, 1666–1888," Princeton University, Princeton, NJ.

Chapter One

1. Odin W. Anderson, "The Lynching of Hans Jakob Olson: The Story of a Norwegian-American Crime," *Norwegian American Studies* 29 (Summer 1983), 159–85; the lynching received widespread coverage in newspapers that variously described Olson as a victim, a possible murderer, demented, a half idiot, and insane. Johnson was convicted of first-degree murder, sentenced to life in prison, but pardoned five years later; Norman K. Risjord, *The WPA Guide to Wisconsin* (Minneapolis: Minnesota Historical Society Press, 1941), 418.

2. Angela Hornsby-Gutting and Charles Reagan Wilson, "Politics of Respectability," in *The New Encyclopedia of Southern Culture*. Vol. 13: *Gender*, ed. Nancy Bercaw and Ted Ownby (Chapel Hill: University of North Carolina Press, 2009), 238–42; Kathryn Lofton, "Everything Queer?" in *Queer Christianities: Lived Religion in Transgressive Forms*, ed. Kathleen T. Talvacchia, Michael F. Pettinger, and Mark Larrimore (New York: NYU Press, 2015), 195–204; Fredrick C. Harris, "The Rise of Respectability Politics," *Dissent* 61 (Winter 2014), 33–37.

3. Ben McJunkin, "Rank among Equals," *Michigan Law Review* 113 (April 2015), 855–76; Michael D. Gilbert, "The Problem of Voter Fraud," *Columbia Law Review* 115 (April

2015), 739–75; Fredrick Harris, *Price of the Ticket: Barack Obama and Rise and Decline of Black Politics* (New York: Oxford University Press, 2012).

4. W. Caleb McDaniel, "The Fourth and the First: Abolitionist Holidays, Respectability, and Radical Interracial Reform," *American Quarterly* 57 (March 2005), 129–51.

5. Jeffrey J. Lange, *Smile When You Call Me a Hillbilly: Country Music's Struggle for Respectability, 1939–1954* (Athens: University of Georgia Press, 2004).

6. Woodruff D. Smith, *Consumption and the Making of Respectability, 1600–1800* (New York: Routledge, 2002); Janice Hume, *Obituaries in American Culture* (Jackson: University Press of Mississippi, 2000).

7. For example, Peter Thal Larsen, "Tough Guys Step Out from the Shadows," *Financial Times,* April 11, 2002; John T. Landry, "Wheels of Fortune: The History of Speculation from Scandal to Respectability," *Harvard Business Review* 80 (December 2002), 26.

8. Krishna S. Dhir and Denis Vinen, "Managing Corporate Respectability: Concept, Issues, and Policy Formulation," *Corporate Communications* 10 (2005), 5–23.

9. Calvin White Jr., *The Rise to Respectability: Race, Religion, and the Church of God in Christ* (Fayetteville: University of Arkansas Press, 2012); Pamela E. Klassen, "The Robes of Womanhood: Dress and Authenticity among African American Methodist Women in the Nineteenth Century," *Religion and American Culture* 14 (Winter 2004), 39–82.

10. James S. Coleman, "Social Capital in the Creation of Human Capital," *American Journal of Sociology* 94 (1988), S95–S120, for example, grounds the discussion of trust and trustworthiness in the language of role performance, stating, "If A does something for B and trusts B to reciprocate in the future, this establishes an expectation in A and an obligation on the part of B" (S102). Role-specific trust is also the basis for considering trust as confidence in taking cooperative risks, as in Russell Hardin, *Trust and Trustworthiness* (New York: Russell Sage Foundation, 2002). The overlap with respect is evident in context specific approaches, as in Karen S. Cook, Margaret Levi, and Russell Hardin, eds., *Who Can We Trust? How Groups, Networks, and Institutions Make Trust Possible* (New York: Russell Sage Foundation, 2009).

11. Following Bourdieu, Michele Lamont and Annette Lareau, "Cultural Capital: Allusions, Gaps and Glissandos in Recent Theoretical Developments," *Sociological Theory* 6 (Autumn 1988), 153–68, note that respectable is sometimes regarded as "good but not prestigious," quote on 157.

12. "Reading Character from Inspection of the Vulva and Vagina," *Atlanta Journal Record of Medicine* 1 (August 1, 1899), 388–90; I. M. Rutkow, "Edwin Hartley Pratt and Orificial Surgery: Unorthodox Surgical Practice in Nineteenth Century," *Surgery* 114 (September 1993), 558–63. Pratt also believed that insanity and a propensity to engage in sexual crimes could be inferred from orificial examinations, and that the effects of telling lies ramified through every cell of the body; E. H. Pratt, "Editorial," *Journal of Orificial Surgery* 2 (1894), 275–82.

13. Melvin L. Kohn, "Social Class and Parental Values," *American Journal of Sociology* 64 (January 1959), 337–51; quote on 350.

14. John C. Ball, *Social Deviancy and Adolescent Personality* (Knoxville: University Press of Kentucky, 1962), provides examples of research in this vein.

15. Evelyn Brooks Higginbotham, *Righteous Discontent: The Women's Movement in the Black Baptist Church, 1880–1920* (Cambridge, MA: Harvard University Press, 1993); the "talented tenth" are described on 19–46 and the politics of respectability is the focus of 185–230.

16. The relational approach offered here builds on sociological studies concerned with the phenomenology of deviance; for example, Jack D. Douglas, ed., *Deviance and Respectability: The Social Construction of Moral Meanings* (New York: Basic Books, 1970);

Darrell J. Steffensmeier and Robert M. Terry, "Deviance and Respectability: An Observational Study of Reactions to Shoplifting," *Social Forces* 51 (June 1973), 417–26; Mary S. Hartman, "Murder for Respectability: The Case of Madeleine Smith, " *Victorian Studies* 16 (June 1973), 381–400; Keith M. Macdonald, "Building Respectability," *Sociology* 23 (February 1989), 55–80. On architecture and respectability, see also Karin Aguilar-San Juan, *Little Saigons: Staying Vietnamese in America* (Minneapolis: University of Minnesota Press, 2009), who discusses how community leaders constructed the Asian Garden Mall to counter prevailing negative ideas about Vietnamese immigrants.

17. Amy Laura Hall, "Respectability," in Stan Goff, *Borderline: Reflections on War, Sex, and Church* (London: Lutterworth Press, 2015), 261–70, quote on 264.

18. Émile Durkheim, *Elementary Forms of the Religious Life* (New York: Free Press, 1915); Mary Douglas, *Purity and Danger: An Analysis of Concepts of Pollution and Taboo* (New York: Routledge, 1966); Clifford Geertz, *The Interpretation of Cultures* (New York: Basic Books, 1973); Susanne K. Langer, *Philosophy in a New Key: A study in the Symbolism of Reason, Rite, and Art* (Cambridge, MA: Harvard University Press, 1941), 14; Norman O. Brown, *Love's Body* (New York: Random House,1966); Pierre Bourdieu, *Distinction: A Social Critique of the Judgement of Taste* (Cambridge, MA: Harvard University Press, 1979).

19. Mustafa Emirbayer, "Manifesto for a Relational Sociology," *American Journal of Sociology* 103 (September 1997), 281–317, quote on 287; Viviana A. Zelizer, "How I Became a Relational Economic Sociologist and What Does that Mean?" *Politics and Society* 40 (June 2012), 145–74; Ann Mische, "Relational Sociology, Culture, and Agency," in *The Sage Handbook of Social Network Analysis*, ed. John Scott and Peter Carrington (London: Sage Publications, 2011), 80–97.

20. Pierre Bourdieu, *Outline of a Theory of Practice* (New York: Cambridge University Press, 1977); Pierre Bourdieu, *The Logic of Practice* (Stanford, CA: Stanford University Press, 1990); Alasdair MacIntyre, *After Virtue: A Study in Moral Theory* (Notre Dame, IN: Notre Dame University Press, 1981); Jeffrey Stout, *Ethics after Babel* (Princeton, NJ: Princeton University Press, 1988); and Theodore R. Schatzki, Karin Knorr Cetina, and Eike von Savigny, eds., *The Practice Turn in Contemporary Theory* (New York: Routledge, 2000).

21. Helmut R. Wagner, ed., *Alfred Schutz on Phenomenology and Social Relations* (Chicago: University of Chicago Press, 1970), 321–22.

22. Donna T. Andrew, *Aristocratic Vice: The Attack on Duelling, Suicide, Adultery, and Gambling in Eighteenth-Century England* (New Haven, CT: Yale University Press, 2013), 220–21.

23. Erving Goffman, *Relations in Public* (New York: Penguin, 1972), 385.

24. Harvey Sacks, *Lectures on Conversation* (Cambridge, MA: Blackwell, 1992), 32–66.

25. Brian P. Luskey, *On the Make* (New York: NYU Press, 2010); on bodies, Catherine Bell, *Ritual Theory, Ritual Practice* (New York: Oxford University Press, 1992), 94–117; and on discourse about bodies, Christina Simmons, "'I Had to Promise . . . Not to Ask 'Nasty' Questions Again': African American Women and Sex and Marriage Education in the 1940s," *Journal of Women's History* 27 (Spring 2015), 110–35.

26. Item posted on Facebook by David Battiste, March 1, 2016.

27. Edward W. Morris, *Learning the Hard Way: Masculinity, Place, and the Gender Gap in Education* (New Brunswick, NJ: Rutgers University Press, 2012), 20–34.

28. Lorena Garcia, *Respect Yourself, Protect Yourself: Latina Girls and Sexual Identity* (New York: NYU Press, 2012), 84.

29. Liza G. Steele, "'A Gift from God': Adolescent Motherhood and Religion in Brazilian Favelas," *Sociology of Religion* 72 (January 2011), 4–27.

30. Mitchell Duneier, *Slim's Table: Race, Respectability, and Masculinity* (Chicago: University of Chicago Press, 1992).

31. Robert Wuthnow, *Small-Town America: Finding Community, Shaping the Future* (Princeton, NJ: Princeton University Press, 2013).

32. Mikhail Bakhtin, *The Dialogic Imagination: Four Essays* (Austin: University of Texas Press, 1981); Michael Holquist, *Dialogism: Bakhtin and His World*, 2nd ed. (New York: Routledge, 2002). The emphasis on cognitive schemas as a different approach is exemplified in the work of Roy D'Andrade, *The Development of Cognitive Anthropology* (New York: Cambridge University Press, 1995). On narrative as relational discourse, see Margaret R. Somers, "The Narrative Constitution of Identity: A Relational and Network Approach," *Theory and Society* 23 (October 1994), 605–49.

33. David Goodhew, "Working-Class Respectability: The Example of the Western Areas of Johannesburg, 1930–55," *Journal of African History* 41 (June 2000), 241–66, quote on 242.

34. Morris, *Learning the Hard Way*, 32.

35. Vanesa Ribas, *On the Line: Slaughterhouse Lives and the Making of the New South* (Berkeley: University of California Press, 2016), 65

36. Robert Wuthnow, *Acts of Compassion: Caring for Others and Helping Ourselves* (Princeton, NJ: Princeton University Press, 1991).

37. Jennie Chapman, *Plotting Apocalypse: Reading, Agency, and Identity in the Left Behind Series* (Jackson: University Press of Mississippi, 2013), 57.

38. Fiona C. Ross, "Raw Life and Respectability: Poverty and Everyday life in a Post-apartheid Community," *Current Anthropology* 56 (October 2015), S97–S107; Claude Lévi-Strauss, *The Raw and the Cooked: Introduction to a Science of Mythology* (New York: Harper & Row, 1969).

39. Beth Bailey, "Patsy Cline and the Problem of Respectability," in Warren R. Hofstra, ed., *Sweet Dreams: The World of Patsy Cline* (Urbana: University of Illinois Press, 2013), 67–85, quote on 68.

40. Grace Yukich, "Boundary Work in Inclusive Religious Groups: Constructing Identity at the New York Catholic Worker," *Sociology of Religion* 71 (Summer 2010), 172–96.

41. Quoted in Andrew C. Holman, *Sense of Their Duty: Middle-Class Formation in Victorian Ontario Towns* (Montreal: McGill-Queen's University Press, 2000), 4–5.

42. The relationship of organizations to symbolic boundaries is examined in Elizabeth Cherry, "Shifting Symbolic Boundaries: Cultural Strategies of the Animal Rights Movement," *Sociological Forum* 25 (September 2010), 450–75; Joshua Gamson, "Messages of Exclusion: Gender, Movements, and Symbolic Boundaries," *Gender and Society* 11 (April 1997), 178–99; and Rachel Sherman, "Producing the Superior Self: Strategic Comparison and Symbolic Boundaries among Luxury Hotel Workers," *Ethnography* 6 (June 2005), 131–58. An interesting argument about organizations drawing symbolic boundaries on the basis of appropriate displays of emotion is presented in Amy C. Wilkins, "'Happier than Non-Christians': Collective Emotions and Symbolic Boundaries among Evangelical Christians," *Social Psychology Quarterly* 71(September 2008), 281–301.

43. Paul C. Higgins, "Deviance within a Disabled Community: Peddling among the Deaf," *Pacific Sociological Review* 22 (January 1979), 96–114.

44. Max Weber, "The Protestant Sects and the Spirit of Capitalism," in *From Max Weber: Essays in Sociology*, ed. H. H. Gerth and C. Wright Mills (New York: Oxford University Press, 1946), 302–22, quote on 305.

45. S. D. Clark, "Economic Expansion and the Moral Order," *Canadian Journal of Economics and Political Science* 6 (May 1940), 203–25, quote on 218–19.

46. Omar M. McRoberts, *Streets of Glory: Church and Community in a Black Urban Neighborhood* (Chicago: University of Chicago Press, 2003).

47. Allison Schnable, "Singing the Gospel: Using Musical Practices to Build Religious and Racial Communities," *Poetics* 40 (May 2012), 278–98.

48. Michel Foucault, *Madness and Civilization* (New York: Random House, 1965), 65.

49. Anne M. Boylan, *Origins of Women's Activism* (Chapel Hill: University of North Carolina Press, 2002), 17–52, quote on 24.

50. Brian Hoffman, *Naked: A Cultural History of American Nudism* (New York: NYU Press, 2015), 48–86.

51. Georg Simmel, "The Stranger," in Kurt Wolff, *The Sociology of Georg Simmel* (New York: Free Press, 1950), 402–8.

52. Sherri Broder, *Tramps, Unfit Mothers, and Neglected Children: Negotiating the Family in Nineteenth-Century Philadelphia* (Philadelphia: University of Pennsylvania Press, 2002).

53. Randall Collins, *The Credential Society: An Historical Sociology of Education and Stratification* (New York: Academic Press, 1979).

54. Anne Kreamer, *Always Personal: Navigating Emotion in the New Workplace* (New York: Random House, 2012); Olga Khazan, "Lean In to Crying at Work," *Atlantic* (March 17, 2016), http://theatlantic.com.

55. This point is emphasized in Howard Becker, *The Outsiders: Studies in the Sociology of Deviance* (New York: Free Press, 1963), 1–18.

56. James W. Trent Jr., *Inventing the Feeble Mind: A History of Mental Retardation in the United States* (Berkeley: University of California Press, 1995).

57. Pierre Bourdieu, "Social Space and Symbolic Power," *Sociological Theory* 7 (Spring 1989), 14–25, quote on 17.

58. Andreas Wimmer, "The Making and Unmaking of Ethnic Boundaries: A Multilevel Process Theory," *American Journal of Sociology* 113 (January 2008), 970–1022.

59. Charles Tilly, *Durable Inequality* (Berkeley: University of California Press, 1998), 10.

60. Hannah Arendt, *The Origins of Totalitarianism* (New York: Harcourt Brace, 1951).

61. Mona Oikawa, *Cartographies of Violence: Japanese Canadian Women, Memory, and the Subjects of the Internment* (Toronto: University of Toronto Press, 2012), 32.

62. Christopher Waldrep, *The Many Faces of Judge Lynch: Extralegal Violence and Punishment in America* (New York: Palgrave Macmillan, 2002); Steward Tolnay and E. M. Beck, *A Festival of Violence: An Analysis of Southern Lynchings, 1882–1930* (Urbana: University of Illinois Press, 1995); Ashraf H. A. Rushdy, *American Lynching* (New Haven, CT: Yale University Press, 2012), especially 94–122.

63. Erving Goffman, "The Nature of Deference and Demeanor," *American Anthropologist* 58 (June 1956), 473–502; Susan Crawford Sullivan, *Living Faith: Everyday Religion and Mothers in Poverty* (Chicago: University of Chicago Press, 2011).

64. Russell Banks, Loïc Wacquant, and Christa Buschendorf, "Casting America's Outcasts: A Dialogue between Russell Banks and Loïc Wacquant," *American Studies* 53 (2008), 209–19.

65. Ari Adut, *On Scandal: Moral Disturbances in Society, Politics, and Art* (New York: Cambridge University Press, 2008), 13.

66. Orrin E. Klapp, "Heroes, Villains and Fools as Agents of Social Control," *American Sociological Review* 19 (February 1954), 56–62, quote on 57.

Chapter Two

1. "His First Great Victory," *Daily Cairo Bulletin* [Cairo, IL], April 16, 1880. Company A's recruits, also known as Dresser's Battery, were nearly all from Perry County. Of the 209 who served in the company between 1861 and 1865, 42 were killed or died of wounds; 7 were killed or died of wounds incurred at Fort Donelson.

2. Chauncey Herbert Cooke, *Soldier Boy's Letters to His Father and Mother, 1861–65* (New York: News Office, 1915), letter dated September 10, 1864.

3. Literary interest in hucksters and peddlers extends from the huckster in *Aesop's Fables* whose salt-laden ass falls into the stream, to the wicked queen disguised as a peddler in Snow White and the Seven Dwarfs, and to Horatio Alger's plucky *Paul the Peddler*. It includes the crafty hawker of echoes in Mark Twain's "Canvasser's Tale," the Dublin advertising canvasser purveying conspicuous consumption in *Ulysses*, the Persian peddler in *Oklahoma!*, and the defeated Brooklyn traveling salesman Willy Loman. One of the few historical treatments is Walter A. Friedman, *Birth of a Salesman: The Transformation of Selling in America* (Cambridge, MA: Harvard University Press, 2004).

4. Samuel M. Huey, "Affidavit of Claimant," Johnson County, Kansas, November 10, 1890, Civil War Pension File, Application 602394, Certificate 605812, U.S. National Archives and Records Administration. The uncle at whose house Huey convalesced was Samuel Pressly, the husband of Nancy Jane Huey, who was the younger sister of Huey's father John C. Huey. One of Pressly's ancestors, Reverend John T. Pressly of the Associate Reformed Presbyterian Church, had been one of the denomination's opponents of slavery in South Carolina in the 1820s. The cousin with whom Huey traveled to Kansas was Alexander Craig, who was the same age as Huey, and whose father James Craig was a relative of Huey's mother. Although the 1880 U.S. Census listed the occupation of numerous residents as hucksters or peddlers, Huey's Civil War Pension File provides an unusual window into the life and reputation of one such ordinary person, some of the details of which were possible to augment from family-tree postings on Ancestry.com.

5. Robert L. Ardrey, *American Agricultural Implements: A Review of Invention and Development in the Agricultural Implement Industry of the United States* (Chicago: R. R. Ardrey, 1894), 103–15. Advertisements in 1867 for threshing machines in the *Prairie Farmer*, which circulated widely in southern Illinois, included the Sweepstakes Threshing Machine, manufactured in Chicago, and the Star Thresher and Cleaner, manufactured in Albany, New York. Teams of horses that walked in circles, turning the central cogwheel that operated the thresher's tumbling rods, drove both. The advertisements claimed that both machines operated faster and with less friction than older machines, thus taxing the horses less and threshing more wheat in less time. Numerous patents for small improvements on threshing machines were filed with the U.S. Patent Office from 1850 to 1880.

6. William H. Marvin, "Neighbor's Affidavit," Topeka, Shawnee, Kansas, July 5, 1890; C. J. Pressly, "Neighbor's Affidavit," Sparta, Randolph County, Illinois, May 24, 1890, in Civil War Pension File, Application 602394, Certificate 605812, U.S. National Archives and Records Administration. William H. Marvin was four years older than Huey and had grown up in the same county. By 1887 Marvin and Huey were living in the same small town of Eskridge in Kansas (in 1905 a relative of Marvin's married one of Huey's daughters); Marvin's affidavit said of Huey that he "has tried to make a living by canvassing for books and huxtering and any light work he could stand" and explained that "he has been at my house often when he was canvassing and also when huxtering." C. J. (Cephus Jason) Pressly was the son of Samuel Pressly (and thus a cousin of Huey's) and had done canvassing with Huey. He wrote that Huey engaged in "soliciting orders or canvassing for books or other light employment" and "worked at canvassing and other light work."

7. "The Peddler," *Sandusky Daily Register* [Sandusky, OH], December 11, 1890.

8. "Grocers' Criterion," *Le Mars Semi Weekly Sentinel* [Le Mars, IA], January 20, 1891.

9. "The Peddler," *Sandusky Daily Register* [Sandusky, OH], December 11, 1890; the account was probably based on a story by the French diplomat and travel writer Marie Eugène Melchior de Vogüé, which circulated in serialized translation about the same time.

10. John Camden Hotten, *The Slang Dictionary; or, The Vulgar Words, Street Phrases, and "Fast" Expressions of High and Low Society* (London: J. C. Hotten, 1865); Maximilian Schele de Vere, *Studies in English; or, Glimpses of the Inner Life* (New York: Charles Scribner, 1867), 278.

11. Milo M. Hastings, *The Egg Trade of the United States* (Washington, DC: United States Department of Agriculture, 1909), Circular 140.

12. R. H. Hilton, "Lords, Burgesses, and Hucksters," *Past and Present* 97 (November 1982), 3–15; David Pennington, "Taking It to the Streets: Hucksters and Huckstering in Early Modern Southampton, circa 1550–1652," *Sixteenth Century Journal* 39 (Autumn 2008), 657–79.

13. Thomas F. DeVoe, "The Public Markets: True Value of the Markets to the City," *New York Times*, January 23, 1855.

14. "Markets within the City of New York," *New York Weekly Journal*, June 12, 1738.

15. "A Small Account Concerning the Market House at Philadelphia and How the Markets Are Managed," *Weekly Newsletter* [Boston], September 26, 1728.

16. "Legislative Acts," *New York Gazette*, October 8, 1750.

17. Helen Bullock, "Market Square Tavern Historical Report, Block 12, Building 13," *Colonial Williamsburg Foundation Library Research Report Series* (1990), no. 1254.

18. Martha A. Zierden and Elizabeth J. Reitz, "Animal Use and the Urban Landscape in Colonial Charleston, South Carolina, USA," *International Journal of Historical Archaeology* 13 (September 2009), 327–65.

19. Candice L. Harrison, "'Free Trade and Hucksters' Rights!' Envisioning Economic Democracy in the Early Republic," *Pennsylvania Magazine of History and Biography* 137 (April 2013), 147–77.

20. "The Subject of a Market House in Providence Continued," *Providence Gazette and Country Journal*, September 23, 1769.

21. *Revised Ordinances of the City of Saint Louis* (St. Louis: Missouri Argus, 1836), 193.

22. "Getting a Living," *New York Union*, September 22, 1842.

23. "The Huckster Women," *New York Tribune*, September 13, 1845.

24. "The Want of Employment," *New York Tribune*, July 14, 1843.

25. "Proceedings of the City Council," *Baltimore Sun*, February 2, 1843.

26. "Interesting to Cheese Vendors," *Baltimore Sun*, August 6, 1841.

27. "Local Intelligence," *Evening Star* [Washington, DC], November 14, 1854.

28. "Excitement at Cincinnati," *New York Times*, September 20, 1853.

29. "Ordinance No. 25," *Cumberland Civilian and Telegraph* [Cumberland, MD], March 1, 1860.

30. John Gilbert, *The Curious Adventures, Painful Experience, and Laughable Difficulties of a Man of Letters While Traveling as a Peddler in the South during the Late Harper's Ferry Excitement* (Baltimore: John Gilbert and Company, 1860), 3.

31. Ann S. Stephens, *Fashion and Famine* (Philadelphia: T. B. Peterson and Brothers, 1854).

32. My analysis of electronic data files for samples from the 1850–1920 U.S. Federal Censuses courtesy of Steven Ruggles, J. Trent Alexander, Katie Genadek, Ronald Goeken, Matthew B. Schroeder, and Matthew Sobek. *Integrated Public Use Microdata Series: Version 5.0* [Machine-readable database] (Minneapolis: University of Minnesota, 2010).

33. Samuel Rush Watkins, *Memoir of Samuel Rush Watkins* (Chattanooga, TN: Times Printing Company, 1900), 164.

34. Samuel Calvin Jones, *Reminiscences of the Twenty-Second Iowa Volunteer Infantry* (Iowa City: Samuel Calvin Jones, 1907), 23.

35. Gilbert, *Curious Adventures*, 14.

36. "Life on the Farm," *Hagerstown Exponent* [Hagerstown, IN], October 12, 1881.

37. Senator John J. Ingalls, "Address Delivered at the State University at Lawrence," *Emporia News*, June 27, 1873.

38. "Trip on a Huckster Wagon," *Washington Reporter* [Washington, PA], August 4, 1875.

39. John Frank Turner, "The Hoosier Huckster," *Indiana Magazine of History* 50 (March 1954), 51–60. The center of Turner's circuit was Fincastle, a town of approximately 125 people with no rail service, forty-five miles west of Indianapolis.

40. James C. Malin, "The Turnover of Farm Population in Kansas," *Kansas Historical Quarterly* 4 (May 1935), 339–72. The information about Kansans employed as hucksters was obtained from federal and Kansas census records archived in Ancestry.com.

41. "A Clever Canvasser's Monologue," *Kansas City Star*, March 29, 1888.

42. Annie Nelles, *Life of a Book Agent*, 5th ed. (St. Louis: Annie Nelles Dumond, 1892), 275, 449. Details about Nelles' actual life, variations in the editions of her book, and an assessment of the parts that were fictionalized and those that seemed historically factual are discussed in James L. Murphy, "From Atlanta to Alberta: The 'Unbelievable' Odyssey of Annie Nelles Dumond; A Minor Literary Mystery Solved," *Ohio Genealogical Society Quarterly* 50 (Summer 2010), 179–86.

43. "Worse than the Grippe," *Lawrence Journal World* [Lawrence, KS], January 22, 1890.

44. *Character: A Discourse to Young Men* (Rochester, NY: Darrow & Brother, 1856), 5.

45. Winfield Scott, "My Ideal of a Model Teacher," *Jackson Standard* [Jackson, OH], February 5, 1874.

46. "The Test," *Wyoming Democrat* [Tunkhannock, WY], September 11, 1867.

47. "They Have the Gift of Gab," *St. Paul Daily Globe* [St. Paul, MN], July 26, 1885.

48. *Character: A Discourse to Young Men*, 7.

49. George Peck, *Formation of a Manly Character* (New York: Carlton and Phillips, 1853), 190–99; William Greenleaf Eliot, *Lectures to Young Men* (Boston: Crosby and Nichols, 1853), 31–32.

50. "The Cheap Mania," *New York Tribune* (September 2, 1857).

51. Jesse B. Thomas, "Address to the Second Annual Fair of the Ottawa County Agricultural Society," *Grand River Times* [Eastmanville, MI], October 21, 1857.

52. Lewis Masquerier, *Sociology* (New York: Lewis Masquerier, 1877), 13, 18.

53. "The Book Canvasser," *Crawford County Bulletin* [Denison, IA], June 4, 1874.

54. Samuel L. Clemens, "The Canvasser's Tale," *Atlantic Monthly* 38 (December 1876), 673–76.

55. M. M. Murdock, "Shoveling Smoke," *Wichita Daily Eagle*, March 6, 1901.

56. Lee Shai Weissbach, *Jewish Life in Small-Town America: A History* (New Haven, CT: Yale University Press, 2005), quotes 272, 274.

57. "A Clever Canvasser's Monologue," *Kansas City Star*, March 29, 1888.

58. "A Rich Old Maid," *Baltimore Sun*, March 24, 1843.

59. Mary Emily Bradley, "Mabel's New Year," *Watchman and State Journal* [Montpelier, VT], January 12, 1855; reprinted in Mary Emily Bradley, *Mabel's New Year and Other Stories* (New York: Sheldon, 1866).

60. "Modern Sirens," *New York Herald*, March 4, 1886.

61. "Book Canvassers," *Lawrence Journal World* [Lawrence, KS], October 23, 1885.

62. "The Book Canvasser," *Lawrenceburgh Register* [Lawrenceburgh, IN], October 4, 1877.

63. Lu Ann Jones, *Mama Learned Us to Work: Farm Women in the New South* (Chapel Hill: University of North Carolina Press, 2002), 79.

64. Melissa Walker, *Country Women Cope with Hard Times: A Collection of Oral Histories* (Columbia: University of South Carolina Press, 2012), 69.

65. June Bear Ritchie, *The Great Depression Put to Music, Song and Dance* (Bloomington, IN: Trafford Publishing, 2011), 76.

66. Frank L. McVey, "The Work and Problems of the Consumers League," *American Journal of Sociology* 6 (May 1901), 764–77, quote on 765.

67. Warren H. Wilson, "Social Life in the Country," *Annals of the American Academy of Political and Social Science* 40 (January 1912), 119–30, quote on 122.

68. Albion W. Small, "Review of *The Political Economy of Humanism*," *American Journal of Sociology* 7 (July 1901), 133.

69. Enda Bonacich, "A Theory of Middleman Minorities," *American Sociological Review* 38 (October 1973), 583–94.

70. Huey, "Affidavit of Claimant"; correspondence from family members through 1952 in Civil War Pension File, Application 602394, Certificate 605812, U.S. National Archives and Records Administration; additional information from Robert Nye, *Nye Huey Tree*, Ancestry Library, October 11, 2014.

Chapter Three

1. "An Insane Man Kills Two of His Children," *Baltimore Sun*, October 10, 1868; "Tragedy in Kansas," *Chicago Tribune*, September 9, 1871; "Terrible Murder by an Insane Man in Kansas," *New York Times*, September 8, 1872; "Horace Greeley Dead," *New York Tribune*, November 28, 1872; "Attempted Assassination of Senator Pomeroy," *Atlanta Constitution*, October 16, 1873.

2. William A. Hammond, *A Treatise on Diseases of the Nervous System* (New York: D. Appleton, 1871).

3. The literature includes landmark studies such as David J. Rothman, *The Discovery of the Asylum: Social Order and Disorder in the New Republic*, rev. ed. (New Brunswick, NJ: Aldine Transaction, 2002); David J. Rothman, *Conscience and Convenience: The Asylum and Its Alternatives in Progressive America*, rev. ed. (New Brunswick, NJ: Aldine Transaction, 2012); Andrew Scull, *Social Order / Mental Disorder: Anglo-American Psychiatry in Historical Perspective* (Berkeley: University of California Press, 1989); Michel Foucault, *Madness and Civilization: A History of Insanity in the Age of Reason* (New York: Random House, 1965); Erving Goffman, *Asylums: Essays on the Social Situation of Mental Patients and Other Inmates* (Garden City, NY: Anchor Books, 1961); and Thomas Szasz, *Insanity: The Idea and Its Consequences* (New York: John Wiley & Sons, 1987); and more recently Andrew Scull, *Madness in Civilization: A Cultural History of Insanity, from the Bible to Freud, from the Madhouse to Modern Medicine* (Princeton, NJ: Princeton University Press, 2015).

4. David Wright, "Getting Out of the Asylum: Understanding the Confinement of the Insane in the Nineteenth Century," *Social History of Medicine* 10 (January 1997), 137–55; Geoffrey Reaume, "Mental Hospital Patients and Family Relations in Southern Ontario, 1880–1930," in *Family Matters: Papers in Post-Confederation Canadian Family History*, ed. Lori Chambers and Edgar-André Montigny (Toronto: Canadian Scholars Press, 1998), 271–88; and James Moran, David Wright, and Mat Savelli, "The Lunatic Fringe: Families, Madness, and Institutional Confinement in Victorian Ontario," in *Mapping the Margins: The Family and Social Discipline in Canada, 1700–1975*, ed. Nancy Christie and Michael Gauvreau (Montreal: McGill-Queen's University Press, 2004), 277–304.

5. Hall emerged as a particularly interesting case for the purpose of exploring respectability because of the extensive information included in his Civil War pension file about his family, the affidavits they and their neighbors filed at the time of his institutionalization and again upon his death, as well as his medical diagnosis; with this information it became possible through other sources to reconstruct additional details about him and his family and to make comparisons with other cases for which fewer details were available.

6. Hall's parents were Jesse Hall (1793–1858) and Sarah Bryan Hall (1791–1861). Known earlier as Sand Ridge, Scotch Hill took its name from the Scotch workmen who labored

in the mines that opened near Newburg around 1855. Settlement of the area is briefly described in James Morton Callahan, *Genealogical and Personal History of the Upper Monongahela Valley*, vol. 2 (New York: Lewis Historical Publishing Company, 1912), 458.

7. Oren F. Morton, *A History of Preston County, West Virginia*, part 1 (Kingwood, WV: Journal Publishing Company, 1914), 104, 357; A. C. Barnes, "Ashford Hall," *Minutes of the Central Ohio Conference of the Methodist Episcopal Church* 49 (1907), 840. The obituary of Ashford Hall also states that his "father was an ardent patron of the press, being a subscriber to the Pittsburg *Christian Advocate* from 1834 all the rest of his life."

8. U.S. Civil War Draft Registration Records on file at the National Archives in Washington, DC, show that William A. Hall, a laborer age thirty-four, was listed as being "subject to do military duty" in the Second Congressional District, which included Preston County, West Virginia, in October, 1863, as recorded on January 20, 1864, and that he was "now in 6 months service." Military papers at the National Archives show that William Hall joined the West Virginia Cavalry, Company B, 4th regiment on July 13, 1863, at Independence, West Virginia, for an expected six months of service and was discharged nine months later at Wheeling, West Virginia, on March 17, 1864. The papers described him as being six feet tall, dark complexion, with grey eyes and dark hair and as being a farmer. Muster rolls for the West Virginia Cavalry show him present on July 21, 1863, and again on March 7, 1864.

9. Cynthia Ann Scott was the fourth of thirteen children; her grandfather, Winfield Scott, was a Revolutionary War soldier who hailed from an "old Shenandoah Valley family," and her uncle, Sanford Scott, was a minister. Her parents relocated to Preston County in 1835 and were known to have extensive "agricultural operations," including three thousand sheep (Callahan, *Genealogical and Personal History of the Upper Monongahela Valley*, 1112).

10. Cynthia Scott Hall's death occurred at Simpson in Taylor County, West Virginia, approximately twenty-five miles from Independence, where William and Cynthia had been living in 1864.

11. Ann Gallahue Hall was born on April 30, 1832, in Monongalia County, West Virginia, and died November 11, 1926, in Kansas City, Missouri; the Halls' daughter Kate was born at Chanute, Kansas, May 2, 1869 (Missouri Division of Health, file number 59–009586).

12. Henry W. Talcott, "Editorial History of Allen County, Kansas," *Neosho Valley Register* [Iola, KS], January 27, 1869. A history of Wilson County, Kansas, where the Halls lived in the 1870s, indicates that the first white settlers arrived in 1864, squatting on the Osage Indian Reservation. Within a few years other settlers came, and by 1870 there were more than 6,000 people of European ancestry living in the county, a number that more than doubled by 1880. Pleasant Valley Township, where the Halls settled, had 470 residents in 1870 and grew to 848 by 1880. Railways came to the area in 1872. By the mid-1870s, 20,000 acres of the county were in wheat and another 50,000 were in corn. William G. Cutler, *History of the State of Kansas* (Chicago: A. T. Andreas, 1883), 900–901.

13. William Speedy, "Correspondence: Effingham, Kansas, July 18, 1868," *Blairsville Press* [Blairsville, PA], August 7, 1868.

14. John S. Gilmore, "History of Wilson County, Kansas," in *Historical Atlas of Wilson County, Kansas*, ed. John P. Edwards (Philadelphia: F. Bourquin, 1881), http://www.kansasmemory.org.

15. Declaration for an Original Invalid Pension, filed by Ann Hall, October 14, 1889; included in the pension file of William A. Hall, National Archives, Washington, DC.

16. David Detzer, *Donnybrook: The Battle of Bull Run, 1861* (New York: Harcourt, 2004); Horace H. Cunningham, *Field Medical Services at the Battles of Manassas* (Athens: University of Georgia Press, 2008), 18–20. Happening as early in the war as it did (June 21, 1861), the First Battle of Bull Run was nevertheless preceded by months of conflict in the western part of the state where Hall lived. Having long felt that interests in their part of

the state were not well represented in Richmond, the western delegates were further aggrieved by the Virginia Ordinance of Secession on April 17, 1861. Remote as it was, the area where the Halls lived was of strategic military importance. In May 1861 "malcontents" at Kingwood who disagreed with Virginia's secession seized a supply of munitions and Union officers in Washington suggested making use of the arms, arming others in the area, and doing all that might be necessary to secure the B&O railroad that ran from Wheeling to Washington. "Very near this date," according to another source, "great alarm was caused by a report that 1,500 Confederates were about to march from Grafton to Kingwood to arrest and hang the Union leaders." Local militias formed in preparation for the worst. In the days leading to armed conflict at Bull Run, hastily organized militias and interested men gravitated toward the nation's capital. "Gov. Letcher, Wheeling, Malcontents," *Wheeling Intelligencer* [Wheeling, WV], May 25, 1861; Morton, *A History of Preston County*, 148. Although the rumor was soon proven to be false, a militia loyal to the Union assembled at a wooded hill, "formed a hollow square, and in a kneeling posture took the oath of allegiance to the United States. The scene was impressive, and has never been forgotten by those who witnessed it." Some of the volunteers went east a few days later to join federal troops. In all, 1,594 men from Preston County served on the Union side during the Civil War. Enlistment documents also show a number of men having "gone to Dixie." Three weeks after Bull Run, Union troops in Preston County routed a large force of rebel soldiers. "Official Particulars of the Battle near St. Georges, Va.," *Commercial Advertiser* [New York, NY] (July 15, 1861); Dorothy B. Snyder, "Reliving Lives: Prestonians and the Civil War," *Preston County Journal* [Kingwood, WV], November 19, 2003.

17. Another brother-in-law, William Sanford Scott, served in Company A of the 7th Regiment, West Virginia Cavalry.

18. The Western Virginia Conference of the Methodist Protestant Church met at Independence, Preston County, on Wednesday, September 3, 1862, and unanimously took an oath of allegiance to the government of the United States; "Western Virginia Conference," *Fairmont National* [Fairmont, WV], September 11, 1862. Reverend Simpson would likely have participated in this meeting. Although the Halls belong to the Methodist Episcopal Church, they could hardly have been unaware of this action by the other Methodist conference.

19. The engagement at Moorefield, which involved a critical bridge and section of the B&O railroad, took place on February 4, 1864, and involved approximately a thousand cavalry and two pieces of artillery; American Civil War Research Database, online.

20. The Civil War Archive: Union Regimental Histories, West Virginia (http://www.civilwararchive.com); National Archives Civil War Pension Files, Certificate 26911 for Caleb Zinn and Certificate 32269 for Michael Bradshaw.

21. Dr. M. A. Alexander, born in Kentucky in 1834, was living in Pomona, Franklin County, Kansas, in 1889 when he filed the affidavit but was living near the Halls in Pleasant Valley, Wilson County, Kansas, when the 1870 U.S. Census and 1875 Kansas Census were taken.

22. Affidavit in the pension file of William A. Hall, National Archives, November 18, 1889.

23. *Probate Journal, 1873–74*, vol. B (Fredonia, KS: Wilson County Probate Court, 1874), 45–57, handwritten entries, February 21, 1874; February 24, 1874. The three witnesses were C. C. Baum, Silas Coates, and Sevis Coates. The 1875 Kansas Census shows Sevis Coates, a farmer age forty-four, living with his wife and children, and Silas Coates, a farmer age forty-three, living with his wife and children, in Pleasant Valley township near where the Halls lived; C. C. Baum was not listed but is shown on an 1881 map owning land a mile north of the Halls; the person who posted bond as Hall's guardian was Amos F.

Krizer, a farmer who lived two miles west of the Halls. The probate records do not indicate who initiated the proceedings or whether Hall was present and do not include a transcription of the testimony.

24. Numbers compiled from the names, locations, and founding dates of asylums in John Curwen, *History of the Association of Medical Superintendents of American Institutions for the Insane* (Philadelphia: Association of Medical Superintendents of American Institutions for the Insane, 1874), 105–20.

25. Lowell Gish, *Reform at Osawatomie State Hospital: Treatment of the Mentally Ill, 1866–1970* (Lawrence: University of Kansas Press, 1972); subsequent growth in numbers of persons hospitalized at Osawatomie is consistent with arguments that rates of insanity were influenced upward by the availability of asylums; however, the fact that Osawatomie was some eighty miles from the Halls' farm suggests that Hall's institutionalization was probably not dictated simply by the convenience of its location.

26. Ibid., 50–51; in her seventies at the time, Dix had been leading the reform effort since 1840.

27. This information is taken from the 1870 United States Federal Census.

28. As the leaders of asylums across the country expressed when they convened in 1874, "The safety of the community requires the personal liberty of the insane [to] be restrained." Quoted in John B. Chapin, "Duty of States toward Their Insane Poor," *Journal of Social Science* (July 1, 1874), 60–65.

29. "Revolt at the Kansas Insane Asylum," *Sumner County Press* [Wellington, KS], January 3, 1874.

30. A. H. Knapp, "Ninth Annual Report of the Asylum for the Insane of the State of Kansas: 1873," *American Journal of Insanity* 31 (1874–1875), 378–79.

31. *Probate Journal, 1873–74*, vol. B (Fredonia, KS: Wilson County Probate Court, 1874), 57, handwritten entry dated March 16, 1874; April 8, 1874.

32. *Probate Journal, 1878–83*, vol. C (Fredonia, KS: Wilson County Probate Court, 1883), 12–13. 19, handwritten entries dated May 24, 1978; August 20, 1878.

33. *Probate Journal*, 129–34; handwritten entries dated July 28, 1879; July 29, 1879; August 6, 1879; August 20, 1879.

34. No evidence in the Wilson County Probate Court records or the Johnson County (where Ann Hall lived in 1880) Probate Court records indicates that a hearing before a judge and jury was conducted concerning Hall's admission to the Kansas State Insane Asylum at Topeka; the absence of a hearing may have been because of the recent timing of the July 1879 court proceedings.

35. William E. Connelley, *A Standard History of Kansas and Kansans* (Chicago: Lewis Publishing Company, 1918).

36. John M. Price, ed., *The General Statutes of the State of Kansas* (Lawrence, KS: John Speer, 1868), 552–59.

37. *Revised Statutes of the State of Illinois* (Springfield, IL: Walters & Weber, 1845), 276.

38. *The General Statutes of the State of Missouri* (Jefferson City, MO: Emory S. Foster, 1866), 234–39.

39. *The Revised Laws of Indiana* (Indianapolis, IN: Douglass and Maguire, 1831), 287; *Statute Laws of the Territory of Iowa* (Dubuque, IA: Russell & Reeves, 1839), 35; Tennessee's was similar but provided for an idiot or lunatic with no property to be placed under the maintenance of the lowest bidder. R. L. Caruthers and A.O.P. Nicholson, *A Compilation of the Statutes of Tennessee* (Nashville, TN: James Smith, 1836), 378.

40. *The Probate Directory* (Concord, NH: George Hough, 1829), 350–68.

41. John F. Montignani, *The Insanity Law of the State of New York* (Albany, NY: State Commission on Lunacy, 1896), 28–31.

42. "Minor Notes," *Iola Register* [Iola, KS], December 22, 1877.

43. *Manual for the Use of the Board of Health, Lunacy, and Charity of Massachusetts* (Boston: Rand, Avery, 1880), 32.

44. "The Revival at Lawrence," *New York Evangelist* 43 (March 28, 1872), 4; "The Great Work in Kansas," *The Advance* 5 (April 18, 1872), 2; "Revivals and Their Results," *The Independent* 24 (March 28, 1872), 4.

45. G. S. Dearborn, "Kansas Correspondence," *Zion's Herald* 51 (March 5, 1874), 79.

46. "Letter from Kansas," *Zion's Herald* 54 (May 3, 1877), 138.

47. "The Peculiar Children," *Iola Register*, September 5, 1879.

48. Examples are discussed in Leah Greenfeld, *Mind, Modernity, Madness* (Cambridge, MA: Harvard University Press, 2013), 522–613. An insightful nineteenth-century description is *Bodily Effects of Religious Excitement* (Belfast: Phillips & Sons, 1859), a tract that was widely circulated, cited, and republished in American Protestant circles.

49. "Horrible Religious Fanaticism," *Republican Daily Journal* [Lawrence, KS], May 3, 1879.

50. A valuable discussion of religion's relation to insanity during this period, although in a different context, is Elspeth Knewstubb, "'Believes the Devil Has Changed Him': Religion and Patient Identity in Ashburn Hall, Dunedin, 1882–1910," *Health and History* 14 (January 2012), 56–76.

51. L. Wallace Duncan and Charles F. Scott, *History of Allen and Woodson Counties* (Iola, KS: Iola Register, 1901), 69; Cutler, *History of the State of Kansas*, 651.

52. "Geneva Jottings," *Iola Register*, July 29, 1881.

53. Ephraim Fisk, "The War and the Dirty Swindle," *Iola Register*, August 12, 1881.

54. *Probate Directory*, 356–58; Horace Chase, *The New Hampshire Probate Directory* (Concord, NH: G. Parker Lyon, 1845), 261–68.

55. Bernard Douglass Eastman, "The Rights of the Insane" (1895), quoted in Barbara Hauschild, *On the Avenue of Approach* (Topeka, KS: Topeka State Hospital, 1979), 15. Eastman had come out from Worcester, Massachusetts, where he had superintended the asylum there since 1875, to be the Topeka asylum's founding director on April 1, 1879. *Transactions of the Kansas State Historical Society* (Topeka, KS: W. Y. Morgan, 1900), 455; "Notes and Comment," *American Journal of Insanity* 66 (1910), 322. Although "insanity" was the commonly used term in these proceedings, admission papers for Adalade A. Hawley (http://www.dmarlin.com/hawley) show that the term "lunacy" was still in use in 1906. Juries may not have been convened in all cases, and later legislation made them optional.

56. My tally from the information included in the U.S. Federal Census, 1880 Supplemental Schedules, Nos. 1 to 7, for the Defective, Dependent, and Delinquent Classes.

57. The Kansas State Historical Society, which archived records of the asylum at Topeka when it closed, is by law prohibited from disclosing any of the medical records; the medical information provided by Superintendent Eastman, which I discuss in the chapter, and included in Hall's pension file is thus invaluable.

58. Judging from average yields and prices for Wilson County in 1875 as shown in the *Fourth Annual Report of the State Board of Agriculture* (286), gross income from the crops, had they all been sold, would have been $460. Cutler's *History of Kansas* indicates that approximately the same acreage of wheat and corn was planted in 1874 as in 1875 but does not report yields and prices.

59. "A view of single causation of mental illness prevailed. . . . 'Loss of farm,' 'disappointment in love,' and 'death of a child' were typical of the causes listed" (Gish, *Reform*, 27).

60. State Board of Agriculture, *Third Annual Report to the Legislature of Kansas* (Topeka, KS: State Printing Works, 1874), 12; figures for Wilson County (207) suggest that the average yield per acre for corn was at least a third lower than in the following year.

Countywide statistics do not indicate that yields and prices were seriously depressed, although weather affected particular farmers differently, as did other circumstances such as arrangements on mortgages.

61. T. F. Rager, *History of Neosho and Wilson Counties* (Fort Scott, KS: Monitor Printing, 1902), 32. This is also the source (809) that mentions Hall's nephew Jesse Wilkins coming to Miami County, Kansas, in 1868 and then moving to Wilson County in 1870.

62. Register of Deeds, Wilson County, Kansas, April 8, 1874, Township 28, Range 16, Northwest Quarter, Section 12.

63. Hauschild, *On the Avenue of Approach*, 15. The lawn mowing, other activities, and rocking chairs are captured in photos on file at the Kansas State Historical Society.

64. Kansas State Historical Society, *The Annals of Kansas, 1886–1925*. Vol. 1, *1886–1910* (Topeka: Kansas State Historical Society, 1954), selected pages.

65. "The Topeka Asylum," *The Advocate* [Topeka, KS], September 19, 1894; "Charitable Institutions," *The Advocate*, October 10, 1894.

66. "More Redeeming," *Kansas Agitator* [Garnett, KS], August 2, 1895.

67. "Still More Disgraceful," *Dodge City Globe* [Dodge City, KS], November 3, 1898; State Board of Charities, *Sixth Biennial Report of the State Board of Charities* (Topeka: Kansas Publishing House, 1888), 44. Among items listed on the steward's report were 41 gallons of whisky. The report also listed 93½ gallons of alcohol (most likely for medical purposes).

68. B. D. Eastman, "Correspondence," *American Journal of Insanity* 52 (July1895), 133–35.

69. State Board of Charities, *Sixth Biennial Report*, 24.

70. Hauschild, *On the Avenue of Approach*, 40–42; "Insane Asylum Horrors," *The Advocate* [Topeka, KS] (October 7, 1896).

71. Dr. W. Ray, "An Examination of the Objections to the Doctrine of Moral Insanity," *Journal of Insanity* (October 1861), 113.

72. James W. Trent Jr., *Inventing the Feeble Mind: A History of Mental Retardation in the United States* (Berkeley: University of California Press, 1994), 98.

73. George L. Harrison, *Legislation on Insanity: A Collection of All the Lunacy Laws of the States and Territories of the United States to the Year 1883* (Philadelphia: Globe Printing House, 1884), 230–46; John Koren, *Summaries of Laws Relating to the Commitment and Care of the Insane in the United States* (New York: National Committee for Mental Hygiene, 1912), 86–93.

74. My tally from information included in the 1880 U.S. Census. Information included in the State Board of Charities, *Sixth Biennial Report* (27) for 1888 shows a similar pattern: of 575 patients at the Topeka asylum, only 106 (18 percent) were married men; among the 313 male patients, 34 percent were married, while among the 262 female patients, 67 percent were married.

75. Board of Managers, *Fifth Biennial Report of the Board of Managers of State Lunatic Asylum No. 2* (Jefferson City, MO: Tribune Printing Company, 1885), 23.

76. U. S. Bureau of the Census, *Insane and Feeble-Minded in Institutions, 1910* (Washington, DC: Government Printing Office, 1914), 47–48.

77. The possibility that William and Ann's daughter Mame suffered from mental illness may have weighed on the family as well.

78. Perhaps indicative of how the family was regarded in Wilson County, all the children from both marriages moved away, and none of the affidavits about William's illness were from local residents.

79. National Archives Civil War Pension Files, Certificate 375645. Kirkland died in 1911, having returned repeatedly to the asylum at Topeka, sometimes kept under restraint, and requiring constant care and supervision while at home.

80. These case histories were assembled from U.S. Census, Kansas Census, and military pension records.

81. National Archives, Civil War Pension Files, Certificate 564411.

82. Theda Skocpol, *Protecting Soldiers and Mothers: The Political Origins of Social Policy in the United States* (Cambridge, MA: Harvard University Press, 1992), 109, based on Glasson, *Federal Military Pensions*, 144, 271, 272.

83. Robert W. Fogel, *Aging of Veterans of the Union Army: Military, Pension, and Medical Records, 1820–1940* (Ann Arbor, MI: Inter-University Consortium for Political and Social Research, 2011), codebooks and electronic data files, based on standard service and medical records. Analysis of the 35,570 Union infantry veterans sampled identified only 135 for whom insanity (or mental illness, mania, or melancholia) was included among up to fifteen illnesses or wounds for each veteran, all of whom also suffered from other disabilities, but not all of whom were institutionalized. Sixty-two had been institutionalized at least once between 1865 and 1912 at one of fifty-two asylums. Projecting the 0.38 percent the number of 135 represents indicates that as many as 3,500 to 4,000 Union veterans may have suffered from insanity. Among the 135 in the sample, 75 percent were married, 36 percent received invalid pensions, and 43 percent of the widows received widows' pensions.

84. Glasson, *Federal Military Pensions*, 238, notes the problems of cost and administration.

85. Eric T. Dean Jr., *Shook over Hell: Post-Traumatic Stress, Vietnam, and the Civil War* (Cambridge, MA: Harvard University Press, 1997), 86–87, 135–79, which presents evidence from Indiana. R. Gregory Lande, *Madness, Malingering and Malfeasance* (Dulles, VA: Brassey's, 2003), 157–92, provides further evidence of the reasoning and circumstances behind the government's skepticism toward insanity claims.

86. Glasson, *Federal Military Pensions*, 166, and elsewhere discusses the role of pension attorneys.

87. Articles of Agreement between Ann Hall and Noah Mason, signed January 27, 1890, in William Hall's file at the National Archives. A brief account of Moser and his associates is given in *Living Leaders: An Encyclopedia of Biography, Special Edition for Daviess and Martin Counties, Indiana* (New York: American Publishing Company, 1897), 49. Moser's hometown newspaper, the *Loogootee Martin County Tribune* [Loogootee, IN], posted numerous articles in its social column about Moser, including an item on October 3, 1890: "Our hustling pension attorneys, Noah Moser and C. S. Wood, are holding forth at the Daviess County fair grounds this week, where they may be consulted at any time in regard to pension matters. Theirs is one of the most successful agencies in southern Indiana and we cheerfully recommend them to the old soldiers of Daviess County." Several cases in which Moser was involved are included in John W. Bixler, ed., *Decisions of the Department of the Interior in Appealed Pension and Bounty-Land Claims* (Washington, DC: Government Printing Office, 1904).

88. Letter from Noah Moser, pension attorney, to Commissioner of Pensions, July 5, 1891.

89. Among William Hall's fellow veterans in Company B of the 4th West Virginia Cavalry, the number applying for pensions rose from four in 1886 to seven in 1887, ten in 1888, twelve in 1889, and twenty-one in 1890.

90. "The Big Meeting Begins: Milwaukee G.A.R. Encampment Opened," *Kansas City Star*, August 28, 1889; Glasson, *Federal Military Pensions*, details the legislative events leading to the 1890 Pension Act.

91. Eastman letter to Moser, January 27, 1890.

92. Bureau of Pensions letter, April 15, 1890.

93. The document misstated Hall's age as four years older than he was; the weight, if accurate, suggests that his physical health was not good.

94. Ibid., 138.

95. U.S. Census Bureau, Special Schedule—Surviving Soldiers, Sailors, and Marines, and Widows, 1890; courtesy of Ancestry.com. Earlier provisions for war-related pensions from the state of Kansas were less expansive, suggesting that William Hall would not have qualified if he had applied; of 125 male pensioners in Wilson County in 1883, 95 had been wounded or lost limbs or vision, 9 suffered from heart or lung disease, 7 were listed as having chronic diarrhea, and 3 had rheumatism; Kansas 1883 List of Pensioners on the Roll, contributed by Bill Bentley.

96. Judging from a pension voucher at the time of William Hall's death that states "insanity" as his disability, the claim on his behalf based on insanity appears to have been honored. Other data suggest that successful pension claims based on insanity were rare; for example, Sven E. Wilson and Louis L. Nguyen, "Secular Trends in the Determinants of Disability Benefits," *American Economic Review* 88 (1998), 227–31, include data from 1,410 Union Army Pension beneficiaries in 1891–92 whose disability status was "severe," of whom only 0.6 percent were classified as having "mental/psychological" disease, compared with 25.4 percent with "gastrointestinal" disease, 23.3 percent with "arthritis," and 12.4 percent with "cardiovascular" disease.

97. Letter to Moser with copy to Ann Hall, June 30, 1891.

98. Letter from Moser to commissioner of pensions, July 5, 1891.

99. *Probate Journal, 1891*, vol. 11 (Olathe, KS: Johnson County Probate Court, 1891), 46–47; handwritten record dated July 24, 1891.

100. Letter from T. C. Biddle to Emma Hall, October 26, 1899. William Hall was one of fifty-eight patients who died that year. Although he most likely died from heart disease, as Biddle claimed in a letter "to whom it may concern" on June 4, 1900, the fact that "exhaustion" and "paresis" were listed in more than half the cases as cause of death poses doubts about how carefully these determinations were made. Although the correspondence states clearly that William Hall died on July 20, a record book from the Kansas State Hospital from which the Kansas State Historical Society in Topeka took information erroneously listed the date as July 18.

101. Ann Hall, 420 West 15th Street in Kansas City, Missouri, affidavit to the Pension Office on November 1, 1899.

102. Affidavit to the Pension Office sworn to on October 31, 1899, by William's daughters Kate and Emma. On October 31, 1899, daughter Elinor Hall of 420 West 15th Street, Kansas City, Missouri, also filed an affidavit, which stated: "I am the daughter of William A. Hall and Ann Hall above referred. When I signed and swore on the 4th day of August 1899 to the Pension Voucher of Ann Hall as wife and Guardian of William A. Hall that he was alive I did not have a doubt in my mind but that I was swearing to the truth as we were all morally certain that if there was the least trouble out of the ordinary with my father that we would be notified at once by wire and letter so we could go to him. We certainly did not presume on a delay of twenty-four hours hence I felt safe in what I did. I did not for a moment think I could be wrong and my intentions toward the government were and always have been honorable. I never intentionally swore falsely." The reference to a delay of twenty-four hours is unclear, given the other correspondence, unless it may have been meant to read twenty-four days.

103. In conjunction with an application to the Pension Office for a pension as a widow of a Civil War soldier, on July 10, 1900, in an affidavit filed in Jackson County, Missouri, Ann Hall, age sixty-six, of 2016 Belleview Avenue, Kansas City, Missouri, stated: "I was married to the above named soldier May 17, 1868, near Palatine, West Virginia, and it was my first and only marriage to date. My late husband William A. Hall had been once previously married to Cynthia Scott, who died April 12th, 1867, at Independence, West Virginia. I was

acquainted with her family but not with her. There is no public record of her death as the county records containing the same were all destroyed by fire, including the courthouse in March 1869. I have absolutely no real, personal, or mixed property whatever—no stocks, lands, or other investments and no one is legally bound for my support. I have no income from any source. I did have an interest in a farm in Wilson Co. Kansas, which I sold for a net amount of $1300, nearly all of which has been expended. But before selling out my interest, I had rented the farm for $150, which amount belonged to me and ten children by Mr. Hall's first and second wife. After deducting $10 for repairs I have settled with everybody and having nothing left and no source of income." The transaction is not described in sufficient detail to ascertain if $1,300 represented the total value of the 160-acre farm, net of taxes and fees, and $150 was the agreed amount of annual rent. According to the *Tenth Biennial Report of the Kansas State Board of Agriculture* (49), farmland in Wilson County in 1896 was valued at $30 an acre and rented for $3 per acre. The reason Ann kept the farm was that she as William's court-appointed guardian was not legally allowed to sell it until the children were all at least eighteen years of age. Elinor would have turned eighteen in 1896, which meant that Ann rented the land to someone else, as she noted, for $150 a year. The renter was William's nephew, Jesse Wilkins, who had settled only a mile away in 1870, married a local girl (Julia Halstead) in 1876, had two children (Camma and Cyrus), and by 1880 was on his way to becoming one of the most prominent farmers in the township. As character witnesses, James and Irene Leonard filed an affidavit from Marion County, West Virginia, stating that they had been personally and intimately acquainted with Hall's first wife, knew that she died, and knew that Ann was his widow. Irene Leonard (nee Scott), born April 1852 and married to James H. Leonard in 1872, was Cynthia Scott Hall's younger sister. Ann's sister Catharine from the same county in West Virginia also submitted an affidavit stating that she had known William and Ann all her life and had been present at their wedding. Catharine Hall, age sixty-seven, affidavit dated September 4, 1900, Marion County, West Virginia.

104. *Twelfth Biennial Report of the Kansas State Insane Asylum at Topeka* (Topeka, KS: W. Y. Morgan, 1900), 3. The insane asylum became known as the Topeka State Hospital. It closed in 1997, and over the next decade all the buildings were torn down. The grounds were eventually declared a historical site, and a monument was erected listing the names of some of the eleven hundred people buried there.

Chapter Four

1. Stanley Milgram, "The Social Meaning of Fanaticism," *ETC: A Review of General Semantics* 34 (March 1977), 58–61.

2. Among the many studies of mainstream religious groups, R. Laurence Moore, *Religious Outsiders and the Making of Americans* (New York: Oxford University Press, 1986), is especially relevant.

3. Jon Butler, "The Revocation of the Edict of Nantes and Huguenot Migration to South Carolina," in *The Huguenot Connection: The Edict of Nantes, Its Revocation, and Early French Migration to South Carolina*, ed. R. M. Golden (Norwell, MA: Kluwer Academic Publishers, 1988), 63–82, especially the discussion on 80; David Lovejoy, *Religious Enthusiasm in the New World: From Heresy to Revolution* (Cambridge, MA: Harvard University Press, 1985), 172–75, offers a similar interpretation.

4. Bertrand Van Ruymbeke, *From New Babylon to Eden: The Huguenots and Their Migration to Colonial South Carolina* (Columbia: South Carolina University Press, 2006), quote on 143.

5. James O'Kane, *Wicked Deeds: Murder in America* (New Brunswick, NJ: Transaction Publishers, 2005), 117; Mark R. Jones, *Wicked Charleston: The Dark Side of the Holy City*

(Charleston, SC: History Press, 2005), 37–39, also cast the story as an episode of "free love," providing a more detailed but embellished account focusing on incest and adultery.

6. Jeffrey Robert Young, ed., *Proslavery and Sectional Thought in the Early South, 1740–1829: An Anthology* (Columbia: University of South Carolina, 2006), 75–76. Whitefield's appeal was part of wider evangelical Protestant dissent that had negative financial implications for the Anglican churches under Garden's care, according to Thomas J. Little, "The Origins of Southern Evangelicalism: Revivalism in South Carolina, 1700–1740," *Church History* 75 (December 2006), 768–808. The Great Awakening as a shift toward recognizing emotional experience as a source of knowing is from Rhys Isaac, *The Transformation of Virginia, 1740–1790* (Chapel Hill: University of North Carolina Press, 1982).

7. Alexander Garden, "The Case of the Dutartres," July 13, 1740, reprinted in *Gospel Messenger and Southern Christian Register* 1 (1824), 268–70.

8. David Hume, "Essay XII: Of Superstition and Enthusiasm," in Hume, *Essays Moral, Political, and Literary* (Edinburgh: Fleming and Alison, 1741), 144–45.

9. The differences are evident in Jon Butler, "Enthusiasm Described and Decried: The Great Awakening as Interpretive Fiction," *Journal of American History* 69 (September 1982), 305–25; and Douglas L. Winiarski, "Souls filled with Ravishing Transport: Heavenly Visions and the Radical Awakening in New England," *William and Mary Quarterly* 61 (January 2004), 3–46.

10. "A Singular and Fatal Instance of Religious Enthusiasm," *Columbian Magazine* 2 (1788), 195–98; "Striking Instance of the Shocking Effects of Fanaticism," *Universal Magazine* 6 (1789), 82–85.

11. "Zealous of Good Works," *New York Evangelist* (December 28, 1839), 206.

12. "Chapter XV," *The Christian History, Containing Accounts of the Revival and Propagation of Religion in Great Britain and America* 18 (July 2, 1743), 137.

13. Selection reprinted in Thomas Jefferson, "The State of Religion in Virginia," *Columbian Magazine* (February 1788), 86.

14. "The Vermont Pilgrims," *Hallowell Gazette* [Hallowell, ME], February 9, 1820.

15. "A Vindication of the Moravians against the Aspersions of Their Enemies," *Independent Reflector* 6 (1753), 21–24, quotes on 22.

16. Robert Owen, "Address: Delivered in the Hall of Science, New York, on the Fourth of July, 1829," *Gospel Advocate and Impartial Investigator*, August 22, 1829.

17. Alexis de Tocqueville, *Democracy in America*, trans. George Lawrence (New York: Harper Perennial, 1966), 534–35.

18. Simon Stone, "The Miller Delusion: A Comparative Study in Mass Psychology," *American Journal of Psychiatry* 91 (November 1934), 593–623.

19. "A Millerite in a Quandary," *Maine Cultivator* [Hallowell, ME], November 9, 1844.

20. "Zeal without Knowledge," *Boston Recorder*, January 19, 1843.

21. "Mere Zeal," *Berkshire County Whig* [Pittsfield, MA], August 3, 1843.

22. "Zeal in the Cause of Religion," *Farmers' Cabinet* [Amherst, NH], October 2, 1845.

23. Isaac Taylor, *Fanaticism* (London: Holdsworth and Ball, 1833).

24. Ibid., 357.

25. Abel Stevens, *The History of the Religious Movement of the Eighteen Century Called Methodism* (London: Wesleyan Conference, 1878), 320–21; Sydney G. Dimond, *The Psychology of the Methodist Revival: An Empirical and Descriptive Study* (Oxford: Oxford University Press, 1926); Ronald L. Numbers and Janet S. Numbers, "Millerism and Madness: A Study of 'Religious Insanity' in Nineteenth-Century America," in *The Disappointed: Millerism and Millenarianism in the Nineteenth Century*, ed. Ronald L. Numbers and Jon Butler (Bloomington: Indiana University Press, 1987), 92–117.

26. "Extravagant Expressions and Actions," *Christian Advocate and Journal* 8 (December 13, 1833), 16.

27. "Abolition vs. Christianity and the Union," *United States Magazine* 27 (July 1850), 1–16, quote on 2.

28. Amariah Brigham, *Observations on the Influence of Religion upon the Health and Welfare of Mankind* (Boston: Marsh, Capen and Lyon, 1835); Eric T. Carlson, "Amariah Brigham: Life and Works," *American Journal of Psychiatry* 112 (April 1956), 831–36; Brigham's comments about the Millerite following are included in Stone, "The Miller Delusion," 600.

29. S. Hanbury Smith, *Sketch of the Epidemic Religious Monomanie Which Occurred in Sweden in the Year 1841 and 1842* (Columbus, OH: Medary's Steam Press, 1850), quotes on 485, 490, and 495.

30. Church Dedication," *Kansas State Record* [Topeka, KS], August 14, 1871.

31. "Religious Fanaticism," *San Francisco Bulletin*, January 25, 1875.

32. "Religious Fanaticism," *Cincinnati Daily Gazette*, April 29, 1875.

33. James C. Howden, "The Religious Sentiment in Epileptics," *Journal of Mental Science* 4 (January 1873), 99–102, quote on 102.

34. Joseph Workman, "Insanity of the Religious-Emotional Type, and Its Occasional Physical Relations," *American Journal of Insanity* 26 (July 1869), 33–48, quotes on 36, 37, and 39.

35. J. C. Jackson, "A Warning Needed in Methodism," *Methodist Review* 7 (May 1891), 471.

36. James Mudge, "Fanaticism a Present Peril," *Zion's Herald* 63 (May 26, 1886), 1. Reason and common sense were prominent themes in Mudge's later work as well; for example, James Mudge, *The Perfect Life in Experience and Doctrine* (Cincinnati, OH: Jennings and Graham, 1911), and James Mudge, *Religious Experience Exemplified in the Lives of Illustrious Christians* (Cincinnati, OH: Jennings and Graham, 1913).

37. "Became Violent," *St. Louis Republic*, October 9, 1898; "Incendiaries," *Wheeling Register* [Wheeling, WV], March 22, 1895.

38. "The Cobb Fanaticism," *Cincinnati Enquirer*, September 5, 1876; "The Cobbite Religion," *Sacramento Daily Union*, September 4, 1876; "The White County Horror," *Daily Arkansas Gazette*, September 3, 1876.

39. As examples of the many news accounts, see "They Think Heaven Is Near an Illinois Town," *New York Times*, April 30, 1889; "Schweinfurth's Fanaticism," *Daily Inter Ocean* [Chicago], April 14, 1890; "Schweinfurth Did It," *Rockford Daily Register* [Rockford, IL], June 16, 1890; James Mooney, "The Ghost Dance Religion and the Sioux Outbreak of 1890," *Fourteenth Annual Report of the Bureau of Ethnology* (Washington, DC: Government Printing Office, 1896), 641–1110, quote on 945.

40. M. M. Mangasarian, "Minds Out of Tune," *Chicago Herald*, June 4, 1893.

41. John Gilmary Shea, "Vagaries of Protestant Religious Belief," *American Catholic Quarterly Review* 10 (July 1885), 432–44, quote on 433.

42. "Abilene, Kansas," *Lutheran Evangelist* 13 (March 1, 1889), 5.

43. "Steel versus Cast Iron," *American Artisan* 50 (July 8, 1905), 1.

44. H. A. Bushnell, "The Evils of Superficial Christianity," *The Advance* 31 (June 4, 1896), 828.

45. "The Religious Club," *Zion's Herald* 71 (February 1, 1893), 36–37; Nathaniel Hawthorne, "The Celestial Railroad" (1843), in *Complete Novels and Selected Tales of Nathaniel Hawthorne*, ed. Norman Holmes Pearson (New York: Modern Library, 1937), 1070–82.

46. William James, *The Varieties of Religious Experience* (Cambridge, MA: Harvard University Press, 1985; originally published in 1902), quotes on 271, 272, and 273.

47. Charles Monroe Sheldon, "Sermon for February 14, 1904" (handwritten text), Charles Monroe Sheldon Sermons and Notes, 1887–1938, Kansas State Historical Society, Topeka, Kansas.

48. James Monroe Buckley, *Faith-Healing: Christian Science and Kindred Spirits* (Cambridge, MA: Harvard University Press, 1892); James Monroe Buckley, "Fanaticism in the United States," *Century Illustrated Magazine* 67 (June 1903), 196–206.

49. Quotes from Chapman at a revival campaign in Chicago as reported by William Bernard Norton, "Fanaticism and Emotionalism Obstacles to Religious Reform," *Chicago Daily Tribune*, October 20, 1910; biographical information from Papers of John Wilbur Chapman, Billy Graham Center Archives, Wheaton, Illinois.

50. Dowie's Christian Catholic Church at Zion City is briefly discussed in Samuel Kincheloe, "The Prophet: A Study in the Sociology of Leadership," PhD dissertation, University of Chicago, 1929, 198; and Edith L. Blumhofer, *The Assemblies of God: A Chapter in the Story of American Pentecostalism* Springfield, MO: Gospel Publishing House, 1989), 31–34; and received a passing mention in James Joyce, *Ulysses* (New York: Oxford University Press, 1922), 144. Contemporary accounts are given in George Grantham Bain, "Zion City via Chicago," *The Sphere* (December 27, 1902), 318; "Dowie's Zion City," *Los Angeles Times*, January 11, 1903; "Death in Zion City," *New York Times*, January 29, 1905; "Woman Tortured to Death in Zion City," *St. Louis Dispatch*, September 20, 1907; "Zion City at a Crisis," *New York Times*, May 20, 1907; and in numerous articles from 1900 to 1920 in the *Chicago Daily Tribune*.

51. Bain, "Zion City via Chicago"; John Swain, "Wonderful 'Zion City' Which Dowie Has Built within 12 Months," *Atlanta Constitution*, May 4, 1902.

52. "New Overseer of Zion City Is an Industrial Expansionist," *Indianapolis Morning Star*, April 3, 1906.

53. "Voliva Hates Germs More than He Does the Germans," *Chicago Daily Tribune*, October 17, 1917.

54. Maynard Shipley, "The Forward March of the Anti-Evolutionists," *Current History* 29 (January 1, 1929), 578–82.

55. "Faith without Fanaticism," *Zion's Herald*, October 21, 1896.

56. Margaret Mead, "Fanaticism: The Panhuman Disorder," *ETC: A Review of General Semantics* 71 (April 2014; originally published March 1977), 201–204, quote on 204.

57. Matt Hills, *Fan Cultures* (London: Routledge, 2002); Randall Collins, *Violence: A Micro-sociological Theory* (Princeton, NJ: Princeton University Press, 2008), especially chapter 8 on sports violence (282–384); and James Hellings, "Precautions against Fan(atic)s: A Reevaluation of Adorno's Uncompromising Philosophy of Popular Culture," *New German Critique* 118 (Winter 2013), 149–74, which draws an interesting comparison between fans and fanatics' strategic performative uses of fanaticism.

58. William T. Cavanaugh, "The Invention of Fanaticism," *Modern Theology* 27 (April 2011), 226–37; and Thomas F. Gieryn, "Boundary-Work and the Demarcation of Science from Non-science: Strains and Interests in Professional Ideologies of Scientists," *American Sociological Review* 48 (December 1983), 781–95, discuss the construction of religion as irrational from philosophical and sociological approaches, respectively.

Chapter Five

1. Will Herberg, *Protestant, Catholic, Jew: An Essay in American Religious Sociology* (Garden City, NY: Doubleday, 1959); H. Richard. Niebuhr, *The Social Sources of Denominationalism* (New York: H. Holt, 1929); Ruby Jo Reeves Kennedy, "Single or Triple Melting Pot," *American Journal of Sociology* 49 (January 1944), 331–39; John Higham, *Strangers in the Land: Patterns of American Nativism, 1860–1925* (New Brunswick, NJ: Rutgers University Press, 1955). Critical examination of the concept is presented in Philip Gleason, "The Melting Pot: Symbol of Fusion or Confusion?" *American Quarterly* 16 (Spring 1964),

20–46; and Sarah Wilson, *Melting-Pot Modernism* (Ithaca, NY: Cornell University Press, 2010).

2. Milton M. Gordon, *Assimilation in American Life* (New York: Oxford University Press, 1964); and for a critique, Richard Alba and Victor Nee, "Rethinking Assimilation Theory for a New Era of Immigration," *International Migration Review* 31 (Winter 1997), 826–74; Richard Alba and Victor Nee, *Remaking the American Mainstream: Assimilation and Contemporary Immigration* (Cambridge, MA: Harvard University Press, 2003); and Michael J. White and Jennifer E. Glick, *How New Immigrants Do in American Schools, Jobs, and Neighborhoods* (New York: Russell Sage Foundation, 2009).

3. Rubén G. Rumbaut, "The Crucible Within: Ethnic Identity, Self Esteem, and Segmented Assimilation among Children of Immigrants," *International Migration Review* 28 (Winter 1994), 748–94; Alejandro Portes and Jozsef Borocz, "Contemporary Immigration: Theoretical Perspectives on Its Determinants and Modes of Incorporation," *International Migration Review* 23 (Fall 1989), 606–30; Alejandro Portes and Rubén G. Rumbaut, *Immigrant America: A Portrait, Updated and Expanded* (Berkeley: University of California Press, 2014).

4. Census Bureau, Tangstedt Parish Schleswig-Holstein Copenhagen: National Archives of Denmark, 1860, http://www.danishfamilysearch.dk, lists Hinrich Kohman as age seventeen, single, and working as *diensbote* (servant). Horst Beckerhouse, *Die Namen der Hamburger Stadtteile: Woher Sie Kommen Und Was Sie Bedeuten* (Hamburg, Germany: Sabine Groenewold Verlage, 2002), observes that Lemsal, where the Kohmans lived, was under Danish rule in 1860, brought under Austrian rule in 1864, and then annexed by Prussia in 1867, which would have made young men like Kohman subject to German military service.

5. Larry Potter, "History of Hope," unpublished manuscript, 1997; courtesy of the Dickinson County Historical Society, Abilene, Kansas.

6. "Rev. H. H. Nottorf, a Pioneer," *Hope Dispatch* [Hope, KS], January 4, 1906; *100th Anniversary of the First Baptist Church of Dickinson County, Hope, Kansas* (Hope: First Baptist Church, 1966), courtesy of the Germans from Russia Heritage Society Library, Bismarck, North Dakota. Opinion differs as to whether they donated the land or sold it to the church for $7 an acre.

7. Obituary, passport, and citizenship certificate, private collection, courtesy of John Newcomer.

8. The Kohmans and Kruses as illustrative cases reveal the complexities of relationships and social networks that were present so often when wives died young, husbands remarried, and families were large and intermarried within congregations, as well as how congregations' internal solidarity and external relationships were formed; the challenge of reconstructing the details of the Kohman and Kruse families and their congregations and communities was facilitated by having done research for a previous book on religion in Kansas, exploring possible archival sources for a number of other congregations, benefiting from the capable assistance of Chase Sachs, who was a student at Washburn University conveniently located near the Kansas State Historical Society Archive, and being able to visit the locations of both congregations and secure information from members and former members. The research was also facilitated by the many historical sources that have been digitized and made available online.

9. Christopher A. Bail, "The Configuration of Symbolic Boundaries against Immigrants in Europe," *American Sociological Review* 73 (February 2008), 37–59, discusses symbolic boundaries as modes of ethnic exclusion.

10. An extensive literature has emphasized religion's role in preserving ethnic identities; reviewed in Pyong Gap Min, *Preserving Ethnicity through Religion in America:*

Korean Protestants and Indian Hindus across Generations (New York: NYU Press, 2010), 15–28.

11. Surveys of the extensive literature on varying approaches to social cohesion include Noah E. Friedkin, "Social Cohesion," *Annual Review of Sociology* 30 (2004), 409–25; Helen Sullivan, "Evaluating Social Cohesion," in *Promoting Social Cohesion: Implications for Policy and Evaluation*, ed. Peter Ratcliffe and Ines Newman (Bristol, UK: Policy Press, 2011), 41–59; and Joseph Chan, Ho-Pong To, and Elaine Chan, "Reconsidering Social Cohesion: Developing a Definition and Analytical Framework for Empirical Research," *Social Indicators Research* 75 (January 2006), 273–302.

12. Changing patterns of geographic concentration among immigrants are described in Richard Alba and Nancy Denton, "Old and New Landscapes of Diversity: The Residential Patterns of Immigrant Minorities," in *Historical and Contemporary Perspectives on Immigration, Race, and Ethnicity in the United States*, ed. Nancy Foner and George M. Fredrickson (New York: Russell Sage Foundation, 2004), 237–61.

13. Research on the social significance of geographic proximity includes Mark G. Herander and Luz A. Saavedra, "Exports and the Structure of Immigrant-Based Networks: The Role of Geographic Proximity," *Review of Economics and Statistics* 87 (May 2005), 323–35; and Andrew V. Papachristos, David M. Hureau, and Anthony A. Braga, "The Corner and the Crew: The Influence of Geography and Social Networks on Gang Violence," *American Sociological Review* 78 (June 2013), 417–47.

14. Carl F. Bowman, *Brethren Society: The Cultural Transformation of a "Peculiar People"* (Baltimore: Johns Hopkins University Press, 1995), provides a rich illustration of the role of extensive kinship ties.

15. Factors influencing religious endogamy are discussed in Ruth Shonie Cavan, "Concepts and Terminology in Interreligious Marriage," *Journal for the Scientific Study of Religion* 9 (Winter 1970), 311–20; evidence on the extent of religious endogamy is provided in Michael J. Rosenfeld, "Racial, Educational and Religious Endogamy in the United States: A Comparative Historical Perspective," *Social Forces* 87 (September 2008), 1–31.

16. Trust and enforceable norms (norm observance) are key elements in Portes's conceptualization of membership in groups that provide social capital; Alejandro Portes, *Economic Sociology: A Systematic Inquiry* (Princeton, NJ: Princeton University Press, 2010), 27–47.

17. Michèle Lamont and Virag Molnar, "The Study of Boundaries in the Social Sciences," *Annual Review of Sociology* 28 (2002), 167–95. Suzanne Keller, *Community: Pursuing the Dream, Living the Reality* (Princeton, NJ: Princeton University Press, 2005), 264–90, emphasizes rituals, celebrations, myths, beliefs, and values in discussing communal solidarity.

18. William Least Heat-Moon, *PrairyErth* (New York: Houghton, 1992).

19. Mary Alice Sies, "History of Lorraine, Kansas: Little Town on the Prairie," unpublished manuscript, 1987, courtesy of the Kansas State Historical Society, Topeka.

20. Marcus Lee Hansen, *The Immigrant in American History* (Cambridge, MA: Harvard University Press, 1940), 61–62; Sonya Salamon, *Prairie Patrimony: Family, Farming, and Community in the Midwest* (Chapel Hill: University of North Carolina Press, 1992), 21–23.

21. Frederick Ernest Nottorf, "Reminiscences of a Pioneer," undated typescript, courtesy of Linda Ihde. Potter, "History of Hope," incorrectly identifies the brother-in-law (Dorothy Henning Nottorf's brother) as "Chris Hemming" instead of Chris Henning.

22. *Grundriss der Geschichte unserer Gemeinde: Souvenir Program of the Fifty Year Jubilee of the German Baptist Church of Dickinson County, Kansas* (Hope, KS: First Baptist Church, 1916), courtesy of Linda Ihde.

23. Janzen's academy at Monee, Illinois, and the opposition it received from church leaders is discussed in Herman Von Berge, *These Glorious Years: The Centenary History*

of German Baptists of North America, 1843–1943 (Providence, RI: Roger Williams Press, 1943), 76; and Frank H. Woyke, *Heritage and Ministry of the North American Baptist Conference* (Forest Park, IL: North American Baptist Conference, 1979), 158.

24. C. B. Schmidt to Colonel A. S. Johnson, June 9, 1877; courtesy of Kansas State Historical Society.

25. "125th Anniversary, First Baptist Church, Lorraine, Kansas," unpublished church history, 2003, courtesy of Steve Janssen. The agreement stated: "Whatever of the lands marked in blue on the within plat are purchased before the end of March, 1877, or land purchased in this neighborhood outside the reserved land by members of the German Baptist Colony of Ellsworth, an amount equal to the quantity purchased will be reserved for six months from March 31st, 1877; and as the latter reservation is purchased by the Colony amounts will be added thereto to keep up the full quantity. When ten sections have been purchased, eighty acres of fair average quality will be donated for church purpose." *Dedication Program of the First Baptist Church of Lorraine, Kansas*, November 28, 1937, First Baptist Church of Lorraine Kansas Archives.

26. An account of Oncken's baptism is given in "Baptists in Germany," *Boston Recorder*, November 27, 1833; Oncken's previous work with the Lower Saxony Tract Society is discussed in "Foreign Intelligence," *Boston Recorder and Religious Telegraph*, June 13, 1828, and "Brief History of the Continental Society," *Christian Register*, June 3, 1826.

27. Rudolf Donat, *Das Wachsende Werk (The Growing Work)*, trans. Marianne Lengefeld; online at Robert Schulz, "The Baptists in Germany," http://archiver.rootsweb .ancestry.com.

28. "Letter of Mr. Oncken: Results of Political Changes," *Baptist Missionary Magazine* 29 (August 1849), 302; "Mission to Germany," *Annual Report of the Board of Managers of the American Baptist Missionary Union* (Boston: American Baptist Missionary Union, 1850), 89; "Dr. Oncken," *New York Evangelist*, July 28, 1853.

29. "Oncken to Preach," *Sangamo Journal* [Sangamo, IL], November 1, 1853; "Rev. J. G. Oncken," *Christian Watchman and Reflector*, June 2, 1853.

30. "German Baptist Church," *Burlington Hawkeye* [Burlington, IA], November 11, 1869. The inaugural meeting was held at the First English Baptist Church with Rev. E. J. Deckmann of the German Baptist Church at Burlington giving the sermon and Rev. John Wilkens of the Baptist Church at Racine giving the official charge to Rev. John Kohrs. The church had thirty-eight members. In 1879 Kohrs was the pastor at the German Baptist Church in Kekoskee, Wisconsin, where Henry and Mary Kohman had been married in 1872.

31. Karl August Kemnitz, "Letter," *Baptist Missionary Magazine* 54 (September 1874), 328–29.

32. "Letter of Mr. Oncken: The Gospel in Mecklenburg," *Baptist Missionary Magazine* 29 (January 1849), 19.

33. "Baptists in Germany," *Boston Recorder*, November 27, 1833.

34. "Adults" for this purpose are persons age eighteen and over; the Hope church's records suggest that in addition to the 69 adults as many as 55 of those under age eighteen were baptized members.

35. William G. Cutler, *History of the State of Kansas* (Chicago: A. T. Andreas, 1883), 685.

36. Michael R. Haines, "Estimated Life Tables for the United States, 1850–1900," *Historical Methods* 31 (1998), 149–69.

37. Samuel H. Preston and Michael R. Haines, *Fatal Years: Child Mortality in Late Nineteenth-Century America* (Princeton, NJ: Princeton University Press, 1991), 89–114.

38. "Descendants Erect Marker to Honor Woman," *Salina Journal* [Salina, KS], November 9, 1996.

39. Brian Young, *Respectable Burial: Montreal's Mount Royal Cemetery* (Montreal: McGill-Queen's University Press, 2003).

40. Rev. C. A. Kemnitz, "Sketch of Persecutions at Templin," *Missionary Magazine* 34 (September 1853), 395.

41. Families varied in size, meaning that these figures give only a rough indication of the extent to which children's deaths affected some families more than others. Based on the total pool of 109 different surnames represented at the two congregations, each of the 75 families for this comparison had at least four matching surnames.

42. Cutler, *History of the State of Kansas*, 685.

43. Carolyn Jones, *The First One Hundred Years: A History of the City of Manhattan, Kansas, 1855–1955* (Manhattan, KS: Manhattan Centennial Committee, 1955); excerpts from Griffing's letters are included in Linda S. Johnston, *Hope amid Hardship: Pioneer Voices from Kansas Territory* (Guilford, CT: Globe Pequot Press, 2013).

44. "The Spirit and Mission of Methodism," *Methodist Quarterly Review* 6 (January 1854), 68.

45. Potter, "History of Hope."

46. Maury Klein, *Union Pacific: The Birth of a Railroad, 1862–1893* (Garden City, NY: Doubleday, 1987).

47. Early difficulties growing wheat in and around Dickinson County are described in James C. Malin, "Beginnings of Winter Wheat Production in the Upper Kansas and Lower Smoky Hill River Valleys: A Study in Adaptation to Geographical Environment," *Kansas Historical Quarterly* 10 (1941), 227–59; a later statistical study conducted for other purposes that happened to include Green Garden Township in Ellsworth County in its sample is reported in Kenneth Sylvester and Geoff Cunfer, "An Unremembered Diversity: Mixed Husbandry and the American Grasslands," *Agricultural History* 83 (2009), 352–83.

48. Kansas State Board of Agriculture, *Special Report of the Kansas State Board of Agriculture for the Information of Home-Seekers* (Topeka: Kansas Publishing House, 1886), 7–10. The 1895 Agricultural Census (Kansas State Census Collection, 1855–1925, Kansas State Historical Society) reported twice as many acres planted to corn (4,942) as planted to wheat (2,552) in Banner Township of Dickinson County, whereas in Green Garden Township in Ellsworth County acreage in corn (3,915) was about a third the acreage planted in wheat (10,974). Large, flat, adjacent fields suitable for wheat in the Lorraine area reinforced the colony's geographic concentration, while smaller, scattered fields along creeks separated by hills were less conducive to geographic concentration in the vicinity of Hope.

49. *A Biographical History of Central Kansas* (New York: Lewis Publishing Company, 1902), 574–75, 627–28.

50. "Killed by Lightning," *Abilene Reflector* [Abilene, KS], July 14, 1887.

51. "Pottawatomie Colony," *Herald of Freedom* [Lawrence, KS], December 20, 1856.

52. Ellsworth County Kansas, Index of Deeds, Townships 16 and 17; Register of Deeds Office, Ellsworth, Kansas.

53. *History of the First Baptist Church of Frederick*, 1958, unpublished manuscript and photos, courtesy of the Geneseo Museum, Geneseo, Kansas, and the Rice County Historical Society, Lyons, Kansas.

54. Frank J. Klingberg, "Memoirs of Frank J. Klingberg," *Historical Magazine of the Protestant Episcopal Church* 29 (March 1960), 106–35, quote on page 114.

55. "Dillon Recents," *Abilene Reflector*, November 7, 1889.

56. Cindy K. Wesley, "The Pietist Theology and Ethnic Mission of the General Conference of German Baptists in North America, 1851-1920," PhD dissertation, McGill University, 2000, especially 253–314.

57. First Baptist Church of Lorraine, Kansas, Church Minutes, First Baptist Church of Lorraine Archive, courtesy of Steve Janssen.

58. First Baptist Church of Dickinson County, Church Minutes, Box No. 2 A07-4 DJH, Dickinson County Historical Society, Abilene, Kansas, 51, 52, 54, 55, 59.

59. Jacob C. Ruppenthal, "The German Element in Central Kansas," *Collections of the Kansas State Historical Society* 13 (1913–14), 513–35, argued that the strong regional, religious, and linguistic differences among Kansas Germans were a principal deterrent to them forming larger organizations and political movements; Katja Wustenbecker, "German-Americans during World War I," *Immigrant Entrepreneurship: German-American Business Biographies, 1720 to the Present*, vol. 3, ed. Giles R. Hoyt (Berlin: German Historical Institute, 2014), 1–14, suggests that language was the most important unifying element among German Americans.

60. Gerlof D. Homan, "Mennonites and Military Justice in World War I," *Mennonite Quarterly Review* 66 (July 1992), 365–75.

61. "Kansas Farmer Raises the Teuton Flag," *Chicago Livestock World*, March 24, 1917.

62. Registration in Kansas began on February 4, 1918; *Annals of Kansas, 1886–1925* (Topeka: Kansas State Historical Society, 1956), 209.

63. "Kansas Invaded by Nonpartisan League Workers," *Topeka State Journal*, December 28, 1917; "Nonpartisan Stand Upheld by Vrooman," *Baxter Springs News* [Baxter Springs, KS], November 29, 1917; "Nonpartisan League: Farmers' Union of Nebraska and Kansas Do Not Look with Favor upon New Movement," *Lindsborg News-Record* [Lindsborg, KS], September 26, 1917; "Says League Is Disloyal," *Kansas City Star*, April 17, 1918; "Capper Hears of Disloyalty," *Kansas City Star*, April 23, 1918.

64. Ralph Voss, "The Immigrant," 2007, courtesy of Ralph Voss.

65. "John Rumold Obituary," *Hope Dispatch*, January 11, 1917; Klingberg, "Memoirs," 123, 126.

66. "Jacob J. Rumold," *Portrait and Biographical Record of Dickinson, Saline, McPherson, and Marion Counties* (Chicago: Chapman Brothers, 1893), 601. September 1893 is given as the date of Rumold's death according to an obituary published at the time, although the date on the gravestone, which was put up some years later, is 1898.

67. Untitled news article *Hope Dispatch* [Hope, Kansas], May 9, 1918; "Rumold in Bad Again," *Hope Dispatch*, October 24, 1918.

68. Letter from W. J. Rumold to the Adjutant General, Topeka, Kansas, March 11, 1918; courtesy of the Kansas State Historical Society. Minutes of the First Baptist Church of Dickinson County give no indication of sentiment toward the war or the Nonpartisan League and make no mention of the controversy; Rev. P.C.A. Menard's generally favorable standing in the denomination is suggested by his preaching the annual sermon at the Baptists' Southwestern Conference in St. Louis on August 23, 1916, on the theme "The Power of the Gospel." Menard graduated from Rochester Theological Seminary in 1900, was a popular speaker at Baptist youth conferences, and preached in English as well as in German.

69. Moderate versus extreme strictness as aspects of religious organizations is notably associated with the argument in Laurence R. Iannaccone, "Why Strict Churches Are Strong," *American Journal of Sociology* 99 (1994), 1180–1211.

70. The importance of distinguishing national, regional, and local levels of competition among religious organizations is discussed in Adam Goldstein and Heather A. Haveman, "Pulpit and Press: Denominational Dynamics and the Growth of Religious Magazines in Antebellum America," *American Sociological Review* 7, 8 (2013), 797–827.

Chapter Six

1. "Arrest Gimbel Head and Agents," *New York Times*, June 20, 1920.

2. U.S. Bureau of Labor Statistics, "CPI Inflation Calculator," U.S. Department of Labor, 2015; http://www.bls.gov.

3. Theodore H. Price, "The Index Number Wage," *Outlook*, April 30, 1919.

4. U.S. Bureau of Labor Statistics, Consumer Expenditure Survey, figures for 1901 and 1918; *100 Years of U.S. Consumer Spending: Data for the Nation, New York City, and Boston*, BLS Report 991 (2006), 16.

5. President Woodrow Wilson, "Address to Congress on the High Cost of Living," August 8, 1919; American Presidency Project, University of California, Santa Barbara.

6. Sam Pizzigati, *The Rich Don't Always Win: The Forgotten Triumph over Plutocracy That Created the American Middle Class, 1900–1970* (New York: Seven Stories Press, 2012), 73–97; Steve Fraser, *The Age of Acquiescence: The Life and Death of American Resistance to Organized Wealth and Power* (Boston: Little, Brown, 2015).

7. A. Michael Palmer, *Report of the Attorney General*, Department of Justice, Washington, DC, December 11, 1920.

8. Stanley Coben, *A. Mitchell Palmer: Politician* (New York: Columbia University Press, 1963), 171–78.

9. "'Flying Squadron' Opens War on Food Hoarding in Strike," *New York Tribune*, April 14, 1920.

10. "Senior Class, 1904," *Bric a Brac*, 1904, 34; "204 Clansmen Attend 25th Reunion," *Class of 1904, 25th Yearbook*, Princeton University Alumni Archives, 1929, 215; U.S. Congress, House of Representatives, *Hearings before the Committee on Agriculture, Lamborn Sugar Resolution* (Washington, DC: Government Printing Office, 1922), 31–32; U.S. Department of Justice, Office of the Attorney General, *Report of the Attorney General* (Washington, DC: Government Printing Office, 1920), 48, U.S. Attorney General and Department of Justice Collection. In 1935 Riley served as a division administrator for the National Industrial Recovery Board and in that role advocated for the Canning Code, which required canners and packers to adopt uniform standards for grading and labeling the quality of canned goods; Persia Campbell, "Consumer Representation in the New Deal," PhD dissertation, Columbia University, 1940, 177–79.

11. "The Profiteer," *San Jose Mercury News*, August 19, 1919.

12. *Life*, June 17, 1920, 1126; June 3, 1920, 1043; July 29, 1920, 204; June 3, 1920, 1043; November 25, 1920, 1; March 10, 1919, 349; George Creel, "Message of the United States Government to the American People: A Warning to Food Profiteers," *The Independent* 94 (May 11, 1918), 254; George Creel, *How We Advertised America* (New York: Harper and Brothers, 1920).

13. Palmer, *Report of the Attorney General*, 185.

14. "Flying Squadron Makes an Arrest," *New York Times*, April 11, 1920; "Brooklyn Man Held for Trial as a Profiteer," *New York Tribune*, April 11, 1920; "Profiteer Kills Self," *New York World*, April 12, 1920; "Arrested on Profiteering Charge, Ends His Life with a Bullet," *New York Tribune*, April 12, 1920. The possibility of domestic difficulties is suggested by Nichthauser's will, which left amounts of $2,000 to $5,000 to a sister, several nieces, and several Jewish organizations and divided the remainder of the estate between the two daughters but stated, "I make no provision for my wife or my son for reasons well known to them"; Kings County Surrogate's Court, Will and Probate Record, May 18, 1920.

15. "Suicide Won't Retard Hunt for Profiteers," *New York Tribune*, April 13, 1920; "Arrest Gimbel Head and Agents," *New York Times*, June 20, 1920; "Fred A. Gimbel Is Arrested as a Profiteer," *New York Tribune*, June 20, 1920.

16. Paul H. Geenen, *Schuster's & Gimbels: Milwaukee's Beloved Department Stores* (Charleston, SC: History Press, 2012); Michael J. Lisicky, *Gimbels Has It!* (Charleston, SC: History Press, 2011).

17. U.S. Fuel Administration, *General Orders, Regulations and Rulings* (Washington, DC: Government Printing Office, 1920), 9.

18. William B. Marvin, "Food and Fuel Control," *Michigan Law Review* 17 (February 1919), 310–30; William Clinton Mullendore, *History of the United States Food*

Administration, 1917–1919 (Stanford, CA: Stanford University Press, 1941); Thomas Fleming, *The Illusion of Victory: America in World War I* (New York: Basic Books, 2003), 125–27.

19. Palmer, *Report of the Attorney General*, 180.

20. Eugene Campbell, "A.W. Riley Analyzes the Profiteer's Art," *New York Herald*, April 25, 1920; "Urges Jail for Greed," *Kansas City Star*, January 24, 1920; "The Greed of the Profiteer," *Kansas City Advocate*, July 2, 1920; U.S. Senate, *Congressional Record*, April 23, 1920, 6109.

21. Rae Katherine Eighmey, *Food Will Win the War: Minnesota Crops, Cooks, and Conservation during World War I* (St. Paul: Minnesota Historical Society, 2010); Jerry W. Markham, *Law Enforcement and the History of Financial Market Manipulation* (New York: Routledge, 2015), 37–39; Rachel Moloshok, "Saving for Victory!" *Pennsylvania Legacies* 12 (November 2012), 3–5.

22. Arthur Lamb, "Interview on Experiences in World War II," September 27, 2007; courtesy of Kansas State Historical Society, Topeka.

23. Robert S. Lynd and Helen Merrell Lynd, *Middletown: A Study in Modern American Culture* (New York: Harcourt Brace Jovanovich, 1929), 85.

24. Mark Twain, letter to Carolyn Wells, April 15, 1906, http://www.twainquotes.com.

25. F. Scott Fitzgerald, "The Rich Boy," in F. Scott Fitzgerald, *All the Sad Young Men* (New York: Scribner's, 1926), 1.

26. "Must, Can, and Should Money Be Taxed?" *Overland Monthly* 4 (October 1873), 351–64, quote on 351. The same point about the ambiguities of wealth is emphasized in Karen Rowlingson and Stephen McKay, *Wealth and the Wealthy: Exploring and Tackling Inequalities between Rich and Poor* (Bristol, UK: Policy Press, 2011), 53–80.

27. Pierre Bourdieu, *Distinction: A Social Critique of the Judgment of Taste* (Cambridge, MA: Harvard University Press, 1979); Michèle Lamont, *Money, Morals, and Manners: The Culture of the French and the American Upper-Middle Class* (Chicago: University of Chicago Press, 1992).

28. George K. Holmes, "The Concentration of Wealth," *Political Science Quarterly* 8 (1893), 1–12.

29. Charles B. Spahr, *An Essay on the Present Distribution of Wealth in the United States* (New York: Thomas V. Crowell, 1896); Herman E. Taubeneck, "The Concentration of Wealth, Its Cause and Results," *Arena* 18 (1897), 289–301.

30. Hugh Blair, "Necessity of Forming Religious Principles at an Early Age," *Massachusetts Magazine* (January 1789), 37–38.

31. Max Weber, *The Protestant Ethic and the Spirit of Capitalism* (New York: Scribner's, 1958).

32. "The Fragment," *Columbian Gazetteer* [New York, NY], September 30, 1793.

33. "New York," *Independent Ledger*, March 1, 1784.

34. Reprinted in Thomas Reese, "Essay on the Influence of Religion in Civil Society," *American Museum* 8 (1790), 46–47.

35. "Family Sermon," *Christian Observer* 10 (1811), 407–11.

36. Benjamin Williams, *The Book of Psalms as Translated, Paraphrased, or Imitated by Some of the Most Eminent English Poets* (Salisbury, England: Collins and Johnson, 1781), 407; also published as "A Request to the Divine Being," *New Hampshire Gazette*, May 12, 1791; and as "Hermina's Request to the Divine Being," *Independent Gazetteer*, April 24, 1793, in which "human prudence" is substituted for "humane pleasure."

37. "On Wealth," *American Magazine* 1 (1816), 369–71.

38. Moses Y. Beach, *Wealth and Biography of the Wealthy Citizens of New York City* (New York: Sun Office, 1845).

39. Mark Twain and Charles Dudley Warner, *The Gilded Age: A Tale of Today* (New York: American Publishing Company, 1873).

40. Charles Henry Jones, "Editor's Table," *Appleton's Journal* 10 (1873), 409.

41. Henry Ward Beecher, "The Battle of Money," *Christian Union* 7 (February 5, 1873), 110.

42. "The New York Panic," *Religious Magazine and Monthly Review* 50 (October 1873), 374–76.

43. William Graham Sumner, "Politics in America, 1776–1876," *North American Review* 122 (January 1876), 47–87, quotes on 57.

44. Ibid., 87.

45. William Graham Sumner, *What Social Classes Owe to Each Other* (New York: Harper & Brothers, 1884), 41–43.

46. Ibid., 104, 108.

47. Ibid., 149.

48. William A. Peffer, *The Farmer's Side: His Troubles and Their Remedy* (New York: D. Appleton, 1891), 167, 258.

49. Ibid.,167.

50. Ibid., 122; and similarly argued during the 1893 House Committee on Ways and Means discussion; George Tunell,"The Legislative History of the Second Income Tax Law," *Journal of Political Economy* 3 (1895), 311–37.

51. G. H. Fish, *Hew to the Line: A Master or a Slave* (Winfield, KS: H. and L. Vincent, 1891), 2, 12; courtesy of Kansas State Historical Society.

52. William Allen White, "Vanity of Vanities," *Emporia Daily Gazette*, November 16, 1905.

53. Andrew Carnegie, "The Gospel of Wealth," *North American Review* 148 (June 1889), 653–64.

54. "Carnegie on Wealth," *Zion's Herald* 70 (February 17, 1892), 52–53.

55. Joseph Epstein, *Snobbery: The American Version* (Boston: Houghton Mifflin, 2002); Edgar Fawcett, "Plutocracy and Snobbery in New York," in *The Arena*, ed. B. O. Flower (Boston: Arena Publishing, 1891), 142–51; Sven Beckert and Julia B. Rosenbaum, *The American Bourgeoisie: Distinction and Identity in the Nineteenth Century* (New York: Palgrave, 2010); W. D. Howells, "Are We a Plutocracy?" *North American Review* 158 (February 1894), 185–95.

56. Charles H. Parkhurst, *Our Fight with Tammany* (New York: Charles Scribner's Sons, 1895).

57. Ibid., 274, 276.

58. Franklin Henry Giddings, *The Principles of Sociology: An Analysis of the Phenomena of Association and of Social Organization* (New York: Macmillan, 1896). One of the more nuanced discussions of this perspective as it applied to wealth and power was that of sociologist Lester F. Ward, "Plutocracy and Paternalism," *Forum* 20 (November 1895), 300–310.

59. On soulless corporations, essays such as "Great Corporations," *Herald of Gospel Liberty* 96 (July 14, 1904), 433–35, and novels such as Frank Norris, *The Pit: A Story of Chicago* (New York: Doubleday, 1903).

60. Robert Herrick, *The Common Lot* (New York: Macmillan, 1904); Blake Nevius, *Robert Herrick: The Development of a Novelist* (Berkeley: University of California Press, 1962), especially 139–53; quote from Jules Eckert Goodman, "Review of *The Common Lot*," *Current Literature* 38 (February 1905), 182.

61. William Allen White, *A Certain Rich Man* (New York: Macmillan, 1909), 403; Washington Gladden, "Washington Gladden on World Greed," *New York Observer and Chronicle*, December 30, 1909.

62. William Jennings Bryan, *Speeches of William Jennings Bryan* (New York: Funk and Wagnalls, 1913), 75.

63. Ibid.

64. William Jennings Bryan, "The Commoner," *The Commoner*, January 23, 1901.

65. Theodore Roosevelt, *Realizable Ideals* (San Francisco: Whitaker & Ray-Wiggin, 1912), 21, 24, 25.

66. Theodore Roosevelt, *An Autobiography* (New York: Macmillan, 1916), 80, 81.

67. Quotes from "World Greed Is Deplored," *Oregonian* [Portland, OR], August, 25, 1919; related arguments in Allan Hoben, "Moral Problems of Industrial Reconstruction," *Biblical World* 54 (July 1920), 437–48; and Susan Curtis, *A Consuming Faith: The Social Gospel and Modern American Culture* (Columbia: University of Missouri Press, 2001), 19–22.

68. N. D. Cochran, "One Man's Opinions," *The Day Book*, July 29, 1914.

69. For example, "Voice of the People against 'Preparedness,'" *The Commoner*, January 1, 1916.

70. Untitled, *Nonpartisan Leader*, May 19, 1919; Mary M. Cronin, "Fighting for the Farmers: The Pacific Northwest's Nonpartisan League Newspapers," *Journalism History* 23 (1997), 126–36.

71. Amos Pinchot, "Letter of Amos Pinchot to the Honorable Claude Kitchin," *Willmar Tribune* [Willmar, MN], August 10, 1918. The letter expanded on arguments in a September 18, 1917, letter to Kitchin, a portion of which was included in U.S. House of Representatives, Hearings before the Special Committee on Victor L. Berger (Washington, DC: Government Printing Office, 1919), 419–20; and on Pinchot's arguments against profiteering, Pizzigati, *The Rich Don't Always Win*, 73–86.

72. Among the many comparative studies are Werner Sombart, *Why Is There No Socialism in the United States?* (White Plains, NY: International Arts and Sciences Press, 1976; initially published in 1906); Seymour Martin Lipset, *Agrarian Socialism: The Cooperative Commonwealth Federation in Saskatchewan* (Berkeley: University of California Press, 1971); and Daniel Bell, *Marxian Socialism in the United States* (Ithaca, NY: Cornell University Press, 1996).

73. Thorstein Veblen, "The Modern Point of View and the New Order, VIII: The Vested Interests and the Common Man," *The Dial* 66 (January 25, 1919), 75–82, quotes on 76 and 81.

74. T. Jackson Lears, *Fables of Abundance: A Cultural History of Advertising in America* (New York: Basic Books, 1994); Leigh Eric Schmidt, *Consumer Rites: The Buying and Selling of American Holidays* (Princeton, NJ: Princeton University Press, 1995).

75. Mary Doane Shelby, "The Housewife and the High Cost of Living," *Outlook* 123 (September 3, 1919), 13–15.

76. Anne Martin, "If I Were a Senator: In Which the First Woman Candidate Speaks Her Mind," *The Independent* 101 (May 1, 1920), 162–64.

77. Carson C. Hathaway, "Millionaire Army Has 74 Classed as 'Multi,'" *New York Times*, October 3, 1926.

78. Ibid.

79. Arthur Train, "The Billionaire Era: Part I—The Vanderbilts and Andrew Carnegie," *Forum* 72 (November 1924), 617–28, and "The Billionaire Era: Part II—The Rockefellers and Henry Ford," *Forum* 72 (December 1924), 746–59.

80. "Where Are the Kings of Yesteryear?" *The Independent* 114 (January 10, 1925), 32. Country retreats of wealthy Boston residents provided a similar illustration in James C. O'Connell, *The Hub's Metropolis: Greater Boston's Development from Railroad Suburbs to Smart Growth* (Cambridge, MA: MIT Press, 2013), 17–40.

81. "Frozen Assets Blamed for Failure of Old Institution," *Kansas City Star*, October 7, 1925; Comptroller of the Currency, *Annual Report* (Washington, DC: Government

Printing Office, 1927), 614; Carl Felsenfeld and David L. Glass, *Banking Regulation in the United States* (Huntington, NY: Juris Publishing, 2011), 261–74.

82. "Mrs. Snowden Robbed," *New York Tribune*, August 29, 1927; "Wealthy Autoists Robbed," *Los Angeles Times*, January 31, 1925.

83. R. F. Brown, "Twelve International Movements," *Herald of Gospel Liberty* 117 (February 5, 1925), 129–30; "Peggy's Fortune," *Youth's Companion* 97 (November 22, 1923), 712; Thyra Samter Winslow, "My Daughter in the City," *The Bookman* 68 (November 1928), 290–99; F. Scott Fitzgerald, *The Great Gatsby* (New York: Scribner's, 1925); Harold Bloom, *The American Dream* (New York: Infobase Publishing, 2009), 67–80.

84. C. H. Claudy, "Pat Prentiss's Fortune," *Youth's Companion* 103 (January 1929), 3, 37–38, quote on 38; Gertrude Mack, "Rising above the Market," *Forum* 4 (April 1931), 228–34.

85. Lewis H. Haney, "Who Gets the Money?" *North American Review* 229 (January 1930), 59–65, quotes on 59.

86. William Deloach quoted in Geoff Cunfer, "The Dust Bowl," *EH.Net Encyclopedia*, ed. Robert Whaples, August 18, 2004, http://eh.net/encyclopedia; Robert Santelli and Emily Davidson, eds., *Hard Travelin': The Life and Legacy of Woody Guthrie* (Hanover, NH: University Press of New England, 1999), 131. John Steinbeck, *The Grapes of Wrath* (New York: Viking, 1939), of course captured these sentiments in describing landowners' and banks' eviction of tenant farmers.

87. U.S. Senate, *Congressional Record*, March 13, 1933, 262, 268; James E. Sargent, "Roosevelt's Economy Act: Fiscal Conservatism and the Early New Deal," *Congressional Studies* 7 (Winter 1980), 33–51.

88. "New Social Policy Urged on Wealthy," *New York Times*, December 8, 1934; Arthur Schlesinger Jr., "Who Was Henry A. Wallace?" *Los Angeles Times*, March 20, 2000.

89. L. H. Robbins, "White Hails a 'Revolt' of the Middle Class," *New York Times*, November 20, 1938.

90. Robert Smith Bader, *The Great Kansas Bond Scandal* (Lawrence: University Press of Kansas, 1982).

91. William L. White, *What People Said* (New York: Viking, 1938), 516. The assault incident is discussed in Loren E. Pennington, "Interview with Everett Ray Call," July 2007; Flint Hills Oral History Project Collection, Kansas State Historical Society, Topeka.

92. Wallace Stegner, "Chronicles of the West," *Virginia Quarterly Review* (Autumn 1938), 596–601, quotes on 601.

93. Franklin D. Roosevelt, "Message to Congress on Tax Revision," June 19, 1935; online at http://www.presidency.ucsb.edu; Jason Scott Smith, *A Concise History of the New Deal* (New York: Cambridge University Press, 2014), 92–94.

94. Gallup Organization, Gallup Polls, January 13–18, 1936, and August 1937; courtesy of the Roper Center for Public Opinion Research, Storrs, Connecticut, 2015.

95. "Hoover Asks Help for Middle Class," *New York Times*, October 27, 1937; "Disheartening Times," *New York Herald Tribune*, June 11, 1938; "Swill Deal for Poor Man," *Richmond Times Dispatch* [Richmond, VA], February 27, 1936.

96. Robert Lynd and Helen Merrell Lynd, *Middletown in Transition: A Study in Cultural Conflicts* (New York: Harcourt, Brace, 1937), 489.

97. Among others, Wendy L. Wall, *Inventing the 'American Way': The Politics of Consensus from the New Deal to the Civil Rights Movement* (New York: Oxford University Press, 2008); Joseph E. Lowndes, *From the New Deal to the New Right: Race and the Southern Origins of Modern Conservatism* (New Haven, CT: Yale University Press, 2008); and Ira Katznelson, *Fear Itself: The New Deal and the Origins of Our Time* (New York: Norton, 2013).

Chapter Seven

1. Monika Elbert, *Enterprising Youth: Social Values and Acculturation in Nineteenth-Century American Children's Literature* (New York: Routledge, 2008); Ruth Miller Elson, *Guardians of Tradition: American Schoolbooks of the Nineteenth Century* (Lincoln: University of Nebraska Press, 1964); Gretchen A. Adams, *Children and Youth in a New Nation* (New York: NYU Press, 2009); Pat Pflieger, "A Visit to *Merry's Museum*; or, Social Values in a Nineteenth-Century American Periodical for Children," PhD dissertation, University of Minnesota, 1987. A succinct overview of the cultural changes shaping understandings of children and childhood in the nineteenth century is Stephen Kline, "The Making of Children's Culture," in *The Children's Culture Reader*, ed. Henry Jenkins (New York: NYU Press, 1998), 95–109.

2. The three genres are roughly parallel to the ones identified in Daniel Rodgers, "Socializing Middle-Class Children: Institutions, Fables, and Work Values in Nineteenth-Century America," *Journal of Social History* 13 (Spring 1980), 354–67. The popular literature, as Karen Sánchez-Eppler, "Childhood," in *Keywords for Children's Literature* , ed. Philip Nel and Lissa Paul (New York: NYU Press, 2011), 35–41, observes, is informative about the cultural understandings of what childhood should be more so than about what children themselves experienced.

3. The influence of Philippe Ariès, *Centuries of Childhood* (New York: Penguin, 1960), is of course both important and controversial in framing the broader discussion of childhood, about which Patrick H. Hutton, *Philippe Ariès and the Politics of French Cultural History* (Amherst: University of Massachusetts Press, 2004), 92–112, is helpful. Philip J. Greven, *Child Rearing Concepts, 1628-1861* (Itasca, IL: F. E. Peacock, 1973), and Janet Leigh Barker, "From Punishment to Discipline: Strategies of Control in 18th and 19th Century Children's Fiction," PhD dissertation, Texas A&M University, 2001, are useful sources on shifts in parenting styles. Viviana A. Zelizer, *Pricing the Priceless Child: The Changing Social Value of Children* (New York: Basic Books, 1985), focuses on the rising emotional significance of children. The moral messages communicated about neatness, orderliness, and discipline in the selection and care of household furnishings are emphasized in Amy G. Richter, ed., *At Home in Nineteenth-Century America* (New York: NYU Press, 2015).

4. William Bardwell, *Healthy Homes and How to Make Them* (London: Dean and Son, 1854); Annmarie Adams, *Architecture in the Family Way: Doctors, Houses, and Women, 1870-1900* (Montreal: McGill-Queen's University Press, 1996); and, on the refinement of middle-class houses, Richard Lyman Bushman, *The Refinement of America: Persons, Houses, Cities* (New York: Vintage, 1992).

5. "Of the Nursery," *Philadelphia Journal of the Medical and Physical Sciences* 2 (1825), 6–19.

6. "Oliver," *Juvenile Miscellany* 2 (May 1829), 153–67.

7. "The Wicked Girl Changed," *Youth's Companion* 8 (June 28, 1834), 23–24.

8. "Youth's Department," *Christian Watchman* 13 (March 30, 1832), 52.

9. "The Brothers," *Juvenile Miscellany* 3 (November 1827), 209–10.

10. "Wicked Company," *Episcopal Recorder* 11 (May 4, 1833), 20.

11. "End of the Good and Bad Boy," *Christian Advocate* 6 (September 16, 1831), 12.

12. "An Address to Children: At a Prayer Meeting of the Church on Their Behalf at Greensborough, Vermont, June 1819," *Youth's Religious Instructor* 1 (September 1, 1819), 306–10, quotes on 306 and 309.

13. "The Infant Preacher; or, The Story of Henrietta Smith," *Youth's Religious Instructor* 1 (July 1, 1819), 229–34, quotes on 233.

14. Tayler Lewis, "My Old School-Master," in *Proceedings of the Eleventh Anniversary of the University Convocation of the State of New York* (Albany, NY: Weed, Parsons, and Company, 1875), 95–109, quotes on 98 and 99. Tayler Lewis (1802–1877) taught Greek and Hebrew at Union College in Schenectady, New York, was an abolitionist, and authored *Six Days of Creation*, published in 1855, and *Science and the Bible*, published in 1856; Jean Fagan Yellin, ed., *The Harriet Jacobs Family Papers* (Chapel Hill: University of North Carolina Press, 2008), 701.

15. "An Essay on Lying," *South Carolina Weekly Museum and Complete Magazine of Entertainment and Intelligence* (February 25, 1797), 235–37, quote on 235.

16. *Good Advice for Boys and Girls* (Worcester, MA: Henry J. Howland, 1853), 9.

17. "Little Henry and His Bearer," *Weekly Recorder* 7 (November 22, 1820), 100. The *Weekly Recorder* was a Presbyterian newspaper published at Chillicothe, Ohio, from 1814 to 1821.

18. "Ripe Cherries," *Youth's Companion* 2 (October 17, 1828), 83.

19. "The First Lie," in *The Infant's Annual or A Mother's Offering* (New York: Peabody, 1834), 32–56, quote on 47.

20. "The Spoilt Child," *Parley's Magazine* (January 1, 1839), 144.

21. "Children's Friend: The Angry Child," *Episcopal Recorder* 11 (June 1, 1833), 36; the story was reprinted as a specimen of subjects about children "awakened to virtue and deterred from vice" in "The Infant Annual," *Museum of Foreign Literature, Science, and Art* 22 (March 1833), 2.

22. "The Awful Death of a Profane Actress," *Zion's Herald* 2 (February 18, 1824), 4.

23. "The Little Girl That Beat Her Sister," in *Rhymes for the Nursery*, ed. Jane Taylor (London: Harvey and Darton, 1824), 8; "Eliza and Her Little Brother," *Youth's Companion* 3 (March 17, 1830), 170.

24. "Little Jane," *Youth's Companion* 4 (September 22, 1830), 71.

25. "Scene in a Nursery," in *The Word Book, or Stories Chiefly in Three Letters Written for Children under Four Years of Age* (London: John Harris, 1825), 7–8.

26. "Memoir of Mary Ann Clap," *Youth's Religious Instructor* 1 (February 1, 1819), 43–50, quote on 45.

27. "Visits to a Cottage," *Youth's Companion* 14 (September 4, 1840), 65.

28. "The Little Goodwins," *Juvenile Miscellany* 1 (September 1828), 78–98.

29. "The Cruel Boy and the Kittens," in *Rhymes for the Nursery*, ed. Jane Taylor (London: Harvey and Darton, 1824), 46–47; "Little Frederic," *Youth's Companion* 11 (1837), 63.

30. "Softly," *Youth's Companion* 34 (July 12, 1860), 111.

31. "The Naughty Little Girl," *Ohio Farmer* 20 (November 4, 1871), 701.

32. "A Prayer for a Little Child," *Christian Monitor* 1 (August 26, 1815), 58.

33. "Mary the Milk-Maid," *Christian Herald* 3 (May 31, 1817), 155–58, quote on 155; "A Bad Boy," *Episcopal Recorder* 10 (December 15, 1832), 148.

34. "On Man's Depravity," *Washington Theological Repertory* 1 (August 1, 1819), 5–12, quote on 8. The *Washington Theological Repertory* was an Episcopal periodical published in the nation's capital from 1819 to 1830.

35. Isaac Watts, "Obedience to Parents," in *The Nursery Garland* (London: Crowdeer and Hemsted, 1801), 1–2.

36. John Witherspoon, "Letters on Education," *New York Missionary Magazine* 2 (January 5, 1801), 348–57, quote on 350.

37. For example, "Bad Tempers," *Christian Advocate* 5 (October 15, 1830), 28–29.

38. "The Little Goodwins," *Juvenile Miscellany* 1 (September 1828), 78–99, quote on 85.

39. "Memoir of Rebecca M. Coit," *Christian Herald* 5 (February 20, 1819), 696–704; "An Account of the Last Speeches, Prayers, and Exhortations of Mrs. Betsy Henderson," *New York Missionary Magazine* 3 (January 7, 1802), 262–67.

40. Mark Twain, "The Story of the Bad Little Boy That Led a Charmed Life," in Samuel L. Clemens, *Mark Twain's Sketches New and Old* (Chicago: American Publishing Company, 1875), 51–58, originally published in 1865 in *The Californian*.

41. Alice Corkran, "Down the Snow Stairs," in *Alternative Alices: Visions and Revisions of Lewis Carroll's Alice Books*, ed. Carolyn Sigler (Lexington: University Press of Kentucky, 1997), 223–32.

42. Among the most notable example of parents themselves engaged in evil activity was the chapbook account by British moralist Hannah More, "Black Giles the Poacher," *Cheap Repository* 16 (January 16, 1800), 1–34 (originally published in 1796), which was said to have been in the hands of several hundred thousand readers and was reprinted numerous times for American as well as British readers; Laura Kelly Paprocki, "Hannah More and *Cheap Repository Tracts*: Lessons in 'Religious and Useful Knowledge,'" MA thesis, University of Waterloo, 2010. The racial meanings of the story are explored in Karen Sands-O'Connor, *Soon Come Home to This Island: West Indians in British Children's Literature* (New York: Routledge, 2013), 18–19.

43. "New Work on the Management of Children," *Atheneum* 2 (March 14, 1818), 460–62; other examples are discussed in Rima D. Apple, *Perfect Motherhood: Science and Childrearing in America* (New Brunswick, NJ: Rutgers University Press, 2006).

44. Tayler Lewis, "Memoir of the Rev. Cyrus Comstock," in *Proceedings of the Eleventh Anniversary of the University Convocation of the State of New York* (Albany, NY: Weed, Parsons, 1875), 110–14; Cyrus Comstock, *Essays on the Duty of Parents and Children* (Hartford, CT: O. D. Cooke, 1810); Comstock was born in 1765 and died in 1852.

45. "A Warning to Wicked Parents," *Zion's Herald* 12 (November 21, 1828), 48. The bad children bad parenting produced were also sometimes described in colorful and interesting details that would likely have drawn readers' attention; for example, the story of Sophia who peevishly attempts to persuade her mother to let her drink wine, "The Spoilt Child," *The Friend* 4 (April 30, 1831), 227–28.

46. Stephen Wilkinson Dowell, *A Catechism on the Services of the Church of England* (London: Francis and John Rivington, 1852), 172, which includes the catechetical instruction pertaining to each clause of the renunciation.

47. Louisa Hoare, "Hints for the Improvement of Early Education and Nursery Discipline," *American Journal of Education* 2 (March 1827), 169–77, quote on 172.

48. "Early Management of Children," *Christian Index* 5 (December 30, 1831), 422–23.

49. "Children's Friend: Godly Parents," *Philadelphia Recorder* 4 (November 11, 1834), 132, for example, observed, "The parents of many children are wicked and take no pains to teach their children to read and spell, neither do they endeavor to inspire them with the fear and love of God. Nay, some parents are so wicked as to teach their children to lie and swear, and steal."

50. Lydia Maria Child, *The American Frugal Housewife* (New York: Samuel S. and William Wood, 1841), 94; Nancy M. Theriot, *Mothers and Daughters in Nineteenth-Century America: The Biosocial Construction of Femininity* (Louisville: University Press of Kentucky, 1996).

51. "To Parents," *The Evidence; or, Religious and Moral Gazette* 1 (February 7, 1807), 31.

52. "On Education and Manners," *Juvenile Port-Folio, and Literary Miscellany* 1 (May 15, 1813), 122–23.

53. Benjamin Parham Aydelott, *The Duties of Parents, a Discourse, Preached in Christ Church, Cincinnati, January 17, 1831* (Cincinnati, OH: Williamson and Wood, 1831), 7,

italics in the original. Aydelott (1785–1880) taught moral and political philosophy and served as president of Woodward College in Cincinnati.

54. Gardiner Spring, *Hints to Parents on the Religious Education of Children* (New York: Taylor and Gould, 1835), 14–16. Spring (1785–1873) was educated at Yale and Andover Theological Seminary.

55. John Witherspoon, "Letters on Education," *New York Missionary Magazine* 2 (January 2, 1801), 107–14, quote on 111–12. Lest it be concluded that the problems were economic rather than moral, though, other writers stressed the distinction; for example, a story about a boy imprisoned for theft explained, "It was not because he was a poor ignorant boy, but because he was a bad boy," "Wicked Boy in Prison," *Youth's Companion* 5 (February 29, 1832), 162.

56. Otis Ainsworth Skinner, *Letters on the Moral and Religious Duties of Parents* (Boston: B. B. Mussey, 1844), 9. Skinner (1807–1861) taught and preached in Maryland, Massachusetts, New York, and Illinois.

57. "On Domestic Management of Children," *American Journal of Education* 4 (September/October 1829), 400–414, quote on 402.

58. Susan Huntington, "Management of Children," *Western Luminary* 3 (July 5, 1826), 3; Susan Huntington, *Memoirs of Mrs. Susan Huntington of Boston, Mass., Designed for the Young* (New Haven, CT: A. H. Maltby, 1831), quotes on 49. Huntington (1791–1823) was the daughter, granddaughter, and wife of Congregational clergy.

59. Catharine E. Beecher, *A Treatise on Domestic Economy for the Use of Young Ladies at Home and at School* (New York: Harper & Brothers, 1845), 233. Beecher's influence is amply described in Kathryn Kish Sklar, *Catharine Beecher: A Study in American Domesticity* (New Haven, CT: Yale University Press, 1973). Sarah A. Leavitt, *From Catharine Beecher to Martha Stewart: A Cultural History of Domestic Advice* (Chapel Hill, NC: University of North Carolina Press, 2002) and Nicole Tonkovich, *Domesticity with a Difference: The Nonfiction of Catharine Beecher, Sarah J. Hale, Fanny Fern, and Margaret Fuller* (Jackson, MS: University of Mississippi Press, 1997) place Beecher in the larger context of antebellum middle-class domesticity.

60. Carl F. Kaestle, "Social Change, Discipline, and the Common School in Early Nineteenth-Century America," *Journal of Interdisciplinary History* 9 (Summer 1978), 1–17.

61. Jacob Abbott, *The Duties of Parents, in Regard to the Schools Where Their Children Are Instructed* (Boston: Tuttle and Weeks, 1834), 13–14; Barker, *From Punishment to Discipline*, 163–67.

62. John Hall, *Education of Children While under the Care of Parents or Guardians* (New York: John P. Haven, 1835), 18. John Hall (1783–1847) and the Ellington School for boys of age ten and older, which he founded in 1829, are described in Lynn Kloter Fahy, *Ellington* (Charleston, SC: Arcadia, 2005).

63. Sylvanus Urban, "Domestic Economy: The Management of Children," *New York Mirror* 6 (April 18, 1829), 324.

64. Abbott, *Duties of Parents*, 16, capitalization in the original.

65. Spring, *Hints to Parents*, 20–21.

66. Skinner, *Letters on Moral Duties*, 69–70.

67. Thomas Condie, "On Deceit," in *Juvenile Portfolio* (Philadelphia: Thomas Condie, 1812), 10.

68. An example that would have been familiar to many churchgoers in the 1820s was W. B. Tappan's poem the first lines of which were "I saw the outcast—an abandoned boy, Whom wretchedness, debased, might call its own"; "Poetry," *Sabbath School Repository* 1 (February 1, 1823), 47. To be outcast was also to be a person or category of people regarded

as morally or spiritually inferior, as in the case of references in Christian literature to Jews and African Americans as nature's outcasts. Late nineteenth- and early twentieth-century examples are discussed in Claudia Nelson, *Little Strangers* (Bloomington: Indiana University Press, 2003).

69. James D. Schmidt, "Willful Disobedience: Young People and School Authority in the Nineteenth-Century United States," in *Children and Youth During the Gilded Age and Progressive Era*, ed. James Marten (New York: NYU Press, 2014), 125–44.

70. De Witt Clinton, "To the Public," *Evening Fireside* 1 (August 24, 1805), 294.

71. David Floyd, *Street Urchins, Sociopaths and Degenerates: Orphans of Late-Victorian and Edwardian Fiction* (Cardiff, UK: University of Wales Press, 2014), 1–36.

72. Paul Boyer, *Urban Masses and Moral Order in America, 1820-1920* (Cambridge, MA: Harvard University Press, 1978), 68.

73. Hall, *On the Education of Children*, 151.

74. "Charity and Sabbath Schools," *Religious Remembrancer* 12 (November 16, 1816), 48.

75. "Remarks on Sabbath School Discipline," *Pittsburgh Recorder* 6 (March 27, 1827), 26.

76. "Juvenile Beggars," *Daily National Intelligencer* (Washington, DC), May 14, 1855.

77. Sherri Broder, *Tramps, Fallen Women, and Neglected Children: Political Culture and the Urban Poor in the Late Nineteenth Century* (Philadelphia: University of Pennsylvania Press, 2002).

78. Society for the Prevention of Pauperism in the City of New York, *Report of a Committee Appointed by the Society for the Prevention of Pauperism in the City of New York on the Expediency of Erecting an Institution for the Reformation of Juvenile Delinquents* (New York: Mahlon Day, 1824); Cadwallader D. Colden, "Juvenile Delinquents," *National Advocate* (New York, NY), July 23, 1824.

79. "Improved Discipline for Boys," *Boston Recorder* 13 (July 4, 1828), 105; "House of Industry," *Boston Recorder* 11 (September 15, 1826), 148.

80. Charles Dickens, *American Notes for General Circulation* (London: Chapman & Hall, 1842), 116.

81. "Law for Juvenile Vagrants," *Salem Observer*, February 14, 1852; "Juvenile Offenders," *Daily Picayune* (New Orleans), October 21, 1851; "Second Annual Report of the Children's Aid Society," *Christian Inquirer* 23 (March 10, 1855), 1.

82. "Juvenile Department," *Christian Herald* 1 (September 21, 1816), 411.

83. "Juvenile Antislavery Societies," *Philadelphia National Enquirer*, January 7, 1837; "Juvenile Temperance Band," *Newark Sentinel*, September 12, 1843; New York Religious Tract Society, *Fifth Annual Report* (New York: J. Seymour, 1817), 11–12.

84. "From the Christian Herald," *Weekly Recorder* (Chillicothe, OH), October 9, 1816.

85. Horatio Alger, Jr., *Ragged Dick; or, Street Life in New York with the Boot Blacks* (New York: A. K. Loring, 1868), which the author hoped would encourage readers to support the work of the Children's Aid Society of New York and other charitable organizations; Carol Nackenoff, *Fictional Republic: Horatio Alger and American Political Discourse* (New York: Oxford University Press, 1994).

86. For example, New York's officials debated stricter law enforcement against the "infamy" and "vicious indulgences" of street children in the city; "The Juvenile Asylum," *Commercial Advertiser* (New York, NY), April 12, 1850. As another example, proponents of stiffer penalties in Massachusetts argued that boys as young as thirteen or fourteen "have all the evil of brutal passions" of older criminals; "The Westborough Reform School," *Boston Daily Advertiser*, March 24, 1877.

87. Charles Loring Brace, *The Dangerous Classes of New York, and Twenty Years' Work among Them* (New York: Wynkoop and Hallenbeck, 1880); Nicole Han Rafter, ed., *White Trash: The Eugenic Family Studies, 1877-1919* (Boston: Northeastern University Press, 1988).

88. "Wise and Unwise Mothers," *Arthur's Home Magazine* 64 (1894), 222.

89. "On Being Naughty," *Life* 77 (May 5, 1921), 639; "Bad Boys," *Parry's Monthly Magazine* 3 (August 1, 1887), 345; Bert Roller, "The 'Bad Boy' in American Literature," *Peabody Journal of Education* 8 (March 1931), 291–96; George F. Weston, Jr., "Making the Bad Boy Good," *Journal of Education* 81 (February 18, 1915), 173–74. Spirited girls were featured in such works as Sophie May, *Janet* (New York: Lee and Shepard, 1883), and William Black, *Madcap Violet* (London: Macmillan, 1876).

90. Quoted in "Alfred Stieglitz and His Latest Work," *Photographic Times* 28 (April 1, 1896), 160–69, quote on 160.

91. J. S. Crawford, "The Farm Boy's Triumph," *Gunton's Magazine* (October 1902), 43–51, quotes on 45.

92. "Children and Their Country Birthright," *The Independent* 55 (November 5, 1903), 2644–45.

93. Continuities between earlier childrearing practices and twentieth-century parenting are discussed in Philip Greven, *Spare the Child: The Religious Roots of Punishment and the Psychological Impact of Physical Abuse* (New York: Knopf, 1991); Murray A. Straus, *Beating the Devil Out of Them: Corporal Punishment in American Families and Its Effects on Children* (Boston: Lexington Books, 1994); and Michael Donnelly, "Putting Corporal Punishment of Children in Historical Perspective," in *Corporal Punishment of Children in Theoretical Perspective*, ed. Michael Donnelly and Murray A. Straus (New Haven, CT: Yale University Press, 2005), 41–54.

94. Peter N. Stearns, *Anxious Parents: A History of Modern Childrearing* (New York: NYU Press, 2003).

95. L. B. Hessler, "On 'Bad Boy' Criticism," *North American Review* 240 (September 1935), 214–24, quote on 217.

Chapter Eight

1. Julia Kristeva, *Strangers to Ourselves*, trans. Leon Roudiez (New York: Columbia University Press, 1991), 1.

2. Michael Barber and Nolan McCarty, "Causes and Consequences of Polarization," in *Political Negotiation: A Handbook*, ed. Jane Mansbridge and Cathie Jo Martin (Washington, DC: Brookings Institution Press, 2016), 37–89, especially fig. 2–1, p. 40, which shows that polarization on positions in the U.S. House and Senate has risen steadily since the 1970s and was higher in 2010 than at any time since the 1890s. Alan I. Abramowitz, *The Disappearing Center: Engaged Citizens, Polarization, and American Democracy* (New Haven, CT: Yale University Press, 2010); Kyle Dodson, "The Return of the American Voter? Party Polarization and Voting Behavior, 1988 to 2004," *Sociological Perspectives* 53 (Fall 2010), 443–49; and Alan I. Abramowitz and Walter J. Stone, "The Bush Effect: Polarization, Turnout, and Activism in the 2004 Presidential Election," *Presidential Studies Quarterly* 36 (June 2004), 141–54, show that strong partisanship and polarization appear to increase voter turnout. Alan I. Abramowitz and Steven Webster, "The Only Thing We Have to Fear Is the Other Party," *Center for Politics Report*, June 4, 2015, online at http://www.centerforpolitics.org, shows rising unfavorability toward the opposition party in election surveys; and Jaime Fuller, "Partisans of the Two Parties Hate Each Other," *Washington Post*, June 12, 2014, suggests that at least among Republicans, likelihood of voting was higher among those with very unfavorable views of Democrats than among those with very favorable views of Republicans.

3. Ruth Lister, *Poverty* (Malden, MA: Polity Press, 2004), especially 99–123 on the discursive construction of othering and respect.

4. Robert A. Orsi, *Between Heaven and Earth: The Religious Worlds People Make and the Scholars Who Study Them* (Princeton, NJ: Princeton University Press, 2005), 177–204.

5. Roger M. Keesing, "Theories of Culture," in *Assessing Cultural Anthropology*, ed. Robert Borofsky (New York: McGraw-Hill, 1994), 301–10; Lila Abu-Lughod, "Writing against Culture," in *Recapturing Anthropology: Working in the Present*, ed. Richard G. Fox (Santa Fe, NM: School of American Research, 1991), 137–60; Edward Said, *Orientalism* (New York: Pantheon, 1978); Herbert S. Lewis, "The Misrepresentation of Anthropology and Its Consequences," *American Anthropologist* 100 (September 1998), 716–31; Michelle Fine, "Working the Hyphens: Reinventing Self and Other in Qualitative Research," in *Handbook of Qualitative Research*, ed. Norman K. Denzin and Yvonne S. Lincoln (Thousand Oaks, CA: Sage, 1994), 70–82; Michal Krumer-Nevo, "Researching against Othering," in *Qualitative Inquiry and the Politics of Advocacy*, ed. Norman K. Denzin and Michael D. Giardina (New York: Routledge, 2009), 185–264.

6. Stuart Hall, "The Spectacle of the 'Other,'" in *Representation: Cultural Representations and Signifying Practices*, ed. Stuart Hall (Thousand Oaks, CA: Sage, 1997), 223–90.

7. Eduardo Bonilla-Silva, "The Essential Social Fact of Race," *American Sociological Review* 64 (December 1999), 899–906, for instance, asserts that race "is assigned externally" and "is intrinsically connected to power relations and hierarchy" and "is a way of otherizing, of excluding," whereas "ethnicity is a way of asserting distinctiveness and creating a sense of commonality" (903); Stephen Cornell and Douglass Hartmann, *Ethnicity and Race* (Thousand Oaks, CA: Pine Forge Press, 1998).

8. G. Cristina Mora, *Making Hispanics: How Activists, Bureaucrats, and Media Constructed a New American* (Chicago: University of Chicago Press, 2014); Mari Carmen Ramírez, "The Multicultural Shift," in *Resisting Categories: Latin American and/or Latino?*, ed. Héctor Olea and Melina Kervandjian (New Haven, CT: Yale University Press, 2012), 944–56; and as a contrasting case study, Sune Quotrup Jensen, "Othering, Identity Formation and Agency," *Qualitative Studies* 2 (December 2011), 63–78, in which young ethnic minority men in Denmark are shown to embrace and capitalize in some instances on being the "other."

9. Laura P. Alonso Gallo, "Latino Culture in the U.S.: Using, Reviewing, and Reconstructing *Latinidad* in Contemporary Latino/a Fiction," *KulturPoetik* 2 (2002), 236–48; Paul Sant Cassia, "Exoticizing Discoveries and Extraordinary Experiences: 'Traditional' Music, Modernity, and Nostalgia in Malta and Other Mediterranean Societies," *Ethnomusicology* 44 (Spring–Summer 2000), 281–301; Ivan Karp, "How Museums Define Other Cultures," *American Art* 5 (Winter–Spring 1991), 10–15.

10. Ferdinand de Saussure, *Course in General Linguistics*, ed. Charles Bally and Albert Sechehaye (LaSalle, IL: Open Court Press, 1983).

11. Kai T. Erikson, *Wayward Puritans: A Study in the Sociology of Deviance* (New York: John Wiley & Sons, 1966).

12. Albert James Bergesen, "Political Witch Hunts: The Sacred and the Subversive in Cross-National Perspective," *American Sociological Review* 42 (April 1977), 220–33; Robert Wuthnow, *Be Very Afraid: The Cultural Response to Terror, Pandemics, Environmental Devastation, Nuclear Annihilation, and Other Threats* (New York: Oxford University Press, 2010).

13. Émile Durkheim, *The Division of Labor in Society*, trans. George Simpson (New York: Free Press, 1933), 287.

14. Émile Durkheim, *The Elementary Forms of the Religious Life* (New York: Free Press, 1915), 337–56.

15. Quoted in Peter McLaren, *Critical Pedagogy and Predatory Culture: Oppositional Politics in a Postmodern Era* (New York: Routledge, 2002), 134.

16. G. K. Chesterton, *What I Saw in America* (London: Hodder and Stoughton, 1922), 12; Sidney E. Mead, "The 'Nation with the Soul of a Church,'" *Church History* 36 (September 1967), 262–83; Sidney E. Mead, *The Nation with the Soul of a Church* (New York: Harper & Row, 1975); James Nolan, *What They Saw in America: Alexis de Tocqueville, Max Weber, G. K. Chesterton, and Sayyid Qutb* (New York: Cambridge University Press, 2016).

17. Jeffrey A. Becker, *Ambition in America: Political Power and the Collapse of Citizenship* (Knoxville: University Press of Kentucky, 2014), 149, develops the contrast between the positive implications of this limited view of citizenship and what he calls the celebration of individual ambition.

Abbott, Jacob. *The Duties of Parents, in Regard to the Schools Where Their Children Are Instructed.* Boston: Tuttle and Weeks, 1834.

Abramowitz, Alan I. *The Disappearing Center: Engaged Citizens, Polarization, and American Democracy.* New Haven, CT: Yale University Press, 2010.

Abramowitz, Alan I., and Walter J. Stone. "The Bush Effect: Polarization, Turnout, and Activism in the 2004 Presidential Election." *Presidential Studies Quarterly* 36 (June 2004), 141–54.

Abu-Lughod, Lila. "Writing against Culture." In *Recapturing Anthropology: Working in the Present.* Edited by Richard G. Fox. Santa Fe, NM: School of American Research, 1991, 137–60.

Adams, Annmarie. *Architecture in the Family Way: Doctors, Houses, and Women, 1870–1900.* Montreal: McGill-Queen's University Press, 1996.

Adams, Gretchen A. *Children and Youth in a New Nation.* New York: NYU Press, 2009.

Adams, James Truslow. *The Epic of America.* Boston: Little, Brown, 1931.

Adut, Ari. *On Scandal: Moral Disturbances in Society, Politics, and Art.* New York: Cambridge University Press, 2008.

Aguilar-San Juan, Karin. *Little Saigons: Staying Vietnamese in America.* Minneapolis: University of Minnesota Press, 2009.

Alba, Richard, and Nancy Denton. "Old and New Landscapes of Diversity: The Residential Patterns of Immigrant Minorities." In *Historical and Contemporary Perspectives on Immigration, Race, and Ethnicity in the United States.* Edited by Nancy Foner and George M. Fredrickson. New York: Russell Sage Foundation, 2004, 237–61.

Alba, Richard, and Victor Nee. *Remaking the American Mainstream: Assimilation and Contemporary Immigration.* Cambridge, MA: Harvard University Press, 2003.

———. "Rethinking Assimilation Theory for a New Era of Immigration." *International Migration Review* 31 (Winter 1997), 826–74.

Alger, Horatio, Jr. *Ragged Dick; or, Street Life in New York with the Boot Blacks.* New York: A. K. Loring, 1868.

Anderson, Odin W. "The Lynching of Hans Jakob Olson: The Story of a Norwegian-American Crime." *Norwegian American Studies* 29 (Summer 1983), 159–85.

Andrew, Donna T. *Aristocratic Vice: The Attack on Duelling, Suicide, Adultery, and Gambling in Eighteenth-Century England.* New Haven, CT: Yale University Press, 2013.

Apple, Rima D. *Perfect Motherhood: Science and Childrearing in America.* New Brunswick, NJ: Rutgers University Press, 2006.

Ardrey, Robert L. *American Agricultural Implements: A Review of Invention and Development in the Agricultural Implement Industry of the United States.* Chicago: R. R. Ardrey, 1894.

Arendt, Hannah. *The Origins of Totalitarianism.* New York: Harcourt Brace, 1951.

Ariés, Philippe. *Centuries of Childhood.* New York: Penguin, 1960.

Aydelott, Benjamin Parham. *The Duties of Parents, a Discourse, Preached in Christ Church, Cincinnati, January 17, 1831.* Cincinnati: Williamson and Wood, 1831.

Bader, Robert Smith. *The Great Kansas Bond Scandal.* Lawrence: University Press of Kansas, 1982.

Bail, Christopher A. "The Configuration of Symbolic Boundaries Against Immigrants in Europe." *American Sociological Review* 73 (February 2008), 37–59.

Bailey, Beth. "Patsy Cline and the Problem of Respectability." In *Sweet Dreams: The World of Patsy Cline*, Edited by Warren R. Hofstra. Urbana: University of Illinois Press, 2013.

Bain, George Grantham. "Zion City via Chicago." *The Sphere* (December 27, 1902), 318.

Bakhtin, Mikhail. *The Dialogic Imagination: Four Essays*. Austin: University of Texas Press, 1981.

Ball, John C. *Social Deviancy and Adolescent Personality*. Knoxville: University Press of Kentucky, 1962.

Banks, Russell, Loïc Wacquant, and Christa Buschendorf. "Casting Ameica's Outcasts: A Dialogue between Russell Banks and Loïc Wacquant." *American Studies* 53 (2008), 209–19.

Barber, Michael, and Nolan McCarty. "Causes and Consequences of Polarization." In *Political Negotiation: A Handbook*. Edited by Jane Mansbridge and Cathie Jo Martin. Washington, DC: Brookings Institution Press, 2016, 37–89.

Bardwell, William. *Healthy Homes and How to Make Them*. London: Dean and Son, 1854.

Barker, Janet Leigh. "From Punishment to Discipline: Strategies of Control in 18th and 19th Century Children's Fiction." PhD dissertation, Texas A&M University, 2001.

Barnes, A. C. "Ashford Hall." *Minutes of the Central Ohio Conference of the Methodist Episcopal Church* 49 (1907), 840.

Beach, Moses Y. *Wealth and Biography of the Wealthy Citizens of New York City*. New York: Sun Office, 1845.

Becker, Howard. *The Outsiders: Studies in the Sociology of Deviance*. New York: Free Press, 1963.

Becker, Jeffrey A. *Ambition in America: Political Power and the Collapse of Citizenship*. Knoxville: University Press of Kentucky, 2014.

Beckerhouse, Horst. *Die Namen der Hamburger Stadtteile: Woher Sie Kommen Und Was Sie Bedeuten*. Hamburg, Germany: Sabine Groenewold Verlage, 2002.

Beckert, Sven, and Julia B. Rosenbaum. *The American Bourgeoisie: Distinction and Identity in the Nineteenth Century*. New York: Palgrave, 2010.

Beecher, Catharine E. *A Treatise on Domestic Economy for the Use of Young Ladies at Home and at School*. New York: Harper & Brothers, 1845.

Beecher, Henry Ward. "The Battle of Money." *Christian Union* 7 (February 5, 1873), 110.

Bell, Catherine. *Ritual Theory, Ritual Practice*. New York: Oxford University Press, 1992.

Bell, Daniel. *Marxian Socialism in the United States*. Ithaca, NY: Cornell University Press, 1996.

Bellah, Robert N. *The Broken Covenant: American Civil Religion in Time of Trial*, 2nd ed. Chicago: University of Chicago Press, 1992.

Bergesen, Albert James. "Political Witch Hunts: The Sacred and the Subversive in Cross-National Perspective." *American Sociological Review* 42 (April 1977), 220–33.

Bixler, John W., ed. *Decisions of the Department of the Interior in Appealed Pension and Bounty-Land Claims*. Washington, DC: Government Printing Office, 1904.

Black, William. *Madcap Violet*. London: Macmillan, 1876.

Blair, Hugh. "Necessity of Forming Religious Principles at an Early Age." *Massachusetts Magazine* (January 1789), 37–38.

Bloom, Harold. *The American Dream*. New York: Infobase Publishing, 2009.

Blumhofer, Edith L. *The Assemblies of God: A Chapter in the Story of American Pentecostalism*. Springfield, MO: Gospel Publishing House, 1989.

Board of Managers. *Fifth Biennial Report of the Board of Managers of State Lunatic Asylum No. 2*. Jefferson City, MO: Tribune Printing Company, 1885.

Bonacich, Edna. "A Theory of Middleman Minorities." *American Sociological Review* 38 (October 1973), 583–94.

Bonilla-Silva, Eduardo. "The Essential Social Fact of Race." *American Sociological Review* 64 (December 1999), 899–906.

Bourdieu, Pierre. *Distinction: A Social Critique of the Judgement of Taste*. Cambridge, MA: Harvard University Press, 1979.

———. *The Logic of Practice*. Stanford, CA: Stanford University Press, 1990.

———. *Outline of a Theory of Practice*. New York: Cambridge University Press, 1977.

———. "Social Space and Symbolic Power." *Sociological Theory* 7 (Spring 1989), 14–25.

Bowman, Carl F. *Brethren Society: The Cultural Transformation of a "Peculiar People."* Baltimore: Johns Hopkins University Press, 1995.

Boyer, Paul. *Urban Masses and Moral Order in America, 1820–1920*. Cambridge, MA: Harvard University Press, 1978.

Boylan, Anne M. *Origins of Women's Activism*. Chapel Hill: University of North Carolina Press, 2002.

Brace, Charles Loring. *The Dangerous Classes of New York, and Twenty Years' Work among Them*. New York: Wynkoop and Hallenbeck, 1880.

Bradley, Mary Emily. *Mabel's New Year and Other Stories*. New York: Sheldon, 1866.

Brandon, Joseph D. *America A Staggering Nation: A Vision of the Future, Recovery or Demise*. Bloomington, IN: WestBow Press, 2010.

Brigham, Amariah. *Observations on the Influence of Religion upon the Health and Welfare of Mankind*. Boston: Marsh, Capen and Lyon, 1835.

Broder, Sherri. *Tramps, Unfit Mothers, and Neglected Children: Negotiating the Family in Nineteenth-Century Philadelphia*. Philadelphia: University of Pennsylvania Press, 2002.

Brown, Norman O. *Love's Body*. New York: Random House, 1966.

Brown, R. F. "Twelve International Movements." *Herald of Gospel Liberty* 117 (February 5, 1925), 129–30.

Bryan, William Jennings. *Speeches of William Jennings Bryan*. New York: Funk and Wagnalls, 1913.

Buckley, James Monroe. *Faith-Healing: Christian Science and Kindred Spirits*. Cambridge, MA: Harvard University Press, 1892.

———. "Fanaticism in the United States." *Century Illustrated Magazine* 67 (June 1903), 196–206.

Bullock, Helen. "Market Square Tavern Historical Report, Block 12, Building 13." *Colonial Williamsburg Foundation Library Research Report Series* (1990), no. 1254.

Bushman, Richard Lyman. *The Refinement of America: Persons, Houses, Cities*. New York: Vintage, 1992.

Bushnell, H. A. "The Evils of Superficial Christianity." *The Advance* 31 (June 4, 1896), 828.

Butler, Jon. "Enthusiasm Described and Decried: The Great Awakening as Interpretive Fiction." *Journal of American History* 69 (September 1982), 305–25.

———. "The Revocation of the Edict of Nantes and Huguenot Migration to South Carolina." In *The Huguenot Connection: The Edict of Nantes, Its Revocation, and Early French Migration to South Carolina*. Edited by R. M. Golden. Norwell, MA: Kluwer Academic Publishers, 1988, 63–82.

Callahan, James Morton. *Genealogical and Personal History of the Upper Monongahela Valley*. Vol. 2. New York: Lewis Historical Publishing Company, 1912.

Campbell, Persia. "Consumer Representation in the New Deal." PhD dissertation, Columbia University, 1940.

Carlson, Eric T. "Amariah Brigham: Life and Works." *American Journal of Psychiatry* 112 (April 1956), 831–36.

Carnegie, Andrew. "The Gospel of Wealth." *North American Review* 148 (June 1889), 653–64.

Caruthers, R. L., and A.O.P. Nicholson. *A Compilation of the Statutes of Tennessee.* Nashville: James Smith, 1836.

Cassia, Paul Sant. "Exoticizing Discoveries and Extraordinary Experiences: 'Traditional' Music, Modernity, and Nostalgia in Malta and Other Mediterranean Societies." *Ethnomusicology* 44 (Spring–Summer 2000), 281–301.

Cavan, Ruth Shonie. "Concepts and Terminology in Interreligious Marriage." *Journal for the Scientific Study of Religion* 9 (Winter 1970), 311–20.

Cavanaugh, William T. "The Invention of Fanaticism." *Modern Theology* 27 (April 2011), 226–37.

Chan, Joseph, Ho-Pong To, and Elaine Chan. "Reconsidering Social Cohesion: Developing a Definition and Analytical Framework for Empirical Research." *Social Indicators Research* 75 (January 2006), 273–302.

Chapin, John B. "Duty of States toward Their Insane Poor." *Journal of Social Science* (July 1, 1874), 60–65.

Chapman, Jennie. *Plotting Apocalypse: Reading, Agency, and Identity in the Left Behind Series.* Jackson: University Press of Mississippi, 2013.

Chase, Horace. *The New Hampshire Probate Directory.* Concord, NH: G. Parker Lyon, 1845.

Cherry, Conrad, ed. *God's New Israel: Religious Interpretations of American Destiny*, 2nd ed. Chapel Hill: University of North Carolina Press, 1998.

Cherry, Elizabeth. "Shifting Symbolic Boundaries: Cultural Strategies of the Animal Rights Movement." *Sociological Forum* 25 (September 2010), 450–75.

Chesterton, G. K. *What I Saw in America.* London: Hodder and Stoughton, 1922.

Child, Lydia Maria. *The American Frugal Housewife.* New York: Samuel S. and William Wood, 1841.

Clark, S. D. "Economic Expansion and the Moral Order." *Canadian Journal of Economics and Political Science* 6 (May 1940), 203–25.

Clarke, Erskine. *Our Southern Zion: A History of Calvinism in the South Carolina Low Country, 1690–1990.* Tuscaloosa: University of Alabama Press, 1996.

Claudy, C. H. "Pat Prentiss's Fortune." *Youth's Companion* 103 (January 1929), 3, 37–38.

Clemens, Samuel L. "The Canvasser's Tale." *Atlantic Monthly* 38 (December 1876), 673–76.

Coben, Stanley. *A. Mitchell Palmer: Politician.* New York: Columbia University Press, 1963.

Coleman, James S. "Social Capital in the Creation of Human Capital." *American Journal of Sociology* 94 (1988), S95–S120.

Collins, Randall. *The Credential Society: An Historical Sociology of Education and Stratification.* New York: Academic Press, 1979.

———. *Violence: A Micro-sociological Theory.* Princeton, NJ: Princeton University Press, 2008.

Comstock, Cyrus. *Essays on the Duty of Parents and Children.* Hartford, CT: O. D. Cooke, 1810.

Connelley, William E. *A Standard History of Kansas and Kansans.* Chicago: Lewis Publishing Company, 1918.

Cook, Karen S. Margaret Levi, and Russell Hardin, eds. *Who Can We Trust? How Groups, Networks, and Institutions Make Trust Possible.* New York: Russell Sage Foundation, 2009.

Cooke, Chauncey Herbert. *Soldier Boy's Letters to His Father and Mother, 1861–65.* New York: News Office, 1915.

Corkran, Alice. "Down the Snow Stairs," in *Alternative Alices: Visions and Revisions of Lewis Carroll's Alice Books.* Edited by Carolyn Sigler. Lexington: University Press of Kentucky, 1997, 223–32.

Cornell, Stephen, and Douglass Hartmann. *Ethnicity and Race*. Thousand Oaks, CA: Pine Forge Press, 1998.

Crawford, J. S. "The Farm Boy's Triumph." *Gunton's Magazine* (October 1902), 43–51.

Creel, George. *How We Advertised America*. New York: Harper and Brothers, 1920.

———. "Message of the United States Government to the American People: A Warning to Food Profiteers." *The Independent* 94 (May 11, 1918), 254.

Cronin, Mary M. "Fighting for the Farmers: The Pacific Northwest's Nonpartisan League Newspapers." *Journalism History* 23 (1997), 126–36.

Cunningham, Horace H. *Field Medical Services at the Battles of Manassas*. Athens: University of Georgia Press, 2008.

Curtis, Susan. *A Consuming Faith: The Social Gospel and Modern American Culture*. Columbia: University of Missouri Press, 2001.

Curwen, John. *History of the Association of Medical Superintendents of American Institutions for the Insane*. Philadelphia: Association of Medical Superintendents of American Institutions for the Insane, 1874.

Cutler, William G. *History of the State of Kansas*. Chicago: A. T. Andreas, 1883.

D'Andrade, Roy. *The Development of Cognitive Anthropology*. New York: Cambridge University Press, 1995.

Dean, Eric T. Jr., *Shook Over Hell: Post-Traumatic Stress, Vietnam, and the Civil War*. Cambridge, MA: Harvard University Press, 1997.

Detzer, David. *Donnybrook: The Battle of Bull Run, 1861*. New York: Harcourt, 2004.

Dhir, Krishna S., and Denis Vinen. "Managing Corporate Respectability: Concept, Issues, and Policy Formulation." *Corporate Communications* 10 (2005), 5–23.

Dickens, Charles. *American Notes for General Circulation*. London: Chapman & Hall, 1842.

Dodson, Kyle. "The Return of the American Voter? Party Polarization and Voting Behavior, 1988 to 2004." *Sociological Perspectives* 53 (Fall 2010), 443–49.

Donnelly, Michael. "Putting Corporal Punishment of Children in Historical Perspective," in *Corporal Punishment of Children in Theoretical Perspective*. Edited by Michael Donnelly and Murray A. Straus. New Haven, CT: Yale University Press, 2005.

Douglas, Jack D., ed. *Deviance and Respectability: The Social Construction of Moral Meanings*. New York: Basic Books, 1970.

Douglas, Mary. *Purity and Danger: An Analysis of Concepts of Pollution and Taboo*. New York: Routledge, 1966.

Dowell, Stephen Wilkinson. *A Catechism on the Services of the Church of England*. London: Francis and John Rivington, 1852.

Dubois, W.E.B. *The Philadelphia Negro: A Social Study*. Philadelphia: University of Pennsylvania, 1899.

Duncan, L. Wallace, and Charles F. Scott, *History of Allen and Woodson Counties*. Iola, KS: Iola Register, 1901.

Duneier, Mitchell. *Slim's Table: Race, Respectability, and Masculinity*. Chicago: University of Chicago Press, 1992.

Durkheim, Émile. *The Division of Labor in Society/*. Translated by George Simpson. New York: Free Press, 1933.

———. *Elementary Forms of the Religious Life*. New York: Free Press, 1915.

Eastman, B. D. "Correspondence," *American Journal of Insanity* 52 (July1895), 133–35.

Eighmey, Rae Katherine. *Food Will Win the War: Minnesota Crops, Cooks, and Conservation during World War I*. St. Paul: Minnesota Historical Society, 2010.

Elbert, Monika. *Enterprising Youth: Social Values and Acculturation in Nineteenth-Century American Children's Literature*. New York: Routledge, 2008.

Eliot, William Greenleaf. *Lectures to Young Men*. Boston: Crosby and Nichols, 1853.

Elson, Ruth Miller. *Guardians of Tradition: American Schoolbooks of the Nineteenth Century*. Lincoln: University of Nebraska Press, 1964.

Emirbayer, Mustafa. "Manifesto for a Relational Sociology." *American Journal of Sociology* 103 (September 1997), 281–317.

Epstein, Joseph. *Snobbery: The American Version*. Boston: Houghton Mifflin, 2002.

Erikson, Kai T. *Wayward Puritans: A Study in the Sociology of Deviance*. New York: John Wiley & Sons, 1966.

Fahy, Lynn Kloter. *Ellington*. Charleston, SC: Arcadia, 2005.

Fawcett, Edgar. "Plutocracy and Snobbery in New York." In *The Arena*. Edited by B. O. Flower. Boston: Arena Publishing, 1891, 142–51.

Feingold, Henry L. *Zion in America: The Jewish Experience from Colonial Times to the Present*. New York: Dover Publications, 2002.

Felsenfeld Carl, and David L. Glass. *Banking Regulation in the United States*. Huntington, NY: Juris Publishing, 2011.

Fine, Michelle. "Working the Hyphens: Reinventing Self and Other in Qualitative Research." In *Handbook of Qualitative Research*. Edited by Norman K. Denzin and Yvonne S. Lincoln. Thousand Oaks, CA: Sage, 1994, 70–82.

Fish, G. H. *Hew to the Line: A Master or a Slave*. Winfield, KS: H. and L. Vincent, 1891.

——. "The Rich Boy," in F. Scott Fitzgerald, *All the Sad Young Men*. New York: Scribner's, 1926, 1.

Fleming, Thomas. *The Illusion of Victory: America in World War I*. New York: Basic Books, 2003.

Floyd, David. *Street Urchins, Sociopaths and Degenerates: Orphans of Late-Victorian and Edwardian Fiction*. Cardiff, UK: University of Wales Press, 2014.

Fogel, Robert W. *Aging of Veterans of the Union Army: Military, Pension, and Medical Records, 1820–1940*. Ann Arbor, MI: Inter-University Consortium for Political and Social Research, 2011.

Foucault, Michel. *Madness and Civilization: A History of Insanity in the Age of Reason*. New York: Random House, 1965.

Fraser, Steve. *The Age of Acquiescence: The Life and Death of American Resistance to Organized Wealth and Power*. Boston: Little, Brown, 2015.

Friedkin, Noah E. "Social Cohesion." *Annual Review of Sociology* 30 (2004), 409–25.

Friedman, Walter A. *Birth of a Salesman: The Transformation of Selling in America*. Cambridge, MA: Harvard University Press, 2004.

Gallo, Laura P. Alonso. "Latino Culture in the U. S.: Using, Reviewing, and Reconstructing *Latinidad* in Contemporary Latino/a Fiction." *KulturPoetik* 2 (2002), 236–48.

Gamson, Joshua. "Messages of Exclusion: Gender, Movements, and Symbolic Boundaries." *Gender and Society* 11 (April 1997), 178–99.

Garcia, Lorena. *Respect Yourself, Protect Yourself: Latina Girls and Sexual Identity*. New York: NYU Press, 2012.

Geenen, Paul H. *Schuster's & Gimbels: Milwaukee's Beloved Department Stores*. Charleston, SC: History Press, 2012.

Geertz, Clifford. *The Interpretation of Cultures*. New York: Basic Books, 1973.

Giddings, Franklin Henry. *The Principles of Sociology: An Analysis of the Phenomena of Association and of Social Organization*. New York: Macmillan, 1896.

Gieryn, Thomas F. "Boundary-Work and the Demarcation of Science from Non-science: Strains and Interests in Professional Ideologies of Scientists." *American Sociological Review* 48 (December 1983), 781–95.

——. "A Space for Place in Sociology." *Annual Review of Sociology* 26 (2000), 463–96.

Gilbert, John. *The Curious Adventures, Painful Experience, and Laughable Difficulties of a Man of Letters While Traveling as a Peddler in the South During the Late Harper's Ferry Excitement*. Baltimore: John Gilbert, 1860.

Gilbert, Michael D. "The Problem of Voter Fraud." *Columbia Law Review* 115 (April 2015), 739–75.

Gish, Lowell. *Reform at Osawatomie State Hospital: Treatment of the Mentally Ill, 1866–1970*. Lawrence: University of Kansas Press, 1972.

Gitlin, Todd, and Liel Leibovitz. *The Chosen Peoples: America, Israel, and the Ordeals of Divine Election*. New York: Simon & Schuster, 2010.

Gleason, Philip. "The Melting Pot: Symbol of Fusion or Confusion?" *American Quarterly* 16 (Spring 1964), 20–46.

Goffman, Erving. *Asylums: Essays on the Social Situation of Mental Patients and Other Inmates*. Garden City, NY: Anchor Books, 1961.

———. "The Nature of Deference and Demeanor." *American Anthropologist* 58 (June 1956), 473–502.

———. *Relations in Public*. New York: Penguin, 1972.

Goldstein, Adam, and Heather A. Haveman. "Pulpit and Press: Denominational Dynamics and the Growth of Religious Magazines in Antebellum America." *American Sociological Review* 78 (2013), 797–827.

Goodhew, David. "Working-Class Respectability: The Example of the Western Areas of Johannesburg, 1930–55." *Journal of African History* 41 (June 2000), 241–66.

Goodman, June Eckert. "Review of *The Common Lot*." *Current Literature* 38 (February 1905), 182.

Gordon, Milton M. *Assimilation in American Life*. New York: Oxford University Press, 1964.

Greenfeld, Leah. *Mind, Modernity, Madness*. Cambridge, MA: Harvard University Press, 2013.

Greven, Philip J. *Child Rearing Concepts, 1628–1861*. Itasca, IL: F. E. Peacock, 1973.

———. *Spare the Child: The Religious Roots of Punishment and the Psychological Impact of Physical Abuse*. New York: Knopf, 1991.

Haines, Michael R. "Estimated Life Tables for the United States, 1850–1900." *Historical Methods* 31 (1998), 149–69.

Hall, Amy Laura. "Respectability." In *Borderline: Reflections on War, Sex, and Church*. Edited by Stan Goff. London: Lutterworth Press, 2015, 261–70.

Hall, John. *Education of Children While Under the Care of Parents or Guardians*. New York: John P. Haven, 1835.

Hall, Stuart. "The Spectacle of the 'Other.'" In *Representation: Cultural Representations and Signifying Practices*. Edited by Stuart Hall. Thousand Oaks, CA: Sage, 1997, 223–90.

Hammond, William A. *A Treatise on Diseases of the Nervous System*. New York: D. Appleton, 1871.

Haney, Lewis H. "Who Gets the Money?" *North American Review* 229 (January 1930), 59–65.

Hansen, Marcus Lee. *The Immigrant in American History*. Cambridge, MA: Harvard University Press, 1940.

Hanson, Sandra L., and John Zogby. "Attitudes about the American Dream." *Public Opinion Quarterly* 74 (2010), 570–84.

Hardin, Russell. *Trust and Trustworthiness*. New York: Russell Sage Foundation, 2002.

Harrington, Michael. *The Other America*. New York: Macmillan, 1973.

Harris, Fredrick C. *Price of the Ticket: Barack Obama and Rise and Decline of Black Politics*. New York: Oxford University Press, 2012.

———. "The Rise of Respectability Politics." *Dissent* 61 (Winter 2014), 33–37.

Harrison, Candice L. "'Free Trade and Hucksters' Rights!' Envisioning Economic Democracy in the Early Republic." *Pennsylvania Magazine of History and Biography* 137 (April 2013), 147–77.

Harrison, George L. *Legislation on Insanity: A Collection of All the Lunacy Laws of the States and Territories of the United States to the Year 1883*. Philadelphia: Globe Printing House, 1884.

Hartman, Mary S. "Murder for Respectability: The Case of Madeleine Smith." *Victorian Studies* 16 (June 1973), 381–400.

Hastings, Milo M. *The Egg Trade of the United States*. Washington, DC: United States Department of Agriculture, 1909.

Hauschild, Barbara. *On the Avenue of Approach*. Topeka, KS: Topeka State Hospital, 1979.

Hawthorne, Nathaniel. "The Celestial Railroad" (1843). In *Complete Novels and Selected Tales of Nathaniel Hawthorne*. Edited by Norman Holmes Pearson. New York: Modern Library, 1937, 1070–82.

Heat-Moon, William Least. *PrairyErth*. New York: Houghton, 1992.

Hellings, James. "Precautions against Fan(atic)s: A Reevaluation of Adorno's Uncompromising Philosophy of Popular Culture." *New German Critique* 118 (Winter 2013), 149–74.

Hendler, Glenn. "Pandering in the Public Sphere: Masculinity and the Market in Horatio Alger." *American Quarterly* 48 (September 1996), 415–38.

Herander, Mark G., and Luz A. Saavedra. "Exports and the Structure of Immigrant-Based Networks: The Role of Geographic Proximity." *Review of Economics and Statistics* 87 (May 2005), 323–35.

Herberg, Will. *Protestant, Catholic, Jew: An Essay in American Religious Sociology*. Garden City, NY: Doubleday, 1959.

Herrick, Robert. *The Common Lot*. New York: Macmillan, 1904.

Hessler, L. B. "On 'Bad Boy' Criticism." *North American Review* 240 (September 1935), 214–24.

Higginbotham, Evelyn Brooks. *Righteous Discontent: The Women's Movement in the Black Baptist Church, 1880–1920*. Cambridge, MA: Harvard University Press, 1993.

Higgins, Paul C. "Deviance within a Disabled Community: Peddling among the Deaf." *Pacific Sociological Review* 22 (January 1979), 96–114.

Higham, John. *Strangers in the Land: Patterns of American Nativism, 1860–1925*. New Brunswick, NJ: Rutgers University Press, 1955.

Hills, Matt. *Fan Cultures*. London: Routledge, 2002.

Hilton, R. H. "Lords, Burgesses, and Hucksters." *Past and Present* 97 (November 1982), 3–15.

Hoare, Louisa. "Hints for the Improvement of Early Education and Nursery Discipline." *American Journal of Education* 2 (March 1827), 169–77.

Hoben, Allan. "Moral Problems of Industrial Reconstruction." *Biblical World* 54 (July 1920), 437–48.

Hochschild, Jennifer L. *Facing Up to the American Dream: Race, Class, and the Soul of the Nation*. Princeton, NJ: Princeton University Press, 1995.

Hoffman, Brian. *Naked: A Cultural History of American Nudism*. New York: NYU Press, 2015.

Holman, Andrew C. *Sense of Their Duty: Middle-Class Formation in Victorian Ontario Towns*. Montreal: McGill-Queen's University Press, 2000.

Holmes, George K. "The Concentration of Wealth." *Political Science Quarterly* 8 (1893), 1–12.

Holquist, Michael. *Dialogism: Bakhtin and His World*. 2nd ed. New York: Routledge, 2002.

Homan, Gerlof D. "Mennonites and Military Justice in World War I." *Mennonite Quarterly Review* 66 (1992), 365–75.

Hood, J. Larry. *Visions of Zion: Christianity, Modernization and the American Pursuit of Liberty Progressivism in Rural Nelson and Washington Counties Kentucky*. Lanham, MD: University Press of America, 2005.

Hornsby-Gutting, Angela, and Charles Reagan Wilson. "Politics of Respectability." In *The New Encyclopedia of Southern Culture*. Vol. 13: *Gender*. Edited by Nancy Bercaw and Ted Ownby. Chapel Hill: University of North Carolina Press, 2009, 238–42.

Hotten, John Camden. *The Slang Dictionary; or, The Vulgar Words, Street Phrases, and "Fast" Expressions of High and Low Society*. London: J. C. Hotten, 1865.

Howden, James C. "The Religious Sentiment in Epileptics." *Journal of Mental Science* 4 (January 1873), 99–102.

Howells, W. D. "Are We a Plutocracy?" *North American Review* 158 (February 1894), 185–95.

Hume, Janice. *Obituaries in American Culture*. Jackson: University Press of Mississippi, 2000.

Hume, David. "Essay XII: Of Superstition and Enthusiasm." In Hume, *Essays Moral, Political, and Literary*. Edinburgh: Fleming and Alison, 1741, 144–45.

Huntington, Susan. "Management of Children." *Western Luminary* 3 (July 5, 1826), 3.

———. *Memoirs of Mrs. Susan Huntington of Boston, Mass., Designed for the Young*. New Haven, CT: A. H. Maltby, 1831.

Hutton, Patrick H. *Philippe Ariès and the Politics of French Cultural History*. Amherst: University of Massachusetts Press, 2004.

Iannaccone, Laurence R. "Why Strict Churches Are Strong." *American Journal of Sociology* 99 (1994), 1180–1211.

Isaac, Rhys. *The Transformation of Virginia, 1740–1790*. Chapel Hill: University of North Carolina Press, 1982.

Jackson, J. C. "A Warning Needed in Methodism." *Methodist Review* 7 (May 1891), 471.

James, William. *The Varieties of Religious Experience*. Cambridge, MA: Harvard University Press, 1985; originally published in 1902.

Jensen, Sune Quotrup. "Othering, Identity Formation and Agency." *Qualitative Studies* 2 (December 2011), 63–78.

Johnston, Linda S. *Hope amid Hardship: Pioneer Voices from Kansas Territory*. Guilford, CT: Globe Pequot Press, 2013.

Jones, Carolyn. *The First One Hundred Years: A History of the City of Manhattan, Kansas, 1855–1955*. Manhattan, KS: Manhattan Centennial Committee, 1955.

Jones, Lu Ann. *Mama Learned Us to Work: Farm Women in the New South*. Chapel Hill: University of North Carolina Press, 2002.

Jones, Mark R. *Wicked Charleston: The Dark Side of the Holy City*. Charleston, SC: History Press, 2005.

Jones, Samuel Calvin. *Reminiscences of the Twenty-Second Iowa Volunteer Infantry*. Iowa City, IA: Samuel Calvin Jones, 1907.

Joyce, James. *Ulysses*. New York: Oxford University Press, 1922.

Kaestle, Carl F. "Social Change, Discipline, and the Common School in Early Nineteenth-Century America." *Journal of Interdisciplinary History* 9 (Summer 1978), 1–17.

Kansas State Board of Agriculture. *Special Report of the Kansas State Board of Agriculture for the Information of Home-Seekers*. Topeka: Kansas Publishing House, 1886.

Kansas State Historical Society. *The Annals of Kansas, 1886–1925*. Vol. 1: *1886–1910*. Topeka: Kansas State Historical Society, 1954.

Karp, Ivan. "How Museums Define Other Cultures." *American Art* 5 (Winter–Spring 1991), 10–15.

Katznelson, Ira. *Fear Itself: The New Deal and the Origins of Our Time*. New York: Norton, 2013.

Keesing, Roger M. "Theories of Culture." In *Assessing Cultural Anthropology*. Edited by Robert Borofsky. New York: McGraw-Hill, 1994, 301–10.

Keller, Suzanne. *Community: Pursuing the Dream, Living the Reality*. Princeton, NJ: Princeton University Press, 2005.

Kennedy, Ruby Jo Reeves. "Single or Triple Melting Pot." *American Journal of Sociology* 49 (January 1944), 331–39.

Kincheloe, Samuel. "The Prophet: A Study in the Sociology of Leadership." PhD dissertation, University of Chicago, 1929.

Klapp, Orrin E. "Heroes, Villains and Fools as Agents of Social Control." *American Sociological Review* 19 (February 1954), 56–62.

Klassen, Pamela E. "The Robes of Womanhood: Dress and Authenticity among African American Methodist Women in the Nineteenth Century." *Religion and American Culture* 14 (Winter 2004), 39–82.

Klein, Maury. *Union Pacific: The Birth of a Railroad, 1862–1893*. Garden City, NY: Doubleday, 1987.

Kline, Stephen. "The Making of Children's Culture." In *The Children's Culture Reader*. Edited by Henry Jenkins. New York: NYU Press, 1998, 95–109.

Klingberg, Frank J. "Memoirs of Frank J. Klingberg." *Historical Magazine of the Protestant Episcopal Church* 29 (March 1960), 106–35.

Knewstubb, Ellspeth. "'Believes the Devil Has Changed Him': Religion and Patient Identity in Ashburn Hall, Dunedin, 1882–1910." *Health and History* 14 (January 2012), 56–76.

Kohn, Melvin L. "Social Class and Parental Values." *American Journal of Sociology* 64 (January 1959), 337–51.

Koren, John. *Summaries of Laws Relating to the Commitment and Care of the Insane in the United States*. New York: National Committee for Mental Hygiene, 1912.

Kreamer, Anne. *Always Personal: Navigating Emotion in the New Workplace*. New York: Random House, 2012.

Kristeva, Julia. *Strangers to Ourselves*. Translated by Leon Roudiez. New York: Columbia University Press, 1991.

Krumer-Nevo, Michal. "Researching against Othering." In *Qualitative Inquiry and the Politics of Advocacy*. Edited by Norman K. Denzin and Michael D. Giardina. New York: Routledge, 2009, 185–264.

Lamont, Michèle. *Money, Morals, and Manners: The Culture of the French and the American Upper-Middle Class*. Chicago: University of Chicago Press, 1992.

Lamont, Michèle, and Annette Lareau. "Cultural Capital: Allusions, Gaps and Glissandos in Recent Theoretical Developments." *Sociological Theory* 6 (Autumn 1988), 153–68.

Lamont, Michèle, and Virag Molnar. "The Study of Boundaries in the Social Sciences." *Annual Review of Sociology* 28 (2002), 167–95.

Lande, R. Gregory. *Madness, Malingering and Malfeasance*. Dulles, VA: Brassey's, 2003.

Landry, John T. "Wheels of Fortune: The History of Speculation from Scandal to Respectability." *Harvard Business Review* 80 (December 2002), 26.

Lange, Jeffrey J. *Smile When You Call Me a Hillbilly: Country Music's Struggle for Respectability, 1939–1954*. Athens: University of Georgia Press, 2004.

Langer, Susanne K. *Philosophy in a New Key: A Study in the Symbolism of Reason, Rite, and Art*. Cambridge, MA: Harvard University Press, 1941.

Lears, T. Jackson. *Fables of Abundance: A Cultural History of Advertising in America*. New York: Basic Books, 1994.

Leavitt, Sarah A. *From Catharine Beecher to Martha Stewart: A Cultural History of Domestic Advice*. Chapel Hill: University of North Carolina Press, 2002.

Lévi-Strauss, Claude. *The Raw and the Cooked: Introduction to a Science of Mythology*. New York: Harper & Row, 1969.

Lewis, Herbert S. "The Misrepresentation of Anthropology and Its Consequences." *American Anthropologist* 100 (September 1998), 716–31.

Lewis, Tayler. "Memoir of the Rev. Cyrus Comstock." In *Proceedings of the Eleventh Anniversary of the University Convocation of the State of New York*. Albany, NY: Weed, Parsons, 1875, 110–14.

———. "My Old School-Master." In *Proceedings of the Eleventh Anniversary of the University Convocation of the State of New York* (Albany, NY: Weed, Parsons, , 1875), 95–109.

Lipset, Seymour Martin. *Agrarian Socialism: The Cooperative Commonwealth Federation in Saskatchewan*. Berkeley: University of California Press, 1971.

Lisicky, Michael J. *Gimbels Has It!* Charleston, SC: History Press, 2011.

Lister, Ruth. *Poverty*. Malden, MA: Polity Press, 2004.

Little, Thomas J. "The Origins of Southern Evangelicalism: Revivalism in South Carolina, 1700–1740." *Church History* 75 (December 2006), 768–808.

Lobao, Linda M., Gregory Hooks, and Ann R. Tickamyer. "Introduction: Advancing the Sociology of Spatial Inequality." In *The Sociology of Spatial Inequality*. Edited by Linda M. Lobao, Gregory Hooks, and Ann R. Tickamyer. Albany: State University of New York Press, 2007), 1–27.

Lofton, Kathryn. "Everything Queer?" In *Queer Christianities: Lived Religion in Transgressive Forms*. Edited by Kathleen T. Talvacchia, Michael F. Pettinger, and Mark Larrimore. New York: NYU Press, 2015, 195–204.

Lovejoy, David. *Religious Enthusiasm in the New World: From Heresy to Revolution*. Cambridge, MA: Harvard University Press, 1985.

Lowndes, Joseph E. *From the New Deal to the New Right: Race and the Southern Origins of Modern Conservatism*. New Haven, CT: Yale University Press, 2008.

Luce, T. James. *New Jersey's Sourland Mountain*. Hamilton, NJ: White Eagle Printing, 2001.

Luskey, Brian P. *On the Make*. New York: NYU Press, 2010.

Lynd Robert S., and Helen Merrell Lynd. *Middletown: A Study in Modern American Culture*. New York: Harcourt Brace Jovanovich, 1929.

———. *Middletown in Transition: A Study in Cultural Conflicts*. New York: Harcourt, Brace, 1937.

Macdonald, Keith M. "Building Respectability." *Sociology* 23 (February 1989), 55–80.

MacIntyre, Alasdair. *After Virtue: A Study in Moral Theory*. Notre Dame, IN: Notre Dame University Press, 1981.

Mack, Gertrude. "Rising bove the Market." *Forum* 4 (April 1931), 228–34.

Malin, James C. "Beginnings of Winter Wheat Production in the Upper Kansas and Lower Smoky Hill River Valleys: A Study in Adaptation to Geographical Environment." *Kansas Historical Quarterly* 10 (1941), 227–59.

———. "The Turnover of Farm Population in Kansas." *Kansas Historical Quarterly* 4 (May 1935), 339–72.

Markham, Jerry W. *Law Enforcement and the History of Financial Market Manipulation*. New York: Routledge, 2015.

Martin, Anne. "If I Were a Senator: In Which the First Woman Candidate Speaks Her Mind." *The Independent* 101 (May 1, 1920), 162–64.

Marvin, William B. "Food and Fuel Control." *Michigan Law Review* 17 (February 1919), 310–30.

Masquerier, Lewis. *Sociology*. New York: Lewis Masquerier, 1877.

May, Sophie. *Janet*. New York: Lee and Shepard, 1883.

McDaniel, W. Caleb. "The Fourth and the First: Abolitionist Holidays, Respectability, and Radical Interracial Reform." *American Quarterly* 57 (March 2005), 129–51.

McJunkin, Ben. "Rank among Equals." *Michigan Law Review* 113 (April 2015), 855–76.

McLaren, Peter. *Critical Pedagogy and Predatory Culture: Oppositional Politics in a Post-modern Era*. New York: Routledge, 2002.

McRoberts, Omar M. *Streets of Glory: Church and Community in a Black Urban Neighborhood*. Chicago: University of Chicago Press, 2003.

McVey, Frank L. "The Work and Problems of the Consumers League." *American Journal of Sociology* 6 (May 1901), 764–77.

Mead, Margaret. "Fanaticism: The Panhuman Disorder." *ETC: A Review of General Semantics* 71 (April 2014), 201–4 (originally published March 1977).

Mead, Sidney E. "The 'Nation with the Soul of a Church.'" *Church History* 36 (September 1967), 262–83.

———. *The Nation with the Soul of a Church*. New York: Harper & Row, 1975.

Milgram, Stanley. "The Social Meaning of Fanaticism." *ETC: A Review of General Semantics* 34 (March 1977), 58–61.

Min, Pyong Gap. *Preserving Ethnicity through Religion in America: Korean Protestants and Indian Hindus across Generations*. New York: NYU Press, 2010.

Minor, DoVeanna S. Fulton, and Reginald H. Pitts, eds. *Speaking Lives, Authoring Texts: Three African American Women's Oral Slave Narratives*. Albany: State University of New York Press, 2010.

Mische, Anne. "Relational Sociology, Culture, and Agency." In *The Sage Handbook of Social Network Analysis*. Edited by John Scott and Peter Carrington. London: Sage Publications, 2011, 80–97.

Moloshok, Rachel. "Saving for Victory!" *Pennsylvania Legacies* 12 (November 2012), 3–5.

Montignani, John F. *The Insanity Law of the State of New York*. Albany, NY: State Commission on Lunacy, 1896.

Mooney, James. "The Ghost Dance Religion and the Sioux Outbreak of 1890." *Fourteenth Annual Report of the Bureau of Ethnology*. Washington, DC: Government Printing Office, 1896, 641–1110.

Moore, R. Laurence. *Religious Outsiders and the Making of Americans*. New York: Oxford University Press, 1986.

Mora, G. Cristina. *Making Hispanics: How Activists, Bureaucrats, and Media Constructed a New American*. Chicago: University of Chicago Press, 2014.

Moran, James, David Wright, and Mat Savelli. "The Lunatic Fringe: Families, Madness, and Institutional Confinement in Victorian Ontario." In *Mapping the Margins: The Family and Social Discipline in Canada, 1700–1975*. Edited by Nancy Christie and Michael Gauvreau. Montreal: McGill-Queen's University Press, 2004, 277–304.

More, Hannah. "Black Giles the Poacher." *Cheap Repository* 16 (January 16, 1800), 1–34 (originally published in 1796).

Morris, Edward W. *Learning the Hard Way: Masculinity, Place, and the Gender Gap in Education*. New Brunswick, NJ: Rutgers University Press, 2012.

Morton, Oren F. *A History of Preston County, West Virginia*, part 1. Kingwood, WV: Journal Publishing Company, 1914.

Mudge, James. "Fanaticism a Present Peril." *Zion's Herald* 63 (May 26, 1886), 1.

———. *The Perfect Life in Experience and Doctrine*. Cincinnati: Jennings and Graham, 1911.

———. *Religious Experience Exemplified in the Lives of Illustrious Christians*. Cincinnati: Jennings and Graham, 1913.

Mullendore, William Clinton. *History of the United States Food Administration, 1917–1919*. Stanford, CA: Stanford University Press, 1941.

Myrdal, Gunnar. *An American Dilemma: The Negro Problem and Modern Democracy*. New York: Harper & Row, 1944.

Nackenoff, Carol. *Fictional Republic: Horatio Alger and American Political Discourse*. New York: Oxford University Press, 1994.

Nelles, Annie. *Life of a Book Agent*. 5th edition. St. Louis: Annie Nelles Dumond, 1892.

Nelson, Claudia. *Little Strangers*. Bloomington, IN: Indiana University Press, 2003.

Nevius, Blake. *Robert Herrick: The Development of a Novelist*. Berkeley: University of California Press, 1962.

Niebuhr, H. Richard. *The Social Sources of Denominationalism*. New York: H. Holt, 1929.

Nolan, James. *What They Saw in America: Alexis de Tocqueville, Max Weber, G. K. Chesterton, and Sayyid Qutb*. New York: Cambridge University Press, 2016.

Norris, Frank. *The Pit: A Story of Chicago*. New York: Doubleday, 1903.

Numbers, Ronald L., and Janet S. Numbers. "Millerism and Madness: A Study of 'Religious Insanity' in Nineteenth-Century America." In *The Disappointed: Millerism and Millenarianism in the Nineteenth Century*. Edited by Ronald L. Numbers and Jon Butler. Bloomington: Indiana University Press, 1987, 92–117.

O'Connell, James C. *The Hub's Metropolis: Greater Boston's Development from Railroad Suburbs to Smart Growth*. Cambridge, MA: MIT Press, 2013.

O'Foran, Shelly. *Little Zion*. Chapel Hill: University of North Carolina Press, 2006.

O'Kane, James. *Wicked Deeds: Murder in America*. New Brunswick, NJ: Transaction Publishers, 2005.

Obama, Barack. *The Audacity of Hope: Thoughts on Reclaiming the American Dream*. New York: Random House, 2006.

Oikawa, Mona. *Cartographies of Violence: Japanese Canadian Women, Memory, and the Subjects of the Internment*. Toronto: University of Toronto Press, 2012.

Orsi, Robert A. *Between Heaven and Earth: The Religious Worlds People Make and the Scholars Who Study Them*. Princeton, NJ: Princeton University Press, 2005.

Otley, J. W., L. Van Derveer, and J. Keily. *Map of Somerset County New Jersey Entirely from Original Surveys*. Camden, NJ: Lloyd Van Derveer, 1850.

Palmer, A. Michael. *Report of the Attorney General*. Department of Justice, Washington, DC, December 11, 1920.

Papachristos, Andrew V., David M. Hureau, and Anthony A. Braga. "The Corner and the Crew: The Influence of Geography and Social Networks on Gang Violence." *American Sociological Review* 78 (June 2013), 417–47.

Paprocki, Laura Kelly. "Hannah More and *Cheap Repository Tracts*: Lessons in "Religious and Useful Knowledge." MA thesis, University of Waterloo, 2010.

Parkhurst, Charles H. *Our Fight with Tammany*. New York: Charles Scribner's Sons, 1895.

Peck, George. *Formation of a Manly Character*. New York: Carlton and Phillips, 1853.

Peffer, William A. *The Farmer's Side: His Troubles and Their Remedy*. New York: D. Appleton, 1891.

Pennington, David. "Taking It to the Streets: Hucksters and Huckstering in Early Modern Southampton, circa 1550–1652." *Sixteenth Century Journal* 39 (Autumn 2008), 657–79.

Pflieger, Pat. "A Visit to *Merry's Museum*; or, Social Values in a Nineteenth-Century American Periodical for Children." PhD dissertation, University of Minnesota, 1987.

Pitofsky, Alex. "Dreiser's *The Financier* and the Horatio Alger Myth." *Twentieth Century Literature* 44 (Fall 1998), 276–90.

Pizzigati, Sam. *The Rich Don't Always Win: The Forgotten Triumph over Plutocracy that Created the American Middle Class, 1900–1970*. New York: Seven Stories Press, 2012.

Portes, Alejandro. *Economic Sociology: A Systematic Inquiry*. Princeton, NJ: Princeton University Press, 2010.

Portes, Alejandro, and Jozsef Borocz. "Contemporary Immigration: Theoretical Perspectives on Its Determinants and Modes of Incorporation." *International Migration Review* 23 (Fall 1989), 606–30.

Portes, Alejandro, and Rubén G. Rumbaut. *Immigrant America: A Portrait, Updated and Expanded*. Berkeley: University of California Press, 2014.

Pratt, E. H. "Editorial." *Journal of Orificial Surgery* 2 (1894), 275–82.

Preston, Samuel H., and Michael R. Haines. *Fatal Years: Child Mortality in Late Nineteenth-Century America*. Princeton, NJ: Princeton University Press, 1991.

Price, John M., ed. *The General Statutes of the State of Kansas*. Lawrence, KS: John Speer, 1868.

Rafter, Nicole Han, ed. *White Trash: The Eugenic Family Studies, 1877–1919*. Boston: Northeastern University Press, 1988.

Rager, T. F. *History of Neosho and Wilson Counties*. Fort Scott, KS: Monitor Printing, 1902.

Ramírez, Mari Carmen. "The Multicultural Shift." In *Resisting Categories: Latin American and/or Latino?*. Edited by Héctor Olea and Melina Kervandjian. New Haven, CT: Yale University Press, 2012, 944–56.

Reaume, Geoffrey. "Mental Hospital Patients and Family Relations in Southern Ontario, 1880–1930." In *Family Matters: Papers in Post-Confederation Canadian Family History*. Edited by Lori Chambers and Edgar-André Montigny. Toronto: Canadian Scholars Press, 1998, 271–88.

Ribas, Vanesa. *On the Line: Slaughterhouse Lives and the Making of the New South*. Berkeley: University of California Press, 2016.

Richter, Amy G., ed. *At Home in Nineteenth-Century America*. New York: NYU Press, 2015.

Risjord, Norman K. *The WPA Guide to Wisconsin*. Minneapolis: Minnesota Historical Society Press, 1941.

Ritchie, June Bear. *The Great Depression Put to Music, Song and Dance*. Bloomington, IN: Trafford Publishing, 2011.

Rodgers, Daniel. "Socializing Middle-Class Children: Institutions, Fables, and Work Values in Nineteenth-Century America." *Journal of Social History* 13 (Spring 1980), 354–67.

Roosevelt, Theodore. *An Autobiography*. New York: Macmillan, 1916.

———. *Realizable Ideals*. San Francisco: Whitaker & Ray-Wiggin, 1912.

Rosenfeld, Michael J. "Racial, Educational and Religious Endogamy in the United States: A Comparative Historical Perspective." *Social Forces* 87 (September 2008), 1–31.

Ross, Fiona C. "Raw Life and Respectability: Poverty and Everyday life in a Postapartheid Community." *Current Anthropology* 56 (October 2015), S97–S107.

Rothman, David J. *Conscience and Convenience: The Asylum and Its Alternatives in Progressive America*. Rev. ed. New Brunswick, NJ: Aldine Transaction, 2012.

———. *The Discovery of the Asylum: Social Order and Disorder in the New Republic*. Rev. ed. New Brunswick, NJ: Aldine Transaction, 2002.

Rowlingson, Karen, and Stephen McKay. *Wealth and the Wealthy: Exploring and Tackling Inequalities between Rich and Poor*. Bristol, UK: Policy Press, 2011.

Rumbaut, Rubén G. "The Crucible Within: Ethnic Identity, Self Esteem, and Segmented Assimilation among Children of Immigrants." *International Migration Review* 28 (Winter 1994), 748–94.

Ruppenthal, Jacob C. "The German Element in Central Kansas." *Collections of the Kansas State Historical Society* 13 (1913–14), 513–35.

Rushdy, Ashraf H. A. *American Lynching*. New Haven, CT: Yale University Press, 2012.

Rutkow, I. M. "Edwin Hartley Pratt and Orificial Surgery: Unorthodox Surgical Practice in Nineteenth Century." *Surgery* 114 (September 1993), 558–63.

Sacks, Harvey. *Lectures on Conversation*. Cambridge, MA: Blackwell, 1992.

Said, Edward. *Orientalism*. New York: Pantheon, 1978.

Salamon, Sonya. *Prairie Patrimony: Family, Farming, and Community in the Midwest*. Chapel Hill: University of North Carolina Press, 1992.

Sánchez-Eppler, Karen. "Childhood." In *Keywords for Children's Literature*. Edited by Philip Nel and Lissa Paul. New York: NYU Press, 2011, 35–41.

Sands-O'Connor, Karen. *Soon Come Home to This Island: West Indians in British Children's Literature*. New York: Routledge, 2013.

Santelli, Robert, and Emily Davidson, eds. *Hard Travelin': The Life and Legacy of Woody Guthrie*. Hanover, NH: University Press of New England, 1999.

Sargent, James E. "Roosevelt's Economy Act: Fiscal Conservatism and the Early New Deal." *Congressional Studies* 7 (Winter 1980), 33–51.

Saussure, Ferdinand de. *Course in General Linguistics*. Edited by Charles Bally and Albert Sechehaye. LaSalle, IL: Open Court Press, 1983.

Schatzki, Theodore R., Karin Knorr Cetina, and Eike von Savigny, eds. *The Practice Turn in Contemporary Theory*. New York: Routledge, 2000.

Schele de Vere, Maximillian. *Studies in English; or, Glimpses of the Inner Life*. New York: Charles Scribner, 1867.

Schmidt, James D. "Willful Disobedience: Young People and School Authority in the Nineteenth-Century United States." In *Children and Youth during the Gilded Age and Progressive Era*. Edited by James Marten. New York: NYU Press, 2014, 125–44.

Schmidt, Leigh Eric. *Consumer Rites: The Buying and Selling of American Holidays*. Princeton, NJ: Princeton University Press, 1995.

Schnable, Allison. "Singing the Gospel: Using Musical Practices to Build Religious and Racial Communities." *Poetics* 40 (May 2012), 278–98.

Schwartzman, Roy. "Recasting the American Dream through Horatio Alger's Success Stories." *Studies in Popular Culture* 23 (October 2000), 75–91.

Scull, Andrew. *Madness in Civilization: A Cultural History of Insanity, from the Bible to Freud, from the Madhouse to Modern Medicine*. Princeton, NJ: Princeton University Press, 2015.

———. *Social Order / Mental Disorder: Anglo-American Psychiatry in Historical Perspective*. Berkeley: University of California Press, 1989.

Shea, John Gilmary. "Vagaries of Protestant Religious Belief." *American Catholic Quarterly Review* 10 (July 1885), 432–44.

Shelby, Mary Doane. "The Housewife and the High Cost of Living." *Outlook* 123 (September 3, 1919), 13–15.

Sherman, Rachel. "Producing the Superior Self: Strategic Comparison and Symbolic Boundaries among Luxury Hotel Workers." *Ethnography* 6 (June 2005), 131–58.

Shipley, Maynard. "The Forward March of the Anti-Evolutionists." *Current History* 29 (January 1, 1929), 578–82.

Simmel, Georg. "The Stranger." In Kurt Wolff, *The Sociology of Georg Simmel*. New York: Free Press, 1950, 402–8.

Simmons, Christina. "'I Had to Promise . . . Not to Ask 'Nasty' Questions Again': African American Women and Sex and Marriage Education in the 1940s." *Journal of Women's History* 27 (Spring 2015), 110–35.

Skinner, Otis Ainsworth. *Letters on the Moral and Religious Duties of Parents*. Boston: B. B. Mussey, 1844.

Sklar, Kathryn Kish. *Catharine Beecher: A Study in American Domesticity*. New Haven, CT: Yale University Press, 1973.

Skocpol, Theda. *Protecting Soldiers and Mothers: The Political Origins of Social Policy in the United States*. Cambridge, MA: Harvard University Press, 1992.

Small, Albion W. "Review of *The Political Economy of Humanism*." *American Journal of Sociology* 7 (July 1901), 133.

Smith, Dale Edwyna. *The Slaves of Liberty: Freedom in Amite County, Mississippi, 1820–1868*. New York: Routledge, 2012.

Smith, Jason Scott. *A Concise History of the New Deal*. New York: Cambridge University Press, 2014.

Smith, S. Hanbury. *Sketch of the Epidemic Religious Monomanie Which Occurred in Sweden in the Year 1841 and 1842*. Columbus, OH: Medary's Steam Press, 1850.

Smith, Woodruff D. *Consumption and the Making of Respectability, 1600–1800*. New York: Routledge, 2002.

Sombart Werner. *Why Is There No Socialism in the United States?* White Plains, NY: International Arts and Sciences Press, 1976; first published in 1906.

Somers, Margaret R. "The Narrative Constitution of Identity: A Relational and Network Approach." *Theory and Society* 23 (October 1994), 605–49.

Spahr, Charles B. *An Essay on the Present Distribution of Wealth in the United States*. New York: Thomas V. Crowell, 1896.

Spring, Gardiner. *Hints to Parents on the Religious Education of Children*. New York: Taylor and Gould, 1835.

State Board of Agriculture. *Third Annual Report to the Legislature of Kansas*. Topeka, KS: State Printing Works, 1874.

State Board of Charities. *Sixth Biennial Report of the State Board of Charities*. Topeka: Kansas Publishing House, 1888.

Stearns, Peter N. *Anxious Parents: A History of Modern Childrearing*. New York: NYU Press, 2003.

Steele, Liza G. "'A Gift from God': Adolescent Motherhood and Religion in Brazilian Favelas." *Sociology of Religion* 72 (January 2011), 4–27.

Steffensmeier, Darrell J., and Robert M. Terry. "Deviance and Respectability: An Observational Study of Reactions to Shoplifting." *Social Forces* 51 (June 1973), 417–26.

Stegner, Wallace. "Chronicles of the West." *Virginia Quarterly Review* (Autumn 1938), 596–601.

Steinbeck, John. *The Grapes of Wrath*. New York: Viking, 1939.

Stephens, Ann S. *Fashion and Famine*. Philadelphia: T. B. Peterson and Brothers, 1854.

Stevens, Abel. *The History of the Religious Movement of the Eighteen Century Called Methodism*. London: Wesleyan Conference, 1878.

Stone, Simon. "The Miller Delusion: A Comparative Study in Mass Psychology." *American Journal of Psychiatry* 91 (November 1934), 593–623.

Stout, Jeffrey. *Ethics after Babel*. Princeton, NJ: Princeton University Press, 1988.

Straus, Murray A. *Beating the Devil Out of Them: Corporal Punishment in American Families and Its Effects on Children*. Boston: Lexington Books, 1994.

Sullivan, Helen. "Evaluating Social Cohesion." In *Promoting Social Cohesion: Implications for Policy and Evaluation*. Edited by Peter Ratcliffe and Ines Newman. Bristol, UK: Policy Press, 2011, 41–59.

Sullivan, Susan Crawford. *Living Faith: Everyday Religion and Mothers in Poverty*. Chicago: University of Chicago Press, 2011.

Sumner, William Graham. "Politics in America, 1776–1876." *North American Review* 122 (January 1876), 47–87.

———. *What Social Classes Owe to Each Other*. New York: Harper & Brothers, 1884.

Sylvester, Kenneth, and Geoff Cunfer. "An Unremembered Diversity: Mixed Husbandry and the American Grasslands." *Agricultural History* 83 (2009), 352–83.

Szasz, Thomas. *Insanity: The Idea and Its Consequences*. New York: John Wiley, 1987.

Taylor, Isaac. *Fanaticism*. London: Holdsworth and Ball, 1833.

Taylor, Jane, ed. *Rhymes for the Nursery*. London: Harvey and Darton, 1824.

Theriot, Nancy M. *Mothers and Daughters in Nineteenth-Century America: The Biosocial Construction of Femininity*. Louisville: University Press of Kentucky, 1996.

Tilly, Charles. *Durable Inequality*. Berkeley: University of California Press, 1998.

Tocqueville, Alexis de. *Democracy in America*. Translated by George Lawrence. New York: Harper Perennial, 1966.

Tolnay, Steward, and E. M. Beck. *A Festival of Violence: An Analysis of Southern Lynchings, 1882–1930*. Urbana: University of Illinois Press, 1995.

Tonkovich, Nicole. *Domesticity with a Difference: The Nonfiction of Catharine Beecher, Sarah J. Hale, Fanny Fern, and Margaret Fuller*. Jackson: University of Mississippi Press, 1997.

Train, Arthur. "The Billionaire Era: Part I—The Vanderbilts and Andrew Carnegie." *Forum* 72 (November 1924), 617–28.

———. "The Billionaire Era: Part II—The Rockefellers and Henry Ford." *Forum* 72 (December 1924), 746–59.

Trent, James W., Jr. *Inventing the Feeble Mind: A History of Mental Retardation in the United States*. Berkeley: University of California Press, 1994.

Tunell, George. "The Legislative History of the Second Income Tax Law." *Journal of Political Economy* 3 (1895), 311–37.

Tupper, H. A. *Two Centuries of the First Baptist Church of South Carolina*. Baltimore: R. H. Woodward, 1889.

Turner, John Frank. "The Hoosier Huckster." *Indiana Magazine of History* 50 (March 1954), 51–60.

Tuveson, Ernest Lee. *Redeemer Nation: The Idea of America's Millennial Role*. Chicago: University of Chicago Press, 1968.

Twain, Mark. "The Story of the Bad Little Boy That Led a Charmed Life." In Samuel L. Clemens, *Mark Twain's Sketches New and Old* (Chicago: American Publishing Company, 1875), 51–58; originally published in 1865 in *The Californian*.

Twain, Mark, and Charles Dudley Warner. *The Gilded Age: A Tale of Today*. New York: American Publishing Company, 1873.

U. S. Bureau of the Census. *Insane and Feeble-Minded in Institutions, 1910*. Washington, DC: Government Printing Office, 1914.

U.S. Bureau of Labor Statistics. "Consumer Expenditure Survey," figures for 1901 and 1918; *100 Years of U.S. Consumer Spending: Data for the Nation, New York City, and Boston*. BLS Report 991 (2006), 16.

———. "CPI Inflation Calculator." U.S. Department of Labor, 2015; http://www.bls.gov.

U.S. Congress, House of Representatives. *Hearings before the Committee on Agriculture, Lamborn Sugar Resolution*. Washington, DC: Government Printing Office, 1922.

U.S. Department of Justice, Office of the Attorney General. *Report of the Attorney General*. Washington, DC: Government Printing Office, 1920.

U.S. Fuel Administration. *General Orders, Regulations and Rulings*. Washington, DC: Government Printing Office, 1920.

U.S. House of Representatives. Hearings before the Special Committee on Victor L. Berger. Washington, DC: Government Printing Office, 1919.

Urban, Sylvanus. "Domestic Economy: The Management of Children." *New York Mirror* 6 (April 18, 1829), 324.

Van Ruymbeke, Bertrand. *From New Babylon to Eden: The Huguenots and Their Migration to Colonial South Carolina*. Columbia: South Carolina University Press, 2006.

Veblen, Thorstein. "The Modern Point of View and the New Order, VIII: The Vested Interests and the Common Man." *The Dial* 66 (January 25, 1919), 75–82.

Von Berge, Herman. *These Glorious Years: The Centenary History of German Baptists of North America, 1843–1943*. Providence, RI: Roger Williams Press, 1943.

Wagner, Helmut R., ed. *Alfred Schutz on Phenomenology and Social Relations*. Chicago: University of Chicago Press, 1970, 321–22.

Waldrep, Christopher. *The Many Faces of Judge Lynch: Extralegal Violence and Punishment in America*. New York: Palgrave Macmillan, 2002.

Walker, Melissa. *Country Women Cope with Hard Times: A Collection of Oral Histories*. Columbia: University of South Carolina Press, 2012.

Wall, Wendy L. *Inventing the "American Way": The Politics of Consensus from the New Deal to the Civil Rights Movement*. New York: Oxford University Press, 2008.

Ward, Lester F. "Plutocracy and Paternalism." *Forum* 20 (November 1895), 300–10.

Watkins, Samuel Rush. *Memoir of Samuel Rush Watkins*. Chattanooga, TN: Times Printing Company, 1900.

Weber, Max. *The Protestant Ethic and the Spirit of Capitalism*. New York: Scribner's, 1958.

———. "The Protestant Sects and the Spirit of Capitalism." In *From Max Weber: Essays in Sociology*. Edited by H. H. Gerth and C. Wright Mills. New York: Oxford University Press, 1946, 302–22.

Weissbach, Lee Shai. *Jewish Life in Small-Town America: A History*. New Haven, CT: Yale University Press, 2005.

Wesley, Cindy K. "The Pietist Theology and Ethnic Mission of the General Conference of German Baptists in North America, 1851–1920." PhD dissertation, McGill University, 2000.

Weston, George F., Jr. "Making the Bad Boy Good." *Journal of Education* 81 (February 18, 1915), 173–74.

White, Calvin, Jr. *The Rise to Respectability: Race, Religion, and the Church of God in Christ*. Fayetteville: University of Arkansas Press, 2012.

White, Michael J., and Jennifer E. Glick. *How New Immigrants Do in American Schools, Jobs, and Neighborhoods*. New York: Russell Sage Foundation, 2009.

White, William Allen. *A Certain Rich Man*. New York: Macmillan, 1909.

White, William L. *What People Said*. New York: Viking, 1938.

Wilkins, Amy C. "'Happier than Non-Christians': Collective Emotions and Symbolic Boundaries among Evangelical Christians." *Social Psychology Quarterly* 71 (September 2008), 281–301.

Williams, Benjamin. *The Book of Psalms as Translated, Paraphrased, or Imitated by Some of the Most Eminent English Poets*. Salisbury, England: Collins and Johnson, 1781.

Wilson, Sarah. *Melting-Pot Modernism*. Ithaca, NY: Cornell University Press, 2010.

Wilson, Warren H. "Social Life in the Country." *Annals of the American Academy of Political and Social Science* 40 (January 1912), 119–30.

Wimmer, Andreas. "The Making and Unmaking of Ethnic Boundaries: A Multilevel Process Theory." *American Journal of Sociology* 113 (January 2008), 970–1022.

Winiarski, Douglas L. "Souls Filled with Ravishing Transport: Heavenly Visions and the Radical Awakening in New England." *William and Mary Quarterly* 61 (January 2004), 3–46.

Winslow, Thyra Samter. "My Daughter in the City." *The Bookman* 68 (November 1928), 290–99.

Witherspoon, John. "Letters on Education." *New York Missionary Magazine* 2 (January 5, 1801), 107–14, 348–57.

Workman, Joseph. "Insanity of the Religious-Emotional Type, and Its Occasional Physical Relations." *American Journal of Insanity* 26 (July 1869), 33–48.

Woyke, Frank H. *Heritage and Ministry of the North American Baptist Conference*. Forest Park, IL: North American Baptist Conference, 1979.

Wright, David. "Getting Out of the Asylum: Understanding the Confinement of the Insane in the Nineteenth Century." *Social History of Medicine* 10 (January 1997), 137–55.

Wustenbecker, Katja. "German-Americans during World War I." In *Immigrant Entrepreneurship: German-American Business Biographies, 1720 to the Present*. Vol. 3. Edited by Giles R. Hoyt. Berlin: German Historical Institute, 2014.

Wuthnow, Robert. *Acts of Compassion: Caring for Others and Helping Ourselves*. Princeton, NJ: Princeton University Press, 1991.

———. *Be Very Afraid: The Cultural Response to Terror, Pandemics, Environmental Devastation, Nuclear Annihilation, and Other Threats*. New York: Oxford University Press, 2010.

————. *Small-Town America: Finding Community, Shaping the Future.* Princeton, NJ: Princeton University Press, 2013.

Yellin, Jean Fagan, ed. *The Harriet Jacobs Family Papers.* Chapel Hill: University of North Carolina Press, 2008.

Young, Brian. *Respectable Burial: Montreal's Mount Royal Cemetery.* Montreal: McGill-Queen's University Press, 2003.

Young, Brigham. *Discourses of Brigham Young,* edited by John A. Widtsoe. Salt Lake City, UT: Deseret Book Company, 1954.

Young, Jeffrey Robert, ed. *Proslavery and Sectional thought in the Early South, 1740–1829: An Anthology.* Columbia: University of South Carolina, 2006.

Yukich, Grace. "Boundary Work in Inclusive Religious Groups: Constructing Identity at the New York Catholic Worker." *Sociology of Religion* 71 (Summer 2010), 172–96.

Zelizer, Viviana A. "How I Became a Relational Economic Sociologist and What Does That Mean?" *Politics and Society* 40 (June 2012), 145–74.

————. *Pricing the Priceless Child: The Changing Social Value of Children.* New York: Basic Books, 1985.

Zierden Martha A., and Elizabeth J. Reitz. "Animal Use and the Urban Landscape in Colonial Charleston, South Carolina, USA." *International Journal of Historical Archaeology* 13 (September 2009), 327–65.

A NOTE ON THE TYPE

{≈≈≈≈≈}

THIS BOOK has been composed in Miller, a Scotch Roman typeface designed by Matthew Carter and first released by Font Bureau in 1997. It resembles Monticello, the typeface developed for The Papers of Thomas Jefferson in the 1940s by C. H. Griffith and P. J. Conkwright and reinterpreted in digital form by Carter in 2003.

Pleasant Jefferson ("P. J.") Conkwright (1905–1986) was Typographer at Princeton University Press from 1939 to 1970. He was an acclaimed book designer and AIGA Medalist.

The ornament used throughout this book was designed by Pierre Simon Fournier (1712–1768) and was a favorite of Conkwright's, used in his design of the *Princeton University Library Chronicle*.

financial products secured against mortgages. *Second* was a more general set of market failures to correctly price risk in relation to the growth of credit that helped sustain a major financial upswing. As in 1929, an asset price bubble had burst, and the sub-prime crisis and the contraction of liquidity it created also led to a stock market collapse.

A *third* dimension to the GFC was a far more intensified development of financial globalization than was present in 1929. While cross-border trade and capital flows were present in the earlier crisis, the scale of finance within the global economy was far less. Since 2007, the interconnections between global financial centres and finance markets have been far greater, leading to a more rapid and intense global crisis.

A *fourth* dimension to the GFC involved the system of international payments. Unlike the gold standard operating in 1929, the contemporary system adjusted trade imbalances through fluctuating exchange rates and huge flows of finance across borders. While the gold standard required a credit contraction in the USA to adjust to its perennial trade deficit, within the current financial system, the imbalance has remained intact, financed through the transfer of funds to the USA from countries with trade surpluses such as China and the oil-producers. These new characteristics of the system meant that the USA avoided a currency crisis or the need to deflate the home economy because of the availability of funds from other countries.

A *fifth* feature of the GFC was a more highly developed regulatory system than in 1929–31. This had given central bankers a greater role in monetary policy and prudential regulation of global banks than existed in the gold standard system. It also involved a wider set of regulatory bodies, a number of them originally established in the aftermath of 1929–31. Governments were now more happy to intervene in crises rather than simply to wait for markets to revive. Nonetheless, policy and regulatory failure was still evident in the recent crisis, partly because older regulatory arrangements such as the US separation of commercial and investment banking had been reversed, and partly because the climate of loose-touch regulation had inhibited tougher capital adequacy requirements limiting credit creation to sustainable levels.

Sixth, and as in 1929–31, a sovereign debt crisis became superimposed on crises of banking, credit, and liquidity. This initially became pronounced in Europe, notably in the peripheral economies of Greece, Ireland, and Portugal, but also affected the Euro block as a whole.

Historical analysis suggests periodic financial crises do not take an entirely standard form. Although common features may include market failure to correctly discern risk in the context of asset price bubbles, structural changes in the shape and functioning of the global economy and the regulatory architecture also matter a great deal.

Conclusion

This chapter draws on insights from sociology and economic history to establish a broader approach to global finance than is usually found within economics. It shows how and why history and geography matter to the development of finance. Instead of the rational pursuit of self-interest and economic individualism alone, the approach demonstrates how finance markets are necessarily bound up with states, warfare, questions of risk and social legitimacy, together with inequalities in economic power. These broader considerations provide essential elements both in the history and contemporary functioning of credit and in recent processes of financialization. Structures of power matter. This is why the broader concept of capitalism remains valuable as a way of recognizing the overarching framework in which markets operate. Equally, inequalities of power between financial institutions and nation-states indicate a profound democratic deficit in the way public policy emerges.

Much more is needed, however, than a focus on power and inequality in tracing issues in the history and geography of global finance and financial crisis. In this chapter, particular attention has been given to inherent challenges in worlds of credit provision that cross boundaries, requiring new financial instruments and a stable and effective international monetary system. Risk and uncertainty abound, and processes of credit provision and insurance against default are particularly vulnerable to them. And while crisis is an over-used term, financial crises punctuate history in such an endemic manner that it is not clear that they can ever be avoided.

In the following chapter, the broader focus developed here is further extended to an examination of the cultural worlds of global finance.

4

THE SOCIAL ACTORS IN GLOBAL FINANCE

Market culture and financial knowledge

There is one key aspect to global finance that generally gets little attention, in spite of its centrality to the topic. And that centres on the people who inhabit the world of finance, their cultural dispositions, and the kinds of knowledge and assumptions that they bring to financial markets. In the light of the GFC, bankers, share dealers, and financial traders are typically seen in terms of stereotypes, as rapacious speculators bloated by multi-million bonuses. Such images are mollified only by the sober faces of ineffectual central bankers and public regulators charged with clearing up the mess, appearing on television or in parliamentary committees to explain why they failed to prevent crisis, and what can be done about it.

These stereotypes may reflect public anger, but they are inadequate in their grasp of the cultural worlds that traders and bankers inhabit. And beyond these prominent occupations lie a more elaborate and significant, yet often neglected, set of actors concerned with finance. These include hedge fund managers, bond dealers, commodity brokers, foreign exchange dealers, actuaries in life insurance, financial analysts and journalists, private sector lawyers and public regulators, economists and statisticians. They inhabit a range of financial worlds rather than a single integrated financial system. These multiple worlds include trading rooms, confidential client-centred transactions, boardroom decision-making, central bank deliberations, and regulatory engagements with financial corporations. This is a world tied together by interpersonal networks of interaction that link private and public sectors, as well as electronic trading networks which often involve automatic trading programmes.

Financial actors certainly deploy evidence-based economic and statistical analysis. But they also build in a range of experience-based judgements, gut feelings, and, in the case of traders, raw emotions such as fear, uncertainty, confidence, hope, and even euphoria. These may all be found within global finance, though they are not evenly spread among the various financial sectors and occupational communities. They do, nonetheless, have to be taken into account in any analysis of the financial world, rather than being relegated to the status of marginal, ideological or irrational intrusions into essentially rational processes. This applies, as we shall see later in the chapter, whether we are talking about public policy-making, decisions about investment strategy, credit policies, risk management or governance processes.

The cultural characteristics of global finance have not generally been of interest to economists, corporate managers, or policy-makers, nor did early generations of sociologists give much thought to such questions. This neglect arose from one of two reasons.

The first of these assumes financial markets are populated by acquisitive ego-centred economic-rationalists, relentlessly pursuing financial returns through economic self-interest. This approach fitted well with the expansion of global finance in the last quarter of the twentieth century when a more sophisticated and mathematical approach to financial markets led to a greater adoption of financial theory by financial traders. It also fitted well with an epoch of apparent on-going economic success. Periodic crises and panics brought subsidiary views about the world of finance markets into play, notably the presence of psychological traits such as greed and fear. This has generated an interest among behavioural economists in the psychology of market behaviour, including phenomena such as confidence, mimicry, and herding. Yet this tended to focus on sets of individual psychological dispositions, rather than the collective organizational features of market cultures.

The second reason for neglect of cultural dimensions to finance, more prevalent among earlier generations of sociologists, arose from an excessively structural approach to institutions considered from the top-down. Finance, as analysed by radical political economists, is seen as part of global capitalism, understood as a system founded on capital accumulation in pursuit of private economic advantage operating through markets for land, labour, and capital. Analysts influenced by Marxist political economy have observed both the dynamic and the crisis-ridden features of capitalism for 150 years or so, but have not taken much time to explore how cultures of finance operate, how and why financial innovation takes place, and how different forms of knowledge create new financial products and new risks. Social actors in finance are simply assumed to be driven by the system imperatives of the over-arching economic system.

This kind of sociological neglect has been overcome in the last two decades with the growth of economic sociology and social studies of knowledge. Economic sociology, unlike most of the earlier production-centred work by political economists, embraced first the sphere of consumption and then finance. Books such as Jocelyn Pixley's *Emotions in Financial Markets: Distrust and Uncertainty in Global Markets* (2004) and Donald McKenzie's *An Engine, Not a Camera: How Financial Models Shape Markets* (2006) have helped revolutionize the study of financial cultures. Pixley claims that financial worlds have to deal with the consequences of radical uncertainty about the future. This necessarily builds emotional anchorages around trust, reputation, and confidence into the far-from rational worlds of financial transactions and governance. McKenzie, meanwhile, deepens understandings of the discursive contribution of knowledge to economic life, focusing on the ways in which economic and financial thought has constituted new types of financial markets rather than simply observing and describing them.

While the theoretical dimensions underlying these trends will be explored further in Chapter 5, attention here is given to several key elements in the cultures of global finance, dealing first with traders and then with central bankers.

Traders, electronic transactions, and trading rooms

Financial traders are the very visible manifestation of global finance, dealing in colossal volumes of financial instruments, and placed in positions where they can make huge profits and personal bonuses – as well as huge losses. As is well known, a single trader, Nick Leeson, a leading trader in London in the 1990s, made such huge losses that he brought down the long-established Barings Bank single-handed. But what kind of social actors are traders, and what are the most central cultural features of traders' worlds?

This question requires analysis of very recent changes in financial trading. These involve a shift away from face-to-face market transactions involving networks of traders to flows of computer-generated financial data interpreted by traders sitting at screens, communicating through text or voice. In contrast to traditional stock and bond markets based on the physical presence of traders in the one space, within open-outcry markets such as the New York Stock Exchange and the Chicago Board of Trade, many now emphasize a trend towards private trading rooms dominated by screen-based communication. For the Swiss sociologist Karen Knorr-Cettina and her associates, the continuous market flow represented on screens has become the dominant aspect of traders' work. Traders' realities are now enveloped in visual attention to fast-flowing forms of information that require both observing and trading, forms of action lacking deliberation and calculation. Conversation-based trading certainly happens, though it is often mediated through text-based communication systems, as in the massive daily volumes in excess of $4 trillion traded in the global spot market for foreign exchange. In global financial markets in general, however, much trading is organized through pre-programmed trading systems that automatically execute trades when the conditions envisaged in the programming arise.

In contrast with the almost visceral and highly competitive interpersonal engagements experienced in the so-called trading pits of commodity futures or bond dealers in the Chicago Board of Trade, the argument here is that electronic trading creates very thin levels of social contact. Accordingly, the human relationships that lie behind screen-based flows of information and trading seem minimal and perhaps post-social. Rather than the rich interpersonal interactions of open outcry networks, screen technology somehow isolates the trader from wider social contexts. For critics of financial cultures, this kind of social introversion helps explain why global finance ends up playing out socially destructive forms of market behaviour that create business bankruptcy and unemployment.

The wider impact of shifts towards electronic communication within global finance are, however, far less clear-cut than such arguments imply.

There are several reasons for this. One is that not all markets have abandoned 'open-outcry' systems in favour of electronic trading. This sets limits to theories of the post-social evolution of finance. Interpersonal interactions still matter, as do networks, in which particular traders gain and lose reputation for their capacity to make profitable deals. Reliable information remains a major feature of financial networks, and this depends to a significant degree on the personal sources associated with it.

Pixley sees this world as far more than an exercise in economic rationality geared to self-interest. Since economic futures are profoundly uncertain and hence unpredictable, rationality needs an emotional anchorage to assure financial actors that expectations about the future have some degree of reliability. This anchorage is provided by trust – a social quality beyond rational self-interest. Trust, however, is not limited to the personalized trust of networks of financial actors which some analysts see as in decline. This is because there is a heavy investment in the financial sector in what she calls impersonal trust. Although markets are full of distrust, the relations of credit and indebtedness, embodied in finance, require some sense of trust between lenders and borrowers. Promises to repay debt at some time in the future can never be guaranteed but the emotional uncertainties that this creates can be provisionally softened by trust that institutions will perform what is required of them. Such 'emotions' of trust are not, however, to be seen as irrational and embarrassing in an otherwise rational world. Rather, they are as it were adjuncts to economic rationality, addressing the future-oriented form that credit relations take, and the uncertainties built into it. The time-dimension of finance markets therefore matters a great deal to the social relations and cultural world financial actors inhabit. Instantaneous electronically mediated spot markets may indeed only be thinly social, but this model is less relevant to future-oriented markets, whether interpersonal or electronic. Here trust matters alongside rational calculation.

A second kind of criticism of the post-social theory of financial trading, which reinforces the sociological approach outlined here, is that trading rooms are more interesting social settings than is often supposed. Thus alongside and in the midst of the battery of screens are conversations between traders of different kinds, commenting on aspects of market behaviour that they encounter. This amounts to a 'space of sociability' (in the words of Buenza and Stark (2004)) organized in an open-plan format without cubicles or partitions. Physical space and physical closeness still matter.

One way of understanding the milieu of the trading room is to emphasize that traders' main task is to select and interpret which aspects of the information on the multiplicity of screens before them is significant. This kind of activity may be regarded as involving the links between persons and instruments, akin in some ways to the operation of scientists in a laboratory. Traders are generally highly educated, and trading rooms rely on a considerable degree of mathematical and economic knowledge. While screens are important, interactions in cyberspace do not get sufficiently close to the sense in which trading rooms operate more like 'interpretive communities'. These large rooms include spaces for discussion and white boards on which formulae and mathematical relationships may be presented and discussed. There is also interaction between the denizens on different trading desks, typically organized in terms of different specialist areas such as merger arbitrage, convertible bond arbitrage, derivatives, and so forth.

An additional way of thinking about traders is to consider their broader social worlds and how these may influence their thinking and performance as market players. Such issues demand a more anthropological than economistic approach. Some observers suggest that traders are like engineers, technically adept but socially inept. Others, looking at the elite of Wall Street traders in arbitrage, report a rich world of external cultural reference points in cinema, literature, and philosophy. Such traders are clearly not one-dimensional screen-focused 'nerds', at least in their private lives. And yet the impression remains of a sharp divide or differentiation between economic 'workplace' activities and wider interests. In the introverted highly competitive worlds of trading, the language of success and failure all too often lapses into a coarse vocabulary of sex and violence. Failure involves being 'shafted', 'bent over' or 'stuffed', success involves 'fucking' or 'killing' others. While success may mean bonuses, failure leads to redundancy.

Focus on financial transactions and trading rooms explains a good deal about the day-to-day worlds of traders, yet this by no means exhausts an understanding of the wide range of activities and locales within which global finance operates. The elite of traders may operate autonomously, but many trades are executed on behalf of the institution that employs traders or for other external clients. In the former case, what matters most are the proprietary investment strategies of institutions rather than the workplace milieu of traders. It is of course the case that traders may combine both roles and may seek to maximize autonomy, especially in relation to new and complex financial instruments that higher level managers and institutional clients may not understand.

Nonetheless, financial institutions contain hierarchies of authority and experience which creates priorities and limits for trading activities. Pixley cites the chief financial officer of a Swiss bank, who would meet with the bank's chief economist and head of trading each Monday morning to review proprietary trading positions in areas such as bond futures, in the light of current economic and political developments. In such circumstances within investment banks, institutional factors are clearly highly relevant in setting the parameters within which the mass of traders operate.

Market knowledge – practical and abstract

Market knowledge clearly plays a crucial part in the culture of global financial trading and this is where formal economic and mathematical knowledge enters the picture. Rather than seeing traders as exclusively practical in orientation, a number of analysts have demonstrated the key role that highly abstract economic reasoning has played in financial markets over the last three or four decades. Economics, and more especially the economics of finance, has been an intrinsic part not simply in the analysis of markets, but also in the development and in some cases the inception of specialist financial markets of various kinds. Academia and global trading have been closely interlinked, especially in the USA.

The leading example of this kind of connection is the Black–Scholes formula as further elaborated by Merton, developed in the early 1970s as a means of understanding and predicting the price of options, a particular kind of financial derivative. This class of financial instruments gives the owner the right (but not the obligation) to buy or sell assets at a set price up to a specific date in the future. It is not necessary to own such assets or to buy them in the future, only to be interested in trading rights to buy and sell. While the general public may have very little if any knowledge of these instruments, they have come to represent a significant element in global finance and, in particular, in arbitrage trading by investment banks and hedge funds. The following paragraph attempts a summary of the basic features of the formula.

The aim of the Black–Scholes–Merton approach was to resolve the problem of how to calculate the present value of projected future income and expenditures involved in trading in a range of financial assets. Share trading clearly had intrinsic risks in dealing with future unknowns. How could these risks be avoided or minimized (or in technical parlance, hedged)? The model indicated that, under certain (heroic) assumptions, risks could be hedged by buying both shares and call options, which gave the right to buy the share. The formula, based on an understanding of the relative volatilities of shares against that of the market as a whole, also gave a precise answer to the ratio of the two assets that needed to be held to achieve effective hedging, a ratio that could be constantly adjusted. The hedged position was then seen as largely riskless.

This formula, while highly technical, was put into use in a practical way by market traders. Many went into the physical open-outcry markets of the 1970s and 1980s equipped with Black–Scholes formulae for the assets in which they were interested. Market strategists now based portfolio construction on the model to maximize returns while minimizing risks. In addition, new markets for derivatives were themselves created over the opposition that they represented mere speculation. An example is the Chicago Board Options Exchange. In this way, the economics of finance, and many of the leading economists within this field, who established private companies to supply share-data based on their analyses, entered into the development of the financial sector. Theory and practice were united, or, put more sociologically, economists were intimately involved in the inception and performance of finance markets, alongside traders, advancing extreme forms of social differentiation between finance markets and society. These arrangements, however, only had legitimacy insofar as they were able to convince others that the markets created were efficient and able to contain risk. If these two key elements were not met, the extreme social differentiation involved would, and as it happened did, start to unravel.

While the mathematization of finance has persisted as a cultural feature of markets and market analysis, it has receded in significance and plausibility with episodes of market instability and crisis. The 1987 stock market crash represented the first of these episodes, where share price fluctuations and volatility were far in advance of that predicted in financial models that assumed markets typically priced in risk in an effective manner. One of the heroic assumptions underlying the new financial economics is the efficient market thesis. This argues that markets price new information into share prices because if they did not there would be endless opportunities for highly lucrative arbitrage. This thesis assumes perfect information, which is a debatable one in the light of insider trading and differential access to information sources between large institutions and private investors, on the one hand, and small retail investors, on the other. However, the challenge of the 1987 crash for this thesis was to explain how markets fell so much without any new injection of information.

Further shocks in the late 1990s occurred with the fall of the giant hedge fund Long Term Capital Management (LTCM), with catastrophic losses for its investors and negative effects on the global financial system. These arose, at least in part, from the large number of derivatives contracts that could no longer be fulfilled and were thus 'left hanging'. LTCM was basically in the business of arbitrage, identifying very temporary price differences that could be used to make money. It also used current risk management practices that sought to identify and minimize potential losses and believed it had taken a conservative stance towards risk. When it failed, the question was why? It had significantly leveraged its market trading but not excessively so for the sector as a whole. The 1998 Russian default on its rouble–debt and a subsequent shift by investors to 'quality' investments was one major contributing problem for the market as a whole, and this helped fuel a panic withdrawal of investors' funds to such an extent that it exceeded the assumptions about worst-case outcomes on which LTCM's arbitrage operated. While its own investors' funds were locked in beyond the short term, other financial institutions' funds were not. A more sociological way of understanding the flight of funds is to say that many investment houses imitated the strategies of large players such as LTCM, and their withdrawals constituted such an extreme event that it was not catered for in the mathematical modelling used by traders. This in turn suggests the limits of purely economistic reasoning in understanding global finance, something again demonstrated in the recent GFC.

Put another way, the competitive but uncertain worlds of financial trading cannot simply be understood as exercises in calculation and rational strategies of self-interest, whether by individuals or institutions. This is not to downplay the importance of mathematical and statistical disciplines in the strategic shift to arbitrage trading. But it is to emphasize a wide-ranging set of extra-economic modes of market behaviour and performance that are not simply about individual psychological dispositions of greed and feed. Such extra-economic factors include a range of component parts. These include social or collective psychological processes such as imitation and 'herd' behaviour. But they also include ways of dealing with the uncertainties and periodic crises of the financial world, by reference to qualities such as reputation, judgement, and experience, which set quantitative methodologies of market analysis within a wider set of qualitative social judgements.

Central bankers

Central bankers represent important social actors within global finance, located as they are within the interface between nation-states and global financial processes. While they have recently gained considerable autonomy from government, they remain a crucial element within public policies with respect to the economy. At the core of their work is the setting of official short-term interest rates to create the conditions for economic growth without either excessive inflation or recession. Alongside interest rate policy, central banks may also create liquidity in the system, when recession deepens. Finally, there are on-going supervisorial responsibilities over financial markets in most jurisdictions, whereby private sector behaviour can be influenced in varying ways, if central banks wish to do so.

Central bank policy settings are therefore crucial to market expansion of an orderly kind. Yet there are considerable tensions and dilemmas in performing this role. Some of these centre on the kind of balance to be struck between fighting inflation and allowing rapid growth to proceed unchecked. Others centre on the problem that stabilization in one area of the economy, such as prices, may create instability in others, such as employment. In the last three decades, central banks have tended to focus on inflation-fighting, leaving employment levels for governments to regulate.

These concerns are, moreover, global as much as national. Central banks are key institutions within nation-states, yet processes of economic globalization such as the growing mobility of capital and increased cross-border interdependence mean that they play an important role within global deliberations, centred on the Bank for International Settlements and the feeding through of policy advice to intergovernmental bodies such as the G8 and G20.

In the light of these considerations, it is not surprising to find that the cultural world of central bankers is rather different to that of traders. A former Swiss banker puts the contrast as follows:

> If you see a trading pit, emotional energy is expended and people are acting on gut instinct and emotion. ... When you get to a central bank ... every effort is made to suppress any of that. ... They are aloof, cloistered away.

Such characteristics of sober deliberation are linked in part to time-frames. Whereas traders may need to take decisions in split sections, central bankers can be more deliberative. The committees that debate and set interest rates typically meet on a monthly basis, and seek consensus based on analysis of evidence, past history, and, in the words of participants, 'the art of judgement'. Whereas trading floors have little or no need of market memory, central bankers draw on memory of past events and decisions extensively. They may take a number of months to ascertain whether inflationary trends are becoming potentially dangerous. They must also bear in mind the serious impact that may be made both by their decisions and by the way that they publicly express them. This applies especially to the US Federal Reserve whose policies influence bond rates, stock markets, and global confidence. This undoubtedly breeds a kind of public reticence, especially as to the dangerous potential created by future uncertainties, over issues such as the adequacy of bank deposits to meet highly leveraged loans.

However, the aloofness and relatively time-consuming procedures of central banking also raise wider criticism that these key financial actors are out of touch – albeit in a way that is different to traders. This criticism recurs even though central bank deliberation is now more transparent with the publication of the proceedings of committees that deal with the setting of interest rates. In an interesting panel discussion organized by the *American Journal of Economics and Sociology*, a group of panellists were asked to consider whether the personality of central bankers matters to the conduct of policy. One striking way of putting this is to ask whether policy would be better, 'If the leader of the central bank did card tricks and told jokes?' This question arose in part through the US experience of central bankers addressing the Banking Committee of the US Senate. Could criticism of bankers' aloofness and reticence be partly overcome if they were perceived to share more everyday personal qualities such as humour?

For Pixley, a participant in this panel, jokes might make things worse. Given the ignorance of the public as to the global operations of credit and debt markets, let alone the more esoteric world of derivatives, jokes about uncertainty might simply magnify fear. Yet the refusal to take on a greater element of financial education suggests central bankers are far more oriented to financial markets than any other audience. Fear of making mistakes may encourage a habitual reticence that at best speaks in a coded language to other professionals and at worse amounts to a kind of 'leadership from behind' through impression management.

Summing up, we may say that the worlds of traders and of central bankers are as much a cultural as a technically rational world. Analysis, statistical inference, and techniques of risk assessment matter to both, yet they are in their different ways characterized by cultural dispositions, which in many cases take the form of emotions – cool as well as hot. Culture – in terms of prevailing forms of identity, trust between market participants, and the valuation of autonomous markets as socially legitimate ways of behaving – feeds into the ways in which global traders do business. Participants watch and study each other, sometimes directly, sometimes mediated through network intelligence and gossip – not simply the decontextualized flows of numbers on the screens before them. Central bankers, meanwhile, rely on appeals to long-term experience of previous episodes of crisis, and on the intangible 'reputation' of those such as Alan Greenspan, long-time chairman of the US Federal Reserve Bank, in responding to challenges, largely because uncertainty and the indeterminacy of statistical analysis creates a need for alternative cultural supports such as 'trust'.

This cultural dimension often lies below the surface and is either taken for granted or unacknowledged by participants. Yet it remains important, as demonstrated in crises when things go wrong, when unforseen events make implicit features of finance explicit and the subject of social and political commentary, conflict, and political attention. Herd behaviour among traders is barely noticed except when the consensus position is wrong and vast sums of money are lost. Bankers' worlds are based on cooler emotions around the preservation of a reputation for riding success-fully through crises without rocking the boat. The dilemma for a democracy here is whether underlying financial processes and problems should require a greater degree of transparency from central bankers in the light of the GFC, or whether this function is better left to politicians, academics, educators, and specialist journalists.

Global finance and the wider society

In spite of the autonomy that finance markets claim from close forms of cultural and political control, there remain many points of connection between global finance and the wider social domains of which they are part. These, however, take a particular form in an epoch of globalization, where the 'society' that finance is linked with is not simply that of indi-vidual nation-states and national finance sectors, but also of a wider array of global and regional forms of cultural connection and governance.

How then should connections between markets and society be best understood? The over-arching approach of economic sociology is to speak of the social construction of markets. At least three broad perspectives have been used to identify what 'social construction' means; namely, the political, the network and the framing approach. These are not necessarily mutually exclusive and can be combined to a degree as indicated below.

The political approach to markets is broader than government and legislation, being concerned with the deployment of power to shape the rules which govern markets. Many initiatives from within the global financial sector seek to set such rules as far as possible without external political legislation, or at least through political governance mechanisms closely linked to markets. In the important global derivatives market, for example, the International Swaps and Derivatives Association (ISDA) brings together all significant market players in a series of committees that have drawn up a master agreement to which all subscribe. Most nation-states see the issues involved as technical and regard such processes as a matter of financial expertise. Beyond this there is a more public overview of derivatives and other financial markets through the central bankers' Bank for International Settlements in Basel. This is largely concerned with issues of potential instability within the sector and in redesigning the architecture of private capital markets to prevent crises. In cycles of financial development and expansion, governments largely rely on central banks to exercise macroprudential governance. It is only in crises that they become more centrally involved, supporting broad policy initiatives through intergovernmental bodies such as the G8 and G20. A major example is the periodic moves to tighten banks' capital reserve requirements in the series of Basel agreements.

The second approach to the social construction of markets focuses on networks, an issue already raised in the analysis of market trading and trading rooms. The value of network analysis may have been over-stated in particular markets such as the spot market for foreign exchange considered above. This is because spot markets require little of their participants other than a very brief exchange of immediate prices offered and sought out. The kind of trust involved in longer-term transactions is not really required.

Yet in other forms of trading, networks remain significant, and extend beyond actual trading to governance processes. Thus in the example of derivatives, already mentioned, the ISDA engages its members and associated professional experts in a decentralized network to influence or bend national rules to maximize the autonomy of derivatives markets. This approach meshes with the political approach insofar as networks are a means through which power circulates. The emphasis here remains on governance linking networks of bankers and traders, more than government through representative parliamentary organizations and state fiat. Market regulation across the board typically takes this form, with networks of industry associations, experts, and professional bodies linked with a wider set of international bodies such as the EU and WTO, as well as the BIS. Central banks such as the US Federal Reserve, Bank of England, and the European Central Bank are also key players here, with executive powers to set national or regional interest rates in the interest of financial stability, as well as an overview of global trends. Since the GFC, a greater awareness of the desirability of global co-ordination has intensified global regulatory networks.

The third approach to the social construction of markets has been termed a 'framing approach'. Associated with analysts such as the French sociologist Michel Callon, this represents an application of actor network theory to social studies of finance. Markets, in this perspective, are constructed through forms of understanding linked with technologies and objects. Markets are 'framed' in this cognitive sense, through the interaction of persons and objects that are free from social and moral obligations, and structured through processes of calculation (e.g. the Scholes–Black equation) and calculation machines (Bloomberg trading terminals) that identify predictable, sustainable, and legitimate sequences of prices that form the basis for trading. In terms of derivative markets, this approach refers not simply to trading rooms, but also to governance processes which legitimate particular ways of framing markets. The most notable of these are the ideas that finance markets can be scientifically demonstrated to be efficient, and thus require little external regulation. Those such as economists and leading traders seeking to create markets for new financial products represent epistemic communities around markets. They are differentiated from alternative ways of framing markets, whether as hotbeds of greed or unstable forms of speculation parasitical on the 'real' economy of producers and consumers.

Market framing of these various kinds produces debates, new forms of understanding, and changing forms of governance, in which external policy processes are significant. Even though global financial markets over the last thirty years were able for much of the time to persuade regulators and public policy-makers of the desirability of largely unregulated specialist markets for products such as derivatives, this broader climate no longer prevails, whether we look at politics, networks, and cognitive understandings of markets.

Andrew Haldane indicates how circumstances have changed in a number of senses. First, the complexity and profound interconnections of global finance have to be better understood among traders, public regulators, and government. This requires better understanding of risk, and uncertainty. Second, drawing on analogies from epidemiological understandings of the dynamics of disease, regulators need to develop ways of controlling or 'vaccinating' super-spreaders of financial risk against financial risk contagion. Third, system–wide financial architecture requires serious review in the light of its vulnerability to the complex interaction of financial claims and obligations. Global finance has hitherto assessed risk atomistically, at the level of the firm or node within a firm, rather than the system as a whole. In the crisis, official agreement to let Lehman Brothers fail, given the huge irredeemable gap between its assets and liabilities, created complicated and negative effects for trading partners that were not fully appreciated and which took months to unravel. For

Haldane, policy-makers navigated in a dense fog when they came to tackle the dynamics of the failing financial system.

Conclusion

This chapter has covered the social processes that finance markets often take for granted. In the light of the GFC, these are now evident for all to see. In other words, the focus moves beyond exclusive reliance on the structures of global finance and financial markets to the broader but hitherto neglected theme of the cultures of finance. These are explored by examining the social actors involved, moving beyond the stereotypes about traders and bankers that abound in popular culture. This alternative focus may not suit populist appetites for stories about bankers and traders that portray them simplistically as greedy demonic figures. Yet it is necessary to go beyond stereotypes if we are to understand the micro-level interactions that constitute markets.

This world is also of little analytical interest to economists who retain a conventional focus on rationality and calculation, centred only on those processes that can be measured. The alternative cultural emphasis evident in the sociology of finance gives a broader account of the practical worlds of traders and bankers, worlds which are constituted both through new information technology and through interpersonal networks of judgement and trust. These are central to any understanding of global finance. They extend the macro-level focus on financial institutions and power discussed in Chapter 3, with a micro-level focus that brings people back into the picture. This peopling of global finance, discussed here in relation to traders and central bankers, helps explain the meanings financial actors give to their actions, moving beyond simple psychological propensities, to a broader sociology of motives, emotions, trust, and judgement.

We turn in the following chapter to a general re-statement of why a new start is required in understanding how finance works, and why this requires abandonment of the utopian expectations that surround market ideology.

5

SOCIETY AND FINANCE

An alternative theoretical approach

A fundamental revision of the way economic life is popularly understood is well overdue. While the theoretical basis for this revision has been around for many years, and grown in stature and coherence over the last twenty years, public debates around the GFC still remain wedded to older inadequate ways of thinking. The social and political trauma of the GFC does, however, create an opportunity to push this revision forward. So in this short chapter an attempt will be made to summarize and assess what a new approach could add to an understanding of global finance.

The theoretical starting point

A key move in re-thinking finance is the choice of analytical starting point. Where theories start from, privileges some ways of thinking so fundamentally that it is very difficult to modify or re-think such theories further down the track. Theoretical habits die hard, especially when allied with cherished values. This is especially the case with values that are so deeply held that they are rarely made explicit or seriously scrutinized.

In the case of markets, the conventional starting point among economists is a set of actors invested with rationality and self-interest, and sensitive to price signals. Market processes play out in terms of patterns of supply and demand, and processes of competition between suppliers of desired commodities. The assumption is made that market players can rationally determine their interests and order their preferences. The markets that arise on this basis are seen as an efficient means of matching a range of individual preferences, using money as a sensitive measure of value and means of exchange. This picture is of course deliberately simple to identify the logic of markets. Generations of economists have complicated the simple picture, bringing in firms as organizations, problems of imperfect information, limits to rationality, and challenges posed by risk.

Where then do deeply-held values enter the picture? What kind of problems are created thereby? And how does this relate to global finance?

The value-assumptions underlying this depiction of markets are grounded in the philosophy of liberalism as applied to economic life. Taken in its broadest sense, liberalism values the freedom and autonomy of individuals as rational self-governing actors. Further, the relationships which individuals enter should protect and nurture this autonomy or freedom. Economic relationships in the marketplace should therefore be indifferent to the particular values and wants that individuals have. Markets are seen, in the words of Adam Smith, as systems of natural liberty, in that they are neutral between individual wants. Individual freedom and autonomy, and the indifference of institutions to particular wants, are the ultimate values that ideologists of free markets draw upon to criticize state intervention and heavy-handed regulation of markets. The moral struggle is reduced to two basic positions. On the one hand are the supporters of economic freedom and efficiency, individual autonomy, and a liberal world of free-standing actors. On the other, external forms of control that tend to subordinate individual freedom and efficiency to state-centred objectives that are both coercive and inefficient.

There is no doubt that liberalism, in its moral and political as well as economic forms, has been and continues to be a major social reference point in the modern world. Moral and political forms of liberalism tend to be critical of the atomistic assumptions of economic liberalism, displacing markets as an exclusively privileged mode of social life in favour of political citizenship rights, welfare-rights, and constraints on excessive market power. Liberalism has been a major force in both the struggle for the vote and the welfare state, alongside socialism. More radical criticisms of economic liberalism for its neglect of the coercive elements in market power obviously represent an enduring line of Socialist criticism, often couched in terms of theories of capitalism rather than the more neutral language of markets.

Criticisms of markets from many quarters have intensified both during the recent expansion of economic globalization and, as we have seen, during the GFC. Markets now and in the past have failed at key points to secure steady and orderly economic development with social justice, as indicated by recurrent crises discussed in the previous chapter. And finance markets involving banking and public sector debt have usually been disproportionately involved in crisis.

Why then has the liberal view of markets not been displaced as an intellectual starting point? Why, indeed, is the very idea of 'market failure' relatively unused in public discourse? And how is it that in the very midst of crisis, market ideologues reject revival strategies based on tighter market regulation and public policy intervention?

It is perhaps not surprising that market ideologues committed to markets as part of a fundamentalist world-view seek ways in which to wriggle out of the challenges posed by market failure. One response, typical during the cold war, was to argue that there are only two options for economic policy: markets or command economies on the Soviet model. Since the latter were both inefficient and coercive, they fail as an alternative, leaving markets, however problematic, in command of the ideological battlefield. The assumption that there are only two options is, however, most unsatisfactory, given the complex reality of public policy and regulatory arrangements. Leaving aside whether there is a coherent 'third way' between markets and command economies, it is preferable to see multiple choices being available in terms of different modes and levels of market regulation. In the financial sector, for example, public regulation of banking at national, regional, and/or global levels is a reality, but one in which the ground is constantly shifting between different combinations of multi-level governance. Within this sphere, regulation takes different forms in different sectors of finance, and has recently been stronger in relation to some products rather than others. Meanwhile, central banks may take somewhat different views of policy objectives, and have differing relationships with government over time. To speak in terms of stark choices between regulation or de-regulation is far too simplistic a way of dealing with the range of options possible. It is how you regulate, not whether you regulate, that lies at the heart of the issue.

Market ideologues typically bypass all of this. Markets seem not to fail. When they go wrong, it is because they are too heavily or clumsily regulated. Thus the GFC occurred not because of any problems with markets, but because bodies such as the US Federal Reserve did not do their job properly, or because regulatory environment is too complex a jigsaw of multiple jurisdictions.

This line of objection has more credibility because regulatory arrangements may and have had faults, the precise details of which are sketched in the next chapter. For current purposes though, the main difficulty with this defence is that it wriggles away once again from the question of market failure and market inefficiency, leaving de-regulated markets as the default setting for analysis and policy choice. The probability that certain regulatory processes failed does not entail the view that markets did all right after all. It speaks rather to combinations of market and regulatory failure.

Let us then re-state the direct criticism that can be made of market ideologies in relation to finance. It is that finance markets have failed repeatedly through the history of modern capitalism, reflected in banking crises, corporate failure, bankruptcy, and most recently huge bail-outs from the public sector to recapitalize corporations regarded as too big to fail. And there are theoretical reasons why this is so. These are connected to problems of risk and uncertainty that are endemic to credit, the lynchpin of finance in general, and global finance in particular. Credit is necessarily future-oriented. It requires a set of promises to repay at some future point, and acceptance of payment. This future-oriented dimension is not adequately captured in depictions of markets as a series of completed transactions at a given moment in time based on rationally discerned information.

Frank Knight, as has previously been pointed out, famously distinguished between risk and uncertainty. Risk relates to future contingencies, the probability of which may be calculated. Uncertainty deals with those that cannot. Finance markets have always been prone to both risk and uncertainty. However, recent advances in financial theory seemed to suggest that the sphere of calculable risk could be mastered, and thus be priced effectively into markets. In this way, uncertainty could be minimized and the future-oriented nature of credit, now organized on a global scale, could be controlled. This re-affirmed the idea of market actors as knowledgeable, and markets as efficient. The reasoning here is that it is in everyone's interest to find under-priced assets and buy them before others catch up and prices rise, while over-priced assets can be sold on the same logic. This practice of arbitrage, based on widely dispersed information, so it is supposed, makes markets necessarily efficient.

Market actors may deploy rational calculation and sophisticated statistical analysis, but this is no guarantee that this enables them to correctly price risk. Whereas the conventional starting point of market economics presumes that rationality applied to information-gathering combined with self-interest are adequate means of disciplining market behaviour to achieve efficient outcomes, this scenario breaks down when rational calculations are not sufficient. This could be because knowledge is not widely available, though if so this may be regarded as a market imperfection that can in principle be corrected. An alternative possibility is that there are epistemological limits to what can be known about the future, or, as put colloquially by Donald Rumsfeld, we don't know what we don't know.

A minority of economists including Keynes, and more recent thinkers such as Shackle, have been aware that uncertainty is a bigger problem than most market analysts presumed. It is, however, a recent string of financial crises culminating in the GFC that have brought home problems with innovations in financial theory that promised to control risk and minimize uncertainty. This process has been brilliantly analysed by Donald Mckenzie in *An Engine Not a Camera* (2006). He shows how financial theory appeared to have overcome a good deal of the problem of risk by a series of mathematical innovations. These treated stock price movements as random, but identified patterns in the volatility of individual stocks vis-à-vis the market as a whole. As we saw in Chapter 4, the innovative Black–Scholes–Merton equations appeared to solve the difficult problem of calculating the current value of the projected future income and expenditure flows involved in trading assets. Using the formula in its early years seemed to work. Future-oriented action seemed, at least within these technical parameters, to be risk-free.

But as we also saw in Chapter 4, the continuing incidence of financial stress – especially in the 1990s and 2000s – has rendered this apparent victory over risk dubious. An underlying problem with the approach was the underestimation of the probability of extreme events and this derived in large measure from the assumption that the distribution of such events followed the pattern of a normal distribution. In statistical theory, a normal distribution means that the probability of extreme, highly atypical events is very rare. The French mathematician Mandlebrot had already shown this was not the case for financial markets, but financial theorists were not convinced. The GFC, following on from previous events such as the collapse of the hedge fund LTCM in 1996, proved their scepticism to be ill-founded. Extreme events are not so rare after all.

What theoretical implications does all this have for an understanding of finance markets?

First, it suggests that rational calculation is not enough to prevent financial crisis and the destructive consequences that follow from it. This is partly for epistemological reasons. Epistemology involves the theory of knowledge, or put another way, how sure can we be that particular claims to knowledge are valid. The epistemological problems in finance are to do with the existence of limits to our capacity to calculate and hedge against risk. These problems were ignored during the heyday of financialization over the twenty years when the confident hubris of market players carried regulators with it, multiplying risk and undermining prudence.

Second, it suggests that financial markets are neither entirely rational nor necessarily efficient either. Just because markets may tend to factor in new information very quickly for fear of missing out on profitable opportunities does not mean that markets are necessarily efficient. Information, as we saw in the previous chapter, is limitless, and thus has to be both perceived and interpreted as relevant to transactions. It may be that potentially relevant information is known but not deemed relevant. The huge leverage ratios where institutions lent out funds up to thirty times the value of their deposits was clearly known on the eve of recent crisis but not considered a significant risk. Another indication of the weaknesses of the market efficiency argument is that crises can emerge, such as the stock market collapse of 1987, even without new information entering the market.

Rational calculation combined with self-interest is not an adequate starting point for an understanding of the dynamics of markets in general, and finance markets in particular. This point may be put more strongly than that. Such assumptions are a very weak starting point because they leave out so much. Among the omissions are first the structures of power and influence that markets generate that undermine the ideal of a system of natural liberty shared by free-standing individuals. These include structures of economic power, reflected in the capacity of financial interests to create new forms of lucrative financial markets and to lobby governments to regulate (or de-regulate) markets in ways that suit investors. Bond-holders are currently able to exercise financial power over the fate of indebted nation-states, by demanding such high interest rates from newly issued government bonds that the interest payments required come close to bankrupting state finances – unless other remedial actions such as savage expenditure cuts are made.

In an epoch of financialization, the centre of gravity of economic power involves investors in a range of financial institutions linked not simply with banks, but also hedge funds and private equity firms linked with bond markets as well as share markets, and with a host of financial derivatives. This suggests the bottom-up micro foundations of market theory are incomplete because they are inadequate to deal with top-down macro-level asymmetries of power between the finance sector, governments, and households. Finance, for example, through the bond-market, can determine medium to long-term interest rates on government debt, while households are vulnerable to global financial crises that undermine the values of savings and pensions, and increase unemployment.

In the worlds of public fiscal crises of expenditure or downward pressure on household welfare, the underlying normative ideals of market freedom based on free-standing and autonomous social actors seems out of place and irrelevant.

Beyond this, a second set of omissions surround the endemic problems of risk and uncertainty. Following the analysis of Jocelyn Pixley, finance markets build emotions and other kinds of intuitive dispositions into their operations precisely to handle the uncertainties of the future which render trust in others problematic. Calculation can only work reliably in relation to the past. It is far more difficult to apply successfully and over the medium to long term to the future. This argument is worthy of further elaboration because the role of emotions in markets is often misconceived.

Recent developments in sociological theory suggest that the place of the emotions in social and economic life has often been misconceived. A major problem here is a false dichotomy between rationality, on the one hand, and emotions on the other. Whereas rationality is seen as cold and calculating, emotions are seen as necessarily hot, passionate, and irrational.

This approach is typically linked with a second argument in which emotions are removed from any social context and regarded either as matters of innate personal psychology or 'animal spirits' – the term famously used by Keynes to depict the spontaneous rush to action characteristic of speculation.

Sociology diagnoses two major problems here. The first is that the span of emotions has a wider range than the conventional emphasis on passions implies. Hope, grief, sadness, optimism, and gut feeling may all be regarded as emotions, in that they are dispositions distinct from calculations of self-interest and abstract processes of cognition. The sharp dichotomy between rationality and emotionality tends to obscure that part of the register of feelings that is neither impulsive nor strictly calculative. It is, however, precisely within this register that many of the dispositions of financial traders and central bankers operate.

Traders, for example, tend to imitate each other, assuming that success will breed success, rather than being moved simply by statistical calculation, leading to the so-called 'herd' behaviour evident in both the periodic heady peaks and the dismal collapses that markets generate. As Pixley demonstrates, central bankers, even Alan Greenspan of the US Federal Reserve, combine analysis of evidence with hope and gut feeling. Even if many bankers reject the idea that there is an emotional element in their financial dealings, they do recognize both the problem of future uncertainty and the role of non-calculative dispositions. These were described variously in Pixley's interviews with bankers, in terms ranging from intuitive feelings linked to an 'inner voice', 'gut feeling', and 'prognostications about the future'. One of the most interesting examples draws on the German word *entschiedungsfreudig*, which may be translated as the joy in making decisions. This was used by a former bank official now providing advice to financial executives as a 'filter' for dealing with fear and uncertainty in financial transactions.

A second related area of misconception in the handling of emotions in finance surrounds the source of emotions. The conventional way of interpreting these is either as products of individual psychology or basic features of human nature. This approach neglects the social contexts in which emotions arise as means of dealing with the exigencies of life ranging from bereavement and suffering to financial uncertainty and fear of failure. Behavioural psychology has made a start in suggesting a broader framework, though it does not take the analysis far enough. Robert

Shiller, for example, in *Market Volatility* (1989) and *Irrational Exuberance* (2000), provides plentiful survey evidence of emotional feelings among investors. However, these feelings are seen as strongest among those prone to herd behaviour, swayed by the financial media. So-called 'smart' investors have a different psychology. Yet in Pixley's account, even the smartest are not immune from the social challenges of uncertainty which are endemic in future-oriented transactions based on promises. From a sociological viewpoint, variations in individual psychological propensities are therefore less significant than the social characteristics of the relationships that finance promotes and tries to reproduce.

We spoke above about a set of omissions in the typical starting point in economic analysis that focused on rational calculation and self-interest alone. Two types of omission involved first structures of power and domination in economic life, and second, problems of risk and uncertainty. A third level of omissions in conventional accounts of markets, that has been stressed throughout this study, involves the ways in which politics and culture constitute and contribute to the reproduction of markets. This occurs through security of property rights, legal regulation, public policy support for infrastructure and the training of human capital, and bail-outs to cope with market failure. These inputs may be seen as contextual to markets rather than essential to its functioning. Yet to argue in this way encourages a slippage from acknowledging the social and political preconditions for markets, back to the idealized starting point of rational self-interested actors jealous of their freedom and autonomy.

It is therefore time to replace the language of market freedom contrasted with external intervention with a new language that is more sensitive to what may be called social-economics or economic sociology. In this discourse, markets, states, and cultures interact in a complex set of ways, often articulated through public policy. To refuse this new language is to leave in place an ideologically loaded world view masquerading as powerful and relevant analysis. So why hasn't this occurred before?

The answer is a mixture of two considerations. One is the continuing normative force of the utopia of free markets. The other is scepticism that an alternative approach to economic analysis, based on a new starting point, is possible.

Utopias are widespread in social life, and show no sign of receding. They include visions of a harmonious and peaceful cosmopolitan world, an environmentally sustainable way of life, global religious community to end suffering, and the restoration of authentic national communities of like-minded citizens. Yet dystopias are also present, from endemic wars of civilizations without end, to the collapse of inner cities into violence, and the abject failure of states to guarantee security and an orderly life in the face of crime, corruption, and rampant poverty.

Market freedom, in this context, gains most of its utopian force from the presumption that self-interest is a universal human attribute, but that its operation can be civilized. Following the analysis of Adam Smith, this occurs through a combination of the spontaneous order that markets bring – the famous invisible hand – and public regulation of a market-complementing kind. It is arguable that financial markets do not and cannot approach this utopia, both because of their tremendous power and because the problem of uncertainty renders them crisis-prone and destructive. If the free market utopia persists, in spite of all evidence to its lack of accord with evidence, it must either be because other dystopia induce greater horror than that of financial crisis, or because financial utopians believe that pragmatic public authorities will always come to the rescue.

The dystopian foil that ideals of market freedom presuppose relies on some notion of coercive authoritarianism. If markets are either abolished or rigidly controlled as in command economies, then individual freedom and autonomy is undermined. But what if markets have coercive or authoritarian effects, whether in the abuse of cheap labour or reckless lending that ends in bankruptcy and loss of savings? That it seems is not enough to destroy the utopia. However, regulation to ratchet up labour standards or regulate speculation is very often portrayed as such a threat. The utopia is thus founded on arbitrary presumptions and forms of implausible rhetoric. It should be abandoned freeing economic analysis from its utopian anchorage and starting again.

This new start requires the abandonment of utopias of the two alternative free markets and perfect regulation. Each leads to unexpected failure and periodic crisis. Making a new start also means adopting options that are philosophically more sophisticated in that they recognize the intrinsic uncertainties and limits to knowledge that constitute the future-oriented uncertainties of finance markets. This alternative approach requires pragmatism rather than utopianism. It also benefits from a less economistic, more sociological approach.

The economy and finance: a sociological and interdisciplinary approach

Finance and the economy are part of society. This seems obvious. Yet it currently makes little real sense to the way 'insiders' in financial worlds understand the industry, or to the way most policy-makers and regulators typically justify their actions. This is partly because of the scientific reputation of economics, and partly, as I have argued here, because of the moral and utopian foundations underpinning pro-market ideologies. Unless this utopian world view is cut down to size, finance markets are destined to fail repeatedly in the future, creating adverse social as much as economic consequences. The finance sector will become even less legitimate than it is now and populist pressure on governments to rein in bankers will increase the likelihood of knee-jerk policy reactions. Such pressures do not, however, mean that global finance markets should be abandoned and finance de-globalized. Rather, it means that the policy and regulatory options should try to maximize prudence in relation to risk, and bridge the growing gulf between finance and society.

Concrete policy and regulatory measures are discussed in the following chapter. I concentrate here on further dimensions to a sociological understanding of global finance.

A key element of this approach is that the study of finance needs to be re-cast in a systematic manner to take account of the interaction of social and economic processes. Law, politics, culture, and social psychology matter to the foundation of markets, to their internal operation, and to their creative performance, dynamics, and limitations. Applying a sociological approach is not simply to do with enriching a sense of market mentalities, including greed, fear, panic, imitation, gut feeling, prudence, and joy in making a good deal, alongside rational calculation – though this broader psychology is very helpful to the understanding of the complex worlds of traders and bankers. Sociology, however, can do more than this.

Building on a more complex social psychology offers ways of understanding how cultural expectations, and senses of trust and legitimacy, perform a number of functions within financial markets. Above all, they assist market actors to meet challenges associated with both the uncertainties and the future-oriented characteristics of finance. The possibility of radical uncertainty and crisis could paralyse market actors. Yet this generally does not happen. This is partly because market players have to trust each other – at least enough to complete transactions. It is also because market actors trust the calculative methods they employ. They also assume that their activities are legitimate because they meet wider expectations that increase shareholder value for financial institutions, which is a desirable end – not least because it maximizes their income and welfare, as well as that of others. In normal times, all this is taken for granted and becomes a habitual feature of financial worlds. But in crises, these underlying foundations of finance are starkly revealed. What is also revealed is a weak sense of responsibility for the failures of finance markets.

Whereas in normal times, the autonomy and differentiation of markets from the worlds of culture and politics is taken for granted, in a major crisis such as the GFC, it becomes problematized. Traders and bankers are seen as greedy and selfish, unethical, and too cut-off from public and community concerns and anxieties. Calls for their bonuses to be extinguished, their taxes to be increased, and for their priorities to be more ethical and socially responsible abound. While for economists these are so to speak 'noises off stage', for sociologists, these calls speak both to the continuing location of finance in society and to crises of the dysfunctional or pathological effects of financial freedom. The senses of dysfunction occur within nations, but they are also very much a response to the globalization of financial markets, beyond the apparent control of democratic politics which is primarily expressed at national or (in the case of Europe) regional levels. Differentiation of global finance from society, therefore, has national and global dimensions, and both of these spill over into politics, where policy and public regulatory deliberations are centred. And again in a deep crisis such as the GFC, politics intervenes, with bail outs of public money to keep institutions afloat.

The conceptual repertoire of sociology also describes problems of differentiation and integration through metaphors of embedding and disembedding. The embedding of economy in society is reflected in closer relations between markets, politics, and culture, characteristic of pre-industrial and pre-modern worlds. It is reflected in doctrines such as just prices and moral responsibilities to individuals and groups adversely affected by economic change. The disembedding of markets from society is associated with modern processes of market autonomy and doctrines of laissez-faire economics. Karl Polanyi, the Hungarian economic historian and social philosopher, author of *The Great Transformation* (1944), thought laissez-faire impossible to sustain since societies would always demand a sense of social responsibility from markets. Welfare states represent one form this could take in modern societies. Polanyi has proven a great inspiration to the development of economic sociology. Yet financialization tied to late twentieth-century globalization created, as we have seen, a new phase of laissez-faire akin to the nineteenth-century phases of market-based economic globalization that Polanyi thought of almost as a historical aberration. It seems then that modern economies have a more cyclical dynamic, with waves of market-led economic expansion followed by crisis, disembedding followed by calls to re-embed, differentiation followed by challenges of re-integration.

In a general sense, then, sociology encourages accounts of how economy, culture, and polity interact. This is built around three elements: theories of social action under conditions of uncertainty, concepts of the embedding and disembedding of the economy in society, and theories of social differentiation and re-integration. These apply both across phases of apparently normal market-operation and phases of crisis when the pathologies of social differentiation apply are clearly manifest. Equally, they embrace both the structures of financial power and financialization, discussed in Chapter 3, and the cultural worlds of traders and bankers.

Sociology offers broader insights than economics alone, but it is equally the case that global finance demands an even wider interdisciplinary focus. This embraces history and geography so as to integrate time and space within the analysis of finance markets. Without history, it would not be possible to fully gauge the repeated patterns of global financial boom and bust, nor compare and contrast the performance of policy options tried in the past. Meanwhile a greater awareness of spatial patterns indicates both how varied are the origins of financial innovations and how far global cities and global networks linked by new information technology are involved in the complex sets of nodes and links that constitute global finance. And beyond this, mathematics and statistics are necessary to an understanding of measurable features of global finance. Whereas the insights of sociology have hitherto been primarily qualitative, it is clear that finance is inseparable from quantification. Sociology can nonetheless add to the repertoire of quantifiable questions that may be asked of finance, including 'How far are financial arrangements socially legitimate?', 'What forms of market differentiation are dysfunctional to social arrangements?', and 'What properties of financial networks increase system risk?'

What is more debatable though is the meaning and reliability of conventional statistical analysis of finance markets, especially when applied to the valuation of risk and calculation of the present value of cash flows projected into the future. Here an element of epistemological caution is required, the significance of which extends far beyond philosophy to practical questions of the efficiency of markets. This suggests that the statistical orderliness of normal distributions may be inappropriate to the analysis of extreme events.

Without a sociological and even broader interdisciplinary approach to global finance it is simply not possible to understand how far finance markets are efficient, just, pathological or dysfunctional. Such considerations also feed into questions of policy reform and regulatory responses raised by the GFC, the theme of the concluding chapter.

6

GLOBAL FINANCE AND PUBLIC POLICY

The global financial crisis (GFC) dramatized failures and dilemmas in the way public policy has approached global finance. Just as financial markets failed, so too did the policy and regulatory framework surrounding finance. This 'double failure' has been partly obscured by an ideological stand-off between free marketers who blame regulators, and supporters of public regulation who blame finance markets and the laissez-faire culture of bankers. In this chapter, we ask whether there are better ways for public policy to regulate global finance. Can the endemic risks and uncertainties of this sector be approached in more effective ways? And if so, what changes are required in the institutional architecture of global finance to bring them into being?

Such questions are of course complicated by the intensification of financial globalization in recent years. This has not destroyed the nation-state and national regulation as predicted by some of the earlier theorists of globalization. But it has, nonetheless, magnified the scale of cross-border flows of finance transmitted increasingly through electronic channels and through complex sets of financial instruments. This context does not spell the end of national regulation through agencies such as the US Federal Reserve or the Bank of England that set interest rates, or through national policies on the regulation of banking, or prudential regulation of the entire finance sector. But having said this, it is equally the case that financial globalization demands better co-operation between nations in bodies such as the G20 and especially the EU. And beyond this, improvements are also required in the functioning of global institutions such as the International Monetary Fund, or the Bank for International Settlements, in the way that the global financial system is monitored and supervised and crises averted or minimized in their consequences.

Such challenges of public regulation should not of course obscure problems with de-regulated markets and the inadequate self-regulation by the finance industry of sectors such as derivatives, or processes such as credit rating. In this sense, it is improvements in the relationship between market processes and players, on the one hand, and public regulation, on the other, that matters most rather than public policy reform alone.

This chapter is also informed by the broad sociological view of finance elaborated in earlier chapters. This extends the analysis beyond finance markets bringing together investors and credit-seekers of various kinds mediated through the price of credit. Finance markets embody the pursuit of rational self-interest, but they are also arenas of risk and uncertainty, of social emotions such as trust, imitation, and panic, and places where culture and politics influence and shape judgements and the operation of financial institutions. The belief that financial players should be left alone by the rest of society so they can generate economic goods and improved welfare by operating efficient money markets is a cultural belief that many dispute, including many friends of market mechanisms.

A theoretical problem with laissez-faire assumptions of this kind is that of excessive social differentiation of economy from society. This involves a mismatch between wider cultural and political expectations of the economy and the self-centred and often self-serving world of financial traders and bankers. The sub-culture of global finance appears so differentiated from society because its denizens, particularly those at the top are buffered against the uncertainties and risks of everyday life through large salaries and bonuses and an irrational belief that market processes can be fully understood through mathematical modelling. The faltering and embarrassed stance of bankers appearing recently at televised meetings of parliamentary committees under tough questioning by parliamentarians provides an important public indication of a clash of different worlds, reflected in a severe reputational crisis for the finance industry and its leaders.

We raise this wider sociological framework here to provide a broader basis for the evaluation of the various reforms that have been proposed for global finance in the light of the GFC. Public policy initiatives may be assessed in terms of a broad range of economic objectives from their contribution to financial stability and avoidance of inflation, to economic growth and increased employment. However, broader criteria matter too, including contributions to social cohesion, the cultural legitimacy of finance, and the democratic accountability of financial markets and institutions to political processes. These criteria are partly a matter of the public reputation of bankers and the legitimacy of the finance industry, but in more extreme circumstances, of the capacity of social life and governance to continue in a sustainable way. More dire crises of this kind are evident at the time of writing in many parts of Europe, where a fiscal crisis of the state has combined with the general adverse impact of the earlier banking crisis. There are never solely market-based solutions to such crises, whether organized through cuts to public expenditure to satisfy creditors – current and future – or in terms of increased taxation to help balance books. Market problems become political problems, and political problems move beyond legislative and regulatory form, when deep-seated questions of fairness and social justice become involved. Questions therefore arise as to how various recipes for reform might assist social cohesion and restore public legitimacy and confidence.

In the light of these general considerations, we now turn to public policy initiatives proposed in the light of the GFC.

Causes of the global financial crisis

To sort out what should be done, in the light of the GFC, depends on what is taken to be the leading causes of the crisis. This is not such an easy or straightforward exercise. Howard Davies, former head of the Financial Services Authority, in his review of the GFC identifies around thirty-eight causes that have been canvassed by observers. These range from macro-economic imbalances in global trade and financial flows, through dysfunctional properties of financial markets for derivatives and regulatory failure, to broader possibilities such as an excess of testosterone in trading rooms. If trade imbalances were the key reason for crisis, then public policy responses in the field of global trade policy would be appropriate, whereas if excess testosterone were the problem, then perhaps trading rooms should operate according to a more explicit code of professional ethics designed to curb irrational exuberance and create a culture more open to women traders. Analysis does, however, have to move away from single-factor explanations and long lists of multiple causes to get very far. A more discriminating approach is to select the more important causes and consider interactions between them.

One way of doing this is to group contributory causes into three categories (see Box 6.1). These may be considered in turn.

BOX 6.1 CONTRIBUTORY CAUSES OF GFC

1. Macro-economic imbalances.
2. Market failure.
3. Policy and regulatory failure.

Macro-economic imbalances

One of the fundamental underlying causes of the GFC is widely thought to be the trade imbalance between the USA, which is the leading deficit country, and China, the leading surplus country. The existence of this imbalance means that the USA, together with some other advanced European countries, run their national economies in deficit and must rely on flows of finance into deficit countries from countries of surplus, such as China, Japan, and the oil-producing nations. Such flows are forthcoming because the USA has been seen as a safe haven for finance, and because the dollar is the leading trading currency. Such funding flows into apparently safe assets create a kind of self-insurance for surplus countries held against future uncertainties. Much of this finance is used to purchase US government debt, in the form of Treasury bonds. China has accumulated well in excess of $1 trillion of these. Global inflows of funds finance both the US trade deficit and the US government's large budget deficit.

Financial globalization in this sense keeps the US economy and government afloat. Without these financial inflows, the USA would have to increase export earnings relative to imports in a global climate of increased competition in manufacturing, and increase domestic savings, or try to resort to protectionist policies. Curtailment of imports relative to exports would also tend to limit consumer spending. Making the necessary adjustments here would be very painful economically and socially including downward pressure on employment levels, but adjustment has been inhibited by funding inflows. Even more significantly perhaps, funding inflows also underwrite two further processes: one is the government budget deficit; the other, low interest rates which in turn means cheap credit.

East Asian savings have therefore allowed the USA to postpone serious attempts to re-balance budgets, while allowing cheap credit to further boost consumption and borrowing – whether to purchase housing or financial investments. There is a clear connection here between global trade imbalances, inflows of cash to the USA, and the easy credit availability that fuelled both the sub-prime mortgage crisis in US housing and the boom in new financial investments financed by cheap money. This state of affairs is no longer sustainable and requires serious policy re-adjustment.

Policy responses to trade imbalances

Trade imbalances are seen by most observers as a crucial element behind the GFC. Insofar as this is the case, what policy responses would address this issue? Several strands of thinking are evident. The first involves trade policy and relationships between currencies. US observers regard Chinese trade surpluses, in particular, as a product of cheap global Chinese exports. Chinese products are kept cheap, by the Chinese authorities refusing to allow the Chinese *yuan* to appreciate significantly against the dollar. The USA therefore looks to Chinese policy initiatives to rectify trade imbalances, while the Chinese argue that following their own national interest requires a more cautious and less radical currency appreciation. China does not regard itself as a cause of the GFC and argues that policy adjustments and reform must occur elsewhere.

Yet it is clear to all, including China, that its continuing economic development cannot simply be sustained through export-led strategies given the size of the country. Expansion of the domestic market is therefore crucial, and some shifts in this direction are evident, though previous phases of cheap domestic credit have created an asset price bubble in Chinese real estate. Tighter fiscal policies in China have a negative global effect on

Chinese imports from the rest of the world but they do not address the problem of global imbalances. In the longer term, only a reduction in surpluses arising from greater reliance on domestic growth would assist global financial re-adjustment, and this at best would only be part of any solution.

Another way of looking at the problem of structural imbalances takes a more multilateral approach, centred on alternative mechanisms for handling the trade surpluses of developing countries. Such countries, as we have seen, look for safe havens in which to place surpluses as a form of self-insurance for future financial and economic security. Location of much these surpluses in the USA in dollar denominated assets, however, creates an artificially high level for the US dollar, again making US trade re-adjustment difficult. What then if pressures to amass self-insurance surpluses were abated?

The financial journalist Martin Wolf, amongst others, has supported initiatives directed towards support for developing countries facing trade deficits and currency crises that would reduce the search for surplus and security. These include a greater role for the IMF in providing short-term non-conditional liquidity at an early stage in crises to ward off greater financial instability, building on the IMF scheme 'New Arrangements to Borrow' begun in 2008. This would need an expansion in the resources of the IMF, including an expansion in the special drawing rights (SDR) scheme run by the IMF which acts as a quasi-currency. Far more radical ideas of working towards a single world currency that would offer alternative mechanisms for re-balancing of trade relationships without financial instability have been canvassed but are not at this stage seen as politically practical. This reflects the unevenness of globalization which is far more extensive in terms of cross-border financial transactions than in monetary policy-making and financial governance.

Another way of looking at these issues argues that global imbalances may only be problematic if they inhibit sounder macro-economic policies. If US policies encouraged greater economic flexibility in response to trade competition, and if public expenditure deficits were lessened, then a more effective policy environment would better enable the USA to deal with the stresses inherent in finance markets. Neither seems likely, hence the need to perpetuate huge flows of finance.

Policy criteria here may well be seen as too focused on particular national policy settings, and insufficiently directed to more multilateral ways of thinking about how to achieve world development and poverty-reduction without financial dislocation. Martin Wolf puts it well when he argues that global finance in the lead up to the GFC had the effect of funding a rich-country real estate boom at a point when it could have been far better invested in infrastructural development in poorer countries. International monetary policy would, however, need to be reformed significantly if this were to happen.

The rise of the G20 with its wider representation of developing countries, in the aftermath of the GFC, certainly offers the possibility of a more widely drawn global debate and improved global action. In the absence of effective global macro-economic agreement among powerful economic forces such as the USA and China, the more mundane discussions at G20 level on co-ordinated approaches to global imbalances are likely to get nowhere. This, by itself, does not mean that global financial instability will continue unabated, because there are a number of additional causes of crisis that need to be taken into account. Global imbalances may therefore have helped pave the way for crisis, but they are not sufficient as an explanation for it. Even without global imbalances, financial crisis may still have occurred because of weaknesses in financial markets and in the regulatory framework surrounding it.

And the relationship between democratic accountability and global financial operations remains a fraught one. The so-called 'democracy deficit' between elite-based global institutions and democratic processes is manifest especially clearly in the area of global finance. Ordinary citizens oriented to national democratic structures feel excluded from deliberations in the G20 or IMF. There are few if any transnational democratic structures that parallel the global financial architecture. The problem of democratic deficit here is made worse by two further associated problems. One is the tendency of national politicians to operate as if unconditional national sovereignty remained intact when in reality sovereignty remains highly conditional on international processes and agreements, as well as being limited by the autonomy of global capital markets. The second problem is a lack of public education in the current shape, architecture, dynamic, and weaknesses of the global financial order. There is a huge information gap here in capacity of the general public to grasp the relevance and significance of global trade imbalances for everyday life. The void is filled by populist calls to blame the bankers and reliance on the integrity of sovereign nations to fix the mess. Blaming bankers is not, however, a solution, while individual nations are unable to produce effective policy responses without achieving higher levels of co-operative agreement than is currently evident.

Market failure

Global trade imbalances are not the only macro-economic or structural factor at work in creating financial crisis. Some analysts hold laissez-faire models of global capitalism responsible instead. This argument may be connected with the financialization of the global economy discussed in Chapter 3. This process increased the relative importance of finance within the global economy, and hence increased the potential seriousness of market failure should anything go badly wrong. Short-term financial objectives, including the maintenance of shareholder value, also came to dominate the development of many non-financial corporations against increasing vulnerability to financial volatility. Underlying such developments, as we have seen above, was the development of a mathematically sophisticated economics of finance that treated perfect markets as necessarily efficient and claimed that risks could be identified and managed, stimulating investment strategies based on short-run arbitrage in self-regulated market arenas.

De-regulated or self-regulated markets have a long history of crisis and depression, boom and bust. Throughout recent history, a pattern of de-regulation and re-regulation is evident. This is especially true for finance because processes of credit expansion contain high levels of uncertainty over the future. Over-confidence and speculation leads to asset price 'bubbles', where the price of assets such as housing takes off in an unsustainable way. Risk is endemic in this sector, even though this is obscured during economic upswings and financial 'bubbles' when all is seen to be going well, and ideological defenders of laissez-faire look to be right – at least for those with short memories. It is this fundamental uncertainty that undermined the economics of finance and with it the whole edifice of risk-free trading in efficient markets.

Thus, the structural problem here is not simply that global finance is uncertain and unstable, but also that it is not necessarily efficient. The GFC proved once again that finance markets failed to price risk effectively into their transactions. Credit was extended by financial institutions at high rates of leverage where loans might exceed thirty times the value of assets, and where mortgages were extended to home-buyers with little realistic chance of re-payment if house prices ceased to rise each year.

When markets fail, financial value is lost, profits collapse, credit is withdrawn, and businesses collapse or go into administration. Manufacturing industry is adversely affected alongside finance. Unemployment then rises. All this happened between 2008 and 2009, at levels that were worse in the USA and Western Europe than other regions such as the Asia-Pacific. While pro-market ideologues dispute that market failure was the product of causes internal to markets, it is difficult to sustain attempts to claim that state failures are really to blame. Regulatory deficiencies are undoubtedly part of the story, as we shall see below, but it is quite unacceptable to deny that market failure happened or that finance markets have repeated problems with risk and uncertainty. They are part of the story too.

There are two major themes linking market failure in finance with wider social and economic crisis. One, as already stressed, is the endemic problem of risk and uncertainty within financial markets. The second is connected with financialization, in the sense that finance and capital markets, oriented to the short term, have had a distorting effect on product markets, oriented to the longer term. The social costs of indulging the market utopias of financial ideologues may be measured in terms of economic volatility, diminished growth rates, crises in housing finance in countries such as the USA, and post-crisis restrictions on creditworthiness.

Responses to market failure

How then may market failure be addressed in policy reform?

One obvious response is better regulation – something that we shall move on to consider below. Before doing that, it is worthwhile looking briefly at a more general sociological perspective, to identify some of the broader social aspects of the problem.

Sociology views the ideological notion of free-standing markets and laissez-faire policy as encouraging a profound and pathological differentiation of economy from society. Rather than markets always providing the goods which are then allocated according to the cultural preferences of consumers, there are occasions when markets generate economic bads that generate political and cultural instability, which, in turn disrupts social cohesion. If markets under certain conditions produce pathological outcomes, they should not be written off altogether because under other conditions they may generate economic growth, advancing the aggregate social welfare of the planet more efficiently than other systems – if efficiency is measured in terms of levels of productivity. So what conditions work?

One way of thinking about this is to consider the embedding or re-embedding of markets into society, that is, through the creation of social markets. These have been defined in different ways, but a common thread running through them is the idea that social considerations should exist alongside economic imperatives. While it is conventional to think of political systems intervening in already existing markets, to meet social obligations funded through taxation and borrowing, this may be insufficient to permit re-embedding of markets into society. This is often when markets directly and manifestly produce bads, such as low wages, abusive work conditions or environmental pollution, bads that should be directly tackled at source. But it is also where characteristic structures and cultures of market-based decision-making fail to recognize antisocial practices, which are more latent and less manifest in their operations. Short-term profit-seeking based on highly risky investment practices is one example. Another is the creation of personal incentive arrangements that simply reward profit when made, but do not penalize loss on a proportionate and reciprocal basis when it is incurred.

Responses to market failure, therefore, may operate at the level of changing not only social and cultural norms but also expectations about what should be done and how it should be achieved, as well as at the more conventional level of institutional re-structuring.

Relevant examples of social and cultural change involve matters such as the curriculum of business school training, professional codes of conduct in financial trading, and governance processes within financial institutions. Cultural change is not irrelevant to averting market failure, because it is clearly of importance to issues such as the lack of sufficient emphasis on business ethics within the curriculum of business schools over the last two decades, or the limited scope of corporate social responsibility schemes within the short-term worlds of finance markets and market players. Yet one perennial problem with this kind of thinking is that it is often vague and exhortatory, lacking a specific normative thrust that institutions and financial actors may take up.

Paul Woolley, writing in *The Future of Finance* (2010), an important volume published by the London School of Economics, provides a more specific and elaborate example of desirable normative reform in finance. This involves what he calls 'a manifesto for giant funds'. The aim is to produce a normative strategy for large institutional investors that is designed both to stabilize markets and increase long-term returns by avoiding high-risk investments that lead to market failure. His interpretation of where finance went wrong focuses on the familiar themes of the mispricing of risk, but he links this with a structural feature of finance to do with the relationship between principals (i.e. investors) and agents (i.e. financial intermediaries such as traders).

This relationship went wrong during the period of financialization because agents gained excessive autonomy from investors, allowing them to devise and trade in complex derivative financial products that few investors understood. The vast fees paid to agents therefore amount to rent capture by agents rather than an efficient market-based allocation of returns to successful trading firms. A key remedy to prevent this happening again is therefore a more pro-active stance by investors, especially those giant 'public, pension, and charitable' funds that have an interest in long-term returns.

Woolley's manifesto offers a way of promoting this agenda around a number of key principles. These include the following:

- Adopt a long-term approach to investing based on long-term dividend flows, rather than momentum-based strategies that rely on short-term price changes.
- Cap annual turnover of portfolios at 30 per cent.
- Understand that all the tools currently used to determine (investment) policy objectives and implementation are based on the discredited theory of efficient markets.
- Do not sanction the purchase of 'structured', untraded or synthetic products.
- Do not pay performance fees (or only pay on long-term performance).
- Insist on total transparency by managers with respect to their strategies, costs, leverage, and trading.
- Allow public scrutiny of fund compliance with these policies.

This manifesto is worth quoting at some length because it indicates some ways in which the pathological and dysfunctional separation of finance from broader considerations such as long-term financial sustainability, trust in managers' trading procedures and public transparency may be addressed and reformed. Markets are neither efficient left to themselves, nor do they guarantee the social legitimacy of global finance. However, it is possible to conceive of specific normative and procedural changes that could be implemented within finance that do not wholly rely on external political regulation. This means that advocates of such changes bypass the obvious criticism that states and state-regulation can 'fail' too.

This does not mean that regulation always fails, any more than markets always fail. Nor does it mean that regulation could not help underwrite normative and procedural change. Woolley gives two examples. One involves the approval of new financial products. These should not be approved simply because they claim to increase liquidity or complete markets. The second involves taxable treatment of funds. In the UK, at least, these may be tax exempt, providing they invest rather than trade. When a high proportion of the portfolio is turned over by fund managers in any given year, this begins to look suspiciously like trading, yet is rarely penalized through loss of tax exemption. Regulators in his view should be more pro-active in this area, and the norm of a cap of 30 per cent turn-over each year would seem a reasonable indicator of an investment strategy geared to long-term returns rather than short-run speculation.

Woolley's argument that performance fees should not be paid to traders and fund managers engages with a matter of huge public interest; namely, the remuneration of financial service providers. While much populist anger has been directed against levels of pay, it may be more relevant for the prevention of market failure to consider the structure of pay. There are two interrelated issues here. One is the incentive to engage in high-risk but potentially high-return activity created by reward of short-term investment success rather than long-term economic returns. A second closely linked problem is the tendency to reward success but not to penalize failure. While leading traders have made huge bonuses in good times through risky behaviour, the losses incurred in the GFC did not generate a corresponding direct penalty – rather the public purse picked up most of the losses. The perverse incentives in this structure of pay create dangers for global finance as a whole and are distinct from the issue of levels of pay, which may violate community notions of fairness, and which can be dealt with through the tax system.

The problem of uncertainty-induced market failure is therefore an issue that requires recognition not only by public investment and pension funds, but also in wider public policy debates. This is partly a question of identifying ways of anticipating and averting failure, and partly a question of allowing broader social and political considerations into the worlds of global finance. This is perhaps easier for central bankers, who, as we have seen, may bring historical memory and intuitive judgements of what works into play. It may be far harder for traders whose increasingly screen-based trading horizons are very short term, backed up by automatic trading programmes. In between these two layers of the financial world are the various financial institutions such as banks, insurance companies, and pension funds. Some of these fit into Woolley's category of principals who have the capacity to mandate investment goals and procedures. However, for investment banks, or mixed-function banks who perform commercial and trading activities, the position is very different.

The highest profits in banking in the lead-up to the GFC came precisely from short-run arbitrage using derivatives that are targeted by Woolley as short term and based on the false promise of risk-free trading in efficient markets. Remedies against a repeat of market-failure in global finance have therefore extended to questions of how to limit the disruptive consequences of investment banking failures as manifest in the GFC with the demise of Lehman Brothers and huge bail-outs for other banks such as Goldman Sachs.

The most widely canvassed remedy is to somehow separate commercial and investment banking in order to protect the credit extended to households and smaller business from the consequences of credit collapse brought on by investment banking failures. Since this is unlikely to arise spontaneously from the banking system itself, it looms large as a major feature of regulatory reform to which we now turn.

Policy and regulatory failure

Poor public policy and poor regulation have been canvassed as major causes of the GFC requiring policy re-think and regulatory reform. Some balance is therefore required in combining an awareness of market failure with policy and regulatory failure as co-present causes of crisis rather than opting for one or the other to fit ideological prejudices. And the corollary of this kind of balance is a parallel recognition that not everything about finance markets is bad or dysfunctional, just as not everything about monetary policy and financial regulation is fundamentally defective.

Finance market intermediation has had a large measure of success in creating long-term credit from the typically shorter-term perspectives of investors. This in turn has helped stimulate economic growth and technological innovation through the continuing evolution of capital markets. Policies of low interest rates, other things being equal, have made a contribution to the avoidance of inflation preserving the value of savings and pensions, while equally lowering cost burdens on business loans and mortgages. Financial regulation meanwhile has learnt something from previous crises in terms of identifying institutional weakness in banking structures associated with inadequate capital reserves, as well as beginning the reform of these processes. That regulation in this area ultimately failed to prevent crisis is in part because financial institutions did not implement prudential regulation, as much as any fault in the regulatory structure itself.

The leading candidate for public policy failure in the lead up to the GFC is that monetary policy set by central bankers was too easy. This charge is laid especially at the door of the US Federal Reserve led up until 2006 by Alan Greenspan and more recently by Ben Bernanke. The argument here is that short-term interest rates were kept low in a manner that was too inflexible. While positive in many respects, this orientation to monetary policy meant that little attempt was made to use policy levers to prevent or at least put a check to asset price bubbles. Rather than a pro-active policy of 'leaning against the wind' as practised, for example by the Australian Reserve Bank in relation to potential real estate bubbles, Greenspan preferred to use monetary policy to 'mop up' after markets had come much closer to bubble-induced crisis. Bernanke seems to be continuing in this mould, looking more to regulation to avert future volatility and crisis than to stepping in earlier.

In essence, this approach reduces central bank policy to price stability. It represents a kind of minimalist policy perspective. The rationale behind it is that excessive intervention to prick asset price bubbles before they reach extreme proportions could potentially weaken growth and impose unnecessary economic costs. Yet the obvious criticism of this position is that merely mopping up after bubbles burst fails to avert costs of asset price collapse, which in the case of the GFC far exceeded the costs of an earlier pre-emptive move. The point here is that the cost to growth of some monetary tightening before asset price bubbles gain too much momentum may be rather limited, and most probably less than when momentum is greater and bubbles have burst.

A broader approach to monetary policy is, however, unlikely to be a sufficient remedy by itself to avert future crisis, especially as so many regulatory failures are evident in the lead up to the GFC.

The sociologist John Braithwaite (2008) has characterized the contemporary global economy not in terms of financialization, but as regulatory capitalism. Cutting through debates about the need for greater regulation as against de-regulation, his argument is that markets never generate spontaneous order by themselves but rely on some kind of regulation, whether public or private in form. This perspective provides a way of cutting through misleading ideologically debates that use highly rhetorical language about regulation, including the conceptual sleight of hand that regards de-regulation as no regulation, and the conflation of regulation with public initiative alone. As it happens, the GFC witnessed regulatory failure both with respect to public agencies and with private self-regulatory initiatives, the two of which are often closely interconnected.

Regulatory failure associated with the GFC has been associated with both general features of global finance and specific features of the regulatory framework in particular nations, notably the USA, but also the UK. One of the most serious general problems was a lack of adequate capital in the banking system. This under-capitalization of banks was reflected both by the scale of losses entailed and by the huge size of public bail-outs to keep many major global banks afloat. Under-capitalization might be thought to represent a private failure of inadequate provisioning by banks in relation to the liabilities they took on. Sole focus on this argument would, however, understate problems of public regulatory failure in the global rules of capital adequacy for banks developed through the so-called Basel Accords.

Basel is the home of the central bankers' bank – the Bank for International Settlements which has been tasked over the last thirty-five years with greater monitoring and supervision of cross-border capital movements, including a sense of the capital it is prudent for banks to have available to weather crises. This initiative represented a belated global regulatory response to the globalization of banking and financial markets which previously were left to national regulators. After a period of deliberating over the principles of banking regulation, the Basel Committee for banking supervision developed three successive Accords. Basel 1 dating from 1988 emerged in the aftermath of the stock market collapse of 1987. This first Accord focused on problems of inadequate capital held by banks, which reduced their capacity to weather crisis. Basel 1 determined capital adequacy in terms of a set ratio of the securest kind of bank capital (such as shareholders equity or home government bonds) to its total assets (taking into account the risk profile in the various types of assets). This ratio was broadly determined at 8 per cent.

This kind of regulation, designed to secure adequate capital reserves taking risk into account, was largely evaded by many banks. Further attempts to produce more effective capital adequacy requirements led to Basel 2 dating from 2004. This new Accord emerged after further financial crises in the 1990s. It now gave financial regulators greater flexibility in making judgements about the adequacy of capital held by particular banks, but did not revise the basic ratio or the kinds of capital that could be counted. This meant significant regulatory weaknesses were still intact as the GFC was to demonstrate.

A key weakness of the system was a pro-cyclical bias. This means that this structure of supervision encouraged banks to hold too little capital in an upswing when risks appeared lower, and too much capital in a down-swing when risks appeared more evident. The net effect of pro-cyclicality was that credit expansion in an upswing was not backed by sufficient assets, while in an economic downswing credit was contracted too sharply to meet risk-based capital adequacy ratios. In this latter case, the scale of downswings was made worse by the capital adequacy regime. These arrangements were therefore a contributory cause to the worsening of the depth and severity of the GFC.

Underlying such weaknesses are several further problems. First, capital adequacy levels were still too low. Second, assessment of the quality of capital in relation to risk was inadequate. This relates to a third major problem; namely, that risk was assessed on an individual basis – bank by bank – using a variety of procedures, rather than at the level of the system as a whole. Amongst other things, this individualistic approach failed to take into account the complex web of risks involved in dealings between banks and financial institutions, through instruments such as credit default swaps, discussed in Chapter 2. However, the failure to take a system-wide approach to risk is clearly a problem of public regulation that contributed to the GFC.

Further problems of regulation involve variable compliance with Basel 2, which US banks had not signed up to. Their own capital adequacy ratios were often far lower than 8 per cent, as low as 4 per cent in some cases. Problems of low compliance are a product of weak public supervision as well as private avoidance of a broader social responsibility to play their part in securing financial stability.

Another important dimension to the GFC is the distinction between capital adequacy and liquidity. An everyday way of thinking of liquidity is 'ready money', that is, assets immediately available to make transactions, such as servicing debts. Global finance based on credit requires both adequate capital reserves in financial institutions and liquidity so that day-to-day transactions can be met. In the GFC, liquidity dried up as institutions found they could not re-finance short-term loans when they expired and fresh loans were needed. In the USA, Bear Stearns had to be saved when its cash ran dry, Lehman Brothers then collapsed, and Goldman Sachs came close to running out of money.

A key problem here is that regulators have spent far more time thinking about capital adequacy and too little about liquidity. In a sense, financial institutions left it to central bankers to ensure liquidity, especially since holding assets in liquid form offers institutions a very low return. Regulators, however, had not included liquidity within the Basel Accords, and this clearly reduced the buffers that might otherwise have been put in place to secure greater financial resilience. Even so, inadequate liquidity was not a fundamental cause of the GFC, since it was the high rates of leverage on loans that created much of the difficulty, itself linked as we have seen to the culture of finance.

In addition to these general problems of global regulation, other more specific problems emerged in particular national settings. Many elements of finance continue to be regulated at a national, and sometimes even a sub-national level, such as the state jurisdictions in federally organized nations.

National regulation may not always be the optimal level for addressing key features of global finance which require co-operation and co-ordination, such as capital adequacy ratios for banks engaged in cross-border transactions. However, key nations such as the USA and UK had not, by the eve of the GFC, developed integrated or co-ordinated systems of domestic financial regulation. This mattered greatly because both were the home of world-leading financial centres in Wall Street and the City of London.

The regulatory system in the USA has generally been singled out as having the most significant levels of weakness. This is largely because it did not function as a co-ordinated system. It was composed rather as a complex set of separate regulatory domains, further weakened by holes in sectors such as insurance where federal public regulation was non-existent. The US preference for separate regulators for each sub-section of finance made it almost impossible to co-ordinate action to prevent crisis, in terms of both information-sharing and co-ordination of action. Banks, insurance, stock markets, and the public housing mortgage system operated by Freddie Mac and Fannie Mae, were regulated separately, sometimes at state level and sometimes federally. This partly explains why the full significance of finance sector exposures to the sub-prime mortgage crisis was not appreciated earlier, and why system-level risk in the financial sector as a whole was not evident to most observers until too late.

If public regulators failed in the various ways indicated above, this does not necessarily mean that the market would have done all right if only regulation had been better. This is because market self-regulation failed too. This is partly a matter of poor corporate governance and oversight of banking and credit practices. Many corporate leaders did not fully understand the new complex derivative products or systems of insurance surrounding them, partly because lending policies operated on leverage ratios that far exceeded prudent levels. Derivatives were themselves both poorly self-regulated and poorly regulated, if at all by public regulators. While it may be true that money gravitates to the least well-regulated sectors, both private and public regulators bear responsible for the dire consequences. In the private sector, the debt-rating agencies, seemed to perceive nothing much going wrong until crisis hit, while the lucrative momentum behind leveraged derivative trading was not properly scrutinized by managers or accountants. Public scrutiny and regulation was largely non-existent.

Towards more effective regulation

What fresh regulatory initiatives are therefore required to deal with the GFC and the future economic sustainability of global finance?

A unifying theme in the discussion of both market and regulatory failure is the lack of any system-wide capacity to understand the build-up of risk. This failure applies to the mathematical models that traders believed could price-risk into market transactions, to the practice of corporations to calculate risks for their own firm alone, and to the failure of public regulators at national and global levels to understand risk. To put the problem in the more technical language discussed in Chapter 5, the problem for finance markets is one of uncertainty as much as risk. The distinction between uncertainty and risk, as we have seen in earlier chapters, makes it possible to assess how far problems derive from unknowable contingencies that we cannot measure or predict, as against those contingencies whose probability can be reliably calculated and managed. The priority then for more effective regulation is not simply a better structure for the management for risk, but also to determine how to plan for uncertainty.

Andrew Haldane of the Bank of England argues that global finance operating as a cross-border network of nodes and linkages is particularly vulnerable to extreme and uncertain events. This is partly because of the intense scale of inter-connections across the globe, and also because risk hitherto has been calculated on an atomistic level within the nodes rather than across the linkages.

Re-stabilizing a vulnerable system of this kind requires a range of initiatives. Some require better information of network-wide risk rather than risk within particular nodes. After the collapse of hedge fund Long Term Capital Management (LTCM) in 1998, the Bank for International Settlements began to collect cross-border banking statistics. After the GFC, there is a need to extend this to financial flows in general, including non-bank institutions. This would, however, have to have a better grasp of the many off-balance sheet financial transactions that securitization has spawned. And beyond better information, the improved analysis of risk requires new forms of analysis that operate beyond the level of individual firms to that of financial networks and the financial system as a whole. Haldane looks here to network theory in general, and measures of robustness developed by statisticians around characteristic patterns of network interaction. But he also looks to epidemiology in biology, noting that disease epidemics feature a relatively few high-risk super-spreaders with high numbers of network linkages, which are disproportionately responsible for contagion. This model might well be applied in finance where a few large financial institutions, such as Lehman Brothers, may play a disproportionate role in spreading crisis.

These analytical points have great implications for reform of global financial regulation. Much emphasis has been placed here on tightening the capital adequacy ratios to which global banks are subject. The BIS and the Financial Stability Board, as expert regulatory advisors to the G20 nations, have recently been involved in the development of Basel Accord 3. The latest regulatory changes included higher and more robust levels of capital adequacy, including an increase from 2 per cent to 7 per cent in the highest quality (tier one shareholder equity) capital – albeit phased in over eight years. There are also encouragements to operate a higher level of provision in the good years as a counter-cyclical strategy against future crisis. Surprisingly, however, there is far less regulation of the leverage ratios banks may operate. Under Basel 3, these may still be as high as 33.33 times tier one capital.

It is also not clear that Basel 3 addresses Haldane's point that particular institutions may need specific regulatory attention due to the scale and vulnerability of their activities. Macro-prudential regulation does not address this problem. Historical problems with individual institutions were handled privately by other bankers, while in the twentieth-century central banks have played a more major role. Indeed, there is some indication that larger banks in the run up to the GFC expected public help if they ever got into difficulty and operated inadequate capital buffers accordingly. This in turn raises the problem of whether some institutions are too big to fail, and whether it was a mistake to let Lehman Brothers go under. The case for allowing failure, at least on rare occasions, centres on problems of moral hazard and wider political and social considerations, including finite limits to the public purse.

The moral hazard argument is that financial institutions should not be encouraged to pursue unduly risky courses of action, confident that they will always be bailed out if things go very wrong. Private sector institutions, especially the larger ones, must accept market penalties for faulty decision-making including the mis-pricing of risk. Public support cannot be unlimited. Excessive levels of support, as recently provided by the Irish state to its own banks, risk bringing on a fiscal crisis of the state on top of the GFC. This in turn creates highly politicized dilemmas for democratic nations. Adequate state expenditure to support banks may require cut-backs to other kinds of public expenditure, risking social conflict. Recourse to increased taxation would be extremely unpopular, and make crises worse, at a time that risks of default make borrowing on the sovereign debt market more expensive for governments. Once again there is need for a sociology of finance that goes beyond the internal economics of markets in order to analyse the linkages between markets, states, citizens, and cultural expectations made of financial institutions and governments.

Conclusion

In this chapter we have applied a broader sociological to the analysis of the GFC and what should be done about it. At the time of writing, the sovereign debt crises in European countries is still spreading and stock markets remain volatile and fearful. While each displays features particular to the nation in question – such as the chaotic state of Greek public finances across recent history – there are common themes in play. The GFC, which began as a sub-prime mortgage crisis, and developed into a full-scale crisis of global credit and capital markets, now continues as a crisis of sovereign indebtedness. In Greece, though not Ireland, this spills over beyond parliamentary conflict into social conflict in the streets. Changes in economic policy and regulatory structures discussed above may offer some longer-term success in averting or limiting the impact of future crises but they will not resolve short-term socio-political discontent or restore the reputation of the finance industry, bankers, and regulators.

The re-legitimization of global finance is not simply a matter of waiting for street conflict to subside, but requires a greater awareness of the democracy deficit and information divide that separates the worlds and cultures of finance from wider populations. This divide applies to all aspects of globalization, as much as the globalization of finance in particular. The world of trading rooms, arbitrage, and derivatives, and the interest-rate setting and macro-prudential activities of central bankers are not well understood in the world outside by legislators let alone citizens. Bridging this gap is not only a matter of demonstrating market and regulatory success in achieving economic advance without crisis, but also requires a better architecture of democratic transparency to allow more informed democratic deliberation about its purposes, its strengths, and limits.

Underlying this endeavour is a set of critical questions, namely 'is economic globalization compatible with democracy? If so, is this democracy as practised in the slow-moving worlds of national politics, or is greater democratization of global regulatory bodies required?'.

One aspect of this that demands greater and more urgent attention than hitherto is improved education – in terms of both public education of citizens and specialist education in schools and universities. Improved public education would require continuous disclosure requirements in relation to all capital and money markets on the model of the disclosure requirements imposed on many share markets. It also requires a greater emphasis on finance – corporate and governmental as well as household – within curricula. If citizens were better aware of the relationships between government expenditure and bond markets, or of the intrinsic risks and uncertainties involved in credit provision, their expectations and capacities to realize their objectives would be greatly enhanced. To the objection that this is simply too technical or hard to achieve, the obvious rejoinder is that analysis of improved information flows would be enhanced if the education of graduates and school-leavers provided a greater emphasis on finance in the curriculum. This, in turn, following the analysis offered in this book, should be inter-disciplinary, placing economic insights in a broader sociological and scientific framework.

This book is written precisely to advance these educative functions, demonstrating that finance need not be technically complex, and that analytical depth need not be sacrificed in the search to write accessibly. This volume is dedicated then to the principle of deliberative democracy and to the hope that its practitioners may feel emboldened to restructure global finance, even in the midst of its darkest days.

GLOSSARY

Bonds:
Financial products based on the payment of a sum of money to a government or business in return for future regular income streams. Bonds can be sold on by purchasers to others.

Collateralized Debt Obligations:
An investment product backed by a pool of financial assets, such as bonds or loans, that vary in the risks associated with them.

Credit Default Swaps:
Financial institutions can take out insurance against the failure of debtors to repay loans, that is, default. This credit default insurance can, however, be traded or swapped, such that institutions may hold credit default instruments applying to potential defaults on the loan book of other institutions.

Derivatives:
Financial products whose value is derived from the value of some other financial entity, such as a stock market index, or an estimate of the future value of a particular share price derived from its current value.

Embeddedness/Embedding:
Sociological concepts that refer to the way in which economic processes are set within and dependent on wider social processes, even if this is not necessarily acknowledged by market participants.

Financialization:
An increase in the importance of finance within the economy as a whole.

Investment Banking:
This is where banks conduct investment activity on their own account, as distinct from commercial banking, based on the provision of loans and transaction services for customers. Investment banking, especially where it is based on high rates of leverage (see below), is more high risk and high return, but can, in a crisis, jeopardize the retail banking deposits of small depositors taken during the course of normal commercial banking.

Legitimacy:
A sociological concept referring to acceptance of the authority of particular institutions (such as banks), or of ways of organizing social life (such as markets, payment of bankers bonuses and so forth). Acceptance can fall short of complete agreement with the institution or practice in question, but minimally must involve practical compliance.

Leverage:
Technically, this means the taking on or issuing of loans to finance economic activity, usually secured against a set of assets. De-leveraging means reduction in loans previously taken on or issued.

Risk:
The term carries a number of meanings. As used in this study, it is contrasted with uncertainty. Risk refers to future contingencies that it is possible to anticipate and whose probability can in some sense be calculated, allowing planning for the future. If markets can measure risk, they can then price risk into the market value of financial products. Risk here is distinct from uncertainty which cannot be measured. It is also distinct from the uses of risk by the sociologist Ulrich Beck, who sees risk as combining adverse contingency with environmental and species hazard.

Securitization:
The process whereby financial flows (e.g. loan payments) received by a financial institution secured on some asset, such as houses or a car, can be packaged together into a pool and then sold on to other investors.

Social Differentiation:
A sociological concept referring to the separation of distinct spheres or component parts of society from one another, usually reflected in specialized institutions performing distinct functions. This study deals with the differentiation of economy from society. Differentiation generally raises problems of system integration and social cohesion.

Sub-prime mortgages:
Mortgages extended to high-risk clients; for example, those with no assets and/or no job.

Uncertainty:
In a technical sense, this refers to future contingencies that cannot be predicted or anticipated, and thus reliably integrated into the planning and management of businesses and governments. Extreme events are an example. (See also *Risk*.)

FURTHER READING

The concept of a financial system is defined in R.C. Merton and Z. Bodie (1995) 'A Conceptual Framework for Analyzing the Financial Environment', in D.B. Crane *et al.* (eds), *The Global Financial System: A Functional Perspective*, Boston: Harvard University Business School Press, pp. 3–33.

The contemporary operations of global finance, up to and including the global financial crisis, are ably discussed in A. Turner (2010) 'What Do Banks Do?', in A. Turner *et al.* (ed.) *The Future of Finance: The LSE Report*, London: London School of Economic and Political Science, pp. 3–63.

D. McKenzie (2006) *An Engine, Not a Camera: How Financial Models Shape Markets*, Boston: MIT Press.

Important contributions to the study of regulation include: J. Braithwaite and P. Drahos (2000) *Global Business Regulation*, Cambridge: Cambridge University Press.

J. Braithwaite (2008) *Regulatory Capitalism*, Cheltenham: Elgar.

Important studies in the history of global finance include N. Ferguson (2008) *The Ascent of Money*, London: Allen Lane.

C. Kindleberger (1978) *Manias, Panics and Crashes: A History of Financial Crises*, London: Macmillan.

C.M. Reinhart and K. Rogoff (2009) *This Time is Different: Eight Centuries of Financial Folly*, Princeton: Princeton University Press.

Aspects of financialization are explored in G. Epstein (ed.) (2005) *Financialization and the Global Economy*, Cheltenham: Elgar.

A range of publications including: S. Sassen (1996) *Losing Control? Sovereignty in an Age of Globalization*, New York: Columbia University Press.

——(2005) *Cities in a World Economy*, Thousand Oaks: Pine Forge Press, explores both the social geography of global finance and the problems of loss of democratic sovereignty.

A broad set of essays covering many aspects of the sociology of financial markets is available in K. Knorr Cetina and A. Preda (eds.) (2005) *The Sociology of Financial Markets*, Oxford: Oxford University Press.

Sociological insights into the worlds of financial traders may be obtained from the work of K. Knorr Cetina and U. Bruegger (2002) 'Global Microstructures: the Virtual Societies of Financial Markets', *American Journal of Sociology*, 107(4), 905–50.

D. Buenza and D. Stark (2004) 'Tools of the Trade: the Socio-Technology of Arbitrage in a Wall Street Trading Room', *Industrial and Corporate Change*, 13(2), 369–400.

Central bankers' worlds are very ably explored in J. Pixley (2004) *Emotions in Finance*, Cambridge: Cambridge University Press, with particular reference to uncertainty and trust.

Key theoretical resources in the understanding of how markets, states, and cultures interconnect are available in M. Weber (1968) *Economy and Society*, 2 vols, Berkeley: University of California Press.

K. Polanyi (1944) *The Great Transformation*, Boston: Beacon Press.

M. Granovetter (1985) 'Economic Action and Social Structure: The Problem of Embeddedness', *American Journal of Sociology*, 89, 481–510.

For the analytical scope of economic sociology, see R. Swedberg (2003) *Principles of Economic Sociology*, Princeton: Princeton University Press.

Insights into the psychology of markets are available in R. Shiller (2000) *Irrational Exuberance*, Princeton: Princeton University Press.

Very helpful introductions in the causes and policy options available to resolve problems highlighted in the GFC are available in M. Wolf (2009), *Fixing Global Finance: How to Curb Financial Crises in the 21st Century*, Newhaven: Yale University Press.

H. Davies (2010) *The Financial Crisis: Who Is To Blame?* Cambridge: Polity Press.

P. Woolley (2010) 'Why are Financial Markets Inefficient and Exploitative – And a Suggested Remedy', in A. Turner *et al.* (eds) see above, Chapter 3.

WEB RESOURCES

The general dimensions of cross-border financial flows are available from the Bank for International Settlements (www.bis.org/statistics/index.htm).

Individual financial institutions also provide information on their own global activities, though some offer a far more direct and transparent approach than others.

The most helpful websites include the leading global bond dealers, Pimco (www.pimco.com/en/Pages/default.aspx), banks such as Barclays (www.barclays.com), then navigate to 'Barclays Worldwide', and Credit Suisse (www.credit-suisse.com/who_we_are/en). Morgan Stanley Smith Barney provide interesting information on investment banking (see www.morganstanley.com/institutional/invest_bank/index.html).

Global insurance is well represented by Lloyds of London (www.lloyds.com) whose website also provides interesting insights into challenges posed by global risk. While Moodys, the debt ratings agency, in its own website (www.moodys.com) outlines its thinking on the risks involved in the sovereign debts of nations.

Corporate websites clearly try to represent their activities in the most favourable light possible. More independent judgements are available in some specialist financial journalism, though it is always worth checking whether particular writers make explicit where they hold financial interests in companies under review. Specialist websites of the Financial Times of London (www.ft.com) and the Australian Financial Review (www.afr.com.au) offer well-informed analytical material, but much of this is on a subscription basis only. Reuters (www.reuters.com) and the *Wall Street Journal* (www.wsj.com) are more accessible.

The personal websites of economists and financial journalists are very useful. Good examples include those of the economist John Kay (www.johnkay. com), fellow economist Joseph Stiglitz (www.josephstiglitz.com) and the world's pre-eminent financial journalist Martin Wolf, whose columns appear within the Financial Times of London (www.ft.com). There are also tens of thousands of financial blogs offering varying degrees of expertise, many focused on individual day traders rather than large professional traders. The best site for financial commentary is Reuters (www.reuters.com – select 'opinion').

Financial regulation at a global level is available within the International Monetary Fund (www.imf.org) and the Bank for International Settlements (www.bis.org). The key role of the Federal Reserve Bank in the USA may be tracked in its website (www.federalreserve.gov). Other important central bank websites include the Bank of England (www.bankofengland.co.uk) and the European Central Bank (www.ecb.int). These sites include discussion and execution of policy and regulatory decisions as well as analytical observations. On the Bank of England website, the papers by Andrew Haldane, director of financial stability, are particularly interesting on questions of risk and uncertainty, see for example 'The $100 Billion Question' (www.bankofengland.co.uk/ publications/speeches/2010/speech433.pdf).

INDEX